Adventuring with Books

3 68 ̄3

2

Adventuring with Books

A Booklist for Pre-K–Grade 6

New Edition

Mary Lou White, Editor

and the Committee on the Elementary School Booklist
of the National Council of Teachers of English

National Council of Teachers of English
1111 Kenyon Road, Urbana, Illinois 61801

NCTE Editorial Board: Paul T. Bryant, Marilyn Hanf Buckley, Thomas J. Creswell, C. Kermeen Fristrom, Jane Hornburger, Robert Hogan, *ex officio*, Paul O'Dea, *ex officio*

Book Design: Tom Kovacs

NCTE Stock Number 00759

Library of Congress Cataloging in Publication Data

National Council of Teachers of English. Committee
  on the Elementary School Booklist.
  Adventuring with books.
  Includes indexes.
  1. Children's literature—Bibliography.
I. White, Mary Lou   II. Title.
Z1037.N265 1978 [PN1009.A1]   011.62   81-11179
ISBN 0-8141-0075-9   AACR2

Contents

Contents

Introduction

The 1981 edition of *Adventuring with Books* is a selective booklist designed primarily for teachers of preschool through sixth-grade children and also for the use of librarians, educational media specialists, parents, students of children's literature, and, on occasion, children. Approximately 2500 new children's trade books are annotated in this list, selected from the 10,000 books published from 1977 through 1980.

The current Committee on the Elementary School Booklist of the National Council of Teachers of English followed the same two criteria for book selection that previous committees used. One basis for selection was high potential interest for children. The other was a significant degree of literary merit; popularity alone was not enough to qualify books for the compilation. Two other factors were of concern to this committee: the equitable treatment of minorities and the recognition of quality books of the past. Eventually, children's literature about minorities might not need to be dealt with as a separate topic, but the committee felt that it must be reflected in the books selected for the 1981 list.

In addition to soliciting books from major publishers, the committee sought books from the multitude of alternative presses that publish books for children. These books were subjected to the same criteria of selection as those of long-established publishers. When we saw reviews of noteworthy books not sent to us by publishers, we tried to locate library copies for consideration. These were not always available. Almost all the books recommended in this edition were published between the end of 1976 and the end of 1980. A few award-winning books published in 1976 that did not appear in the 1977 edition are included. A few selected older books have been retained from previous booklists to add balance to the collection. Because the booklist's focus is on newness, the outstanding older books are listed at the end of each major category without annotations. In general, reissues of classics are not included unless the format is particularly outstanding.

The purpose of the booklist is to inform teachers of recently published good books to share with children. It can be used to help find appropriate books for children who want a good story about a particular theme. It can also serve as an aid when teachers need books for an instructional unit and want to know what recent books are available on the topic.

Annotations provide brief summaries of the books. All the books selected are recommended; in some cases strengths are noted and other

1

evaluative comments are given. When books contain language or explicit scenes that might be offensive to some readers, annotations so indicate. Occasional suggestions are made for class use and for integrating the books into various areas of the curriculum. Newbery and Caldecott Award and Honor Books are identified. Age levels are indicated as a matter of paramount interest. It is possible, as in the case of picture books, that books noted for ages 5–8 could be used with older children to initiate discussions or to stimulate creative writing. Likewise, well-illustrated non-fiction books with texts and concepts for ages 8–12 might be used with younger children. While the range of the booklist is kindergarten through grade six, some annotations suggest more difficult reading by the designation "12–up." In some instances, books in series or sequels that were similar in content or style are referred to within the annotation rather than annotated separately. Each annotation lists bibliographic information. Where annotated books were translated into Spanish, the titles are listed. A list of publishers' addresses is appended for book ordering purposes. All books listed were in print at the time of publication.

During the four-year period that the committee worked on the book, we asked teachers about the usefulness of *Adventuring with Books* and similar bibliographies. Most wanted more help in selecting books on specific topics. The contents was consequently made more specific, which required assigning a particular topic to each book, rather than simply classifying it by genre. As a committee we realized the difficulty of making such a judgment; many books have multiple themes and could be classified into several categories. We decided that the guidance offered through a multi-categorized table of contents outweighed unequivocal categorization. For example, a book of realistic fiction might be considered mainly a "family story," but the central character might do a great deal of "growing up" while "facing problems." Such a book would be placed in the category that suggested the most central theme as decided by the committee member, realizing that the judgment might not be shared by all. Although teachers can be assured of finding many good books in the appropriate categories, they will also benefit from checking related categories. The category assignments are teacher-oriented rather than arranged by standard library subject headings. Always, the teacher's use was the paramount consideration in categorizing a book. The expanded table of contents, therefore, is intended to help teachers find a certain type of book more readily. Specific titles can most easily be found, of course, in the title index.

Picture books and easy-to-read books have been integrated into the fiction content areas. The philosophy of the committee was that picture books should be used at all levels and the likelihood would be increased if the books were integrated throughout the compilation. To make picture books easily identifiable for the primary grade teacher, the phrase (Picture book) is at the end of each appropriate fiction annotation.

This edition includes a list of recently published professional books about children's literature. More and more professional books are being published as the field of children's literature grows. These books are valuable to teachers as they seek specialized listings, critical viewpoints, and suggestions for teaching.

Wordless books have been published in growing numbers over the past four years. Those that tell stories are listed in the Wordless Book category, while those that relate to specific content areas are under those categories. Traditional Literature, including folk literature from nursery rhymes to world mythology, is available for preschool to intermediate age children.

The fiction books are grouped according to genre. Modern Fantasy is divided into categories based primarily on characters. Science Fiction constitutes a separate genre, perhaps suggesting that this class of novels is coming into its own in children's books. Historical Fiction is divided according to time and place. Contemporary Realistic Fiction is classified according to themes, some of which reflect the concern of contemporary children's literature for social issues, notably "facing problems," "handicaps," and "young and old." These are balanced by the less controversial standard fare of "animals," "humor," "mystery," and "sports."

The Poetry section is divided into thematic groupings; Holiday books are listed according to individual holidays. A section on Concepts includes the very basic beginnings of concepts such as color, time, and the alphabet. The Social Studies, Biography, and Sciences sections are categorized according to names used in most school curricula. Here once again, the teaching aspect is emphasized in the classification.

Nonfiction books of Sports and Games are abundant and popular, so the committee felt they should be singled out as a separate category. Some might wonder about the "circus" category as one of The Arts, but primary grade teachers will benefit from a separate listing of nonfiction books about this performing art. Books on Language, Crafts, and Hobbies are also categorized by various content areas. The Amusement section will be popular with children; we were especially selective about these books, which are interesting as well as amusing. The new Professional Books section rounds out the listing.

The help of many persons was necessary for the preparation of *Adventuring with Books*. The committee members are most grateful to all of them. Publishers generously provided review copies during the past four years. Four graduate assistants served superbly: Sharon Callahan, now Community Relations Representative, McDonald's Corp., Dallas, Texas; Jeralyn Clayton, now Reading Teacher Specialist, Fairbanks, Alaska; Sylvia B. Bernstein and Robin Kemp, currently at Wright State University. Charlotte Leonard, Director of Children's Services of the Dayton and Montgomery County Public Library, provided initial suggestions and long-term support through her fine library staff and holdings. Barbara Fultz, Wright State University, assisted far beyond the regular duties of a secretary. Students and teachers at many institutions read and commented on books, providing additional insights for the committee members. All these people supported our continued goal of identifying high quality, enjoyable literature for children.

Mary Lou White
College of Education
Wright State University

Wordless Books

Arnosky, Jim. **Nathaniel.** Addison-Wesley Publishing, 1978. 5–8.

Nathaniel baches it on a Vermont farm. His funny adventures, imaginatively exaggerated, are told in the uncluttered, humorous ink drawings of three wordless picture stories, and in two diary memoirs penned in black ink highlighted by miniature drawings. Humorous stories that broaden life-style concepts.

Briggs, Raymond. **The Snowman.** Random House, 1978. 5–8.

A little boy makes a snowman who comes to life at night. They explore household things such as television, ice cubes, and skateboards; then the snowman flies the boy above Brighton-by-the-Sea during the snowstorm. In the morning the snowman is gone. Cartoon format; beautiful drawings.

Crews, Donald. **Truck.** Greenwillow Books, 1980. 3–5.

The big red trailer-truck moves from the loading dock to its destination. The author's vivid illustrations carry the reader along the truck's route. 1981 Caldecott Honor Book.

Degen, Bruce. **Aunt Possum and the Pumpkin Man.** Harper & Row, Publishers, 1977. 4–7.

This wordless picture book shows an indomitable Aunt Possum refusing to be frightened by a Halloween prank played by neighborhood children. Colorful illustrations.

deGroat, Diane. **Alligator's Toothache.** Illus. by author. Crown Publishers, 1977. 4–7.

Alligator takes a taste of the icing he is putting on cupcakes and the painful expression on his face is evidence of a toothache. His friends arrive with more treats to find him wrapped in a bandage and suffering. Treatment by a dentist is rejected until his friends trick him and the party begins.

de Paola, Tomie. **Pancakes for Breakfast.** Harcourt Brace Jovanovich, 1978. 3–7.

A little old lady living in the country tries to make pancakes. Although her pets greedily interfere, this determined lady doesn't give up and comically finds a way to have her pancakes. The colorful and humorous illustrations present information about supplying ingredients needed to make pancakes.

Emberley, Ed. **A Birthday Wish.** Little, Brown, 1977. 4–7.

A humorous series of events leads to the granting of a small mouse's birthday wish. The oblong format is perfect for the cumulative chain story; the meticulous details of the illustrations encourage readers to observe the unfolding story carefully.

Giovannetti. **Max.** Atheneum, 1977. All ages.

Max is a hamster. His captivating antics are told through a series of highly expressive line drawings. Max was first introduced in *PUNCH,* the British humor magazine. His curiosity brings laughter to his many admirers.

Goodall, John S. **Paddy's New Hat.** Atheneum, 1980. 5–8.

Paddy Pork buys a handsome new hat, only to see it blown into the police recruiting office. He joins the police force and inadvertently captures a thief in the royal apartment. His rewards are a royally bestowed medal, dismissal from the force, and his retrieved hat with an added plume. Half pages; delightful illustrations.

Goodall, John S. **The Surprise Picnic.** Atheneum, 1977. 4–7.

The cat family spreads their picnic lunch on a smooth stone. This improvised table is actually a turtle, who waddles away with their meal on his back, the first of many surprises. Another of Goodall's wordless books of cozy Edwardian scenes painted in soft colors on full and half pages.

Hartelius, Margaret A. **The Birthday Trombone.** Doubleday, 1977. 4–7.

Little girl monkey is delighted with her parents' gift of a trombone for her birthday! However, she repeatedly makes trouble for the other animals with her noisy practice sessions, until one loud blast actually helps someone. The well-characterized illustrations stimulate children to verbalize about the humorous tale.

Heller, Linda. **Lily at the Table.** Macmillan Publishing, 1979. All ages.

Lily doesn't want to eat her dinner. As she stares at her plate, she escapes into a fantasy world where spaghetti stretched between spoons becomes a tightrope. A chicken leg becomes a violin, and a celery stalk, a slide. This wordless picture book will elicit a smile from everyone who has ever toyed with food.

Hughes, Shirley. **Up and Up.** Prentice-Hall, 1979. 7–10.

One little girl makes everyone's dream come true: she flies. The townspeople chase, an entire classroom of students follows, and a man in a balloon tries to catch her. She escapes them all and yet returns to earth, unscathed and still dreaming.

Krahn, Fernando. **Catch That Cat!** E. P. Dutton, 1978. 4–7.

A little boy chases his runaway cat through the dock area of a Mediterranean port. The chase ends aboard a freighter where the cat releases the boy from a locked stateroom and the boy saves the cat from being thrown overboard. Expressive black and white illustrations tell the wordless story.

Krahn, Fernando. **The Mystery of the Giant Footprints.** E. P. Dutton, 1977. 6–9.

The giant footprints in the snow are very mysterious. All of the people in the village join together to trail the giant. They find a giant surprise. Black and white drawings.

Lisowski, Gabriel. **The Invitation.** Holt, Rinehart and Winston, 1980. 3–5.

Little Pig weeps and sulks because he is the only one not invited to a party. Trying to get even, he plays a mean trick on the partygoers, only to discover, to his chagrin, that the party is for him. Appealing illustrations, full of expression and action, carry the story line effectively.

Mayer, Mercer. **Oops.** Dial Press, 1977. 3–5.

Young children giggle over the humorous antics of Ms. Hippo as she goes about doing her shopping and visits a museum. The town is left in shambles because of her thoughtless gestures. Cartoonlike illustrations capture the humor of the story.

Turkle, Brinton. **Deep in the Forest.** E. P. Dutton, 1976. 4–7.

A small bear enters an empty cabin, samples three bowls of porridge, tries out three chairs and breaks one, then settles down for a nap in the smallest of three beds, where he is discovered by the owner, a little girl with yellow sausage curls. A delightful turnabout tale with warm and expressive illustrations.

Wetherbee, Holden. **The Wonder Ring: A Fantasy in Silhouette.** Doubleday, 1978. 7–10.

Clear-cut silhouettes tell a wordless story of fantasy. A poor abused boy is given a magic ring when he shares his food with a stranger. The 136 pictures provide excellent challenges for children to follow the story line. An interesting history of silhouette-making is appended.

Winter, Paula. **Sir Andrew.** Crown Publishers, 1980. 3–6.

Meet Sir Andrew, an unusual and vain donkey, who dresses elegantly and then takes an eventful stroll on a windy day. Funny, pastel illustrations show that Andrew's self-admiration leads him to disaster. Giggles are guaranteed.

Additional Wordless Books

Bolliger-Savelli, Antonella. *The Knitted Cat*. Macmillan Publishing, 1971. 4–7.
Goodall, John S. *The Adventures of Paddy Park*. Harcourt Brace Jovanovich, 1968. 4–6.
Krahn, Fernando. *A Flying Saucer Full of Spaghetti*. E. P. Dutton, 1970. 4–12.
Mayer, Mercer. *One Frog Too Many*. Dial Press, 1975. 4–8.
Ringi, Kjell. *The Winner*. Harper & Row, Publishers, 1969. 4–6.
Ueno, Noriko. *Elephant Buttons*. Harper & Row, Publishers, 1973. 4–up.
Ward, Lynd. *The Silver Pony*. Houghton Mifflin, 1973. 8–12.
Winters, Paula. *The Bear and the Fly*. Crown Publishers, 1976. 5–8.

Traditional Literature

Fables

Aesop. **The Lion and the Mouse.** Illus. Ed Young. Doubleday, 1979. 7–10.

Restraint in words and pictures typifies this retelling of the fable about the tiny mouse who repays the mighty lion by freeing him from a rope net in which the lion is captured. Expressive black and white sketches are bordered in red. An outstanding book.

Aesop. **The Town Mouse and the Country Mouse.** Illus. T. R. Garcia. Troll Associates, 1979. 4–7.

The country mouse visits his cousin in the city and finds that city life is difficult. This age-old tale is illustrated in fresh, vivid colors. One of twenty-two books in Troll's Fables and Fairy Tales series.

Franko, Ivan (translator Bohdan Melnyk). **Fox Mykyta.** Illus. William Kurelek. Tundra Books, 1978. 10-up.

This classic collection of Ukranian Fox tales is enriched with folklore and humor. Fox is a lovable, independent rogue who outwits his enemies, using their moral flaws to triumph. Spirited illustrations match the author's commentary. Sophisticated readers can discuss the satirical, social, and political elements.

Rice, Eve, adapter. **Once in a Wood: Ten Tales from Aesop.** Illus. by adapter. Greenwillow Books, 1979. 7–10.

Favorite fables including "The Lion and the Mouse," "Belling the Cat," and "The Frog and the Ox" are retold in easy-to-read wording. In most cases the moral is given in rhyme. Handsome black and white pen sketches grace this beautifully designed collection. A read-alone book.

Soyer, Abraham (translators Rebecca S. Beagle and Rebecca Soyer). **The Adventures of Yemima.** Illus. Raphael Soyer. Viking Press, 1979. 3–5.

A young girl outwits a sly fox, greed gets its comeuppance, and coins literally fly away from a miser in these tales translated from the Hebrew. The stories are warm and satisfying, and the format is outstanding.

9

Stevens, Bryna, editor. **Borrowed Feathers and Other Fables.** Illus. Freire Wright and Michael Foreman. Random House, 1977. 4–7.

Seven of Aesop's best-known fables are retold in simplified prose for reading aloud and younger readers. Includes "The Fox and the Crow," "The North Wind and the Sun," "The Milkmaid." Full-color illustrations.

Weil, Lisl, adapter. **Gillie and the Flattering Fox.** Atheneum, 1978. 4–8.

Gillie the Cock is so vain that he foregoes caution in order to be admired by everyone, including the hungry fox. His friends save him and teach him a lesson in this clever retelling of a familiar fable.

Ziner, Feenie, retold by. **Cricket Boy.** Illus. Ed Young. Doubleday, 1977. 12–up.

Scholar Hu lived long ago in the village of Yung Ping. There began the strange tale of a champion cricket, the death of Hu Sing, the scholar's son, and the emperor's cricket match. Full-color luminous illustrations create an Oriental setting for this retold fable.

Folktales

Aardema, Verna, retold by. **Half-a-Ball-of-Kenki.** Illus. Diane Stanley Zuromskis. Frederick Warne, 1979. 6–9.

This Ashanti tale tells how the Leopard gets his spots, his cry, and his comeuppance (a half-a-ball of cornmeal mush called kenki), from Dokonfa. Excellent to read aloud and for dramatic play.

Aardema, Verna, retold by. **Who's in Rabbit's House? A Masai Tale.** Illus. Leo Dillon and Diane Dillon. Dial Press, 1977. 6–9.

In this humorous read-aloud folktale, rabbit can't get into her house because Long One is inside and threatens her. Rabbit rejects her friend's help, but the problem is unexpectedly resolved. The story is presented in play form including animal masks that change expressions.

Anderson, Bernice G., compiler. **Trickster Tales from Prairie Lodgefires.** Illus. Frank Gee. Abingdon Press, 1979. 7–10.

Trickster sometimes plays good tricks, sometimes bad tricks. On occasion his tricks backfire and he is tricked. All the people of the prairie lodges tell the stories of trickster but they tell them only at night so trickster doesn't come back and play tricks again. A delightful collection.

Aronin, Ben. **The Secret of the Sabbath Fish.** Illus. Shay Rieger. Jewish Publication Society of America, 1978. 7–10.

In this retelling of a Jewish folktale, the story of gefilte fish is told. Two hundred years ago a poor Russian woman known as a fine cook had a magical encounter with the prophet Elijah. She was instructed to prepare a fish according to what had been happening to the Jewish people. Her method became the recipe for gefilte fish.

Asian Cultural Centre for UNESCO, editors. **Folk Tales from Asia for Children Everywhere: Book One and Book Two.** John Weatherhill, 1975. 8–12.

Authentic and less familiar folktales from sixteen Asian nations have been selected, retold, and illustrated by writers and artists in each country. Stories are from Indonesia, Japan, Khmer, Malaysia, Nepal, Pakistan, Philippines, Sri Lanka, Bangladesh, India, Iran, Korea, Laos, Singapore, Thailand, and Vietnam. Colorful illustrations.

Bang, Molly Garrett, adapter. **Wiley and the Hairy Man.** Macmillan Publishing, 1976. 6–9.

Humor and suspense abound in this trickster tale from American folklore, when Wiley's mother and his own quick thinking save him from the hairy monster who lives in the swamp beside the Tombigbee River. Both writing style and illustrations are of a quality seldom found in easy readers.

Belpre, Pura. **The Rainbow-Colored Horse.** Illus. Antonio Martorell. Frederick Warne, 1978. 6–9.

Pio, the youngest of three brothers, frees a rainbow-colored horse. In return, the horse grants Pio three wishes, which he uses to gain the hand of a beautiful girl, much to the chagrin of his two older brothers. Striking woodcuts in full-color illustrations make this Puerto Rican folktale a visual sensation.

Bere, Rennie, retold by. **Crocodile's Eggs for Supper and Other Animal Tales from Northern Uganda.** Illus. John Paige. Andre Deutsch, 1979. 7–10.

This collection of folktales from the Acholi tribal society of Northern Uganda features clever animals, a trickster hare, and dramatic situations, frequently amusing. Echoes of Uncle Remus and other folktales will be found. Black and white illustrations.

Berson, Harold, adapter. **Kassim's Shoes.** Illus. by adapter. Crown Publishers, 1977. 5–8.

Kassim's neighbors give him a fine new pair of shoes to replace his old comfortable ones. Kassim's efforts to get rid of his beloved old shoes bring chaos to the village and laughter to the picture-book audience. Muted wash illustrations.

Bible, Charles, adapter. **Hamdaani: A Traditional Tale from Zanzibar.** Illus. by adapter. Holt, Rinehart and Winston, 1977. 7–10.

Strong illustrations capture the mood of this African tale about the lessons of ingratitude. A gazelle brings fortune to Hamdaani, a beggar who soon forgets his humble beginnings. When he refuses to help the animal, he loses his wife and wealth and becomes again a poor man scratching for food.

Boegehold, Betty. **Small Deer's Magic Tricks.** Illus. Jacqueline Chwast. Coward, McCann & Geoghegan, 1977. 4–10.

Four folktales of Borneo, all about how a small deer outwits the larger, pompous, and aggressive animals, are wittily presented. Large print and brief text assist early readers. This is a good read-aloud book with engaging drawings.

Bowden, Joan Chase. **The Bean Boy.** Illus. Sal Murdocca. Macmillan Publishing, 1979. 6–9.

An old woman sets out to make her fortune with a little boy carved out of a bean. A rooster swallows the bean boy, a cat swallows the rooster, and so forth until the woman reaches the king and good fortune. This retelling of an Italian folktale, with clever illustrations and well-paced repetitions, makes an enjoyable first reader.

Bowden, Joan Chase. **Why the Tides Ebb and Flow.** Illus. Marc Brown. Houghton Mifflin, 1979. 5–8.

In the world's beginning, a stubborn old woman holds Sky God to his promise that she may have any rock she wants, even the one that plugs the hole at the bottom of the sea. The heartwarming solution to the dilemma of a fast-draining sea results in the ebb and flow of the tides. Exceptional artwork.

Brenner, Barbara. **Little One Inch.** Illus. Fred Brenner. Coward, McCann & Geoghegan, 1977. 7–10.

A Japanese couple who have prayed to the gods for a child are happy to accept a very tiny baby. Issun Boshi, Little One Inch, grows up to have many adventures, outsmarting both demons and mortals. The soft Oriental illustrations bring the reader into close contact with Japanese culture.

Briggs, Katharine. **Abbey Lubbers, Banshees and Boggarts.** Illus. Yvonne Gilbert. Pantheon Books, 1979. All ages.

A delightful encyclopedia for all lovers of fantasy. Not only are such creatures as Habetrot, Fenodree, and Capelthwaite identified, but groups of fairy folk are categorized. This charming book is filled with fascinating detail and tales of the strange creatures.

Briggs, Katharine. **British Folk Tales.** Pantheon Books, 1977. 12-up.

Scholarship and readable style combine to make a rich resource of folk literature for teachers and students. Cultural concepts will be enriched by reading and hearing the tales in dialect. Briggs' introduction and her comments preceding each category of tale are integral to the book's value.

Briggs, Katharine. **The Vanishing People: Fairy Lore and Legends.** Illus. Mary I. French. Pantheon Books, 1978. All ages.

Various types of fairies and their wide-ranging habits are discussed in this scholarly study. Included are such diverse topics as fairy sports and morality. A glossary of fairies is one of several useful appendices.

Bryan, Ashley, retold by. **Beat the Story-Drum, Pum-Pum.** Illus. by reteller. Atheneum, 1980. 7-10.

Five African tales are retold with melodic language that invites reading aloud. The animals in these stories are like people who have little problems that get them into big troubles. Many handsome, bold black and white drawings and several bright two-color plates.

Bryan, Ashley, retold by. **The Dancing Granny.** Illus. by reteller. Atheneum, 1977. 8-12.

In this folktale from the Antilles, Granny Anika, who loves best of all to dance, even while working, has a duel of wits with singing Spider Ananse. The elegant prose captures the rhythms of the wheeling, whirling native dance illustrated by gracefully flowing pen and ink drawings.

Carlson, Bernice Wells. **Quick Wits and Nimble Fingers.** Illus. Dolores Marie Rowland. Abingdon Press, 1979. 8-12.

Ten brief and little-known folktales from many parts of the world are retold. Following each tale are several craft activities related to the theme. The projects are especially interesting and are complete with easy-to-follow instructions. They include baker's clay ornaments, aluminum foil relief, sand painting, and origami.

Carlson, Natalie Savage. **King of the Cats and Other Tales.** Illus. David Frampton. Doubleday, 1980. 7-10.

Mam Marig relates eight fascinating stories of Breton folklore to her godchild Yvette. She has taught her how to knit and as the needles fly, the tales continue to unwind. Werewolves, goblins, and korrigans perform magic tricks. Strong woodcuts complement these hearty tales.

Carrick, Malcolm, retold by. **Happy Jack.** Harper & Row, Publishers, 1979. 5-7.

Foolish, lazy Happy Jack must go to work because his mother has no money. His hilarious adventures culminate in the traditional happy ending. This new version of a folktale for beginning readers has handsome two-color illustrations that are highly amusing and perfectly complement the simplified text.

Clark, Ann Nolan. **In the Land of Small Dragon: A Vietnamese Folktale.** Illus. Tony Chen. Viking Press, 1979. 7-10.

A traditional Vietnamese version of the Cinderella story, complete with cruel stepmother, ugly half-sister, fairy godmother, lost slipper, and handsome prince. Only the pumpkin is missing. Outstanding full-page watercolor illustrations.

Cohen, Barbara, retold by. **Lovely Vassilisa.** Illus. Anatoly Ivanov. Atheneum, 1980. 7–10.

The Russian Cinderella story is retold in a spirited version with the wicked Baba Yaga portrayed in a terrifying manner. When Vassilisa confronts Baba Yaga with an even greater spirit, she is granted her request. Vassilisa's doll, given to her by her dying mother, helps her through all her tribulations.

Coombs, Patricia. **Tillabel.** Lothrop, Lee & Shepard Books, 1978. 6–9.

Tillabel, a rather lazy groundhog, is the despair of her mother, who wishes that she would act like other groundhogs. The queen overhears her as she scolds her daughter and invites Tillabel to the castle. This delightful German tale is reminiscent of Rumplestiltskin. Appealing, soft pencil illustrations.

Craig, M. Jean, adapter. **The Donkey Prince.** Illus. Barbara Cooney. Doubleday, 1977. 6–9.

In this familiar tale, a variant of Beauty and the Beast, a greedy king deceives the wizard and must accept his punishment: a son who looks like a donkey. Only the love of someone who accepts him as he is will break the evil spell. Exquisite color illustrations enhance this lovely retelling.

Curley, Daniel. **Billy Beg and the Bull.** Illus. Frank Bozzo. Thomas Y. Crowell, 1978. 7–10.

A marvelous retelling and expansion of the Irish tales of Billy Beg and his magical talking bull. Disillusioned by his new mother, Catelinn of the Broken Nose (who insists on clean shirts every day and no bulls by the fireside), Billy sets out and eventually finds his true mother, Brigid the Lovely. A natural read-aloud tale.

Curtis, Edward S., compiler (editor John Bierhorst). **The Girl Who Married a Ghost and Other Tales from the North American Indian.** Photographs by compiler. Four Winds Press, 1978. 10–up.

These selected tales are considered to be authentic materials representative of Native Americans west of the Mississippi. The translation maintains much of the flavor of the original language and allows the reader to savor somewhat incomprehensible events. Illustrations are copies of photos done in the early 1900s. Excellent.

Cutt, Nancy, and W. Towrie Cutt. **The Hogboon of Hell and Other Strange Orkney Tales.** Illus. Richard Kennedy. Andre Deutsch, 1979. 8–12.

Hogboons or goblins, demons, talking stones, and selkie folk abound in this fine collection of little-known tales from the Orkney Islands off the Scottish coast. Superstition, magic, mystery, and humor are part of the legends collected by contemporary folklorists. Black and white line drawings complement the tales.

Darling, Kathy. **Pecos Bill Finds a Horse.** Illus. Lou Cunette. Garrard Publishing, 1979. 8–12.

Pecos Bill, legendary cowboy hero of America's wild West, has no horse to ride. He tries a giant mountain lion, lightning, and a huge grizzly bear, with fantastic but frustrating results. But the great golden stallion, ah, there's a *horse*! Satisfying illustrations in watercolor.

Dawood, N. J., retold by. **Tales from the Arabian Nights.** Illus. Ed Young. Doubleday, 1978. 10–12.

Translated from the Arabic by a Middle East scholar, this collection includes familiar and not-so-familiar tales that Shahrazad told for a thousand and one nights in order to avoid being slain by her husband, King Shahriyar. Although told in modern idiom, the Middle East flavor has been preserved.

de Beaumont, Madame (translator Diane Goode). **Beauty and the Beast.** Illus. by translator. Bradbury Press, 1978. 8–12.

The stuff of dream and magic, virtue truly valued, courage rewarded, and selfishness and deceit appropriately recompensed are combined in this beautiful translation of the old folktale. The exquisite line and watercolor paintings portray emotion and fantasy, with authentic detailing of eighteenth-century French culture.

Demi, retold by. **Under the Shade of the Mulberry Tree.** Prentice-Hall, 1979. 7–10.

A rich man enjoys sitting under his mulberry tree until a poor man joins him. The latter buys the tree's shade and goes into the house whenever it is shaded. The rich man becomes angry; he finally leaves the house. A Chinese folktale with handsomely rendered color over line drawings.

de Paola, Tomie, retold by. **The Prince of the Dolomites.** Illus. by reteller. Harcourt Brace Jovanovich, 1980. 6–9.

How the Dolomite Mountains became so bright is explained in this Italian folktale. The illustrations help sustain the mood and fascination of the story of how Prince Pazzo of the Dolomites fell in love with Princess Lucia of the Moon.

de Regniers, Beatrice Schenk. **Everyone is Good for Something.** Illus. Margot Tomes. Clarion Books, 1980. 6–9.

Jack, a kind-hearted boy, is considered by his mother to be good for nothing. A cat, whose life Jack saves, helps him to clear an island overrun with mice, proving to his mother as well as to himself that he is "good for something." Based on a Russian folktale.

Domanska, Janina. **King Krakus and the Dragon.** Greenwillow Books, 1979. 7–10.

King Krakus and his beautiful daughter are loved by the people of Krakow. People are happy and life is pleasant until a frightful monster comes to live in the river Vistula. The brave apprentice shoemaker finds a plan to save the king, the town, and the people. A Polish folktale.

dos Santos, Joyce Audy, retold by. **The Diviner.** Illus. by reteller. J. B. Lippincott, 1980. 7–10.

Jean-Pierre is both lazy and lucky. He not only persuades the king that he can solve riddles and foretell the future, but he actually succeeds in doing so. A clever twist at the end makes this French Canadian trickster tale a natural for story time. Young audiences will enjoy responding to the question, "What happened next?"

Duff, Maggie, retold by. **Rum Pum Pum.** Illus. Jose Aruego and Ariane Dewey. Macmillan Publishing, 1978. 4–7.

The blackbird sets out to rescue his wife, who was stolen by the king. Along the way he meets other animals who are angry at the king and they journey together. How the blackbird wins his wife back is color- fully depicted in this retelling of a folktale from India.

Galdone, Joanna. **The Tailypo: A Ghost Story.** Illus. Paul Galdone. Clarion Books, 1977. 7–10.

This eerie Tennessee folktale tells of an old man who cuts off the tail of a strange little creature. Suspense builds as the tailless creature comes back again and again to call for the return of his "tailypo." Illustrations in pencil and soft colors capture the mountain setting and humor.

Galdone, Paul. **Cinderella.** McGraw-Hill, 1978. 5–8.

Perrault's tale is retold with delightful touches of humor. While Cinderella is helping her sisters get ready for the ball, the author suggests, "Anyone but Cinderella would have tangled their hair for them." The illustrations, luminous and delicate, have an appropriate French flavor.

Gauch, Patricia Lee, retold by. **Once upon a Dinkelsbuhl.** Illus. Tomie de Paola. G. P. Putnam's Sons, 1977. 6–9.

The medieval village of Dinkelsbuhl is invaded by Swedish soldiers who eat all the food and take everything they want. They plan to burn the town but are stopped by the brave actions and planning of Lora and the other children. Humorous and sensitive illustrations.

Ginsburg, Mirra, compiler and adapter. **The Twelve Clever Brothers and Other Fools.** Illus. Charles Mikolaycak. J. B. Lippincott, 1979. 7–10.

These fourteen brief, entertaining Russian folktales about clever and silly fools will appeal to a wide range of readers. Fools may be young or old, clever or stupid, rich or poor; whatever the type, they will be met in these appealing tales. Attractive illustrations.

Goble, Paul. **The Girl Who Loved Wild Horses.** Illus. by author. Bradbury Press, 1978. 6–9.

A young Native American girl loves horses and understands them in a special way. A thunderstorm drives the girl and horses far from home to live with a leader of wild horses, a beautiful stallion. Award-winning illustrations sweep the reader through this symbolic story. 1978 Caldecott winner.

Grimm, Jakob, and Wilhelm Grimm (translator Lore Segal). **The Bear and the Kingbird.** Illus. Chris Conover. Farrar, Straus & Giroux, 1979. 6–9.

Read aloud this Grimm's tale about a curious bear who visited a nest of baby kingbirds and rudely called them no-good children. This caused a revengeful conflict between the birds and the animals. Bright, very detailed illustrations highlight the humor of this sense of justice story.

Grimm, Jakob, and Wilhelm Grimm. **The Bearskinner.** Illus. Felix Hoffman. Atheneum, 1978. 8–12.

Due to a bargain with the devil, a young soldier is to live clad in a bearskin, unwashed and unshaven for seven years in return for an endless supply of gold. Published posthumously, the book is illustrated by the artist's preliminary color studies that are dramatically beautiful.

Grimm, Jakob, and Wilhelm Grimm (translators Anne Rogers and Anthea Bell). **The Best of Grimm's Fairy Tales.** Illus. Svend Otto S. Larousse, 1979. 6–9.

The artwork makes this volume a unique treasure: characters and old European country scenes are at once realistically and enchantingly painted in vivid colors. Tales include Snow White, Four Musicians of Bremen, Tom Thumb, Puss in Boots, and the Wolf and the Seven Little Kids. Fine paper and print.

Grimm, Jakob, and Wilhelm Grimm (translator Anthea Bell). **The Brave Little Tailor.** Illus. Svend Otto S. Larousse, 1979. 7–10.

The little tailor kills flies, seven at a blow, and decides to tell the world of his prowess. His cleverness enables him to outwit a giant, kill two giants, capture a unicorn, marry the king's daughter, and gain half a kingdom. Full-color humorous illustrations.

Grimm, Jakob, and Wilhelm Grimm (translator Brian Alderson). **The Brothers Grimm: Popular Folk Tales.** Illus. Michael Foreman. Doubleday, 1978. 6–9.

Thirty-one of the best-loved folktales told by the Brothers Grimm are newly translated in this volume in speech modes refreshingly true to the original language. Illustrations combine authentic detail with fairyland mood in colorplates and sketches. Fine quality paper and print add to the aesthetic pleasure. Good to read aloud.

Grimm, Jakob, and Wilhelm Grimm (retold by Eric Carle). **Eric Carle's Storybook.** Illus. by reteller. Franklin Watts, 1976. 7–10.

Modernized versions of seven Grimm tales include "Tom Thumb," "Seven with One Blow," and "The Fisherman and His Wife."

Grimm, Jakob, and Wilhelm Grimm (translator Randall Jarrell). **The Fisherman and His Wife.** Illus. Margot Zemach. Farrar, Straus & Giroux, 1980. 6–9.

When the fisherman catches an enchanted prince in the form of a flounder, his wife urges him to ask for a nice little cottage to replace their hovel. Humorous watercolors depict the couple as they ask for more and more until they end up right back in their shack.

Grimm, Jakob, and Wilhelm Grimm. **Hansel and Gretel.** Illus. Susan Jeffers. Dial Press, 1980. 6–9.

A magnificently illustrated version of an old gruesome story, with a literal translation of the original Grimm text. A benign-looking witch and two plumpish youngsters mitigate the horror of this classic tale of evil.

Grimm, Jakob, and Wilhelm Grimm. **Rapunzel.** Illus. Bert Dodson. Troll Associates, 1979. 6–9.

The wicked witch imprisons Rapunzel in the tower, but the handsome prince rescues the beautiful maiden with the long golden hair. One of twenty-two titles in the Troll Fables and Fairy Tales series that includes "Rumplestiltskin," "Cinderella," and "Jack and the Beanstalk." Full-color artwork.

Grimm, Jakob, and Wilhelm Grimm (retold by Donna Diamond). **The Seven Ravens.** Illus. by reteller. Viking Press, 1979. 6–9.

A timeless tale familiar to many is given a new look with outstanding black and white drawings. A family with seven sons wishes most earnestly for a daughter. Finally, their wish is granted. The rejoicing is short-lived, for her brothers are turned into ravens.

Grimm, Jakob, and Wilhelm Grimm (retold by Trina Schart Hyman). **The Sleeping Beauty.** Illus. by reteller. Little, Brown, 1977. 7–10.

The king ignores the oldest fairy, who retaliates by putting a curse on his infant daughter, somewhat tempered by another fairy so that the princess will not die, but will sleep for one hundred years. Handsome drawings contrast light and dark on each double-page spread, paralleling the story of good and evil.

Grimm, Jakob, and Wilhelm Grimm. **The Twelve Dancing Princesses.** Illus. Errol Le Cain. Viking Press, 1978. 6–9.

The twelve princesses are locked up by the king each night. Each morning their shoes are worn. A soldier solves the mystery by trailing the princesses and discovering their secret dancing place. Lavishly illustrated, this is a worthy successor to Le Cain's *Thorn Rose* and *Cinderella.*

Grimm, Jakob, and Wilhelm Grimm (translator Wanda Gág). **Wanda Gág's Jorinda and Joringel.** Illus. Margot Tomes. Coward, McCann & Geoghegan, 1978. 6–9.

While strolling through the woods Jorinda and Joringel are unaware that they have gone too far and are held within the magic circle of the enchantress. Joringel discovers a clever plan to outwit the witch. Illustrations enhance the appealing version of the old folktale.

Grimm, Jakob, and Wilhelm Grimm (adapter Wanda Gág). **Wanda Gág's The Sorcerer's Apprentice.** Illus. Margot Tomes. Coward, McCann & Geoghegan, 1979. 6–9.

A clever boy, apprenticed to a sorcerer, reads books on magic at night. The sorcerer discovers that the boy knows the secrets of magic and trickery. The boy cleverly uses his knowledge to escape the evil master.

Hall, Malcolm. **And Then the Mouse . . .** Illus. Stephen Gammell. Four Winds Press, 1980. 6–9.

Three simple stories in the folklore tradition tell about a clever mouse who uses trickery to outwit others. Based on ancient Indo-Persian lore, the short stories can be compared with other trickster tales in which the small, weak character triumphs.

Harris, Christie. **The Trouble with Princesses.** Illus. Douglas Tait. Atheneum, 1980. 10–12.

Princesses of the Old World clothed in silks, satins, and jewels are compared with the princesses of the Northwest Coast in these fascinating stories. Customs and cultural heritage are revealed. Could be used with units on American folklore. Strong black and white illustrations enhance the well-written text.

Horn, Geoffrey, and Arthur Cavanaugh, retold by. **Bible Stories for Children.** Illus. Arvis Stewart. Macmillan Publishing, 1980. 10–up.

Major stories of the Old and New Testament approved by a review board of Catholic, Jewish, and Protestant scholars are retold in simple language with explanations integrated into the text. The watercolor illustrations on each page are vivid and suited to the tales. A well-designed book.

Hou-tien, Cheng. **Six Chinese Brothers: An Ancient Tale.** Illus. by author. Holt, Rinehart and Winston, 1979. 8–12.

Six look-alike brothers of ancient China save their father and themselves from execution through use of their unique magical abilities. This satisfying tale is beautifully illustrated with scissor cuts, a venerable Chinese form of art. In classroom study, compare with *The Five Chinese Brothers* by Bishop.

Jacobs, Joseph (retold by Rodney Peppé). **Three Little Pigs.** Illus. by reteller. Lothrop, Lee & Shepard Books, 1979. 4–7.

A fresh retelling of the wolf and the three little pigs folktale. Young readers will delight in the sparkling pictures and simple text.

Jagendorf, M. A., and Virginia Weng. **The Magic Boat and Other Chinese Folk Stories.** Illus. Wan-go Weng. Vanguard Press, 1980. 12–up.

The colorful introduction and illustrated map comprising the end pages invite the reader to examine the thirty-three delightful tales in this collection. Each chapter heading indicates the location where the story originated. Magic tales of boats, shrimp, earthworms, birds, and waterfalls make up this book. Graceful, appealing pen drawings complement the text.

Keithahn, Edward L. (editor Kenneth Gilbert). **Alaskan Igloo Tales.** Illus. George Aden Ahgupuk. Alaska Northwest Publishing, 1979. 10–up.

A collection of tales gathered from the Eskimos who live along the Arctic coast and rivers of the Seward Peninsula. These explanations of natural phenomena and recounting of experiences written in the oral style give fresh insight into this American minority culture.

Kendall, Carol, and Yao-wen Li, retold by. **Sweet and Sour: Tales from China.** Illus. Shirley Felts. Seabury Press, 1979. 8–12.

These twenty-four carefully selected Chinese tales from different periods of history have warm appeal. The wide variety of plots and length of the tales provide a significant reading or listening experience. Graceful black and white drawings blend well with these lively stories.

Kovalik, Tibor, editor. **From Tale to Tale: An International Collection of Children's Stories.** Illus. by editor. Mosaic Press/Valley Editions, 1979. 8–12.

This attractive collection, published with the assistance of the Ontario, Canada, Arts Council contains ten stories from Europe, Asia, and North and South America. Although some are available in other collections, this book, illustrated with beautiful full-color paintings, is useful for studying the universality of folklore.

Lang, Andrew (editor Kathleen Lines). **The Rainbow Fairy Book: A Selection of Outstanding Fairy Tales from the Color Fairy Books.** Illus. Margery Gill. Schocken Books, 1977. 7–10.

Thirty-seven tales from the famous color fairy-tale books published at the turn of the century make up this choice collection.

Lobel, Anita. **The Pancake.** Greenwillow Books, 1978. 6–9.

This easy-reading version of the Danish tale has the pancake eluding a woman, seven children, a farmer, goose, cat, sheep, and goat only to be gobbled up by a pig. They go home with the woman who cooks another wonderful pancake. They all eat it and the farmer does the dishes.

Löfgren, Ulf, retold by (translator Sheila LaFarge). **The Boy Who Ate More Than the Giant and Other Swedish Folktales.** Illus. by reteller. William Collins Publishers, 1978. 6–9.

Included besides the title tale are "The Master Tailor" and "The Three Billy Goats Bruse." The detailed illustrations are large and humorous and just grotesque enough to amuse young readers. Published in cooperation with the U.S. Committee for UNICEF.

Lurie, Alison, retold by. **Clever Gretchen and Other Forgotten Folktales.** Illus. Margot Tomes. Thomas Y. Crowell, 1980. 7–10.

This excellent collection of fifteen folktales from various European countries focuses on young heroines. Helpful notes at the end of each tale mention other variants of the same tale that could be read, compared, and discussed. Illustrations complement the tales.

Luzzatto, Paola Caboara, retold by. **Long Ago When the Earth Was Flat.** Illus. Aimone Sambuy. William Collins Publishers, 1980. 7–10.

Three African folktales related to the creation theme are beautifully illustrated in a large book handsomely designed by Bruno Munari. "A Visit from Mister Sea" is a version of the well-known "Why the Sun and the Moon Live in the Sky." Elegant book.

McGovern, Ann. **Half a Kingdom: An Icelandic Folktale.** Illus. Nola Langner. Frederick Warne, 1977. 8–12.

Prince Lini disappears in an icy fog, stolen by troll girls who want him to marry one of them. Signy, a clever peasant girl, hears the King's desperate offer of half the kingdom for Lini's rescuer, and accepts the challenge. Down-to-earth humor mixed with common sense and courage.

McLenighan, Valjean. **Three Strikes and You're Out.** Illus. Laurie Hamilton. Follett Publishing, 1981. 5–8.

A poor boy seeks help from his aunt and is given a magic hen, which he loses, and a magic cloth, which is also lost. Finally, a

magic stick solves his problems. This easy-to-read book with charming old-fashioned illustrations is told comic-book style in modern
vernacular.

The Magic Castle Fairytale Book. Illus. Dale Payson and Ib Penick.
Random House, 1978. 6–9.

Four much-loved fairy tales are told in an attached booklet; a
tagboard castle pops up when the opposite part is folded out.
The centerfold of removable tagboard characters is reminiscent of
the nineteenth-century toy theater booklets. Useful for puppet
dramatization.

Maher, Ramona. **When Windwagon Smith Came to Westport.** Illus. Tom
Allen. Coward, McCann & Geoghegan, 1977. 8–12.

Windwagon Smith, a dapper bachelor, tries to attract backers for his
scheme to build a fleet of wind-powered wagons. Illustrated with
sepia pen and ink drawings, this book would be useful with language
arts activities in United States social studies.

Maitland, Anthony, retold by. **Idle Jack.** Illus. by reteller. Farrar, Straus &
Giroux, 1979. 8–10.

The familiar noodlehead tale about Jack, the boy who could not do
anything right, is adapted by an award-winning artist. Bold ink
drawings with delicate watercolors enhance this humorous tale.

Manniche, Lise, translator. **How Djadja-em-ankh Saved the Day.** Illus. by
translator. Thomas Y. Crowell, 1977. 8–12.

Bored King Seneferu of ancient Egypt watches young maidens row-
ing. When one drops her amulet it is recovered by Djadja-em-ankh's
magic. Illustrations are copies of Egyptian drawings, hieratic and
hieroglyphic texts on papyrus-like paper in folded scroll form. The
story is printed Egyptian style from right to left. The commentary,
printed from left to right, describes Egyptian life around 4500 BC.

Manning-Sanders, Ruth, retold by. **A Book of Kings and Queens.** Illus.
Robin Jacques. E. P. Dutton, 1978. 8–12.

Kings, queens, fair maidens, handsome princes, and lazy oafs, all
with various enchantments or tricks, inhabit these ten folktales from
nine different countries, all well-suited for reading aloud. This is
another skillful and felicitous collaboration of author and illustrator.

Manning-Sanders, Ruth. **A Book of Spooks and Spectres.** Illus. Robin
Jacques. E. P. Dutton, 1980. 12–up.

The author, who has many earlier volumes on demons, goblins,
wizards, and the like, now brings together twenty-three ghostly tales,
sometimes fearsome, sometimes humorous. Most of the folktales
included in this exciting volume are little-known stories, most of
them from Europe but a few from other parts of the world.

Manton, Jo, and Robert Gittings. **The Flying Horses: Tales from China.**
Illus. Derek Collard. Holt, Rinehart and Winston, 1977. 8–12.

This is a collection of short Chinese legends dating from the twenty-
second century BC to the twentieth century. Each story is told in a
style that helps to retain its Oriental feeling. The black and white
pen drawings capture many Chinese symbols and attitudes toward
life and art.

Mayer, Mercer. **East of the Sun & West of the Moon.** Illus. by author.
Four Winds Press, 1980. All ages.

This is the retelling of the old fairy tale of an assertive heroine who,
to win back her handsome youth's love, must rescue him from his
troll princess captor. Seventeen full-page, full-color illustrations make
this book a visual delight and invite lingering and looking. Excellent
for reading aloud.

Mitchnik, Helen, retold by. **Egyptian and Sudanese Folk-tales.** Illus. Eric
Fraser. Oxford University Press, 1978. 8–12.

A fine addition to a folktale collection. These tales enlighten the
reader concerning the Egyptian and Sudanese cultures, their mores,
social customs, and humor. They could be used for enjoyment, comparison with other cultures, or be included in a unit of work. Black
and white pen drawings enhance the tales.

Obrist, Jürg, retold by. **They Do Things Right in Albern.** Illus. by reteller.
Atheneum, 1978. 6–9.

In Albern, people are solid and hardworking, but not very smart.
When a mole is found, no one knows what it is or what to do with it
until a quiet little man suggests a solution. A Swiss folktale done
with black and white illustrations.

Perrault, Charles (translator David Walker). **The Sleeping Beauty.** Illus.
by translator. Thomas Y. Crowell, 1977. 6–9.

This French version of the classic tale differs in several aspects from
its German counterpart and can be compared for variations in the
retellings. Walker's illustrations make strong use of light and color to
evoke the romantic tradition of the tale.

Phelps, Ethel Johnston, editor. **Tatterhood and Other Tales.** Illus. Pamela
Baldwin Ford. Feminist Press, 1978. 8–up.

A collection of traditional tales from Europe, Africa, and Asia. All
stories have as the central character a strong active woman. A
welcome addition with new and interesting stories from the oral
tradition.

Plume, Ilse, retold by. **The Bremen-Town Musicians.** Illus. by reteller.
Doubleday, 1981. 6–9.

The donkey, the cat, the dog, and the rooster band together when

their masters try to get rid of them. They start off for the city of
Bremen, braying, barking, meowing, and crowing, practicing to
become street musicians. Distinctly stylized color illustrations add to
the humor of the animals' tale. 1981 Caldecott Honor Book.

Riordan, James, retold by. **Tales from Tartary: Russian Tales, Volume
Two.** Illus. Anthony Colbert. Viking Press, 1979. 8–12.

Tartary is the vast Asian land, now a part of Russia, that was the
domain of Genghis and Kubla Khan; it was the land where Marco
Polo journeyed eight hundred years ago. The tales have a touch of
Oriental flavor; many are quite brief. The characters are quick-witted
and the language is rich. This is a sequel to *Tales from Central
Russia: Russian Tales, Volume One.* Well illustrated.

Rockwell, Anne. **The Old Woman and Her Pig and 10 Other Stories.**
Illus. by author. Thomas Y. Crowell, 1979. 6–9.

Ten familiar folktales and fables are retold in simple style and rich
language. Humorous bright watercolor illustrations fill each page.
Included are "The Three Sillies," "Lambikin," "The Shepherd Boy,"
"The Lad Who Went to the North Wind," "The Milkmaid and the
Bucket of Milk," and "The Bremen Town Musicians."

Rose, Anne, retold by. **Akimba and the Magic Cow: A Folktale from
Africa.** Illus. Hope Meryman. Four Winds Press, 1976. 6–9.

Poor Akimba has nothing left to eat and goes out to seek his fortune.
An old man in the forest helps him, but attempts are made to trick
him out of his newly found magic animals. The simple woodcut
illustrations are appropriate for the setting and flavor of this folktale.

Rose, Anne. **The Triumphs of Fuzzy Fogtop.** Illus. Tomie de Paola. Dial
Press, 1979. 6–9.

Fuzzy Fogtop is a lovable, absent-minded character who loses himself in bed, attempts an unsuccessful trip from Pinsk to Minsk, and
mistakes a stranger for his friend. Illustrations thoughtfully and
richly portray the village of Chelm and its traditionally foolish
inhabitants.

Ross, Blanche, translator. **A Strange Servant: A Russian Folktale.** Illus.
Paul Galdone. Alfred A. Knopf, 1977.

A poor Russian peasant, Nassir-Yedin, tricks three rich merchants
into believing he has a talented rabbit as a valet. Bidding for the
valet's services begins. A charming tale enhanced by colorful illustrations.

Schwartz, Alvin, compiler. **Kickle Snifters and Other Fearsome Critters.**
Illus. Glen Rounds. J. B. Lippincott, 1976. 6–9.

The goofus bird flies backward; the billdad catches his fish by
smacking it with his tail; the timberdoodle bites. This collection of
strange creatures from tall tales and folklore is a sure-fire introduc-

tion to both genres. Each creature is fearsomely illustrated by a line drawing.

Scribner, Charles, Jr., retold by. **The Devil's Bridge.** Illus. Evaline Ness. Charles Scribner's Sons, 1978. 5–8.

This French folktale tells how the villagers trick the Devil after he agrees to rebuild a bridge over a gorge leading to their marketplace. Masterful woodcuts add to the delightful story. A good book for sharing.

Sewell, Marcia, adapter. **The Little Wee Tyke: An English Folktale.** Illus. by adapter. Atheneum, 1979. 4–7.

A wee dog, "smaller than a house cat," is wanted by no one. A little girl saves him from drowning and takes him to her bewitched farm. His courage breaks the spells and banishes the witch and the tyke becomes a treasured pet. Size isn't everything! Illustrations complement style.

Shulevitz, Uri. **The Treasure.** Farrar, Straus & Giroux, 1978. 7–10.

Isaac has a dream commanding him to look for treasure under the bridge in the capital city. He trudges there but finds the bridge heavily guarded. The captain laughingly tells him his own dream. Isaac goes back to his modest home and finds his treasure there. 1980 Caldecott Honor Book.

Still, James. **Jack and the Wonder Beans.** Illus. Margot Tomes. G. P. Putnam's Sons, 1977. 8–12.

This Appalachian version of Jack and the Beanstalk uses the language and setting of the region. The giant's chant is, "Fee, fie, chew tobaccer, I smell the toes of a tadwhacker!" Great fun and matched with delightful illustrations.

Titiev, Estelle, and Lila Pargment, translators and adapters. **How the Moolah Was Taught a Lesson.** Illus. Ray Cruz. Dial Press, 1976. 7–10.

The Moolah, the richest man in the village, covets the beautiful wife of poor Khameed. A simple, funny trick foils the Moolah's sly scheme. In each of these four little-known Russian folktales a fearsome crisis is resolved with wit and courage, preserving human values. Illustrations are distinct and charming.

Travers, P. L., retold by. **Two Pairs of Shoes.** Illus. Leo Dillon and Diane Dillon. Viking Press, 1980. 8–12.

Elegant full-color illustrations reflect the mystique of the ancient Near Eastern kingdoms from which these stories come. Two men who wear worn, battered slippers learn vastly different, yet universal truths about life. The two separate Persian tales are linked together in the retellings.

Van Woerkom, Dorothy O., retold by. **The Friends of Abu Ali.** Illus.
    Harold Berson. Macmillan Publishing, 1978. 4–7.

In each of three noodlehead stories, Abu Ali uses strange logic to
solve his problems or those of his friends. Detailed illustrations
reflect the humor in the stories as well as their Turkish origin. An
easy-to-read book, a sequel to *Abu Ali.*

Wolkstein, Diane, compiler. **The Magic Orange Tree and Other Haitian
    Folktales.** Illus. Elsa Henriquez. Alfred A. Knopf, 1978. All ages.

These stories collected from the *maitre-conte* or professional storyteller of Haiti are rich in humor and rhythm. Wolkstein's foreword
and the notes that precede each story give insights into Haitian
culture and the art of storytelling. Music for the songs, a part of
many of the stories, is included.

Wolkstein, Diane, retold by. **The Red Lion: A Tale of Ancient Persia.**
    Illus. Ed Young. Thomas Y. Crowell, 1977. 7–10.

Prince Azged, afraid to fight the fierce Red Lion as dictated by
tradition, runs away. Only after he finds other lions awaiting him
wherever he goes does he realize that it is his fear that makes the
beasts ferocious. This ancient Persian tale has a lesson for today's
children.

Young, Ed, adapter (retold by Leslie Bonnet). **The Terrible Nung Gwama:
    A Chinese Folktale.** Illus. by adapter. William Collins Publishers,
    1978. 7–9.

As she carries a gift of cakes to her parents, a poor young woman
meets a terrible monster. Nung Gwama delights in eating humans
and promises to visit her that evening. Taking the suggestions of
peddlers, she outwits the monster. A cumulative tale beautifully illustrated with fan-shaped pictures.

Zemach, Margot, retold by. **It Could Always Be Worse: A Yiddish Folk-
    tale.** Illus. by reteller. Farrar, Straus & Giroux, 1976. 4–7.

A distraught man seeks help from the Rabbi to deal with his large
quarrelsome family. When he follows the surprising advice and
brings the animals and relatives inside the house, things get so
chaotic that he wishes only to return to normal. Funny illustrations
enliven this familiar Yiddish folktale. 1978 Caldecott Honor Book.

Myths and Legends

Anderson, Lonzo. **Arion and the Dolphins.** Illus. Adrienne Adams. Charles
    Scribner's Sons, 1978. 6–9.

Arion's life is threatened because of his huge winnings in a musical
contest. On the return voyage he leaps from the boat where his
friends, the dolphins, change the course of the story. Simply retold,

the story can be read independently. The sea is beautifully illustrated in blues and greens.

Aylesworth, Thomas G. **The Story of Dragons and Other Monsters.** McGraw-Hill, 1980. 8–12.

Fascinating bits of lore about monsters and dragons from Greek, Roman, Norse, and Egyptian mythology. Black and white photos and reproductions of old prints and engravings along with good type size overcome some possible vocabulary obstacles poor readers might encounter. Includes an index and a listing of other books about monsters.

Aylesworth, Thomas G. **The Story of Vampires.** McGraw-Hill, 1977. 10–12.

Vampire lore from different parts of the world includes material from ancient Greece to the twentieth century, including information on Vlad Tepes and Countess Elizabeth Bathory, bloody historical figures who were thought to be vampires by superstitious people. Numerous photographs and old prints illustrate the text.

Barth, Edna, retold by. **Balder and the Mistletoe: A Story for the Winter Holidays.** Illus. Richard Cuffari. Seabury Press, 1979. 10–12.

Balder, god of light and joy, was the favorite of all Norse gods and goddesses. All was well until he was awakened by a horrifying dream of his own death. His mother, Frigga, and the others tried to protect him. Explanation of the symbolic mistletoe is given. Well illustrated.

Bernstein, Margery, and Janet Kobrin, retold by. **The First Morning: An African Myth.** Illus. Enid Warner Romanek. Charles Scribner's Sons, 1976. 7–10.

Before there was light in the world, all the animals bumped into each other and continually fell into holes. This intriguing African tale relates how the mouse, the spider, and the fly brought back light from the sky.

Bernstein, Margery, and Janet Kobrin, retold by. **The Summer Maker.** Illus. Anne Burgess. Charles Scribner's Sons, 1977. 6–9.

This easy-to-read text relates how Otter, Beaver, Wolverine, Lynx, and Bear journeyed in search of summer and found it, although Bear was unable to return and still remains in the sky. Black and white pen sketches accompany each text page. A good retelling of an Ojibway Indian myth.

Blumberg, Rhoda. **The Truth about Dragons.** Illus. Murray Tinkelman. Four Winds Press, 1980. 8–12.

This examination of dragon lore fascinates the reader with its facts concerning both the western dragon and the eastern dragon. The differences between the two are striking and are enhanced by full-page, black and white illustrations. For dragon lovers of all ages.

Brodsky, Beverly. **Jonah: An Old Testament Story.** J. B. Lippincott, 1977. 7-10.

Jonah hears a call from God but does not obey him. When he tries to escape his duty, he is shipwrecked and swallowed by a whale. There he repents. After he is saved, he follows God's command but cannot resist questioning God's judgment. Bold drawings make this an outstanding book.

Brown, Dee, retold by. **Tepee Tales of the American Indian.** Illus. Louis Mofsie. Holt, Rinehart and Winston, 1979. 8-11.

This collection of memory stories of North American Indians is written in the language of a modern-day storyteller. Included are legends relating different groups' first contacts with white people.

Brown, Marcia. **The Blue Jackal.** Charles Scribner's Sons, 1977. 7-10.

In this tale from India's *The Panchatantra,* Fierce-Howl, the jackal, runs from a pack of dogs and hides in a vat of indigo. The other animals are fearful of this strange blue animal and make him their king. When he howls like a jackal, his true identity is discovered. Handsome prints.

Campbell, Maria. **Little Badger and the Fire Spirit.** Illus. David Maclagan. McClelland and Stewart, 1977. 8-12.

Ahsinee, an eight-year-old Indian girl, gets to spend the summer with her grandparents in present-day Alberta, Canada. Her grandfather tells her the ancient story of how Little Badger, a blind Indian boy, brings fire to the human race. Strong, vivid illustrations give power to the classic legend.

Chaikin, Miriam. **The Seventh Day: The Story of the Jewish Sabbath.** Illus. David Frampton. Doubleday, 1980. 8-12.

The story of the Jewish Sabbath is beautifully explained in the text and artistic black and white woodcuts. It is a joyous time for celebration. Worries and cares are set aside to praise God. An excellent book for parents to use with children.

Coatsworth, Emerson, and David Coatsworth, compilers. **The Adventures of Nanabush: Ojibway Indian Stories.** Illus. Francis Kagige. Atheneum, 1980. 7-10.

Nanabush is one of the most powerful spirits of the Ojibway Indians. He uses his magic and trickery to create much mischief in all sixteen of these stories, many of which are *pourquoi* tales. Handsomely illustrated in stylized full-color drawings; a beautifully designed book.

Cohen, Barbara. **The Binding of Isaac.** Illus. Charles Mikolaycak. Lothrop, Lee & Shepard Books, 1978. 7–10.

Isaac's grandchildren gather around him to listen to a story. He tells them of the time God told his father Abraham to offer him, Isaac, as a sacrifice. Told from the point of view of a person remembering a frightening childhood event. Full-page color illustrations.

de Paola, Tomie, retold by. **The Clown of God.** Illus. by reteller. Harcourt Brace Jovanovich, 1978. 7–10.

An old Italian legend tells of the traveling juggler who offered his gift of talent before the statue of the Christ Child on Christmas Eve, and of the miracle that happened. The beauty and artistry of the watercolor illustrations enhance the authenticity by showing early Renaissance life and scenery.

de Wit, Dorothy, editor. **The Talking Stone: An Anthology of Native American Tales and Legends.** Illus. Donald Crews. Greenwillow Books, 1979. 9–12.

Tales from the Native Americans were told after the season's work was finished, when people relaxed together. The time to tell stories was regulated by beliefs and customs. These twenty-seven stories reflect the culture before and after European influence. They represent nine geographic regions of North America.

Edwards, David L., adapter. **The Children's Bible from the Good News Bible in Today's English Version.** Illus. Guido Bertello. William Collins Publishers, 1978. 8–up.

Written in a simple and direct style, the meaning of the stories from the Old and New Testaments is made clear to the young reader. Many colorful and appealing illustrations accompany the text. Map and index are included. A treasure to be shared with many.

Erdoes, Richard, translator and editor. **The Sound of Flutes and Other Indian Legends.** Illus. Paul Goble. Pantheon Books, 1976. 10–up.

This collection of North American Plains Indian tales, edited and transcribed over a twenty-five-year period, represents a great oral tradition. In their present format, the legends provide us with valuable insights into Native American life. The vibrant illustrations complement the text.

Farmer, Penelope, compiler and editor. **Beginnings: Creation Myths of the World.** Illus. Antonio Frasconi. Atheneum, 1979. 10–up.

Over eighty creation stories and poems from many parts of the world make up this collection. Materials are grouped under the headings of earth, man, flood, fire, death, food plants, and the end of the world. Strong woodcuts capture the intensity of the areas. Includes source list and bibliography for further study.

Fregosi, Claudia, adapter. **Snow Maiden.** Illus. by adapter. Prentice-Hall, 1979. 6–9.

A Russian adaptation of the Greek myth of Persephone. Lovely Snow Maiden is allowed by her parents to go to live on the earth, but only after she promises to stay out of sunlight and never to let her heart be warmed by love. Warm, folk art illustrations.

Fritz, Jean. **Brendan the Navigator: A History Mystery about the Discovery of America.** Illus. Enrico Arno. Coward, McCann & Geoghegan, 1979. 7–10.

Unusual and breathtaking incidents occur the day of St. Brendan's birth and continue to take place throughout his life. His nephew's successful voyage spurs him on to build his own ship and voyage to the New World. Grey-blue stylized drawings accentuated with black illustrate this lighthearted story.

Goble, Paul. **The Gift of the Sacred Dog.** Illus. by author. Bradbury Press, 1980. 7–10.

This legend of Indians of the Great Plains tells of the gift of the horse. When his people could find no buffalo and were starving, a boy climbed high on the mountain and prayed to the Great Spirit. The horse, Sacred Dog, was the answer to his prayers. Outstanding illustrations.

Haley, Gail E. **The Green Man.** Illus. by author. Charles Scribner's Sons, 1979. 7–10.

Claude, the spoiled son of a wealthy squire, ridicules others' beliefs, such as the peasants' tales of the Green Man who protects them and their crops. Claude becomes lost while hunting and is forced to survive alone, taking on the role of the Green Man. Richly colored illustrations capture the texture and mood of medieval tapestries.

Hall, Lynn. **Dog of the Bondi Castle.** Follett Publishing, 1979. 12–up.

Aubry, a young knight, is adored by Isabelle, favored by his liege, and has the steadfast devotion of his dog, Griffon. His good fortune arouses the envy of Richard Mecaire. Based on a legend and set in fourteenth-century France, this tale recounts how Isabelle and Griffon see that justice is done.

Harris, Christie. **Mouse Woman and the Mischief-Makers.** Illus. Douglas Tait. Atheneum, 1977. 8–12.

Seven legends of humor and horror, based on Pacific Northwest Indian lore, feature a tiny narnauk, a supernatural being that watches for those who disturb the proper order of things. She becomes involved in the mischief makers' inherent problems and always comes up with just solutions. Stark black and white illustrations. Companion books are *Mouse Woman and the Muddleheads* and *Mouse Woman and the Vanished Princesses.*

Highwater, Jamake. **Anpao: An American Indian Odyssey.** Illus. Fritz Scholder. J. B. Lippincott, 1977. 12–up.

The author calls his story "an alternative vision of the world, and an alternative process of history," yet it reads like a glorious epic tale as one man journeys through the history of his people. Traditional North American Indian tales are woven into one story as Anpao grows through his heritage to manhood. 1978 Newbery Honor Book.

Jagendorf, M. A. **Stories and Lore of the Zodiac.** Illus. Anne Bevans. Vanguard Press, 1977. 8–12.

In Polynesia, they are called the Seven Sisters. The Onondagas see them as dancing children. We call them the Pleiades, part of the constellation Taurus. A master storyteller has collected zodiacal lore from all over the world and accompanied it with both astronomical and astrological information. Stylized black and white drawings enhance the text.

Leach, Maria. **The Lion Sneezed: Folktales and Myths of the Cat.** Illus. Helen Siegl. Thomas Y. Crowell, 1977. 8–12.

How did the cat come to be? According to folklorists it was sneezed from a lion on Noah's ark. This collection includes humorous tales (some dating back centuries) about cats from various countries. The scholarly introduction supplies an excellent background. Black and white illustrations.

Leech, Jay, and Zane Spencer. **Moon of the Big-Dog.** Illus. Mamoru Funai. Thomas Y. Crowell, 1980. 7–10.

At the trading fair, all the people of the plains come together to exchange goods. When three Sioux hunters who do the trading for their people see horses for the first time, they must have them for their people. A retelling of the legend of how the Brule Indians got their name.

Lorimer, Lawrence T., retold by. **Noah's Ark.** Illus. Charles E. Martin. Random House, 1978. All ages.

Selected portions of the Old Testament account of Noah and the Great Flood. The colorful illustrations make clear to the youngest reader the size of the ark, both inside and out, and the magnitude of the flood.

Lurie, Alison, retold by. **The Heavenly Zoo: Legends and Tales of the Stars.** Illus. Monika Beisner. Farrar, Straus & Giroux, 1979. 8–12.

Tales from all corners of the earth show the intriguing differences and surprising similarities among the explanations people have

invented for the "pictures in the sky," the Great Bear, the Great
Dog, the Bull, the Lion, and eleven other constellations. Lively and
literate, with outstanding full-color illustrations.

McDermott, Beverly Brodsky. **The Golem: A Jewish Legend.** Illus. by
author. J. B. Lippincott, 1976. 8–12.

A powerful retelling of the legend of the Golem, the man-like
monster created from clay by Rabbi Lev to protect the Jews of
the ghetto. When it starts destroying the enemy, it cannot stop,
and must be returned to clay. Large, vivid, sometimes terrifying
illustrations, filled with symbolism. Not for the tender-minded. 1977
Caldecott Honor Book.

McDermott, Gerald, retold by. **The Knight of the Lion.** Illus. by reteller.
Four Winds Press, 1979. 8–12.

Young Gawain sets out from King Arthur's court on a quest for
glory. Along his path are adventure, danger, love, failure, and, at
last, success as Knight of the Lion. This skillful retelling of an ancient
tale is strengthened by the bold black and white illustrations.

McDermott, Gerald. **Sun Flight.** Four Winds Press, 1980. All ages.

The Greek myth of Daedalus and Icarus is retold with simple text
and exquisite illustrations. Daedalus makes wax wings so that he
and his son Icarus can escape from the Labyrinth of King Minos of
Crete, but Icarus ignores his father's warning about the wings.

McDermott, Gerald, retold by. **The Voyage of Osiris: A Myth of Ancient
Egypt.** Illus. by reteller. E. P. Dutton, 1977. 10–up.

This ancient myth could easily be followed from the brilliant, luminous illustrations. Through the trickery of his evil brother, Osiris is
entrapped in a large coffer and cast into the Nile. The love and
devotion of his wife Isis and the compassion of Ra restore him to
life.

McKinley, Robin. **Beauty: A Retelling of the Story of Beauty & the Beast.**
Harper & Row, Publishers, 1978. 12–up.

A superb retelling of the old tale of enchantment, this is a fascinating, skillfully written novel. Characterizations of depth and sensitivity, warm family relationships, and a love story of developing
strength and sensuousness all contribute to the reader's pleasure. The
author's sense of humor and unique concept of enchanted castles are
an added bonus!

Miles, Bernard. **Robin Hood: His Life and Legend.** Illus. Victor G.
Ambrus. Rand McNally, 1979. 10–up.

Historical background of England is woven throughout this excellent
modern version of the Robin Hood story. The language is easy to
understand and very descriptive. Slightly different twists to events

add to the episodes with a religious tone in some of the references. Colorful, exciting illustrations and endpaper maps.

Naden, C. J. **Jason and the Golden Fleece.** Illus. Robert Baxter. Troll Associates, 1981. 7–10.

Jason is presented as a strong and fearless god living on earth among humans, accomplishing heroic tasks. This tale and three others are part of a series: *Pegasus the Winged Horse, Perseus and Medusa,* and *Theseus and the Minotaur.* All four books have a similar appealing format with an interesting, easy-to-read content, making mythology attractive and understandable. The colorful illustrations are meaningful and extend the stories. Helpful pronunciation keys are supplied.

Prather, Ray. **The Ostrich Girl.** Charles Scribner's Sons, 1978. 7–10.

Based on a Kenyan legend, this is the story of an infant found under a tree who first learns of her origin from the village children. Oster searches for her true identity and becomes involved with a witch, dwarf, and giant. At last she returns to her loving parents.

Reeves, James, retold by. **The Shadow of the Hawk and Other Stories by Marie de France.** Illus. Anne Dalton. Seabury Press, 1977. 12–up.

Marie de France was a twelfth-century poet whose verse legends are exciting stories of courtly love and adventure during the Middle Ages. Reeves has maintained the vivid language of these spoken tales, which reflect their Arthurian and Celtic sources. The book is useful for studying literature of the medieval period.

Rose, Anne, adapter. **Spider in the Sky.** Illus. Gail Owens. Harper & Row, Publishers, 1978. 6–9.

An American Indian *pourquoi* tale. All the animals in the forest agree that heat and light would make their lives more comfortable. Several animals try to bring back a piece of the sun. All fail and are left with visible effects of their attempts. The title identifies the successful creature.

San Souci, Robert, adapter. **The Legend of Scarface: A Blackfeet Indian Tale.** Illus. Daniel San Souci. Doubleday, 1978. 6–9.

He is poor, he has a facial scar, and he is taunted by the other braves. Scarface loves Singing Rain and she loves him, but she has promised the Sun never to wed. Scarface faces danger when he attempts to get Singing Rain released from her vow. Twelve exquisite paintings catch the action.

Silverthorne, Elizabeth. **I, Heracles.** Illus. Billie Jean Osborne. Abingdon Press, 1978. 10–12.

The first-person account of the twelve exciting tasks assigned to Heracles by his jealous cousin permits the reader to be close at hand during the hero's fantastic accomplishments. Two maps identify the places of his great feats. An excellent introduction to Greek mythology.

Skurzynski, Gloria. **What Happened in Hamelin.** Four Winds Press, 1979. 10–up.

Fourteen-year-old Geist, a mistreated baker's assistant, meets the Pied Piper in 1284 and is promised a new life in a faraway place. His gripping adventures include the children's rat massacre, the festival of ergot buns, and the exodus to the Piper's music. Geist, realizing the children's fate, does not go and has to live with the knowledge of his involvement in the Piper's plot.

Spier, Peter, translator. **Noah's Ark.** Illus. by translator. Doubleday, 1977. All ages.

Jacobus Revius' poem, "The Flood," introduces this version of the Bible story. Spier's illustrations recording the events inside and the appointments of the ark are visual delights. Aside from the poem, the book is wordless. 1978 Caldecott Award.

Sutcliff, Rosemary. **The Light beyond the Forest: The Quest for the Holy Grail.** E. P. Dutton, 1979. 12–up.

This is a retelling of that section of the romance of King Arthur that speaks of Sir Galahad and the search for the Holy Grail, the final quest of the knights of the Round Table. The author's language reflects superbly the early medieval period without sacrificing lucidity, a real gift to the reader.

Synge, Ursula. **The Giant at the Ford and Other Legends of the Saints.** Illus. Shirley Felts. Atheneum, 1980. 8–12.

The lives of a number of saints are told in a way that is in turn funny, exciting, and moving. Along with the adventures of such well-known saints as Saint Christopher and Saint George are lesser known saints such as Mochae, who listened to a bird sing and let 150 years slip by! Inspiring and enjoyable.

van der Land, Spike, retold by. **Stories from the Bible.** Illus. Bert Bouman. William B. Eerdmans Publishing, 1979. 8–12.

Bible stories are told in modern language and style. Each one is introduced by a short paragraph to orient the reader to the story or to relate it to the reader in the modern context. Pictures are full page and well detailed.

Wildsmith, Brian. **The True Cross.** Oxford University Press, 1977. 7–10.

Legend tells that the cross upon which Christ died descended from a sprig of the Tree of Life in the Garden of Paradise. Centuries later St. Helena, the mother of Constantine, set out to find the true cross.

Williams, Jay. **The Surprising Things Maui Did.** Illus. Charles Mikolaycak. Four Winds Press, 1979. 6–9.

This beautiful Hawaiian myth about Maui and his wonderful gifts is told in a slow, unhurried manner so that the extraordinary, richly colored illustrations can be enjoyed. Incorporation in a Polynesian unit would add interest and appreciation of another culture.

Wilson, Karen, retold by. **Agha the Terrible Demon.** Illus. Marie Thérèse Dubois. Bala Books, 1977. 7–10.

This story from Hindu mythology tells of Krishna as a young boy who takes part in the usual child play with his young friends. When Agha, the terrible demon, attempts to swallow all the children, Krishna outwits him and saves his friends. Brilliantly colored stylistic illustrations.

Yellow Robe, Rosebud, retold by. **Tonweya and the Eagles and Other Lakota Indian Tales.** Illus. Jerry Pinkney. Dial Press, 1979. 6–9.

Chano is the name of a real-life Indian boy who was educated during his teens in a white man's school, and treasured the ancient stories of his people, the Lakota (Sioux) Indians. Chano's daughter retells these authentic animal tales. Beautifully and authentically illustrated.

Nursery Rhymes

Ahlberg, Janet, and Allan Ahlberg. **Each Peach Pear Plum: An 'I Spy' Story.** Viking Press, 1978. 3–5.

Familiar nursery figures like Jack and Jill and Mother Hubbard are appealingly illustrated in this read-aloud book. Youngsters will enjoy finding the hidden figures tucked throughout the pictures and delight in the continuity of the rhyme from page to page. All the hidden figures appear in the last illustration.

Blegvad, Erik, retold by. **Burnie's Hill: A Traditional Rhyme.** Illus. by reteller. Atheneum, 1977. 4–7.

The question-and-answer format of the traditional rhyme is extended and enhanced by illustrations that portray gradual seasonal changes beginning with summer and culminating in spring. The rhyme is cumulative without the familiar repetitive pattern.

Fiddle-I-Fee: A Traditional American Chant. Illus. Diane Stanley. Little, Brown, 1979. 3–5.

The traditional American chant about a young girl giving a tea party for her animal friends is delightfully illustrated. The cumulative rhyme will amuse young readers.

If Wishes Were Horses and Other Rhymes. Illus. Susan Jeffers. E. P. Dutton, 1979. 3–7.

A collection of well-known rhymes about horses illustrated with lively, colorful, full-page pictures. Beginning readers and very young children will enjoy both the pictures and the rhymes.

Kessler, Leonard. **Hey Diddle Diddle.** Garrard Publishing, 1980. 5–8.

The old nursery rhyme has been expanded to include some silly new characters such as, "Hey diddle doodle, the goat ate some noodles," and now ends with, "The men on the moon were very surprised when the cow flew away on a spoon!" An easy-to-read book.

Livermore, Elaine. **Three Little Kittens Lost Their Mittens.** Illus. by author. Houghton Mifflin, 1979. 4–7.

This new rhyming version of a familiar story gets the reader involved in a clever way. The youngster is asked to help find the mittens by going back and looking for them hidden among the black and yellow sketches. Fun and helpful for visual discrimination.

Lobel, Arnold, compiler. **Gregory Griggs and Other Nursery Rhyme People.** Illus. by compiler. Greenwillow Books, 1978. 4–7.

Soft pastel illustrations make the humorous, less-known nursery characters come to life. There's Gregory Griggs with his twenty-seven different wigs, Little Miss Tuckett, Giant Jim, Punch and Judy, and thirty-two other entertaining rhymes. Table of contents and an interesting afterword that explains the author's choices.

Marshall, James. **James Marshall's Mother Goose.** Farrar, Straus & Giroux, 1979. 3–7.

Familiar and less well-known nursery rhymes are included in this collection. The unique illustrations give these Mother Goose verses a fresh and humorous look.

Tarrant, Margaret, compiler. **Nursery Rhymes.** Thomas Y. Crowell, 1978. 4–7.

Tarrant first illustrated Mother Goose rhymes over sixty years ago. This reissue has the quaint appeal of the old-fashioned characters and muted colors and is as charming for today's young children as it was for their grandparents.

Tripp, Wallace, compiler. **Granfa' Grig Had a Pig and Other Rhymes without Reason from Mother Goose.** Illus. by compiler. Little, Brown, 1976. 4–7.

A lively, colorful, and earthy collection of Mother Goose rhymes, in which most of the characters are animals. Miss Muffett, for example, is a rabbit, and Old King Cole a bear. Includes old favorites and some authentic but unfamiliar verses.

Riddles

Aardema, Verna. **Ji-Nongo-Nongo Means Riddles.** Illus. Jerry Pinkney. Four Winds Press, 1978. 8–12.

This book is delightful for riddle-loving children, but its deeper value lies in the insights into African culture it provides. Eleven African tribes are represented. Through the riddles one can see what is valued and enjoyed in another culture. Beautifully detailed sepia pencil drawings enrich the cultural understandings.

Schwartz, Alvin, compiler. **Flapdoodle: Pure Nonsense from American Folklore.** Illus. John O'Brien. J. B. Lippincott, 1980. 8–12.

This collection of outrageous puns, riddles, spoonerisms, sight gags, and just pure nonsense draws on sources from folklore archives to recent issues of *Boys' Life,* and is sure to tickle the funny bones of jokesters of all ages. Copious notes, extensive bibliography, and clever illustrations.

Schwartz, Alvin. **Ten Copycats in a Boat and Other Riddles.** Illus. Marc Simont. Harper & Row, Publishers, 1980. 6–9.

Here is a collection of old and not-so-old riddles for the beginning reader selected from folklore around the world. The humorous illustrations add to the fun.

Young, Ed, compiler. **High on a Hill: A Book of Chinese Riddles.** Illus. by compiler. William Collins Publishers, 1980. 8–12.

This collection of authentic Chinese riddles, printed in both Chinese and English, will intrigue riddle fans. Exquisite pencil drawings by the author enhance the text.

Additional Traditional Literature

Asbjørnsen, P. C., and J. E. Moe. *The Three Billy Goats Gruff.* Illus. Marcia Brown. Harcourt Brace Jovanovich, 1957. 4–8.
Belting, Natalia. *The Sun Is a Golden Earring.* Illus. Bernarda Bryson. Holt, Rinehart and Winston, 1962. 8–12.
Brown, Marcia. *Once a Mouse.* Charles Scribner's Sons, 1961. 5–8.
Bryson, Bernarda. *Gilgamesh: Man's First Story.* Holt, Rinehart and Winston, 1967. 6–11.
Chase, Richard. *Grandfather Tales.* Houghton Mifflin, 1948. 9–up.
Chase, Richard. *The Jack Tales.* Illus. Berkeley Williams, Jr. Houghton Mifflin, 1943. 8–12.
Colum, Padraic. *The Children's Homer: The Adventures of Odysseus and the Tales of Troy.* Illus. Willy Pogany. Macmillan Publishing, 1965. 10–12.
Courlander, Harold. *The Piece of Fire and Other Haitian Tales.* Illus. Beth Krush and Joe Krush. Harcourt Brace Jovanovich, 1964. 9–12.
Dayrell, Elphinstone. *Why the Sun and Moon Live in the Sky.* Illus. Blair Lent. Houghton Mifflin, 1968. 5–8.
Domanska, Janina. *The Turnip.* Macmillan Publishing, 1969. 5–9.

Graham, Lorenz. *God Wash the World and Start Again.* Illus. Clare R. Ross. Thomas Y. Crowell, 1971. 7–11.

Grimm Brothers. *King Grisly-Beard.* Translated by Edgar Taylor. Illus. Maurice Sendak. Farrar, Straus & Giroux, 1973. 6–10.

Grimm Brothers. *The Seven Ravens.* Illus. Felix Hoffman. Harcourt Brace Jovanovich, 1963. 5–8.

Grimm Brothers. *Snow White.* Translated by Paul Heins. Illus. Trina Schart Hyman. Little, Brown, 1974. 6–8.

Grimm Brothers. *Snow White and the Seven Dwarfs.* Translated by Randall Jarrell. Illus. Nancy Ekholm Burkert. Farrar, Straus & Giroux, 1972. 6–12.

Hodges, Margaret. *The Wave.* Illus. Blair Lent. Houghton Mifflin, 1964. 6–10.

Hogrogian, Nonny. *One Fine Day.* Macmillan Publishing, 1971. 5–8.

Jameson, Cynthia. *The Clay Pot Boy.* Illus. Arnold Lobel. Coward, McCann & Geoghegan, 1973. 5–8.

Kent, Jack. *The Fat Cat: A Danish Folktale.* Parents Magazine Press, 1971. 5–8.

La Fontaine, Jean de. *The North Wind and the Sun.* Illus. Brian Wildsmith. Franklin Watts, 1963. 4–8.

McDermott, Gerald. *Anansi the Spider.* Holt, Rinehart and Winston, 1972. 4–8.

Mosel, Arlene. *The Funny Little Woman.* Illus. Blair Lent. E. P. Dutton, 1972. 4–8.

Mosel, Arlene. *Tikki Tikki Tembo.* Illus. Blair Lent. Holt, Rinehart and Winston, 1968. 6–8.

Perrault, Charles. *Cinderella.* Illus. Marcia Brown. Charles Scribner's Sons, 1953. 5–9.

Pyle, Howard. *Story of King Arthur and His Knights.* Charles Scribner's Sons, 1903. 12–up.

Sherlock, Sir Philip. *Anansi, the Spider Man.* Illus. Marcia Brown. Thomas Y. Crowell, 1954. 9–up.

Singer, Isaac Bashevis. *Zlateh the Goat and Other Stories.* Illus. Maurice Sendak. Translated by the author and Elizabeth Shub. Harper & Row, Publishers, 1966. 6–12.

Sturton, Hugh. *Zomo the Rabbit.* Illus. Peter Warner. Atheneum, 1966. 8–up.

Yolen, Jane. *The Emperor and the Kite.* Illus. Ed Young. William Collins Publishers, 1967. 6–11.

Zemach, Harve. *Duffy and the Devil.* Illus. Margot Zemach. Farrar, Straus & Giroux, 1973. 8–up.

Modern Fantasy

Animals

Picture Books

Alexander, Martha. **I Sure Am Glad to See You, Blackboard Bear.** Dial Press, 1976. 4–7.

Faithful Blackboard Bear again comes to the rescue of his young friend Anthony when a neighborhood bully takes his ice-cream cone. Illustrations perceptively capture a small child's frustrations. Other Blackboard Bear stories relate to a small child's sensibilities. (Picture book)

Allamand, Pascale (translator Elizabeth Watson Taylor). **The Animals Who Changed Their Colors.** Lothrop, Lee & Shepard Books, 1979. 6–9.

A polar bear, whale, tortoise, and two crocodiles want to be as colorful as the parrot. After they have painted themselves different colors, the parrot points out that they will be very conspicuous and easy prey for their enemies. They swim home and wash away the paint. (Picture book)

Asch, Frank. **The Last Puppy.** Prentice-Hall, 1980. 3–7.

The last of Momma's nine puppies to be born is the last in everything. When the owners decide to sell the puppies, he is afraid he will be the last to be chosen. Soft color illustrations add to the poignant text. (Picture book)

Asch, Frank. **MacGooses' Grocery.** Illus. James Marshall. Dial Press, 1978. 4–7.

This easy-to-read story finds the MacGoose family getting tired of watching their grocery store and their new goose egg, so the egg looks after himself. Illustrations add greatly to the silliness of the egg's adventures, as he impatiently waits to become a new member of the growing goose family. (Picture book)

Asch, Frank. **Moon Bear.** Charles Scribner's Sons, 1978. 4–7.

Bear loves the moon. He is very upset when he sees the moon getting thinner and thinner. How Bear tries to help save the moon and what he finally discovers make a good read-aloud story. The illustrations catch the mood of Bear's concern. (Picture book)

Augarde, Steve. **Pig.** Bradbury Press, 1977. 5–8.

A funny, impossible story of barnyard life. All the animals wonder what Pig's job is until one day he makes an unexpected contribution to their well-being. Color illustrations add zest and humor. Young children will enjoy this as a read-aloud story. (Picture book)

Bach, Alice. **The Most Delicious Camping Trip Ever.** Illus. Steven Kellogg. Harper & Row, Publishers, 1976. 5–8.

When the twin bears prepare for an overnight outing with Aunt Bear, Ronald comes up with an idea that accommodates his scientific interests and Oliver's love of food. Anticipating the "worst hike in history," they are surprised how Aunt Bear provides the comforts of home. Brown and white illustrations. (Picture book)

Baker, Alan. **Benjamin and the Box.** Illus. by author. J. B. Lippincott, 1977. 3–5.

Ingenious Benjamin Hamster attempts to open a padlocked box with a screwdriver, a hammer, magic, and finally dynamite. The story ends with Benjamin discovering that the box contains a delightful surprise. Detailed and action-filled illustrations make the determined hamster a hit. (Picture book)

Baker, Alan. **Benjamin Bounces Back.** Illus. by author. J. B. Lippincott, 1978. 4–7.

Benjamin, a nearsighted hamster, cannot read a "no entry" sign on a door and unexpectedly takes a joy ride through a fun house. Few words and detailed colorful illustrations make this a good read-aloud book for preschoolers. (Picture book)

Berends, Polly Berrien. **Ladybug and Dog and the Night Walk.** Illus. Cyndy Szekeres. Random House, 1980. 4–7.

This is a gentle story of a dog and a ladybug who take Ladybug's seven cousins for a night nature walk on the farm. They enjoy their nighttime discoveries until one ladybug is lost. Captivating illustrations blend with this adventure for the young listener. (Picture book)

Barrett, John M. **Oscar the Selfish Octopus.** Illus. Joe Servello. Human Sciences Press, 1978. 4–7.

A modern morality tale. When self-centered and therefore lonely Oscar is caught inside the mouth of a shark, he is rescued by two small starfish who also deliver a sermon on being selfish. Oscar learns that his arms can be used to hug others and not just himself. (Picture book)

Berenstain, Stan, and Jan Berenstain. **The Berenstain Bears and the Missing Dinosaur Bone.** Beginner Books, 1980. 6–9.

The Bear Detectives are on a case to find the missing dinosaur bone before the Bear Museum opens. They find it but not without the help of hound dog. An easy-to-read book in rhyme. (Picture book)

Berger, Terry, adapter. **The Turtles' Picnic and Other Nonsense Stories.** Illus. Erkki Alanen. Crown Publishers, 1977. 6–9.

Three humorous short stories for beginning readers include a suspicious baby turtle who doesn't trust his parents, a fussy dog who wants his cake baked just so, and a proud, young lion who criticizes every animal he meets until the mouse leaves him speechless. Hilarious color illustrations. (Picture book)

Berson, Harold. **Truffles for Lunch.** Macmillan Publishing, 1980. 6–9.

An unhappy pig wishes to be like other animals. Quite unexpectedly he meets a wizard who can grant his wishes. Being a lion isn't everything he thought it would be, but a happy surprise awaits him. Amusing pen sketches with exaggerated expressions carry the action. Good for independent reading. (Picture book)

Bohdal, Susi. **Tom Cat.** Doubleday, 1977. 4–7.

Understanding the language of other animals makes Tom Cat quite remarkable. He's labeled peculiar by fellow cats because he doesn't hunt. After visiting with a wise old hen, he cleverly outwits his friends and becomes accepted. Outstanding black and white etchings enrich the text. (Picture book)

Bond, Michael. **Olga Carries On.** Illus. Hans Helweg. Hastings House, Publishers, 1979. 6–9.

Olga, a wiry guinea pig, makes things happen in her own backyard in nine episodic stories. She speaks French, sounds a fire alarm, and enjoys telling tall tales to Noel the cat, Graham the tortoise, and Fangio the hedgehog. Humorous illustrations provide delightful entertainment. (Picture book)

Bond, Michael. **Paddington at the Seaside.** Illus. Fred Banbery. Random House, 1978. 5–7.

When Paddington visits the seashore, exciting things happen for the whole family. Punch and Judy shows need to be explained to the lovable bear. A good introduction to the harder series of Paddington Books. (Picture book)

Boynton, Sandra. **Hester in the Wild.** Harper & Row, Publishers, 1979. 4–7.

Hester, the pig, sets off on a camping trip only to face a variety of problems: a hole in her canoe, a hole in her tent, a rainstorm, and an invasion of gophers! Hester approaches each problem with creativity and aplomb. The lively illustrations add to the fun. (Picture book)

Brandenberg, Franz. **Nice New Neighbors.** Illus. Aliki. Greenwillow Books, 1977. 6–8.

The Fieldmouse children are having trouble making friends with their new neighbors. Discouraged at first, they soon create their own fun and the tables are turned. A read-alone book. (Picture book)

Brandenberg, Franz. **Six New Students.** Illus. Aliki. Greenwillow Books, 1978. 6–8.

It's the first day of school and the six little Fieldmice get ready for the big day. Little first-grader Ferdinand isn't so sure he's going to like it. Who wants arithmetic, calligraphy, botany, art, and physical education? A read-alone book with appealing pink and green pen illustrations. (Picture book)

Brown, Marc. **Arthur's Nose.** Little, Brown, 1976. 4–7.

Arthur, an aardvark, decides to change his problem nose, which stops up, gets red, and makes him feel unaccepted by classmates. After trying many other kinds of noses, he makes a surprising decision. This amusingly illustrated book is easy to read. Good for discussion of self-acceptance. (Picture book)

Brown, Margaret Wise. **Fox Eyes.** Illus. Garth Williams. Pantheon Books, 1977. 4–7.

A sly fox steals about the forest spying on the animals to obtain their secrets. Along the way he encounters opossums, rabbits, bears, tree toads, and children. His sneeze, "Whiskerchew," makes his presence known. Unaware of the commotion he is causing, he cozily falls asleep. Good for reading aloud. (Picture book)

Brown, Palmer. **Hickory.** Harper & Row, Publishers, 1978. 6–9.

Hickory, a mouse, leaves the security of his family home to build his own home in the meadow. Lonely at first, he soon develops a close friendship with a grasshopper. As winter approaches, he realizes that he will soon lose his friend. Soft illustrations complement the warm mood of the story. (Picture book)

Browne, Anthony. **Bear Hunt.** Atheneum, 1980. 3–5.

An unsuspecting little bear goes for a walk in the forest. Hunters, wild animals, and even capture await him, but he escapes because of the little pencil he carries with him. Colored, stylized illustrations complement the story. (Picture book)

Burningham, John. **The Shopping Basket.** Thomas Y. Crowell, 1980. 4–7.

Steven is sent to the store to buy six eggs, five bananas, four apples, three oranges, two doughnuts, and a package of crisps. He gets to the store, but coming home is quite difficult. Strange animals meet him at every turn, but Steven is clever. Amusing, colored, cartoonlike illustrations. (Picture book)

Calhoun, Mary. **Cross-Country Cat.** Illus. Erick Ingraham. William Morrow, 1979. 6–9.

A spunky cat, Henry, is using his unusual skill of walking on his hind legs when the family inadvertently leaves him behind at the ski cabin. He wears the cross-country skis made especially for him and catches up with the family as they are searching for him. Outstanding illustrations. (Picture book)

Carle, Eric. **The Grouchy Ladybug.** Thomas Y. Crowell, 1977. 6–9.

Bright illustrations and half-pages show a ladybug's pursuit of someone to fight. Each challenge is countered with the ladybug's sneer, "Oh, you're not big enough." After meeting progressively larger animals, the bug meets a whale who slaps her back to her starting point, a leaf she now shares willingly. (Picture book)

Carlson, Natalie Savage. **Runaway Marie Louise.** Illus. Jose Aruego and Ariane Dewey. Charles Scribner's Sons, 1977. 4–7.

When Marie Louise, a little brown mongoose, is punished for being naughty, she decides to run away and find a new home. To her dismay, no other mother wants her. She finally finds a nice lady who loves her, none other than her own mother. (Picture book)

Carlson, Natalie Savage. **Time for the White Egret.** Illus. Charles Robinson. Charles Scribner's Sons, 1978. 6–9.

The white cattle egret is impatient to find her own host cow to forage food for her. A wise cow tells her that time will solve her problem. The author presents a gentle lesson in patience in this story of the egret who is searching for time. (Picture book)

Carrick, Malcolm. **Today Is Shrew's Day.** Harper & Row, Publishers, 1978. 4–8.

A cheerful little shrew and a disgruntled bullfrog spend an adventurous day by the river. Children will identify with the small shrew who convinces the bullfrog that, despite her size, she can have worthwhile ideas. Real characterization is developed in the exchanges between the animals. An easy-to-read book. (Picture book)

Cartlidge, Michelle. **The Bears' Bazaar: A Story/Craft Book.** Lothrop, Lee & Shepard Books, 1979. 4–7.

Eric and Lucy Bear must make something to sell for the coming bazaar. With the guidance of Mother and Father Bear, they make mobiles, paint rocks, decorate boxes, and design a mural. Directions for the projects are given at the end of the book. Attractive illustrations weave together the story and crafts. (Picture book)

Cartlidge, Michelle. **Pippin and Pod.** Pantheon Books, 1978. 5–8.

The mouse world of Pippin and Pod makes for fascinating exploration. When the brothers wander off from their mother they find exciting adventures and just enough danger and fear to make them need to find her. Miniature, detailed illustrations create a pleasant illusion of a world populated by mice. (Picture book)

Cauley, Lorinda Bryan. **The Bake-Off.** G. P. Putnam's Sons, 1978. 5–7.

Before hibernating, the forest creatures hold an "Autumn Bake-Off" as a way of fattening up for winter. Parents compete and children brag on their folks' baking prowess. Conflict between vegetables and sugars might add spice to nutrition studies. Pen and ink drawings add charm. Prize-winning recipe included. (Picture book)

Chukovsky, Kornei (adapters William Jay Smith and Max Hayward). **The Telephone.** Illus. Blair Lent. Seymour Lawrence, 1977. 5–8.

An entertaining classic of nonsense verse by a popular Soviet children's poet. The amusing illustrations of the animals by Blair Lent portray their personalities delightfully. The animals constantly inconvenience the author with their calls about their problems. Visual clues add the right touch to this Russian treasure. (Picture book)

Clymer, Eleanor. **Horatio Solves a Mystery.** Illus. Robert Quackenbush. Atheneum, 1980. 4–7.

Horatio, the cat, lives alone with Mrs. Casey. He has a great life until one day things start to disappear. Mrs. Casey blames him until he solves the mystery of the next-door thief. Another tale is found in *Horatio Goes to the Country.* (Picture book)

Crowe, Robert L. **Tyler Toad and the Thunder.** Illus. Kay Chorao. E. P. Dutton, 1980. 4–7.

Tyler Toad is afraid of the impending thunder and hides in a hole. Other animals tell him their view of what thunder is, but Tyler refuses to believe them. When the thunder clap finally comes, Tyler follows all the other fearless animals into the hole! Charming full-color illustrations. (Picture book)

Crowley, Arthur. **Bonzo Beaver.** Illus. Annie Gusman. Houghton Mifflin, 1980. 5–8.

Older brother Boo Beaver doesn't like babysitting for his little brother, Bonzo, and he lets him know it. When Bonzo runs away, he meets Mrs. Grisley, who collaborates with him on a way to give Boo his comeuppance. Delightful illustrations enhance this rhymed story. (Picture book)

Dahl, Roald. **The Enormous Crocodile.** Illus. Quentin Blake. Alfred A. Knopf, 1978. All ages.

In spite of his secret plans and nasty tricks, Enormous Crocodile is foiled at every turn in his efforts to eat some juicy boys and girls. Humorous dialogue and delightful watercolors are enchanting. (Picture book)

Dauer, Rosamond. **Bullfrog and Gertrude Go Camping.** Illus. Byron Barton. Greenwillow Books, 1980. 4–7.

This is the third episode of Bullfrog's adventures. As Bullfrog and friend Gertrude are camping, they meet a lonely snake Itsa, whom they decide to adopt. This funny, easy-to-read story is complemented by bright illustrations. Other books are *Bullfrog Grows Up* and *Bullfrog Builds a House.* (Picture book)

Dauer, Rosamond. **Bullfrog Builds a House.** Illus. Byron Barton. Greenwillow Books, 1977. 6–8.

Bullfrog decides to build a home, but he isn't sure where to begin. His friend Gertrude offers suggestions and Bullfrog builds the house, but something is missing. Only Gertrude can supply the answer. Amusing, colored, cartoonlike illustrations in this read-alone book. (Picture book)

de Brunhoff, Laurent. **Babar's Mystery.** Random House, 1978. 5–8.

This twenty-fourth book of the Babar series proves to be as attractive and appealing as the previous stories. King Babar and Celeste are vacationing at Celesteville-on-the-Sea with their three children. One by one their belongings begin to disappear, and Babar discovers an ingenious plan. Cartoon drawings. (Picture book)

Delaney, Ned. **Rufus the Doofus.** Houghton Mifflin, 1978. 6–7.

Rufus, an energetic animal, attends school. Most of the time he is shunned, but he longs to be noticed. Through a freak accident when the teacher is out of the room, he rescues one of his classmates. (Picture book)

Delaney, Ned. **A Worm for Dinner.** Illus. by author. Houghton Mifflin, 1977. 5–8.

Mole and Bird are hungry at the same time and see the same worm. In the ensuing struggle and quarrel, the worm gets away. A big cooperative dinner effort almost results in a disaster and does result in lost appetites. The illustrations are bright, bold, and comical. (Picture book)

Delton, Judy. **Penny-Wise, Fun-Foolish.** Illus. Guilio Maestro. Crown Publishers, 1977. 6–9.

Ostrich clips coupons, saves string, and hoards her money so that she can travel to America with her friend Elephant. Tired of not having fun because his friend is so thrifty, Elephant tricks Ostrich into spending some of her money to enjoy life. A lesson on economy for early readers. (Picture book)

Delton, Judy. **Rabbit's New Rug.** Illus. Marc Brown, Parents Magazine
Press, 1979. 4–7.

Rabbit admires his beautiful new flowered rug. Fox, Owl, and
Raccoon come to see, but they aren't allowed to step on it so they
stay away. Rabbit gets lonely and decides to have a party. But what
about the rug? The ending is happy for all. Delightfully illustrated in
vibrant color. (Picture book)

Delton, Judy. **Three Friends Find Spring.** Illus. Guilio Maestro. Crown
Publishers, 1977. 5–8.

Rabbit and Squirrel try many ways to cheer Duck, who hates winter.
Nothing helps, including Easter eggs, bright yellow paint, and
shoveled snow. Finally it is Duck who finds a true sign of spring and
shares it with his friends. Full-color illustrations. (Picture book)

de Paola, Tomie. **Bill and Pete.** Illus. by author. G. P. Putnam's Sons,
1978. 5–8.

Bill, the crocodile, is very happy with his toothbrush friend, Pete,
and with school. When he has difficulty writing his name, Pete
comes to the rescue. Later, Bill is caught off guard and captured by
a crocodile collector, but cleverly frees himself. A read-aloud book
for preschoolers with humorous, colorful illustrations. (Picture book)

Dragonwagon, Crescent. **Your Owl Friend.** Illus. Ruth Bornstein. Harper
& Row, Publishers, 1977. 6–10.

An unusual story of the strong bond of friendship between a boy
and an owl. In lyrical language the owl and the boy share their
special feelings about the night. The pink and lavender chalk illustrations and the short length would make this a good book for reading
aloud. (Picture book)

Dumas, Philippe (adapter Michael Rosenbaum). **Caesar: Cock of the
Village.** Prentice-Hall, 1979. 6–9.

Caesar, a vivacious cock, leaves his post as a weathervane and goes
for a walk in the village. He lands in a church garden and is spied by
the priest who tries to capture him. In cumulative style he visits
many craftsmen who in turn join the crowd pursuing him. (Picture
book)

Dumas, Philippe (translator Michael Rosenbaum). **Lucie: A Tale of a
Donkey.** Prentice-Hall, 1977. 6–9.

Lucie, a naughty little donkey from the woods, befriends Louis, a
small boy, and goes to Paris with him. Many escapades, her father's
rescue of them, and a race lead Lucie to realize that there still are
some good people in the world. Illustrations add dimension to the
subtly humorous text. (Picture book)

Duvoisin, Roger. **Crocus.** Alfred A. Knopf, 1977. 4–7.

The animals of Sweetpea farm think highly of Crocus, the crocodile, until calamity strikes. His severe toothaches result in the dentist's decision to pull his four long rows of beautiful teeth. An unusual solution cheers him and restores his self-image. Children will enjoy listening to the story. (Picture book)

Duvoisin, Roger. **Snowy and Woody.** Alfred A. Knopf, 1979. 4–7.

Snowy, a polar bear, and Woody, a woodland bear, are befriended by Kitty, a gull. All three help each other when hunters come. The concept of protective coloring is clearly observable in the colored illustrations. (Picture book)

Freeman, Don. **Bearymore.** Illus. by author. Viking Press, 1976. 4–7.

Bearymore, a lovable circus bear, runs into trouble while trying to hibernate and plan a new circus act at the same time. He accidentally solves his problems and achieves spectacular success. Soft illustrations complement this high interest story. (Picture book)

Freschet, Berniece. **Bernard of Scotland Yard.** Illus. Gina Freschet. Charles Scribner's Sons, 1978. 7–10.

When Aunt Hilly tells the family that her son, Foster, is an Inspector with Scotland Yard, Bernard's mouse ears perk up. Off he goes to London where he joins in the search for a notorious jewel-thieving Mole Gang. Adventure and intrigue delight read-aloud audiences. (Picture book)

Freschet, Berniece. **Elephant & Friends.** Illus. Glen Rounds. Charles Scribner's Sons, 1977. 6–9.

Elephant and his friends must leave the desert because there is little food or water. After a perilous journey to the forest, they come upon their greatest enemy. The friends summon all that is left of their courage and determination. In a surprise move they frighten away the hunters. (Picture book)

Freschet, Berniece. **Five Fat Raccoons.** Illus. Irene Brady. Charles Scribner's Sons, 1980. 4–7.

Father, Mother, Little Sister, Little Brother, and Uncle Rocky all live in the same hollow tree. They are hungry all the time and spend hours hunting and fishing for food. Uncle Rocky is a bit daring and has a narrow escape. Beautiful sepia-colored illustrations with appeal. (Picture book)

Freschet, Berniece. **The Happy Dromedary.** Illus. Glen Rounds. Charles Scribner's Sons, 1977. 6–9.

When the camel chose to live in the desert, he soon found that he lacked certain physical characteristics, so he approached the Animal

King for help. The author creates a tale to explain why the camel
has a hump. Humorous and sensitive drawings show the camel's
changes. (Picture book)

Freschet, Berniece. **Where's Henrietta's Hen?** Illus. Lorinda Bryan Cauley.
G. P. Putnam's Sons, 1980. 3–6.

Henrietta's hen faithfully gives her an egg for her breakfast every
morning. But one day the hen disappears. Henrietta searches with
help from the other animals and finally finds not only her hen but
eight baby chicks. A simple counting tale that will delight younger
readers. (Picture book)

Gackenbach, Dick. **Crackle Gluck and the Sleeping Toad.** Seabury Press,
1979. 6–9.

The Glucks are strong believers in luckbringers, especially in a toad
that sleeps in their barn. It is pampered and fussed over until Crackle
Gluck, a perceptive young girl, sees the foolishness of her superstitious family and takes action. Amusing three-color illustrations.
(Picture book)

Gackenbach, Dick. **Hattie Be Quiet, Hattie Be Good.** Harper & Row,
Publishers, 1977. 4–7.

Although Hattie Rabbit is determined to be helpful, she is loud
when she tries to be quiet and she makes a sick friend feel worse. All
ends well when the Doctor prescribes ice cream for friend Shirley
Rabbitfoot, and Hattie gets to share the "medicine." Easy to read.
(Picture book)

Gackenbach, Dick. **More from Hound and Bear.** Clarion Books, 1979.
4–7.

Sensible Bear rescues his silly friend, Hound, who falls in a hole. In
a second story he shows Hound how to be a good friend. However,
in the third episode, Hound teaches Bear a lesson. Funny pen and
ink illustrations add to the text. (Picture book)

Gackenbach, Dick. **Mother Rabbit's Son Tom.** Harper & Row, Publishers, 1977. 6–9.

Young Tom Rabbit is full of tricks in these two high interest, easy-
to-read stories. Tom refuses all vegetables from his worried mother
and eats only his favorite, hamburgers. Next, mother says no to a
pet, but he comes home with a surprise. Humorous and warm illustrations add chuckles. (Picture book)

Gantos, Jack. **Worse Than Rotten, Ralph.** Illus. Nicole Rubel. Houghton
Mifflin, 1978. 4–7.

Sarah's cat, Rotten Ralph, decides to reform. His life becomes so
dull that he is easily enticed by a gang of alley cats to join them as
they create mayhem. Ralph ends up safely back in Sarah's arms, but
dreaming of another encounter with the alley cats. (Picture book)

Getz, Arthur. **Humphrey, the Dancing Pig.** Illus. by author. Dial Press, 1980. 7–10.

Humphrey, the pig, wants to be slim like the cat. So he dances and dances and dances until one day he is so thin that the farmer doesn't recognize him. A humorous tale with softly colored watercolors. (Picture book)

Godden, Rumer. **A Kindle of Kittens.** Illus. Lynne Byrnes. Viking Press, 1978. 5–8.

She-Cat walks alone in her English village until she meets He-Cat and gives birth to a kindle of kittens. Loving homes must be found for each kitten; the fond mother chooses carefully among the villagers whose dustbins she knows. Exquisite color illustrations of cats and an English village. (Picture book)

Grahame, Kenneth. **The Open Road.** Illus. Beverley Gooding. Charles Scribner's Sons, 1979. 8–12.

Toad goes off in his fantastic new horse-drawn caravan accompanied by Rat and Mole. This adventure from *The Wind in the Willows* is illustrated with detailed full-color illustrations. (Picture book)

Grahame, Kenneth. **The River Bank.** Illus. Adrienne Adams. Charles Scribner's Sons, 1977. 7–10.

This first chapter of *The Wind in the Willows* is a complete story in itself and introduces wise Rat and bashful Mole. This is an enchanting book and an exceptionally good read-aloud story. Many magical full-color illustrations. (Picture book)

Hall, Malcolm. **CariCatures.** Illus. Bruce Degen. Coward, McCann & Geoghegan, 1978. 7–10.

Claws and Paws, the world's leading animal newspaper, is in trouble; sales are down. Something fresh is needed to regain its readers. The staff brainstorms for a solution. Wasn't Hank Raccoon a cartoonist? Weren't his lively caricatures just the thing? A lively, humorous story with enjoyable pictures. (Picture book)

Harris, Dorothy Joan. **The School Mouse and the Hamster.** Illus. Judy Clifford. Frederick Warne, 1979. 5–8.

Jonathan's mouse, who appeared in *The House Mouse* and *The School Mouse,* returns. Jonathan helps him share adventures with the school hamster. The hamster gets to explore the mouse's trails and the mouse frolics on the hamster's swings and wheels. Beautifully detailed illustrations lend a strong note of realism to this tale. (Picture book)

Hayes, Geoffrey. **The Secret Inside.** Harper & Row, Publishers, 1980. 4–9.

Bear has a secret. He is lonely because his friends don't understand. Mother Bear hugs away the loneliness, but it is in a wonderful dream that Bear recognizes the value of his secret. Small homelike pictures in warm, gentle colors. (Picture book)

Herz, Irene. **Hey! Don't Do That.** Illus. Lucinda McQueen. Prentice-Hall, 1978. 4–7.

This brief story is told in the first person by a little girl who goes to the playground with her brother. Huge animals invade the playground and use the children's equipment. The sister and brother warn the animals as the title implies. Colorful illustrations. (Picture book)

Hiller, Catherine. **Argentaybee and the Boonie.** Illus. Cyndy Szekeres. Coward, McCann & Geoghegan, 1979. 4–7.

Emily Kitten is happy and helpful until imaginary friends Argentaybee and the Boonie come to stay. Things get difficult for Emily and Mother. But the first day of school brings a real friend and Argentaybee moves to Paris. Delightful two-color illustrations. (Picture book)

Hoban, Lillian. **Arthur's Pen Pal.** Illus. by author. Harper & Row, Publishers, 1976. 6–9.

Arthur thinks that his pen pal would be a better playmate than his little sister. After all, his sister is a girl and can't do much. A great surprise for Arthur comes when he receives a letter back from his pen pal. An easy-to-read book. (Picture book)

Hoban, Lillian. **Arthur's Prize Reader.** Harper & Row, Publishers, 1978. 6–8.

Arthur, the chimp, returns in this warm brother-sister story. He and his little sister, Violet, discover that to read "hard" words is not enough; they must understand the meaning of the words. Beginning readers will relate to and enjoy this easy-to-read book that is expressively illustrated. (Picture book)

Hoban, Lillian. **Mr. Pig and Family.** Harper & Row, Publishers, 1980. 6–9.

When Mr. Pig marries Selma Pig, they need to move into one house. Their house-moving ends up in a rainy day tea party. Then Mr. Pig tries to plant a garden and he ends up with a hole full of seeds and water. More easy-reading humorous adventures of silly Mr. Pig. (Picture book)

Hoban, Russell. **Arthur's New Power.** Illus. Byron Barton. Thomas Y. Crowell, 1978. 6–9.

Energy problems confront the Crocodile family. The entire family has to rely on extension cord electricity from the neighboring Boa household until Arthur generates an unusual solution. They all discover something about being plugged in and plugged out. Bright illustrations and a fast-moving story. (Picture book)

Hoff, Syd. **Walpole.** Harper & Row, Publishers, 1977. 6–8.

Walpole, the biggest and strongest walrus, does not want to become the leader of his herd until one day when he saves the herd from a polar bear. This easy-to-read book will appeal to the beginning reader. The cartoon-like illustrations are bold and humorous. (Picture book)

Houghton, Eric. **The Mouse and the Magician.** Illus. Faith Jaques. Andre Deutsch, 1979. 4–7.

The mouse looks longingly through the magician's window as the snow falls about him. Food and warmth are worth the risk. But the mouse is clumsy, the magician frightened, and all ends happily in this clever tale. Full-color illustrations add to the pleasure. (Picture book)

Hyman, Robin, and Inge Hyman. **Casper and the Rainbow Bird.** Illus. Yutaka Sugita. Barron's Educational Series, 1978. 4–7.

One day Casper's daddy tells him that he is old enough to fly to town by himself. Thrilled with this new privilege, he leaves immediately. Along the way he discovers Rainbow Bird in a cage and a lasting friendship is begun. Appealing, colorful pictures. (Picture book)

Joerns, Consuelo. **The Lost & Found House.** Four Winds Press, 1979. 6–9.

Here's a story about the adventures of a resourceful and courageous mouse, Cricket, who loses his comfortable house. After many mishaps, the mouse and the house are reunited and find an exciting new life with a boy and his model train. Small book size and watercolor illustrations are bonuses for young independent readers. (Picture book)

Keenan, Martha. **The Mannerly Adventures of Little Mouse.** Illus. Meri Shardin. Crown Publishers, 1977. 3–5.

Little Mouse needs constant reminders to say thank you and please, but when he joins Uncle Cheddar on a food hunt, he proves that he has the best manners of all. The loving closeness of the mouse family comes through in the delicately colored pencil drawings. (Picture book)

Kennedy, Richard. **The Mouse God.** Illus. Stephen Harvard. Little, Brown, 1979. 4–7.

In order to earn his keep, a large lazy barnyard cat is expected to catch the mice. He makes himself a complete outfit of mouse skins. The mice mistake him for a mouse god and find themselves in a dangerous situation. Excellent illustrations and endpages add to the entertaining story. (Picture book)

Kessler, Leonard. **Do You Have Any Carrots?** Illus. Lori Pierson. Garrard Publishing, 1979. 6–8.

As two bunnies hop about in search of carrots, their favorite food, they discover what dogs, foxes, raccoons, and other animals eat. They are disappointed until they meet a kind farmer. Full-color illustrations combine with the text to make an appealing book for the beginning reader. (Picture book)

Kimmel, Eric. **Why Worry?** Illus. Elizabeth Cannon. Pantheon Books, 1979. 4–7.

Cricket always worries. Grasshopper never does. Yet they are the best of friends. The two share a series of improbable, exciting, amusing adventures one summer day and get home in time for tea. Handsome full-color illustrations are carefully designed to match text. (Picture book)

Krahn, Fernando. **The Family Minus.** Illus. by author. Parents Magazine Press, 1977. 6–9.

An ordinary day in the lives of Mr. Harry Minus, Mrs. Mary Minus, and their eight children is combined with the description of Mrs. Minus's extraordinary household inventions in this humorous picture book. The author's full-page colorful illustrations add to the fun. (Picture book)

Kraus, Robert, and Bruce Kraus. **The Detective of London.** Illus. Robert Byrd. E. P. Dutton, 1977. 4–7.

While being transported to London for Queen Victoria's Jubilee, newly discovered dinosaur bones are stolen. The Detective of London is given the case. His adventures take him on a tour of the city as he eats his way to a solution. Charming black and white illustrations of Victorian London. (Picture book)

Kraus, Robert. **The Good Mousekeeper.** Illus. Hilary Knight. E. P. Dutton, 1977. 4–7.

The good mousekeeper knows exactly what to do for the little mice in her care. Her work is never finished until late at night. Oval-shaped illustrations show the kindly mouse feeding the mice, washing their clothes, and reading to them at bedtime. A good read-aloud book. (Picture book)

Kwitz, Mary DeBall. **Rabbits' Search for a Little House.** Illus. Lorinda Cauley. Crown Publishers, 1977. 5–8.

Mother Rabbit and Little Rabbit search for a wee little, warm little, snug little winter home. They just miss renting several places but finally find a hollow stump and furnish it to their liking. Rhythmic flowing language; attractive illustrations. (Picture book)

Lawson, Annetta. **The Lucky Yak.** Illus. Allen Say. Parnassus Press, 1980. 7–10.

Edward, a successful yak who has everything, is depressed and unhappy. At his psychiatrist's suggestion, Edward reluctantly agrees to baby-sit for young Muffin Puffin, who eats a bar of soap and dents the refrigerator with her tricycle. Edward quickly appreciates his life and finds happiness. Detailed ink drawings capture the humor. (Picture book)

Le Guin, Ursula K. **Leese Webster.** Illus. James Brunsman. Atheneum, 1979. 8–12.

Leese is a spider who weaves beautiful intricate webs that rival the paintings and carvings that are in her castle home. Her webs are so unique that many people come to see them and Leese is thrown into the garden where a whole new world of web-making awaits her. (Picture book)

Lesikin, Joan. **Down the Road.** Illus. by author. Prentice-Hall, 1978. 3–5.

A snake and a box turtle set out to seek a suitable home. They soon discover that what is good for one is not quite right for the other. Well-drawn black and tan pictures illustrate and carry the action of the story. (Picture book)

Lionni, Leo. **Geraldine, the Music Mouse.** Pantheon Books, 1979. 4–7.

✓ Another large picture book for story hour. Geraldine nibbles an enormous piece of Parmesan cheese and uncovers a statue of a mouse holding a flutelike object. Wonderful things happen. Soft and subdued color illustrations. (Picture book)

Lobel, Arnold. **Days with Frog and Toad.** Harper & Row, Publishers, 1979. 6–8.

An amusing and humorously illustrated easy-to-read book. Frog and Toad fly kites, enjoy telling spooky stories, and decide that sometimes they like to be alone. Brown and green pictures. (Picture book)

Lobel, Arnold. **Grasshopper on the Road.** Harper & Row, Publishers, 1978. 6–8.

Grasshopper's pleasant adventures with other personified insects are gently and affectionately reminiscent of human foibles. They deal with everyday, comfortable matters. The softly colored watercolor and ink illustrations authentically detail flora and fauna. An easy-to-read book. (Picture book)

Lobel, Arnold. **Mouse Soup.** Harper & Row, Publishers, 1977. 5–8.

An easy-to-read book containing four stories from which the ingredients of mouse soup are taken. The mouse convinces a weasel that he needs all the items to make the soup tasty. The amazing stories are charmingly illustrated in muted colors. (Picture book)

Low, Joseph. **Mice Twice.** Illus. by author. Atheneum, 1980. 4–7.

Cat was hungry and decided to invite Mouse to dinner and eat him. Therein begins a battle of wits between the two with hilarious results. The author's colorful graphic illustrations capture the humor of this tale. 1981 Caldecott Honor Book. (Picture book)

McClure, Gillian. **Prickly Pig.** Andre Deutsch, 1976. 4–7.

As the cold winds begin to blow and bring the leaves to the ground, the hedgehog is reminded that he must find a home for the winter. None of the animals welcome him into their cozy homes. Where will he go? Appealing illustrations make this a fine read-aloud book. (Picture book)

McNulty, Faith. **The Elephant Who Couldn't Forget.** Illus. Marc Simont. Harper & Row, Publishers, 1980. 6–8.

Congo, the baby elephant, has a good memory. He remembers all the things the older, wiser elephants have taught him about lions and manners and rules. But one day he forgets the most important thing of all. An easy-to-read book. (Picture book)

McPhail, David. **Bumper Tubbs.** Illus. by author. Houghton Mifflin, 1980. 7–10.

Three tales about Bumper Tubbs, the alligator, and his good friend and neighbor, Hornsby, will delight readers. The author has depicted his characters and their humorous adventures in brightly colored full-page illustrations that add to the reading enjoyment. (Picture book)

McPhail, David. **Captain Toad and the Motorbike.** Illus. by author. Atheneum, 1978. 5–7.

Captain Toad may well be the great-grandson of the memorable Toad from *The Wind in the Willows.* Instead of hankering for a motorcar, the more modern Toad is more interested in possessing a motorbike. An exciting book illustrated with pencil and soft washes. (Picture book)

McPhail, David. **Pig Pig Grows Up.** E. P. Dutton, 1980. 4–7.

Despite the pleas of his weary mother, Pig Pig does not want to grow up. He clings to his high chair, sleepers, and stroller. One day, when faced with an emergency, he grows up and likes it. Illustrations capture the humor of a very large pig acting like a very small baby. (Picture book)

McPhail, David. **Those Terrible Toy-Breakers.** Parents Magazine Press, 1980. 4–7.

Walter thinks he lives near the jungle. When he finds his tricycle all bent and other toys broken, his friend Bernie insists it was done by a lion, a tiger, and an elephant, so the boys set a trap. Surprisingly, Bernie is right! Good for creative art and story stimulation; colorful illustrations. (Picture book)

Mack, Stan. **Where's My Cheese?** Pantheon Books, 1977. 4–7.

A cat, accused of stealing a piece of cheese, is chased through the town and becomes part of an incredible chain of events. There is little text; the story is told through bright, humorous illustrations done in comic strip style. This is a book that invites children to read along. (Picture book)

Marshall, James. **George and Martha: Tons of Fun.** Houghton Mifflin, 1980. 4–7.

There are five easy-to-read, humorous stories about two hippo friends, George and Martha. Each brief story is introduced with a numbered cover page. Bright, full-page illustrations contribute to the hilarity of the problems of this friendship. Another favorite book is *George and Martha One Fine Day.* (Picture book)

Marshall, James. **Portly McSwine.** Houghton Mifflin, 1979. All ages.

Portly McSwine worries so about the success of a party he is planning for National Snout Day that he nearly makes himself sick. Younger readers will enjoy the full-page color illustrations, older readers will find even more subtle chuckles hidden within. (Picture book)

Meddaugh, Susan. **Maude and Claude Go Abroad.** Houghton Mifflin, 1980. 6–9.

Maude promises to take care of her brother as the two fox children sail to France on the S.S. *Reynard.* When Claude falls overboard, Maude rescues him and they hitch a ride with a friendly whale. Told in rhyme, this is a humorous read-aloud book. (Picture book)

Meddaugh, Susan. **Too Short Fred.** Houghton Mifflin, 1978. 4–7.

In five brief tales, Fred learns to accept his short stature and even finds that being short can be an advantage. The colored-pencil illustrations of the cats express with warmth the sensitive but humorous content of the stories. (Picture book)

Miklowitz, Gloria D. **Save that Raccoon!** Illus. St. Tamara Kolba. Harcourt Brace Jovanovich, 1978. 6–9.

A forest fire destroys Raccoon's home and causes him to move to a town to forage for food. The tale, told from Raccoon's point of view, presents some interesting perspectives. Delicate drawings in brown ink with a red wash add much to this simply told, unsentimental story. An easy-to-read book. (Picture book)

Miles, Miska. **Mouse Six and the Happy Birthday.** Illus. Leslie Morrill. E. P. Dutton, 1978. 4–7.

Mother Mouse warns all her children not to tell anyone that today is her birthday. Mouse Six sets out to find a suitable gift. When the neighbors see him they think he is running away. The result of their plan and Six's day make a happy story. (Picture book)

Miles, Miska. **Noisy Gander.** Illus. Leslie Morrill. E. P. Dutton, 1978. 5–7.

Little gosling isn't the only one in the barnyard who wonders why his father honked when there was nothing to honk about. This amusing picture book gives the solution and makes little gosling proud of his father. Soft pencil drawings add to the delight of this easy-to-read story. (Picture book)

Miles, Miska. **Small Rabbit.** Illus. Jim Arnosky. Little, Brown, 1977. 7–10.

Small rabbit leaves the burrow to play after warnings from father and mother rabbit about foxes, hawks, and humans. Readers will identify with the small rabbit's heady feelings of adventure, delicious fear, bravery, and pleasure when she meets a friend at last. Charming ink and water wash illustrations. (Picture book)

Miles, Miska. **This Little Pig.** Illus. Leslie Morrill. E. P. Dutton, 1980. 3–5.

The runt of the litter is tired of being last. The other pigs shove her aside at mealtime, and she never has a chance to wallow. She aims to have *one* nice day when she won't be pushed or shoved. Gray-shaded pencil drawings enhance this read-aloud book. (Picture book)

Miller, Edna. **Jumping Bean.** Illus. by author. Prentice-Hall, 1979. 4–7.

The answer to one of nature's puzzling wonders is revealed in this explanation of why the jumping bean jumps. Precise watercolor illustrations combine with a lively text to demonstrate the jumping bean's metamorphosis from larva to moth. (Picture book)

Ness, Evaline. **Fierce: The Lion.** Illus. by author. Holiday House, 1980. 4–7.

Isobel's lion-tamer parents give her a cub for a pet. She carefully nurtures Fierce, who becomes the star of the circus show, arousing jealousy among other performers. Saddened by their attitude, Fierce asks Isobel to find him another job. Quaint, imaginative illustrations extend the action of the story. (Picture book)

Oakley, Graham. **The Church Mice at Bay.** Atheneum, 1979. 6–9.

When a new vicar comes to the village of Wortlethorpe, the cat Sampson moves to save the resident church mice from almost certain doom. Mice, cats, dogs, and a startled naked vicar stage a mass chase through town in this very funny book. One of a series that uses understated text and riotous hilarity. (Picture book)

Oneal, Zibby. **Turtle and Snail.** Illus. Margot Tomes. J. B. Lippincott, 1979. 4–7.

Turtle and snail are friends because they both have something: a shell. They share good times and bad, have funny misunderstandings, and learn to laugh together. Delightful illustrations enhance the five episodes in this easy-to-read book. (Picture book)

Pape, Donna Lugg. **Where Is My Little Joey?** Illus. Tom Eaton. Garrard Publishing, 1978. 4–7.

Mother Kara Kangaroo loses her little Joey in a park. People try many uses for her pocket as she wanders in search of her baby, but Kara rejects them all, insisting that her pocket is for Joey! The story ends happily with Joey asleep in his mother's pocket. Cartoon illustrations. (Picture book)

Parker, Nancy Winslow. **Love from Uncle Clyde.** Illus. by author. Dodd, Mead, 1977. 4–7.

Charlie's birthday present from Uncle Clyde in Africa is a lovely big purple hippopotamus named Elfreda. Charlie learns to take care of her and Elfreda learns to love him. Bold, full-color, full-page illustrations. (Picture book)

Pavey, Peter. **I'm Taggarty Toad.** Bradbury Press, 1980. 4–7.

There's a different view of the bragging, adventurous toad at the end of the book than is seen on the title page. He boasts to the animals of the forest of his daring escapades only to have one of his victims find sweet revenge during the boasting. Outstanding illustrations. (Picture book)

Pearson, Susan. **Molly Moves Out.** Illus. Steven Kellogg. Dial Press, 1979. 4–7.

Ten rabbits living in one house are nine rabbits too many for elder sister Molly, who finally moves away. She revels in peace and quiet until loneliness sets in. A new friendship and a surprise visit from her obstreperous family resolve all problems in this appealing easy reader. The illustrations are pure delight. (Picture book)

Peet, Bill. **Big Bad Bruce.** Houghton Mifflin, 1977. 6–9.

Big Bruce, a bear, is the bully of Forevergreen Forest and revels in scaring smaller animals. One day he antagonizes Roxy, a witch, who shrinks him to the size of a chipmunk. Roxy, really a kindly witch, rescues Bruce from predators and keeps him for a pet. Colorful, humorous illustrations. (Picture book)

Peet, Bill. **Cowardly Clyde.** Houghton Mifflin, 1979. 4–7.

Clyde looks like a great, brave war-horse but isn't. He's a coward and knows it. When his courageous knight Sir Galavant is attacked by a fierce ogre, Clyde rides to a spectacular rescue. Bold, big full-color illustrations. (Picture book)

Pinkwater, Daniel M. **The Wuggie Norple Story.** Illus. Tomie de Paola. Four Winds Press, 1980. 6–9.

Wuggie Norple is growing! Lunchbox Louie mentions this fact to his wife and son but they disagree. Each day Louie brings home another animal to compare in size with the kitten. Soon Wuggie Norple is as big as an elephant and the family has acquired quite a menagerie. Delightful illustrations. (Picture book)

Provensen, Alice, and Martin Provensen. **A Horse and a Hound, a Goat and a Gander.** Atheneum, 1980. 4–7.

Four special animals live on Maple Hill Farm. They are Bashful Boy, a horse; a big brown bloodhound, John; Goat Dear, the nanny goat; and Evil Murdock, the biggest, crankiest goose. Colorful, humorous illustrations bring these characters to life for the young reader. (Picture book)

Rayner, Mary. **Garth Pig and the Ice Cream Lady.** Atheneum, 1977. 4–7.

On a bicycle built for the ten little pigs of *Mr. and Mrs. Pig's Evening Out,* nine of his siblings rescue Garth Pig, who has gone to buy Whooshes from the lady wolf on the "Volfswagon" ice-cream truck. Adventure plus delightfully piggy illustrations mark this bit of British whimsy. (Picture book)

Rice, Eve. **Sam Who Never Forgets.** Greenwillow Books, 1977. 4–7.

Every day at three o'clock Sam feeds the animals in the zoo the things they like best to eat: greens for giraffe, red berries for bear. He never forgets anyone, even the elephant who is so big. Bold, full-color, full-page illustrations. (Picture book)

Roche, P. K. **Webster and Arnold and the Giant Box.** Dial Press, 1980. 3–5.

Webster and Arnold, two little mice, find a large box. They like to pretend and the box soon becomes a cave, a train, a restaurant, a rocket, and a submarine. This amusing story is just right for beginning readers. Soft blue, yellow, and green illustrations. Another story with these two delightful characters is *Good-bye, Arnold!* (Picture book)

Rockwell, Anne. **Honk Honk!** E. P. Dutton, 1980. 3–5.

Gray Goose earns the title "bad," as she nips the farm animals and Billy Boy, who chase her across the countryside. The about-to-read child or preschooler can laugh at the story's conclusion. Lively, amusing illustrations suit the very brief text. (Picture book)

Rockwell, Anne. **Willy Runs Away.** E. P. Dutton, 1978. 4–7.

Willy, a little dog, lives comfortably with his family. When he decides to leave his secure but small world, he becomes lost. His family anxiously searches for their lost pet. Black and white illustrations enhance this read-alone adventure. (Picture book)

Romanek, Enid Warner. **Teddy.** Illus. by author. Charles Scribner's Sons, 1978. 4–7.

Little children will identify with Teddy as he goes about his everyday experiences that are so much like theirs. He plays in the park, eats his meals, and goes to bed. The love he experiences from his safe, secure homelife will be most satisfying. Exceptional etched illustrations. (Picture book)

Rose, Gerald. **The Tiger-Skin Rug.** Illus. by author. Prentice-Hall, 1979. 4–7.

A very old, very hungry tiger looks longingly through the window of the Rajah's house. By pretending to be a tiger-skin rug, he secures food and company until the night when robbers attack. A delightfully humorous story complemented by bold and amusing full-color illustrations. (Picture book)

Roy, Ron. **Old Tiger, New Tiger.** Illus. Pat Bargielski. Abingdon Press, 1978. 7–10.

Old Tiger is blind and dying of starvation. His death will mean that new swift tigers will take over the territory and threaten the small animals. Wise Monkey's successful plan to help Old Tiger demonstrates the value of interdependence. Satisfying illustrations in yellow and sepia. (Picture book)

Roy, Ron. **Three Ducks Went Wandering.** Illus. Paul Galdone. Seabury Press, 1979. 4–7.

Three little ducks wander away from their mother and, oblivious to danger, encounter an angry bull, some hungry foxes, a hawk, and a snake. All of the foes meet undesirable fates but the little ducks return home tired and ready for their naps. (Picture book)

Ruck-Pauquèt, Gina (translator Anthea Bell). **Mumble Bear.** Illus. Erika Dietzsch-Capelle. G. P. Putnam's Sons, 1980. 4–7.

Mumble Bear is a dear bear because he does favors on demand for everybody. But he never has time to play his violin. Then self-assertion brings changes. Colorful cuddly-bear illustrations. Good for discussing human relationships. (Picture book)

Ruck-Pauquèt, Gina. **Oh, That Koala!** Illus. Anna Mossakowska. McGraw-Hill, 1979. 4–7.

A cheerful little Koala is accepted as a new neighbor in a sedate bear community. Then he upsets their routine life with rowdy sleep-walking escapades. Young listeners and readers delight in Koala's need to be himself and laugh at his jaunty singing. Large colorful illustrations are very effective. (Picture book)

Ruskin, John. **Dame Wiggins of Lee and Her Seven Wonderful Cats.** Illus. Patience Brewster. Thomas Y. Crowell, 1980. 4–7.

This nineteenth-century tale, which bears resemblance to the traditional "Dame Trot and Her Comical Cat," is a cumulatve verse about the marvelous antics of seven cats who sing, spell, dance, and care for sick animals. Soft pencil drawings add humor to the gentle rhyme. (Picture book)

Scarry, Patsy. **Patsy Scarry's Big Bedtime Storybook.** Illus. Cyndy Szekeres. Random House, 1980. 3–5.

Sixteen humorous brief stories for very young children are illustrated attractively in full color with much detail. The animal characters are childlike in thinking; the rewards of their adventures are enormous, in their unsophisticated esteem. (Picture book)

Schneider, Rex. **The Wide-Mouthed Frog.** Illus. by author. Stemmer House Publishers, 1980. 4–7.

A conceited wide-mouthed frog, feeling above the lowly fare of bugs, seeks advice from different animals concerning what foods are grand enough for him. Encountering an alligator who likes only wide-mouthed frogs, the frog is satisfied with a mosquito. Illustrations in subdued colors create the atmosphere of the Okefenokee Swamp. (Picture book)

Seuling, Barbara. **The Great Big Elephant and the Very Small Elephant.** Crown Publishers, 1977. 6–9.

The Great Big Elephant and the Very Small Elephant are best friends. They boost each other's spirits and help each other through diffficult times; the best gifts are the intangible ones. Pleasant illustrations in ink and pastel watercolor. (Picture book)

Sharmat, Marjorie Weinman. **Grumley the Grouch.** Illus. Kay Chorao. Holiday House, 1980. 4–7.

When J. Grumley Badger's home becomes flooded, he seeks help from other animals, but he is too grouchy for them to befriend him. Finally he meets Brunhilda, a badger of like disposition, and both lives undergo change. Action and mood are expressed well in finely detailed illustrations. (Picture book)

Sharmat, Marjorie Weinman. **I'm Terrific.** Illus. Kay Chorao. Holiday House, 1977. 4–7.

Jason Everett Bear is so good. He eats his spinach, helps his mother, and brushes his hair. However, when he tells his friends how terrific he is, they tell Jason that he is a "Mama's Bear." Rejected and dejected, Jason tries to cut the apron strings. A warm story. (Picture book)

Sharmat, Marjorie Weinman. **Mooch the Messy.** Illus. Ben Shecter. Harper & Row, Publishers, 1976. 6–9.

Mooch the rat lives happily under a hill in Boston even though his hole is a mess. Then his father, who likes everything neat, comes for a visit and Mooch must compromise. Warm family feeling in this easy-to-read book with lively illustrations. (Picture book)

Sharmat, Marjorie Weinman. **Mooch the Messy Meets Prudence the Neat.** Illus. Ben Shecter. Coward, McCann & Geoghegan, 1978. 6–9.

Mooch, who enjoyed being the messiest rat in Boston, meets his new neighbor, Prudence, who is extremely neat. Mooch's wonderful mess causes a problem when he does not invite his new neighbor for a visit. Illustrations add humor to the simple text. (Picture book)

Sharmat, Marjorie Weinman. **Mr. Jameson and Mr. Phillips.** Illus. Bruce Degen. Harper & Row, Publishers, 1979. 6–9.

Two animal friends, a writer and an artist, escape the rush of the city and find refuge on a beautiful, uninhabited tropical island. There they enjoy solitude until visitors in increasing numbers come to the island and the friends must seek a new home away from the rush and pollution. (Picture book)

Sharmat, Marjorie Weinman. **Say Hello, Vanessa.** Illus. Lillian Hoban. Holiday House, 1979. 4–7.

Vanessa Mouse is very bashful. Each day in school she tries a different way to make friends. Nothing works. How she finally overcomes her shyness and finds a friend is a delightful story. Black and white illustrations. (Picture book)

Sharmat, Marjorie Weinman. **Taking Care of Melvin.** Illus. Victoria Chess. Holiday House, 1980. 4–7.

How much help is too much help? Melvin Dog helps everyone but himself until the day he is ordered to bed, where he becomes as demanding of his friends as he was generous. Expressive gray and white pictures on a shocking pink background add just the right note of incongruity. (Picture book)

Sharmat, Marjorie Weinman. **Thornton the Worrier.** Illus. Kay Chorao. Holiday House, 1978. 4–7.

All the other animals are busy with their various tasks. However, Thornton Rabbit worries about everything: toothaches, bad weather, mosquito bites, assorted disasters. After meeting an old man who does not worry about anything, Thornton gets a new perspective on life. Detailed illustrations are gentle and amusing. (Picture book)

Sharmat, Marjorie Weinman. **The Trip and Other Sophie and Gussie Stories.** Illus. Lillian Hoban. Macmillan Publishing, 1976. 6–9.

In these four humorous, easy-to-read Sophie and Gussie stories, the clever squirrel-ladies bustle about packing for a trip Gussie plans to take, cleaning Sophie's house, coping with a leak in Gussie's ceiling, and sharing a forest flower. The watercolors catch the comfortable warmth of their give-and-take friendship. (Picture book)

Sharmat, Mitchell. **Gregory, the Terrible Eater.** Illus. Jose Aruego and Ariane Dewey. Four Winds Press, 1980. 5–8.

Gregory Goat prefers eggs and juice to the diet of junk that is normal for goats. His parents take him to a doctor and entice him to eat more jackets and boxes. After a terrible stomachache, Gregory finally teaches his parents about what makes a good meal. Outstanding illustrations. (Picture book)

Sharmat, Mitchell. **Reddy Rattler and Easy Eagle.** Illus. Marc Simont. Doubleday, 1979. 6–9.

Reddy Rattler feels down because everyone thinks rattlesnakes are bad. His friend, Easy Eagle, urges him to put to *good* use his greatest talent, rattling. A humorous easy-to-read book. (Picture book)

Shecter, Ben. **The Hiding Game.** Illus. by author. Parents Magazine Press, 1977. 4–7.

Henri Hippopotamus gets tired of waiting for Pierre Rhinoceros to find him during their game of Hide and Seek. When the two finally catch up with each other they decide that it's more fun playing together than looking for each other. Humorous illustrations add to this warm story about friendship. (Picture book)

Smith, Jim. **The Frog Band and the Onion Seller.** Illus. by author. Little, Brown, 1976. 7–10.

Marvelous full-color illustrations highlight this story of an aristocratic frog, Duke de Buffo Buffo, who enlists the aid of the eminent Alphonse le Flic to track down a treasure chest. Hindered, but not stopped by the infamous Frog Band, the detective leads a riotous chase through a monastery. (Picture book)

Steig, William. **Tiffky Doofky.** Farrar, Straus & Giroux, 1978. 7–10.

Tiffky Doofky, a garbage collector, spends a day of perilous adventures after he seeks advice from Madam Tarsal, a fortune teller, and her enemy, a chicken witch. Witty illustrations fit this silly animal fantasy's ending that will delight readers and listeners. (Picture book)

Steiner, Jörg, adapter. **The Bear Who Wanted to Be a Bear.** Illus. by adapter. Atheneum, 1977. 6–9.

A bear emerging from hibernation finds a factory built over his den. He is mistaken for a lazy worker and, despite his protests that he is a bear, is made to shave, punch a time clock, and sit daily turning a light on and off. A satire on automation and corporate business. (Picture book)

Steiner, Jörg (translator Ann Conrad Lammers). **Rabbit Island.** Illus. by author. Harcourt Brace Jovanovich, 1978. All ages.

Two rabbits escape from the rabbit factory. Little Brown remembers the taste of clover, the feel of the sun. Big Gray does not. Little Brown accepts the perils of freedom; Big Gray trembles and returns to his cage. Muted full-color illustrations contrast the artificial light of the factory with sun of the countryside. (Picture book)

Stevens, Carla. **Pig and the Blue Flag.** Illus. Rainey Bennett. Seabury Press, 1977. 6–9.

Pig experiences the pangs felt by many youngsters when his lack of athletic ability makes him the last one chosen for team sports. A game of Capture the Flag and the encouragement of his friends enable him to succeed in this fun, easy-to-read story. (Picture book)

Stevenson, James. **Howard.** Greenwillow Books, 1980. 5–8.

Howard, a duck, misses his flight south with his flock. He tries to follow them, but accidentally lands in New York City. His adventures with a frog and three mice acquaint him with the Big Apple. When his flock returns in the spring, Howard opts for the big city and his new-found friends instead. (Picture book)

Stone, Bernard, in collaboration with Alice Low. **The Charge of the Mouse Brigade.** Illus. Tony Ross. Pantheon Books, 1980. 6–9.

This clever spin-off from Tennyson's "The Charge of the Light Brigade" pictures well-fed, well-dressed mice in battle. The cats steal the cheese and the mice must recover it. The story is told in lively prose and poetry. Appealing colored pictures provide delightful entertainment. (Picture book)

Stren, Patti. **Hug Me.** Harper & Row, Publishers, 1977. 4–7.

Elliot Kravitz is a porcupine in search of love who finds himself hugging everything in sight. The illustrations make Elliot a very lovable creature, and the happy ending confirms the belief that two porcupines can really fall in love, carefully. Simple pen drawings enhance the book's unique quality. (Picture book)

Tether, Graham. **Skunk and Possum.** Illus. Lucinda McQueen. Houghton Mifflin, 1979. 4–7.

Skunk is foolish and Possum is practical; yet they are good friends. Four short, humorous tales relate how friendship survives the animals' apparent differences. Warm, expressive illustrations enhance the episodes. (Picture book)

Tompert, Ann. **Badger on His Own.** Illus. Diane de Groat. Crown Publishers, 1978. 6–8.

A badger seeks independence by moving to his own house. He learns he still has to make his own decisions when his neighbor, Owl, convinces him to go to the fair rather than unpack. This lighthearted lesson on choice and responsibility can be read by beginning readers. (Picture book)

Tompert, Ann. **Little Otter Remembers and Other Stories.** Illus. John Wallner. Crown Publishers, 1977. 4–7.

Preschool listeners and beginning readers can sympathize with Little Otter's three adventures. He experiences indecisiveness trying to select a gift for his mother, forgetfulness when losing his favorite pine cone, and disappointment about a coasting party. Soft, three-color pencil drawings support gentle, nature-filled stories. (Picture book)

Van Leeuwen, Jean. **Tales of Oliver Pig.** Illus. Arnold Lobel. Dial Press, 1979. 6–8.

Oliver Pig and his loving family are introduced in this new easy-to-read series. Oliver is the oldest and his little sister Amanda is learning to talk. Mother and Father Pig are very understanding. Appealing pictures illustrate the five tales of this special family. (Picture book)

Waber, Bernard. **Good-Bye, Funny Dumpy-Lumpy.** Houghton Mifflin, 1977. 6–9.

Five short episodes show a Victorian feline family coping with everyday life. Common foibles and problems are explored with warmth and humor. Natural dialogue adds to the immediacy of the stories. (Picture book)

Wagner, Jenny. **Aranea: A Story about a Spider.** Illus. Ron Brooks. Bradbury Press, 1978. 4–7.

Aranea, the spider, is a hardworking artist, trying to weave her web perfectly. Although everything from school boys to thunderstorms breaks her art apart, she survives. The story weaves for the young reader an appreciation for this industrious worker. Pen and ink drawings exquisitely portray Aranea's encounters. (Picture book)

Wahl, Jan. **Carrot Nose.** Illus. James Marshall. Farrar, Straus & Giroux, 1978. 4–7.

After a bunny grumbles, "Not one more carrot," a displeased carrot elf gives bunny a carrot nose. The funny problems Carrot Nose has with this troublesome nose bring giggles from all young readers. Black, white, and orange illustrations greatly add to the humor. (Picture book)

Wahl, Jan. **Doctor Rabbit's Foundling.** Illus. Cyndy Szekeres. Pantheon Books, 1977. 6–8.

Doctor Rabbit unexpectedly becomes the guardian of Tiny Tadpole. Helpless at first, Tiny quickly grows into an adventurous young toad, the darling of the forest. Detailed pictures enhance the fantasy and create a warm homey community. (Picture book)

Wahl, Jan. **Doctor Rabbit's Lost Scout.** Illus. Cyndy Szekeres. Pantheon Books, 1979. 3–5.

When Spotty Chipmunk sleepwalks away from camp, Doctor Rabbit and Miss Mouse form a search party. The simple text gently calls attention to nature's beauty as the lushly colored drawings concentrate on the animals' reactions of concern, fatigue, grief, and joy. (Picture book)

Wahl, Jan. **Who Will Believe Tim Kitten?** Illus. Cyndy Szekeres. Pantheon Books, 1978. 5–8.

Tim Kitten doesn't exactly fib but he does tell stories; the other kittens laugh at him. With the help of his ball-playing sisters, one story comes true and he learns to tell the truth. Captivating black and white illustrations of cat family and friends. Read-aloud/read-alone book. (Picture book)

Watanabe, Shigeo. **What a Good Lunch!** Illus. Yasuo Ohtomo. William Collins Publishers, 1978. 3–5.

Bear tries to feed himself for the first time and finally overcomes several difficulties. This second book in the "I can do it myself" series will delight the young. (Picture book)

Watson, Pauline. **Wriggles: The Little Wishing Pig.** Illus. Paul Galdone. Seabury Press, 1978. 4–7.

Wriggles the pig likes to wish he had the characteristics of other animals he sees. One day the wishes come true and he turns into a gator-monster. He discovers it is better to be a little pig. Bold, full-color illustrations. (Picture book)

Wild, Robin, and Jocelyn Wild. **Spot's Dogs and the Alley Cats.** J. B. Lippincott, 1979. 6–9.

Four tales of conflict between a gang of tough-looking but law-abiding dogs and the sinister Alley Cats, who have tender feelings after all, at least at a Christmas party for orphans. The cartoon-strip drawings are outrageously funny in the best British fashion. Cor, the whole thing's a lark! (Picture book)

Williams, Barbara. **Never Hit a Porcupine.** Illus. Anne Rockwell. E. P. Dutton, 1977. 3–5.

When Fletcher Fox's birthday comes around, he decides that he is old enough to leave home and seek his fortune. Mother packs a lunch while father gives him several survival tactics to outwit the other animals. An amusing picture book with comical illustrations. (Picture book)

Winthrop, Elizabeth. **Sloppy Kisses.** Illus. Anne Burgess. Macmillan Publishing, 1980. 5–8.

Emmy Lou's family just loves to kiss when leaving or arriving or any time at all. This is fine until Emmy Lou's friend, Rosemary, says kissing is for babies. Soft watercolor illustrations. (Picture book)

Wolkstein, Diane. **The Visit.** Illus. Lois Ehlert. Alfred A. Knopf, 1977. 3–5.

Clear, brilliant colors and simple shapes are used to portray the journey of an ant's visit to her friend. She makes her way step by step, over twig and leaf and stone. The repetitive text will appeal to the young child. (Picture book)

Yolen, Jane. **Mice on Ice.** Illus. Lawrence Di Fiori. E. P. Dutton, 1980. 4–7.

Horace Hooper, mouse inventor and owner of Mice Capades, a dazzling ice show starring Rosa Burrow-Minder, is threatened by Gomer Rat King and the Mouse Mafia. Suspense, adventure, and great good humor are all delightfully illustrated in an easy-to-read format. (Picture book)

Yolen, Jane. **Spider Jane.** Illus. Stefen Bernath. Coward, McCann & Geoghegan, 1978. 6–9.

Spider Jane keeps her web so clean that she has nothing left to eat. Her problem is solved after developing a friendship with a bluebottle fly. These four easy-to-read episodes provide simple, interesting language for primary readers. Humorous illustrations are a bonus. (Picture book)

Zalben, Jane Breskin. **Will You Count the Stars without Me?** Illus. by author. Farrar, Straus & Giroux, 1979. 4–7.

Two animal friends, Saba and Shana, share everything until Shana leaves their island to look for food. While Shana is gone, Saba feels very lonely and dull until he begins helping his friends. Large illustrations capture this tender account of friendship and female resourcefulness. (Picture book)

Zemach, Kaethe. **The Beautiful Rat.** Illus. by author. Four Winds Press, 1979. 5–7.

Mr. and Mrs. Rat, a Japanese couple, are very anxious that their beautiful daughter Yoshiko marry, but not a rat. As they search, the sun, a cloud, and the wind refuse their invitation. Upon their return a surprise awaits them. Outstanding bright, bold two-color illustrations. (Picture book)

Longer Stories

Alexander, Lloyd. **The Town Cats and Other Tales.** Illus. Laszlo Kubinyi. E. P. Dutton, 1977. 10–12.

Pescato is a town cat with many relatives. When he needs help in resolving a crisis in the town, they respond most effectively. This story and seven others about cats are delightfully told. Even non-cat-lovers will appreciate the wit, humor, and skill in this collection.

Cunningham, Julia. **A Mouse Called Junction.** Illus. Michael Hague. Pantheon Books, 1980. 6–9.

Junction, a poor little rich mouse, deserts his plush life to seek the love he has been denied and finds the best in unexpected places. Detailed, expressive illustrations add much to the reader's concern for Junction.

Donovan, John. **Family.** Harper & Row, Publishers, 1976. 10–12.

Sasha tells the story of his escape with three other apes from the university lab where he was sure they were being prepared for a final and horrifying experiment. An unusual book, with endless discussion possibilities.

du Bois, William Pène. **The Forbidden Forest.** Harper & Row, Publishers, 1978. 7–10.

A witty account of how Adelaide, a boxing kangaroo; her owner, Spider Max; and Buckingham, the bulldog, put a stop to World War I. Illustrations of exploding shells and flaming airplanes point up the futile horror of war; the portrayal of the antics of Adelaide, the agile heroine, are delightful.

Hayes, Geoffrey. **The Alligator and His Uncle Tooth.** Harper & Row, Publishers, 1977. 10–12.

Corduroy Alligator discovers that his old Uncle Tooth, the family ne'er-do-well, can tell fascinating stories of his adventures at sea. He persuades Uncle Tooth to set out one more time. Drawings are like neatly detailed old black and white photographs.

Howe, Deborah, and James Howe. **Bunnicula: A Rabbit-Tale of Mystery.** Illus. Alan Daniel. Atheneum, 1979. 8–12.

How could Chester the cat convince the family that the cute little abandoned rabbit they had found was really a sinister creature? Chester stars in the delicate line drawings as well as in the story, but everyone wins in the end, including the reader.

Pinkwater, Daniel M. **Return of the Moose.** Illus. by author. Dodd, Mead, 1979. 7–10.

A very humorous spoof on the tribulations of being an author or a publisher. The blue moose, a waiter in a forest-side restaurant, writes the best book ever written by man or moose and experiences the anguish and the joys of writing. A sequel to *Blue Moose.*

Schaffner, Val. **Algonquin Cat.** Illus. Hilary Knight. Delacorte Press, 1980. 8–12.

Hamlet is a cat living at the Hotel Algonquin in New York City, a favorite meeting place of literary and theatrical people. One day Hamlet becomes involved in the disappearance of a diamond. A contemporary setting with lapses into cat dreams, this funny book is liberally sprinkled with delightful drawings of cats.

Sharp, Margery. **Bernard into Battle.** Illus. Leslie Morrill. Little, Brown, 1978. 7–10.

It all comes about because a Waterworks Board man carelessly leaves a manhole cover ajar, permitting the despicable rats to enter the Embassy and spread disease. Bernard, a mouse, realizes the gravity of the situation and begins training the troops. Lighthearted reading with appropriate illustrations. One of the Miss Bianca series.

Tomlinson, Jill. **Hilda: The Hen Who Wouldn't Give Up.** Illus. Fernando Krahn. Harcourt Brace Jovanovich, 1980. 6–9.

Hilda, the hen, wants to see her Aunt Emma's new brood of chicks. Her misadventures in traveling the five miles to Emma's farm are described with great humor. Good read-aloud book.

Wyeth, Betsy James. **The Stray.** Illus. Jamie Wyeth. Farrar, Straus & Giroux, 1979. 8–12.

This story, slightly reminiscent of Grahame's *The Wind in the Willows,* centers on a society of animals whose peaceful existence is threatened by violence and blackmail. Lynch, the stray of the title, befriends the unnamed narrator and together they thwart the evil Sour Kraut. Black and white line drawings add humor to the amusing tale.

Fantasy Worlds

Alexander, Lloyd. **The First Two Lives of Lukas-Kasha.** E. P. Dutton, 1978. 10–12.

Lukas finds a new life when a traveling magician creates a new kingdom for him. He learns that being king is work and that friends can be found anywhere in any world. A fantasy of exquisite dimension and balance.

Cuneo, Mary Louise. **Inside a Sand Castle and Other Secrets.** Illus. Jan Brett. Houghton Mifflin, 1979. 5–8.

This creative fantasy about the interior of a sand castle, the house in the haystack, and the little village under the pine tree's lowest branches awaits the venturesome reader. Blue and tan illustrations blend with the text in this story of fascinating miniature worlds.

Eldridge, Roger. **The Shadow of the Gloom-World.** E. P. Dutton, 1978. 12–up.

This masterful tale of courage concerns a young boy, Fernfeather, who rebels against a society marked by suppression and conformity. Banished to the Gloom-World because he dares to question the power of Olden, Fernfeather discovers truth and realizes that he can help his people escape the darkness of their underground world.

Farris, Stella. **The Magic Castle.** Illus. by author. Harper & Row, Publishers, 1978. 4–7.

Surprises are in store when readers follow Scott as he explores the castle of his dream; colorful, exciting illustrations pop up to add three-dimensional realism to the fantasy. Last to appear is a teddy-bear—Scott's own—a most comforting discovery. Sturdy, attractive construction; good to stimulate creative writing.

Hamilton, Virginia. **Dustland.** Greenwillow Books, 1980. 12–up.

Justice, her twin brothers Thomas and Levi, and their friend Dorian are intricately linked by their supersensory powers into a special unit that travels through time and space. In this sequel to *Justice and Her Brothers,* the children encounter much danger in their quest to unravel the secret of Dustland.

Hamilton, Virginia. **Justice and Her Brothers.** Greenwillow Books, 1978. 12–up.

Justice, her identical twin brothers, and a neighbor friend have supersensory powers. They are able to move about in each others' thoughts. Excellent character study and unique plot enhance this fantasy that is grounded in a realistic setting. First of a trilogy.

Jones, Diana Wynne. **Cart and Cwidder.** Atheneum, 1977. 10–12.

Clennen is a licensed musician whose traveling takes him and his family from North to South Dalemark. When he is killed, young Moril inherits the big, ancient, lute-like cwidder said to be charmed by an ancient ancestor. For exceptional readers with a taste for mystery and fantasy.

Jones, Diana Wynne. **Drowned Ammet.** Atheneum, 1978. 12–up.

Concerned about unfair and repressive conditions of poor people living in Dalemark, Mitt attacks the ruler. His plans have adverse effects; he looks for safety and stows away on a boat owned by Hildy and Ynen, who are runaway children. Mitt, soon discovered, is mistrusted, but they travel together to the Holy Islands.

Karl, Jean E. **Beloved Benjamin Is Waiting.** E. P. Dutton, 1978. 8–12.

Abandoned by her mother and harassed by a teenage gang, Lucinda, a sixth-grader, lives in the cemetery. Her sensitive presence plus an iron statue of "Beloved Benjamin," a young boy who had died years earlier, allow the transmission of messages from outer space.

Keele, Luqman, and Daniel Pinkwater. **Java Jack.** Thomas Y. Crowell, 1980. 10–up.

Jack goes on a mysterious journey to Indonesia to find his missing anthropologist parents. With conflicting information on whether they are dead or alive, he searches for the truth in this world and beyond. A puzzling tale of action and intrigue.

Pittaway, Margaret. **The Rainforest Children.** Illus. Heather Philpott. Oxford University Press, 1980. 6–9.

A boy and a girl, Rufous and Lantana, journey from the Australian rainforest through grasslands, plantations, and swamps to their destination, the bright gold world beside the sea. They love it, but after a while little things begin to bother them so they return to the lush rainforest. Exquisite illustrations. (Picture book)

Snyder, Zilpha Keatley. **Until the Celebration.** Illus. Alton Raible. Atheneum, 1977. 10–12.

The final volume of the Green-Sky trilogy reunites the Kindar and the Erdlings through the discovery of the truth concerning their mutual past, two holy children, and the sacrifice of young Raamo. For devotees of fantasy.

Ghosts, Magic, the Supernatural

Aiken, Joan. **The Shadow Guests.** Delacorte Press, 1980. 12–up.

When Cosmos comes to England to stay with his cousin at the old mill house, he learns about the family curse. His days at school are miserable being the new boy, but his weekends at home are filled with great fun until unexplained happenings begin to occur.

Ainsworth, Ruth. **The Phantom Fisherboy: Tales of Mystery and Magic.** Illus. Shirley Hughes. Andre Deutsch, 1974. 10–12.

The fourteen stories of unusual occurrences, ghosts, and magic powers capture the imagination of the readers. The stories include a water spirit, a weeping witch, a boy who drowned a hundred years ago, a shivering orphan from the past, an invisible rope. Insightful, imaginative drawings capture the magic and mystery.

Alexander, Sue. **Witch, Goblin, and Sometimes Ghost.** Illus. Jeanette Winter. Pantheon Books, 1976. 4–7.

Three friends, Witch, Goblin, and Ghost, share daily experiences about being afraid, grumpy, and bewildered. Gentle pencil drawings match the mood of these six easy-to-read short stories. Beginning writers may be inspired to compose a book about a friend after reading "Goblin's Book." (Picture book)

Allard, Harry. **Bumps in the Night.** Illus. James Marshall. Doubleday, 1979. 6–12.

Dudley the stork is scared by a ghost in his house one night. The next midnight, Madame Kreepy holds a seance for Dudley and his friends. The ghost's arrival presages a surprising turn of events. Good to read aloud and help allay fears. Humorous pictures add to enjoyment. (Picture book)

Bellairs, John. **The Letter, the Witch, and the Ring.** Illus. Richard Egielski. Dial Press, 1976. 10–12.

As thirteen-year-old Rose Rita vacations with her neighbor Mrs. Zimmerman, who is a genuine witch, unexpected mysteries await them. Looking for a magic ring brings danger to both and they narrowly escape harm. This suspenseful story of black and white magic is well-paced and is the last of a trilogy.

Briggs, K. M. **Hobberdy Dick.** Greenwillow Books, 1977. 12–up.

Hobberdy Dick is a good hobgoblin of the seventeenth century. His loyal care of Widford Manor and his devotion to the family are crucial when evil forces try to prevent the betrothal of gentle Joel Widdison to his beloved Anne Seckar and to steal the manor treasure. Suspenseful story.

Chapman, Carol. **Barney Bipple's Magic Dandelions.** Illus. Steven Kellogg. E. P. Dutton, 1977. 5–8.

Barney Bipple has many wishes, but most of all he wants to be eight instead of six. Why? Life would be more exciting. A special kind of magic changes things overnight and then he has second thoughts about making complicated wishes. Appealing drawings complement this lively story. (Picture book)

Clyne, Patricia Edwards. **Strange and Supernatural Animals.** Illus. Ted Lewin. Dodd, Mead, 1979. 10–12.

A sequel to the author's *Ghostly Animals of America.* Based upon American historical fact and legend, fifteen tales tell of such strange phenomena as the Demon Cat, who stalks the corridors of the United States Capitol, and the phantom wolves, who are said to appear to campers in Indiana. Bibliography.

Coombs, Patricia. **Dorrie and the Screebit Ghost.** Lothrop, Lee & Shepard Books, 1979. 7–10.

In this thirteenth of the Dorrie books, Dorrie finds a slip of paper that was dropped by her mother witch. She follows the directions

and conjures up a friendly ghost. Screebit gives Dorrie many exhil-
arating experiences. An entertaining story illustrated with soft pencil
sketches. Good for reading aloud.

Cooper, Susan. **Jethro and the Jumbie.** Illus. Ahsley Bryan. Atheneum,
1979. 6–9.

Jethro wants to go fishing on his eighth birthday with his big brother,
Thomas, who reneges on his promise. Jethro gets so angry that when
he encounters the magical jumbie, he is unafraid of the fearsome
creatures the jumbie conjures. The jumbie helps Thomas have a
change of heart and all is well. Caribbean setting and language.
(Picture book)

Demi. **Liang and the Magic Paintbrush.** Holt, Rinehart and Winston,
1980. 5–10.

Liang is a poor boy whose one wish is to paint. One day he is given
a magic paint brush and all that he paints comes to life. Unfortunately this is noticed by an evil emperor! The delicately detailed
watercolors capture the texture of life in ancient China in glowing
colors. (Picture book)

Elwood, Roger, and Howard Goldsmith, editors. **Spine-Chillers.** Doubleday, 1978. 10–up.

True to its title, this collection of twenty-three stories of the occult
will keep the reader on the edge of the chair. Witchcraft, the werewolf, the zombie, and magic, universal subjects found throughout
the world, are included. Brief accounts of authors, mostly nineteenth-
century, are appended. Easy reading.

Farber, Norma. **There Goes Feathertop!** Illus. Marc Brown. E. P. Dutton,
1979. 5–8.

Feathertop is a scarecrow brought to life by Mother Rigby's witchcraft. He captivates a town and a lady until a mirror reflects the
truth. Excellent for reading aloud, this is a charming retelling of
Hawthorne's story in verse, handsomely illustrated in black and
white. (Picture book)

Fleischman, Paul. **The Half-a-Moon Inn.** Illus. Kathy Jacobi. Harper &
Row, Publishers, 1980. 10–12.

Aaron, a mute boy, searches for his mother during a blizzard. He
falls into the clutches of the weird Miss Grackle, the proprietress
of a mysterious old inn. After many strange experiences under her
spell, he is reunited with his mother, who in turn has long searched
for him. Gloomy, haunting drawings.

Flora, James. **Grandpa's Ghost Stories.** Illus. by author. Atheneum, 1978.
8–12.

During a frightening thunderstorm, Grandpa holds the boy in his lap and tells about how he, himself, lost in the woods on a stormy night, found a bag of old bones in a deserted cabin. One hair-raising adventure leads to another. Funny ink drawings in blue, black, and white. (Picture book)

Gage, Wilson. **Mrs. Gaddy and the Ghost.** Illus. Marylin Hafner. Greenwillow Books, 1979. 4–7.

Mrs. Gaddy has a real problem as she tries to oust a ghost. None of her plans are successful, no matter how cleverly she carries them out, but there was one plan that she didn't consider. The story and rose-tinted illustrations are humorous and satisfying. Good for reading aloud. (Picture book)

Hirsh, Marilyn. **Deborah the Dybbuk: A Ghost Story.** Illus. by author. Holiday House, 1978. 6–9.

In Jewish folklore, a dybbuk is a ghost who inhabits another person's body. When Deborah, an extremely naughty little girl, drowns as a result of a prank, she enters the body of Hannah, whose most exciting activity is embroidering. A rollicking tale with action-packed illustrations portraying life in a nineteenth-century Hungarian village. (Picture book)

Hoffman, Elizabeth P. **Here a Ghost, There a Ghost.** Illus. David Kingham. Julian Messner, 1978. 8–12.

All kinds of ghosts—old, new, noisy, real, and imaginary—are discussed in an anecdote-filled, calm style. The author suggests asking questions before accepting stories as true. Charcoal drawings add to the eerie quality.

Hopkins, Lee Bennett, compiler. **Monsters, Ghoulies and Creepy Creatures.** Illus. Vera Rosenberry. Albert Whitman, 1977. 6–12.

A guaranteed child-pleaser! This collection of stories and poems, both old and new, is often hilarious. Colorful cover and black and white line drawings put faces on the monsters, ghoulies, and creepy creatures of the title. This book would be fun for reading aloud.

Johnston, Tony. **Four Scary Stories.** Illus. Tomie de Paola. G. P. Putnam's Sons, 1978. 6–9.

One night an imp, a goblin, and a scalawag meet in a dark place, and each one tells a scary *boy* story. When a boy really comes, they are at first frightened, then intrigued by his scary story, and all become friends. Full-page illustrations increase the reader's delight. (Picture book)

Kotzwinkle, William. **Dream of Dark Harbor.** Illus. Joe Servello. Doubleday, 1979. 12–up.

Jack leaves home with his shadow and flute, and follows the lure of the Big Water until he climbs far out on the harbor's edge to an abandoned fishing shack. Nearly drowned by tide and storm, Jack's despair changes to courage with the highspirited help of three old seamen's ghosts.

Krensky, Stephen. **The Dragon Circle.** Illus. A. Delaney. Atheneum, 1977. 10–12.

Magic was a Wynd family tradition, practiced for countless generations and now being carried on in a modern-day Massachusetts community. With little call for sorcery, the five Wynd children conjure harmless enchantments until something interferes with their spells and a family of dragons begins to cause problems for everyone.

Kroll, Steven. **Amanda and the Giggling Ghost.** Illus. Dick Gackenbach. Holiday House, 1980. 4–7.

Amanda is awakened by a crash and is startled by a huge ghost demanding her favorite baseball hat. Being refused, the ghost grabs other prize possessions and zooms out the door. She follows it and is blamed for the ghost's thievery. Illustrations in pink, brown, and gray washes. (Picture book)

McGraw, Eloise Jarvis. **Joel and the Great Merlini.** Illus. Jim Arnosky. Pantheon Books, 1979. 7–10.

Joel knows that if he is to become a great magician, he must practice, practice, practice. When a wizard-like magician, the Great Merlini, transmits magical powers to Joel, the boy feels guilty because it is all too easy. A humorous story with a thoughtful ending.

Myers, Steven J. **The Enchanted Sticks.** Illus. Donna Diamond. Coward, McCann & Geoghegan, 1979. 7–10.

A simple Japanese woodcutter is threatened by a band of outlaw samurai warriors. Enchanted sticks help him rescue a kidnapped princess. When danger is over, the sticks lose their magic and serve to cook the old man's fish. Soft line drawings enhance this satisfying tale of innocence rewarded. (Picture book)

Owen, Dilys. **Leo Possessed.** Illus. Stephen Gammell. Harcourt Brace Jovanovich, 1979. 10–12.

When thirteen-year-old Leonora moves with her widowed mother, a brother, and a sister into an old Georgian townhouse in England, she becomes disturbed with the haunting presence of previous occupants. An emotional, dramatic climax forces her to accept herself and her changing family. Illustrations enhance drama of story.

Pearce, Philippa. **The Shadow Cage and Other Tales of the Supernatural.** Illus. Ted Lewin. Thomas Y. Crowell, 1977. 10–14.

This collection of supernatural tales is firmly rooted in present-day, middle-class English family life. The central figures are children and the more successful tales are haunting indeed. There is an occasional fillip of humor. The black and white illustrations are especially effective.

Peck, Richard. **Ghosts I Have Been.** Viking Press, 1977. 12–up.

Blossom Culp has the disturbing ability to communicate with ghosts and the habit of turning Bluff City upside down. Set in the early 1930s, our heroine's adventures climax in London's Madame Taussaud's Museum and Buckingham Palace. An appealing and strong heroine, an intriguing plot, and eccentric characters make an excellent novel.

Postma, Lidia. **The Witch's Garden.** McGraw-Hill, 1979. 7–10.

One rainy day, when a group of children try to frighten a witch with their homemade monster, she surprises them with her kindness. They reluctantly accept an invitation to her secret garden, which holds many bewitching surprises. Beautiful detailed illustrations hauntingly enchant young readers. (Picture book)

Ricks, Charlotte Hall. **Look at Me.** Illus. Annie Gusman. Houghton Mifflin, 1979. 4–7.

When lonely Catherine consistently fails to get her busy mother's attention, she threatens to disappear and does. The understated text is extended by colorful, stylized illustrations. (Picture book)

Roberts, Nancy. **Appalachian Ghosts.** Photographs by Bruce Roberts. Doubleday, 1978. 12–up.

In a collection of thirteen short tales, old ghost stories of the region are merged into modern settings and events. In each story, people long dead haunt the living and test their reasoning and imagination.

Rockwell, Anne. **Walking Shoes.** Doubleday, 1980. 6–9.

This easy-to-read story tells of a sad little red house in search of a family to live in it. A goblin helps the house by giving it magical walking shoes to go looking for a family. Bright child-like illustrations blend with this happy-ending adventure. (Picture book)

Slater, Jim. **Grasshopper and the Unwise Owl.** Illus. Babette Cole. Holt, Rinehart and Winston, 1980. 8–12.

Being a miniature figure in the real world can be exciting and dangerous. That's what happens to Grasshopper, a young boy, after he eats magic candy that causes him to shrink. He makes friends with many animals and is able to solve his mother's problems. Pen drawings and a glossary are included.

Sleator, William. **Into the Dream.** Illus. Ruth Sanderson. E. P. Dutton, 1979. 10–12.

Paul and Francine are linked by a recurring nightmare. They search for and find a small boy, the key to their dream, who possesses amazing powers of the mind. The three share extrasensory mental abilities that make them the focus of a kidnapping plot. A unique chiller that raises thought-provoking questions.

Van Allsburg, Chris. **The Garden of Abdul Gasazi.** Illus. by author. Houghton Mifflin, 1979. 5–8.

A small boy, Alan, a bad tempered dog, Fritz, and a mean magician, Abdul Gasazi, together make a story of enchantment. The strength is in the haunting, wonderfully conceived black and white illustrations. Each detailed drawing speaks of mystery and magic. 1980 Caldecott Honor Book. (Picture book)

Wuorio, Eva-Lis. **Escape If You Can: 13 Tales of the Preternatural.** Viking Press, 1977. 12–up.

Thirteen stories set in Canada, London, and Finland provide an eerie reading experience in the tradition of Edgar Allan Poe. A few display a humorous twist; most revel in the bizarre. For readers who delight in the supernatural, these well-constructed tales are a feast.

Humor

Allard, Harry. **It's So Nice to Have a Wolf around the House.** Illus. James Marshall. Doubleday, 1977. 5–8.

The Old Man and his three old pets advertise for a charming companion. Cuthbert Q. Devine arrives, a wolf disguised as a German shepherd. He does wonders for the household until they learn his true identity: a wolf bank robber. He reforms and they all move to Arizona for the wolf's health. Humorous illustrations. (Picture book)

Barrett, Judi. **Cloudy with a Chance of Meatballs.** Illus. Ron Barrett. Atheneum, 1978. 7–10.

Surreal illustrations set the scene for this tale of calamity in the town of Chewandswallow. The weather sends all the food to the town. It rains soup and snows mashed potatoes. When the tomato tornado ensues, the townspeople set sail on peanut butter sandwiches to a new town. Flashback style. (Picture book)

Brittain, Bill. **All the Money in the World.** Illus. Charles Robinson. Harper & Row, Publishers, 1979. 8–12.

Quentin catches a leprechaun and wishes for all the money in the world. Of course, that means that no one else has any money at all. Quentin visits the White House and the world reaches the brink of war before a way is found to stop Quentin's Midas touch. A funny story with some lighthearted lessons in economics and racial prejudice.

Burningham, John. **Come Away from the Water, Shirley.** Thomas Y. Crowell, 1977. 4–7.

Unnoticed by her parents, who are relaxing at the beach, Shirley ensures herself an exciting day as she imaginatively embarks on an adventure of fighting pirates and buried treasure. Most of the information about her two worlds is found in the illustrations, accompanied by only brief text. (Picture book)

Burningham, John. **Time to Get Out of the Bath, Shirley.** Thomas Y. Crowell, 1978. 4–7.

Mother is tidying the bathroom while Shirley is taking her bath. Unknown to her, the little girl sets off on an imaginary journey. Bright colors show Mother's real-life activities on one page and Shirley's fantasy adventures on the opposite. (Picture book)

Craft, Ruth. **The King's Collection.** Illus. Elisa Trimby. Doubleday, 1978. 4–7.

The king collects everything: tea cups, keys, buttons, toothbrushes, and shoelaces. When he gets the flu, he finds himself bored with his usual collections, but finally wafts off to dreamland collecting pleasant sounds. A charming collection of pictures for identifying and comparing.

Cole, Brock. **No More Baths.** Illus. by author. Doubleday, 1980. 4–7.

Jessie McWhistle runs away because she doesn't want to take a bath. She tries living with Mrs. Chicken, Mrs. Pig, and Mrs. Cat but decides home is best. Good read-aloud book. (Picture book)

Collins, David R. **If I Could, I Would.** Illus. Kelly Oechsli. Garrard Publishing, 1979. 6–9.

An imaginative young boy wishes he could do magical and marvelous things with his mother. Since few books are available for Mother's Day, this one might serve as a model for a class project on making wish books. Colorful and easy to read. (Picture book)

Cressey, James. **Fourteen Rats & a Rat-Catcher.** Illus. Tamasin Cole. Prentice-Hall, 1977. 5–8.

The problems of sharing a house together are viewed by both the nice old lady in her parlor and the happy rat family beneath the floor. A handsome rat-catcher provides satisfying answers for everyone. The simple colorful illustrations yield fresh delights with each perusal. (Picture book)

Cunliffe, John. **The King's Birthday Cake.** Illus. Faith Jaques. Andre Deutsch, 1979. 4–7.

Grandmother Gooseberry bakes a cake for the king's birthday. As it passes from one traveler to another on its journey, unbelievable misfortune accompanies it. This amusing story with brightly colored pictures reminds one of an old-fashioned picture book. Primary children will enjoy this cumulative tale. (Picture book)

Fleischman, Sid. **McBroom Tells a Lie.** Illus. Walter Lorraine. Little, Brown, 1976. 8–12.

How is McBroom going to keep the magical marvelous one-acre farm from evil Heck Jones? Easy. Just mix eleven children, a popcornmobile, self-flipping eggs, and homemade sunshine. This good read-aloud story offers excellent possibilities for creative dramatics. Black and white illustrations.

Gackenbach, Dick. **Harry and the Terrible Whatzit.** Seabury Press, 1977. 4–8.

Determination to protect Mother, who doesn't return from the cellar, gives Harry the courage to attack the thing that he knows is hiding behind the furnace. Under Harry's fierce blows, the terrible thing shrinks, as all fears do when stoutly encountered. Attractive drawings in brown, bright orange, black, and white. Surprise ending. Available in Spanish: *Harry y el Terrible Quensabeque.* (Picture book)

Gackenbach, Dick. **Ida Fanfanny.** Harper & Row, Publishers, 1978. 6–9.

The mountains of Yurt are so high that no weather reaches them until a peddler sells Ida Fanfanny four magic paintings: Summer, Fall, Winter, and Spring. She enjoys the seasons they bring and learns to appreciate the good and bad of each one. Good read-aloud picture book for discussion of weather. (Picture book)

Gantos, Jack. **The Werewolf Family.** Illus. Nicole Rubel. Houghton Mifflin, 1980. 6–10.

The elegantly dressed, attractive Werewolf family sets out for a family reunion, but as the full moon rises their features begin to change. Their teeth become fangs and their faces get quite hairy. The Werewolves' behavior at the party is as wild as their appearance. Brightly patterned illustrations add to the hilarity. (Picture book)

Gibbons, Gail. **The Too-Great Bread Bake Book.** Frederick Warne, 1980. 4–7.

Missy Tilly likes to bake bread and send it to Mr. Simon's store. One day she prepares the dough and places it on the windowsill for the yeastie beasties to do their work. She falls asleep and then the action begins. A lively story with brown and tan folk art illustrations. (Picture book)

Gilchrist, Theo E. **Halfway up the Mountain.** Illus. Glen Rounds. J. B. Lippincott, 1978. 6–8.

An old couple lives in the mountains. The old man becomes tired of eating beef every day, but after his wife scares off Bloodcoe the bandit he learns that there are worse things than a lackluster diet. A clever plot with appropriate illustrations for this easy-to-read book. (Picture book)

Ginsburg, Mirra. **Ookie-Spooky.** Illus. Emily McCully. Crown Publishers, 1979. 5–8.

Masha's mother gave her a drawing book. Each page shows the reader what she's drawn. Gradually something less recognizable begins to take shape and Masha's imagination is off and running! Delightful child-like drawings. Fun for use with primary art classes. Told in rhyme; based on a story by Korney Chukovsky. (Picture book)

Hoban, Russell. **The Twenty Elephant Restaurant.** Illus. Emily Arnold McCully. Atheneum, 1978. 7–10.

After testing one sturdy table, strong enough for an elephant to dance on, an old man and woman open a restaurant with twenty sturdy tables for twenty dancing elephants. Illustrations blend with this ridiculous, humorous tale. Recommended for the reader or listener with sophisticated imagination. (Picture book)

Hurd, Edith Thacher. **Dinosaur My Darling.** Illus. Don Freeman. Harper & Row, Publishers, 1978. 5–10.

Everybody needs somebody to love, and lonely Joe, operator of a steam-powered backhoe, decides to care for the live dinosaur he and his hoe discovered in the depths of the earth. This fantastic odd couple story is illustrated delightfully with line drawings and soft shades of green watercolor. (Picture book)

Kessler, Leonard. **The Pirates' Adventure on Spooky Island.** Garrard Publishing, 1979. 5–8.

Captain Ben of the pirate ship *Jolly Molly* finds a note in a bottle from prisoners begging for rescue from Spooky Island. With the aid of his parrot Polly and his brave crew, he defeats Bad Bart and saves the captives. Easy reading; full-color illustrations. (Picture book)

Krensky, Stephen. **The Perils of Putney.** Illus. Jürg Obrist. Atheneum, 1978. 10–12.

Giant Putney, an apple farmer, has had no experience in rescuing Fair Damsel, who has disappeared. He is unprepared for dealing with sorcerers, witches, ogres, dwarfs, and dragons, but he has no choice. Fantasy lovers will enjoy this spoof. Could be a discussion-starter for contrasts and parallels of characters.

Kuskin, Karla. **Herbert Hated Being Small.** Houghton Mifflin, 1979. 5–8.

Herbert doesn't want to spend his life looking at other people's knees. He sets out with his teddy bear to travel the world. Philomel, who is tall, too tall according to her, does the same. What they find when they meet each other is what the reader will find, short or tall. (Picture book)

LeSieg, Theo. **Please Try to Remember the First of Octember!** Illus. Art Cumings. Random House, 1977. 6–8.

You can have any frabjous, far-out, marvelous, or plain common thing you want, if you'll just wait till the First of Octember. March is too dusty, April's too gusty. This fun-filled beginner's book in rhyme will stimulate reading interest and laughter. Colorful, humorous drawings. (Picture book)

Lööf, Jan. **Uncle Louie's Fantastic Sea Voyage.** Random House, 1977. 8–12.

Rusty is sent to visit Uncle Louis in time to help him and his friend Millpond, a would-be magician, finish their junk-parts paddle steamer. Rusty stows away to sail to Africa; Millpond conjures up a terrific storm! Detailed watercolor drawings. (Picture book)

McGovern, Ann. **Mr. Skinner's Skinny House.** Illus. Mort Gerberg. Four Winds Press, 1980. 4–7.

Humorous reading for a change of pace is offered in this comical story. Mr. Skinner's house is very narrow and his big concern is to find someone to share his new home. Although he does have pets, he wants a real friend. Cartoon-style drawings complement the energetic story. (Picture book)

Martinband, Gerda. **Bing Bong Bang and Fiddle Dee Dee.** Illus. Anne Rockwell. Doubleday, 1979. 6–8.

The old man squeaks too much with his new fiddle, so his wife bangs on a pan to drown out the noise. When the farm animals all run away, the chase leads the old couple through storm and fright, but to a happy ending. An easy-to-read book. (Picture book)

Parker, Nancy Winslow. **The Ordeal of Byron B. Blackbear.** Illus. by author. Dodd, Mead, 1979. 8–12.

Dr. Clothears and colleagues tranquilize a northwoods black bear and attach electronic equipment to him for hibernation research. Byron Bear thwarts science and maintains bear autonomy. Intriguing illustrations also show simple scientific drawings, labelled. Excellent corollary to class nature study or discussion of values in animal research. (Picture book)

Paterson, Diane. **The Bathtub Ocean.** Dial Press, 1979. 5–8.

Henry imagines his bathtub is the bottom of the ocean. What he sees and does there will delight the reader. Colorful lighthearted drawings add whimsy to this easy-to-read book. While the ending is excellent, this book might also be used to allow youngsters to suggest a different conclusion. (Picture book)

Pinkwater, D. Manus. **The Hoboken Chicken Emergency.** Prentice-Hall, 1977. 10–12.

When young Arthur Bobowicz discovers that there are no Thanksgiving turkeys left in the stores, he brings home a 266-pound chicken. Henrietta becomes a pet instead of dinner and the difficulties of keeping her are explored to the zany utmost. Simple black and white drawings add to the wild humor.

Platt, Kin. **Big Max in the Mystery of the Missing Moose.** Illus. Robert Lopshire. Harper & Row, Publishers, 1977. 6–8.

Big Max, who is reminiscent of Sherlock Holmes on a smaller scale, travels by umbrella to find Marvin the missing moose. His expertise as a detective enables him to get on the right track within a short time. A funny story complemented with hilarious pictures. An easy-to-read book. (Picture book)

Poochoo (translator Nelly Segal). **Methuselah's Gang.** Illus. Hank Blaustein. Dodd, Mead, 1980. 8–12.

A group of children befriend Methuselah, an old man with an extremely long beard. Methuselah's gang becomes notorious because of their hilarious adventures in their quest to find the old man's long lost son. Good read-aloud book.

Quin-Harkin, Janet. **Peter Penny's Dance.** Illus. Anita Lobel. Dial Press, 1976. 4–7.

There's no question about it. Peter Penny likes to dance. In fact, he dances when he should be working and the captain of the ship tells him to leave. He sets out to dance around the world in five years and then expects to claim his prize. Appealing illustrations. (Picture book)

Quin-Harkin, Janet. **Septimus Bean and His Amazing Machine.** Illus. Art Cumings. Parents Magazine Press, 1979. 3–5.

Septimus Bean's wonderful machine is impressive but quite useless, despite the king and queen's enthusiastic suggestions. At last the perfect solution is found, much to everyone's delight. Clever rhymed verse that is fun to read; colorful cartoon illustrations. (Picture book)

Rose, Anne. **The Talking Turnip.** Illus. Paul Galdone. Parents Magazine Press, 1979. 6–9.

An old woman is amazed and frightened when her cat, spoon, turnip, and floor start talking to her. She runs off to tell the king only to find more talking objects on the way. Good to read aloud or for dramatic play. (Picture book)

Rounds, Glen. **Mr. Yowder, the Peripatetic Sign Painter.** Holiday House, 1980. 7–10.

Mr. Xenon Zebulon Yowder bills himself as "The World's Bestest and Fastest Sign Painter." In three separate tall tales, he capsulizes a lion's roar in hopes of becoming wealthy, drives a steamboat through the streets of New York City, and develops a giant bull snake by means of body-building exercises. The stories are also published in separate volumes.

Salus, Naomi Panush. **My Daddy's Mustache.** Illus. Tomie de Paola. Doubleday, 1979. 4–7.

Not penguins, not tigers, not cows, but elephants inhabit Daddy's mustache in this imaginative, funny, warmhearted, offbeat picture story. Large, open black and white illustrations are a delight. (Picture book)

Sharmat, Marjorie Weinman. **A Big Fat Enormous Lie.** Illus. David McPhail. E. P. Dutton, 1978. 6–9.

A small boy experiences deep pangs of guilt when he tells a fib. A small green monster, the Lie, lurks behind a bush and grows to enormous proportions as the youngster struggles with his feelings. He finally tells the truth, the Lie shrinks, and a lesson is gently and humorously imparted. (Picture book)

Smath, Jerry. **But No Elephants.** Parents Magazine Press, 1979. 4–10.

Grandma Tildy buys a lot of different animals to become her pets. She does not want an elephant, but she gets one. The elephant saves the day by performing a neat trick. The story is made even funnier through the illustrations. (Picture book)

Wiseman, Bernard. **Morris Has a Cold.** Illus. by author. Dodd, Mead, 1978. 4–7.

Morris the Moose gets a cold and his friend Boris the Bear becomes exasperated trying to make his confused, sick friend well. Cartoon illustrations match the silly humor. Youngsters heartily enjoy this easy-to-read book. (Picture book)

Wiseman, Bernard. **Morris Tells Boris Mother Moose Stories and Rhymes.** Illus. by author. Dodd, Mead, 1979. 4–7.

Boris requests a bedtime story to put him to sleep. Morris tells his version of a Mother Moose story. Boris becomes so frustrated with the story he cannot sleep. The humorous illustrations and text, plus easy vocabulary, will appeal to beginning readers. (Picture book)

New Tales in Folktale Form

Andersen, Hans Christian (compiler Edward Ardizzone and translator Stephen Corrin). **Ardizzone's Hans Andersen.** Illus. by compiler. Atheneum, 1979. 7–10.

Fourteen of Hans Andersen's beloved tales, including well-known ones like "The Steadfast Tin Soldier" and "The Emperor's New

Clothes" and lesser-known ones such as "The Darning Needle" and "The Flying Trunk" are collected in this unique volume. Beautiful full-color illustrations catch the mood and flavor of the tales. (Picture book)

Andersen, Hans Christian (translator Erik Haugaard). **Hans Andersen: His Classic Fairy Tales.** Illus. Michael Foreman. Doubleday, 1978. 7–10.

Eighteen favorite Andersen tales are newly translated into highly readable, elegant prose, accompanied by handsome full-color and black and white illustrations. Included are "Tinderbox," "Princess and the Pea," "Snow Queen," "Emperor's New Clothes," "Wild Swans," "Little Mermaid." Excellent for reading aloud.

Andersen, Hans Christian. **The Princess and the Pea.** Illus. Paul Galdone. Seabury Press, 1978. 7–10.

The test of a real princess is nearly as classic as this Andersen tale. The princess in this version is bent over with pain after sleeping on the pea, even though it was separated from her by twenty mattresses and twenty featherbeds. Full-color humorous illustrations. (Picture book)

Andersen, Hans Christian (adapter Naomi Lewis). **The Snow Queen.** Illus. Errol Le Cain. Viking Press, 1979. 4–7.

Hans Christian Andersen's tale of how Kay is taken away by the Snow Queen and how his playmate Gerda searches for him is exquisitely illustrated in full color. Gerda finally finds her friend and her love frees him from the Snow Queen's spell. (Picture book)

Andersen, Hans Christian. **The Steadfast Tin Soldier.** Illus. Paul Galdone. Clarion Books, 1979. 8–12.

The tin soldier watches the beautiful ballerina who stands on one foot without falling. His admiration for her is resented by the goblin, who casts a spell. The soldier has a series of adventures before he and the ballerina are reunited, sadly, forever. Illustrations are well-detailed, in bright, clear colors. (Picture book)

Andersen, Hans Christian (retold by Amy Ehrlich). **Thumbelina.** Illus. Susan Jeffers. Dial Press, 1979. 7–10.

The sensitivity in this retelling is matched by the delicacy of the illustrations. The book is large in size, which allows Thumbelina to appear dwarfed by the birds, animals, and flowers. An elegant tale of the tiny girl who is rescued by the loving swallow and finally finds her king. (Picture book)

Andersen, Hans Christian. **Ugly Duckling.** Illus. Jennie Williams. Troll Associates, 1979. 5–7.

The ugly duckling is ignored and teased until he realizes that he is a beautiful swan. One of a series of twenty-two books in the "Fables and Fairy Tales" collection. Other Andersen tales in the series are *Emperor and the Nightingale, The Emperor's New Clothes,* and *Thumbelina.* Fresh, vivid, full-color illustrations. (Picture book)

Bedini, Silvio A. **The Spotted Stones.** Illus. Richard Erdoes. Pantheon Books, 1978. 7–10.

When Brother Magro and Brother Grasso embark to visit a faraway shrine they don't anticipate getting lost, being suspected as spies, and worst of all, being thrown into a dungeon. To while away the dreary hours Brother Grasso collects spotted stones; eventually this becomes the enticing game of dominoes.

Bomans, Godfried (translator Patricia Crampton). **The Wily Witch and All the Other Fairy Tales and Fables.** Illus. Wouter Hoogendijk. Stemmer House Publishers, 1977. 8–12.

The collection contains forty-five tales by the modern Dutch master whose works have been compared with those of Hans Christian Andersen, the Brothers Grimm, James Thurber, and Oscar Wilde. Detailed pen and ink drawings extend the text.

Bornstein, Ruth. **The Dancing Man.** Illus. by author. Seabury Press, 1978. 6–9.

Joseph, an orphan in a Baltic Sea village, meets an old man who gives him a gift of silver dancing shoes. Joseph's dancing brings joy to his village and throughout the region. Finally, his life complete, he passes the shoes on to another little boy. Softly shaded black and white illustrations. (Picture book)

Bulla, Clyde Robert. **My Friend the Monster.** Illus. Michele Chessare. Thomas Y. Crowell, 1980. 7–10.

Prince Hal is considered plain and ordinary by the King and Queen, but his forbidden friendship with the young monster Humbert and the exciting adventures they share transform him. Youth, loyalty, and love triumph in a satisfying way over pompous, thoughtless convention. Sensitive, evocative black and white wash drawings.

Bunting, Eve. **Demetrius and the Golden Goblet.** Illus. Michael Hague. Harcourt Brace Jovanovich, 1980. 7–10.

A young prince's passion for the sea is tantalized by a blind old mystic who tells him of the ocean's beauties. When the prince becomes king, he commissions Demetrius, a young sponge diver, to describe the undersea panorama. Demetrius tells only unembellished reality and the king learns a major lesson. (Picture book)

Chapman, Carol. **The Tale of Meshka the Kvetch.** Illus. Arnold Lobel. E. P. Dutton, 1980. 4–7.

The "kvetch" of the village was Meshka. She complained about everything until one day her pseudocomplaints turned into real ones.

This humorous tale about the village complainer is delightfully illustrated. Yiddish flavor. (Picture book)

Coville, Bruce, and Katherine Coville. **Sarah's Unicorn.** J. B. Lippincott, 1979. 6–9.

Sarah's Aunt Mag is a wicked witch and Sarah is lonely until she becomes friends with the unicorn. But Aunt Mag has plans for the special magic of the unicorn's horn; Sarah and her animal friends foil the evil plot. Excellent black and white illustrations in this easy-to-read book. (Picture book)

Cunliffe, John. **The Giant Who Swallowed the Wind.** Illus. Faith Jaques. Andre Deutsch, 1980. 7–10.

When the giant yells for food, people take him all they have, to save themselves from harm. Young Bob proves a way to change the intolerable situation. In retaliation, the giant swallows all their wind. Bob's courageous solution brings good results, even for the giant! Bright illustrations. (Picture book)

Cunliffe, John. **The Great Dragon Competition and Other Stories.** Illus. Alexy Pendle. Andre Deutsch, 1980. 8–12.

Ten stories about dragons, knights, princesses, clever fishermen, and brave girls are told with wit and style. Fun to read. Black and white illustrations.

de Paola, Tomie. **Big Anthony and the Magic Ring.** Illus. by author. Harcourt Brace Jovanovich, 1979. 7–10.

Spring has come to Calabria and Big Anthony moves very slowly. Strega Nona thinks a little night life might make him more speedy. Her magic ring does the trick but it also brings trouble for handsome Big Anthony. Full-page color pictures and gentle, funny text create a good story. (Picture book)

de Paola, Tomie. **The Knight and the Dragon.** Illus. by author. G. P. Putnam's Sons, 1980. 6–12.

A youthful knight has never fought a dragon; nearby lives a dragon who has never fought a knight. Both read up on the subject and practice with dummies. The Big Fight, however, is a glorious fizzle, so the castle librarian starts them on a cooperative project. Full-color illustrations. (Picture book)

Farber, Norma. **A Ship in a Storm on the Way to Tarshish.** Illus. Victoria Chess. Greenwillow Books, 1977. 4–7.

A ship crashes through stormy seas. The narrator, exclaiming in barking verse, is sure all is over, especially when a whale bumps the ship. Narrator Jonah turns navigator and leads the lonely whale home. Illustrated with black and white drawings, this poetic retelling is fun to read aloud. (Picture book)

Fleischman, Sid. **Jim Bridger's Alarm Clock and Other Tall Tales.** Illus. Eric von Schmidt. E. P. Dutton, 1978. 7–12.

The real Jim Bridger, who was a nineteenth-century mountain explorer in the American West, is recast into a legendary figure resembling Pecos Bill or Paul Bunyan. Clever stories and delightful illustrations combine to create innocent humor in these three tall tales.

Flory, Jane. **The Lost and Found Princess.** Illus. by author. Houghton Mifflin, 1979. 6–9.

A plump old woman is joined by a civilized dragon and a cat of superior intellect in a bumbling, but finally successful, attempt to locate a kidnapped princess. Humorous black and white drawings and decorated pages enhance an already appealing story.

Foreman, Michael. **All the King's Horses.** Bradbury Press, 1977. 7–10.

Watercolors evoke a dreamlike Asiatic Steppe setting for this amusing tongue-in-cheek tale of a princess who will marry only a man who can outwrestle her. Will the handsome son of a woodcutter succeed? The unexpected outcome is likely to be especially satisfying to today's girls. (Picture book)

Fox, Paula. **The Little Swineherd and Other Tales.** Illus. Leonard Lubin. E. P. Dutton, 1978. All ages.

These six witty and entertaining stories are a real treat for a variety of ages. One meets ducks, horses, roosters, crickets, raccoons, and the swineherd. All are unique characters and each story is complete in itself. Excellent, elegant illustrations.

Garrison, Christian. **The Dream Eater.** Illus. Diane Goode. Bradbury Press, 1978. 6–9.

Little Yukio experiences troublesome dreams and soon learns that other members in his village are suffering from the same plight. Quite surprisingly, he discovers a baku, an eater of bad dreams, who really needs his help. Ink-on-parchment paintings complete this beautifully told story inspired by a Japanese legend. (Picture book)

Greaves, Margaret. **A Net to Catch the Wind.** Illus. Stephen Gammell. Harper & Row, Publishers, 1979. 7–10.

Princess Mirabelle knows that the silver colt in the forest must always run free. Her father covets the colt for his stable and tricks Mirabelle into luring the colt to capture. After losing both he understands the net that can catch the wind. A fine retelling of the unicorn legend. (Picture book)

Haley, Gail E. **Go Away, Stay Away.** Illus. by author. Charles Scribner's Sons, 1977. 7–10.

People in many parts of the world hold festivals in the spring to lure away any evil spirits that still might be lurking from winter. Villagers join with masks, chants, and dances to free themselves of the *Bunshees* and *Hobble Goblins.* Bold prints done in full color. (Picture book)

Hunter, Mollie. **A Furl of Fairy Wind.** Illus. Stephen Gammell. Harper & Row, Publishers, 1977. 8–10.

Four stories in folktale tradition tell of a Brownie who would not be ignored, a boy who was put under an enchantment by the fairies, a peddler who found the secret of happiness from the fairy queen, and a plain girl who saved a baby from becoming a changeling.

Kennedy, Richard. **The Blue Stone.** Illus. Ronald Himler. Holiday House, 1976. 7–10.

Jack and Bertie, a loving couple, find a blue stone. Bertie swallows it and turns into a chicken. In turn, Jack becomes a rooster, pigs become loaves, and loaves become pigs. Only after the couple solves a musical riddle does life return to normal. A humorous, modern morality tale.

Kennedy, Richard. **The Dark Princess.** Illus. Donna Diamond. Holiday House, 1978. 8–12.

The princess is so beautiful that all who look upon her are blinded by her radiance. Though many seek her hand, none are willing to risk looking at her directly. She doubts love. The jester finally helps the princess to know the true meaning of love. The illustrations illuminate the ethereal mood. (Picture book)

Kent, Jack. **Clotilda.** Random House, 1978. 4–7.

Clotilda, a spunky fairy godmother, turns unbelieving Tommy into a donkey. Tommy's sister Betty, who finds magic in her everyday world, is granted three wishes. Preschool listeners will find the magic enjoyable, not threatening. Humorous, colorful illustrations complement the easy-to-read text. (Picture book)

Krensky, Stephen. **Castles in the Air and Other Tales.** Illus. Warren Lieberman. Atheneum, 1979. 7–10.

Five short stories are based on cliches that are developed into humorous tales. Castles in the air, a fine kettle of fish, the last straw, too clever for words, and a barrel of fun are the themes. These are brief stories that are fun to read.

Krensky, Stephen. **Woodland Crossings.** Illus. Jan Brett Bowler. Atheneum, 1978. 8–11.

A series of five modern fables, delightfully written, portray life's cycles and questions. Black and white sketches of woodland plants and animals are imaginative and detailed. Will fit with philosophy, nature study, ecology units, and fantasy. (Picture book)

Kroeber, Theodora. **Carrousel.** Illus. Douglas Tait. Atheneum, 1977. 7–10.

After the children and Keeper of the Carrousel have gone home, the carrousel animals, descendants of mythological beings, leave their pole positions to gambol on Green Knoll. Proud Pegason flies too high and plummets into the world of Man, who threatens to cement him in place as a statue.

Langton, Jane. **The Fledgling.** Illus. Erik Blegvad. Harper & Row, Publishers, 1980. 10–12.

Georgie, a wisp of a child, wishes more than anything to fly. A migrating Canada goose teaches her, and the two spend many happy hours around and above Walden Pond. The philosophy of Henry Thoreau is interwoven in the plot. 1981 Newbery Honor Book.

Lisowski, Gabriel. **Miss Piggy.** Holt, Rinehart and Winston, 1977. 4–7.

The wolf brothers invite Miss Piggy to a picnic in this delightful spoof on the traditional tale. Miss Piggy leads them on a wild chase that ends when she pushes them out an attic window to a stream below. Humorous black and white line drawings highlight the nearly wordless story. (Picture book)

Lobel, Arnold. **Fables.** Illus. by author. Harper & Row, Publishers, 1980. 10–up.

Animal characters, from crocodile to ostrich, are depicted in richly colored illustrations and their tales are humorously told as modern fables with fresh, new morals. Good for class discussion. 1981 Caldecott Award. (Picture book)

Lobel, Arnold. **How the Rooster Saved the Day.** Illus. Anita Lobel. Greenwillow Books, 1977. 4–8.

A robber, wishing to plunder in the protection of the dark, threatens to kill the rooster who crows up the sun. The rooster tricks the robber into accomplishing the task for him. Framed illustrations provide a stage-like setting for the story. (Picture book)

Lobel, Arnold. **A Treeful of Pigs.** Illus. Anita Lobel. Greenwillow Books, 1979. 7–10.

Each morning the lazy farmer tells his wife he'll help her when the pigs do some preposterous thing. The wife makes the pigs do the feat, but the husband always reneges. At last she outwits him. Outstanding full-color illustrations depict a European peasant setting with much humor. (Picture book)

MacLachlan, Patricia. **Moon, Stars, Frogs, and Friends.** Illus. Tomie de Paola. Pantheon Books, 1980. 7–10.

What happens to a frog prince when he joins real frogs in a pond?

Prince Rupert got sick eating bugs, but he made friends with Randall the frog and had long talks about the moon and stars and friendship. A funny book with a delightful twist at the end. Illustrations underline the humor. (Picture book)

Maestro, Betsy. **Lambs for Dinner.** Illus. Giulio Maestro. Crown Publishers, 1978. 5–9.

Mama Sheep leaves home, warning her four lambs not to let Mr. Wolf in, for he wants them for dinner. But Mr. Wolf, after two unsuccessful tries, captures three lambs. However, this story ends with a happy surprise for Mrs. Sheep and the reader. Delightfully illustrated. (Picture book)

McClenathan, Louise. **My Mother Sends Her Wisdom.** Illus. Rosekrans Hoffman. William Morrow, 1979. 7–10.

The moneylender collects rubles every month for loans made long ago. Widow Petrovna must pay regularly and include a high rate of interest. Finally she works out a plan that finishes the paying. Katya carries out the plan to perfection. All the other peasants benefit from Katya's courage.

Mobley, Jane. **The Star Husband.** Illus. Anna Vojtech. Doubleday, 1979. 8–12.

A girl admires the beauty of the stars and wishes to have one for a husband. Her wish is granted. She goes to live in the sky with her star husband and her son, the Moon. Soon she becomes lonely and wishes to return to mortal life.

Myers, Walter Dean. **The Golden Serpent.** Illus. Alice Provensen and Martin Provensen. Viking Press, 1980. 6–9.

The wise man, Pundabi, lives on a high mountain with Ali, a young boy. One day the King demands that Pundabi solve a mystery but doesn't tell him what the mystery is. Richly colored illustrations accompany this philosophic tale. (Picture book)

Newman, Winifred Barnum. **The Secret in the Garden.** Illus. by author. Baha'l Publishing Trust, 1980. 4–7.

All the people in the village are squabbling over their differences. An old woman comes and plants a garden full of many different flowers to show the villagers how beautiful differences can be. How the villagers learn about love and stop their quarreling makes a delightful tale. (Picture book)

Noble, Trinka Hakes. **The King's Tea.** Dial Press, 1979. 6–9.

The milk is sour so the king's tea isn't perfect. He blames the servant, who blames the cook, who blames the next person, etc. When the

king overhears the cow being blamed, he stops the blaming and
everyone has a wonderful tea party. A funny cumulative tale. (Picture
book)

Parish, Peggy. **Zed and the Monsters.** Illus. Paul Galdone. Doubleday,
1979. 8–12.

Zed leaves his rockin' chair, with a lunch from Ma in his handy bag,
and ambles away to work for a little money. The governor promises
Zed a bag of gold for killing four monsters. Whimsical illustrations
complement Zed's spunky adventures. Good read-aloud book.

Ruskin, John. **The King of the Golden River.** Illus. Krystyna Turska.
Greenwillow Books, 1978. 8–12.

In Treasure Valley live three brothers. Two are cruel and greedy
while the youngest one is kind and loving. Though his brothers are
as harsh to him as they are to the neighbors, Bluck remains loving.
The King of the Golden River rewards him and punishes the older
brothers. (Picture book)

Sage, Alison. **The Ogre's Banquet.** Illus. Gian Calvi. Doubleday, 1978.
7–10.

Tom, the seventh son of a seventh son, is sent to serve the ogre. His
task of turning a disreputable-looking, gravelly-voiced gryphon into
a sleek and beautiful songster proves impossible. However, Tom
manages to charm the ogre and make a better life for the townspeople. Humorous, colorful illustrations. (Picture book)

Stearns, Pamela. **The Fool and the Dancing Bear.** Illus. Ann Strugnell.
Little, Brown, 1979. 8–12.

A curse by a spiteful queen, a young king in love with a beautiful
princess, a faithful jester, and a mysterious bear are all included in a
fantasy adventure with elements of the classic fairy tale. Well written;
beautifully detailed illustrations. Highly recommended for fantasy
readers.

Steele, Mary Q. **The Owl's Kiss.** Greenwillow Books, 1978. 8–12.

In the title story, the first of three short allegorical stories, a girl
overcomes her fear of owls when she admits to a dishonest act. "The
Last Great Smoke" tells of a man who regains his honor by making
restitution for a crime he did not commit. In "Dita's Story" a girl
resists using her powers of witchcraft for personal gain.

Tompert, Ann. **Charlotte & Charles.** Illus. John Wallner. Crown Publishers, 1979. 4–7.

Charles and Charlotte live alone on an island. When settlers arrive,
Charlotte is delighted and Charles is wary. Doubts and superstitions

among the settlers threaten the gentle way of life of the original inhabitants, reflecting the wide range of human behavior. Detailed colored illustrations. (Picture book)

van der Meer, Ron, and Atie van der Meer. **Oh Lord!** Crown Publishers, 1980. 7–10.

Using quantities of paint and clay, the Lord creates the world in seven hectic days with the help of two enthusiastic cherubs. A funny book, but not for those who would be offended by a Lord who looks like Santa, takes showers, eats chocolates, and spanks naked cherubs. (Picture book)

Van Woerkom, Dorothy O. **Harry and Shellburt.** Illus. Erick Ingraham. Macmillan Publishing, 1977. 5–8.

An old fable, the tortoise and the hare, is creatively and amusingly retold. The young reader will relate to the well-defined personalities of friends Harry and Shellburt. Large illustrations capture the gentle spirit of this easy-to-read tale. (Picture book)

Wetterer, Margaret. **Patrick and the Fairy Thief.** Illus. Enrico Arno. Atheneum, 1980. 5–8.

Patrick lives in a thatched cottage in Ireland with his mother. His prize possession is his little brown cow. Trouble appears when the fairy folk steal his mother and try to steal his cow. Patrick's courage manages to thwart the fairies' evil designs and break the spell that holds his mother. (Picture book)

Wilde, Oscar (abridged by Jennifer Westwood). **The Star Child.** Illus. Fiona French. Four Winds Press, 1979. 6–9.

The mysterious child found in the forest by woodcutters grows up to be beautiful, vain, and cruel. Denying his old mother, he suddenly becomes hideously ugly and is forced to learn compassion in a hard world before assuming his rightful place. Glowing, luminous, full-color illustrations. (Picture book)

Williams, Jay. **The Water of Life.** Illus. Lucinda McQueen. Four Winds Press, 1980. 7–10.

A kind-hearted young fisherman, Pilchard, sets out to find the Water of Life for the king. His adventures along the way, and the secret he eventually finds, are told in a simple, eloquent style. Full-color paintings add humor and warmth to the story with a familiar theme. (Picture book)

Wolkstein, Diane. **White Wave.** Illus. Ed Young. Thomas Y. Crowell, 1979. 6–9.

In China a young farmer, poor and shy, lives alone. One day he finds a Moon snail and the Goddess White Wave comes to care for him.

His life is transformed. A beautiful tale, delicately and sensitively told. Exquisite, monochromatic drawings. (Picture book)

Yolen, Jane. **Dream Weaver.** Illus. Michael Hague. William Collins Publishers, 1979. 10–up.

The dream weaver, a blind gypsy storyteller, weaves dreams for the price of a penny. Seven people seek her stories and she tells haunting, imaginative tales of love, life, and death. Good for class discussions.

Yolen, Jane. **The Hundredth Dove and Other Tales.** Illus. David Palladini. Thomas Y. Crowell, 1977. 10–12.

Seven haunting tales make up this unique collection of short stories for the reader with a taste for the unusual and the imaginative. Superbly written, each story has a flavor of the past with a touch of modern myth. Elegant, handsome charcoal drawings.

Yolen, Jane. **The Seeing Stick.** Illus. Remy Charlip and Demetra Maraslis. Thomas Y. Crowell, 1977. 7–10.

An old man shows a blind princess how to see with her fingers when he carves scenes and figures on a golden stick. The gentle wisdom of this tale, set in Ancient China, is made even more dramatic by exquisite pastel drawings. (Picture book)

Yolen, Jane. **The Simple Prince.** Illus. Jack Kent. Parents Magazine Press, 1978. 4–7.

The prince decides to lead the simple life. He claps his hands and his servants prepare his plain clothes and lunch. He finds a farm where he learns that simple means hard work; his attitude changes, so that he becomes a much simpler, nicer prince. Colorful illustrations; good for choral reading. (Picture book)

Yoo, Edward Yushin, retold by. **Bong Nam and the Pheasants.** Illus. Demi. Prentice-Hall, 1979. 6–9.
A young Korean boy rescues some baby pheasants from a giant snake. Days later the snake, disguised as a beautiful young girl, captures the boy and threatens to kill him unless he accomplishes a seemingly impossible task. Delicately tinted line drawings capture the mood of the tale. (Picture book)

Strange and Unique Creatures

Ahlberg, Janet, and Allan Ahlberg. **Jeremiah in the Dark Woods.** Viking Press, 1978. 4–7.

Jeremiah sets out to find the thief of his grandma's strawberry tarts and meets many unusual characters. The action is fast paced, and the illustrations whimsical. The total production adds up to fun. (Picture book)

Baker, Betty. **Latki and the Lightning Lizard.** Illus. Donald Carrick. Macmillan Publishing, 1979. 7–10.

Latki, a young girl, loves her home in Red Rock Canyon, but she must leave to rescue her imprisoned sister from a giant lizard. She's assisted by her animal friends, the ant, the lion, and the eagle. Illustrations contribute to the magical quality of the story. (Picture book)

Balian, Lorna. **Leprechauns Never Lie.** Illus. by author. Abingdon Press, 1980. 6–9.

Lazy Ninny Nanny tells Gram she'll catch a leprechaun to make them rich for life. Ninny Nanny catches the leprechaun, but the little imp tricks her into much more than finding his hidden gold. Illustrations are in soft browns except for the leprechaun's green hat. (Picture book)

Barrett, Judi. **The Wind Thief.** Illus. Diane Dawson. Atheneum, 1977. 4–7.

The wind wants to keep his cold head from getting goose bumps, so he chooses a special hat to blow off and pull down over his ears. His blowing causes confusion and surprise. Children will relate to the ridiculous fun the wind causes. Detailed pen and ink illustrations add humor. (Picture book)

Brooks, Gregory. **Monroe's Island.** Illus. by author. Bradbury Press, 1979. 4–7.

In the midst of a bath, Monroe is transported to a desert island and back again by his imagination, a blue beastie with two horns on its nose and a little smile on its face. Through fresh, clear colors, economical lines, and a sparse text, the adventurous spirit of childhood is captured in this deceptively simple book. (Picture book)

Brown, Marc. **Witches Four.** Parents Magazine Press, 1980. 4–7.

A delightful picture book for any time of year, and especially for Halloween. Four little witches, flying upside down, lose their hats. Four lucky cats use those hats as houses—until the Kerbooms! Outstanding art work. (Picture book)

Cameron, Ann. **Harry (the Monster).** Illus. Jeanette Winter. Pantheon Books, 1980. 4–7.

Harry, a forty-foot monster, is afraid of children. Only when he bravely rescues his bullfrog friend, does he discover that children are more afraid of him than he is of them. Soft, detailed illustrations nicely balance the sensitive subject of being afraid. (Picture book)

Carle, Eric. **Watch Out! A Giant!** William Collins Publishers, 1978. 4–7.

Two children go out to play and are caught by a ferocious giant who plans to eat them. They escape through a die-cut trapdoor, and the story has a satisfactory ending. The clever die-cut illustrations will appeal to young children. (Picture book)

Coville, Bruce, and Katherine Coville. **The Foolish Giant.** J. B. Lippincott, 1978. 4–7.

The good deeds of Harry, a friendly giant, get him into trouble, and the mayor sends him from town. A wicked wizard threatens the villagers, but Harry returns and surprises them all. Preschoolers will enjoy listening to the story and sharing its comical pencil illustrations. (Picture book)

Cunliffe, John. **Sarah's Giant and the Upside Down House.** Illus. Hilary Abrahams. Andre Deutsch, 1980. 4–7.

When Sarah's mother scolds her because the house is upside-down, Sarah enlists the aid of her giant friend, Mr. Zub, who actually turns the house upside-down. Children will enjoy watching Sarah and her parents cope with upside-down sinks, stoves, television sets, and stairs. (Picture book)

Cushman, Doug, compiler. **Giants.** Illus. by compiler. Platt & Munk, Publishers, 1980. 6–9.

This oversized book—appropriately so—contains two poems and four stories about giants. Along with the well-known giant who lived atop Jack's beanstalk and Oscar Wilde's selfish giant are Fergus McGrath, the Connemara giant, and the giant who built an enormous hill near Shrewsbury. (Picture book)

de Paola, Tomie. **Helga's Dowry.** Illus. by author. Harcourt Brace Jovanovich, 1977. 5–8.

Helga is a lovely troll who has no dowry. To keep the affection of handsome Lars, she uses her troll cunning and skill to win a dowry in the world of people—and a new suitor. Charming illustrations. (Picture book)

Fleischman, Sid. **The Hey Hey Man.** Illus. Nadine Bernard Westcott. Little, Brown, 1979. 8–12.

A thief has overheard the farmer burying his gold beneath the Hey Hey Man's tree and sneaks out to steal the money. How the Hey Hey Man pursues him and recovers the gold make a hilarious tall tale. (Picture book)

Fujikawa, Gyo. **Come Follow Me . . . to the Secret World of Elves and Fairies and Gnomes and Trolls.** Grosset & Dunlap, 1979. 4–7.

"Come, follow, follow me . . . " invites the reader to the magical world of elves, fairies, gnomes, and trolls. The delightful variety of poems and brief stories is enhanced by the numerous colored and occasional black and white illustrations. Appealing book. (Picture book)

Harrison, Sarah. **In Granny's Garden.** Illus. Mike Wilks. Holt, Rinehart and Winston, 1980. 6–10.

A young boy in his Granny's "jungly wild" garden discovers a Brontosaurus with eyes as "bosky and benign as warm night skies." The careful details of the vivid illustrations make this fantasy seem quite real. (Picture book)

Hearne, Betsy Gould. **Home.** Illus. Trina Schart Hyman. Atheneum, 1979. 10–12.

A companion book to the author's *South Star* is the story of Megan, daughter of giants, who tries to find the lost King Brendan, her sister's husband. Aided by a sun bird and a boy, she locates Brendan, who is held captive by lionlike men on an island far out to sea. The exciting story is enhanced by vivid imagery and several levels of interpretation.

Hearne, Betsy Gould. **South Star.** Illus. Trina Schart Hyman. Atheneum, 1977. 10–12.

Megan, daughter of the giants, flees for her life when the Screamer attacks her home. The haunting tale of her escape with the help of the boy Randall and the south star is illustrated with pen and ink drawings.

Hunter, Mollie. **The Wicked One.** Harper & Row, Publishers, 1977. 10–up.

The Grollican is a creature who picks on feisty-tempered people. Colin is bothered by its nasty magic and tries to outwit it. When he leaves Ireland for New York City, he is sure he is rid of it. Alas, the wicked one is there also. A rollicking tale.

Huygen, Wil. **Gnomes.** Illus. Rien Poortvliet. Harry N. Abrams, Publishers, 1977. 12–up.

A glorious feast of color, this book is rich in imagination and fun. The tongue-in-cheek documentary examination of gnomes—their history, their sociological and physiological data, their folklore and daily life—provides endless pleasure for readers and browsers.

Janosch (translator Klaus Flugge). **Hey Presto! You're a Bear!** Little, Brown, 1977. 4–7.

A little boy has the magic ability to change people into animals. When he changes his father into a bear, a wild romp begins: furniture is overturned, rooms are flooded, and a circus performance takes place. The illustrations are rich in humorous detail. (Picture book)

Kellogg, Steven. **The Mysterious Tadpole.** Dial Press, 1977. 4–7.

Alphonse, the "tadpole" that Louis received from his uncle in Scotland, outgrows not only the bathtub but the apartment as well. Louis realizes that Alphonse needs a swimming pool and the problem of providing one is solved with the help of the librarian. Large color illustrations and short text make this a good read-aloud book. (Picture book)

Kennedy, Richard. **Inside My Feet: The Story of a Giant.** Illus. Ronald Himler. Harper & Row, Publishers, 1979. 8–12.

Giant boots appear mysteriously outside the door. First the father disappears while investigating the noise made by the boots, then the mother. Only the boy remains to solve the mystery and to find his parents. A fantasy with a different twist.

Kennedy, Richard. **The Leprechaun's Story.** Illus. Marcia Sewall. E. P. Dutton, 1979. 6–9.

A tradesman walking along a country road spies a leprechaun who, according to tradition, must lead the person who discovers him to a pot of gold. The leprechaun tries to fool the wise tradesman, who is determined that he won't be tricked. (Picture book)

Krensky, Stephen. **A Troll in Passing.** Atheneum, 1980. 8–12.

Morgan senses that he is not like the other trolls. More interested in the life of the village, he becomes a forager who steals from the local people to learn more about them. His knowledge about the world ultimately enables him to save the troll community.

Lodge, Bernard. **Rhyming Nell.** Illus. Maureen Roffey. Lothrop, Lee & Shepard Books, 1979. 5–8.

Nell, a witch who casts spells in rhymes, can change adders into ladders and flowers into showers. Her mistake is finding a rhyme for her own name. Delightful drawings on full- and half-page formats allow the spells to be surprises. (Picture book)

MacKellar, William. **The Witch of Glen Gowrie.** Illus. Ted Lewin. Dodd, Mead, 1978. 8–12.

Gavin Fraser doesn't believe in witches until he meets Meg Leckie and watches her heal an injured dog. The mystery of Meg's disappearance and Gavin's discovery of his own talents further the suspense of this novel, reminiscent of a Scottish folktale. Black and white illustrations.

Mayne, William. **A Year and a Day.** E. P. Dutton, 1976. 10–12.

Two little girls find a strange, naked male child on a Midsummer Eve in Cornwall. Christened Adam, the boy doesn't speak or need to eat or sleep. In spite of the loving care of the Polwarne family, the child dies in a year and a day as the local witch had predicted. When a boy is born to the family, he is named Adam.

Miles, Patricia. **The Gods in Winter.** E. P. Dutton, 1978. 10–12.

Twelve-year-old Adam Bramble senses a strangeness about the new home-help the moment she arrives. His account of the mysterious, occasionally frightening, events that surround his lively family during an unusually bitter English winter is a fascinating story that involves a retelling of the classic myth of Demeter and Persephone.

Murphy, Shirley Rousseau. **The Pig Who Could Conjure the Wind.** Illus. Mark Lefkowitz. Atheneum, 1978. 6–9.

Miss Folly is a witch pig whose delight is riding the wind. When a demon casts a spell that causes Miss Folly to crash to earth, she is saved by those whom she has aided. The poetic text and pen and ink drawings capture the joy of swirling above the earth.

Myers, Amy. **I Know a Monster.** Illus. by author. Addison-Wesley Publishing, 1979. 4–7.

Each child sitting in a circle adds to the story of the horrible monster the group is creating. When the monster begins to eat children, the group discovers that they are afraid of their own creation. One of the youngsters saves the day and eliminates the monster! Scary pictures. (Picture book)

Ness, Evaline. **Marcella's Guardian Angel.** Illus. by author. Holiday House, 1979. 6–9.

Marcella has a guardian angel who is a pest. She hovers over Marcella and comments on her behavior, muttering words like "Rude!" or "Stingy!" Marcella's dislike of the angel grows until she learns the game of flip-flop. Bold illustrations in reds, greens, and browns capture Marcella's knobby-kneed charm. (Picture book)

Polushkin, Maria. **The Little Hen and the Giant.** Illus. Yuri Salzman. Harper & Row, Publishers, 1977. 5–8.

Fiery Kurochka, the little hen, has one ambition, "to kill that fool Giant who takes my eggs!" Little but mighty, she succeeds. This humorous tale with a decided Russian flavor has large pictures that make it an excellent choice for reading aloud. (Picture book)

Robb, Brian. **The Last of the Centaurs.** Andre Deutsch, 1979. 6–9.

Achilles, the last of the centaurs, needs new clothes and is fitted by an English tailoring firm. When the fitting fails, Roderick, the tailor, is fired. The children help him and, with Achilles' timely aid, all turns out well. A whimsical tale, colorfully illustrated. (Picture book)

Robison, Nancy. **Izoo.** Illus. Edward Frascino. Lothrop, Lee & Shepard Books, 1980. 6–9.

An ice girl lures a boy and a girl into an igloo, which then flies to the far North. There she leads them into an icy cave from which they must escape or be frozen as specimens of earth children in an ice zoo. Clever wordplay enlivens the conversations and cartoon illustrations add to the fun. (Picture book)

Sargent, Sarah. **Weird Henry Berg.** Crown Publishers, 1980. 8–12.

A baby dragon pops up in Henry Berg's life. An older dragon is sent from Wales to bring back the baby dragon. An old lady helps in the rescue, and Henry Berg learns a lesson about dragons and himself. An unusual and interesting story.

Steig, William. **The Amazing Bone.** Farrar, Straus & Giroux, 1976. 4–7.

A talking bone, fed up with being owned by a nasty witch, takes up with a plump and pretty pig and then saves her from the clutches of a suave fox. Large watercolor illustrations are rich in humor. (Picture book)

Stevenson, James. **The Worst Person in the World.** Greenwillow Books, 1978. 6–9.

The worst person in the whole world has a change of heart when he meets the ugliest creature in the world. The story is humorously told and is an excellent choice for reading aloud. (Picture book)

Sundgaard, Arnold. **Jethro's Difficult Dinosaur.** Illus. Stan Mack. Pantheon Books, 1977. 5–8.

Jethro finds a large egg in the park and takes it home to hatch. Much to his surprise it turns out to be a dinosaur that grows at a rapid rate. Rhyme as well as humorous drawings make this easy-to-read book especially enjoyable. (Picture book)

Towne, Mary. **Goldenrod.** Atheneum, 1977. 12–up.

Goldenrod answers the Madden's ad for a baby-sitter and is hired. On the very first day of her employment, the five children discover she has extraordinary powers. Exciting adventures are in store for the Madden family as their friend transports them through space.

Wagner, Jenny. **The Bunyip of Berkeley's Creek.** Illus. Ron Brooks. Bradbury Press, 1977. 4–7.

A muddy creature crawls out of Berkeley's Creek and asks, "What am I?" The responses are puzzling and disturbing until he meets another creature like himself, a bunyip, an Australian folk-monster. Australian terms such as *billabong* and *billy* will need explanations; otherwise, the story is simply written and appealing.

Williams, Jay. **Everyone Knows What a Dragon Looks Like.** Illus. Mercer Mayer. Four Winds Press, 1976. 7–10.

A Great Cloud Dragon is the only hope to save the city of Wu from attack. When a fat old bald man claims to be the dragon, no one believes him. Only Han, the poor gatekeeper, treats him with respect and kindness. For Han, the dragon saves the city. (Picture book)

Williams, Leslie. **A Bear in the Air.** Illus. Carme Solé Vendrell. Stemmer House Publishers, 1980. All ages.

A boy lying on his back watching a cloud-filled summer sky spots a bear in the air. The bear becomes real and speaks in rhyme, which eventually exasperates the boy. The book is useful for word play and imagination-stretching activities. (Picture book)

Yolen, Jane. **The Giants Go Camping.** Illus. Tomie de Paola. Seabury Press, 1979. 4–7.

On a hot summer day at Fe-Fi-Fo-Farm, five giants decide to go on vacation. Dab, the smallest giant, organizes a fun-filled camping trip at a mountain lake. Lively drawings contribute to the appeal of this easy-to-read book. (Picture book)

Yolen, Jane. **The Mermaid's Three Wisdoms.** Illus. Laura Rader. William Collins Publishers, 1978. 8–12.

Melusina, a mermaid who cannot speak, violates the merfolk's code and is seen by Jess, a twelve-year-old girl with a hearing impairment. Melusina must leave the sea and live on land, where the two become close friends. A skillfully written tale that blends fantasy and reality.

Zolotow, Charlotte. **I Have a Horse of My Own.** Illus. Yoko Mitsuhashi. Thomas Y. Crowell, 1980. 5–8.

A small girl tells of the horse with whom she rides at night to beautiful and wonderful places. In the morning she eats breakfast and goes to school. The book is sensitive to the role imagination plays in the lives of children, and the illustrations complement the poetic mood. The book is useful for discussions of imaginary playmates. (Picture book)

Talking Toys

Bornstein, Ruth. **Annabelle.** Illus. by author. Thomas Y. Crowell, 1978. 3–5.

Annabelle, a lonely toy chimpanzee, feels left out when Sarah, her owner, goes to the park. While searching for her owner, Annabelle has a number of action-packed adventures. This is a story of caring and the love children have for toys. (Picture book)

Hoffmann, E. T. A., (adapter Janet Schulman). **The Nutcracker.** Illus. Kay Chorao. E. P. Dutton, 1979. 8–12.

Here is the fanciful tale of a toy nutcracker who comes to life, fights a battle with the seven-headed mouse king, escorts a little girl through the Land of Sweets, and in the end becomes her true love.

Delicate illustrations reflect the nineteenth-century German setting of this story, which was used by Tchaikovsky in his famous Nutcracker ballet.

Howe, Deborah, and James Howe. **Teddy Bear's Scrapbook.** Illus. David S. Rose. Atheneum, 1980. 4–7.

Teddy Bear recounts his colorful past to a little girl on a rainy afternoon as they look at the pictures in his scrapbook: cowboy, circus performer, even a Hollywood actor. An appealing story with pen illustrations. (Picture book)

Jones, Harold. **There & Back Again.** Atheneum, 1977. 4–7.

Bunby, a stuffed rabbit, doesn't like being left alone and sets off in a toy sailboat to seek adventure. After a wet mishap he shares a glorious afternoon with the forest animals before returning home to the playroom. A gentle story for the youngest believer. (Picture book)

Manley, Seon, and Gogo Lewis, compilers. **The Haunted Dolls.** Doubleday, 1980. 10–up.

This nicely illustrated anthology of eerie tales about dolls with unique powers and lives of their own will attract readers of all ages. Among the authors are Agatha Christie, Algernon Blackwood, Jerome K. Jerome, and Hans Christian Andersen.

Virin, Anna. **Elsa's Bears.** Harvey House, Publishers, 1978. 3–5.

Little Elsa's three stuffed bears have a way of getting lost and finding themselves in mischievous situations. Preschoolers will enjoy the exciting world presented in these adventures. The text is brief and encourages listening. Bright, clear pictures enhance this tiny, appealing book, the first in a series of six. (Picture book)

Wright, Dare. **Edith and Midnight.** Doubleday, 1978. 5–8.

Lovers of dolls, teddy bears, ponies, farms, and fishing will respond with delight to this summertime adventure. Edith, a doll, and her friend, Little Bear, use apples and kindness to tame a wild pony. This oversize book is illustrated with full-page photographs. (Picture book)

Time Fantasy

Anderson, Margaret. **In the Circle of Time.** Alfred A. Knopf, 1979. 10–up.

This compelling story tells of two Scottish children who visit the ancient stones of Arden and slip into future time. There they discover a world where people with limited resources live in peace, though pursued by a barbaric tribe. Strong characterizations and an interesting exploration of value systems.

Babbitt, Natalie. **The Eyes of the Amaryllis.** Farrar, Straus & Giroux, 1977. 10–12.

Jenny comes to Gran's ocean home to take care of her grandmother, who has a broken ankle. Gran, who has been waiting thirty years for a sign from her dead husband, soon has Jenny watching for a signal from the sea. Jenny, her father, and Gran come to a richer understanding of each other.

Bond, Nancy. **A String in the Harp.** Atheneum, 1977. 12–up.

The Morgans, three American children and their father, arrive in Wales, still grieving over the death of Mrs. Morgan. Mr. Morgan loses himself in work and Jen and Becky slowly adjust, but Peter hates everything until he finds the ancient tuning key of a sixth-century harp. The mystical power of the key opens the past and allows Peter to be reconciled with his family. 1977 Newbery Honor Book.

Bosse, Malcolm J. **Cave beyond Time.** Thomas Y. Crowell, 1980. 12–up.

Fifteen-year-old Ben, recently orphaned, finds himself attached to an archeological team with his uncle in Arizona. Unable to get involved in the dig, Ben wanders off toward a mountain and finds himself in a strange world where sloths and camels roam America. Later, after his return, he offers a theory to interpret certain findings of the team.

Cooper, Susan. **Silver on the Tree.** Atheneum, 1978. 12–up.

It is summer in England when the Dark rises for the last, most dangerous time. The circle gathers: Will Stanton, the Welsh boy Bran, and the Drew children. In the mountains of Wales the Forces of Light, with the aid of the crystal sword, vanquish the Dark. This highly imaginative, myth-laden novel brings to an exciting climax *The Dark Is Rising* sequence. Magic departs, and the mortals' world remains.

Curry, Jane Louise. **Poor Tom's Ghost.** Illus. by author. Atheneum, 1977. 12–up.

Roger's life becomes entwined with that of his seventeenth-century counterpart, so that poor Tom's ghost may rest in peace in the Elizabethan house that Roger's family has discovered under the ugly additions of a later age. Roger acts bravely to save his father from fatal involvement with an actor-ghost. Overtones from *Hamlet* are subtly woven into plot and theme.

Davies, Andrew. **Conrad's War.** Crown Publishers, 1980. 10–12.

Obsessed with war, Conrad is determined to build a tank. He dreams of World War II as a thrilling adventure in which he is an energetic, courageous tank driver. The story shifts from reality to fantasy, leaking back into time as Conrad comes to believe that he is participating in a past war.

Ellerby, Leona. **King Tut's Game Board.** Illus. Susan Hopp. Lerner Publications, 1980. 12–up.

Justin, on vacation in Egypt with his parents, teams up with a mysterious companion, Nathan Alistant. The two boys are history buffs, but their sightseeing trips turn into high adventure as Nate follows a quest from another time and place in this exciting blend of mystery and fantasy.

Freeman, Barbara C. **A Pocket of Silence.** E. P. Dutton, 1978. 12–up.

Caroline has a recurring dream of the cottage where she lived until her mother's death. On her sixteenth birthday she returns to the village, meets a ghost, and solves a riddle about the past and future. A fresh twist to the haunted-house theme.

Greenfield, Eloise. **Africa Dream.** Illus. Carole Byard. John Day, 1977. 8–10.

A black child's dream fantasy of long ago and far away Africa is explored through pictures and narrative. Black and white pictures lend a dreamlike quality to a vision of Africa that includes the familiar and the unknown, the ancient and the modern. (Picture book)

Lively, Penelope. **A Stitch in Time.** E. P. Dutton, 1976. 10–12.

Perhaps because her parents are so reserved, Maria, an only child, talks to trees and animals. On holiday by the sea, she becomes involved with people and events of a hundred years ago. A lively neighbor boy, a formidable landlady, and a sampler contribute to the fantasy story of a girl on the verge of growing up.

Lively, Penelope. **The Voyage of QV 66.** Illus. Harold Jones. E. P. Dutton, 1979. 10–12.

Floods have caused humans to evacuate Earth, leaving it to the animals. Stanley, a small, furry, personlike animal, has never seen another like himself. Aboard a small boat, he and five assorted animals travel to London to find his identity in this anthropomorphic satire on human foibles.

Maguire, Gregory. **The Daughter of the Moon.** Farrar, Straus & Giroux, 1980. 10–up.

Twelve-year-old Erikka longs for escape from her home and family. She is determined to become an artist and create a place of peace and beauty. The magic of a candlestick and a painting transport Erikka to a moonlit mountain where unexpected events help her solve difficult problems and accept herself and her family.

Mäh   lqvist, Stefan. **I'll Take Care of the Crocodiles.** Illus. Tord Nygren. Atheneum, 1978. 5–8.

Papa lies down with little Eric until the youngster falls asleep, and then the action begins. The pictures on the wall become enlarged, and Eric and Papa become part of the scene. Appealing watercolor pictures capture the action of the story.

Stewart, Mary. **A Walk in Wolf Wood.** Illus. Emanuel Schongut. William Morrow, 1980. 12–up.

John and Margaret are picnicking in the woods when they spot a strangely dressed, weeping man. Curious, they follow him into Wolf Woods and find that they have been sent back in time to the fourteenth century to rescue a man under enchantment.

Westall, Robert. **The Wind Eye.** Greenwillow Books, 1977. 12–up.

Vacationing on a desolate section of English coast, Michael finds an ancient Viking ship. He and his two half-sisters soon discover that the *Resurre* has the power to short-circuit time. An extraordinary blending of fact and legend about the medieval Saint Cuthbert. No illustrations; some profanity.

Wibberley, Leonard. **The Crime of Martin Coverly.** Farrar, Straus & Giroux, 1980. 12–up.

Nick's investigation into the strange sounds and odors in his family's old Florida house leads him to a late-night meeting with the ghost of an eighteenth-century pirate. Traveling back in time, Nick finds himself in the midst of the search for the fabled King Solomon's Mines.

Additional Modern Fantasy Books

Alexander, Lloyd. *The High King.* Holt, Rinehart and Winston, 1968. 9–14.
Andersen, Hans Christian. *The Little Match Girl.* Illus. Blair Lent. Houghton Mifflin, 1968. 6–12.
Andersen, Hans Christian. *The Nightingale.* Translated by Eva le Galliene. Illus. Nancy Ekholm Burkert. Harper & Row, Publishers, 1965. 8–up.
Atwater, Richard, and Florence Atwater. *Mr. Popper's Penguins.* Illus. Robert Lawson. Little, Brown, 1938. 9–12.
Babbitt, Natalie. *The Search for Delicious.* Farrar, Straus & Giroux, 1969. 8–12.
Babbitt, Natalie. *Tuck Everlasting.* Farrar, Straus & Giroux, 1975. 10–up.
Barrie, J. M. *Peter Pan.* Illus. Nora Unwin. Charles Scribner's Sons, 1954. 10–12.
Boston, Lucy M. *The Treasure of Green Knowe.* Illus. Peter Boston. Harcourt Brace Jovanovich, 1958. 9–12.
Burningham, John. *Mr. Gumpy's Outing.* Holt, Rinehart and Winston, 1971. 3–6.
Burton, Virginia Lee. *The Little House.* Houghton Mifflin, 1942. 4–7.
Burton, Virginia Lee. *Mike Mulligan and His Steam Shovel.* Houghton Mifflin, 1939. 4–7.
Butterworth, Oliver. *The Enormous Egg.* Illus. Louis Darling. Little, Brown, 1956. 9–12.

Carroll, Lewis. *Alice's Adventures in Wonderland and Through the Looking Glass.* Illus. John Tenniel. Macmillan Publishing, 1963 (1865, 1872). 10–12.

Cleary, Beverly. *Runaway Ralph.* Illus. Louis Darling. William Morrow, 1970. 8–12.

Cooper, Susan. *The Grey King.* Atheneum, 1975. 10–14.

de Regniers, Beatrice Schenk. *May I Bring a Friend?* Atheneum, 1964. 4–8.

du Bois, William Pène. *Bear Circus.* Viking Press, 1971. 5–8.

du Bois, William Pène. *The Twenty-one Balloons.* Viking Press, 1947. 8–12.

Eager, Edward. *Half-Magic.* Illus. N. M. Bodecker. Harcourt Brace Jovanovich, 1954. 9–up.

Freeman, Don. *Dandelion.* Viking Press, 1964. 5–8.

Gág, Wanda. *Millions of Cats.* Coward, McCann & Geoghegan, 1938. 4–7.

Grahame, Kenneth. *The Wind in the Willows.* Illus. E. H. Shepard. Holiday House, 1938. 10–up.

Gramatky, Hardie. *Little Toot.* Putnam Publishing Group, 1939. 4–7.

Hoban, Russell. *Bedtime for Frances.* Illus. Garth Williams. Harper & Row, Publishers, 1960. 4–6.

Hoban, Russell. *The Mouse and His Child.* Illus. Lillian Hoban. Harper & Row, Publishers, 1967. 6–11.

Horwitz, Elinor Lander. *When the Sky Is Like Lace.* Illus. Barbara Cooney. J. B. Lippincott, 1975. 4–6.

Hunter, Mollie. *A Stranger Came Ashore.* Harper & Row, Publishers, 1975. 12–16.

Hutchins, Pat. *Rosie's Walk.* Macmillan Publishing, 1968. 3–6.

Jansson, Tove. *Tales from Moominvalley.* Translated by Thomas Warburton. Henry Z. Walck, 1964. 9–12.

Jarrell, Randall. *The Animal Family.* Illus. Maurice Sendak. Pantheon Books, 1965. 10–14.

Kendall, Carol. *The Gammage Cup.* Illus. Erik Blegvad. Harcourt Brace Jovanovich, 1959. 8–12.

Kipling, Rudyard. *Jungle Book.* Illus. Kurt Wiese. Doubleday, 1952. 12–up.

Kraus, Robert. *Leo the Late Bloomer.* Illus. Jose Aruego. Abelard-Schuman, 1971. 6–9.

Kraus, Robert. *Milton the Early Riser.* Illus. Jose Aruego and Ariane Aruego. E. P. Dutton, 1972. 5–8.

Leaf, Munro. *The Story of Ferdinand.* Viking Press, 1936. 4–up.

Le Guin, Ursula K. *A Wizard of Earthsea.* Illus. Ruth Robbins. Parnassus Press, 1968. 10–up.

Lewis, C. S. *The Last Battle.* Illus. Pauline Baynes. Macmillan Publishing, 1956. 9–12.

Lindgren, Astrid. *Pippi Longstocking.* Illus. Louis S. Glanzman. Viking Press, 1950. 9–11.

Lindgren, Astrid. *The Tomten.* Illus. Harold Wiberg. Coward, McCann & Geoghegan, 1961. 4–8.

Lionni, Leo. *Swimmy.* Random House, 1973. 5–8.

Lobel, Arnold. *Frog and Toad Are Friends.* Harper & Row, Publishers, 1970. 4–8.

McCloskey, Robert. *Make Way for Ducklings.* Viking Press, 1969. 4–8.

Merrill, Jean. *The Pushcart War.* Illus. Ronni Solbert. Scott, Foresman, 1964. 10–14.

Milne, A. A. *Winnie-the-Pooh.* Illus. Ernest H. Shepard. E. P. Dutton, 1926. 5–9.

Minarik, Else H. *Little Bear.* Illus. Maurice Sendak. Harper & Row, Publishers, 1957. 6–8.

Norton, Mary. *The Borrowers.* Illus. Beth Krush and Joe Krush. Harcourt Brace Jovanovich, 1953. 8–12.

Ormondroyd, Edward. *Time at the Top.* Illus. Peggy Bach. Parnassus Press, 1963. 10–14.

Pearce, Philippa. *Tom's Midnight Garden.* Illus. Susan Einzig. J. B. Lippincott, 1959. 10–14.

Piatti, Celestino. *The Happy Owls.* Atheneum, 1964. 5–8.

Potter, Beatrix. *The Tale of Peter Rabbit.* Frederick Warne, 1902. 4–7.

Rayner, Mary. *Mr. and Mrs. Pig's Evening Out.* Atheneum, 1976. 4–7.

Rey, Hans A. *Curious George.* Houghton Mifflin, 1941. 4–7.

Saint-Exupéry, Antoine de. *The Little Prince.* Translator Katherine Woods. Harcourt Brace Jovanovich, 1943. 8–up.

Scheer, Julian. *Rain Makes Applesauce.* Illus. Marvin Bileck. Holiday House, 1964. 4–7.

Sendak, Maurice. *In the Night Kitchen.* Harper & Row, Publishers, 1970. 4–8.

Sendak, Maurice. *Nutshell Library.* Harper & Row, Publishers, 1962. 3–8.

Sendak, Maurice. *Where the Wild Things Are.* Harper & Row, Publishers, 1963. 4–8.

Seuss, Dr. *The 500 Hats of Bartholomew Cubbins.* Random House, 1938. 5–9.

Seuss, Dr. *Horton Hatches the Egg.* Random House, 1940. 5–up.

Steig, William. *Abel's Island.* Farrar, Straus & Giroux, 1976. 8–12.

Steig, William. *Amos and Boris.* Farrar, Straus & Giroux, 1971. 4–9.

Steig, William. *Sylvester and the Magic Pebble.* E. P. Dutton, 1973. 6–10.

Thurber, James. *Many Moons.* Illus. Louis Slobodkin. Harcourt Brace Jovanovich, 1943. 5–8.

Tolkien, J. R. R. *The Hobbit.* Houghton Mifflin, 1938. 12–up.

Ungerer, Tomi. *The Beast of Monsieur Racine.* Farrar, Straus & Giroux, 1971. 6–9.

White, E. B. *Charlotte's Web.* Illus. Garth Williams. Harper & Row, Publishers, 1952. 7–10.

Williams, Margery. *The Velveteen Rabbit.* Illus. William Nicholson. Doubleday, 1922, 1958. 8–11.

Yolen, Jane. *The Girl Who Loved the Wind.* Illus. Ed Young. Thomas Y. Crowell, 1972. 5–9.

Zion, Gene. *Harry, the Dirty Dog.* Illus. Margaret Bloy Graham. Harper & Row, Publishers, 1956. 6–9.

Science Fiction

Bonham, Frank. **The Forever Formula.** E. P. Dutton, 1979. 12–up.

Suppose a secret formula is invented to prolong life forever? What is the world like? Young Evan Clark finds out when he wakes into the year 2164. The revolution of which he becomes a part is violent and raises questions for the reader. For sci-fi buffs.

Bulychev, Kirill (translator and adapter Mirra Ginsburg). **Alice.** Illus. Igor Galanin. Macmillan Publishing, 1977. 8–12.

A father in twenty-first-century Moscow relates six stories about his adventuresome five-year-old daughter Alice. She befriends strange animals, makes interplanetary visits, and finds lost Labutsilians visiting earth. Lively illustrations complement a tale that vicariously transports young readers into a fantastic future.

Corbett, Scott. **The Donkey Planet.** Illus. Troy Howell. E. P. Dutton, 1979. 10–12.

Two young scientists are sent to Vanaris, a planet in another solar system; their mission is to exchange metal samples. Suspense and humor combine when one member of the team is disguised as a donkey. Black and white illustrations.

DeWeese, Gene. **Major Corby and the Unidentified Flapping Object.** Doubleday, 1979. 8–12.

This fast-paced tale includes a bumbling sheriff, the lovable town drunk, a writer of sci-fi potboilers, and an invisible space pilot. The fourteen-year-old narrator uses considerable subterfuge to provide the materials needed to repair the spaceship and prevent it from blowing up and destroying much of the country.

Harding, Lee. **The Fallen Spaceman.** Illus. John Schoenherr and Ian Schoenherr. Harper & Row, Publishers, 1980. 8–12.

Within his giant spacesuit, Tyro is small, weak, and totally helpless. When he crashes in Australia, a young boy crawls inside and is trapped there just long enough to make a strong personal contact with the frightened spaceman. An unusual tale with unusual illustrations.

Hoover, H. M. **The Rains of Eridan.** Viking Press, 1977. 12–up.

A mysterious terror strikes an expedition of scientists on a hauntingly beautiful planet. Young Karen Orlov and biologist Theodora Leslie are protagonists in this well-written novel that portrays the growth of friendship against a background of fear.

Hoskins, Robert. **Jack-in-the-Box Planet.** Westminster Press, 1978. 7–14.

Willie has spent the years after the holocaust in a sealed house under the care of robots. After escaping, he searches for other survivors from his planet. A story of growing up.

Hughes, Monica. **Crisis on Conshelf Ten.** Atheneum, 1977. 10–12.

Fifteen-year-old Kepler, the first child to have been born on Moon, visits relatives in Conshelf Ten, an undersea colony on Earth. Both Moon and Conshelf Ten are taxed without representation, and both are ripe for revolution. A beautiful heroine is diverted from radical violence to passive resistance. A rousing story with social and historical analogies.

Kesteven, G. R. **The Awakening Water.** Hastings House, Publishers, 1979. 12–up.

Set in a regimented twenty-first century, the novel relates how John begins to question life after he has tasted fresh water for the first time. As a result, he runs away to join others who by their own resourcefulness are surviving outside the "Party." The well-developed plot has an optimistic and unexpected ending and encourages readers to think about the quality of life today.

Kotzwinkle, William. **The Ants Who Took Away Time.** Illus. Joe Servello. Doubleday, 1978. 8–10.

Time stands still throughout the world when a tribe of huge ants steals the Great Timepiece. Mr. Feldhammer, the Keeper of Time, chooses the wrong moment to go on vacation, and frantic efforts to locate him follow. Two-color illustrations capture the action of this exciting tale. (Picture book)

L'Engle, Madeleine. **A Swiftly Tilting Planet.** Farrar, Straus & Giroux, 1978. 12–up.

Charles Wallace and Gaudior, the unicorn, travel through space and time to find the missing link that will prevent the start of war. For advanced readers this is a companion volume to *A Wrinkle in Time* and *A Wind in the Door.*

McCaffrey, Anne. **Dragonsinger.** Atheneum, 1977. 12–up.

During fifteen-year-old Menolly's first week as an apprentice in the Harper Hall, she deals with resentment from adults and other students, women and men, who don't believe a woman can become a Harper. Her own feelings of inadequacy must be overcome before she can become the first Harper Journeywoman. Second of a trilogy.

McCaffrey, Anne. **Dragonsong**. Atheneum, 1976. 12–up.

The planet Pern has a rigid society in which it is difficult for Menolly, a novice Harper, to pursue music. Finally, she flees home and discovers a clutch of fire lizards and a Master Harper who accepts her. Well written and inventive with a strong, admirable heroine. First of a trilogy.

Marshall, Edward. **Space Case**. Illus. James Marshall. Dial Press, 1980. 4–8.

When the thing from outer space is first observed, it is taken for a trick-or-treater on Halloween night and then for a robot from Buddy McGee's school space project. A conversational text with red, blue, and yellow illustrations boldly outlined in black. (Picture book)

Murphy, Shirley Rousseau. **The Ring of Fire**. Atheneum, 1977. 12–up.

Thorn possesses the gift of seeing, a power that, if discovered, means death in the countries of Ere. As one of the Children of Ynell, he is charged by Anchorstar with finding others who live in the city of Burgdeeth and leading them to escape. First in a series.

Nostlinger, Christine (translator Anthea Bell). **Konrad**. Illus. Carol Nicklaus. Franklin Watts, 1977. 8–12.

When Konrad, a well-behaved seven-year-old from the Factory, arrives on Mrs. Bartolotti's doorstep, she can't remember ordering him but good-naturedly accepts him. How Konrad learns to adapt to Mrs. Bartolotti's erratic life-style makes a delightful read-aloud story.

Packard, Edward. **The Third Planet from Altair**. Illus. Barbara Carter. J. B. Lippincott, 1979. 8–12.

Aboard the spaceship *Aloha,* the reader heads out on a mission vital to the planet Earth. At each crucial moment in the action, a decision must be made that determines which page is read next and what happens to the spaceship.

Paulsen, Gary, and Ray Peekner. **The Green Recruit**. Independence Press, 1978. 10–12.

With scouts from other basketball teams and syndicate members hot on the trail, Danny has to hide an eight-foot, green-skinned Besumi from the planet Brennah, whom his father has recruited to play pro basketball. A lighthearted story that sinks a few well-placed shots concerning racial prejudice.

Pinkwater, Daniel M. **Alan Mendelsohn, the Boy from Mars.** E. P. Dutton, 1979. 10–12.

Two boys, browsing through bookstores for collectible comic books, purchase occult materials that deal with mind control. With study and practice, the boys not only accomplish mind control but experience a bizarre adventure on the lost continent of Waka-Waka. A humorous, somewhat scary story.

Pinkwater, Daniel Manus. **Fat Men from Space.** Illus. by author. Dodd, Mead, 1977. 10–12.

William goes to the dentist to have a tooth filled. From that moment, life becomes out of this world. The tooth now receives radio programs and other messages, including the news of an invasion from outer space to steal our junk food. Fantastic events portrayed in a humorous vein accompanied by cartoon-like drawings.

Pinkwater, D. Manus. **Lizard Music.** Illus. by author. Dodd, Mead, 1976. 10–up.

Left to take care of himself while his parents are on vacation, Victor watches a late night television program in which a lizard quintet plays music. Through a hidden community of intelligent lizards, Victor learns that Earth is to be invaded by the Pod People. While probing these strange occurrences, he meets Chicken Man, an odd character who holds the key to these mysteries.

Slote, Alfred. **My Trip to Alpha I.** Illus. Harold Berson. J. B. Lippincott, 1978. 10–12.

Jack travels by VOYA-CODE to another planet to visit his aunt; his body stays asleep on Earth while a programmed dummy does the traveling. He discovers that his aunt is a dummy like himself and sets out to locate her real self. A blend of science fiction and mystery with a logical plot.

Watson, Jane Werner. **The Case of the Semi-Human Beans.** Coward, McCann & Geoghegan, 1979. 10–12.

Two twelve-year-old boys discover a strange, slithering, snapping bean plant. One strange encounter after another leads the pair into dangerous adventures and UFO investigations from the Air Force.

Wilder, Cherry. **The Luck of Brin's Five.** Atheneum, 1977. 10–up.

Scott Gale, an earthman, accidentally lands on Torin, a planet inhabited by a society of marsupial beings. This tale, told by Dorn, the son in Brin's Five, tells of a shy mountain people whose lives are altered by contact with Scott.

Wiseman, Bernard. **Bobby and Boo, the Little Spaceman.** Illus. by author. Holt, Rinehart and Winston, 1978. 4–7.

Boo, a spaceman, visits earth and becomes friends with young Bobby. Bobby enjoys seeing how many tricks Boo can do, but Bobby's parents and friends have difficulty believing an alien being is really visiting them. (Picture book)

Yolen, Jane. **The Robot and Rebecca: The Mystery of the Code-Carrying Kids.** Illus. Jürg Obrist. Alfred A. Knopf, 1980. 7–10.

In the year 2121, in the American apartment city of Bosyork, lives adventuresome, preteen Rebecca and her family. She and her robot, Watson II, form a detective team that helps two lost children. Their unusual alien friends and futuristic life-style make for stimulating reading.

Additional Science Fiction Books

Cameron, Eleanor. *Stowaway to the Mushroom Planet.* Illus. Robert Henneberger. Little, Brown, 1956. 9–12.

Christopher, John. *The City of Gold and Lead.* Macmillan Publishing, 1967. 10–14.

Christopher, John. *The Pool of Fire.* Macmillan Publishing, 1968. 10–14.

Christopher, John. *The Prince in Waiting.* Macmillan Publishing, 1970. 10–14.

Christopher, John. *The White Mountains.* Macmillan Publishing, 1967. 10–14.

Engdahl, Sylvia. *This Star Shall Abide.* Illus. Richard Cuffari. Atheneum, 1972. 11–up.

Heinlein, Robert. *Tunnel in the Sky.* Illus. P. A. Hutchinson. Charles Scribner's Sons, 1955. 10–14.

Jackson, Jacqueline, and William Perlmutter. *The Endless Pavement.* Illus. Richard Cuffari. Seabury Press, 1973. 7–12.

Key, Alexander. *Escape to Witch Mountain.* Illus. Leon B. Wisdom, Jr. Westminster Press, 1968. 10–12.

Key, Alexander. *The Forgotten Door.* Westminster Press, 1965. 10–12.

L'Engle, Madeleine. *A Wrinkle in Time.* Farrar, Straus & Giroux, 1962. 10–14.

MacGregor, Ellen. *Miss Pickerell Goes Undersea.* Illus. Paul Galdone. McGraw-Hill, 1953. 10–14.

Norton, André. *The Zero Stone.* Viking Press, 1968. 10–14.

Slobodkin, Louis. *The Space Ship under the Apple Tree.* Macmillan Publishing, 1952. 8–12.

Verne, Jules. *Twenty Thousand Leagues under the Sea.* Charles Scribner's Sons, 1925. 12–up.

Williams, Jay, and Raymond Abrashkin. *Danny Dunn and the Homework Machine.* Illus. Ezra Jack Keats. McGraw-Hill, 1958. 8–12.

Wrightson, Patricia. *Down to Earth.* Illus. Margaret Horder. Harcourt Brace Jovanovich, 1965. 9–12.

Historical Fiction

Prehistoric Times

Fradin, Dennis Brindell. **Beyond the Mountain, beyond the Forest.** Illus. John Maggard. Childrens Press, 1978. 8–10.

Tor, a young cave boy appalled by the cold, hunger, and death among his people, courageously ventures beyond the known. Proving that the land does not end with the forest, he returns to his people, who follow him southward in the hope of finding a warmer land.

Millstead, Thomas. **Cave of the Moving Shadows.** Dial Press, 1979. 10–12.

Before recorded history, when men live in caves and woolly mammoths walk the earth, Kimba is discovered to have the power to conjure up game for the tribe. His desire to hunt, his tribe's need for food, and the mystery of the cave paintings make this a fast paced, exciting novel.

Steele, William O. **The Magic Amulet.** Harcourt Brace Jovanovich, 1979. 10–12.

Abandoned by his family because he was wounded and thus a burden, Tragg, through determination and his belief in a magic bracelet, survives and becomes an important member of another family. An exciting portrayal of the nomadic peoples of prehistoric southeastern America.

The Old World

Bulla, Clyde Robert. **The Beast of Lor.** Illus. Ruth Sanderson. Thomas Y. Crowell, 1977. 8–12.

Lud, an orphan boy in Britain at the time of the Roman conquest, befriends a young elephant that has escaped from a Roman galley. Lud and the beast help and protect each other, and finally are given a permanent home where Lud is greatly rewarded for his courageous act of kindness to a fatally wounded man. Beautifully illustrated, a volume to treasure.

Clements, Bruce. **Prison Window, Jerusalem Blue.** Farrar, Straus & Giroux, 1977. 12–up.

A framed piece of Jerusalem blue glass is their only connection with home after a brother and sister are kidnapped by Viking invaders. Taken to Denmark, they are drawn into a political plot that is certain to involve bloodshed. Set in ninth-century Europe, this is an exciting tale of courage and intrigue.

French, Fiona. **Hunt the Thimble.** Oxford University Press, 1978. 8–12.

Little Edo hides the thimble from older brother and sister Pieter and Anna. There is a rollicking search throughout their house and the streets of Amsterdam. Beautiful full-page color paintings authentically detail life in seventeenth-century Holland. Also useful in the social studies and art curricula. (Picture book)

Haugaard, Erik Christian. **Cromwell's Boy.** Houghton Mifflin, 1978. 12–up.

Oliver Cutler, thirteen, is a good horseman, clever, reliable, and a spy for General Cromwell. He is sent to Oxford to infiltrate the homes and hangouts of King Charles' advocates. In doing so, Oliver develops his own value system, while contributing to the causes of Parliament. Sequel to *A Messenger for Parliament.*

Monjo, F. N. **The House on Stink Alley: A Story about the Pilgrims in Holland.** Illus. Robert Quackenbush. Holt, Rinehart and Winston, 1977. 8–12.

Eight-year-old Love Brewster tells the story of the Pilgrims' stay in Holland before they emigrate to America. His father, William Brewster, is bitter against King James, and many tensions are involved. Illustrated with heavy woodcuts.

Palacios, Argentina. **The Knight and the Squire.** Illus. Ray Cruz. Doubleday, 1979. 10–12.

This lively and literate retelling of Cervantes' *Don Quixote* makes the adventures of the wild-eyed tilter at windmills accessible to young readers without spoiling them for the full-length version. Large black and white illustrations capture the absurdities and touching nobility of the man of La Mancha as well as the more down-to-earth characteristics of Sancho Panza.

Reig, June. **Diary of the Boy King Tut-Ankh-Amen.** Charles Scribner's Sons, 1978. 8–12.

This exciting, imaginary diary of Tutankhamen begins with his eighth year, about 1334 B.C., and continues throughout the events of his colorful life. The background information it provides answers many of the questions children are prone to ask. Diagrams and black and white drawings enliven the entries.

Sutcliff, Rosemary. **Blood Feud.** E. P. Dutton, 1977. 10–up.

Jestyn and Thormod are tenth-century blood brothers bound by oath to avenge the death of Thormod's father. Their search takes them out of the country of the Vikingkind and down Russian rivers to Constantinople. Jestyn finds a home and a new way of life that ends his wanderings.

Sutcliff, Rosemary. **Sun Horse, Moon Horse.** Illus. Shirley Felts. E. P. Dutton, 1978. 12–up.

Lubrin, a chieftain's son of the Iceni, the horse people, is thrust into a leadership he does not seek but must accept—along with the sacrifice of his life for the lives of his people. Set in pre-Roman Britain, the origin of the white horse of Uffington is given plausible explanation.

Van Woerkom, Dorothy. **Pearl in the Egg.** Illus. Joe Lasker. Thomas Y. Crowell, 1980. 10–12.

Pearl and her brother, Gavin, are orphans. To escape a life of serf-dom they join a troup of wandering minstrels. Pearl discovers a love of singing and a gift for composing. A fascinating glimpse of life in thirteenth-century England.

Von Canon, Claudia. **The Moonclock.** Houghton Miffin, 1979. 12–up.

Barbara Cammerloherin married Jacob Schretter on Christmas Day, 1682, in Vienna. Barbara was twenty, Jacob was forty-seven, and the marriage was an arranged one. This fictional account of Barbara's life during 1683 is brilliantly constructed through letters, diaries, municipal records, medical books, and the like. Thus the reader observes Barbara grow from girl to woman against a background of historical accuracy.

Walsh, Jill Paton. **Children of the Fox.** Illus. Robin Eaton. Farrar, Straus & Giroux, 1978. 10–12.

Greek history comes alive in these short stories that show the courage and determination of three young people who risk safety and security to aid Themistokles in the battle to save their country during the Persian Wars.

Exploring the New World

Gray, Genevieve. **How Far, Felipe?** Illus. Ann Grifalconi. Harper & Row, Publishers, 1978. 6–9.

Traveling with his family from Mexico to California, Felipe and his pet burro, Filomena, grow up quickly. Vivid illustrations portray not only the warmth of the boy-pet relationship but also the hardships of the journey. An easy-to-read history book, based on the expedition of Colonel Juan Bautista de Anza in 1775. (Picture book)

O'Dell, Scott. **The Captive.** Houghton Mifflin, 1979. 8–12.

Julian Escobar, a young Sevillian Jesuit seminarian, joins a Spanish expedition and sails for the New World to be a man of God to the natives. Shipwreck, treachery, and greed change his life. He finally must choose between death for himself and the enslavement of others. Set in Mexico in the 1500s.

Rockwood, Joyce. **To Spoil the Sun.** Holt, Rinehart and Winston, 1976. 12–up.

Rain Dove, a strong Cherokee woman, tells of her life across two generations. Through her powerful story, the beginning of the end of the Cherokee way of life unfolds. Their lands were invaded, the Spaniards came, and the invisible fire of smallpox wiped out large numbers. Well researched and magnificently told.

Steele, William O. **The War Party.** Illus. Lorinda Bryan Cauley. Harcourt Brace Jovanovich, 1978. 7–10.

A young warrior learns that war is horror, not glory, and that the enemy is not a beast but a man like himself. The story is authentically told in the context of sixteenth-century Cherokee tribal life. Clear, beautiful line drawings provide much accurate detail. Useful in discussing the social issues raised by war as a solution to human problems. (Picture book)

Eighteenth Century

World

Burton, Hester. **To Ravensrigg.** Thomas Y. Crowell, 1977. 12–up.

In late eighteenth-century England the slave trade has been officially abolished but continues to thrive. Emmie helps a runaway before she sets out with her sea captain father on a dangerous voyage. A ship wreck, secrets about her family's past, and a search for her mother's family add excitement to this fine historical novel.

Cheatham, K. Follis. **Spotted Flower and the Ponokomita.** Illus. by author. Westminster Press, 1977. 8–12.

Spotted Flower is lost on the plains when she finds a horse, or ponokomita, the first any member of her family has seen. She survives the dangers of being among her people's enemy, the Snake, and returns to her Kainan Indian family with the horse. This event marks a change in the life of her tribe.

Parenteau, Shirley. **Secrets of Scarlet.** Illus. Ann Toulmin-Rothe. Childrens Press, 1979. 8–12.

Picking red kermes bugs to sell for making scarlet dye, Marie is cold and discouraged. She sneaks a ride into town in Grandmother's wagon, hoping to find another way for her family to earn money. She doesn't realize that people will notice her lace collar! Set in eighteenth-century France and colorfully illustrated, the story provides interesting information about dye-making.

Paterson, Katherine. **The Master Puppeteer.** Illus. Haru Wells. Thomas Y. Crowell, 1975. 10–14.

Set in eighteenth-century Osaka, the book focuses on the ancient Japanese art of puppetry. A thirteen-year-old boy tells an intriguing and absorbing story of the theater and everyday existence during this lawless period.

Roach, Marilynne K. **Presto or the Adventures of a Turnspit Dog.** Illus. by author. Houghton Mifflin, 1979. 10–up.

Presto's world is narrow and filled with drudgery as he turns the spit that rotates the meat on the blazing hearth in London's Fortune Inn. Then life takes an exciting turn for the turnspit dog when a young puppeteer arrives and Presto joins the exciting street life of eighteenth-century England. Black and white sketches.

Colonial America and the Revolution

Avi. **Captain Grey.** Illus. Charles Mikolaycak. Pantheon Books, 1977. 9–12.

An eleven-year-old boy is captured and taken to a small village on the New Jersey coast following the American Revolution. A bay, hidden by an island, is the center of a pirate operation led by the evil Captain Grey. The boy and his sister overpower the thieves, end the piracy, and escape.

Avi. **Night Journeys.** Pantheon Books, 1979. 10–12.

Peter, a twelve-year-old orphan, is taken into the home of a stern Quaker man in colonial Pennsylvania in 1767. Trying to prove his worth, Peter assists in searching for two runaway indentured servants. When he finds them, he aids them in their escape and in so doing learns of the complexities of the Quaker's personality.

Benchley, Nathaniel. **George the Drummer Boy.** Illus. Don Bolognese. Harper & Row, Publishers, 1977. 6–8.

The start of the American Revolution is seen through the eyes of a British drummer boy at the Battles of Lexington and Concord. Thus this easy-to-read book offers a point of view not generally familiar to young readers.

Burchard, Peter. **Whaleboat Raid.** Illus. by author. Coward, McCann & Geoghegan, 1977. 10–12.

Jud Coleman acts as a guide for the raid made by four companies of revolutionaries against British-held Sag Harbor on Long Island in 1777. The day's events make an indelible mark on the sixteen-year-old Jud. A short, moving story with a two-page glossary of nautical terms.

Monjo, F. N. **A Namesake for Nathan.** Illus. Eros Keith. Coward, McCann & Geoghegan, 1977. 10–12.

The events of 1776 are interestingly portrayed through the eyes of Joanna, the sister of Nathan Hale. The family's grief is poignant when they learn of his capture and death. Documented. Woodcuts.

√ O'Dell, Scott. **Sarah Bishop.** Houghton Mifflin, 1980. 12–up.

Fifteen-year-old Sarah Bishop is left without a surviving member of her family at the time of the American Revolution. Her father had remained loyal to the king while her brother had joined the rebels. Their possessions are completely destroyed in a raid and Sarah is forced to find a new life on her own.

Rockwood, Joyce. **Groundhog's Horse.** Illus. Victor Kalin. Holt, Rinehart and Winston, 1978. 8–12.

Groundhog, an eleven-year-old Cherokee, sets out on a one-boy raid to get back his horse, which had been captured by a Creek raiding party. The story is sensitive and amusing, and the Indian boy is a likable hero. Set in 1750.

Steele, William O. **The Man with the Silver Eyes.** Harcourt Brace Jovanovich, 1976. 8–12.

An eleven-year-old Cherokee boy is ordered by his grandmother and great-uncle to live in an American settlement with a Quaker man. The boy, who hates white Americans, does not understand the new living arrangement. Nor does he understand why the Quaker is kind, even solicitous, to him. Set in 1780.

Nineteenth Century

World

Avi. **The History of Helpless Harry.** Illus. Paul O. Zelinski. Pantheon Books, 1980. 10–12.

In this Victorian-style adventure helpless Harry's parents go away and several people feel they must protect Harry and the family money box. Through deliberate misunderstandings, unrighteous indignation, and simple greed, the plot thickens. In the end, a most unhelpless Harry triumphs. Exaggerated pen and ink drawings complement the vintage text.

Branson, Karen. **The Potato Eaters.** Illus. Jane Sterrett. G. P. Putnam's Sons, 1979. 12–up.

The O'Connor family experiences many hardships in Ireland in 1846. Potatoes come up black and rent and taxes are high, but the family stays together despite increasing difficulties of illness and hunger. Finally, they emigrate to America. Expressive black and white wash illustrations. Suited for advanced readers.

Garfield, Leon. **Footsteps.** Delacorte Press, 1980. 10–14.

Haunted by the sound of his dead father's footsteps and hoping to free himself from the charge of stealing, twelve-year-old William flees to London, where his life is alternately endangered and saved by a cast of unsavory Dickensian characters. Melodrama, high adventure, and humor in an historic setting.

Lewis, Thomas P. **Clipper Ship.** Illus. Joan Sandin. Harper & Row, Publishers, 1978. 6–8.

Captain Murdock is accompanied by his wife and children on the clipper ship *Rainbird* as she voyages from New York around the Horn to San Francisco. This easy-to-read book is based on fact and the illustrations are appealing and well researched. (Picture book)

Lively, Penelope. **Fanny's Sister.** Illus. Anita Lobel. E. P. Dutton, 1980. 7–10.

Fanny is the oldest of six children and with the birth of each, she has lost more attention. Finally, when the seventh baby is born, Fanny prays that God will take it back. Then, fearing that God will answer her prayer, Fanny runs away. Set in Victorian England.

Monjo, F. N. **Prisoners of the Scrambling Dragon.** Illus. Arthur Geisert. Holt, Rinehart and Winston, 1980. 8–12.

Sam seeks adventure when he enlists as a cabin boy aboard his uncle's trading ship bound for China in the early 1800s. When smugglers capture the ship and kidnap thirteen-year-old Sam and another sailor, the boy's excitement turns to terror as the two struggle to escape. First person narrative.

Zei, Alki (translator Edward Fenton). **The Sound of the Dragon's Feet.** E. P. Dutton, 1979. 8–12.

Sasha, age ten, leads the protected life typical of girls in pre-Revolutionary Russia. But Sasha is curious and asks questions, not only about her immediate world but also about the world beyond her microcosm. A compelling view of the effects of oppressive rule.

United States: Early in the Century

Blos, Joan W. **A Gathering of Days: A New England Girl's Journal, 1830–32.** Charles Scribner's Sons, 1979. 12–up.

This journal account of two years in the life of fourteen-year-old Catherine Hall presents the joys and hardships of life in rural New Hampshire in the 1830s. 1980 Newbery Award Book.

Bowen, Gary. **My Village, Sturbridge.** Illus. Gary Bowen and Randy Miller. Farrar, Straus & Giroux, 1977. 8–12.

True Mason submits a portfolio of his work to Isaiah Thomas, hoping to continue his engraving apprenticeship. The accurate black and white wood engravings of Sturbridge Village in 1827 are outstanding, a form of art rarely found in children's books. True's commentaries, from his fifteen-year-old viewpoint, are enjoyable.

Brady, Esther Wood. **The Toad on Capitol Hill.** Crown Publishers, 1978. 8–12.

Sprightly Dorsy McCurdy enjoys her life in Washington City in 1814, until her father remarries. Two undesirable stepbrothers, Tyler and Brandon, attempt to change this eleven-year-old girl into a young lady. When the British troops move into the city, events change the family's spirit. Fast moving and informative.

Burchard, Peter. **Chinwe.** Illus. by author. G. P. Putnam's Sons, 1979. 12–up.

The African village in which Chinwe, a young Ibo maiden, lives is attacked and burned and its inhabitants are captured, transported to the United States, and sold as slaves. Although the horrors of slavery are portrayed in vivid detail, the major focus is on the human determination to maintain dignity and, most of all, hope.

Cross, Helen Reeder. **A Curiosity for the Curious.** Illus Margot Tomes. Coward, McCann & Geoghegan, 1978. 8–12.

In 1800 Hachaliah Bailey brought the first elephant into the United States, delighting his neighbors and infuriating his wife. Based on fact, this story recounts how Bailey, with the help of young Phineas T. Barnum, barnstormed New England with their famed pachyderm, Old Bet. Humorous illustrations recreate the nineteenth-century atmosphere.

Hall, Donald. **Ox-Cart Man.** Illus. Barbara Cooney. Viking Press, 1979. 7–10.

A New Englander gathers the results of his family's work and packs the goods into his ox-cart. He travels to Portsmouth Market, where he sells his wares and buys supplies for the next year. Illustrations capture the day-to-day life of nineteenth-century New Englanders. 1980 Caldecott Award Book. (Picture book)

Irwin, Hadley. **We Are Mesquakie, We Are One.** Feminist Press, 1980. 10–up.

Hidden Doe's life, from her birth in the early 1800s to the beginning of a new generation, is chronicled. The story takes the Mesquakie Indians from their home in Iowa to the reservation in Kansas, showing their struggle to regain their homeland while trying to adopt white ways. The woman's place in Indian society is realistically portrayed.

Mitchell, Barbara. **Cornstalks and Cannonballs.** Illus. Karen Ritz. Carolrhoda Books, 1980. 4–7.

The people of one small town in Delaware outwitted the British soldiers anchored off their coast during the War of 1812 by convincing them that the hoes and blackened cornstalks they carried were guns. Based on a legend, this is a pleasant look at history in an easy-to-read format.

Smucker, Barbara. **Runaway to Freedom.** Illus. Charles Lilly. Harper & Row, Publishers, 1978. 10–12.

Thirteen-year-old Julilly and her crippled friend, both slaves, reach Canada and freedom via the Underground Railroad. Their story is mixed with human cruelty and human kindness and conveys the despair of slavery and the dangerous role of the abolitionist. Charcoal drawings; an excellent read-aloud book.

Turkle, Brinton. **Rachel and Obadiah.** E. P. Dutton, 1978. 6–9.

In this delightful addition to the three other Obadiah picture books, Rachel and Obadiah vie with one another to carry the good news of the *Speedwell's* arrival in Nantucket to the captain's wife. A silver coin is the reward and a surprising solution is reached. An accurate introduction to the Society of Friends. (Picture book)

United States: Civil War and Westward Expansion

Beatty, Patricia. **By Crumbs, It's Mine!** William Morrow, 1976. 10–12.

Damaris Boyd, fifteen, has a traveling tent-hotel bequeathed to her by the man who won her father's money at poker. Thus is the St. Louis family stranded in the Arizona Territory in 1882 rescued, while Mr. Boyd follows the lure of gold. Considerable factual material about this period of American history is included in the lively story of a courageous heroine.

Beatty, Patricia. **Lacy Makes a Match.** William Morrow, 1979. 12–up.

Thirteen-year-old Lacy, abandoned as a baby on the Bingham's doorstep, tires of being their housekeeper and contrives to marry off her adoptive brothers. All the while she follows up clues to her own parentage. A humorous growing-up story set in a California mining town in the 1890s.

Beatty, Patricia. **That's One Ornery Orphan.** William Morrow, 1980. 12–up.

Blanco County, Texas, is no place for an orphan in the 1870s, as Hattie Lee Baker discovers when she is taken to the county orphanage after the death of her grandfather. Her life in the home and her adventures with the "pickers," the families that come to choose the orphans, are humorously told.

Coerr, Eleanor. **Waza Wins at Windy Gulch.** Illus. Janet McCaffery. G. P. Putnam's Sons, 1977. 6–8.

Waza, a pure white camel, is part of the Camel Brigade brought to Texas from Africa by Jefferson Davis in the 1850s. The sneaky plans of Dirtyshirt Dan, a jealous mule driver, backfire, and Waza helps capture the bank robbers. The tale is based on hilarious newspaper stories of the period and illustrated with witty watercolor paintings.

Hickman, Janet. **Zoar Blue.** Macmillan Publishing, 1978. 12–up.

Barbara leaves Zoar, a German pacifist community in Ohio, when the Civil War breaks out to find her only living relative. Her friend, John, also leaves to join the army. Eventually both return, having experienced war and the pains of growing up in the process.

Keith, Harold. **The Obstinate Land.** Thomas Y. Crowell, 1977. 12–up.

Fritz Romberg is thirteen when his family makes the Oklahoma land run in 1893. "Sooners" have claimed the land the Rombergs had selected so they must settle for a less desirable plot. Ranchers resent the intrusion by the farmers, and crops are often threatened or destroyed by the weather. When Fritz's father freezes to death in a blizzard, Fritz assumes responsibility for the farm and the family.

Levitin, Sonia. **The No-Return Trail.** Harcourt Brace Jovanovich, 1978. 10–12.

This fictionalized account of the Bidwell-Bartleson expedition to California in 1841 recreates the hardships and dangers of that journey. The first woman to make the grueling overland passage, seventeen-year-old Nancy Kelsey, stubbornly persists in spite of her husband's illness and the discouragement of the other travelers.

Nixon, Joan Lowery. **If You Say So, Claude.** Illus. Lorinda Bryan Cauley. Frederick Warne, 1980. 6–9.

Coming from Colorado to Texas to build a homestead, Shirley and Claude are presented with many choices. Each place where Claude decides to settle proves disastrous. This easy-to-read story set in pioneer days abounds in contrasts, humor, onomatopoetic words, and effective repetition. Two-tone and full-color illustrations. (Picture book)

Packard, Edward. **Deadwood City.** Illus. Barbara Carter. J. B. Lippincott, 1978. 8–12.

The innovative format of this book involves the reader in a variety of adventures: "You are a cowhand between jobs arriving in Deadwood City; should you decide to visit the saloon, turn to page eight." Each segment allows the reader three choices for further action, and foolhardy bravado and cautious retreat have different consequences.

Reit, Seymour. **Ironclad! A True Story of the Civil War.** Illus. by author. Dodd, Mead, 1977. 8–12.

This exciting account of the first naval battle between ironclad ships, the *Merrimac* and the *Monitor*, is told from the viewpoint of a young member of the *Monitor*'s crew. The book is full of facts and feelings, making it a lively adventure in history.

St. George, Judith. **The Halo Wind.** G. P. Putnam's Sons, 1978. 10–12.

Ella Jane, thirteen, is moving with her family to the Willamette Valley in 1845. Yvette, a Chinook girl, travels with her. When a part of the wagon train takes a shortcut, lack of water slows their travel. Yvette reveals the courage and the sorrow of her people, who have lost their land and their heritage.

Young, Alida E. **Land of the Iron Dragon.** Doubleday, 1978. 12–up.

Lim Yan-sung was fourteen when he and his father came to San Francisco from China. After his father's death during a wanton attack by prejudiced whites, Lim Yan-sung joins a crew building the transcontinental railroad. Again the boy meets prejudice and treachery. First-person narrative with considerable information about the building of the railroad.

Twentieth Century

World: Early in the Century

Anderson, Margaret J. **The Journey of the Shadow Bairns.** Alfred A. Knopf, 1980. 10–12.

In 1903, thirteen-year-old Elspeth and her four-year-old brother Robbie are orphaned and must travel from Scotland to Canada. Many trying situations nearly separate the two, but Elspeth's courage sees them through. The story is filled with tension and makes good reading.

Arthur, Ruth M. **An Old Magic.** Illus. Margery Gill. Atheneum, 1977. 12–up.

Hannah Lakin is young to be a governess when she leaves her mother, sister, and the New Hampshire sheep farm she loves to take up a new life in Wales. But the new life brings David Morgan, Morgan's ground, a farm in the Welsh hills, and an intriguing relationship with gypsies who come to camp. A three-generation story.

Dickinson, Peter. **Tulku.** E. P. Dutton, 1979. 12–up.

The Boxer Rebellion of 1900 hurls thirteen-year-old Theodore from the secure world of his father's mission in China. He escapes with Mrs. Jones, an eccentric botanist, and Lung, her assistant. Experiencing the hospitality and fantastic powers of the Tibetan monks challenges Theo's way of life. Mature readers recommended.

Garner, Alan. **The Aimer Gate.** Illus. Michael Foreman. William Collins Publishers, 1978. 10–up.

Robert discovers a secret within his secret hiding place. In the uppermost section of a bell tower, his great-grandfather, with delicate precision, shaped the interior stones, left his mark, and signed his name even though he knew they could never be seen. Robert's touch with Robert of the past is another link in this four generation story.

Garner, Alan. **Granny Reardun.** Illus. Michael Foreman. William Collins Publishers, 1978. 8–12.

The second book of a quartet by the same author. Joseph, called a "granny reardun" because he is being reared by his grandparents, takes his first step toward independence when he decides not to follow his grandfather's stonemason trade, which he considers crude. Language gives a sense of Victorian England.

Garner, Alan. **The Stone Book.** Illus. Michael Foreman. William Collins Publishers, 1978. 8–12.

Set in Victorian England, this story tells of a girl who wants to learn to read. Her father, a stonemason, sends her into a cave where she learns that there can be reading even when there are no words and no books. First of a quartet that traces four generations of a working class English family. Themes can be discussed at several levels.

Garner, Alan. **Tom Fobble's Day.** Illus. Michael Foreman. William Collins Publishers, 1979. 10–up.

This is the last of a quartet of books that trace the story of a working class family in England. The ties that bind one generation to another are clearly seen in this story of a day in the life of a boy and his grandfather, a day made special by the building of a sledge and of new understandings.

Geras, Adèle. **The Girls in the Velvet Frame.** Atheneum, 1980. 12–up.

The five Bernstein girls live with their mother in an old section of Jerusalem before World War I. Their father is dead and they have lost contact with their brother Isaac, who went to America to seek his fortune. Each character is beautifully portrayed in day-to-day living.

Gutman, Nahum (translator Nelly Segal). **Path of the Orange Peels: Adventures in the Early Days of Tel Aviv.** Illus. by author. Dodd, Mead, 1979. 10–12.

A wise and witty tale of the author's adventures as a boy of fifteen in Palestine during World War I. Caught in the Turkish-British cross fire, he manages to escape in one piece and complete an important mission to Tel Aviv, then a village of fewer than a hundred homes.

Heyman, Anita. **Exit from Home.** Crown Publishers, 1977. 12–up.

The author's search for roots led to this story of her grandfather's early life in the first decade of twentieth-century Russia and his immigration to America at fifteen. The devout Jewish family struggles to keep the faith while children are listening to "outside" ideas. Events leading to the revolution of 1905 are explained.

Steinberg, Fannie. **Birthday in Kishinev.** Illus. Luba Hanuschak. Jewish Publication Society of America, 1978. 8–12.

In 1903 Sarah has a wonderful birthday party in Kishinev, Russia. The guests include the parents of the boy picked for her through the matchmaker. However, the happy day turns into a nightmare when the Jewish population is attacked. Sarah's family survives the pogrom, but they migrate to America. A true story.

Thiele, Colin. **The Shadow on the Hills.** Harper & Row, Publishers, 1977. 12–up.

Set in rural South Australia in the early twentieth century, readers can readily identify with the mischief of Bodo Schneider's childhood. Unusual, however, is Bodo's friendship with Ebenezer, a wild hermit who shouts Biblical quotations from the hilltops where Bodo runs his rabbit traps. When Ebenezer is accused of arson, Bodo must make a mature decision.

Zhitkov, Boris (translator Djemma Bider). **How I Hunted the Little Fellows.** Illus. Paul O. Zelinsky. Dodd, Mead, 1979. 7–10.

Boris is fascinated by the two-masted steamship on the shelf in Grandmother's kitchen. He promises never to touch it but cannot control his curiosity about the little people whom he imagines live in it. He struggles to discover the truth and still keep his promise. A rich, warm, believable tale set in Russia.

World: World War II

Allan, Mabel Esther. **A Lovely Tomorrow.** Dodd, Mead, 1979. 12–up.

The world of fifteen-year-old Frue Allendale, a drama student in London, crashes when her parents are killed by a V2 rocket in the early hours of New Year's Day, 1945. Her sojourn with relatives and at school helps her to rebuild her life and look toward the future.

Anderson, Margaret J. **Searching for Shona.** Alfred A. Knopf, 1978. 9–13.

Two orphaned girls exchange places at the evacuee center in Edinburgh during World War II. Marjorie, the lonely, unhappy, rich girl, assumes the identity of Shona, the determined, poor girl of unknown origin, and is shipped to southern Scotland. Six years of war change far more than destinations for the girls.

Colver, Anne. **Pluto: Brave Lipizzaner Stallion.** Illus. Sam Savitt. Garrard Publishing, 1978. 7–10.

During World War II the famed Lipizzaner horses are taken to the Alps for safekeeping. Thirteen-year-old Max becomes their stable boy. He helps at a Lipizzaner's performance given for General Patton when the American Army comes to the village. Pencil sketches capture the beauty of these remarkable animals. Easy reading.

Fife, Dale. **North of Danger.** Illus. Haakon Sœther. E. P. Dutton, 1978. 10–12.

A terse account of a real incident in World War II in which a twelve-year-old Norwegian boy risks his life during a two-hundred-mile trip by skis to alert his father to the Nazi occupation of Spitzbergen.

Griese, Arnold A. **The Wind Is Not a River.** Illus. Glo Coalson. Thomas Y. Crowell, 1978. 10–12.

When Japanese soldiers invade their remote village in the Aleutian Islands during World War II, Susan and her brother Sidak use the "old ways" of survival to avoid capture. The two find a young wounded Japanese soldier, and the three make their peace in order to survive. Good historical background.

Haugaard, Erik Christian. **Chase Me, Catch Nobody!** Houghton Mifflin, 1980. 12–up.

It is 1937 and fourteen-year-old Erik Hansen is on a school trip from Denmark to Germany. Along with his friend Nikolai, he finds himself inadvertently involved with resistance to Nazism, in danger from the Gestapo, and rescuer of a young Jewish girl. This fast-paced story has the ring of authenticity.

Lingard, Joan. **The File on Fraulein Berg.** Elsevier/Nelson Books, 1980. 12–up.

Three girls in a private school in Northern Ireland in 1944 suspect that their teacher, Fraulein Berg, is a German spy. The girls' harassment of the innocent victim leads to a suspenseful surprise ending. An excellent growing-up story set in a culture unfamiliar to most American readers.

Little, Jean. **Listen for the Singing.** E. P. Dutton, 1977. 10–12.

Anna must go to high school now instead of to the Sight Saving

Class. It is the eve of World War II and Anna and her German-born family, who have emigrated to Canada, must choose sides. Anna's problem of impaired vision enables her to help her brother.

Mazer, Harry. **The Last Mission.** Delacorte Press, 1979. 12–up.

It is 1944 and Jack Raab, a Jew and fifteen years old, lies about his age to enlist in the United States Air Corps. On Jack's "last mission," the plane takes a direct hit; Jack parachutes to safety but is captured by Germans. Based upon the author's experiences, the story is a powerful indictment of the horror and futility of war.

Orgel, Doris. **The Devil in Vienna.** Dial Press, 1978. 12–up.

Inge, a Jewish girl, and Lieselotte, daughter of a Nazi, are thirteen years old and best friends since they began school, but their friendship is sorely tried. The novel, in the form of entries in Inge's journal, is based on experiences of the author, who writes convincingly about life in Vienna in 1938.

Rees, David. **The Exeter Blitz.** Elsevier/Nelson Books, 1978. 12–up.

On May 4, 1942, the city of Exeter, England, was blitzed. This story tells the events as they occurred in the lives of one family. Fourteen-year-old Colin experiences the bombing and its aftermath with quirks and pranks that are familiar to any young teenager.

Rose, Anne. **Refugee.** Dial Press, 1977. 12–up.

Elleke writes in her diary with all the normal feelings of a twelve-year-old girl. But she is a Jew in Belgium in 1939, and her happy life is suddenly changed as hatred of Jews spreads. Elleke is sent alone to an aunt in New York until the war ends. A gripping story based on the author's life.

Westall, Robert. **The Machine Gunners.** Greenwillow Books, 1976. 12–up.

Fourteen-year-old Chas McGill, collecting war souvenirs in his small English hometown, finds the tail section of a German bomber, with machine gun undamaged. Chas and his friends build a fortress, nurse a wounded German, shelter two orphans, and grow up amidst air raids and death. Excellent characterization and compelling plot.

United States: Early in the Century

Cameron, Eleanor. **Julia and the Hand of God.** Illus. Gail Owens. E. P. Dutton, 1977. 10–up.

Eleven-year-old Julia Redfern wants to be a writer. She is deeply sensitive, outspoken, and often in trouble with "sensible" people, particularly her fundamentalist grandmother. A narrow escape from a forest fire that descends on Berkeley, California in 1923 adds excitement. Julia's career is continued in *A Room Made of Windows*. Vivid characterizations; outstanding illustrations.

Constant, Alberta Wilson. **Does Anybody Care about Lou Emma Miller?** Thomas Y. Crowell, 1979. 12–up.

The reader follows the interesting and exciting incidents of fifteen-year-old Lou Emma's high school activities in Gloriosa, Kansas. She assists in helping local suffragettes elect the first woman mayor and becomes more mature in the process.

Eichelberger, Rosa Kohler. **Big Fire in Baltimore.** Illus. Rex Schneider. Stemmer House Publishers, 1979. 10–12.

Tod and his family, including Gerry the dog, are brought closer together by the Baltimore Fire in 1904. Twelve-year-old Tod is given a chance to fulfill his desire to be a Western Union messenger. Excellent characterization. Black and white illustrations.

Jacobs, William Jay. **Mother, Aunt Susan and Me.** Coward, McCann & Geoghegan, 1979. 10–12.

A readable account of Susan B. Anthony's and Harriet Cady Stanton's efforts to win equal rights for women, written from the point of view of Stanton's sixteen-year-old daughter, Harriet. The epilogue reveals that Harriet continues the fight to become another woman of courage and dignity. Illustrated with prints and photographs.

Moskin, Marietta. **Day of the Blizzard.** Illus. Stephen Gammell. Coward, McCann & Geoghegan, 1978. 7–10.

Mother is ill and Katie must assume responsibility for the house and her five-year-old twin brothers. This is the last day to redeem a brooch, a family heirloom, from the pawnbroker. The story of Katie's journey to uptown New York during the Great Blizzard of 1888 is a rewarding look at people helping people.

Newton, Suzanne. **What Are You Up To, William Thomas?** Westminster Press, 1977. 8–12.

When fifteen-year-old William Thomas "reforms," it is merely in preparation for the most elaborate practical joke of his career. Disaster is always right around the corner in this humorous but realistic picture of small town life in the twenties.

Sebestyen, Ouida. **Words by Heart.** Little, Brown, 1979. 12–up.

Lena, a young black girl whose family struggles against prejudice in their small southwestern town in 1910, wins a scripture reciting contest, but she doesn't know that she will soon have to actually live those words about forgiveness and love. Vicious acts of violence force the girl to come to terms with her beliefs when she is faced with her father's killer.

Skolsky, Mindy Warshaw. **Hannah Is a Palindrome.** Illus. Karen Ann Weinhaus. Harper & Row, Publishers, 1980. 7–10.

Hannah is a palindrome, and so is Otto, her worst enemy in the new town where her family has moved in order to run a small restaurant. This quiet story, with very real people, gives a good view of life in the United States in the 1920s. Another story about Hannah, set in the depression, is *Carnival and Kopeck.*

Thayer, Marjorie, and Elizabeth Emanuel. **Climbing Sun: The Story of a Hopi Indian Boy.** Illus. Anne Siberell. Dodd, Mead, 1980. 10–up.

This fictionalized account is based on the reminiscenses of a Hopi Indian, Hubert Honanie, who, in 1928, at age eleven was sent to the Sherman Indian Institute. The simply written story contrasts American Indian and white cultures, dwelling primarily on the young boy's life in a strange environment.

Wallace, Barbara Brooks. **Peppermints in the Parlor.** Atheneum, 1980. 9–12.

Emily Luccock travels to San Francisco to live with an aunt and uncle of whom she has fond memories. However, their once-happy home is now a house of horrors; Aunt Twice and Emily are both prisoners and servants in what has become a sinister home for the aged. Eventually Emily uncovers a blackmail plot.

United States: The Immigrant Era

Blaine, Marge. **Dvora's Journey.** Illus. Gabriel Lisowski. Holt, Rinehart and Winston, 1979. 9–12.

This lively account of Dvora, a twelve-year-old girl, vividly brings to mind the struggles that the Jews endure as they leave their homeland in Russia in 1904. After many hardships Dvora reaches America to pursue her dream of being a teacher. Easy to read.

Curley, Daniel. **Hilarion.** Illus. Judith Gwyn Brown. Houghton Mifflin, 1979. 10–12.

Four tradesmen from Linsk come to New York in the early 1900s to make their fortunes. Finding no work and missing their families, they become discouraged until young, strong Hilarion from the Old Country unexpectedly joins them. Amusing pen sketches illustrate this witty story.

Fisher, Leonard Everett. **A Russian Farewell.** Illus. by author. Four Winds Press, 1980. 10–up.

The third of a trilogy dealing with emigration to the United States focuses on anti-Semitic terror that drove the Shapiro family out of

Czarist Russia in 1906. The scratchboard etchings fittingly illustrate the strength of character and purpose that underlies this novel based on a family saga.

Snyder, Carol. **Ike and Mama and the Block Wedding.** Illus. Charles Robinson. Coward, McCann & Geoghegan, 1979. 8–11.

When Mr. Weinstein loses his job in 1919, everyone on East 136th Street turns out to provide his daughter Rosie with a fine block wedding. A sequel to *Ike and Mama and the Once-a-Year Suit,* this book depicts the warm immigrant neighborhood that refuses to be ground down by poverty.

Taylor, Sydney. **Ella of All of a Kind Family.** Illus. Gail Owens. E. P. Dutton, 1978. 10–up.

This addition to the *All of a Kind Family Series* updates the reader on this entertaining Jewish family while focusing on the eldest girl. The story provides clear insight into the customs of this family in the years following World War I. Expressive pencil drawings.

United States: The Depression Years

Burch, Robert. **Ida Early Comes over the Mountain.** Viking Press, 1980. 9–12.

The four Sutton children of rural Georgia lose their mother during the Great Depression. Ida Early comes over the mountain and into the unhappy Sutton household and changes everything. Her lively spirit and wild stories make tough times bearable. During her seasonal disappearance, the Suttons realize that she is indispensable.

Burch, Robert. **Wilkin's Ghost.** Illus. Lloyd Bloom. Viking Press, 1978. 8–12.

Wilkin doesn't believe in ghosts but he sees something white under the Hanging Tree. When it and Wilkin next meet, in the hayloft at the Todd's house, they become friends with problems to solve together. A story set in rural Georgia in 1935.

Chaikin, Miriam. **Finders Weepers.** Illus. Richard Egielski. Harper & Row, Publishers, 1980. 8–12.

Mollie is thrilled to find a ring, but the ring brings trouble. Mollie is sure that she is being punished for her inability to return the ring when her baby brother is hospitalized. The book beautifully details the life of a Jewish family in New York in the 1930s. Strong characterization.

Engel, Beth Bland. **Ride the Pine Sapling.** Harper & Row, Publishers, 1978. 10–12.

The character of eleven-year-old Ann is clearly drawn as she faces many complex problems during the summer of 1929 in southern

Georgia. Her father is out of work, her mother is pregnant, and she must give up her own room to boarders. Well-written and useful for discussions.

Greene, Constance C. **Dotty's Suitcase.** Viking Press, 1980. 10–up.

Dotty's adventures begin when she and Jud find a suitcase full of money from a bank robbery. They decide to go to Boonville where Olive, Dotty's best friend, has just moved. Olive finds the money changes a lot of things in her life, but not in the way she expected. Set in the depression era.

Peck, Robert Newton. **Soup's Drum.** Illus. Charles Robinson. Alfred A. Knopf, 1980. 8–12.

Soup and Rob discover girls. The town band is trying to make a comeback for the Fourth of July celebration. After Rob totes Soup's huge drum through the parade and realizes Soup hasn't carried his share, he gets even.

Peck, Robert Newton. **Soup for President.** Illus. Ted Lewin. Alfred A. Knopf, 1978. 9–12.

FDR is running for president of the United States; Soup is running for president of the school. Robert Peck, Soup's campaign manager, is involved in tactics only a mother or an understanding teacher could forgive. This humorous account of growing up in rural Vermont has black and white illustrations.

Rabe, Berniece. **The Orphans.** E. P. Dutton, 1978. 10–12.

The depression of the 1930s is the setting in which the orphans, Big Adam and Little Eve, experience many difficulties. Big Adam is determined to find a permanent home for his twin. After many hardships and the intervention of the local sheriff, a satisfying ending ensues. Well-drawn characters.

Skolsky, Mindy Warshaw. **Carnival and Kopeck and More about Hannah.** Illus. Karen Ann Weinhaus. Harper & Row, Publishers, 1979. 7–10.

Eight-year-old Hannah has a special relationship with her grandmother. After Hannah forgets some promises about behaving, they quarrel and she sees another side to her grandmother. Universal childlike concerns occur in this low-keyed, nostalgic 1930s story set in the Bronx. Hannah is also featured in *The Whistling Teakettle and Other Stories about Hannah.*

Thrasher, Crystal. **Between Dark and Daylight.** Atheneum, 1980. 12–up.

A companion book to the author's *The Dark Didn't Catch Me.* Twelve-year-old Seely and her family are finally moving out of the dark, oppressive hills of southern Indiana. Their old truck breaks down before they reach the daylight of a better life. A vivid, moving story of the rural Midwest in the 1930s.

Waldron, Ann. **Scaredy Cat.** E. P. Dutton, 1978. 10–12.

Ten-year-old Jane has been afraid ever since she read about the Lindbergh kidnapping incident. Similar events in Alabama's daily papers add to her fears; eventually, she is a victim. Insight into the depression years is given as the story revolves around two well-rounded characters.

United States: World War II and Aftermath

Asher, Sandy. **Daughters of the Law.** Beaufort Books, 1980. 12–up.

Ruthie Morganthau is as happy as she can ever remember being, but her unknown past keeps coming back to haunt her. The heartbreaking story of her struggle to cope with her mother's grief from a concentration camp experience and to live her own life is sensitively told.

Blume, Judy. **Starring Sally J. Freedman as Herself.** Bradbury Press, 1977. 10–up.

Sally, ten years old, spends the winter of 1947 in Florida. She makes up lots of stories about people she imagines are living near her, including a mystery about Adolf Hitler. The young friends of Sally and her older brother bring the postwar era to life. A funny, realistic tale of a Jewish family.

Hurwitz, Johanna. **Once I Was a Plum Tree.** Illus. Ingrid Fetz. William Morrow, 1980. 7–10.

Geraldine Flam, who lives in the postwar Bronx neighborhood, is troubled because she isn't quite sure where she belongs. She is Jewish, but her parents are nonobservers. Her Catholic friends are secure in their beliefs. An unexpected invitation settles her doubts. Meaningful black and white sketches.

Lowry, Lois. **Autumn Street.** Houghton Mifflin, 1980. 12–up.

Elizabeth spends her sixth year at her grandfather's home during World War II. Her friendship with Charles, the grandson of the black cook, fills her days with joy and adventure. His murder by the town lunatic changes Elizabeth forever. Outstanding characterization and emotion.

Paterson, Katherine. **Jacob Have I Loved.** Thomas Y. Crowell, 1980. 12–up.

Louise saw her relationship with her twin, Caroline, akin to that of Jacob and Esau. Caroline got the most and the best of all things, including parental love, while Louise withdrew behind a facade of independence and contentment, all the while seething with jealousy. Set in the early 1940s on a remote island in Chesapeake Bay. 1981 Newbery Award Book.

Smith, Doris Buchanan. **Salted Lemons.** Four Winds Press, 1980. 10–up.
Eleven-year-old Darby's family moves from Washington, D.C. to
Atlanta during World War II. Darby is a Yankee, taunted by others
for her different ways. She meets other outsiders, Mr. Kaigler, the
German grocer, and Yoka, a Japanese girl who is later interned.
Darby gains understanding of herself in relation to others.

Uchida, Yoshiko. **Journey Home.** Illus. Charles Robinson. Atheneum,
1978. 10–12.
After a year in a concentration camp to which west coast Japanese
Americans were sent during World War II, twelve-year-old Yuki and
her parents resettle in Salt Lake City and then, after the war's end,
back home in Berkeley. Because the war has fostered hatred for
Japanese, the refugees are greeted with distrust and violence. A
sequel to *Journey to Topaz.*

Additional Historical Fiction Books

Alcott, Louisa May. *Little Women.* Illus. Barbara Cooney. Thomas Y. Crowell,
1955. 10–16.
Armstrong, William. *Sounder.* Illus. James Barkley. Harper & Row, Publishers,
1969. 12–up.
Barringer, D. Moreau. *And the Waters Prevailed.* Illus. P. A. Hutchinson. E. P.
Dutton, 1956. 10–14.
Bawden, Nina. *The Peppermint Pig.* J. B. Lippincott, 1975. 8–12.
Benary-Isbert, Margot. *The Ark.* Translated by Richard Winston and Clara
Winston. Harcourt Brace Jovanovich, 1953. 10–up.
Bishop, Claire Huchet. *Twenty and Ten.* Illus. William Pène du Bois. Viking Press,
1952. 10–14.
Brink, Carol Ryrie. *Caddie Woodlawn.* Illus. Kate Seredy. Macmillan Publishing,
1936. 10–12.
Bulla, Clyde Robert. *John Billington, Friend of Squanto.* Illus. Peter Burchard.
Thomas Y. Crowell, 1956. 8–11.
Caudill, Rebecca. *Tree of Freedom.* Illus. Dorothy Morse. Viking Press, 1949.
10–12.
Collier, James L., and Christopher Collier. *My Brother Sam Is Dead.* Four
Winds Press, 1974. 12–up.
Dalgliesh, Alice. *The Bears on Hemlock Mountain.* Illus. Helen Sewell. Charles
Scribner's Sons, 1952. 7–9.
Dalgliesh, Alice. *The Courage of Sarah Noble.* Illus. Leonard Weisgard. Charles
Scribner's Sons, 1954. 6–10.
De Angeli, Marguerite. *The Door in the Wall.* Doubleday, 1949. 9–12.
De Jong, Meindert. *The House of Sixty Fathers.* Illus. Maurice Sendak. Harper &
Row, Publishers, 1956. 9–12.
Edmonds, Walter. *The Matchlock Gun.* Illus. Paul Lantz. Dodd, Mead, 1941. 8–12.
Field, Rachel. *Calico Bush.* Illus. Allen Lewis. Macmillan Publishing, 1931, 1946,
1966. 10–14.
Fleischman, Sid. *Mr. Mysterious and Company.* Illus. Eric von Schmidt. Little,
Brown, 1962. 9–12.
Forbes, Esther. *Johnny Tremain.* Illus. Lynd Ward. Houghton Mifflin, 1943. 12–16.

Fritz, Jean. *The Cabin Faced West.* Illus. Feodor Rojankovsky. Coward, McCann & Geoghegan, 1958. 8–12.

Gauch, Patricia Lee. *This Time, Tempe Wick?* Illus. Margot Tomes. Coward, McCann & Geoghegan, 1974. 6–10.

Gray, Elizabeth Janet. *Adam of the Road.* Illus. Robert Lawson. Viking Press, 1942. 12–up.

Haugaard, Erik. *The Little Fishes.* Illus. Milton Johnson. Houghton Mifflin, 1967. 12–up.

Hunt, Irene. *Across Five Aprils.* Illus. Albert John Pucci. Follett Publishing, 1964. 10–14.

Ish-Kishor, Sulamith. *A Boy of Old Prague.* Illus. Ben Shahn. Pantheon Books, 1963. 10–14.

Keith, Harold. *Rifles for Watie.* Thomas Y. Crowell, 1957. 10–16.

Konigsburg, E. L. *A Proud Taste for Scarlet and Miniver.* Atheneum, 1973. 12–up.

Latham, Jean Lee. *This Dear-Bought Land.* Illus. Jacob Landau. Harper & Row, Publishers, 1957. 10–14.

Monjo, F. N. *The Drinking Gourd.* Illus. Fred Brenner. Harper & Row, Publishers, 1970. 7–10.

O'Dell, Scott. *Sing Down the Moon.* Houghton Mifflin, 1970. 12–up.

Picard, Barbara L. *One Is One.* Holt, Rinehart and Winston, 1966. 11–up.

Reiss, Johanna. *The Upstairs Room.* Thomas Y. Crowell, 1972. 10–16.

Richter, Hans Peter. *Friedrich.* Translated by Edite Kroll. Holt, Rinehart and Winston, 1970. 12–up.

Speare, Elizabeth George. *The Bronze Bow.* Houghton Mifflin, 1961. 11–14.

Speare, Elizabeth George. *The Witch of Blackbird Pond.* Houghton Mifflin, 1958. 12–16.

Steele, William O. *The Perilous Road.* Illus. Paul Galdone. Harcourt Brace Jovanovich, 1958. 9–12.

Sutcliff, Rosemary. *Warrior Scarlet.* Illus. Charles Keeping. Henry Z. Walck, 1958. 12–up.

Taylor, Mildred D. *Roll of Thunder, Hear My Cry.* Dial Press, 1976. 11–up.

Turkle, Brinton. *The Adventures of Obadiah.* Viking Press, 1972. 5–9.

Van Stockum, Hilda. *The Winged Watchman.* Farrar, Straus & Giroux, 1962. 8–12.

Walsh, Jill Paton. *Fireweed.* Farrar, Straus & Giroux, 1969. 12–up.

Wilder, Laura Ingalls. *Little House in the Big Woods.* Illus. Garth Williams. Harper & Row, Publishers, 1953. 8–12.

Yep, Laurence. *Dragonwings.* Harper & Row, Publishers, 1975. 12–up.

Contemporary Realistic Fiction

Adventure

Adkins, Jan. **Luther Tarbox**. Charles Scribner's Sons, 1977. 8–12.

One foggy day Luther, a lobsterman, brings into port not only his lobster pots but a flotilla of boats lost in the fog. This beautifully prepared book has language so rich that the reader can catch a whiff of salt air. Pencil drawings with their varied perspectives are enjoyable. (Picture book)

Bawden, Nina. **Rebel on a Rock**. J. B. Lippincott, 1978. 10–up.

A family's visit to Ithaca, a country similar to Greece that is ruled by a dictator, involves the children in a startling revolutionary secret and leads them to suspect that their stepfather is a spy. Told from the point of view of twelve-year-old Jo, the story recounts the exciting adventures of the children.

Bawden, Nina. **The Robbers**. Lothrop, Lee & Shepard Books, 1979. 10–12.

Philip enjoys living with his grandmother in a castle. When his father remarries and takes the nine-year-old boy to live with him in a cosmopolitan section of London, life changes drastically. Philip's new friend presents a world of altered values and eventually involves Philip in a theft. A thought-provoking book.

Bφdker, Cecil (translator Sheila La Farge). **Silas and the Black Mare**. Seymour Lawrence, 1978. 12–up.

Silas is an agile and clever thirteen year old who is homeless and must survive by his own wits. He wins a high-spirited black mare in a wager, but the horse is stolen from him. The story tells of his adventures in regaining the horse. Excellent character development; European setting.

Bond, Nancy. **The Best of Enemies**. Atheneum, 1978. 12–up.

Charlotte Paige is twelve; suddenly her world seems to fall apart as her close-knit family becomes increasingly preoccupied with individual interests. Feeling left out and alone she begins to face her own growing up during a series of events climaxing on Patriot's Day, 1977, in Concord, Massachusetts. Hometown Minutemen and a motley group of British soldiers contribute to Charlotte's adventure.

Branscum, Robbie. **To the Tune of a Hickory Stick.** Doubleday, 1978. 10–12.

A country schoolhouse provides protection from winter storms and a cruel uncle for thirteen-year-old Nell and younger brother J. D. Humor, loyalty, and love of learning carry the listener or reader through a winter of excitement with two children, a teacher, and an old man and his dog.

Budbill, David. **Bones on Black Spruce Mountain.** Dial Press, 1978. 10–12.

This wilderness adventure story skillfully weaves survival techniques and outdoor information in a well-paced manner. Seth and Daniel climb Black Spruce Mountain to investigate the legend of a runaway orphan who fled to the mountain. Interesting character study and a satisfying plot; helpful map suggests setting.

Bunting, Eve. **The Big Find.** Photographs by Richard Hutchings. Creative Education, 1978. 8–12.

Two boys find $4,200 in a bean can. Louis wants to turn the money in, but Harp claims half and threatens Louis if he tells anyone. Louis is persuaded by both his conscience and his friend Marie's advice to do what is right. Black and white photos; inner city setting.

Bunting, Eve. **Magic and the Night River.** Illus. Allen Say. Harper & Row, Publishers, 1978. 7–10.

Yashi's faith in Grandfather's gentle skill with their cormorant birds is confirmed in this story of a night's fishing on the Great River in Japan. The suspense of whether Grandfather can catch enough fish to keep his boat and livelihood is heightened by the hostility of Kano, the boat owner, and by a threatening accident. Beautiful and precise pictures. (Picture book)

Callen, Larry. **The Muskrat War.** Little, Brown, 1980. 8–12.

Times are tough in Four Corners, and when two swindlers arrive in town things get desperate: chickens disappear from their pens and the money-producing muskrat hides are stolen. Pinch and Charley, heroes of several previous books, use their wits and a great deal of feisty enterprise to catch the crooks.

Calloway, Northern J., and Carol Hall. **Super-Vroomer!** Illus. Sammis McLean. Doubleday, 1978. 4–7.

Enthusiasm grows from the title page to the photograph of Northern J. Calloway, "Sesame Street" star, on the back cover. The story is his true childhood adventure of building a racing car from junk parts to prove he is the champion racing car builder and driver in the world. Written in black English as told by Northern as a child. (Picture book)

Clymer, Eleanor. **A Search for Two Bad Mice.** Illus. Margery Gill. Atheneum, 1980. 7–10.

Sarah doesn't want to go to England and leave Leo, her cat. Older sister Barbara suggests a search for Hunca Munca, Tom Thumb, and the dollhouse in Beatrix Potter's classic story. The trip is a success, friends are made, and the flavor of England suggested. Evocative drawings of England's Lake District.

Cohen, Peter Zachary. **Deadly Game at Stony Creek.** Illus. Michael J. Deas. Dial Press, 1978. 8–12.

Athletic skills assist Cliff and his friend Eddie narrowly to escape great harm. The author suspensefully captures the fright of two teenage boys hunting a pack of wild dogs. Black and white illustrations greatly contribute to the setting and location of the story.

Delton, Judy. **Kitty in the Middle.** Illus. Charles Robinson. Houghton Mifflin, 1979. 7–10.

A lively, humorous story of Kitty and her two nine-year-old friends, Margaret Mary and Eileen. Escapades brighten their days while attending a parochial school. Going uninvited to a strange wedding and discovering the occupant of a haunted house keep the girls busy and the reader entertained. Black and white sketches.

Delton, Judy. **Kitty in the Summer.** Illus. Charles Robinson. Houghton Mifflin, 1980. 7–10.

Every summer Kitty visits in Norwood, Minnesota, with her Aunt Katie, a busy woman whom Kitty helps with many chores. This summer is filled with unexpected events, from "purchasing" a pagan baby to seeing real poverty. A sequel to *Kitty in the Middle.* Entertaining, humorous, and fine characterization; pen drawings.

de Roo, Anne. **Scrub Fire.** Atheneum, 1980. 8–12.

An unexpected fire during a camping trip sends a fourteen-year-old girl and her two younger brothers into the New Zealand Bush to escape the flames. The story concerns their unusual methods of survival. The sense of adventure is everywhere in this story.

Dionetti, Michelle. **The Day Eli Went Looking for Bear.** Illus. Joyce Audy Dos Santos. Addison-Wesley Publishing, 1980. 4–7.

Young Eli sets off with his dog in search of a bear. The snow-covered bushes and trees provide camouflage as his imagination wanders and he sights bears in unusual places. The last "bear" turns out to be his mother, who welcomes her happy adventurer home. Black and white pencil drawings give us a glimpse of Eli's hidden bears. (Picture book)

Ehrlich, Amy. **The Everyday Train.** Illus. Martha Alexander. Dial Press, 1977. 4–7.

A small girl finds delight in waiting for and then watching the freight train that winds through the countryside each day. Simple concepts of the sights and sounds of the train and the gentle expectation of looking foward to a daily event combine to make a pleasing story. (Picture book)

Eiseman, Alberta, and Nicole Eiseman. **Gift from a Sheep: The Story of How Wool Is Made.** Illus. Tracy Sugarman. Atheneum, 1979. 8–12.

Jenny raises a sheep, goes through all the steps of handling the wool, and even wins prizes at the county fair! One section of the book explains how yarn is made and another gives directions for making a poncho.

Everton, Macduff. **Finding the Magic Circus.** Illus. by author. Carolrhoda Books, 1979. 6–9.

Ricky accompanies his father in Yucatan looking for the circus his father had traveled with years before. He learns something about the Mayas, a few Spanish words, and a circus act. Outstanding full-color pictures using a yarn beeswax technique developed in Mexico. (Picture book)

Furchgott, Terry, and Linda Dawson. **Phoebe and the Hot Water Bottles.** Illus. Terry Furchgott. Andre Deutsch, 1977. 4–7.

Phoebe has over one hundred hot water bottles. She loves playing with them but would secretly rather have a puppy. When an emergency arises, Phoebe and her bottles come to the rescue, for which she is satisfyingly rewarded. This tale about a spunky girl is realistically illustrated in lush colors. (Picture book)

George, Jean Craighead. **River Rats, Inc.** E. P. Dutton, 1979. 10–12.

Joe and Crowbar, on a dangerous and illegal run down the Colorado River in the Grand Canyon, flounder in the rapids but manage to escape drowning. They encounter a feral boy who, after Joe painstakingly teaches him human language, guides the boys to an Indian village and safety. A story of physical survival, it also has a strong element of psychological survival and the development of self-image.

George, Jean Craighead. **The Wentletrap Trap.** Illus. Symeon Shimin. E. P. Dutton, 1978. 7–10.

Dennis wants to take care of himself. When his father tells him he can trade a wentletrap shell for all he needs, Dennis works hard to capture one. Hermit crabs and a storm interfere. Then father returns from the sea and Dennis is content to let father care for him. Bimini setting. (Picture book)

Hass, Patricia Cecil. **Windsong Summer.** Illus. Glo Coalson. Dodd, Mead, 1978. 8–12.

Twelve-year-old Tim and his sister Mouse spend their summer in the Caribbean with busy parents who are away on business. The children become involved in adventures with a runaway boy who owns a beautiful sloop. The themes of being free and loneliness are thoughtfully described.

Herold, Ann Bixby. **The Helping Day.** Illus. Victoria de Larrea. Coward, McCann & Geoghegan, 1980. 3–7.

David wants to express his good feelings by helping someone. His dad, brother, and mom don't need helping, but the ants do. And worms need rescuing, as does a baby rabbit, and a butterfly. Best of all, Daddy understands. Warm illustrations extend the concepts of feelings involved. (Picture book)

Houston, James. **Frozen Fire: A Tale of Courage.** Illus. by author. Atheneum, 1977. 10–12.

Matthew and his father move to the Canadian Arctic. His father, a geologist, believes he can locate copper for mining. The predictably severe weather of the Arctic spring delays the mineral search and endangers the lives of Matthew, his father, and Matthew's Eskimo friend. Excellent for social studies curriculum integration.

Levine, Betty K. **Hawk High.** Illus. Louise E. Jefferson. Atheneum, 1980. 8–12.

A young girl wants to show others that she can take care of herself. She sets out to find hawks, but she encounters a thunderstorm in the dark woods instead. Toni does more than survive; she learns an important lesson.

McDaniel, Suellen R. **Serpent Treasure.** John F. Blair, Publisher, 1978. 10–12.

Sixteen-year-old Chris and his father grow concerned about an old friend, Andrew, who lives alone in a canyon that supposedly hides legendary Aztec gold. Mysterious lights, voices, and Andrew's evil nephew add to the excitement of this story. Flashback style.

Mark, Jan. **Under the Autumn Garden.** Illus. Judith Gwyn Brown. Thomas Y. Crowell, 1977. 10–12.

Ten-year-old Matthew wants to make his history assignment interesting so he decides on an archaeological dig in the backyard. No one understands or encourages. His dig fails; he fails. Too late he unearths one treasure. Good characterizations of English family and village life. For better readers.

Mauser, Pat Rhoads. **How I Found Myself at the Fair.** Illus. Emily Arnold McCully. Atheneum, 1980. 7–10.

The Denton family takes Laura, a nine-year-old only child, to the state fair with them. Upon arrival she feels alone and afraid as the Denton children scatter in many directions at the fairgrounds. After a while it occurs to her that she is really lost and is responsible for finding her way back to the Dentons. Pen sketches.

Nobens, C. A. **The Happy Baker.** Carolrhoda Books, 1979. 6–8.

Joseph, the baker, lives a good life in his small town but he longs to see the world. A discovery causes him to redesign his display sign on the bakery shop. Large print, three-color illustrations. (Picture book)

Orgel, Doris. **A Certain Magic.** Dial Press, 1976. 10–12.

When eleven-year-old Jenny accidentally discovers Aunt Trudl's old diary, she learns many things about her aunt's life as a child evacuated from World War II Vienna. During a trip abroad with her parents, Jenny visits places mentioned in the diary and discovers secrets about her aunt's life that explain present-day questions.

Phipson, Joan. **When the City Stopped.** Atheneum, 1979. 12–up.

Thirteen-year-old Nick Lorimer and his younger sister Binkie find out what it is like to be without electricity and water when a chaotic general strike occurs in their Australian city. Fear overtakes them when their mother fails to return home. Interesting reading with excellent character development.

Place, Marian T. **The Boy Who Saw Bigfoot.** Dodd, Mead, 1979. 8–12.

Ten-year-old Joey, placed in one foster home after another, finds a real home at last with Sara and Mike Brown near logging camps in the mountains of western Washington. His affection for Sara grows as the two of them go out hiking, and share the excitement of seeing Bigfoot.

Politi, Leo. **Mr. Fong's Toy Shop.** Charles Scribner's Sons, 1978. 7–10.

Ancient customs are kept alive by Mr. Fong, a Chinatown toymaker who shares both his craft and the legends of his native land with the local children. Together they prepare a shadow puppet play to perform during the annual Moon Festival. (Picture book)

Ross, Pat. **M and M and the Haunted House Game.** Illus. Marylin Hafner. Pantheon Books, 1980. 6–9.

Mimi and Mandy are bored with their old pastimes so they decide to play the haunted house game. They plan to scare someone but the tables turn and they get scared. Humorous black and white illustrations. (Picture book)

Rumsey, Marian. **Carolina Hurricane.** Illus. Ted Lewin. William Morrow, 1977. 10–12.

Morgan knew the hurricane would destroy his father's fishing traps so he and his dog Tater set out to bring them in. The boy, dog, and boat are stranded on a remote marsh island off the South Carolina coast. The desperate fight to survive the fury of the storm is vividly described.

Seabrooke, Brenda. **The Best Burglar Alarm.** Illus. Loretta Lustig. William Morrow, 1978. 6–9.

Belinda visits her aunt and uncle who have just installed a burglar alarm system. Their three pets were given away, since pets set off alarms. Belinda is bored until night brings excitement and surprises. Good for discussions about paranoia vs. sensible home security precautions. This book is fun to read and includes humorous illustrations. (Picture book)

Snyder, Zilpha Keatley. **The Famous Stanley Kidnapping Case.** Atheneum, 1980. 10–up.

A sequel to Snyder's *The Headless Cupid,* the Italian adventures of these five lively children include their kidnapping and subsequent rescue. The family's experiences provide unexpected and maturing rewards, especially for Molly.

Spencer, Zane, and Jay Leech. **Branded Runaway.** Westminster Press, 1980. 8–12.

A young boy is a chronic runaway and is given an alternative by an understanding judge. He becomes a camp counselor for problem children and finds his own courage by helping other boys.

Spier, Peter. **Bored—Nothing to Do!** Doubleday, 1978. 7–10.

Take a lazy summer day, two boys, one good idea, a house, and a yard full of handy materials just waiting to be made into something special, and anything can happen. Full-page pictures and very few words combine to make this book appealing to a wide age range. (Picture book)

Stewart, A. C. **Silas and Con.** Atheneum, 1977. 10–up.

Ten-year-old Silas is abandoned by his parents. With his stray dog Con, he wanders through the wilds of northwestern Scotland until he quite accidentally finds an island home. A quiet, contemplative story.

Stoutenburg, Adrien. **Where to Now, Blue?** Four Winds Press, 1978. 10–12.

Life is dull and unpleasant for twelve-year-old Blueberry when brother Tod leaves their Minnesota home. With a makeshift houseboat, she and an orphan, six-year-old Tilbo, run away. Their trip leads to problems with nature and with people. Fast-paced, contemporary language.

Talbot, Charlene Joy. **The Great Rat Island Adventure.** Illus. Ruth Sanderson. Atheneum, 1977. 8–12.

Joel spends the summer on an island with his father, whom he hasn't seen for two years. He learns to know his father, an ornithologist, and his research team. They experience a hurricane, solve the mystery of the missing tern eggs, and rescue a girl from a neighboring island. Contemporary ideas, life-styles, and language contribute to a strong story.

Waldron, Ann. **The Luckie Star.** E. P. Dutton, 1977. 10–12.

Quincy Luckie, who wants to be an astronomer, is at odds with the rest of her family, who prefer acting, painting, or writing. A summer in Florida, a hurricane, and a search for sunken treasure reveal the individual characters and relationships of a number of talented and attractive people.

Wartski, Maureen Crane. **A Boat to Nowhere.** Illus. Dick Teicher. Westminster Press, 1980. 10–12.

Grandfather, Mai, and her little brother Loc are forced to flee their tiny village in Vietnam when the new government takes over, burns Grandfather's books, and places him under arrest. They are aided by a war orphan who is impudent, street-wise, and, in the end, intensely loyal. The four of them become boat people. A gripping story.

Zimelman, Nathan. **Walls Are to Be Walked.** Illus. Donald Carrick. E. P. Dutton, 1977. 4–7.

The illustrations show a little boy on his way home from school. Within a short distance there are so many exciting discoveries and adventures! Opposite the full-page picture there is an oval-shaped inset with text that brings the illustrated incident into focus. (Picture book)

Animals

Annixter, Jane, and Paul Annixter. **The Last Monster.** Harcourt Brace Jovanovich, 1980. 8–12.

A teenage boy sets out to find the killer grizzly bear that maimed his father and dog, but he finds himself being hunted instead. The action leads to a confrontation with a giant grizzly bear. A nature book with an exciting theme.

Bartoli, Jennifer. **In a Meadow, Two Hares Hide.** Illus. Takeo Ishida. Albert Whitman, 1978. 6–9.

Two young hares, Mimo and Lepo, mature throughout the changing seasons and survive in spite of dangers and natural enemies. Although the animals have names, the content is factual, not fantasy. Double-page, full-color illustrations are as real as the text. (Picture book)

Baylor, Byrd. **Hawk, I'm Your Brother.** Illus. Peter Parnall. Charles Scribner's Sons, 1976. 7–10.

An Indian boy captures a hawk, which he hopes can teach him to fly. After a time the boy realizes that all things must be free to live as they are intended. Only then does he understand that the hawk is his brother. Sweeping black and white scenes complement this poetic text. 1977 Caldecott Honor Book. (Picture book)

Benchley, Nathaniel. **Kilroy and the Gull.** Illus. John Schoenherr. Harper & Row, Publishers, 1977. 8–12.

Kilroy, a killer whale, is captured and trained to be a marineland performer. His sea gull friend escapes with him to the open sea. The illustrations are dramatic and lifelike. The major question throughout this book is that of true freedom.

Bourne, Eulalia "Sister." **Blue Colt.** Illus. Pam Fullerton. Northland Press, 1979. 10–12.

Manuel, an eleven-year-old boy, lives on a poor farm in Arizona with his grandparents. His special friend Bill entrusts his horse to Manuel while he is in the Navy. Excellent character portrayal and descriptions of the land. An appealing story with woodcutlike illustrations. Glossary appended.

Brown, Margaret Wise. **When the Wind Blew.** Illus. Geoffrey Hayes. Harper & Row, Publishers, 1977. 4–6.

A serious problem confronts an old lady who lives alone by the sea with her seventeen cats and one small blue-grey kitten. As the wind blows, the problem becomes intensified. The little kitten comes to the rescue. Text and pictures blend to produce a folktale quality. A lap book. (Picture book)

Brustlein, Janice. **Mr. and Mrs. Button's Wonderful Watchdogs.** Illus. Roger Duvoisin. Lothrop, Lee & Shepard Books, 1978. 4–7.

Mr. and Mrs. Button need a watchdog because their dog and two cats are too friendly to be of much help. Several times they go to the kennel and think they're coming home with the right dog. Finally, they are happily surprised. Vibrant colored illustrations bring the story to life. (Picture book)

Carlson, Natalie Savage. **Jaky or Dodo?** Illus. Gail Owens. Charles Scribner's Sons, 1978. 7–10.

A Parisian mongrel leads a double life, eating scraps Pierre's grandmother saves for him one day and feasting on gourmet meals served at Monsieur Boffu's café the next. Each owner enters him in the same dog show. Then comes the test: Is he really Pierre's Jaky or Monsieur Boffu's Dodo? (Picture book)

Chambers, John W. **Fritzi's Winter.** Illus. Carole Kowalchuk Odell. Atheneum, 1979. 10–12.

The Arnold family is proud of their Siamese cat, Fritzi. Excitement runs high when they discover that she has been left behind at their summer home. During that fall and winter her survival is all that matters. An enjoyable, readable story illustrated with black and white sketches.

Dann, Colin. **The Animals of Farthing Wood.** Elsevier/Nelson Books, 1979. 10–up.

Because humans have destroyed their homes in Farthing Woods, the animals assemble and plan their move to White Deer Park. The journey is fraught with dangers and narrow escapes, but also inspires cooperation, heroism, and love.

Dixon, Paige. **The Loner: A Story of the Wolverine.** Illus. Grambs Miller. Atheneum, 1978. 8–12.

A wolverine is an animal to be feared and respected at all times according to Indian legend. A hunter sets out to destroy this "Carcajou," but the hunter ends up learning a lot about nature, the wolverine, and himself. Several illustrations give the reader a view of the wolverine in its forest home.

Dixon, Paige. **Summer of the White Goat.** Illus. Grambs Miller. Atheneum, 1977. 10–12.

Gordon Mohlen goes to Glacier National Park to observe mountain goats of the region. His science class research is recorded from day to day on his tape recorder. He becomes ill and is left stranded. Detailed informational chart on the mountain goat included. Bibliography.

Dolan, Sheila. **The Wishing Bottle.** Illus. Leslie Morrill. Houghton Mifflin, 1979. 7–10.

Her head full of fairy tales and her heart longing for a pony, Nora finds a magic bottle into which she repeatedly whispers her wish. A pony does appear, though it is not exactly hers. Soft line drawings complement a satisfying story.

Duncan, Jane. **Janet Reachfar and Chickabird.** Illus. Mairi Hedderwick. Seabury Press, 1978. 4–7.

When Janet Reachfar takes out the horses, a chick is injured accidentally and she feels responsible. Her care of the injured hen through the change of Scottish seasons provides a warm, well-told story, beautifully illustrated with elegant, evocative watercolors. (Picture book)

Dunn, Judy. **The Little Lamb.** Photographs by Phoebe Dunn. Random House, 1977. 5–8.

Emmy cares for Timothy, a newborn lamb. All goes well until he grows older and stronger. As he becomes a nuisance, a decision must be reached. Appealing color photographs make this an inviting book for the young reader or listener. (Picture book)

Farley, Walter. **The Black Stallion Picture Book.** Random House, 1979. 6–9.

A simplified adaptation of *The Black Stallion.* Young Alec Ramsay is shipwrecked on a desert island with the black stallion, a wild horse. The two discover that they need one another. Their adventures continue in America after their rescue. Color photographs from the 1979 motion picture. (Picture book)

Feder, Jane. **Beany.** Illus. Karen Gundersheimer. Pantheon Books, 1979. 3–5.

Beany is "the most beautiful cat in the world and the smartest too." That is how the young narrator describes his cat and his interesting day with Beany as his faithful companion. This small, unusually shaped book full of appealing illustrations is not reserved for cat lovers alone. (Picture book)

Fletcher, Elizabeth. **The Little Goat.** Illus. Deborah Niland and Kilmeny Niland. Grosset & Dunlap, 1977. 3–5.

A simply told tale of a farmer who loses one of his ten goats. He searches all night long until he finds the goat and brings it home. He warms it and puts it to sleep at the foot of his bed. Illustrations in color alternate with bold pen and ink drawings. (Picture book)

Gates, Doris. **A Morgan for Melinda.** Viking Press, 1980. 10–12.

Melinda, a ten-year-old girl, isn't fond of horses until her father buys her a Morgan. Her life changes from that day on. Through her friendship with an elderly writer, Melinda overcomes her fear of riding. She tells of her interesting and exciting life in the first person.

George, Jean Craighead. **The Cry of the Crow.** Harper & Row, Publishers, 1980. 10–12.

Mandy's father and crows are real enemies. Crows are pests and must be kept away from his strawberry patch. Mandy secretly keeps a crow in a sheltered spot in the woods and meets with many surprises. A beautiful relationship exists between Mandy and her family.

George, Jean Craighead. **The Wounded Wolf.** Illus. John Schoenherr. Harper & Row, Publishers, 1978. 4–7.

This story of a wolf, whose leg was injured by a caribou, is a scientist's recorded observation of one wolf saving the life of another. A suspenseful account of the wolf's survival is clearly described. Pen and ink sketches complement this poetic text. (Picture book)

Gipson, Fred. **Curly and the Wild Boar.** Illus. Ronald Himler. Harper &
Row, Publishers, 1979. 10–up.

Old Yeller fans and readers of animal stories will welcome another
of this author's books. Curly raises an eighty-pound prize watermelon but it is eaten by a wild boar. Angered by this boldness, Curly
wants to kill this enemy. Excitement runs high as the battle ensues.
Good for reading aloud. Black and white sketches.

Girion, Barbara. **Misty and Me.** Charles Scribner's Sons, 1979. 10–12.

Kim learns more than how to raise a dog when she buys a puppy at
the pound without her parents' permission. She hires Mrs. Mac as a
dogsitter and everything is fine until Mrs. Mac becomes ill. Then
Kim is faced with some hard decisions. Good for class discussion
about responsibility.

Griffiths, Helen. **Blackface Stallion.** Illus. Victor Ambrus. Holiday House,
1980. 10–up.

A sensitive and unsentimental story of a wild horse. Blackface's
mother is a palomino who is lost on a Mexican desert and eventually
accepted by a herd of wild horses. The story follows Blackface from
his birth until he takes his place as leader of the herd. An exciting
story of survival.

Griffiths, Helen. **Grip: A Dog Story.** Illus. Douglas Hall. Holiday House,
1978. 10–12.

Eleven-year-old Dudley's father is a breeder of generations of fighting
dogs in England. He wishes for a dog of his own; his father entrusts
one of Madman's offspring, a bullterrier, to him. Being a loner, the
boy develops a strong attachment to Grip. English terms.

Hall, Lynn. **Owney: The Traveling Dog.** Illus. Barbara Ericksen. Garrard
Publishing, 1977. 8–12.

This is an appealing story of a homeless mutt befriended by post
office workers in the early twentieth century. The dog grew from a
starved, cowering puppy to an alert, curious, world-famous traveling
dog. Soft color washes add to the charm. A good read-aloud book.

Hancock, Sibyl. **Old Blue.** Illus. Erick Ingraham. G. P. Putnam's Sons,
1980. 7–10.

Old Blue, a longhorn steer, helps young Davy and his father and
other cowboys lead a thousand cattle over the Goodnight Trail to
Dodge City. The hardships of a cowboy's life on the trail are evident.
Large print, easy reading, and softly muted illustrations make this
book popular with youngsters. (Picture book)

Hanson, June Andrea. **Winter of the Owl.** Macmillan Publishing, 1980. 10–up.

Thirteen-year-old Janey cannot endure the idea of parting with her beloved colt. She cannot accomplish his gentling alone so she resentfully accepts the help of John Yellowfeather, an Indian boy who has a special way with animals. During the training, Janey learns about cooperation, responsibility, independence, friendship, and prejudice.

Holmes, Efner Tudor. **Amy's Goose.** Illus. Tasha Tudor. Thomas Y. Crowell, 1977. 6–9.

Amy rescues an injured wild goose, but wants to protect and possess it when the goose is ready to leave. Traditional Tudor illustrations make the book beautiful. (Picture book)

Hooks, William H. **The 17 Gerbils of Class 4A.** Illus. Joel Schick. Coward, McCann & Geoghegan, 1976. 8–12.

Rogue brings two gerbils into his classroom, and the students vote to keep them. The two gerbils become the object of science projects, the parents of more gerbils, and the cause of class problems. Many interesting facts about gerbils are included. Good science integration and fun to read.

Hurd, Edith Thacher. **Under the Lemon Tree.** Illus. Clement Hurd. Little, Brown, 1980. 4–7.

One night a donkey makes an awful noise and awakens the farmer and his wife. They decide to move him away from under his favorite lemon tree. The next night a fox comes to steal their chickens and they realize that the donkey's braying was a warning. Soft-colored illustrations. (Picture book)

John, Naomi. **Roadrunner.** Illus. Peter Parnall and Virginia Parnall. E. P. Dutton, 1980. 6–9.

A day in the life of a roadrunner, the story of the desert bird depicts close encounters with jeep and dog, horse and rider, snake, hawk, and bobcat. The Parnalls' measured illustrations in tan, green, and black capture authentic details of the desert and its creatures. (Picture book)

Johnston, Johanna. **The Fabulous Fox: An Anthology of Fact & Fiction.** Dodd, Mead, 1979. All ages.

True to his name, the sly fox slips in and out of the various genres of literature. Fact and fiction, original sketches, and photographs combine to make this select anthology a real treasure for readers. References found in the Bible and other literature throughout the ages contribute to interesting reading.

Kraus, Robert. **Springfellow.** Illus. Sam Savitt. E. P. Dutton, 1978. 6–9.

Springfellow, a young colt, wants more than anything to romp with the one year olds, but his legs aren't strong enough and he continues to fall. His mother encourages him to keep trying. Action-filled wash illustrations accompany this story of overcoming difficulties. Large pictures, excellent for storytelling. (Picture book)

Longman, Harold S. **The Fox in the Ball Park.** McGraw-Hill, 1980. 8–12.

A beautiful red fox discovers how she can live in Yankee Stadium and search for food in the nearby neighborhood. She has a litter of pups in the stadium that are in danger because Jesus Garcia, a Puerto Rican boy, tells a worker at the stadium that a fox is living there. This animal survival story is realistically told.

McNulty, Faith. **Mouse and Tim.** Illus. Marc Simont. Harper & Row, Publishers, 1978. 4–7.

A young boy develops a friendship with a wild mouse. Parallel story lines show the feelings of each as they perceive their worlds. Good for discussion of captivity versus freedom when the boy reluctantly releases his pet. (Picture book)

Miles, Miska. **Jenny's Cat.** Illus. Wendy Watson. E. P. Dutton, 1979. 6–9.

After finding a stray cat, Jenny, who has been lonely, begins to adjust to her home in the new town. When her mother insists the cat cannot stay, Jenny takes the cat and runs away. Black and white illustrations make the author's memories more real for the sympathetic young listener or reader. (Picture book)

Moeri, Louise. **A Horse for X.Y.Z.** Illus. Gail Owens. E. P. Dutton, 1977. 8–12.

This is a fast-moving story involving Solveig, a spirited twelve-year-old girl who is determined to ride Snake Dancer before leaving camp. Her thoughts take action and she finds herself astride the horse; insurmountable difficulties arise. Pen and ink sketches capture the beauty and action of the horse. Map with legend included.

Morey, Walt. **Sandy and the Rock Star.** E. P. Dutton, 1979. 10–12.

Paul Winters, a lonely young teenage singing star who is carefully controlled and protected by others, runs away to a remote island. There a tame cougar named Sandy is being turned into a wild beast to provide the wealthy island owner with a more challenging hunt. Animal lovers will enjoy this riveting read-aloud story.

Parker, Nancy Winslow. **The Crocodile under Louis Finneberg's Bed.** Illus. by author. Dodd, Mead, 1978. 6–9.

The Finnebergs receive a gift of a crocodile. When the crocodile becomes too big to sleep under Louis's bed, it is donated to a zoo. Louis manages to stay with his pet, but in a most unusual manner! The text, written as a newspaper story, is accompanied by humorously detailed pen and ink drawings. (Picture book)

Pender, Lydia. **The Useless Donkeys.** Illus. Judith Cowell. Frederick Warne, 1979. 4–7.

The Quigleys, a family of seven, live on a farm. Among their animals there are two lovable but useless donkeys. Father is determined to get rid of them, but the other family members protest. An unexpected flood changes the situation. Unusually striking illustrations in collage and watercolors. (Picture book)

Pool, Eugene. **The Captain of Battery Park.** Illus. Leslie H. Morrill. Addison-Wesley Publishing, 1978. 10–12.

Melanie, twelve, finds a wounded Arctic tern in New York's Battery Park. Treated by an eccentric vet, the tern has his own recuperative encounters. Bewildering new experiences and unorthodox responses to traditional situations, coupled with the warmth flowing between animals and humans, make this book a must. Sensitive, dignified illustrations complement this quality text.

Rounds, Glen. **Blind Outlaw.** Illus. by author. Holiday House, 1980. 8–12.

A blind range horse is captured and a boy with no name and a speech impediment befriends him. Trust, love, and friendship transform the outlaw to a useful saddle horse. Riveting horse story with black and white ink sketches.

Roy, Ronald. **A Thousand Pails of Water.** Illus. Vo-Dinh Mai. Alfred A. Knopf, 1978. 4–7.

A young Japanese boy finds a whale wedged between two rocks. Knowing that the great animal must be kept wet, he carries pail after pail of sea water until he falls down, exhausted. The village people come to his aid and together they carry water until the incoming tide frees the whale. (Picture book)

Savitt, Sam. **The Dingle Ridge Fox and Other Stories.** Illus. by author. Dodd, Mead, 1978. 10–12.

This collection of six short stories about foxes, cats, dogs, and horses is illustrated with sensitive watercolor washes that depict highlights of the stories. The reader can learn much about animals and their relationships with other animals and humans.

Scott, Jane. **Cross Fox.** Atheneum, 1980. 12–up.

Eleven-year-old Jamie has just moved with his parents to a farm in Pennsylvania. In the process of adjusting to his new home, he discovers and silently watches a cross fox. When neighbors organize to kill the fox, Jamie resolves to save it. An exciting, fast-moving story with carefully developed characters.

Shura, Mary Francis. **Mister Wolf and Me.** Illus. Konrad Hack. Dodd, Mead, 1979. 10–12.

Mister Wolf, a beautiful sable and silver German shepherd that Miles found as a pup and raised, is accused of killing sheep in the neighborhood. Excellent characterizations and believable depictions of parent-child relationships raise this book above the formula boy-dog story.

Stranger, Joyce. **The Fox at Drummers' Darkness.** Illus. William Geldart. Farrar, Straus & Giroux, 1977. 12–up.

A four-year-old fox feels safe in Drummers' Darkness, a dense, isolated forest. Here an army was defeated many years ago and the phantom army passes by his cave. His daily battles and struggles with men and animals are cleverly related. Rather difficult reading.

Thaler, Mike. **My Puppy.** Illus. Madeleine Fishman. Harper & Row, Publishers, 1980. 7–10.

A young boy discovers that he doesn't have enough money to buy the puppy that he wants so he creates one in his imagination. He enters his puppy in a local dog show and to his surprise he wins. (Picture book)

Thayer, Julie, and Ruth Thayer. **The Lamb Who Went to Paris.** Clarkson N. Potter, Publishers, 1980. 7–10.

Three children vacationing in southern France are given a lamb that has been rejected by its mother. Returning to Paris, the children care for the lamb until it is grown and ready to be returned to the country. Much factual information on lambs and sheep is included in the warm, poignant story.

Thiele, Colin. **Storm Boy.** Illus. John Schoenherr. Harper & Row, Publishers, 1978. 7–10.

Storm Boy lives on a deserted beach in Australia with his father Hideaway, a lonely, quiet man. Lack of contact with others causes Storm Boy to be shy. He becomes very attached to a baby pelican that he rescues. Fingerbone Bill, the aborigine, is an added interest. Black and white pen sketches.

Turner, Dona. **My Cat Pearl.** Thomas Y. Crowell, 1980. 3–5.

The short and simple tale of Pearl, the black cat, is a delight for cat lovers. The vividly colored illustrations add spark to the text. (Picture book)

Wallace, Bill. **A Dog Called Kitty.** Holiday House, 1980. 10–up.

When a helpless, homeless pup shows up on the farm, Ricky is adamant about getting rid of it. He is petrified by all dogs since he was attacked by a dog at a very early age. His attachment to this helpless creature grows and eventually the two become inseparable. A really good story.

Yates, Elizabeth. **The Seventh One.** Illus. Diana Charles. Walker, 1978. 10–12.

There is an enduring lifelong friendship between Tom and his dogs, a very important give-and-take relationship. Each of Tom's seven dogs offers him love in a different way. The text is outstanding in describing a dog's ability to show insight, respect, loyalty, and love.

Zimelman, Nathan. **Positively No Pets Allowed.** Illus. Pamela Johnson. E. P. Dutton, 1980. 4–7.

Seymour Goldberg and his mother bring home a gorilla named Irving as a long-term visitor, but their apartment house rules state that no pets are allowed. This unusual pet story is amusingly illustrated with detailed sketches. (Picture book)

Facing Problems

Aaron, Chester. **Catch Calico!** E. P. Dutton, 1979. 10–12.

Three generations are involved in a sensitive novel set in the mountains. Louis, a fourteen-year-old boy, suspects his grandfather is dying. He struggles with loss and separation, haunted by memories of his dead father and a wild cat named Calico.

Angell, Judie. **Ronnie and Rosey.** Bradbury Press, 1977. 10–up.

The new girl in school has a boy's name, Ronnie. She teams up with a chubby, humorous girl and a talented boy with a girl's name, Rosey. Friendship flourishes between Ronnie and Rosey and takes on an added dimension after Ronnie's father is killed. Some profanity.

Ashley, Bernard. **Break in the Sun.** Illus. Charles Keeping. S. G. Phillips, 1980. 12–up.

Patsy Bligh runs away and joins a touring summer theater group to escape the difficulties of adjusting to a new stepfather. Her return to reality is encouraged by people whom society might consider to be outcasts but who exhibit very special human qualities. The children and the adults do some growing up.

Ashley, Bernard. **A Kind of Wild Justice.** Illus. Charles Keeping. S. G. Phillips, 1979. 12–up.

Ronnie feels he is totally alone in the world when his father is jailed and his mother leaves home. His neighborhood lives under the cruel thumb of the Bradshaw thugs. Ronnie seeks revenge;

his isolation increases but two adult figures offer sanctuary and hope. London setting; written in lusty vernacular. Recommended for mature readers.

Barrett, John M. **No Time for Me.** Illus. Joe Servello. Human Sciences Press, 1979. 7–10.

Jimmy's parents have little time to spend with him, although they make many efforts to surround him with a loving extended family. His parents' homecoming provokes a tantrum that results in an honest and fruitful family conference. A good book to promote child and parent discussions.

Bonsall, Crosby. **Who's Afraid of the Dark?** Harper & Row, Publishers, 1980. 4–7.

A young boy has a dog who is afraid of the dark, so he says. The little girl in the story gives good advice to the dog and everyone, including the boy, is reassured. An easy-to-read book. (Picture book)

Bottner, Barbara. **Dumb Old Casey Is a Fat Tree.** Harper & Row, Publishers, 1979. 6–9.

Casey has a lot of spirit and she needs it to compete with other ballet dancers. She's too fat but she wants to be a dancer more than anything in the world. The recital finally takes place and Casey becomes much wiser about herself. Humorous black and white illustrations. (Picture book)

Branscum, Robbie. **The Saving of P.S.** Illus. Glen Rounds. Doubleday, 1977. 10–12.

Priscilla Sue is the youngest child of widowed Preacher Blue, a fire and brimstone minister in the Arkansas hills. Rather than accept her father's remarriage, she runs away with her smelly old hound dog. Twelve-year-old P.S. is a gutsy young girl who learns a great deal about responsibility and life.

Bulla, Clyde Robert. **Daniel's Duck.** Illus. Joan Sandin. Harper & Row, Publishers, 1979. 4–7.

Jeff and Daniel live in a cabin on a mountain in Tennessee. Despite Daniel's protests, Jeff decides to carve a wooden duck for the fair. He soon learns that art is viewed differently by each individual. An easy-to-read book with softly colored illustrations that clearly depict the setting. (Picture book)

Bunting, Eve. **The Big Red Barn.** Illus. Howard Knotts. Harcourt Brace Jovanovich, 1979. 6–9.

The big red barn burns to the ground and the young narrator loses another link with that secure and happy time when Mother was alive. An understanding grandfather helps the child accept the new without forgetting the old. Illustrations reflect the sensitive, natural atmosphere of the text in this easy-to-read book.

Bunting, Eve. **The Empty Window.** Illus. Judy Clifford. Frederick Warne, 1980. 8–12.

C.G. awakens his younger brother Sweeney one gray Saturday morning. This is the day they must capture the wild parrot for C.G.'s friend Joe, who is dying; just a few days are left. Beautiful illustrations in grays and blacks complement the mood of the story. Discussion-starter on death.

Byars, Betsy. **Good-bye, Chicken Little.** Harper & Row, Publishers, 1979. 10–up.

When his fun-loving uncle drowns in a foolish escapade, Jimmie Little has a hard time coping with his own guilt and with the strange way his family reacts. His mother calls all the relatives together and gives a party. After watching and talking to these zany, memorable characters, he knows he can say good-bye to the nickname he had given himself, "Chicken" Little.

Byars, Betsy. **The PINBALLS.** Harper & Row, Publishers, 1977. 10–up.

Carlie, a tough-talking, suspicious teenager, labels herself, Harvey, and Thomas J. "strays" and likens them to pinballs bouncing here and there. This moving story of emotionally and physically abused children could serve as a manual on coping and surviving. Outstanding characterization makes this an excellent read-aloud book.

Carrick, Carol. **The Accident.** Illus. Donald Carrick. Seabury Press, 1976. 4–7.

It is evening. Christopher and his dog Bodger are on their way to the lake when the pickup truck appears. Bodger dashes into its path and is killed; Christopher reacts with anger. Understanding parents help the boy come to terms with grief. Poignant, sensitive color illustrations. (Picture book)

Carrick, Carol. **The Foundling.** Illus. Donald Carrick. Seabury Press, 1977. 4–7.

Christopher's parents think it is time to adopt a new puppy even though there will never be another Bodger. Christopher doesn't agree; he can't bear the thought of a new dog. A stray puppy provides a happy, satisfying solution. Family warmth is reflected in sensitive color illustrations of a coastal village. (Picture book)

Clark, Ann Nolan. **To Stand against the Wind.** Viking Press, 1978. 10–12.

Em, eleven years old and now living in the United States, writes his memories of Vietnam before and during the war. The war, of course, permeates every facet of the story; the real story, however, is how love of family and love of land can survive tragedy.

Colman, Hila. **Tell Me No Lies.** Crown Publishers, 1978. 10–12.

After believing for twelve years that her father is in another country, Angela learns the truth: he lives nearby and he does not know she exists. Determined to meet him, Angela discovers that he does not need a daughter. Useful bibliotherapy for separation of parents.

Cone, Molly. **The Amazing Memory of Harvey Bean.** Illus. Robert Mac Lean. Houghton Mifflin, 1980. 8–12.

Forgetful Harvy has a problem: his parents are separating. Secretly, he spends a happy and unusual summer in a crazy-looking house with two friendly nonconformists, Mr. and Mrs. Katz. Readers relate to Harry's problems and to his warm relationship with his funny hosts.

Cooney, Nancy Evans. **The Wobbly Tooth.** Illus. Marylin Hafner. G. P. Putnam's Sons, 1978. 5–7.

A very loose tooth that won't come out is the problem. Elizabeth Anne tries many devices but all resist her efforts. Finally, in an unexpected way the dilemma is solved. The pictures portray the surprise ending. (Picture book)

Crook, Beverly Courtney. **Fair Annie of Old Mule Hollow.** McGraw-Hill, 1978. 12–up.

The clannish Collins family faces many problems: making a living on a mountain farm, the onslaught of strip-mining by coal companies, a feud with a rival clan, and others. But there are joyous times, too. Seen through Fair Annie's eyes, this is a compelling tale of survival in Appalachia.

Cunningham, Julia. **Come to the Edge.** Pantheon Books, 1977. 12–up.

Gravel Winter is an orphan, unwanted by his father. He feels betrayed when his friend Skin, another orphan, disappears very suddenly from the foster institution. He escapes and meets an understanding sign painter. The other characters he encounters are clothed in symbolism. For special readers; excellent for discussion.

Cunningham, Julia. **Flight of the Sparrow.** Pantheon Books, 1980. 10–12.

A ten-year-old girl is adopted from an orphanage in Paris by a sympathetic street-wise youth. He refers to her as the "little sparrow." She is forced by the gang to steal a cherished painting, thus betraying a valued friendship and causing her to flee Paris. Excellent character portrayal.

Distad, Audree. **The Dream Runner.** Harper & Row, Publishers, 1977. 10–12.

Twelve-year-old Sam takes up long distance running to work off feelings of inadequacy. His friend, half-Indian Clete, tells of an old

Indian vision site in the mountains. After the deaths of his father, who had abandoned him, and his friend, Sam runs away in search of his vision, which he believes will help in self-discovery.

Dragonwagon, Crescent. **Will It Be Okay?** Illus. Ben Shecter. Harper & Row, Publishers, 1977. 4–10.

The normal fears of people, surfacing in the everyday questions of a small girl to her mother, are gently and satisfyingly answered. Pictures are a perfect extension of the simple and creative text. (Picture book)

Estes, Eleanor. **The Lost Umbrella of Kim Chu.** Illus. Jacqueline Ayer. Atheneum, 1978. 8–12.

Kim Chu lives in New York's exciting Chinatown. Her father wins the coveted prize in the New Year's Day parade, a black umbrella with a secret compartment in its handle. She loses it and panic ensues. A suspenseful story to be read for enjoyment. Appropriate pen sketches.

Filson, Brent. **The Puma.** Doubleday, 1979. 12–up.

Sonny Street tells his own story of coming to grips with his strong feelings about his mother's death and anger over an inadequate relationship with his father. The puma, made from a treasured piece of obsidian, symbolizes Sonny's power as a wrestler and the destructive force of his uncontrolled fury. The action is fast and the characterization excellent.

Fradin, Dennis B. **Bad Luck Tony.** Illus. Joanne Scribner. Prentice-Hall, 1978. 7–10.

Young determined Tony, who lives with his divorced, working mother, has a problem to solve. He tries to find a home for a pregnant stray dog. He also wants his visiting grandfather to stay longer. The sensitive story and soft pencil illustrations combine to reveal insights into a contemporary family relationship. (Picture book)

Gardiner, John Reynolds. **Stone Fox.** Illus. Marcia Sewall. Thomas Y. Crowell, 1980. 8–12.

Grandfather, who has always taken care of Little Willy, is ill. Now Little Willy takes care of Grandfather and tries to earn enough money to pay the taxes. With Searchlight, his dog, he enters a dogsled race, determined to win the prize money. Economical writing style and an unexpected ending make this an unusual story.

Gonzalez, Gloria. **Gaucho.** Alfred A. Knopf, 1977. 10–12.

Eleven-year-old Gaucho wants to take Mama with him back to San Juan. His imagination tells him that life will present fewer problems there. Efforts to earn money for this trip lead Gaucho into big city problems and to an understanding of family relationships. Presents a warm picture of Puerto Rican families in New York City.

Gordon, Sheila. **A Monster in the Mailbox.** Illus. Tony De Luna. E. P. Dutton, 1978. 7–10.

A warmhearted, talented family all help young Julius recover from the disillusionment of sending away for a $2.99 "walking, talking monster," only to receive an ugly balloon which pops on first use. Clever line drawings enhance the quiet humor of the story.

Gordon, Shirley. **The Boy Who Wanted a Family.** Illus. Charles Robinson. Harper & Row, Publishers, 1980. 7–10.

Michael has lived in a series of foster homes. At last his social worker takes him to live with Miss Graham, who may decide to adopt him. Good to read aloud in several sessions, and follow up with class discussions about the need to belong and to care for someone. Realistic happy ending.

Greenberg, Barbara. **The Bravest Babysitter.** Illus. Diane Paterson. Dial Press, 1977. 4–7.

Roles reverse in this story when young Lisa realizes that her babysitter is frightened by the thunderstorm. The warm, humorous story will bring a smile of recognition to many faces and serve as a springboard for a discussion of fears. (Picture book)

Greenberg, Jan. **A Season In-Between.** Farrar, Straus & Giroux, 1979. 12–up.

Twelve-year-old Carrie's worries are minimal until her father is stricken with cancer and leaves for the Mayo Clinic. Then there is a period of emotional disturbance at home and school, culminating with the feeling of deep loss after her father's death. Characters are well drawn in this fast-moving, first-person narrative. For mature readers.

Greene, Constance C. **Beat the Turtle Drum.** Illus. Donna Diamond. Viking Press, 1976. 8–12.

With her birthday money eleven-year-old Joss rents a horse for a week. It is one of the best weeks she and her sister Kate can remember. Then, suddenly, Joss is dead. Kate has to learn to live without Joss and to accept that life goes on.

Greene, Constance C. **Getting Nowhere.** Viking Press, 1977. 10–up.

Mark, fourteen, rebels at his father's remarriage. He is taunted by his classmates and becomes very hostile. Mark finally begins to catch hold of his life when he wrecks a car and injures his brother and a friend. A novel of frustrations and reality.

Hahn, Mary Downing. **The Sara Summer.** Clarion Books, 1979. 10–12.

After Emily turns twelve, she experiences a growth spurt but gains no weight. Classmates liken her to a giraffe and her best friend ignores her. Straightforward and domineering Sara becomes a new neighbor and friend, showing Emily how to speak up for herself. Eventually Emily speaks out assertively, even to Sara.

Hann, Jacquie. **Crybaby.** Four Winds Press, 1979. 3–5.

The tot has a disagreement with his mother; once he starts to cry it is difficult for him to stop. Big brother's teasing worsens the situation. This story provides the opportunity for parents or teachers to discuss feelings with the young child. Humorous illustrations. (Picture book)

Hapgood, Miranda. **Martha's Mad Day.** Illus. Emily McCully. Crown Publishers, 1977. 3–5.

When Martha wakes up one Saturday morning she feels mean. She throws her favorite pig across the room and stays mad all day. The expressive pen and ink line drawings capture her angry mood. (Picture book)

Harris, Mark Jonathan. **With a Wave of the Wand.** Lothrop, Lee & Shepard Books, 1980. 10–12.

Marlee is convinced that a little magic, like her friend Mr. Romaro does, is all that's needed to bring her mother and father back together. She enlists her brother's help in carrying out a spell. How Marlee copes with her parents' separation when the "magic" fails is humorously told. California setting.

Harris, Robie H. **Don't Forget to Come Back.** Illus. Tony De Luna. Alfred A. Knopf, 1978. 5–7.

Annie's parents are going out for the evening. Bob is going to baby-sit. Annie tries many ploys, such as hiding, a tummyache, tears, and a tantrum to make her parents stay home. A small child's emotions are realistically portrayed. Illustrations reinforce the text. (Picture book)

Holland, Isabelle. **Alan and the Animal Kingdom.** J. B. Lippincott, 1977. 10–12.

Alan has learned through bitter experience that adults can't always be trusted, so when his guardian aunt dies he resolves to make it on his own. Only when one of his pets gets sick does he venture to seek help. A moving story of a young boy torn between fear and need.

Hopkins, Lee Bennett. **Mama.** Alfred A. Knopf, 1977. 9–12.

Mama is independent, opinionated, and a thief. Her whole life is devoted to providing the best of everything for her two boys. The older boy narrates the story of Mama's adventures, which are often humorous and usually illegal. He vows to keep loving her while trying to get her to change her ways.

Hughes, Shirley. **David and Dog.** Prentice-Hall, 1978. 4–7.

Children understand David's affection for his soft brown toy called Dog. When Dog is lost the whole family joins in the search. David forlornly watches the hilarious events of the school fair until he sees Dog on a toy sale table. The conclusion is entirely satisfying. (Picture book)

Hughes, Shirley. **Moving Molly.** Prentice-Hall, 1979. 4–7.

Molly and her family move from their basement home in the city to a house with a garden in the country. For Molly, it is very lonely until she discovers the hole in the garden wall and excitement on the other side. (Picture book)

Hutchins, Pat. **Happy Birthday, Sam.** Greenwillow Books, 1978. 3–5.

Even though little Sam turns a year older, he is unable to do many things he would like to do, like turning on the light and reaching his clothes. A surprise package from Grandpa settles all of his problems. Complementary, colorful illustrations. (Picture book)

Jacobson, Jane. **City, Sing for Me: A Country Child Moves to the City.** Illus. Amy Rowen. Human Sciences Press, 1978. 8–12.

Jenny moves to the city from the country, but her initial feeling about her new home is not good. A new friend introduces Jenny to the unique places and excitement that exist in major cities.

Jensen, Virginia Allen. **Sara and the Door.** Illus. Ann Strugnell. Addison-Wesley Publishing, 1977. 3–5.

Sara closes the large front door on her coat. She is frustrated as she tries to solve the problem of being caught with no one to help her. Finally she figures out how to unbutton her buttons and triumphantly walks away. Sepia and black drawings clearly show her emotions. (Picture book)

Jones, Penelope. **I'm Not Moving!** Illus. Amy Aitken. Bradbury Press, 1980. 4–7.

Emma does not want to move and most especially she doesn't want to leave her digging hole. So she tries to find somewhere else in her neighborhood to live. In the end she decides the best place to be is with her family. Colorful illustrations. (Picture book)

Keats, Ezra Jack. **Louie's Search.** Four Winds Press, 1980. 4–7.

Louie wants a new father. Barney, the local junkman, accuses Louie of stealing a music box, but later becomes his new father. Large, bold illustrations emphasize the liveliness of this exciting contemporary story. (Picture book)

L'Engle, Madeleine. **A Ring of Endless Light.** Farrar, Straus & Giroux, 1980. 12–up.

Vicki Austin's family has come to stay all summer with Grandfather, who is dying of leukemia, when an accident takes the life of a family friend. Zachary, Vicki's former boyfriend, is responsible. Vicki is torn between her feelings for Zach, for fatherless Leo Rodney, and for Adam Eddington. With Adam, Vicki discovers her gift for joyful telepathic communication with dolphins. She learns that life and death are part of creation's "ring of endless light." 1981 Newbery Honor Book.

Lowry, Lois. **A Summer to Die.** Illus. Jenni Oliver. Houghton Mifflin, 1977. 10–12.

Eleven-year-old Meg is understandably jealous of her older sister Molly, who is beautiful, clever, and organized. As leukemia overtakes Molly, she becomes less clever, less organized, and certainly less beautiful. A moving study of a young girl's reaction to her older sister's illness and death.

Lutters, Valerie A. **The Haunting of Julie Unger.** Atheneum, 1977. 12–up.

Julie's father is dead; the family has moved to Maine with Grandmother, and twelve-year-old Julie spends the summer photographing geese. She is alone now instead of with Papa, who had also been her teacher and friend. The struggle for emotional stability and acceptance of death's permanence are realistically shown.

McCord, Jean. **Turkeylegs Thompson.** Atheneum, 1979. 10–up.

Betty Ann Thompson's twelfth summer is one of despair, following a wretched school year. She fails to make the boys' basketball team and remains friendless and disliked. When her father abandons the family, her mother goes to work and Betty Ann must shoulder responsibility for her younger siblings. A new friend helps her find a brighter outlook on self and life.

Malloy, Judy. **Bad Thad.** Illus. Martha Alexander. E. P. Dutton, 1980. 3–5.

Thad gets into all sorts of mischief at home, in nursery school, at the doctor's office, and elsewhere. But even mischievous boys are loved. Detailed illustrations. (Picture book)

Mann, Peggy. **There Are Two Kinds of Terrible.** Doubleday, 1977. 9–12.

Robbie thinks breaking his arm is terrible until his mother suddenly dies of cancer. He and his father are virtual strangers who now must look to each other for support. They learn to love each other as they cope with the ordeal. Robbie, his parents, and his best friend Jud are portrayed as very real people.

Maury, Inez (translator Anna Muñoz). **My Mother and I Are Growing Strong: Mi mama y yo nos hacemos fuertes.** Illus. Sandy Speidel. New Seed Press, 1978. 6–9.

A child describes her life as she and her mother survive while her father is imprisoned. The mother takes over the father's job, learns to repair mechanical equipment, and is concerned about developing her body through exercise and natural foods. Includes Spanish and English texts. (Picture book)

Mearian, Judy Frank. **Two Ways about It.** Dial Press, 1979. 10–12.

Eleven-year-old Annie resents the intrusion of her bossy older cousin who spends every summer with her and her parents. Only when Annie's mother faces a mastectomy does she turn to cousin Lou, who offers her own kind of strength and comfort to the troubled young girl.

Merriam, Eve. **Unhurry Harry.** Illus. Gail Owens. Four Winds Press, 1978. 6–9.

Everyone is always after Harry to hurry: get up, get out of the bathroom, eat breakfast, and go to school. Only at the end of a busy day can he lie in bed and enjoy the quiet as he slowly drifts off to sleep. A familiar experience in a humorous story. (Picture book)

Miklowitz, Gloria D. **Did You Hear What Happened to Andrea?** Delacorte Press, 1979. 12–up.

What happened to Andrea is rape. The subject is treated openly, honestly, and with sensitivity. Strong characters include Andrea's sister, the Rape Hot Line counselor, a therapist, an understanding boyfriend, and difficult parents. Pertinent questions are asked. Recommended for mature readers.

Milord, Sue, and Jerry Milord. **Maggie and the Goodbye Gift.** Illus. by authors. Lothrop, Lee & Shepard Books, 1979. 4–7.

Maggie and her family must move when Dad is transferred. Everyone is sad until Maggie uses an electric can opener, a gift from Mom's best friend, in an unusual way to help the family to adjust to the new neighborhood. Primitive pen and ink sketches fit the humor of the story. (Picture book)

Moore, Emily. **Something to Count On.** E. P. Dutton, 1980. 10–12.

It's the end of summer when Ma and Daddy tell Lorraine and Jason that Daddy is moving out. Soon school starts and Lorraine's problems multiply. An understanding teacher helps her recognize and deal with her feelings about herself and her parents' divorce. A poignant tale.

Moore, Ruth Nulton. **Tomás and the Talking Birds.** Illus. Esther Rose Graber. Herald Press, 1979. 7–10.

Tomás soon learns that living with his uncle in a Pennsylvania steel town is quite different from living in his home in Puerto Rico. A parrot in a pet shop helps him solve his problems. The Spanish terms are enjoyable in this easy-to-read story. Black and white illustrations. Available in Spanish: *Tomás y los pájaros parlantes.*

Murphy, Barbara Beasley. **No Place to Run.** Bradbury Press, 1977. 12–up.

Fifteen-year-old Billy and his Italian friend participate in a prank that seems to cause a tramp's death. A Spanish-speaking girl becomes involved when Billy reacts with self-imposed silence. Set in Manhattan, this well-written book includes justifiably strong language and violence and realistic family interaction.

Noble, June. **Two Homes for Lynn.** Illus. Yuri Salzman. Holt, Rinehart and Winston, 1979. 6–9.

Six-year-old Lynn's parents divorce and she is provided with a second home, her father's apartment. She now has a key to each and her own things in each, but it is hard to cope with her hurt, angry feelings. When Janelle comes to play, and both parents accept this imaginary friend, Lynn is comforted. (Picture book)

Ofek, Uriel (translator Israel I. Taslitt). **Smoke over Golan.** Illus. Lloyd Bloom. Harper & Row, Publishers, 1979. 10–12.

Eitan's life with his parents on a farm on the Golan Heights is simple and peaceful until one day, home alone, Eitan hears the sounds of war approaching. The Yom Kippur War between Israel and Syria has begun. A dramatic account of the effects of war upon one Israeli family.

Okimoto, Jean Davies. **My Mother Is Not Married to My Father.** G. P. Putnam's Sons, 1979. 10–up.

Life is not easy when all you want is for your family to be like the Waltons on TV and instead your father is living with his girlfriend and your mother is starting to date Sam. In this realistic tale of modern life, with many pointed, sad, and funny observations by the eleven-year-old narrator, everything turns out okay in the end. Not great, not like the Waltons, but okay.

Paterson, Diane. **Wretched Rachel.** Dial Press, 1978. 4–7.

A new treatment of an old theme humorously exposes the suffering that is often behind bad behavior, and reassuringly asserts that Rachel is loved no matter what. The colorful illustrations are simultaneously ugly and funny. Good for self-concept study. (Picture book)

Paterson, Katherine. **The Great Gilly Hopkins.** Thomas Y. Crowell, 1978. 10–12.

Eleven-year-old Gilly, the child of a "Flower Child" and for years a foster child, continually waits for her mother, love, and a happy ending, only to discover too late that she had all this and more in her last foster home. A well-written, poignant story with universal appeal. 1979 Newbery Honor Book.

Perl, Lila. **Pieface and Daphne.** Clarion Books, 1980. 10–12.

Pamela "Pieface" Teitelbaum, an only child, takes seriously her teacher's experiment to cut down on TV viewing and develop a new interest. Her activity is most unusual. To complicate matters, cousin Daphne comes to live with her. Characters are well developed. Excellent for discussion on selfishness. Easy to read.

Pfeffer, Susan Beth. **Awful Evelina.** Illus. Diane Dawson. Albert Whitman, 1979. 7–10.

Meredith hates to go with her parents when they visit her aunt and uncle because her cousin Evelina is a bully. En route, Meredith has several wild, delicious fantasies about emergencies that could intervene. How Meredith discovers that reality is best and bullies can be dealt with makes for good discussion. (Picture book)

Potter, Marian. **The Shared Room.** William Morrow, 1979. 10–up.

Catherine's mother is sick. Everyone except Catherine knows what kind of sickness. Through her own initiative and courage she finds ways to help her mother and herself. Tightly focused with sensitive treatment of a very real problem.

Rinaldi, Ann. **Term Paper.** Walker, 1980. 12–up.

A special term paper is assigned to Nicki by her teacher-brother in order to help her finally release her guilt about her father's death. She feels responsible because he had his fatal heart attack during an argument with her. Good for understanding about strained family relationships.

Roberts, Willo Davis. **Don't Hurt Laurie!** Illus. Ruth Sanderson. Atheneum, 1977. 12–up.

Eleven-year-old Laurie has been abused by her mother as long as she can remember. She's had no friends, no family to help her until now when her nine-year-old stepbrother guesses how she gets bruised, cut, or burned. A painful but most worthwhile story.

Sharmat, Marjorie Weinman. **Gila Monsters Meet You at the Airport.** Illus. Byron Barton. Macmillan Publishing, 1980. 4–7.

The narrator, moving out west from New York City, envisions all the dreadful stereotypes about the region, including buzzards circling overhead while he expires in the desert heat. At the airport he sees no Gila monsters, but he does meet another boy who is moving east and is sure that the place is full of gangsters. Clever illustrations. (Picture book)

Sharmat, Marjorie Weinman. **Octavia Told Me a Secret.** Illus. Roseanne Litzinger. Four Winds Press, 1979. 5–8.

Secrets are hard to keep, especially good secrets. Octavia's secret is good enough to be the King of Secrets. Imagining how to tell it and who might like to hear it creates a problem for the girl in the story. Her solution reflects a growing maturity. (Picture book)

Shreve, Susan. **Family Secrets: Five Very Important Stories.** Illus. Richard Cuffari. Alfred A. Knopf, 1979. 8–12.

Five short stories told by a sensitive, perceptive, eight-year-old boy cover topics like the death of a loved pet, possible divorce of parents, child suicide, cheating, and old people's problems. Fortunately, the adults give wise counsel to difficult questions. Black and white sketches; excellent book.

Shyer, Marlene Fanta. **My Brother, the Thief.** Charles Scribner's Sons, 1980. 12–up.

Curious twelve-year-old Carolyn discovers her older half brother Richard and his shady friend Flim-Flam are involved in stealing. Richard is also painfully dealing with self-acceptance. Meeting these crises tests the entire family's strength and its ability to face the consequences. Realistically and compassionately told.

Silman, Roberta. **Somebody Else's Child.** Illus. Chris Conover. Frederick Warne, 1976. 8–12.

A chance remark by his school bus driver makes ten-year-old Peter question the security he has always enjoyed with his adoptive parents. Only after he joins the older man in the search for two dogs lost in a snowstorm does he gain a new sense of belonging.

Simon, Marcia L. **A Special Gift.** Harcourt Brace Jovanovich, 1978. 8–12.

Peter tries to keep hidden the fact that he takes ballet lessons because he fears he will lose his standing as an athlete. After being selected for a part in the *Nutcracker,* he comes to terms with his talent, assuring himself that a love for ballet is quite all right. Good example for sex roles.

Simon, Norma. **We Remember Philip.** Illus. Ruth Sanderson. Albert Whitman, 1979. 8–12.

Sam has just learned that Philip, the son of his teacher, Mr. Hall, has died in an accident. Sam struggles to understand death and the grief that follows. From his struggles he learns how to help himself, the other children, and Mr. Hall.

Skurzynski, Gloria. **Martin by Himself.** Illus. Lynn Munsinger. Houghton Mifflin, 1979. 5–8.

Martin comes home from school with muddy shoes. Mother isn't home. He makes dirty tracks on the floor and, out of loneliness, invites the neighbor's dog in for company. Havoc results. When Mother returns, she and Martin decide how to solve the problems created by his loneliness. (Picture book)

Stanek, Muriel. **Who's Afraid of the Dark?** Illus. Helen Cogancherry. Albert Whitman, 1980. 7–10.

Kenny is afraid of the dark. But discussion reveals that each member of his family is afraid of something. Kenny finally discovers a way to help conquer his fear. A realistic portrayal of feelings through text and three-color illustrations. (Picture book)

Strete, Craig Kee. **When Grandfather Journeys into Winter.** Illus. Hal Frenck. Greenwillow Books, 1979. 10–12.

Little Thunder's grandfather, Tayhua, rides a wild stallion with a devastating display of strength. Before Tayhua dies, he explains to his grandson his view of death, a gift of a journey into winter. A touching, sensitive story of friendship between old and young on an Indian reservation.

Swetnam, Evelyn. **Yes, My Darling Daughter.** Illus. Laurie Harden. Harvey House, Publishers, 1978. 8–12.

Eleven-year-old Josephine has difficulty adjusting to her fifth foster home. Just beginning to feel accepted, she discovers that a baby will soon be born into the family. Feeling betrayed, she runs away and becomes lost. A friend returns her to her happy parents, who have just learned they can adopt her.

Tennant, Veronica. **On Stage, Please.** Illus. Rita Briansky. Holt, Rinehart and Winston, 1979. 10–up.

Jennifer has an overwhelming desire to be a ballet dancer. Her acceptance into the Professional School of Ballet in Toronto begins a life of tough academic study and ballet training, but the challenge and inspiration of genuine artistic effort sustain her. All the joys and crises of a youngster in serious ballet training are realistically portrayed in this story by a renowned ballerina. Illustrations are true to good dance technique.

Thomas, Ianthe. **Eliza's Daddy.** Illus. Moneta Barnett. Harcourt Brace Jovanovich, 1976. 4–8.

Eliza's daddy is remarried and she wonders about his new daughter.

Surely she is a Wonderful Angel! One Saturday, Eliza persuades him to take her to his new home, where a happy surprise awaits her. Softly colored charcoal drawings portray the black family. (Picture book)

Tobias, Tobi. **Petey.** Illus. Symeon Shimin. G. P. Putnam's Sons, 1978. 6–9.

Emily loves her pet gerbil, Petey, but he is dying and she cannot help him. This beautifully told story treats honestly all aspects of death: denial, anger, grief, final acceptance. There is a believable little girl and an understanding and supportive family. Excellently drawn, monochromatic illustrations capture the grief of the child, the love in the family. (Picture book)

Wallace-Brodeur, Ruth. **The Kenton Year.** Atheneum, 1980. 10–12.

Nine-year-old Mandy McPherson's father was killed in an accident. Her mother rents a cottage in Vermont where Mandy gradually accepts the painful loss. Her new-found friends, Carrie and Shandee, a recluse, bring comfort. Well-defined characters and a sensitive treatment of death make this good for discussion.

Weiss, Joan Talmage. **Home for a Stranger.** Harcourt Brace Jovanovich, 1980. 8–12.

Juana lives in a Mexican orphanage until an American doctor notices her and takes her to California to correct a harelip. Having no recall of her past, Juana is amazed and discouraged as the doctors examine her and find that the deformation is a result of an accident. This discovery unravels Juana's painful past.

Williams, Barbara. **Whatever Happened to Beverly Bigler's Birthday?** Illus. Emily McCully. Harcourt Brace Jovanovich, 1979. 5–7.

Birthdays are big events to a seven year old, but Beverly Bigler's birthday was completely overshadowed by her big sister's wedding day. Poor Beverly! Maybe she should run away to Texas. Felt-tip sketches are used in this easy-to-read book.

Willoughby, Elaine Macmann. **Boris and the Monsters.** Illus. Lynn Munsinger. Houghton Mifflin, 1980. 6–9.

Boris doesn't like to go to bed at night because he thinks there might be monsters in his room. His parents and he decide to buy a fierce watchdog. Young readers will laugh at the turn-about when Boris has to protect his dog. (Picture book)

Wold, Jo Anne. **Tell Them My Name Is Amanda.** Illus. Dennis Hockerman. Albert Whitman, 1977. 6–9.

No one calls shy Amanda by her own name. Realizing she somehow must work her way out of this dilemma, she tries several indirect courses. Finally she speaks out for herself and is surprised and pleased by the results. Episodes in this concept book lend themselves to dramatization. (Picture book)

Wolkoff, Judie. **Where the Elf King Sings.** Bradbury Press, 1980. 12–up.

Twelve-year-old Marcie experiences the agony of the Vietnam War through her father's depression and alcoholism. Two very different elderly women provide stability and help for Marcie in this well-written novel.

Zolotow, Charlotte. **It's Not Fair.** Illus. William Pène du Bois. Harper & Row, Publishers, 1976. All ages.

The Marthas of this world are ever with us. This Martha has black hair, is talented, never freckles, and never gets fat. It's not fair! Martha tells her side in this book that could be used in class discussions on values and fairness. (Picture book)

Family

Alexander, Martha. **When the New Baby Comes, I'm Moving Out.** Illus. by author. Dial Press, 1979. 3–7.

Oliver becomes upset when his mother paints his old high chair so it will be ready for the new baby. He plots revenge. His understanding mother listens to his threats and helps him to see the advantages of being a big brother. (Picture book)

Association for Childhood Education International. **And Everywhere, Children!** Greenwillow Books, 1979. 10–up.

This collection of stories about children in all parts of the world is an excellent resource for encouraging children to read about growing up in other lands. Eleven stories are excerpted and two are given in full.

Bornstein, Ruth Lercher. **Of Course a Goat.** Illus. by author. Harper & Row, Publishers, 1980. 4–7.

During a conversation with his mother, a boy reveals his dream of having a goat. Colorful, luminescent drawings add substance to the boy's imaginary journey up the mountain to find his goat. (Picture book)

Bulla, Clyde Robert. **Keep Running, Allen!** Illus. Satomi Ichikawa. Thomas Y. Crowell, 1978. 4–7.

Poor Allen is always running to keep up with his older brothers and sister. They go too fast, and they never want to stay anywhere long enough to look at things. Finally Allen trips and falls down in the grass where he lies still watching a fuzzy green worm. Of course the others follow suit and at last enjoy staying still. (Picture book)

Byars, Betsy. **The Cartoonist.** Illus. Richard Cuffari. Viking Press, 1978. 10–12.

The attic of their crowded home is Alfie's retreat, and there he draws cartoons by the hour. When his private domain is threatened by the return of his older brother and his expectant wife, he hangs on to it tenaciously. Only his older sister understands why he needs a place and things of his own.

Byars, Betsy. **The Night Swimmers.** Illus. Troy Howell. Delacorte Press, 1980. 10–12.

Retta, who has learned her parenting skills from television viewing, is rearing two younger brothers without much help from her father, a country-western singer. The action, setting, and conversation have a you-are-there quality. Charcoal illustrations.

Caines, Jeannette. **Daddy.** Illus. Ronald Himler. Harper & Row, Publishers, 1977. 4–7.

Young Windy anxiously awaits weekend visits with her father. Weekly rituals of making chocolate pudding and finding daddy's glasses are shared. A tender father-daughter relationship is presented with few words in this story of a black family with separated parents. (Picture book)

Chaffin, Lillie D. **We Be Warm Till Springtime Comes.** Illus. Lloyd Bloom. Macmillan Publishing, 1980. 7–10.

A small boy goes out into the bitter cold to find fuel to warm the cabin he shares with his mother and baby sister. The poetic language of the text and the haunting chill of the black and white paintings celebrate the love and courage of this Appalachian family. (Picture book)

Cleary, Beverly. **Ramona and Her Father.** Illus. Alan Tiegreen. William Morrow, 1977. 8–12.

Ramona's father loses his job during her second-grade year. She tries to help the family by engaging in moneymaking schemes and by conducting no-smoking campaigns. Fortunately, there is humor in her escapades and the family remains intact and loving. Another well-written book about a popular character. 1978 Newbery Honor Book.

Cleaver, Vera, and Bill Cleaver. **Trial Valley.** J. B. Lippincott, 1977. 10–up.

Mary Call Luther, sixteen, knows that life in Trial Valley is not easy. An orphan, she bears responsibility for younger siblings and takes in an abandoned boy. Appalachian setting, myths, values, and lovely mountain language make this an excellent choice for reading aloud.

Clements, Bruce. **Anywhere Else But Here.** Farrar, Straus & Giroux, 1980. 10–12.

Thirteen-year-old Molly's determination to move with her widowed father to a new town and a fresh start is thwarted when a strange woman fanatically devoted to a self-actualization group leaves her painfully backward young son with them.

Clifton, Lucille. **Amifika.** Illus. Thomas DiGrazia. E. P. Dutton, 1977. 4–6.

Little Amifika fears that his father who has been in the army for so long will not remember him. He attempts to hide when he learns of his father's homecoming. Expressive drawings illustrate this touching story of a black family. (Picture book)

Clifton, Lucille. **Everett Anderson's Nine Month Long.** Illus. Ann Grifalconi. Holt, Rinehart and Winston, 1978. 5–8.

Waiting nine months with his mother and stepfather provides time for young Everett Anderson to accept the idea that there's enough love to share, even when a new brother or sister arrives. Soft black and white illustrations sensitively blend with this poetic story of love in a black family. (Picture book)

Clifton, Lucille. **Everett Anderson's 1-2-3.** Illus. Ann Grifalconi. Holt, Rinehart and Winston, 1977. 4–7.

Everett Anderson worries about the addition of a third member to his family: Mr. Perry is going to be his new stepfather and "three can be crowded or can be just right." Readers will recognize the young hero from *Everett Anderson's Friend, Everett Anderson's Year,* and others. (Picture book)

Clifton, Lucille. **The Lucky Stone.** Illus. Dale Payson. Delacorte Press, 1979. 7–10.

Tee has a stone that has been bringing good luck to its owners since the days of slavery. As she listens to her great-grandmother's tales of its previous owners, Tee is sure that her life too will be charmed by the stone. A warm family story. (Picture book)

De Huff, Elizabeth Willis. **Blue-Wings-Flying.** Illus. Dorothea Sierra. Addison-Wesley Publishing, 1977. 7–10.

Blue-Wings-Flying longs for a sister. As he awaits the birth, he observes and participates in family clan life: corn grinding, story-telling in the kiva. When the baby arrives, he plays an important role in naming her. Two-color illustrations add to this warm view of Hopi life.

Delton, Judy. **My Mom Hates Me in January.** Illus. John Faulkner. Albert Whitman, 1977. 5–8.

Preschooler Lee Henry's mother is fighting the midwinter blues, and his behavior is not contributing to good mental health. But relief is spelled *r-o-b-i-n*. The delightful, warm characters ring true, and mothers can readily identify with Lee Henry's mom. Humorous pen and ink drawings. (Picture book)

Dickinson, Mary. **Alex's Bed.** Illus. Charlotte Firmin. Andre Deutsch, 1980. 4–7.

Alex's room is a disaster area and his mother complains. He notes that the only empty space left is near the ceiling. After brainstorming, Mother puts stilts on the bed. But something was overlooked! Appealing illustrations in color. (Picture book)

Galbraith, Kathryn Osebold. **Come Spring.** Atheneum, 1979. 12–up.

Moving from one rental to the next is all that Reenie has known for twelve years. Now she's excited as the family is about to move into a real house.

Gerson, Corinne. **Son for a Day.** Illus. Velma Ilsley. Atheneum, 1980. 8–12.

Fatherless Danny finds companionship, entertainment, and plenty of good food when he makes friends with an assortment of divorced fathers and their sons during weekly outings to the zoo. Before long, however, his scheme to become part of a family leads to hilarious chaos and confusion.

Gerson, Corinne. **Tread Softly.** Dial Press, 1979. 8–12.

Orphaned eleven-year-old Kitten and her brother Peter live with their grandparents, but Kitten yearns for a "normal" family. Her feelings of loneliness and her need to create a secret fantasy family are realistically drawn. As the story progresses, Kitten realizes that the people in her life do indeed make up a family that is rich and satisfying.

Gessner, Lynne. **Malcolm Yucca Seed.** Illus. William Sauts Bock. Harvey House, Publishers, 1977. 8–12.

Malcolm is the white man's name for the young son of a present-day Navajo family. Malcolm loves the traditional life of his people, and the boy longs to earn a true Indian name as he comes home for summer vacation from the white man's school. A tender story with realistic illustrations and much information about Navajo life.

Greene, Constance C. **I and Sproggy.** Illus. Emily McCully. Viking Press, 1978. 10–up.

Adam's plans for a carefree summer are upset when his father's new English wife arrives with her eleven-year-old daughter, Sproggy. His stepsister is taller than Adam, several months older, and unbearable. Overcoming his attitude and developing new feelings toward her are quite a task.

Hazen, Barbara Shook. **Gorilla Wants to Be the Baby.** Illus. Jacqueline Bardner Smith. Atheneum, 1978. 4–7.

Gorilla, a child's pretend companion, understands the youngster's feelings about the new baby who shares the room. The story line is a naturally phrased monologue of child to gorilla, with Mother coming in affectionately at beginning and end. Charcoal and watercolor illustrations accurately show big green gorilla's satisfying responses. (Picture book)

Hazen, Barbara Shook. **If It Weren't for Benjamin I'd Always Get to Lick the Icing Spoon.** Illus. Laura Hartman. Human Sciences Press, 1979. 6–9.

This story, told by an unnamed younger brother, speaks to the envy of the older, bigger brother. Events are realistic, as are the exceptional three-color illustrations. Adults show love and understanding. (Picture book)

Herman, Charlotte. **My Mother Didn't Kiss Me Good-Night.** Illus. Bruce Degen. E. P. Dutton, 1980. 4–7.

Leon lies in bed wondering why his mother didn't kiss him good night. Was it because he let his pet snake loose when Mrs. Minkus came to visit? Was it because he only pretended to take a bath? His questions are finally answered by a sniffly Mother with a cold who blows him a kiss. (Picture book)

Landis, James David. **The Sisters Impossible.** Alfred A. Knopf, 1979. 8–12.

Saundra, the haughty ballerina in the family, is surprised and disturbed when she learns that her younger sister Lily is planning to take ballet lessons. Excellent characterization of the two sisters keeps the reader interested throughout the usual sibling rivalries.

Lowry, Lois. **Anastasia Krupnik.** Houghton Mifflin, 1979. 8–12.

Ten-year-old Anastasia, an only child, has certain things that she thinks are wonderful and others that she hates. Her lists of these likes and dislikes change, sometimes rather rapidly. A baby brother about to be born, a grandmother in a nursing home, and a special boy are all part of her story. Humorous and poignant.

MacLachlan, Patricia. **The Sick Day.** Illus. William Pène du Bois. Pantheon Books, 1979. 4–7.

Emily has a stomachache in her head and a headache in her throat. She also has a father who makes her sick day a special day as he fixes her hair, draws monsters, and puts toy giraffes in her broth. A warm story enriched by delicate and numerous illustrations. (Picture book)

Marzollo, Jean. **Amy Goes Fishing.** Illus. Ann Schweninger. Dial Press, 1980. 4–7.

One by one the family members disappear from the Saturday morning breakfast table until Amy and Dad are left alone. He suggests going fishing. Because her brother and sister had informed her earlier that "fishing is boring," Amy is surprised and delighted by the events of the day. Watercolor illustrations. (Picture book)

Merrill, Susan. **Washday.** Illus. by author. Seabury Press, 1978. 4–8.

Here is the story of remembered Saturdays when a country family did the wash together. The joys of playing under windblown sheets and sharing a task are portrayed. A gentle tale, illustrated in cool blues and greens. (Picture book)

Myers, Walter Dean. **It Ain't All for Nothin'.** Viking Press, 1978. 10–up.

Twelve-year-old Tippy must live with his father in Harlem when his loving, religious grandmother goes to the hospital. His mother had died at Tippy's birth, and Daddy's survival led to crime. Tippy's struggle for identity and acceptance makes a moving story.

Park, W. B. **Jonathan's Friends.** G. P. Putnam's Sons, 1977. 3–5.

Michael decides to inform his little brother about the tooth fairy, Santa Claus, and elves, but Jonathan remains true to his friends. A surprise ending completes the story. This excellent lap book serves nicely to initiate discussions about make-believe characters and events. Appealing watercolors complement the text. (Picture book)

Power, Barbara. **I Wish Laura's Mommy Was My Mommy.** Illus. Marylin Hafner. J. B. Lippincott, 1979. 6–8.

Jennifer enjoys her visits to Laura's home and wishes her mother were more like Laura's. When Jennifer's mother goes back to work, Jennifer begins to understand and appreciate her. Pencil illustrations clarify the emotional context of this contemporary, easy-to-read story. (Picture book)

Ruffins, Reynold. **My Brother Never Feeds the Cat.** Illus. by author. Charles Scribner's Sons, 1979. 4–7.

Anna tells everyone in the neighborhood how hard she works and how little her brother does. Soft, detailed pictures blend with the brief text to share an amusing conclusion that any young child can enjoy. (Picture book)

Seuling, Barbara. **The Triplets.** Clarion Books, 1980. 5–8.

Triplets Mattie, Hattie, and Pattie take refuge in their room because they are tired of being mistaken for one another. Their parents, teacher, and a classmate think up a plan to stop mixing them up. Vivid, childlike illustrations blend with the theme of this creative story—being appreciated for oneself.

Sharmat, Marjorie, and Mitchell Sharmat. **The Day I Was Born.** Illus. Diane Dawson. E. P. Dutton, 1980. 7–10.

On Alexander's sixth birthday he recounts all the wonderful things that happened the day he was born. His tale is intercepted again and again by his older brother, who adds his memories of each event. Enjoyable humor in the two wildly differing recollections in this point-counterpoint story. (Picture book)

Steptoe, John. **Daddy Is a Monster . . . Sometimes.** J. B. Lippincott, 1980. 6–9.

According to Bweela and Javaka, Daddy is a monster when they are messy, noisy, or bothersome at bedtime. But sometimes, really all of the time, the children know that Daddy loves them. Highly stylized illustrations reflect the emotions of the characters in this black family. (Picture book)

Supraner, Robyn. **It's Not Fair!** Illus. Randall Enos. Frederick Warne, 1976. 6–12.

Baby brother gets lots of special privileges, and he doesn't get punished like big sister does. It's not fair! Everyday experiences are presented with an awareness of children's feelings, especially sibling rivalry. Colorful illustrations. (Picture book)

Tate, Eleanora E. **Just an Overnight Guest.** Dial Press, 1980. 8–12.

Nine-year-old Margie Carson is horrified to learn that four-year-old Ethel, the neglected town brat, will live with her family. It falls to Margie to teach this disruptive, embarrassing child everything. Eventually Margie learns to cope with Ethel and comes to accept her presence in the family. The jealousy and love common to all family relationships are compounded by prejudice, for the Carsons are a black family and Ethel is a white child.

Teibl, Margaret. **Davey Come Home.** Illus. Jacqueline Bardner Smith. Harper & Row, Publishers, 1979. 7–10.

Davey is always the last one left playing outside after school because he has no one to call him home. One week when Dad works late, a new baby-sitter comes to stay with Davey. She calls him home for supper before any of the other guys are called. Davey feels good about that.

Vangheli, Spiridon (translator Miriam Morton). **Meet Guguze.** Illus. Trina Schart Hyman. Addison-Wesley Publishing, 1977. 7–10.

Guguze lives his just-before-school-age life creatively and at full tilt.

What he does and feels as a small boy in a Moldavian village will find lively responses in the feelings and imaginations of American children. Charming folk art. (Picture book)

Vestly, Anne-Cath (translator Eileen Amos). **Aurora and Socrates.** Illus. Leonard Kessler. Thomas Y. Crowell, 1977. 7–10.

Gran and Uncle Brande take turns caring for Aurora and her little brother Socrates when both parents must work. Their family adventures make good reading, and life in a modern Norwegian city is shown to be much like that in a city in the United States. Line drawings with soft gray water wash.

Vigna, Judith. **She's Not My Real Mother.** Illus. by author. Albert Whitman, 1980. 4–7.

Miles visits his father, who has remarried. When Miles gets lost, his stepmother comes to his rescue and he wonders if she could become his friend. This book makes an excellent and necessary statement about divorce and how it affects the very young. (Picture book)

Winthrop, Elizabeth. **Are You Sad, Mama?** Illus. Donna Diamond. Harper & Row, Publishers, 1979. 5–7.

A little girl tries a number of ways to cheer up her sad mother and accidentally discovers the best way of all. An easy-to-read book accompanied by mostly black and white sketches, with a touch of blue, naturally. (Picture book)

Yarbrough, Camille. **Cornrows.** Illus. Carole Byard. Coward, McCann & Geoghegan, 1979. 7–10.

While Grandmother makes cornrows for Sister and Brother, she sings the old songs and tells the story of how cornrows for braided hair began. The hairstyle, an ancient African symbol, reflects the courage of today's Afro-Americans. Muted black and white full-page illustrations add warmth and delight. (Picture book)

Zemach, Margot. **To Hilda for Helping.** Farrar, Straus & Giroux, 1977. 4–7.

Hilda helps. When there are chores to be done, she works without complaining. Her father makes a medal that says "To Hilda for Helping." Sister Gladys is jealous and predicts a miserable future for Hilda. Hilda, however, believes in a more positive tomorrow. (Picture book)

Zolotow, Charlotte. **If You Listen.** Illus. Marc Simont. Harper & Row, Publishers, 1980. 6–9.

A mother reassures her daughter that "if you listen" you can know that someone far away loves you. The full-color pictures capture the mood of the story as the mother offers examples of how to perceive things by listening and feeling. (Picture book)

Zolotow, Charlotte. **Say It!** Illus. James Stevenson. Greenwillow Books, 1980. 5–8.

A warm story of the love between mother and daughter is set on a windy autumn day. The story is beautifully phrased, and the prose is matched by full-page, full-color illustrations that catch the spirit of a brisk autumn jaunt and a shared experience.

Friendships

Adler, C. S. **The Magic of the Glits.** Illus. Ati Forberg. Macmillan Publishing, 1979. 8–12.

Twelve-year-old Jeremy must take care of eight-year-old Lynette. He knows his summer at Cape Cod will be ruined. Jeremy fantasizes that the Glits are magical people who grant wishes, but eventually he makes his own wishes come true. In the process, he learns a lot about himself and true friendship.

Ames, Mildred. **What Are Friends For?** Charles Scribner's Sons, 1978. 10–up.

Eleven-year-old Amy and her friend Michelle both live in single-parent families. Michelle is extremely possessive and doesn't want Amy to have other friends. When Amy discovers that her friend is a shoplifter, the definition of friendship is put to the test.

Angell, Judie. **Tina Gogo.** Bradbury Press, 1978. 8–12.

Hiding behind the facade of a tough kid, Tina begins a tumultuous summer living with a foster family. She pretends that her mother is traveling abroad and her father works for the President in Washington, D.C., but when she invites her new friend Sarajane to meet her mother, Tina's defenses crumble. Sarajane's persistent questions and Tina's defensive actions are the prelude to a warm and understanding friendship.

Baylor, Byrd. **Guess Who My Favorite Person Is?** Illus. Robert Andrew Parker. Charles Scribner's Sons, 1977. 7–10.

In the middle of an alfalfa field a man and a farm girl meet for the first time. They quickly establish a rapport through playing the game of naming their favorite things. The mood is one of rapport, and the easy feeling of the text is carried over into the gentle illustrations. (Picture book)

Brooks, Jerome. **Make Me a Hero.** E. P. Dutton, 1980. 10–up.

A Jewish boy in the early 1940s prepares for his Bar Mitzvah. Stepping beyond the boundaries of his neighborhood, he is changed by the people he meets and the challenges he chooses to face.

Child Study Children's Book Committee at Bank Street, compiler. **Friends Are Like That! Stories to Read to Yourself.** Illus. Leigh Grant. Thomas Y. Crowell, 1979. 6–9.

This anthology of short and easy-to-read stories introduces all kinds of friends and explores the reasons for having close friends. Authors include Charlotte Zolotow, Eloise Greenfield, and Astrid Lindgren. Black and white pen drawings.

Goffstein, M. B. **Neighbors.** Harper & Row, Publishers, 1979. 7–10.

Stories can be told in many ways. This time the author conveys the message through simple line drawings. Two bashful neighbors want to get to know one another better, and each season of the year finds them a little closer. (Picture book)

Gordon, Shirley. **Crystal Is the New Girl.** Illus. Edward Frascino. Harper & Row, Publishers, 1976. 6–9.

Each day Crystal, the new girl in 3-B, does something slightly off-beat. Her actions intrigue Susan and often get both girls in trouble. This popular easy reader contains lively and detailed illustrations that depict a middle-class urban environment. (Picture book)

Greene, Constance C. **Your Old Pal, Al.** Viking Press, 1979. 10–12.

Al, the heroine of two previous books, rages with jealousy when her best friend invites another girl to stay with her. The ups and downs of adolescent friendship, divorced parents, and life in New York City are humorously and realistically explored in this popular "girl-like-me" book.

Hansen, Joyce. **The Gift-Giver.** Clarion Books, 1980. 8–12.

Fifth-grader Doris meets Ami, the new boy in her Bronx neighborhood. A gentle loner, he helps her to become her own person and to understand others better. Their story offers a positive perspective on life in the inner city.

Keats, Ezra Jack. **The Trip.** Greenwillow Books, 1978. 4–7.

Louie moves with his family to a new neighborhood and is unhappy because he has no friends. In his imagination he takes a trip to his old home. Vibrant illustrations enhance the poignant story. (Picture book)

Lloyd, Errol. **Nini at Carnival.** Thomas Y. Crowell, 1978. 4–7.

It's carnival time in Jamaica, but poor little Nini has no costume. But there is lots of magic around at carnival time, and lo and behold, a real fairy godmother deftly transforms Nini into a queen, using only a piece of bright cloth.

Malmgren, Ulf (translator Joan Tate). **When the Leaves Begin to Fall.** Harper & Row, Publishers, 1978. 10–12.

Late one summer Lena and Joel, shy, unsure twelve-year-olds, discover a uniquely perfect friendship. They agree that their secret friendship will last until the leaves begin to fall. A sensitive, beautifully conceived evocation of adolescence and first love.

Mark, Jan. **Thunder and Lightnings.** Illus. Jim Russell. Thomas Y. Crowell, 1976. 10–12.

The Norfolk countryside is vastly different from London, and Andrew dreads the first day at a new school. Then he meets Victor, an unconventional youngster with a passion for airplanes and little success in the classroom.

Numeroff, Laura Joffe. **Amy for Short.** Macmillan Publishing, 1976. 7–10.

Amy is different. She's tall, very tall. Her friendship with Mark is threatened when she grows taller than he. Youngsters will enjoy learning the secret of the Captain Crunchy Decoder Ring, and it may set off a craze of code writing. (Picture book)

Paterson, Katherine. **Bridge to Terabithia.** Illus. Donna Diamond. Thomas Y. Crowell, 1977. 10–12.

Leslie, the new girl in school, is worldly in comparison to Jess with his rural Virginia background. Their differences diminish, however, through their love of running. They become friends and create a secret imaginary kingdom of Terabithia. The strength of their shared experiences enables Jess to cope with Leslie's tragic accidental death. 1978 Newbery Award.

Sachs, Marilyn. **A Secret Friend.** Doubleday, 1978. 8–12.

Jessica is unhappy because her best friend won't have anything to do with her. She decides on an unusual plan to make Wendy jealous. It doesn't work, but a happy surprise results.

Slepian, Jan. **The Alfred Summer.** Macmillan Publishing, 1980. 10–up.

Four preteen friends seek to fulfill their dreams by building a boat in the basement of their apartment building. Two of them are handicapped, but the expert characterization done without sentimentality helps young readers to identify with them.

Sorensen, Virginia. **Friends of the Road.** Atheneum, 1978. 10–12.

Cathy and Pippa meet and become good friends in Morocco, where their fathers are with the American and British foreign services respectively. Both are distressed when Pippa must return to England for school. Fine character portrayal and description of setting.

Stolz, Mary. **Cider Days.** Harper & Row, Publishers, 1978. 8–12.

To replace a best friend who has moved is not easy as Polly Lewis discovers. But new neighbor Consuela Christina Machado and her famous artist mother become a special project for Polly and her warm, happy Vermont family in this sequel to *Ferris Wheel.* Friendship results.

Wade, Anna. **A Promise Is for Keeping.** Photographs by Jon Petersson. Childrens Press, 1979. 6–9.

Kathy and Susan find a beautiful bracelet at the beach. When no one claims it, they take weekly turns wearing it. Their friendship snags when Kathy deliberately keeps the bracelet too long. Discussions of honesty and dependability logically follow the reading of this book. Full-page color photographs. (Picture book)

Growing Up

Bridgman, Elizabeth. **If I Were a Horse.** Illus. by author. Dodd, Mead, 1977. 5–7.

Incongruities result when Jenny fantasizes that she is a horse engaging in her everyday activities. She enjoys the idea of fooling people until she realizes that she might go unrecognized. Cartoonlike illustrations catch the changing moods of this story with its be-yourself theme. (Picture book)

Carrick, Malcolm. **Tramp.** Harper & Row, Publishers, 1977. 6–10.

A lonely boy whose only friends exist in his imagination brings food to a tramp he finds near a London railway. After several days the tramp disappears without saying good-bye, leaving the boy saddened but with a new sense of his own worth. (Picture book)

Cleary, Beverly. **Ramona and Her Mother.** Illus. Alan Tiegreen. William Morrow, 1979. 6–9.

Ramona feels unloved and left out when both Mr. and Mrs. Quimby go to work and many household routines are changed. She suffers the trials of learning to deal with growing up in this humorous story, and her mother finds a special way of showing Ramona how much she is loved.

Cohen, Barbara. **The Innkeeper's Daughter.** Lothrop, Lee & Shepard Books, 1979. 10–up.

A young widow in the 1940s ventures into the hotel business, and the story of that enterprise is narrated by her sixteen-year-old daughter. The romantic and sexual needs of both mother and daughter receive tasteful and moderately frank treatment in an appealing book.

Delton, Judy, and Elaine Knox-Wagner. **The Best Mom in the World.** Illus. John Faulkner. Albert Whitman, 1979. 4–7.

Lee Henry's doting mother is the best mom in the world; she does *everything* for him. Suddenly a frightening change takes place: a baby-sitter comes in after school, and Mom begins to ask Lee Henry for help! A useful book for discussions on growing independence and helping others. (Picture book)

Grimes, Nikki. **Growin'.** Illus. Charles Lilly. Dial Press, 1977. 10–15.

Pumpkin Jackson's father understands why she writes poetry. When he dies, it seems that only hatred is left, hatred towards her mother and everyone else. Pump's friendship with Jim Jim, the class bully, enables both young people to accept themselves and the individuals in their neighborhood. Black culture is an important part of the book, but the story is for all growing people.

Hunter, Mollie. **The Third Eye.** Harper & Row, Publishers, 1979. 10–up.

Fourteen-year-old Jinty sees with a third eye, knowing things without knowing how she knows. When she is called to tell what she knows about the Earl of Ballinford, she learns something about herself and her Scottish family.

Hurmence, Belinda. **Tough Tiffany.** Doubleday, 1980. 10–12.

Tiffany, youngest member of a poor black family in a small North Carolina city, thinks of herself as a tough kid, the only one who can stand up to her bossy, stingy grandmother. In spite of her brave front, eleven-year-old Tiffany's fears and dreams are the same as those many young people face.

Iverson, Genie. **I Want to Be Big.** Illus. David McPhail. E. P. Dutton, 1979. 4–7.

A little girl wants to be big, big enough for a second ice-cream cone but not big enough for even one helping of peas. This book of "big enough" comparisons is charmingly illustrated with black and white line drawings. (Picture book)

Johnston, Norma. **The Sanctuary Tree.** Atheneum, 1977. 12–up.

Fifteen-year-old Tish's feelings of displeasure and compulsion are evident as she learns to cope with change. Trying to accept her grandfather's death and the selling of his farm meshed with other personal struggles force her to examine her inner feelings. Understanding one's self is the central theme.

Klein, Norma. **Tomboy.** Four Winds Press, 1978. 8–12.

Toe, who first appeared in *Confessions of an Only Child,* returns, now ten years old and fighting against growing up. Toe hates getting her period and giving up dolls. Her friendships with Libby and

Jimmy undergo changes. Through it all Toe receives warm and loving support from her lawyer mother and housekeeper father.

Konigsburg, E. L. **Throwing Shadows.** Atheneum, 1979. 10–up.

The relationships of five young adolescents with the people around them are explored in five short stories written in first person. Dialect and gentle humor give each story individuality. The problems each character encounters would encourage class discussion if the book were read aloud.

Little, Lessie Jones, and Eloise Greenfield. **I Can Do It by Myself.** Illus. Carole Byard. Thomas Y. Crowell, 1978. 6–9.

Donny grows a little when he completes a task he has set for himself: buying a plant for his mother's birthday. He meets a scary challenge on the way home. Beautiful black and white sketches with muted wash background and a sensitive use of black dialect and syntax. (Picture book)

MacLachlan, Patricia. **Arthur, for the Very First Time.** Illus. Lloyd Bloom. Harper & Row, Publishers, 1980. 9–12.

Arthur's tenth summer is horrible; his mother is expecting a baby and he must stay with an eccentric aunt and uncle. His new friend Moira dubs him "Mouse," but when he acts with maturity in a crisis, she calls him Arthur for the very first time. Gradually, Arthur begins to look at himself and others in a new way.

Rabe, Berniece. **The Girl Who Had No Name.** E. P. Dutton, 1977. 12–up.

Girlie knows something is wrong when, after Mama's death, everyone begins whispering. Then Papa doesn't want her at home, so she moves from one poor sister to another. But twelve-year-old Girlie has determination and talent. Ultimately she works out the mystery of her parentage, copes with the painful facts of growing up, and claims her own identity. Mature readers.

Sachs, Marilyn. **A Summer's Lease.** E. P. Dutton, 1979. 12–up.

At fifteen Gloria is a gifted writer, fiercely competitive, and not at all attractive. A summer in the mountains and a tough-minded English teacher lift her out of a bitter self-absorption that has not allowed her to form normal friendships. A very special book for the special reader.

Schick, Eleanor. **Home Alone.** Dial Press, 1980. 4–7.

Andy must stay by himself from the time school is out until his mother returns from work. Her reassuring note enables him to handle his time nicely and reinforces his mother's confidence in him. If the cat can stay by herself, Andy reasons, so can he. Helpful suggestions. Comforting illustrations. (Picture book)

Stolz, Mary. **Ferris Wheel.** Harper & Row, Publishers, 1977. 9–12.

Polly is without a best friend. Accepting that, learning to get along with brother Rusty, sharing pony Blondel, and welcoming newcomer Consuela are all part of a summer of growing in Vermont. Style and content document contemporary female life-styles and current parenting practices.

Terris, Susan. **Stage Brat.** Four Winds Press, 1980. 10–up.

Thirteen-year-old Linnet grows up while playing her first major role in a repertory theater company. Oddly enough, the role is Peter Pan. The theater detail is excellent, and the plot is simple enough to be readily understood yet complex enough to hold the reader's interest.

Wilkinson, Brenda. **Ludell and Willie.** Harper & Row, Publishers, 1977. 12–up.

Grandmother is changing from the kind loving person who raised Ludell to a sick, mean old lady. Ludell struggles with problems at home and at school, with a job cleaning for white folk, and with the growing awareness of her love for Willie. A poignant story of a young black girl growing up in Georgia.

Yep, Laurence. **Child of the Owl.** Harper & Row, Publishers, 1977. 10–12.

When twelve-year-old Casey's father is hospitalized, she goes to stay with her maternal grandmother in San Francisco's Chinatown. There she learns a whole new way of life. Learning about her Chinese heritage helps her begin to understand her place in the world.

Yep, Laurence. **Sea Glass.** Harper & Row, Publishers, 1979. 10–up.

Craig, a Chinese-American, moves to California and has difficulty making friends and finding value in himself. His father wants him to excel in sports, but overweight Craig has few talents in that direction and little interest. An acquaintance with a sage old Chinese man helps Craig achieve self-understanding.

Young, Helen. **A Throne for Sesame.** Illus. Shirley Hughes. Andre Deutsch, 1979. 4–7.

Sesame and her siblings like the baby's high chair. Just for fun, Sesame squeezes into it and gets stuck. Not one to miss the class party, Sesame and the high chair go to school. Eventually released, she experiences a variety of feelings about growing up. Lively humor, realistic illustrations, and a satisfying ending. (Picture book)

Zolotow, Charlotte. **Someone New.** Illus. Erik Blegvad. Harper & Row, Publishers, 1978. 4–8.

A young boy has mixed feelings as he realizes that he is growing up. Even though everything is in the right place, he senses that something is missing: "Someone's gone. Someone's missing and I know who . . . . I am someone new." A simple, perceptive picture story book about a young child growing up. (Picture book)

Handicaps

Allen, Marjorie N. **One, Two, Three—Ah-Choo!** Illus. Dick Gackenbach. Coward, McCann & Geoghegan, 1980. 5–8.

Wally Springer has an allergy problem. He cannot have the usual pets; they make him sneeze. He tries frogs and snakes without much luck. His final pet is a winner: a hermit crab. The book is valuable for youngsters suffering from allergies because it explores alternatives. (Picture book)

Arthur, Catherine. **My Sister's Silent World.** Photographs by Nathan Talbot. Childrens Press, 1979. 6–9.

Big sister describes what the world is like to her deaf little sister, Heather, just eight years old. Beautiful full-page color photographs show Heather and her family at the zoo. Heather likes what all children like, but others often misunderstand. (Picture book)

Baldwin, Anne Norris. **A Little Time.** Viking Press, 1978. 8–12.

Sarah loves her younger brother and easily repeats her mother's explanation of why he is different. But when Matt almost ruins her birthday party she cannot accept the reality of having a mongoloid brother. Down's Syndrome is openly and sympathetically discussed as Sarah learns to deal with her feelings.

Bates, Betty. **Love Is like Peanuts.** Holiday House, 1980. 10–up.

Marianne, fourteen, has a summer job that leads to romance. Her major responsibility is the care of a brain-damaged girl, whose brother provides the love angle. The story explores these relationships.

Clifton, Lucille. **My Friend Jacob.** Illus. Thomas DiGrazia. E. P. Dutton, 1980. 6–9.

A warm relationship exists between eight-year-old Sam and his mentally retarded friend Jacob, who is sixteen. Jacob's talents—keen aim for basketball and instant recognition of cars—are highlighted. The illustrations extend the mood of the story, and the book makes a fine starter for discussion. (Picture book)

Cookson, Catherine. **Go Tell It to Mrs. Golightly.** Lothrop, Lee & Shepard Books, 1977. 8–12.

Bella Dodd, a blind girl of eight, is sent to visit her cold, abrupt grandfather. Befriended by serious, fourteen-year-old John, whom the grandfather asks to help her, Bella finds exciting adventure, including a kidnapping. Eventually she wins her grandfather's love.

Fanshawe, Elizabeth. **Rachel.** Illus. Michael Charlton. Bradbury Press, 1977. 5–8.

Rachel recounts her daily life in a matter-of-fact, cheerful narrative that includes discussion of her wheelchair and the limitations of being unable to walk. The overall impression conveyed by the book—both text and drawings—is that of a child who enjoys normal activities and who accepts without fuss what she cannot do. (Picture book)

Garrigue, Sheila. **Between Friends.** Bradbury Press, 1978. 10–12.

When Jill leaves California and moves to Massachusetts during the summer, very few girls her age are around. She becomes friendly with Dede, a retarded girl. Her mother and the friends Jill later makes exert pressure on her to abandon the friendship.

Gold, Phyllis. **Please Don't Say Hello.** Photographs by Carl Baker. Human Sciences Press, 1976. 8–12.

The mother of a nine-year-old autistic child describes the frightening and disturbing world of her son so young readers will understand and recognize this childhood disorder. Photographs complement the sensitive, informative text.

Hanlon, Emily. **The Swing.** Bradbury Press, 1979. 10–up.

A swing, a lie, and a bear hunt are significant elements in this story of Beth, an eleven-year-old deaf girl, and Danny, a thirteen-year-old boy with family problems. A moving story of friendship.

Haynes, Henry Louis. **Squarehead and Me.** Illus. Len Epstein. Westminster Press, 1980. 8–12.

Two city boys have a chance to spend some time on a farm. David tries to help Squarehead, who has a learning disability. The story directs attention to the problems of children with handicaps.

Heide, Florence Parry. **Secret Dreamer, Secret Dreams.** J. B. Lippincott, 1978. 12–up.

The story of thirteen-year-old Caroline, told as she would tell it if she could talk, is compassionately written. The reader shares the mentally handicapped girl's frustrations as she attempts to understand the world she lives in. A haunting insight into the life of a silent person.

Hermes, Patricia. **What If They Knew?** Harcourt Brace Jovanovich, 1980. 12–up.

Jeremy's summer with her grandparents has been perfect. When she finds out that her parents won't be returning from England until December, she dreads going to a new school because of her epilepsy. How she and her friends handle her fears is a warm, humorous story.

Jones, Ron. **The Acorn People.** Illus. Tom Parker. Abingdon Press, 1978. 11–up.

This is an unusual and touching story of a camp counselor who works with massively handicapped children. The making of acorn necklaces at Camp Wiggin draws the campers together and gives the children confidence. The reader's love for and understanding of these children grows as the story unfolds.

Kent, Deborah. **Belonging.** Dial Press, 1978. 12–up.

Having attended the Institute for the Blind for nine years, fifteen-year-old Meg Hollis wants to go to a regular high school. Many of her adjustment problems stem from attitudes she encounters. Meg matures as she realizes that instead of trying to be like others, she must value and nourish her own uniqueness. Much of the book is autobiographical.

Kingman, Lee. **Hand over Wheels.** Houghton Mifflin, 1978. 12–up.

Seventeen-year-old identical twins, Kerry and Terry, share everything: hats, sports, thoughts, and the automobile accident that leaves Terry a quadriplegic. This story of a family devastated emotionally and financially but finding strength to pick up life is told with honesty and sensitivity.

Lasker, Joe. **Nick Joins In.** Illus. by author. Albert Whitman, 1980. 6–9.

Nick worries about going to school. How will he get up the stairs in his wheelchair? Will he be liked? Nick's teacher in a friendly and open manner helps his classmates satisfy their natural curiosity about Nick. When Nick retrieves the ball from the roof, he is appreciated by all and gains self-confidence. (Picture book)

Litchfield, Ada B. **Words in Our Hands.** Illus. Helen Cogancherry. Albert Whitman, 1980. 8–12.

Michael's parents are deaf. They talk with their hands and nine-year-old Michael is proud of them. When the family moves to a new town, however, children make fun of his parents. Suddenly, Michael is embarrassed. A sensitive story which offers much information about the deaf.

MacLachlan, Patricia. **Through Grandpa's Eyes.** Illus. Deborah Ray. Harper & Row, Publishers, 1980. 7–10.

A small boy tells of a day with his blind grandpa, conveying how the world is perceived through grandpa's "eyes." The poetic text and softly colored illustrations are an excellent combination that enriches our understanding of blindness and can be used to stimulate classroom activities on "seeing" without eyes. (Picture book)

Reuter, Margaret. **My Mother Is Blind.** Photographs by Philip Lanier. Childrens Press, 1979. 7–10.

A young son describes the daily life of his blind mother. The full-page color photographs and informative text help young readers feel more comfortable with blind persons. (Picture book)

Smith, Lucia B. **A Special Kind of Sister.** Illus. Chuck Hall. Holt, Rinehart and Winston, 1979. 6–9.

Changes occur easily in the feelings of seven-year-old Sarah, whose younger brother is retarded. Sometimes she feels overburdened because she has to do more things than he does; sometimes she is angry with others because they are not nice to him; sometimes she loves him because he loves her. (Picture book)

Stanek, Muriel. **Growl When You Say R.** Illus. Phil Smith. Albert Whitman, 1979. 6–9.

"My name is Wobbie," says Robbie. Therein lies the problem—a difficulty in articulation. A useful book in the best sense of the word, this easy reader can be used for discussion in a variety of situations. (Picture book)

ter Haar, Jaap (translator Martha Mearns). **The World of Ben Lighthart.** Seymour Lawrence, 1977. 10–up.

An accident leaves Ben blind, and he is forced to make a new life for himself. Gradually he comes to terms with his world of darkness and agrees to attend a special school. Told from his point of view, the story conveys the difficulties of his day-to-day adjustments.

Wahl, Jan. **Jamie's Tiger.** Illus. Tomie de Paola. Harcourt Brace Jovanovich, 1978. 5–8.

A sudden hearing loss resulting from German measles leaves young Jamie a lonely stranger in his familiar environment. Love and support from family and professionals help Jamie reestablish his place. The moving story and illustrations sensitize the reader to the struggle of a hearing-impaired child. (Picture book)

Young, Helen. **What Difference Does It Make, Danny?** Illus. Quentin Blake. Andre Deutsch, 1980. 8–12.

Danny, who has epilepsy, is good at sports and loves everything about the gym, even the smell of old plimsolls. Until now, his disability, controlled by medication, has been handled openly by parents, teachers, and classmates. When the new games master bars

Danny from competitive sports, he reacts by retreating from everything and everyone, but all is resolved when he plays truant and
rescues a child from drowning. Youngsters will enjoy the challenge
of the Britishisms in this story published first in Great Britain.

Humor

Adler, David A. **You Think It's Fun to Be a Clown!** Illus. Ray Cruz.
Doubleday, 1980. 4–7.

"Clowning is not fun at all!" exclaims the clown. Clowns are shot
from cannons, cut in half by magicians, chased by wild beasts, and
squirted by elephants. A surprise awaits the reader. Lively, colorful
pictures accompany the energetic rhymed text. (Picture book)

Alexander, Sue. **Marc the Magnificent.** Illus. Tomie de Paola. Pantheon
Books, 1978. 4–7.

Marc's fantasy of being a renowned magician is "ballooned" on
every other page; the intervening scenes offer reality. His attempts
and finally his success in making a coin disappear provide the story
line. Full-color illustrations effectively portray the grandiose dreams,
the failures, and the satisfaction of accomplishment. (Picture book)

Angell, Judie. **In Summertime It's Tuffy.** Bradbury Press, 1977. 10–up.

Tuffy and her companions in Bunk Ten are having a wonderful year
at camp—except for Uncle Otto, the head counselor. The girls devise
a plan to get even and the results are disastrous and unexpected.

Aylesworth, Jim. **Hush Up!** Illus. Glen Rounds. Holt, Rinehart and
Winston, 1980. 4–7.

Taking a nap on a hot afternoon is so easy for lazy Jasper Walker
and his barnyard animals. Then a nasty horsefly bites the mule's
nose and sets off a crazy chain of events. Young listeners especially
will enjoy this silly farm tale enlivened by very comic illustrations.
(Picture book)

Barrett, Judi. **I Hate to Go to Bed.** Illus. Ray Cruz. Four Winds Press,
1977. 4–7.

Humorous drawings help a child envision the many reasons for not
going to bed. Further reflection, however, reveals a pleasant side to
bedtime in this reassuring story. (Picture book)

Blume, Judy. **Superfudge.** E. P. Dutton, 1980. 8–up.

Peter Hatcher is disturbed about the disruptions in family life. As if
having an irritating brother like Fudge isn't enough, Dad quits his
job to write a book, the family moves to the suburbs, and baby sister

is on the way. Eventually family life straightens out to everyone's satisfaction.

Bram, Elizabeth. **Woodruff and the Clocks.** Dial Press, 1980. 6–9.

Four easy-to-read stories tell about Woodruff, an imaginative boy who loves his cats, clocks, and dreams. Happy feelings and good ideas to carry over into classroom or home life abound. (Picture book)

Bridgman, Elizabeth. **How to Travel with Grownups.** Illus. Eleanor Hazard. Thomas Y. Crowell, 1980. 4–7.

The text of this clever book gives sound advice to youngsters traveling with adults, but the hilarious, detailed illustrations show the real story line of twins who do just the opposite. (Picture book)

Bridgman, Elizabeth. **New Dog Next Door.** Harper & Row, Publishers, 1978. 3–5.

The neighbor's new dog likes a little boy so much that he helps with such tasks as taking out the garbage and guarding the house. Much of the humorous story is conveyed through line drawings. (Picture book)

Cresswell, Helen. **Absolute Zero: Being the Second Part of the Bagthorpe Saga.** Macmillan Publishing, 1978. 10–up.

After Uncle Parker wins a Caribbean cruise in a slogan-writing contest, the Bagthorpe family, in their usual deliciously wacky manner, moves into the Era of Competitive Entering. Jack's dog, Zero, becomes the idol of a dog food company. Second of a British series.

Cresswell, Helen. **Bagthorpes Unlimited: Being the Third Part of the Bagthorpe Saga.** Macmillan Publishing, 1978. 10–up.

Even when running smoothly, life in the Bagthorpe household is a fair imitation of bedlam. When Grandma plans a family reunion, things inexorably go from worse to disaster. Third of a British series. Mild profanity.

Cresswell, Helen. **Bagthorpes V. the World: Being the Fourth Part of the Bagthorpe Saga.** Macmillan Publishing, 1979. 10–up.

An overdrawn bank account sets Mr. Bagthorpe on a course of self-sufficiency, and the Bagthorpe estate expands to include a goat, beer making, and vegetable gardens. The situation is complicated by rich Great-aunt Lucy's visit and four-year-old Daisy's "funerals." Fourth of a British series. Mild profanity.

Cresswell, Helen. **Ordinary Jack: Being the First Part of the Bagthorpe Saga.** Macmillan Publishing, 1977. 10–up.

The Bagthorpes are highly volatile geniuses, all except Jack, who is just plain ordinary. With the connivance of a sympathetic uncle, however, Jack begins to foretell the future, and his extraordinary behavior throws the whole family into an uproar. Daisy, a precocious four-year-old incendiary, adds to the hilarious confusion. First of a British series.

Croll, Carolyn. **Too Many Babas.** Harper & Row, Publishers, 1979. 4–7.

Baba decides to make soup and three other babas come to help her. Each decides what is needed in the way of flavoring. How they resolve the dilemma of the spoiled broth makes a delightful story. This easy-to-read book has appealing pictures and a wordless section. (Picture book)

Danziger, Paula. **There's a Bat in Bunk Five.** Delacorte Press, 1980. 10–up.

Fourteen-year-old Marcy from *The Cat Ate My Gymsuit* is a counselor-in-training at Ms. Finney's creative arts camp. Marcy and her fellow campers have delightful escapades as she deals with typical camp problems—and falling in love!

Frascino, Edward. **Eddie Spaghetti.** Harper & Row, Publishers, 1978. 7–10.

Eddie is nine years old and growing up in Yonkers during the 1940s. Except for the setting, the ten episodes are timeless as Eddie goes to the zoo, trains his dog, plays his first piano recital, and outsmarts the neighborhood gang. A humorous look at growing up in the "old days."

Gage, Wilson. **Down in the Boondocks.** Illus. Glen Rounds. Greenwillow Books, 1977. 6–9.

Rhyme, rhythm, and repetition are delightful elements in this story of a farmer who is deaf in one ear. He uses an ear trumpet, but his wife hollers, and the rooster crows loudly. All this noise scares away a would-be robber. Lively illustrations. (Picture book)

Giff, Patricia Reilly. **Next Year I'll Be Special.** Illus. Marylin Hafner. E. P. Dutton, 1980. 5–8.

Marilyn has mean Miss Minch in first grade, but she knows that school will be different when she has Miss Lark as her second-grade teacher. She's sure everyone will send her valentines and invite her to parties—next year she'll be special. (Picture book)

Gilson, Jamie. **Harvey, the Beer Can King.** Illus. John Wallner. Lothrop, Lee & Shepard Books, 1978. 10–up.

Harvey is vying with his friend Quint in the sixth-grade Superkids Contest. He's sure he'll win because he has the greatest beer can collection in town. Exaggerations like this get Harvey in trouble over and over again, but his escapades make hilarious reading.

Greenwald, Sheila. **It All Began with** *Jane Eyre.* Little, Brown, 1980.
12–up.

Franny loves to read, especially in the closet with a bag of chips. She
decides to keep a diary in the hope that exciting adventures will
begin to happen to her, adventures like those experienced by the
heroines in the teenage romances her mother gives her to read.
Curiously, strange things do start to happen.

Hann, Jacquie. **Up Day, Down Day.** Illus. by author. Four Winds Press,
1978. 6–9.

This first-person account tells how one friend caught a fish and the
other caught a cold. Jeremy seems to be on the plus side of life until
a unique turn of events. Simple vocabulary, brief text, and pictures
to make a reader giggle. (Picture book)

Heide, Florence Parry. **Banana Twist.** Holiday House, 1978. 8–12.

Two boys meet in their apartment elevator and a hilarious tale
unfolds. Jonah thinks Goober is weird, but they have some fascinating adventures together. Throughout the story Jonah hopes to be
accepted by a private school. He succeeds, and his roommate is a
real surprise. A laugh-filled story.

Heller, Linda. **Horace Morris.** Macmillan Publishing, 1980. 7–10.

Always-punctual Horace Morris goes to Emmaline's house for dinner, but no one is home. Each of the Pottertons—Emmaline, her
mother, and her father—arrives late and offers preposterous explanations. Horace doesn't believe them until he reads about their escapades in the newspaper. Unusual perspectives in these intriguing
illustrations. (Picture book)

Hirsch, Linda. **The Sick Story.** Illus. John Wallner. Hastings House, Publishers, 1977. 8–12.

Miranda stays home from school with a slight head cold and gets
super room service from Mom and Dad. But when classmate
Rebecca tells her there is one good part left in the school play,
Miranda finds herself in a dilemma. Humorously written and illustrated and excellent for discussions on responsibility.

Hurwitz, Johanna. **Aldo Applesauce.** Illus. John Wallner. William Morrow, 1979. 7–10.

This sequel to *Much Ado about Aldo* is entertaining and easy to
read. Aldo, a vegetarian, has an accident in the lunchroom in his
new school, which gives him the nickname of Applesauce. He also
wins the friendship of Dede, a girl who wears a moustache. (Picture
book)

Hurwitz, Johanna. **Much Ado about Aldo.** Illus. John Wallner. William Morrow, 1978. 6–9.

Eight-year-old Aldo, an animal lover, is intensely interested in school. His teacher announces that their next classroom science project will be the study of crickets in the terrarium. All goes well until chameleons are introduced and the crickets become their prey. Aldo makes a decision. Pencil sketches.

Hutchins, Pat. **Don't Forget the Bacon!** Greenwillow Books, 1976. 4–7.

Colorful drawings illustrate the story in rhyme of a boy sent to the grocery to get four items for his mother. Despite his best efforts to remember the list, experiences along the way lead to confusion for the boy but giggles for the reader. (Picture book)

Inkiow, Dimiter (translator Paula McGuire). **Me and Clara and Snuffy the Dog.** Illus. Traudl Reiner and Walter Reiner. Pantheon Books, 1980. 6–9.

"Me" and Clara and Snuffy have days that are filled with action and mischief. They do good deeds, but they also give their parents' clothes away, break dishes, and count on their fingers and toes to solve math problems. Delightful characters and cartoon-like illustrations—just right for reading aloud to a class. (Picture book)

Kahl, Virginia. **Whose Cat Is That?** Charles Scribner's Sons, 1979. 5–8.

The same white cat becomes the property of seven houses. When a government committee checks on the "seven" cats, the children make sure that a different cat is at each house. The ears become red, the paws are blackened, and so on. A cumulative tale with a happy ending. (Picture book)

Krasilovsky, Phyllis. **The Man Who Tried to Save Time.** Illus. Marcia Sewell. Doubleday, 1979. 6–9.

A man who lives with his cat has developed a good schedule. He eats breakfast, feeds his cat, cleans his house, and gets to work on time. When he decides to be lazy, he has to figure out a way to save time. He has trouble. (Picture book)

Levy, Elizabeth. **Frankenstein Moved In on the Fourth Floor.** Illus. Mordicai Gerstein. Harper & Row, Publishers, 1979. 8–12.

Sam and Robert are on a Frankenstein and Dracula kick: dolls, books, movies, television. When ill-tempered Mr. Frank moves into their apartment building with his boxes of wires and radio tubes, the boys do a little sleuthing. A suspense-filled story good to read aloud by chapters and a springboard to discussions about fears and reality.

Myers, Walter Dean. **Mojo and the Russians.** Viking Press, 1977. 10–12.

While bicycling, Dean upsets an old woman suspected to have Mojo power. To save him, his Harlem friends become involved with the Russian consul, New York's finest, and even the FBI.

Naylor, Phyllis Reynolds. **Eddie, Incorporated.** Illus. Blanche Sims. Atheneum, 1980. 7–10.

Twelve-year-old Eddie wants to operate his own business. Everyone else in his family is gainfully employed, and Eddie decides to test his abilities. He opens a baby-sitting agency and learns about profit, loss, and competition. A humorous story with black and white illustrations.

Naylor, Phyllis Reynolds. **How Lazy Can You Get?** Illus. Alan Daniel. Atheneum, 1979. 8–10.

Miss Brasscoat comes to take care of the three Megglethorp children for the week equipped with everything but a smile. The children attempt to give her one, and their efforts make the reader laugh out loud. Pen and ink wash drawings add to the humor.

O'Connor, Jane. **Yours Till Niagara Falls, Abby.** Illus. Margot Apple. Hastings House, Publishers, 1979. 10–12.

Summer at Camp Pinecrest brings the new recruit, Abby Kimmel, and last year's camp klutz, Roberta Harrison, together. Abby, dreading a two-month ordeal at camp without her best friend, learns to survive with style and to extend her friendship to others.

Orbach, Ruth. **Apple Pigs.** Illus. by author. William Collins Publishers, 1976. 8–10.

With care and attention, an overachieving apple tree produces so much fruit that the family doesn't know how to dispose of the surplus. Even the bunk beds and trunks are filled! What to do? Many answers are given, including directions for making apple pigs. Rhyming text and bright drawings. (Picture book)

Parish, Peggy. **Amelia Bedelia Helps Out.** Illus. Lynn Sweat. Greenwillow Books, 1979. 7–10.

Amelia Bedelia has a helper, niece Effie Lou. Although Effie Lou doesn't quite understand the instructions, she is eager to help "dust" the potato bugs and "sew" the seeds. The double trouble these two make for themselves makes a delightful easy-to-read book. (Picture book)

Parish, Peggy. **Be Ready at Eight.** Illus. Leonard Kessler. Macmillan Publishing, 1979. 6–9.

Today is a special day for absent-minded Miss Molly. She is sure of it because she tied a string around her finger. All day she goes about asking her friends what day it is until finally she remembers the birthday surprise. Humorous illustrations add to the fun. (Picture book)

Parish, Peggy. **Teach Us, Amelia Bedelia.** Illus. Lynn Sweat. Greenwillow Books, 1977. 6–9.

Imagine Amelia Bedelia as a substitute teacher! She leads the children to plant bulbs, practice play, and take away apples in the most literal way. The day is saved and everyone made happy with her taffy apples. (Picture book)

Parker, Nancy Winslow. **Poofy Loves Company.** Illus. by author. Dodd, Mead, 1980. 5–8.

Well-groomed Sally and her mother pay a social call and meet Poofy, a dog who has no social graces. Poofy loves Sally's company because he triumphs in every encounter. A disheveled Sally leaves and Poofy is content with Sally's belongings. Marvelous satire in text and illustrations.

Paterson, Diane. **If I Were a Toad.** Dial Press, 1977. 5–8.

A child imitates the behavior of many creatures. With few words and humorous drawings, this small book will fit tiny hands. Teachers may find it useful for introducing creative movements. (Picture book)

Peck, Robert Newton. **Trig.** Illus. Pamela Johnson. Little, Brown, 1977. 7–10.

Elizabeth Trigman hates her name, loves her Shirley Temple doll named Fred, idolizes Tom Mix, and proudly owns an official junior G-man machine gun. This feisty young Vermont farm girl romps her way through hilarious adventures to the horror of her parents and the embarrassment of the neighborhood bullies.

Phelan, Terry Wolfe. **The Week Mom Unplugged the TVs.** Illus. Joel Schick. Four Winds Press, 1979. 7–10.

Mom pulls the plug on television for a week, and the family experiences television withdrawal symptoms. This amusing story captures the problem of three youngsters held captive by the television set.

Pinkwater, Daniel M. **The Big Orange Splot.** Hastings House, Publishers, 1977. 6–9.

On Mr. Plumbean's street all the houses look alike. One day an orange splot appeared on his roof. "You will have to repaint your house," said his neighbors. Mr. Plumbean did—but not in the manner everyone expected. (Picture book)

Pinkwater, Daniel M. **The Last Guru.** Dodd, Mead, 1978. 10–up.

Twelve-year-old Harold Blatz possesses an extraordinary financial sense, and he soon amasses the world's third largest fortune. Although the story is given a realistic setting, it soon spins into a humorous tall tale.

Prager, Annabelle. **The Surprise Party.** Illus. Tomie de Paola. Pantheon Books, 1977. 6–9.

Nicky wants a surprise birthday party so he asks Al to plan it for him. Nicky, however, keeps telling Al what to do for the party. In the end, Nicky is really surprised! The party is a great success. (Picture book)

Segal, Lore. **Tell Me a Trudy.** Illus. Rosemary Wells. Farrar, Straus & Giroux, 1977. 5–8.

The three "Trudies" in the book stretch from almost possible to fantastic. They deal with going to bed, sharing, and routing the Martians from the bathroom. The stories are simply told and reflect a loving family situation. Watercolor illustrations are warm and appealing. (Picture book)

Sharmat, Marjorie, and Mitchell Sharmat. **I Am Not a Pest.** Illus. Diane Dawson. E. P. Dutton, 1979. 4–7.

Alicia is not a pest, or so she says. Besides, her attempt to discover the bark in her brother's mechanical dog might pay off in some future important invention, or her trumpet blatting could lead to musical fame. Large black and white illustrations add to the humor. (Picture book)

Snyder, Anne. **The Old Man and the Mule.** Illus. Mila Lazarevich. Holt, Rinehart and Winston, 1978. 7–10.

Stubborn Zeke and his old mule, Tully, enjoy a relationship based on mutual bad temper and mean tricks. Inheriting a used tractor gives Zeke his chance to get rid of Tully, only to discover that he is lonely and can't get along without the old mule. Illustrations are large, clear and funny. Good for discussion of human relationships. (Picture book)

Spier, Peter. **Oh, Were They Ever Happy!** Doubleday, 1978. 5–8.

When the sitter doesn't show up, the three Noonan children decide to paint the house. Each page reveals more of the undertaking. The final double-page spread shows the multicolored house. A colorful delight. (Picture book)

Springstubb, Tricia. **My Minnie Is a Jewel.** Illus. Jim Lamarche. Carolrhoda Books, 1980. 4–7.

The theme of an old Scandinavian folktale runs through this humorous tale of a woodcutter and his forgetful wife. Henry and Minnie are very happy with one another, and when the scenes from her window captivate Minnie and she forgets what she is doing, Henry is always understanding. (Picture book)

Stevenson, James. **"Could Be Worse!"** Greenwillow Books, 1977. 5–8.

Grandpa leads a routine life and always gives a routine answer, "Could be worse," to anything that is said. When he overhears Louie say that Grandpa's life is uninteresting, he decides to tell a great whopper. The children's comment is, "Could be worse!" Readers would enjoy trying to top Grandpa's tale. (Picture book)

Ventura, Piero, and Marisa Ventura. **The Painter's Trick.** Random House, 1977. 5–8.

A poor traveling painter in Italy convinces the monks that they need a mural of St. George and the dragon in their monastery. He then tricks five of them into believing that the completed painting will display their likenesses as the courageous Saint. Anticipation runs high. Colorful cartoon-like drawings add to this delightful story. (Picture book)

Viorst, Judith. **Alexander, Who Used to Be Rich Last Sunday.** Illus. Ray Cruz. Atheneum, 1978. 7–10.

Money seems to run through Alexander's pockets like water. Last Sunday he had a dollar but a series of misfortunes befall him and soon the money is gone. Humorous illustrations add to the fun. (Picture book)

Wallace, Barbara Brooks. **The Contest Kid Strikes Again.** Illus. Gloria Kamen. Abingdon Press, 1980. 10–12.

Harvey Small, the contest kid, has won again! And what better to do with his prize chickens than give them to Hawkins, Mrs. Mosley's English butler, to keep. Unfortunately, someone who is trying to get rid of Hawkins uses the chickens for foul purposes. The results are hilarious.

Watson, Pauline. **The Walking Coat.** Illus. Tomie de Paola. Walker, 1980. 3–5.

Little Scott enjoys wearing his older cousin's cast-off-coat, which totally envelops him from head to foot. He also enjoys surprising people who think they are seeing a coat walking about by itself. His humorous adventures will delight young readers as will the cartoon-style illustrations. (Picture book)

Willard, Nancy. **Simple Pictures Are Best.** Illus. Tomie de Paola. Harcourt Brace Jovanovich, 1976. 6–9.

A shoemaker and his wife being photographed for their wedding anniversary add one ridiculous thing after another to the scene, despite the photographer's insistence that "simple pictures are best."

A wild melee with an angry bull results in a very simple picture indeed. Clever and colorful illustrations. (Picture book)

Wolkoff, Judie. **Wally.** Bradbury Press, 1977. 8–12.

When two brothers baby-sit a chuckawalla lizard named Wally without telling their lizard-hating mother, there are bound to be some problems and a lot of laughs. This large-print, easy-to-read book is also a delightful choice for reading aloud.

Mystery

Anderson, Mary. **Matilda's Masterpiece.** Illus. Sal Murdocca. Atheneum, 1977. 10–12.

Twelve-year-old Mattie wants to be a detective. When a painting is stolen while she is visiting the Brooklyn Museum, Mattie decides that it is her case and begins investigating.

Baker, Will. **Chip.** Harcourt Brace Jovanovich, 1979. 8–12.

A young drifter comes to a small Idaho town and meets a new friend. He also finds prejudice and a murder in which he is the prime suspect. The story is fast and filled with an unusual number of true-to-life experiences.

Bellairs, John. **The Treasure of Alpheus Winterborn.** Illus. Judith Gwyn Brown. Harcourt Brace Jovanovich, 1978. 10–12.

Thirteen-year-old Anthony Monday is driven by curiosity in his efforts to solve the riddle left behind in a poem by Alpheus T. Winterborn, a rich eccentric citizen of Anthony's small town. Black and white sketches; some mild profanity.

Bonsall, Crosby. **The Case of the Double Cross.** Illus. by author. Harper & Row, Publishers, 1980. 6–9.

The Wizard's private eye club does not allow girls to become members. The boys have a change of heart when Marigold and her friends help them solve a puzzling mystery. An easy-to-read book. (Picture book)

Cooney, Caroline B. **Safe as the Grave.** Illus. Gail Owens. Coward, McCann & Geoghegan, 1979. 8–12.

Lynn and Victoria are twins but very unlike in temperament. Lynn, the adventuresome one, quite by accident solves the mystery of a treasure lost since the Civil War. A good story with a believable view of twin relationships.

Corcoran, Barbara. **The Person in the Potting Shed.** Atheneum, 1980. 10–12.

Dorothy and Franklin are eager to spend the summer near New

Orleans with their mother, but not with her new husband. The two discover mysterious circumstances but their stepfather won't listen. The suspense builds until a murder is discovered and the murderer confronted. The children are rescued and the family united.

Crayder, Dorothy. **The Riddles of Mermaid House.** Atheneum, 1977. 8–12.

Becky and her family are shunned as newcomers in town. Disappointed, Becky occupies herself by exploring the marsh where she encounters some mysterious people, one of whom may be responsible for the rash of fires in town. Mrs. Hendrix, who lives in the old mansion Mermaid House, enlists Becky's help to defend herself and solve the crimes.

Cunliffe, John. **Mr. Gosling and the Great Art Robbery.** Illus. William Stobbs. Andre Deutsch, 1979. 6–9.

Mr. Gosling and Sara encounter a terrible mix-up and a mysterious Mr. Brown while attempting to deliver a valuable painting. Full-color illustrations combine painting and montage. Amusing, light-hearted mystery. (Picture book)

Curry, Jane Louise. **The Bassumtyte Treasure.** Atheneum, 1978. 10–12.

All the elements of a successful mystery are here: the old ancestral home in England with a secret passageway, a ten-year-old American boy with curiosity and wit, and rumors of a family treasure. The narrative never flags and the outcome is believable.

Curry, Jane Louise. **Ghost Lane.** Atheneum, 1979. 10–12.

Richard's summer with his father turns into an unforgettable adventure when a series of burglaries occur at the manor house near their vacation cottage in England. Richard helps solve the mystery, but not without great danger to one of his new friends.

Dicks, Terrence. **The Baker Street Irregulars in the Case of the Crooked Kids.** Elsevier/Nelson Books, 1978. 10–up.

Dab Robinson and his Baker Street Irregulars have earned the reputation of solving cases that the police can't. Their latest escapade with a kid burglary ring puts them in trouble when the law mistakes them for crooks instead of detectives. Another exciting mystery in this series is *The Case of the Blackmail Boys.*

Elmore, Patricia. **Susannah and the Blue House Mystery.** Illus. John C. Wallner. E. P. Dutton, 1980. 8–12.

Susannah and Lucy are partners in their own detective agency. They haven't had much chance to solve any cases until Juliet's grandfather disappears. With Susannah in the lead, the girls explore Blue House, where Grandpa lived, and follow the clues until the mystery is solved.

Fife, Dale. **Follow That Ghost!** Illus. Joan Drescher. E. P. Dutton, 1979. 7–10.

Chuck and Jason are in business: the following business. Glory hires them to find the ghost who makes noise in her mother's apartment. When the mystery is solved they get their reward, a plate of salty peanut fudge.

Gelman, Rita Golden, and Joan Richter. **Professor Coconut and the Thief.** Illus. Emily McCully. Holt, Rinehart and Winston, 1977. 7–10.

Peter and Sipo, eight-year-old detectives, set ingenious traps for the mysterious thief in an anthropologists' camp. Line drawings illustrate this fast-moving story about a white boy from the States and his African friend. The humorous mystery is appropriate for beginning and reluctant readers.

Godden, Rumer. **The Rocking Horse Secret.** Illus. Juliet Stanwell Smith. Viking Press, 1978. 7–10.

Tibby's mother works for old Mrs. Pomeroy who is very rich. Tibby's best friends are Noble, the Rocking Horse, and Jed, the handyman. Add a missing will and two nasty nieces and all the elements for a very happy ending are present.

Harris, Christie. **Mystery at the Edge of Two Worlds.** Illus. Lou Crockett. Atheneum, 1978. 12–up.

Three teenagers in northwestern Canada set out to discover who has been stealing valuable Indian art. Legends of the Wild Woman of the Woods make their imaginations run wild as they try to solve the mystery.

Hassler, Jon. **Four Miles to Pinecone.** Frederick Warne, 1977. 8–12.

While Tom is cabin-sitting in Minnesota, he is attacked by a gang of thieves, one of whom he knows! How he solves his problem is the key to this book.

Heide, Florence Parry, and Roxanne Heide. **Mystery of the Forgotten Island.** Illus. Seymour Fleishman. Albert Whitman, 1980. 7–10.

Three youngsters find adventure and a mystery while on vacation in the north woods. The trio helps an old man save his island and preserve the environment. A fast-paced story for young mystery readers.

Hicks, Clifford B. **Alvin Fernald, TV Anchorman.** Illus. Laura Hartman. Holt, Rinehart and Winston, 1980. 10–12.

Alvin and his friends develop a local television news show so successful that the children are invited to appear on network television. Alvin manages to unravel the mystery of a long-ago bank robbery, not only cleverly, but on camera and in prime time! Funny and fast-moving.

Hicks, Clifford B. **Alvin's Swap Shop.** Illus. Bill Sokol. Holt, Rinehart and Winston, 1976. 10–12.

Alvin, the "Magnificent Brain," is back again in a sixth adventure. It all begins when he trades an ant for a collection of dead spiders and ends up with a swap shop. He becomes involved with Pim, a Bahamaian boy, and a mystery of a sunken ship develops. Delightful, humorous entertainment.

Hildick, E. W. **The Case of the Phantom Frog.** Illus. Lisl Weil. Macmillan Publishing, 1979. 8–12.

The McGurk detective organization has taken on another case. This one involves baby-sitting seven-year-old Bela, who is part of the mystery. McGurk, Willie, Wanda, Joey, and Brains finally uncover the solution. Humorous black and white drawings.

Hildick, E. W. **The Case of the Snowbound Spy.** Illus. Lisl Weil. Macmillan Publishing, 1980. 8–12.

The McGurk detective organization receives a cryptic message from an unknown client. In solving this case, they need to have sharp wits for more code-cracking and for outwitting a high-level industrial espionage plot. A good read-aloud book.

Hooker, Ruth, and Carole Smith. **The Pelican Mystery.** Illus. George Armstrong. Albert Whitman, 1977. 10–12.

Grant and Patti, a brother and sister, happen on a mysterious-acting diver while searching for a pet pelican and help solve the burglaries on a Florida key. An easy-to-read mystery with large print and black and white drawings.

Hooks, William H. **The Mystery on Bleeker Street.** Illus. Susanna Natti. Alfred A. Knopf, 1980. 6–9.

Chase and his seventy-eight-year-old friend Babette observe strange occurrences at the Star Hotel as they are walking Josephine, Babette's old dog. Before the mystery is solved, Babette and the dog are kidnapped and ten-year-old Chase must use his ingenuity to save them. Black and white illustrations.

Keats, Ezra Jack. **Maggie and the Pirate.** Four Winds Press, 1979. 6–9.

Maggie and her pet cricket Niki spend warm days on the river with friends Paco and Katie until one fateful day Niki is stolen by a mysterious stranger. The unexpected, touching ending appeals to young readers. Brilliant collage and wash illustrations accent action and suspense. (Picture book)

Myers, Walter Dean. **The Black Pearl and the Ghost or One Mystery after Another.** Illus. Robert Quackenbush. Viking Press, 1980. 7–10.

Dr. Aramy, great detective, and his friend, Mr. Uppley, solve the mystery of the missing Black Pearl of Kowloon. Next, Mr. Dibble, famous ghost chaser, rids Bleek Manor of its ghost. Brilliantly colorful pictures add sparkle to these two humorous spoofs. (Picture book)

Naylor, Phyllis Reynolds. **The Witch Herself.** Illus. Gail Owens. Atheneum, 1978. 10–12.

Lynn and Mouse are sure Mrs. Tuggle is a witch. In their search to prove it, some enticing hints about Mrs. Tuggle's past are uncovered. The girls are desperate in their struggle to save Lynn's mother from whatever has been planned for her by the witch. Third volume of a trilogy that includes *Witch's Sister* and *Witch Water.*

Newman, Robert. **The Case of the Vanishing Corpse.** Atheneum, 1980. 10–12.

Andrew and Sara assist Scotland Yard not only in locating a missing corpse but also in recovering stolen diamonds. A finely crafted mystery with the same protagonists as the author's earlier *The Case of the Baker Street Irregulars.*

Norton, Browning. **Wreck of the Blue Plane.** Coward, McCann & Geoghegan, 1978. 8–12.

Alaska becomes the scene for a lost plane containing a small fortune in cash. Fourteen-year-old Mark and his older brother are involved in a dangerous search. Believable characters enrich an exciting plot.

Phipson, Joan. **Fly into Danger.** Atheneum, 1977. 12–up.

Margaret Stewart, living with her father in Australia, loves the beauty of nature and especially the exotic birds in the wilderness areas of her father's land. She is horrified to learn that poachers can profit from capturing wild birds and smuggling them out of the country. On a thirty-hour flight to England to visit her mother, Margaret discovers that there are bird smugglers aboard.

Quackenbush, Robert. **Piet Potter's First Case.** Illus. by author. McGraw-Hill, 1980. 7–10.

Piet Potter, boy detective, moves into a new apartment in New York City and stumbles onto his first case. He helps find a million dollar inheritance for his neighbors in 3B. Mystery fans will also enjoy his further escapades in *Piet Potter Returns.* (Picture book)

Raskin, Ellen. **The Westing Game.** E. P. Dutton, 1978. 12–up.

A group of eccentric and zany heirs must discover the circumstances of a millionaire's death before they can claim their inheritance. The clues are funny, the situations are wild, and the whole book is highly imaginative. 1979 Newbery Award.

Rice, Eve. **The Remarkable Return of Winston Potter Crisply.** Greenwillow Books, 1978. 10–up.

Rebecca and Maxwell spot their older brother in downtown Manhattan when he is supposed to be at Harvard. They follow him discreetly through New York City until they discover his secret. A delightful story that allows the imaginations of children free range.

Roberts, Willo Davis. **More Minden Curses.** Illus. Sherry Streeter. Atheneum, 1980. 10–12.

Danny accepts the dare to capture Killer, one of the Caspitorian cats, in order to earn his membership in a secret club. His attempts at winning over the cat bring him into contact with its owners, Rosa and Anna, and the mysteries that surround them.

Rosenbloom, Joseph. **Maximilian, You're the Greatest.** Elsevier/Nelson Books, 1980. 10–12.

Twelve-year-old Maximilian Augustus Adams is a superior detective. Here is a collection of story puzzles that Max and his friends help the Mid-Manhattan police solve. The reader is invited to solve them along with Max. Solutions are given at the end of the book.

Schulman, Janet. **Jack the Bum and the Haunted House.** Illus. James Stevenson. Greenwillow Books, 1977. 6–11.

Jack the bum gets a new home and almost loses it. A mystery in the house turns out to be more than anyone expected. Jack is lucky to have nice friends. An easy-to-read book. (Picture book)

Sharmat, Marjorie Weinman. **Nate the Great and the Phony Clue.** Illus. Marc Simont. Coward, McCann & Geoghegan, 1977. 4–7.

Nate is challenged by a mysterious clue of four letters. Encouraged by Sludge, his dog, and his friends he proves his prowess as a detective to two doubting acquaintances. Bold, two-color illustrations. (Picture book)

Shecter, Ben. **A Summer Secret.** Harper & Row, Publishers, 1977. 6–9.

During the winter, a young boy tries to learn the summer secret from those living around the pond. A mystery to read aloud and discuss. Black and white drawings and a small, easy-to-handle size make this an interesting selection. Guidance from a teacher or parent will be necessary for developing understanding. (Picture book)

Shire, Ellen. **The Mystery at Number Seven, Rue Petite.** Random House, 1978. 6–9.

An antique dealer in Paris has a secret room that piques the curiosity of his chef and housekeeper. They solve the mystery, uncover a crime, and reap a reward. The bright illustrations completely capture the Parisian atmosphere with charm and humor. (Picture book)

Shreve, Susan. **The Nightmares of Geranium Street.** Alfred A. Knopf, 1977. 10–12.

The "Nightmares" is a gang of children who live in Germantown, a once fashionable section of Philadelphia but now deteriorating rapidly. The children, both girls and boys, come from a variety of home backgrounds. Acknowledging the potential for danger, they seek to solve the mystery of Aunt Tess, a beautiful mysterious lady who lives in a once-elegant house where strangers come and go at all hours of the day and night.

Simon, Seymour. **Einstein Anderson Shocks His Friends.** Illus. Fred Winkowski. Viking Press, 1980. 8–12.

Concepts in electricity, motion, heat, space, biology, and zoology are presented in story format. Readers will want to help solve the science problems that Einstein Anderson encounters daily. An earlier book starring the science superstar is *Einstein Anderson: Science Sleuth.*

Sobol, Donald J. **Encyclopedia Brown Carries On.** Illus. Ib Ohlsson. Four Winds Press, 1980. 10–up.

Mystery fans will enjoy trying to solve the cases in Idaville that Chief Brown encounters. Encyclopedia Brown, his son, is called upon to help but the reader is given a chance to guess the solution before reading it.

Nature

Baylor, Byrd. **If You Are a Hunter of Fossils.** Illus. Peter Parnall. Charles Scribner's Sons, 1980. 8–12.

Following the fossil hunter in these artistic, rather stylized illustrations is enjoyable. At times he appears quite large and then as small as a pinhead. As the fossils are discovered, we can picture the lapping waters that covered the land millions of years ago. (Picture book)

Baylor, Byrd. **Your Own Best Secret Place.** Illus. Peter Parnall. Charles Scribner's Sons, 1979. 7–10.

The author finds her own best private place in the hollow of a cottonwood tree. The spot becomes very special as she realizes that she is sharing it with someone who discovered it before her. The unique integration of text and illustration will invite the reader to share the secret place.

Bram, Elizabeth. **One Day I Closed My Eyes and the World Disappeared.** Dial Press, 1978. 4–7.

Stark line drawings accompany the simple text that describes a small girl's imaginative exploration of her senses. She closes her eyes and can no longer see, but she takes delight as she feels, smells, hears, and tastes the things in her expanding world. (Picture book)

Dabcovich, Lydia. **Follow the River.** E. P. Dutton, 1980. 4–7.

A stream starts in the mountains and the reader follows it as it flows through the countryside as it becomes a river and eventually flows into the ocean. Simple text and soft colored drawings. (Picture book)

dos Santos, Joyce Audy. **Sand Dollar, Sand Dollar.** J. B. Lippincott, 1980. 4–6.

Beautiful silkscreen illustrations flow with the shoreline adventure of a small boy and his dog, Urchin. Peter makes a wish on a new-found sand dollar and discovers that the beach, though quiet, is a satisfying place to spend a day. (Picture book)

Fisher, Aileen. **Anybody Home?** Illus. Susan Bonners. Thomas Y. Crowell, 1980. 4–7.

A small child dreams of being able to peek into a mouse's nest, a bear's lair, a fox's den, and a beaver's lodge. A simple tale told in rich and rhymed language. Softly realistic charcoal illustrations capture the snug coziness of each habitat. (Picture book)

Himler, Ronald. **Wake Up, Jeremiah.** Harper & Row, Publishers, 1979. 6–9.

Jeremiah gets up early and hurries to the hilltop to see something he knows is waiting for him. The sun is beautiful, just as he expected. He hurries home to awaken his parents. Magnificent pictures, few words. (Picture book)

Hurd, Thacher. **The Quiet Evening.** Greenwillow Books, 1978. 4–7.

"Shhhhh. Everything is quiet." Mother and Father are by the fireplace, the sun has set, everyone is quiet. Even nature becomes tranquil as the sun sets and the evening appears. Watercolor illustrations set the mood. A deep blue frame surrounds the pictures. Concept of night is clearly developed. (Picture book)

Knab, Linda Z. **The Day Is Waiting.** Illus. Don Freeman. Viking Press, 1980. 4–7.

A collection of Don Freeman's illustrations has been gathered posthumously. The author describes the lovely pictures through the eyes of a small child looking into the wide wonderful world on a pleasant day.

Lapp, Eleanor J. **In the Morning Mist.** Illus. David Cunningham. Albert Whitman, 1978. 4–8.

Pale watercolor illustrations evoke a gentle mood as a young boy and his grandfather go on an early morning fishing expedition. The mist transforms the countryside into a magical haven for sheep, spiderwebs, rabbits, horses, and deer before the sun breaks through on a clear, bright day. (Picture book)

McGee, Myra. **Willie's Garden.** Illus. by author. Rodale Press, 1977. 4–7.

Little Willie happily plants one plant at a time and before he realizes it, he finds himself in a big garden. An appealing story about gardening for the young child with colorful pictures of the seasons. The names of many fruits and vegetables are introduced to the beginning reader. (Picture book)

Mack, Gail. **Yesterday's Snowman.** Illus. Erik Blegvad. Pantheon Books, 1979. 4–7.

A quiet winter mood book. A mother and two children share the joys of building a snowman. So great is that joy that they do not feel sad when the rain comes and melts their handiwork. Soft, realistic illustrations reflect the mood perfectly. (Picture book)

Norris, Louanne, and Howard E. Smith, Jr. **An Oak Tree Dies and a Journey Begins.** Illus. Allen Davis. Crown Publishers, 1979. 6–9.

This life cycle story is seldom told. An oak tree dies. Part of it falls into a stream where it becomes home for animals and water plants. Eventually, it travels into the ocean and is washed onto a beach where it is claimed as driftwood. Black and white illustrations. (Picture book)

Rice, Eve. **Goodnight, Goodnight.** Greenwillow Books, 1980. 3–5.

Goodnight is creeping through the city. It comes to the police officer, the little girl, and the chestnut vendor. It finally comes to the kitten whose mother takes him home. Outstanding black and white full-page drawings with touches of bright yellow. A charming nighttime story.

Ryder, Joanne. **A Wet and Sandy Day.** Illus. Donald Carrick. Harper & Row, Publishers, 1977. 4–7.

An independent little girl with "sunny feelings" goes to the beach and has a glorious time, quite by herself, despite the rain. The full-page sand and sea colored illustrations capture both the spirit of the text and the spirit of an adventurous, happy child. (Picture book)

Trimby, Elisa. **Mr. Plum's Paradise.** Lothrop, Lee & Shepard Books, 1977. All ages.

Mr. Plum has an idea; why doesn't he make a garden in the backyard? The neighborhood is dingy and unattractive and a garden will transform it into a colorful world of beauty. The neighbors copy his plan. Unusual visitors come to enjoy it. Exceptionally beautiful, intricate illustrations. (Picture book)

Ward, Leila. **I Am Eyes: Ni Macho.** Illus. Nonny Hogrogian. Greenwillow Books, 1978. 7–10.

An African child wakes to the morning marvels of her native land. She sees what the sun sees: sunflowers and skies, giraffes and grasses. Full-page illustrations give a panorama of the Kenyan landscape. (Picture book)

Yano, Shigeko (translator Yukiko Kawakami). **One Spring Day.** Judson Press, 1977. 4–7.

Beautiful soft-colored illustrations depict what a young boy believes. Some things he can see, like the meadow over the hill or the stars in the sky, and other things he cannot, like the song of the bird or the scent of the flowers. These he just believes. (Picture book)

School

Allard, Harry. **Miss Nelson Is Missing!** Illus. James Marshall. Houghton Mifflin, 1977. 8–12.

Nice Miss Nelson's class is the worst behaved in school. They throw spitballs and paper planes. They are rude. Suddenly Miss Nelson disappears and a witchy substitute makes the children work hard. They try unsuccessfully to find Miss Nelson; the surprise ending lets the reader in on the secret. (Picture book)

Atkinson, Mary. **Maria Teresa.** Illus. Christine Engla Eber. Lollipop Power, 1979. 7–10.

Maria Teresa moves to a school where the children laugh at her name and no one speaks Spanish. She is unhappy until she brings her puppet, Monteja, who speaks only Spanish. Monteja tells the children about Maria Teresa and they begin to appreciate her. Useful for discussion on differences; some Spanish words. (Picture book)

Chorao, Kay. **Molly's Lies.** Illus. by author. Seabury Press, 1979. 5–8.

It is Molly's first day at school. She is afraid and hides her fears by lying. She joins other children in taunting the new boy until she realizes he might be as frightened as she is. (Picture book)

Cohen, Miriam. **Lost in the Museum.** Illus. Lillian Hoban. Greenwillow Books, 1979. 4–7.

Danny's enthusiasm to see the dinosaurs leads to half the first-grade class getting lost in the museum. He also saves the day by finding the teacher. Good for class discussion. (Picture book)

Cohen, Miriam. **No Good in Art.** Illus. Lillian Hoban. Greenwillow Books, 1980. 4–7.

First-grader Jim thinks he is no good in art. He makes his grass thick and his people with no necks. One day in art he hides his picture but his friends find it. All the pictures are hung for everyone to see. The children gather around to admire only one. Whose? (Picture book)

Cohen, Miriam. **When Will I Read?** Illus. Lillian Hoban. Greenwillow Books, 1977. 4–7.

Jim is impatient to learn how to read. His first-grade teacher encourages him to be patient and assures him that he will read when he is ready. Good read-aloud book. (Picture book)

Conford, Ellen. **The Revenge of the Incredible Dr. Rancid and His Youthful Assistant, Jeffrey.** Little, Brown, 1980. 10–12.

Jeffrey, the skinniest kid in sixth grade, has an alter ego who comes alive in his secret notebook. In his fantasies he rids the world of his archenemy, Dewey Belasco. But in real life he would never dare stand up to him, or would he?

Delton, Judy. **The New Girl at School.** Illus. Lillian Hoban. E. P. Dutton, 1979. 6–9.

For the first few days at a new school the little girl feels lonely and incompetent. But she and her mother give it time, and good things begin to happen. Well written and sensitively illustrated in soft colors. (Picture book)

de Paola, Tomie. **Oliver Button Is a Sissy.** Illus. by author. Harcourt Brace Jovanovich, 1979. 6–12.

Oliver Button likes to draw pictures, read books, play dress-up, and take dancing lessons, but he messes up at baseball. The boys tease him. "Oliver Button Is a Sissy" gets written on the school wall. How and why the sign and the attitudes get changed makes for good reading and class discussion. Superbly illustrated. (Picture book)

Feder, Paula Kurzband. **Where Does the Teacher Live?** Illus. Lillian Hoban. E. P. Dutton, 1979. 6–9.

In this intriguing easy reader, three classmates become detectives in order to answer the burning question in the title. Perhaps all of the teachers live in school. Not so, they discover. Their teacher lives someplace very special: in a houseboat! Charming illustrations. (Picture book)

Fife, Dale. **Who'll Vote for Lincoln?** Illus. Paul Galdone. Coward, McCann & Geoghegan, 1977. 7–10.

Lincoln's class elections are complicated by modern political strategies and a neighborhood police problem. Lincoln learns something about the pressure of campaigning and about himself. Another worthwhile book about the black child, Lincoln.

Gordon, Shirley. **Me and the Bad Guys.** Illus. Edward Frascino. Harper & Row, Publishers, 1980. 8–12.

Mike Berger, one of the good guys, is angry because his basketball has been stolen by one of the bad guys. Life seems even more unfair when it is returned flat as a pancake. How Mike loses his cool and almost becomes a bad guy is humorously told.

Haywood, Carolyn. **Betsy's Play School.** Illus. James Griffin. William Morrow, 1977. 6–9.

Energetic Betsy decides to organize a play school for the youngsters in the neighborhood. She discovers that teaching school isn't all that easy; there's more to it than passing out milk and cookies. Appealing pencil drawings depict her students and complement the text. Good for reading aloud.

Isadora, Rachel. **Willaby.** Macmillan Publishing, 1977. 6–9.

First-grader Willaby loves to draw. During lessons, recess, and after school, Willaby draws. Instead of copying the get-well poem for her dear teacher, Willaby draws a fire engine and forgets to sign her name! Will Miss Finney be angry? The outcome is satisfying and so are the illustrations. (Picture book)

Mack, Bruce. **Jesse's Dream Skirt.** Illus. Marian Buchanan. Lollipop Power, 1979. 6–9.

Dedicated to all persons who feel out of place, this book tells of a preschool boy who longs to wear a skirt. When he wears one, his daycare classmates tease him. The understanding black male teacher helps Jesse's adjustment by encouraging discussion and dressing up in homemade costumes. Good for building views of differences. (Picture book)

Morrison, Bill. **Louis James Hates School.** Illus. by author. Houghton Mifflin, 1978. 5–8.

Louis James quits first grade to seek his fortune, starting out as a skywriter who can't spell and descending through a series of jobs to end up as a Prune Peeler. He quits in disgust, retrieves his books, and "turns to page one." Cartoony, but a sure-fire hit. (Picture book)

Noble, Trinka Hakes. **The Day Jimmy's Boa Ate the Wash.** Illus. Steven Kellogg. Dial Press, 1980. 4–7.

Jimmy secretly takes his pet boa constrictor on a class field trip to a farm. Havoc ensues, from egg throwing to the boa's eating the farmer's clean clothes. Bright, action-filled illustrations match this silly, cumulative tale. (Picture book)

Peck, Robert Newton. **Mr. Little.** Illus. Ben Stahl. Doubleday, 1979. 8–12.

Drag and Finley look forward to having pretty Miss Kellogg for a teacher, but on the first day of school Mr. Little makes his appearance instead. They plan tricks to make him the spectacle of the town. Two boys learn an important lesson. Black and white illustrations.

Perl, Lila. **Don't Ask Miranda.** Seabury Press, 1979. 10–12.

This realistically-written story is about Miranda, a thirteen-year-old girl who is friendless because of her peripatetic parents. In order to win friends in another new school she soon learns that painful decisions must be made. Characters are well portrayed. Excellent for discussion.

Price, Michelle. **Mean Melissa.** Illus. by author. Bradbury Press, 1977. 4–7.

Three kindergarten children experience the problem of getting along because Melissa is always telling Samantha her pictures are ugly. With the aid of Jonathan's creative and humorous idea, the children work out their own problem. The wash and pencil illustrations add validity and insight. (Picture book)

Thwaite, Ann. **The Chatterbox.** Illus. Glenys Ambrus. Andre Deutsch. 1978. 4–7.

Everyone at Salad Street School liked to talk, except Miss Walters who had the Chatterbox built before she and her class could reach a compromise. Bold and amusing full-color illustrations of a multi-racial English school. (Picture book)

Wolf, Bernard. **Adam Smith Goes to School.** J. B. Lippincott, 1978. 4–7.

Adam begins his first day of school by entering into many new learning experiences. The realistic photography presents an accurate and detailed account of what children can expect when they go to school. (Picture book)

Sports

Bonham, Frank. **The Rascals from Haskell's Gym.** E. P. Dutton, 1977. 8–12.

Sissy Benedict is key gymnast of the Butterflies gymnastics team. But as the grudge match with archrivals Haskell's Raskells approaches, she is distracted by her father's struggle to save a historic hotel landmark. Mystery, suspense, and humor are combined with details of practice sessions and competitions.

Etter, Les. **Get Those Rebounds!** Illus. James Calvin. Hastings House, Publishers, 1978. 10–12.

Basketball is sixteen-year-old Rick's main interest, but what chance does he have? Overshadowed by his older brother, everyone seems to enjoy making comparisons. In a fit of anger he quits the team. An easy-to-read, enjoyable story with well-developed characters. Black and white illustrations.

Fenner, Carol. **The Skates of Uncle Richard.** Illus. Ati Forberg. Random House, 1978. 7–10.

Young Marsha, nine, dreams of becoming an ice-skating champion. Her first day on ice is very discouraging, until her Uncle Richard offers encouragement and sound advice. Dreams being realized and family concern are themes the young reader can understand. Soft black and white illustrations blend with gentle story.

Gault, William Campbell. **Cut-Rate Quarterback.** E. P. Dutton, 1977. 10–up.

Joe Rogers, a 160-pound quarterback, is a superb high school football player. Later, as one of the Chicago Miners, he is faced with problems of many kinds, but his tenacious will urges him on. A fast-paced story illustrated with photographs.

Harris, Robie H. **Rosie's Double Dare.** Illus. Tony DeLuna. Alfred A. Knopf, 1980. 7–10.

Eight-year-old Rosie accepts a dare because she wants to be part of the Willard Street Gang and play baseball with them. She gets into more trouble than she expects. In the end she's a hero when the gang wins the neighborhood championship baseball game with her help.

Kalb, Jonah. **The Goof That Won the Pennant.** Illus. Sandy Kossin. Houghton Mifflin, 1976. 8–12.

This story of a no-win team that becomes league champ is based on a true event in baseball history. The Blazers were a collection of losers until their coach talked them into trying to win and gave them self-confidence. Good read-aloud book.

Knudson, R. R. **Rinehart Lifts.** Farrar, Straus & Giroux, 1980. 7–10.

Rinehart, who can't run or kick a ball, and Zan, who is very sports-minded, are best friends. Together they exchange interests when Zan puts Rinehart on a weight-lifting program, and she takes care of his plants. A funny, high interest story.

Lee, H. Alton. **Seven Feet Four and Growing.** Westminster Press, 1978. 10–up.

Bill Saunders is fifteen years old and tall, *really* tall. Although he is the best player on the school basketball team, he plays only to please his father, his coach, and his friends. Actually, he dislikes basketball and is more interested in animals and the possibility of one day working with them. A veterinarian friend and a tall cheerleader help Bill resolve his dilemma.

Levy, Elizabeth. **The Tryouts.** Illus. Jacquie Hann. Four Winds Press, 1979. 10–12.

When two girls make the eighth-grade varsity basketball team, a popular but fat boy is cut. Girls and boys join forces to pressure the coach into putting him on the team. This humorous book addresses a timely subject.

Love, Sandra. **Melissa's Medley.** Harcourt Brace Jovanovich, 1978. 10–12.

Melissa has a strong competitive streak and vows to beat her long-time rival in an important swim meet. This success would assure her a place on the Olympic team and would attract attention from her estranged father. Shows the tense atmosphere of competitive swimming and the emotional struggles of a teenage girl.

Winthrop, Elizabeth. **Marathon Miranda.** Holiday House, 1979. 10–up.

Asthma-and-allergy-ridden Miranda meets Phoebe, an only child who is lonely, and starts jogging with her. To build up her lungs, Miranda works hard in preparation for running a 6.3 mile marathon. This is an interesting story with good jogging advice. A sequel is *Miranda in the Middle.*

Wiseman, Bernard. **The Lucky Runner.** Garrard Publishing, 1979. 7–9.

Runner Buddy Barnes believes his lucky socks account for his success in races. His coach says the real reason is that Buddy practices hard and wants to win. During the State Junior Championship race, Buddy learns the truth. Large print, three-color illustrations, easy to read. (Picture book)

Young and Old

Adler, C. S. **The Silver Coach.** Coward, McCann & Geoghegan, 1979. 10–12.

Chris, twelve, and her sister, six, do not want to spend the summer with a grandmother they hardly know in a remote woodland cabin. As Chris begins to know and love her grandmother, she learns to accept the truth about each of her parents, their divorce, and her own growing up.

Aliki. **The Two of Them.** Illus. by author. Greenwillow Books, 1979. All ages.

From the day she was born, when Grandfather made a ring for her, the love between this granddaughter and grandfather deepens. When

Grandfather becomes ill, she cares for him; when he dies, she cherishes her memories of him. Realistic description of a beautiful relationship. (Picture book)

Baker, Jeannie. **Grandfather.** Illus. by author. Andre Deutsch, 1979. 4–7.

A little girl whose grandfather owns a junk shop tells her story in the first person. The shop is full of surprises, and she loves to go there to work and play. The disorderly store comes alive in the collage illustrations. (Picture book)

Baker, Jeannie. **Grandmother.** Illus. by author. Andre Deutsch, 1978. 4–7.

A little girl comes to visit her grandmother who lives in a house surrounded by tall bushes. They share a happy loving day doing things together. The warm grandmother-granddaughter relationship is illustrated with handsome full-page collages. Companion volume to *Grandfather* by the same author. (Picture book)

Bosse, Malcolm J. **The 79 Squares.** Thomas Y. Crowell, 1979. 12–up.

Eric, fourteen, is involved with a gang. While on probation, he and an eighty-two-year-old man become friends. Eric spends long hours in the man's garden, carefully observing life in detail. When the man's past as a convicted murderer is revealed, Eric defends him against the townspeople's rejection. A moving story.

Cleaver, Vera, and Bill Cleaver. **Queen of Hearts.** J. B. Lippincott, 1978. 10–12.

Before her stroke, Wilma's seventy-nine-year-old grandmother felt and acted younger than her years. Now Granny scares away housekeeper-companions as fast as they are hired. Although they do not like each other, Wilma is crotchety Granny's choice for a companion. Together they experience what it means to grow old.

Clifford, Eth. **The Rocking Chair Rebellion.** Houghton Mifflin, 1978. 10–up.

Fourteen-year-old Opie visits a former neighbor, Mr. Pepper, who lives at Maple Ridge Home for the Aged. Volunteering to work at the home involves her with the problems of the home's residents. The theme of acceptance and segregation of older people in our society is sensitively presented.

Clymer, Eleanor. **The Get-Away Car.** E. P. Dutton, 1978. 8–12.

Maggie lives with Grandma whose motto is, "Fun first, work later," and fun it is. Maggie takes off with Grandma in an ancient car, thus eluding the authorities who are trying to separate them. A marvelous picture of a witty, intelligent, loving, but slightly disorganized senior citizen and her relationship with her granddaughter. Fun by itself, but great for discussion.

Corcoran, Barbara. **The Faraway Island**. Atheneum, 1977. 10–up.

Painfully shy, Lynn's problems of growing up are compounded when she goes to Nantucket Island to live for a year with a grandmother who is becoming increasingly senile. An enjoyable story.

Craft, Ruth. **Carrie Hepple's Garden**. Illus. Irene Haas. Atheneum, 1979. 4–7.

Luminous shades of green provide a misty background for this gentle mood story of a midsummer evening romp. When their ball sails over the wall into the garden of the mysterious Carrie Hepple, three children venture into the unknown where they meet the eccentric, but enchanting old lady. (Picture book)

Eisenberg, Phyllis Rose. **A Mitzvah Is Something Special**. Illus. Susan Jeschke. Harper & Row, Publishers, 1978. 7–10.

Lisa's two grandmothers are very different from each other. One loves to quilt and cook; the other loves to make music and dance. They both love Lisa and she finds a way to make a mitzvah for both of them. (Picture book)

Girion, Barbara. **Joshua, the Czar, and the Chicken Bone Wish**. Illus. Richard Cuffari. Charles Scribner's Sons, 1978. 8–12.

Joshua is the klutz of the fourth grade, the leftover when sports teams are chosen and, worse, the kid brother of a superstar. His friendship with an elderly man enables Josh to overcome his sense of failure and to develop some much needed self-confidence. The humor appeals to children, both klutzy and athletic.

Goffstein, M. B. **Fish for Supper**. Dial Press, 1976. 7–10.

A twist on the usual: here's a grandma who loves to fish. Her entire day is devoted to either fishing or putting the rest of life's necessities in order to allow more time for fishing. Economical line drawings; the book is a size youngsters love. 1977 Caldecott Honor Book. (Picture book)

Greenfield, Eloise. **Grandmama's Joy**. Illus. Carole Byard. William Collins Publishers, 1980. 6–9.

Young Rhondy, who lives with Grandmama, tries to cheer her up by singing and dancing, but it just doesn't work. Something serious is wrong; they must move. Charcoal drawings blend with this realistic story of binding love between granddaughter and grandmother in this black family. (Picture book)

Härtling, Peter (translator Anthea Bell). **Oma**. Illus. Jutta Ash. Harper & Row, Publishers, 1977. 8–12.

When five-year-old Kalle's parents are killed in an accident, he goes to live with his grandmother, Oma. They have heartwarming and funny adventures for five years. The story is narrated in the third person with Oma's brief italicized first-person account at each chapter's end. German setting.

Holland, Isabelle. **Now Is Not Too Late.** Lothrop, Lee & Shepard Books, 1980. 12–up.

Cathy's summer on a Maine island with her grandmother stretches lazily ahead of her until she meets the lady who moves into the stone cottage. As eleven-year-old Cathy uncovers her secret, she also discovers something about her own past that is both frightening and exciting.

Holmes, Efner Tudor. **Carrie's Gift.** Illus. Tasha Tudor. William Collins Publishers, 1978. 7–10.

Carrie often wonders about Old Duncan, whose vine-covered cabin is across the field from her home. Expressive watercolors illustrate her attempt to become friends when she takes a strawberry shortcake to him. Later, when Heidi, her dog, is caught in a trap, Old Duncan comes to the rescue and strengthens their friendship.

Irwin, Hadley. **The Lilith Summer.** Feminist Press, 1979. 10–12.

Ellen wants a ten-speed bike and agrees to "lady-sit" for Lilith who is seventy-seven; Lilith wants new screens for her house and agrees to "baby-sit" for Ellen. Out of initial misunderstanding and distrust, mutual love and understanding grow. Sensitively written, this book captures the spirit of a young girl and the indomitable gallantry and wisdom of an old woman as they share a lingering summer.

Jewell, Nancy. **Bus Ride.** Illus. Ronald Himler. Harper & Row, Publishers, 1978. 4–7.

A night bus ride alone can be frightening for a little girl. Janie meets Mrs. Rivers, who helps her enjoy the journey to her waiting grandpa. Black and white illustrations enhance the warmth shared between an old woman and a child. Good for stimulating discussion. (Picture book)

Kesselman, Wendy. **Emma.** Illus. Barbara Cooney. Doubleday, 1980. 8–12.

A lonely seventy-two-year-old woman receives a painting of her home town. After analyzing the painting she decides it is not right, so she buys materials and paints her own picture. The hobby continues and her loneliness vanishes. Unique illustrations with two styles of painting. (Picture book)

Kroll, Steven. **If I Could Be My Grandmother.** Illus. Lady McCrady. Pantheon Books, 1977. 3–5.

If Steffie were a grandmother, she would wear long robes, bake cookies, and spend weekends with her granddaughter. Amusing pastel illustrations complement the story, revealing the love of Steffie for her grandmother. (Picture book)

Lasky, Kathryn. **My Island Grandma.** Illus. Emily McCully. Frederick Warne, 1979. 7–10.

This Cape Cod grandmother spends the summer teaching her granddaughter how to sail, swim, float, take down shutters, garden, and make soup and salad from periwinkles and sea herbs. Soft watercolor with ink illustrations help raise readers' consciousness about older people. All grannies do not sit and knit! (Picture book)

Mearian, Judy Frank. **Someone Slightly Different.** Dial Press, 1980. 8–12.

Twelve-year-old Marty is having a hard time at school and at home until her grandmother Flossie arrives and helps her resolve her feelings about growing up without a father. The sensitive quality of both the story and the characters make the book unique.

Pollowitz, Melinda. **Cinnamon Cane.** Harper & Row, Publishers, 1977. 10–12.

Cassie and her grandfather have a very special caring relationship. She refuses to admit that he is growing old and helps him fight those who take away his independence step by step. As grandfather's world becomes more and more circumscribed, Cassie reaches out for a clearer identity.

Roth, David. **The Hermit of Fog Hollow Station.** Beaufort Books, 1980. 12–up.

When twelve-year-old Alex moves to the country, he doesn't seem to fit in or make friends except for Old Man Turner, the hermit of Fog Hollow Station. Here is a poignant story of the friendship between young and old. Each gives of himself until Mr. Turner's death.

Vogel, Ilse-Margret. **Dodo Every Day.** Illus. by author. Harper & Row, Publishers, 1977. 6–9.

This gentle book's chapter headings reflect a range of human emotions: sadness, jealousy, shame, pride, and happiness. The young narrator learns to cope with her feelings through the wise and loving help of Dodo, her grandmother. Self-acceptance and understanding radiate from pages illuminated by soft pencil drawings. (Picture book)

Walter, Mildred Pitts. **Ty's One-man Band.** Illus. Margot Tomes. Four Winds Press, 1980. 4–7.

One hot, humid day Ty goes down to the pond and spies an unusual man. He becomes acquainted with Andro, a one-man band with a washboard, comb, spoons, and pail, who later that evening provides delightful entertainment for the town. Beautifully written and illustrated. (Picture book)

Wittman, Sally. **A Special Trade.** Illus. Karen Gundersheimer. Harper & Row, Publishers, 1978. 3–5.

Little Nellie and elderly Bartholomew, her neighbor, are always together; their friends call them "ham and eggs." Bartholomew takes Nellie for a walk in her stroller every day. As she grows older they trade places, a very special trade. Humorous pen sketches complete this story of contrasts. (Picture book)

York, Carol Beach. **The Look-Alike Girl.** Beaufort Books, 1980. 8–12.

Charlene promotes the friendship of old Mrs. Mayfield and her eight-year-old cousin because she doesn't want Gracie tagging along with her all summer. A special bond grows between the old and the young as Gracie earns a place in the hearts of both Mrs. Mayfield and Charlene.

Additional Contemporary Realistic Fiction Books

Alexander, Martha. *Nobody Asked Me If I Wanted a Baby Sister.* Dial Press, 1971. 4–7.

Ball, Zachary. *Bristle Face.* Holiday House, 1962. 12–up.

Bemelmans, Ludwig. *Madeline.* Viking Press, 1939, 1962. 4–8.

Blue, Rose. *Grandma Didn't Wave Back.* Illus. Ted Lewin. Franklin Watts, 1972. 8–12.

Blue, Rose. *A Month of Sundays.* Illus. Ted Lewin. Franklin Watts, 1972 8–10.

Blume, Judy. *Are You There, God? It's Me, Margaret.* Bradbury Press, 1970. 10–14.

Bødker, Cecil. *The Leopard.* Translated by Gunnar Poulsen. Atheneum, 1975. 10–12.

Bonsall, Crosby. *The Case of the Hungry Stranger.* Harper & Row, Publishers, 1963. 5–10.

Boston, L. M. *A Stranger at Green Knowe.* Illus. Peter Boston. Harcourt Brace Jovanovich, 1961. 9–11.

Burch, Robert. *Queenie Peavey.* Illus. Jerry Lazare. Viking Press, 1966. 10–14.

Burnford, Sheila. *The Incredible Journey.* Illus. Carl Burger. Little, Brown, 1961. 9–up.

Byars, Betsy. *Summer of the Swans.* Illus. Ted Coconis. Viking Press, 1970. 10–up.

Childress, Alice. *A Hero Ain't Nothin' but a Sandwich.* Coward, McCann & Geoghegan, 1973. 12–up.

Christopher, Matt. *The Year Mom Won the Pennant.* Illus. Foster Caddell. Little, Brown, 1968. 9–12.

Clark, Ann Nolan. *In My Mother's House.* Illus. Velino Herrera. Viking Press, 1941. 7–10.

Cleary, Beverly. *Ramona the Brave.* Illus. Alan Tiegreen. William Morrow, 1975. 8–12.

Cleaver, Vera, and Bill Cleaver. *Where the Lilies Bloom.* Illus. James Spanfeller. J. B. Lippincott, 1969. 10–up.

Clifton, Lucille. *My Brother Fine with Me.* Illus. Moneta Barnett. Holt, Rinehart & Winston, 1975. 5–8.

Corbett, Scott. *The Turnabout Trick.* Illus. Paul Galdone. Little, Brown, 1967. 8–12.

Cunningham, Julia. *Dorp Dead.* Illus. James Spanfeller. Pantheon Books, 1965. 10–up.

Dunn, Mary Lois. *The Man in the Box: A Story from Vietnam.* McGraw-Hill, 1968. 12–up.

Estes, Eleanor. *The Hundred Dresses.* Illus. Louis Slobodkin. Harcourt Brace Jovanovich, 1944. 10–12.

Ets, Marie Hall. *Gilberto and the Wind.* Viking Press, 1963. 3–6.

Ets, Marie Hall. *Play with Me.* Viking Press, 1955. 3–6.

Fitzhugh, Louise. *Harriet the Spy.* Harper & Row, Publishers, 1964. 10–14.

Fox, Paula. *How Many Miles to Babylon?* Illus. Paul Giovanopoulos. David White, 1967. 9–12.

Friis-Baastad, Babbis. *Don't Take Teddy.* Translated by Lise McKinnon. Charles Scribner's Sons, 1967. 10–14.

Gates, Doris. *Blue Willow.* Illus. Paul Lantz. Viking Press, 1940. 10–12.

George, Jean Craighead. *Julie of the Wolves.* Illus. John Schoenherr. Harper & Row, Publishers, 1972.

George, Jean Craighead. *My Side of the Mountain.* E. P. Dutton, 1959. 10–14.

Greene, Bette. *Philip Hall Likes Me, I Reckon Maybe.* Illus. Charles Lilly. Dial Press, 1974. 9–12.

Greene, Constance C. *A Girl Called Al.* Illus. Byron Barton. Viking Press, 1969. 8–12.

Hamilton, Virginia. *The House of Dies Drear.* Illus. Eros Keith. Macmillan Publishing, 1968. 10–up.

Hamilton, Virginia. *M. C. Higgins, the Great.* Macmillan Publishing, 1974. 10–up.

Holling, Holling C. *Pagoo.* Houghton Mifflin, 1957. 8–12.

Holman, Felice. *Slake's Limbo.* Charles Scribner's Sons, 1974. 12–up.

Hunt, Irene. *Up a Road Slowly.* Follett Publishing, 1966. 12–up.

Keats, Ezra Jack. *The Snowy Day.* Viking Press, 1962. 3–6.

Keats, Ezra Jack. *Whistle for Willie.* Viking Press, 1964. 3–6.

Kjelgaard, Jim. *Big Red.* Illus. Bob Kuhn. Holiday House, 1956. 10–up.

Konigsburg, E. L. *Father's Arcane Daughter.* Atheneum, 1976. 10–14.

Konigsburg, E. L. *From the Mixed-Up Files of Mrs. Basil E. Frankweiler.* Atheneum, 1967. 8–12.

Lexau, Joan M. *Emily and the Klunky Baby and the Next-Door Dog.* Illus. Martha Alexander. Dial Press, 1972. 5–9.

Little, Jean. *Mine for Keeps.* Illus. Lewis Parker. Little, Brown, 1962. 9–12.

McCloskey, Robert. *Blueberries for Sal.* Viking Press, 1948. 3–6.

McCloskey, Robert. *Homer Price.* Viking Press, 1943. 10–14.

McCloskey, Robert. *The Morning in Maine.* Viking Press, 1952. 5–8.

McCloskey, Robert. *Time of Wonder.* Viking Press, 1957. 5–up.

Mathis, Sharon Bell. *The Hundred Penny Box.* Illus. Leo Dillon and Diane Dillon. Viking Press, 1975. 6–10.

Mazer, Norma Fox. *A Figure of Speech.* Delacorte Press, 1973. 12–up.

Miles, Miska. *Annie and the Old One.* Illus. Peter Parnall. Little, Brown, 1971. 6–9.

Mohr, Nicholasa. *Nilda.* Harper & Row, Publishers, 1973. 10–up.

Morey, Walter. *Gentle Ben.* Illus. John Schoenherr. E. P. Dutton, 1965. 10–14.

Ness, Evaline. *Josefina February.* Charles Scribner's Sons, 1963. 5–9.

Ness, Evaline. *Sam, Bangs and Moonshine.* Holt, Rinehart and Winston, 1966. 4–8.

Neville, Emily. *It's Like This, Cat.* Illus. Emil Weiss. Harper & Row, Publishers, 1963. 10–14.

O'Dell, Scott. *Island of the Blue Dolphins.* Houghton Mifflin, 1960. 11–14.

Raskin, Ellen. *Nothing Ever Happens on My Block.* Atheneum, 1966. 5–9.
Sachs, Marilyn. *The Bears' House.* Illus. Louis Glanzman. Doubleday, 1971. 9–13.
Scott, Ann Herbert. *Sam.* Illus. Symeon Shimin. McGraw-Hill, 1967. 4–7.
Slote, Alfred. *Hang Tough, Paul Mather.* J. B. Lippincott, 1973. 9–12.
Smith, Doris Buchanan. *A Taste of Blackberries.* Illus. Charles Robinson. Thomas Y. Crowell, 1973. 6–10.
Sonneborn, Ruth A. *Friday Night Is Papa Night.* Illus. Emily A. McCully. Viking Press, 1970. 4–8.
Steptoe, John. *Stevie.* Harper & Row, Publishers, 1969. 4–8.
Ullman, James. *Banner in the Sky.* J. B. Lippincott, 1954. 12–up.
Viorst, Judith. *Alexander and the Terrible, Horrible, No Good, Very Bad Day.* Illus. Ray Cruz. Atheneum, 1972. 5–8.
Viorst, Judith. *The Tenth Good Thing about Barney.* Illus. Erik Blegvad. Atheneum, 1971. 5–9.
Ward, Lynd. *The Biggest Bear.* Houghton Mifflin, 1952. 4–8.
Weik, Mary Hays. *The Jazz Man.* Illus. Ann Grifalconi. Atheneum, 1968. 8–12.
Wersba, Barbara. *The Dream Watcher.* Atheneum, 1968. 12–up.
Wier, Esther. *The Loner.* Illus. Christine Price. David McKay, 1963. 11–up.
Wilkinson, Brenda. *Ludell.* Harper & Row, Publishers, 1975. 9–up.
Wojciechowska, Maia. *Shadow of a Bull.* Illus. Alvin Smith. Atheneum, 1964. 10–14.
Yashima, Taro. *Crow Boy.* Viking Press, 1955. 6–12.
Zolotow, Charlotte. *William's Doll.* Illus. William Pène du Bois. Harper & Row, 1972. 4–8.

Poetry

Animals

Adoff, Arnold. **Friend Dog.** Illus. Troy Howell. J. B. Lippincott, 1980. All ages.

A dog, mauled by a pack of wild dogs, is found by a young girl. This story describes the growth of their friendship and the small daily joys of their relationship. A gentle tale illustrated by soft pencil drawings that capture the depth of affection between girl and dog.

Blegvad, Lenore, compiler. **This Little Pig-A-Wig and Other Rhymes about Pigs.** Illus. Erik Blegvad. Atheneum, 1978. 4–7.

This collection of twenty-two poems includes old English and American rhymes that have been favorites for many generations. Pigs are pictured in serious and jovial moods. Energetic ones go to market while others dance a jig and wear a wig. The full-color and pen and ink sketches are complementary.

Cole, William, compiler. **An Arkful of Animals.** Illus. Lynn Munsinger. Houghton Mifflin, 1978. 7–10.

Fifty-three delightful poems about animals, domestic and wild. A few of the entries are old standards but most have not been anthologized widely. Light and humorous, the poems are enhanced by funny black and white illustrations.

Cole, William, compiler. **Dinosaurs and Beasts of Yore.** Illus. Susanna Natti. Putnam Publishing Group, 1979. 7–10.

Fossil fans enjoy these thirty-nine humorous poems by British and American poets. Various poetic forms and black and white sketches add to the amusement of the verses about extinct animals.

Farber, Norma. **Never Say Ugh to a Bug.** Illus. Jose Aruego. Greenwillow Books, 1979. 6–9.

The microscopic world of insects and creeping animals provides an unusual and interesting focus for these twenty poems about snails, crickets, and caterpillars.

Gardner, John. **A Child's Bestiary.** Alfred A. Knopf, 1977. 6–up.

From "The African Wild Dog" to "The Zebra," sixty poems celebrate the alphabet from A to Z. The humor of the poems ranges from nonsense to subtle satire.

Hopkins, Lee Bennett, compiler. **Kits, Cats, Lions and Tigers.** Illus. Vera Rosenberry. Albert Whitman, 1979. 8–12.

This collection of stories, verses, and poems is about all kinds of cats. Some cats are impossibly wise, others impossibly foolish. All are amusing—especially for cat fanciers.

Hopkins, Lee Bennett, compiler. **My Mane Catches the Wind.** Illus. Sam Savitt. Harcourt Brace Jovanovich, 1979. 8–12.

Twenty-two poems about horses, each contributing to a sensitive understanding of this servant and friend of humans, make up this collection. Handsome halftone illustrations enrich each selection. Table of contents and index make selections easy.

Hopkins, Lee Bennett, compiler. **Pups, Dogs, Foxes and Wolves.** Illus. Vera Rosenberry. Albert Whitman, 1979. 9–up.

Stories, poems, and verse on members of the canine family are collected here. Some stories are funny and others may cause the reader to blink back a tear, but all are absorbing. This would be useful for units on dogs or domesticated animals as well as for reading aloud. Black and white sketches.

Lewin, Betsy. **Animal Snackers.** Photographs by Vincent Colabella. Dodd, Mead, 1980. 4–7.

Nearly everyone has a favorite snack, including animals. In catchy four-line rhymes, the reader learns what eleven animals like to eat. Raccoons raid garbage cans while puffins enjoy herring. Creatively illustrated with bread-dough animals; also includes a simple recipe for making them.

Oliver, Robert S. **Cornucopia.** Illus. Frederick Henry Belli. Atheneum, 1978. 8–12.

Witty poems about familiar and fabulous animals are alphabetically conceived. The verses cleverly express common experiences with other living creatures and give ribtickling presentations of animals unusual or rare. Meticulous ink drawings perfectly complement the poet's humorous conceptions.

Everyday Events

Adoff, Arnold. **Eats.** Illus. Susan Russo. Lothrop, Lee & Shepard Books, 1979. 8–12.

A recipe for apple pie, an ode to French toast, and a lament on the paucity of morsels when using chopsticks are the (food) stuff of this poetry collection. The avant-garde nonpunctuated spacing of the lines and the surreal illustrations of food make this a visually pleasing gastronomic experience.

Fisher, Aileen. **Out in the Dark and Daylight.** Illus. Gail Owens. Harper & Row, Publishers, 1980. 7–10.

"Let's pick clovers between our toes out in the yard where the clover grows." Going barefoot, getting presents, and watching birds are but a few of the experiences of a child in this lovely collection of 140 poems by the recipient of the 1978 NCTE Poetry Award. Graceful pencil illustrations.

Greenfield, Eloise. **Honey, I Love, and Other Love Poems.** Illus. Diane Dillon and Leo Dillon. Thomas Y. Crowell, 1978. 8–12.

Sixteen tender, rich, and varied poems make up this book about the wonderful things in a child's life: playing with dolls, jumping rope, and dressing up. The illustrations are an interplay of realism and fantasy that highlight the relationship between sensory word and sensed world. Small in size and scope, a fine format.

Hopkins, Lee Bennett, compiler. **Morning, Noon and Nighttime, Too.** Illus. Nancy Hannans. Harper & Row, Publishers, 1980. 6–9.

These poems reflect everyday happenings, such as early morning "toothpaste foam," school giggles, and "listening to the day shut tight." Soft pencil illustrations are a bonus.

Mitchell, Cynthia. **Playtime.** Illus. Satomi Ichikawa. William Collins Publishers, 1978. 3–7.

Simple rhymes about children playing are exquisitely pictured in full color. The playtime activities encourage children to participate.

Thurman, Judith. **Lost and Found.** Illus. Reina Rubel. Atheneum, 1978. 4–7.

The concept of lost and found is explored in poetry through such illustrations as sand castles lost to the waves but replaced by sea treasures washed to the shore, and ice-cream cones lost to the child but found by a hungry puppy. A fresh perspective on common occurrences.

Worth, Valerie. **More Small Poems.** Illus. Natalie Babbitt. Farrar, Straus & Giroux, 1976. 8–12.

The content of these poems about everyday objects and events appeals to the young, and the clear style leaves definite images in the mind of the reader or listener. Black pen drawings.

Worth, Valerie. **Still More Small Poems.** Illus. Natalie Babbitt. Farrar, Straus & Giroux, 1978. 7–10.

Another fine collection following two similar books, the twenty-five poems are on simple topics like a cat bath, the backyard, and rags. Childlike in theme and form so that they are easily understood, they contain thoughtful kernels. Delicately illustrated.

The Feelings of Children

Adoff, Arnold. **I Am the Running Girl.** Illus. Ronald Himler. Harper & Row, Publishers, 1979. 10–up.

"I am the running girl who runs to win" is how a young girl describes her joy and pride in running. Adoff's use of free verse is artistically interwoven with the black and white drawings.

Adoff, Arnold. **Under the Early Morning Trees.** Illus. Ronald Himler. E. P. Dutton, 1978. 7–10.

A girl walks under a long row of trees early in the morning to awaken and to be alone. The animals, birds, and plants share her solitary moments. The author's skillfully crafted poem helps the reader see and feel the girl's closeness to nature.

Adoff, Arnold. **Where Wild Willie.** Illus. Emily Arnold McCully. Harper & Row, Publishers, 1978. 5–8.

Wild Willie runs away for the day and explores all the exciting places where she can hide. When night comes, Willie is glad to return home to her urban black family and still be free. Strong rhythmic verse and soft pastels add appeal to this small poetry book that stresses alliteration.

Cole, William, compiler. **I'm Mad at You.** Illus. George MacClain. William Collins Publishers, 1978. 6–up.

This anthology of humorous verse centers on feelings of rage and temper. Such poems as Cole's "I'm So Mad I Could Scream" and Merriam's "Mean Song" help children to recognize the fact that frustrations are faced by all and to see how laughable reactions to those trying moments can be.

Grimes, Nikki. **Something on My Mind.** Illus. Tom Feelings. Dial Press, 1978. 10–up.

Poems in a city setting of black and white cover a broad range of feelings: love, isolation, loneliness, and friendship. Unrhymed, the poems evoke powerful images and emotions related to growing up.

Hopkins, Lee Bennett, compiler. **By Myself.** Illus. Glo Coalson. Thomas Y. Crowell, 1980. 8–12.

Black and white drawings add to the expressive mood of this collection of poems about being alone. Poets included are Myra Cohn

Livingston, David McCord, Karla Kuskin, Charlotte Zolotow, Felice Holman, and Lilian Moore.

Hopkins, Lee Bennett, compiler. **Go to Bed!** Illus. Rosekrans Hoffman. Alfred A. Knopf, 1979. 6–9.

A poem to tell of loneliness, or nighttime antics, or just-one-more-minute is just right when bedtime comes. A poem to wonder about stars or tomorrow helps sleep come. Black and white sketches on each page complete a delightful small collection.

Larrick, Nancy, compiler. **Bring Me All of Your Dreams.** Photographs by Larry Mulvehill. M. Evans, 1980. 10–12.

Included in this collection are poems about dreams and dreamers by William Stafford, Langston Hughes, Walter de la Mare, Carl Sandburg, e. e. cummings, David McCord, and others. Illustrated with photographs.

Maher, Ramona. **Alice Yazzie's Year.** Illus. Stephen Gammell. Coward, McCann & Geoghegan, 1977. 8–12.

Twelve free verse poems recount a year in the life of an eleven-year-old Navajo girl. They describe her grandfather's hogan at Black Mountain, the beliefs and customs of her people, and the white world's intrusion. The glowing sepia-colored illustrations are appropriate. A four-page commentary on Navajo life is included.

Marzollo, Jean. **Close Your Eyes.** Illus. Susan Jeffers. Dial Press, 1978. 3–5.

A lullaby is humorously and delicately illustrated, depicting a loving father who has problems putting his young unwilling child to bed. Preschoolers can enjoy and relate to this familiar routine.

Tudor, Tasha, compiler. **The Springs of Joy.** Rand McNally, 1979. 6–9.

A collection of sayings that have brought joy to people has been beautifully illustrated. The verses are from Wilde, Thoreau, Shakespeare, Donne, Wordsworth, Emerson, James, and others.

Watson, Nancy Dingman. **Blueberries Lavender: Songs of the Farmer's Children.** Illus. Erik Blegvad. Addison-Wesley Publishing, 1977. All ages.

Gentle verses that weave a portrait of life in the country: gathering berries ("blueberries high, huckleberries low"), churning butter, and swinging on monkey vines. Quiet pen and wash illustrations capture these special moments.

Wood, Nancy. **War Cry on a Prayer Feather: Prose and Poetry of the Ute Indians.** Doubleday, 1979. All ages.

Here are the laments, paeans, and words of wisdom of the little-known tribe of Ute Indians who now survive on three western reservations. Like the flames of a bright fire being slowly smothered, these Native Americans strive to preserve their spiritual values through poetry and prose, authentically interpreted in this volume. Fine full-page photographs.

Ghosts and Magic

Hopkins, Lee Bennett, compiler. **Elves, Fairies, & Gnomes.** Illus. Rosekrans Hoffman. Alfred A. Knopf, 1980. 6–9.

The common theme throughout this excellent collection of seventeen poems is the belief in elves, fairies, and gnomes. The poems are imaginative without being frightening. Soft black and white illustrations blend with the magical words and mood of the poems.

Prelutsky, Jack. **Nightmares: Poems to Trouble Your Sleep.** Illus. Arnold Lobel. Greenwillow Books, 1976. All ages.

Deliciously shivery poems in a book where the bogeyman is finally pictured, along with a ghoul, an ogre, a werewolf, and others. The verses are spooky and humorous enough to be in constant demand. Excellent for vocabulary enrichment, poetry units, or just fun reading.

Wallace, Daisy, editor. **Fairy Poems.** Illus. Trina Schart Hyman. Holiday House, 1980. 6–9.

This child-sized anthology includes poets ranging from Shakespeare to Prelutsky. Expressive black and white illustrations complement the poetic imagery.

Wallace, Daisy, editor. **Ghost Poems.** Illus. Tomie de Paola. Holiday House, 1979. 6–up.

The "ghoulies and ghosties" of ancient Scotland and the tiger-like ghosts of the Araucanian Indians inhabit this book. There are watery phantoms from the deep, along with a teeny, tiny ghost who can only utter a teeny, tiny boo. A delightful anthology made even better by the illustrations.

Wallace, Daisy, editor. **Giant Poems.** Illus. Margot Tomes. Holiday House, 1978. 6–9.

This picture book anthology includes seventeen poems about giants, such as Blunderbore, Hickenthrift, Momotara, Stanley, and others. Line drawings capture their antics.

Humor

Aiken, Conrad. **A Little Who's Zoo of Mild Animals.** Illus. John Vernon Lord. Atheneum, 1977. 8–12.

The introduction assures the reader that the mixture of creatures met within the book is imaginary. Imagine meeting an Alligatorangutan,

Rhinocerostrich, Chimpanzebra and other fantastic creatures. They are described in humorous verse and striking illustrations. Children enjoy discovering the butterfly hidden in each picture.

Brewton, John E., and Lorraine A. Blackburn, compilers. **They've Discovered a Head in the Box for the Bread and Other Laughable Limericks.** Illus. Fernando Krahn. Thomas Y. Crowell, 1978. 8–12.

The title sets the tone for over two hundred funny limericks about topics as diverse as animals and love. One grouping includes rhymed spellings that need to be deciphered while another set allows the reader to write the last line. Illustrated with humorous black and white sketches.

Carroll, Lewis. **Lewis Carroll's Jabberwocky.** Illus. Jane Breskin Zalben. Frederick Warne, 1977. 10–up.

The classic nonsense poem from *Through the Looking Glass,* where Alice enlists the aid of Humpty Dumpty to help her understand, is recreated with expressive art and imaginative colored drawings. Useful for introducing Alice's other adventures.

Cole, William, compiler. **Oh, Such Foolishness!** Illus. Tomie de Paola. J. B. Lippincott, 1978. 6–up.

A collection of poems designed to make children of all ages chuckle. Included are such well-known poets as John Ciardi, Laura Richards, Shel Silverstein, and Lilian Moore. Ink and pencil drawings add to the merriment.

Dugan, Michael, compiler. **Stuff & Nonsense.** Illus. Deborah Niland. William Collins Publishers, 1977. 8–10.

If one likes animals and humorous poetry, this delightful book is made to order. The rhyming quality of the words and the humorous illustrations make for real "stuff and nonsense." "Where does the elephant keep his trunk, when he becomes a sailor bold?" This book holds the answer to many questions.

Kennedy, X. J. **The Phantom Ice Cream Man: More Nonsense Verse.** Illus. David McPhail. Atheneum, 1979. 8–12.

What great fun lies in store for readers of these poems! Easy rhymes and rhythms make delightful reading and listening. Included are odes to such diverse topics as lasagna, tyrannosaurus rex's teeth, the terrible troll's tollbridge, and mother's pig. Illustrations are as nonsensical and funny as the poems.

Lear, Edward. **The Owl and the Pussy-cat.** Illus. Gwen Fulton. Atheneum, 1977. 4–7.

The detailed and colorful illustrations in this new edition of a familiar humorous verse take the reader to an appealing and unthreatening dreamland. The illustrations beautifully match Lear's verse.

Livingston, Myra Cohn. **A Lollygag of Limericks.** Illus. Joseph Low. Atheneum, 1978. 10–up.

Each of these forty-four nonsense verses and comical drawings is amusing. Many English place names are encountered. An excellent book to use when teaching the structure of the limerick.

Moss, Howard. **Tigers and Other Lilies.** Illus. Frederick Henry Belli. Atheneum, 1977. 7–10.

Here is a collection of humorous poems about plants with animals in their names: catnip, dogwood, cowslip, horse chestnut, cattail, hare-bell, toadstool, and others. The poems delight young readers and invite them to create their own plant-animal verses.

Nash, Ogden (compiler Quentin Blake). **Custard and Company.** Illus. by compiler. Little, Brown, 1980. 10–up.

Some of Ogden Nash's most delightful and amusing verses are humorously illustrated. Selections include favorites such as "The Parent," "The Dog," "The Kitten," and numerous others.

Orgel, Doris, **Merry, Merry FIBruary.** Illus. Arnold Lobel. Parents Magazine Press, 1977. 8–12.

In these nonsense verses, little fibs grow into tall tales because it's FIBruary. Reading aloud is satisfying due to the rhythmic alliteration. Illustrated with watercolor drawings; especially suitable for the good reader.

Prelutsky, Jack. **The Queen of Eene and Other Poems.** Illus. Victoria Chess. Greenwillow Books, 1978. 8–12.

Weird and wacky best describe this assortment of characters created by verse and pictures. The rhymed poems are funny and outlandish, telling of strange persons with even stranger pastimes. Children will enjoy hearing and reading the poems and will chuckle over the zany illustrations.

Rosenbloom, Joseph. **Silly Verse (and Even Worse).** Illus. Joyce Behr. Sterling Publishing, 1979. 7–10.

"I was sitting on a tombstone, when a ghost came by and said, 'I'm sorry to disturb you, but you're sitting on my head.'" This humorous collection of limericks, poems, and parodies is a good investment for home or school. Many illustrations and a subject index are included.

Thayer, Ernest Lawrence. **Casey at the Bat: A Ballad of the Republic, Sung in the Year 1888.** Illus. Wallace Tripp. Coward, McCann & Geoghegan, 1978. 10–up.

This classic colorful narrative poem is illustrated with a cast of animal characters who seem quite at home in their baseball roles.

Contrast is provided by the fast action of the poem and the last page where a tiny mouse is alone in the deserted ballpark.

Yolen, Jane. **How Beastly! A Menagerie of Nonsense Poems.** Illus. James Marshall. William Collins Publishers, 1980. 6–8.

Readers will enjoy this collection of nonsense poems about strange but slightly familiar beasts. The ink and wash illustrations add lots of humor to the already funny verses.

Nature

Adoff, Arnold. **Tornado! Poems.** Illus. Ronald Himler. Delacorte Press, 1977. 8–up.

The terror and aftermath of the tornado that struck Xenia, Ohio is relived with fear and hope in this single-theme poem. The destruction and period of rebuilding are movingly described. Format and style combine to capture the unusual mood.

Atwood, Ann. **Fly with the Wind, Flow with the Water.** Charles Scribner's Sons, 1979. 8–12.

"To fly with the wind, to flow with the water in a dance of light." Haiku verses that highlight the joy of movement are the focus of this beautifully illustrated book.

Atwood, Ann. **Haiku-Vision in Poetry and Photography.** Illus. by author. Charles Scribner's Sons, 1977. 12–up.

A discussion of the meaning and effect of haiku poetry is accompanied by newly written haiku poems and outstanding color photographs. Useful in teaching about the origins and depth of haiku, this is a fine teacher's resource book. It also serves as a beautiful model of illustrated poetry.

Baylor, Byrd. **The Other Way to Listen.** Illus. Peter Parnall. Charles Scribner's Sons, 1978. 8–12.

A child is eager to learn the other way to listen after the old man tells him that, with patience and silence, one can hear the cactus blooming or the hills singing. Lovely illustrations and verse related to nature.

Farber, Norma. **Small Wonders.** Illus. Kazue Mizumura. Coward, McCann & Geoghegan, 1979. 8–up.

Simple woodcuts perfectly illustrate these short poems of common wonders. Poetic allusions are written with wit and skillful use of language. The poems speak to experiences of all ages with delightful metaphors for better readers.

Fox, Siv Cedering. **The Blue Horse and Other Night Poems.** Illus. Donald Carrick. Seabury Press, 1979. 7–10.

Quiet, wandering poems meander like the mind before sleep comes. The blue horse eats grass on the coverlet; the shoes sprout wings and fly; the blanket is warm and covers the head when a bad dream comes. A unified experience. Black and white full-page pictures.

Frost, Robert. **Stopping by Woods on a Snowy Evening.** Illus. Susan Jeffers. E. P. Dutton, 1978. All ages.

The well-known poem is illustrated in gorgeous black and white drawings filled with woodland life. Beautiful depictions of snow scenes.

Hopkins, Lee Bennett, compiler. **Moments.** Illus. Michael Hague. Harcourt Brace Jovanovich, 1980. 8–12.

A rich, thoughtfully selected collection of poems about the seasons. Poems are juxtaposed to let the reader see, touch, taste, and smell the special wonder of each season and to reflect on some special moments: quiet times, funny times, and holidays. Authors include David McCord, Karla Kuskin, and Langston Hughes.

Hopkins, Lee Bennett, compiler. **To Look at Any Thing.** Photographs by John Earl. Harcourt Brace Jovanovich, 1978. All ages.

A beautiful combination of haunting visual scenes of nature and poets' words of celebration creates an outstanding book for browsing. Extension activities are numerous as children are encouraged to look at their world with increased awareness.

Mizumura, Kazue. **Flower Moon Snow: A Book of Haiku.** Illus. by author. Thomas Y. Crowell, 1977. 8–12.

Many aspects of nature throughout the changing seasons are captured in these original haiku poems. Generally, the author has been faithful to the seventeen-syllable pattern of Japanese haiku. The soft gray and brown woodcuts harmonize with the text.

Moore, Lilian. **Think of Shadows.** Illus. Deborah Robison. Atheneum, 1980. 7–10.

All kinds of shadows, frightening and calm, are included in these seventeen poems. Light and filled with imagery, many of the poems have themes that prod thinking. Attractive illustrations.

Russo, Susan, compiler. **The Moon's the North Wind's Cooky.** Illus. by author. Lothrop, Lee & Shepard Books, 1979. 4–7.

Fourteen poems of night for very young children show nighttime in its many guises. Most of the choices are old favorites, some humorous, some thoughtful. Poets include Nikki Giovanni, Myra Cohn

Livingston, Vachel Lindsay, Karla Kuskin, Joan Aiken, Robert
Louis Stevenson, Marchette Chute, and Louis Untermeyer. Handsomely illustrated.

Schweninger, Ann, compiler. **The Man in the Moon as He Sails the Sky
and Other Moon Verse.** Illus. by author. Dodd, Mead, 1979. 4–7.
The moon's special charm is the subject of the twenty-one poems in
this appealing book. Sources of poems include Mother Goose,
Edward Lear, and Vachel Lindsay. Watercolor illustrations complement the lovely verses that are sure to delight the young.

Sun through Small Leaves: Poems of Spring. Illus. Satomi Ichikawa.
William Collins Publishers, 1980. 8–12.
This small collection of poems celebrates spring. Contributors include
renowned authors such as Emily Dickinson, Gerard Manley Hopkins,
Rudyard Kipling, and William Blake. Exquisitely illustrated.

General Collections

Abercrombie, Barbara, editor. **The Other Side of a Poem.** Illus. Harry
Bertschmann. Harper & Row, Publishers, 1977. All ages.
This anthology of twentieth-century American poetry groups poems
into such inviting categories as "Delicious Sounds" and "Secret
Messages." Theodore Roethke, Sylvia Plath, and William Carlos
Williams are among the distinguished poets represented. The poems
included have child appeal. T. S. Eliot, for example, writes of the
difficulties in naming a cat.

Brewton, Sara, John E. Brewton, and John Brewton Blackburn, compilers.
**Of Quarks, Quasars, and Other Quirks: Quizzical Poems for the
Supersonic Age.** Illus. Quentin Blake. Thomas Y. Crowell, 1977.
10–up.
These poems, all commenting on the modern world and the space
age, provide both wry humor and disturbing images. Many favorite authors are included: Nash, Ciardi, McCord, Merriam. The
black and white line drawings make their own amusing and
pointed comments.

Brown, Marc, compiler. **Finger Rhymes.** Illus. by author. E. P. Dutton,
1980. 4–7.
Fourteen nursery rhymes and poems are shown with instructions for
finger rhymes. Handsome double-page spreads of black and white
drawings with orange borders make this an attractive book. Includes
"Where Is Thumbkin?," "There Was a Little Turtle," "Five Little
Pigs," "Fish Story," "Whoops! Johnny," "Clap Your Hands," and
"The Squirrel."

de Regniers, Beatrice Schenk. **A Bunch of Poems and Verses.** Illus. Mary Jane Dunton. Seabury Press, 1977. 4–7.

Here is an excellent collection of contemporary limericks, poems, and verses about time-related experiences and events. Graphic illustrations enhance the vivid, descriptive verses. A good reference for the teacher of young children.

Dickinson, Emily. **I'm Nobody! Who Are You?** Illus. Rex Schneider. Stemmer House Publishers, 1978. 8–12.

Rich-toned, full-color drawings make this a very special collection of forty-five poems especially selected for children. Many are story poems and their themes vary: nature, emotions, unique thoughts. An introduction by Richard B. Sewall is helpful to the study of these works, as is the glossary.

Driz, Ovsei (translator Joachim Neugroschel). **The Boy and the Tree.** Illus. Victor Pivovarov. Prentice-Hall, 1978. 8–12.

This collection of children's poems maintains the quaintly humorous, direct, and imaginative qualities of the original Russian Yiddish version.

Hill, Helen, Agnes Perkins, and Alethea Helbig, compilers. **Straight on Till Morning: Poems of the Imaginary World.** Illus. Ted Lewin. Thomas Y. Crowell, 1977. 8–12.

Nearly 100 poems by modern English and American poets, some seldom anthologized, are arranged in eight imaginative categories including "Fetch Me Far and Far Away" and "Funny and Fabulous Friends." Pencil drawings capture glimpses of the child's world of imagination, which is emphasized in the collection.

Kuskin, Karla. **Dogs and Dragons, Trees and Dreams.** Harper & Row, Publishers, 1980. 8–12.

The 1979 NCTE Poetry Award recipient has collected many of her poems and has added fresh and lively pictures to her notes and comments, inviting the reader to take an enchanting tour of the world of poetry.

Lewis, Claudia. **Up and Down the River: Boat Poems.** Illus. Bruce Degen. Harper & Row, Publishers, 1979. 6–9.

Original poems inspired by boats on a river are simple in style and meaning and full of imagery. Each of the thirteen poems is reminiscent of a particular type of boat, such as a cutter, sailboat, barge, tugboat. Well illustrated.

Livingston, Myra Cohn. **O Sliver of Liver.** Illus. Iris Van Rynbach. Atheneum, 1979. 10–up.

Over forty poems, some thoughtful, some humorous, cover a wide range of topics. Haiku, cinquains, and concrete poetry are included in the variety of forms written and compiled by the 1980 NCTE Poetry Award recipient.

McCord, David. **Speak Up: More Rhymes of the Never Was and Always Is.** Illus. Marc Simont. Little, Brown, 1980. 7–10.

The recipient of the first NCTE Poetry Award has put together a collection of forty new poems to delight old fans and attract new ones. Once again the poet's fascination and skill with words shine through in this group of "rhymes of the never was and always is."

Millay, Edna St. Vincent. **Edna St. Vincent Millay's Poems Selected for Young People.** Illus. Ronald Keller. Harper & Row, Publishers, 1979. 12–up.

This handsomely designed collection provides a fine introduction to the poet. The sixty poems include "Renascence" and "Harp Weaver"; there are also numerous sonnets and nature poems. Well illustrated with striking woodcuts.

Moore, Lilian, compiler. **Go with the Poem.** McGraw-Hill, 1979. 10–12.

Poems reflecting feelings that all of us share have been collected for middle grade students. The ninety poems are chosen from twentieth-century poets such as William Carlos Williams, Lucille Clifton, John Updike, and others to provide a rich, varied anthology.

Morrison, Lillian. **The Sidewalk Racer and Other Poems of Sports and Motion.** Lothrop, Lee & Shepard Books, 1977. 10–12.

Themes of the thirty-eight poems in this collection run the gamut from golf to streetfighting, baseball to biking. Several poems are specifically about women participating in sports, a rarity in children's poetry. Superb black and white photos add interest and appeal for advanced readers.

Pagliaro, Penny, editor. **I Like Poems and Poems Like Me.** Illus. Wendy Kim Chee. Press Pacifica, 1977. 6–9.

This delightful collection from contemporary poets as well as old favorites is good for introducing children to poetry with poems that look at the world and everyday experiences. Enchanting black and white illustrations.

A Poison Tree and Other Poems. Illus. Mercer Mayer. Charles Scribner's Sons, 1977. 12–up.

A collection of twenty thoughtful poems by such poets as William Blake, Langston Hughes, Eve Merriam, and Nikki Giovanni. Full-page illustrations quietly reflect the mood and emotion of each poem.

Starbird, Kaye. **The Covered Bridge House and Other Poems.** Illus. Jim Arnosky. Four Winds Press, 1979. 8–12.

There's something for every child in these sometimes humorous, sometimes serious poems. Vignettes of childhood scenes are clearly depicted in the poems and complementary black and white sketches.

Stevenson, Robert Louis. **A Child's Garden of Verses.** Illus. Ruth Sanderson. Platt & Munk, Publishers, 1977. 4–7.

This large picture book contains ten well-known poems and is a fine introduction to Robert Louis Stevenson's works. The pictures are reminiscent of a past era. Included are favorites such as "The Swing" and "The Land of Counterpane."

Tarbox, Shirley, and Todd Tarbox, editors. **Footprints of Young Explorers by Children from around the World.** Todd Tarbox Books, 1978. 6–up.

Poems, stories, and illustrations by children from around the world have been collected by the editors. Subjects range from animals to sand castles. Use as a springboard for inspiring other young poets and illustrators.

Watson, Clyde. **Catch Me & Kiss Me & Say It Again.** Illus. Wendy Watson. William Collins Publishers, 1978. 3–5.

Rhyme, rhythm, and repetition invite young children to participate in the activities suggested by the thirty-two modern nursery rhymes. The amusing verses are rendered even more appealing by the humorous watercolor illustrations.

Wilner, Isabel, compiler. **The Poetry Troupe: An Anthology of Poems to Read Aloud.** Illus. by author. Charles Scribner's Sons, 1977. All ages.

The compiler read much poetry to children, delighting them so much that they developed a poetry troupe in order to share poems they loved. These are some of their favorites, categorized in a way that makes them especially useful to the teacher who would like to try poetry readings.

Additional Poetry Books

Adoff, Arnold. *I Am the Darker Brother.* Illus. Benny Andrews. Macmillan Publishing, 1968. 9–up.
Aldis, Dorothy. *All Together.* Illus. Helen Jameson, Marjorie Flack, and Margaret Freeman. G. P. Putnam's Sons, 1952. 4–7.
Arbuthnot, May Hill, and Shelton L. Root, Jr., comps. *Time for Poetry.* 3rd ed. Illus. Arthur Paul. Scott, Foresman, 1967. 5–13.
Association for Childhood Education International, comp. *Sung under the Silver Umbrella.* Illus. Dorothy Lathrop. Macmillan Publishing, 1935. 4–14.
Atwood, Ann. *Haiku: The Mood of Earth.* Photographs by author. Charles Scribner's Sons, 1971. 8–up.
Baron, Virginia Olsen, comp. *The Seasons of Time: Tanka Poetry of Ancient Japan.* Illus. Yasuhide Kobashi. Dial Press, 1968. 12–up.
Behn, Harry. *Cricket Songs: Japanese Haiku.* With pictures selected from Sesshu and other Japanese masters. Harcourt Brace Jovanovich, 1964. 9–up.

Bodecker, N. M. *Hurry, Hurry, Mary Dear!* Atheneum, 1976. 9–up.
Brewton, Sara, and John E. Brewton, comps. *Laughable Limericks.* Illus. Ingrid Fetz. Thomas Y. Crowell, 1965. 8–11.
Brooke, L. Leslie. *Ring O'Roses.* Frederick Warne, 1923. 3–7.
Brooks, Gwendolyn. *Bronzeville Boys and Girls.* Illus. Ronni Solbert. Harper & Row, Publishers, 1956. 7–11.
Ciardi, John. *The Reason for the Pelican.* Illus. Madeleine Gekiere. J. B. Lippincott, 1959. 6–10.
Coatsworth, Elizabeth. *Sparrow Bush.* Illus. Stefan Martin. Norton, 1966. 9–11.
Cole, William, ed. *Oh, That's Ridiculous!* Illus. Tomi Ungerer. Viking Press, 1972. All ages.
DeAngeli, Marguerite. *Book of Mother Goose and Nursery Rhymes.* Doubleday, 1952. 3–7.
de Regniers, Beatrice Schenk. *Something Special.* Illus. Irene Haas. Harcourt Brace Jovanovich, 1958. 4–8.
Doob, L. W., comp. *A Crocodile Has Me by the Leg.* Illus. S. I. Wangboje. Walker, 1968. 9–14.
Dunning, Stephen, Edward Lueders, and Hugh Smith, comps. *Reflections on a Gift of Watermelon Pickle . . . and Other Modern Verse.* Lothrop, Lee & Shepard Books, 1967. 12–up.
Field, Rachel. *Poems.* Macmillan Publishing, 1957. 8–up.
Fisher, Aileen. *Feathered Ones and Furry.* Illus. Eric Carle. Thomas Y. Crowell, 1971. 6–12.
Froman, Robert. *Street Poems.* McCall, 1971. 8–up.
Frost, Frances. *The Little Whistler.* Illus. Roger Duvoisin. McGraw-Hill, 1966. 6–10.
Frost, Robert. *You Come Too: Favorite Poems for Young Readers.* Illus. Thomas Nason. Holt, Rinehart and Winston, 1959. 10–up.
Hopkins, Lee Bennett, comp. *I Think I Saw a Snail: Young Poems for City Seasons.* Illus. Harold James. Crown Publishers, 1969. 4–9.
Jordan, June. *Who Look at Me.* Illus. with paintings. Thomas Y. Crowell, 1969. 10–up.
Kuskin, Karla. *Any Me I Want to Be.* Harper & Row, Publishers, 1972. 6–9.
Larrick, Nancy, comp. *On City Streets.* Illus. by David Sagarin. M. Evans, 1968. 10–13.
Lear, Edward. *The Complete Nonsense Book.* Dodd, Mead, 1958. 5–9.
Lewis, Richard, comp. *Miracles: Poems by Children of the English-speaking World.* Simon & Schuster, 1966. 7–12.
Lines, Kathleen, comp. *Lavender's Blue.* Illus. Harold Jones. Franklin Watts, 1954. 4–7.
Livingston, Myra Cohn. *Whispers and Other Poems.* Illus. Jacqueline Chwast. Harcourt Brace Jovanovich, 1958. 4–9.
McCord, David. *Every Time I Climb a Tree.* Illus. Marc Simont. Little, Brown, 1967. 5–9.
McDonald, Gerald D., comp. *A Way of Knowing.* Illus. Clare and John Ross. Thomas Y. Crowell, 1959. 9–16.
Merriam, Eve. *It Doesn't Always Have to Rhyme.* Illus. Malcolm Spooner. Atheneum, 1964. 10–up.
Milne, A. A. *The World of Christopher Robin.* Illus. E. H. Shepard. E. P. Dutton, 1958. 6–up.
Moore, Lilian. *I Feel the Same Way.* Illus. Robert Quackenbush. Atheneum, 1968. 3–8.

Ness, Evaline, comp. *Amelia Mixed the Mustard*. Charles Scribner's Sons, 1975. 6–10.

O'Neil, Mary. *Hailstones and Halibut Bones*. Illus. Leonard Weisgard. Doubleday, 1961. 5–8.

Read, Herbert, comp. *This Way, Delight: A Book of Poetry for the Young*. Illus. Juliet Kepes. Pantheon Books, 1956. 5–9.

Reed, Philip. *Mother Goose and Nursery Rhymes*. Atheneum, 1963. 5–7.

Richards, Laura. *Tirra Lirra*. Illus. Marguerite Davis. Little, Brown, 1955. 5–12.

Rieu, E. V. *The Flattered Flying Fish and Other Poems*. Illus. E. H. Shepard. E. P. Dutton, 1962. 9–12.

Riley, James Whitcomb. *The Gobble-Uns'll Git You ef You Don't Watch Out!* Illus. Joel Schick. J. B. Lippincott, 1975. 6–12.

Rojankovsky, Feodor. *The Tall Book of Mother Goose*. Harper & Row, Publishers, 1942. 3–6.

Rossetti, Christina. *Goblin Market*. Illus. Ellen Raskin. E. P. Dutton, 1970. 12–16.

Sandburg, Carl. *Early Moon*. Illus. James Daugherty. Harcourt Brace Jovanovich, 1930. 12–up.

Silverstein, Shel. *Where the Sidewalk Ends*. Harper & Row, Publishers, 1974. 5–12.

Starbird, Kaye. *Don't Ever Cross a Crocodile*. Illus. Kit Dalton. J. B. Lippincott, 1963. 5–up.

Tudor, Tasha. *Mother Goose*. Henry Z. Walck, 1944. 3–7.

Wallace, Daisy, ed. *Witch Poems*. Illus. Trina Schart Hyman. Holiday House, 1976. 8–12.

Wildsmith, Brian. *Brian Wildsmith's Mother Goose*. Franklin Watts, 1965. 3–6.

Holidays

Christmas

Balian, Lorna. **Bah! Humbug?** Abingdon Press, 1977. 4–7.

Margie's big brother Arthur says there is no Santa. She watches as he plots a trap with bells and string to catch "fat humbug Santa Claus." Arthur falls asleep but wide-awake Margie delightfully witnesses Santa's visit. The humorous illustrations and text beautifully blend to shake even big brother Arthur's disbelief.

Barth, Edna, compiler. **A Christmas Feast: Poems, Sayings, Greetings, and Wishes.** Illus. Ursula Arndt. Clarion Books, 1979. 8–12.

This valuable collection of Christmas poems, sayings, greetings, and wishes is grouped by topic. The anticipation of Christmas is explored as well as the happy events of the Christmas season. An excellent book for home or school because activities are suggested for both. Artistic etchings complement the text.

Berenstain, Stan, and Jan Berenstain. **The Berenstain Bears' Christmas Tree.** Random House, 1980. 3–7.

The Berenstain bears are hunting for a Christmas tree. Papa Bear knows exactly which tree to get. Their search takes them far but they decide against the tree that they came for when they discover that it is the home of several small animals. (Picture book)

Carroll, Theodus C. **The Lost Christmas Star.** Illus. William Hutchinson. Garrard Publishing, 1979. 7–10.

Matthew, jealous of Judy's interest in Tim, the new boy, suspects Tim of stealing the wooden star that Matt had placed on the community Christmas tree. Tim's shyness accentuates the problem until Matt's dog Jingles finds the star. Good to read aloud by chapters; stimulates discussion. (Picture book)

✓ Dasent, George Webbe, Sir, translator. **The Cat on the Dovrefell: A Christmas Tale.** Illus. Tomie de Paola. G. P. Putnam's Sons, 1979. 5–8.

A traveler seeks lodging in a cottage with his white bear. He isn't particularly welcome because the trolls always spend Christmas Eve there, but he stays nonetheless. After the awesome trolls arrive and feast, they mistake the bear for a cat and tease it. The bear frightens them away forever. A Norwegian tale with full-color illustrations. (Picture book)

de Paola, Tomie. **The Family Christmas Tree Book.** Illus. by author. Holiday House, 1980. 7–10.

A family on an outing to select a Christmas tree discusses that particular holiday custom. The author shares many facts in an interesting fashion. Readers learn not only the history of Christmas trees, but such anecdotes as how Theodore Roosevelt's son once hid his Christmas tree in a closet!

Devlin, Wende, and Harry Devlin. **Cranberry Christmas.** Parents Magazine Press, 1976. 6–9.

Mr. Whiskers is troubled and facing a gloomy Christmas. He can't find the deed to the pond and his house is a mess. Then his friends, young Maggie and her grandmother, come to his aid in both a practical and surprising way. Good holiday read-aloud book. (Picture book)

Walt Disney Productions. **The Small One.** Random House, 1979. 7–10.

Small One is an old donkey well loved by the boy who is sent to Nazareth to sell him. The eventual buyer is a kindly man who needs a gentle animal to carry his wife, Mary, to Bethlehem. Large print, colorful Disney illustrations, and reinforced binding; Christmas reading. (Picture book)

Foreman, Michael. **Winter's Tales.** Illus. Freire Wright. Doubleday, 1979. 6–9.

Six magical tales of Christmastime contain love, humor, warmth, and wonder. Secular in content, the essence of each is captured in the softly painted illustrations. The combination of quality text and drawings make this a highly recommended book. (Picture book)

Hodges, C. Walter. **Plain Lane Christmas.** Illus. by author. Coward, McCann & Geoghegan, 1978. 8–12.

The residents of Plain Lane realize that immediate strong action must be taken if their little street is going to escape the wrecking ball of urban renewal. A Christmas celebration followed by a Chinese New Year festival brings remarkable results.

Hoff, Syd. **Merry Christmas, Henrietta!** Garrard Publishing, 1980. 6–9.

An enterprising chicken visits a department store Santa to get suggestions for a present for her owner. After working as Santa's helper for a day, she ends up with presents both for herself and for Farmer Gray. An improbable and very funny easy reader with cartoon illustrations. (Picture book)

Johnston, Tony. **Five Little Foxes and the Snow.** Illus. Cyndy Szekeres. G. P. Putnam's Sons, 1977. 4–7.

Security, love, the joy of living, and old-fashioned family values are implicit in the narration and watercolor drawings of this simple Christmas tale. Gramma Fox knits "click, click" by the fire while each little fox begs to play in the snow, until Christmas morning! Good for choral reading and dramatizing. (Picture book)

Kurelek, William. **A Northern Nativity: Christmas Dreams of a Prairie Boy.** Tundra Books, 1976. 10–up.

A series of paintings show how the Christ Child and His mother might be welcomed in times and places other than Bethlehem. The Holy Family is shown in a railroad car, in a motel, in a fishing village. The masterful pictures are worthy of the text. (Picture book)

✓ Livingston, Myra Cohn, editor. **Poems of Christmas.** Atheneum, 1980. 8–up.

Christmas poems for the young and old include old favorites from the Bible and traditional carols to less-known verses by George MacDonald, T. S. Eliot, W. H. Auden and a host of others. Author, title, and first line indexes.

MacKellar, William. **The Silent Bells.** Illus. Ted Lewin. Dodd, Mead, 1978. 8–12.

For over two hundred years, the bells in a Swiss cathedral had been silent. Legend says that when a pilgrim offers the right gift to the Christ Child, the bells will ring. Anne-Marie, a simple child, is rewarded for her likewise simple gift by the triumphant pealing of the bells. A beautiful, sensitive Christmas story.

Manley, Seon, and Gogo Lewis, compilers. **Christmas Ghosts.** Doubleday, 1978. 12–up.

The ghost story is a Christmas tradition of Dickensian respectability and this fine collection of short stories contains both ghosts and mysteries linked to the holiday season. Authors include Allingham, Walpole, Sayers, and Dickens himself. Stories in the classic tradition for the distinctly older reader.

✓ Moore, Clement. **The Night before Christmas.** Illus. Tomie de Paola. Holiday House, 1980. All ages.

The classic poem is illustrated with an 1840s New Hampshire village setting. Each page is bordered by designs from New England quilts. Large full-color watercolor and ink drawings include a St. Nicholas who is properly plump and jolly. The book is certain to become a Christmas classic itself. (Picture book)

Paterson, Katherine. **Angels and Other Strangers: Family Christmas Stories.** Thomas Y. Crowell, 1979. 10–up.

A fine collection of nine Christmas stories that reveal the true meaning of the day, the birth of the Savior. The problems of everyday life are met in these appealing stories: foster children are taken in by a widow, a boy runs away, and a mother loses her child.

Quackenbush, Robert. **The Most Welcome Visitor.** E. P. Dutton, 1978. 6–9.

Fred Horny Toad has a large family. One by one they come to visit him just when he has moved into a new home. His own special visitor at Christmastime gives a gift that causes the visitors to change their plans and visit their own homes. A funny cumulative tale. (Picture book)

Stevens, Patricia Bunning. **Merry Christmas! A History of the Holiday.** Macmillan Publishing, 1979. 10–up.

A unique look at the Christmas holiday traces its history from ancient pagan festivals to contemporary American customs. Black and white photographs and illustrations are included. Useful bibliography and index.

Theroux, Paul. **A Christmas Card.** Illus. John Lawrence. Houghton Mifflin, 1978. 10–12.

A deceptively simple story of a family lost on its way to spend Christmas in a new home becomes a tale of magic and mystery. A strange old man and a nine-year-old boy meet through a world illustrated on a Christmas card and make possible a joyous Christmas.

Thomas, Dylan. **A Child's Christmas in Wales.** Illus. Edward Ardizzone. David R. Godine, Publisher, 1980. All ages.

The author's remembrances of childhood Christmases in a small Welsh town is a fine read-aloud book. The illustrations make this version unique. Alternate black and white pen sketches and full-color watercolor illustrations add to the charm. (Picture book)

Williams, Vera B. **It's a Gingerbread House: Bake It, Build It, Eat It!** Greenwillow Books, 1978. 7–9.

Grandpa Ben baked and sent a gingerbread house to his grandchildren, who found it irresistible. When they ate the roof, they found Grandpa's letter with complete instructions, necessary patterns, and explicit directions for the house. Three-color diagrams also enable the reader to duplicate the house.

Easter

Gackenbach, Dick. **Hattie, Tom, and The Chicken Witch: A Play and a Story.** Harper & Row, Publishers, 1980. 6–9.

Tom doesn't want any rabbits in his Easter play. Hattie insists that Easter and rabbits go together like peanut butter and jelly. This is an enjoyable easy-to-read story of how Hattie gets to be in the play. A play script is included. (Picture book)

Hopkins, Lee Bennett, compiler. **Easter Buds Are Springing: Poems for Easter.** Illus. Tomie de Paola. Harcourt Brace Jovanovich, 1979. 4–7.

This collection of nineteen poems celebrates Easter, both the secular and religious aspects. Included are poets Elizabeth Coatsworth, Aileen Fisher, Joyce Kilmer, and David McCord. Delightful drawings accompany each poem.

Wahl, Jan. **Old Hippo's Easter Egg.** Illus. Lorinda Bryan Cauley. Harcourt Brace Jovanovich, 1980. 4–7.

When a little duck hatches from an Easter egg left at lonely Mr. Hippo's door, Mr. Hippo happily becomes the baby duck's parent. Large humorous illustrations blend to tell this funny but gentle story of family love and new beginnings. A good read-aloud book. (Picture book)

Halloween

Asch, Frank. **Popcorn: A Frank Asch Bear Story.** Parents Magazine Press, 1979. 3–5.

Mama and Papa Bear leave little Sam all alone on Halloween Eve. He calls his friends, designs a costume, and soon there is a party. Each friend brings a treat: popcorn! The evening proves to be a lot of fun. The simple plot and simple illustrations are just right for preschoolers. (Picture book)

Brewton, John E., Lorraine A. Blackburn, and George M. Blackburn, III. **In the Witch's Kitchen: Poems for Halloween.** Illus. Harriett Barton. Thomas Y. Crowell, 1980. All ages.

Forty-two poems by twenty-seven children's poets will be welcomed by children, teachers, parents, and librarians alike. Black and white illustrations add a childlike charm to the laughs and chills of this scary good fun.

Cavagnaro, David, and Maggie Cavagnaro. **The Pumpkin People.** Sierra Club Books, 1979. 6–9.

Pippin and his father plant pumpkin seeds in the spring. During the summer the plants grow, produce, then wither. The family invites the neighbors in to celebrate the harvest in a way just right for jack-o-lanterns.

Cuyler, Margery. **The All-Around Pumpkin Book.** Illus. Corbett Jones. Holt, Rinehart and Winston, 1980. 8–12.

Little-known facts about the pumpkin, a planting and cultivation guide, recipes, and a variety of party and craft ideas fill this unusual book. Black and white illustrations add interest to the text.

Jasner, W. K. **Which Is the Witch?** Illus. Victoria Chess. Pantheon Books, 1979. 6–8.

Every Halloween Jenny insists on dressing up as a witch. Then she gets a chance to trade places with a *real* witch. Black and white pictures add proper witchiness to this funny story. An easy-to-read book. (Picture book)

Kellogg, Steven. **The Mystery of the Flying Orange Pumpkin.** Dial Press, 1980. 3–7.

Joan, Brian, and Ellis plant a pumpkin seed in their friend Mr. Bramble's yard. Before the pumpkin is large enough, Mr. Bramble moves away and the new neighbor refuses to let the children in his yard. A Halloween "Trick and Treat" provides a happy ending for all. (Picture book)

Kessler, Leonard. **Riddles That Rhyme for Halloween Time.** Garrard Publishing, 1978. 6–10.

Twenty-three Halloween rhyming riddles in which the reader encounters ghosts, witches, cats, and other Halloween characters are cleverly illustrated. The wordplay gives readers an enjoyable treat.

Low, Alice. **The Witch Who Was Afraid of Witches.** Illus. Karen Gundersheimer. Pantheon Books, 1978. 7–9.

Wendy, the youngest of three witches, could do few witchy things and was even afraid of witches! Losing her broomstick just before Halloween helped her make a friend and find powers she didn't know she had. A good Halloween read-aloud story; colorful drawings add to appeal. (Picture book)

Nolan, Dennis. **Witch Bazooza.** Prentice-Hall, 1979. 6–9.

Hoping to win the most spookily decorated house contest, Witch Bazooza uses many poetic incantations. She and Ajax, her red-nosed cat, have difficulty in getting the perfect window centerpiece. Humorous story and drawings in this Halloween read-aloud book. (Picture book)

Prelutsky, Jack. **It's Halloween.** Illus. Marylin Hafner. Greenwillow Books, 1977. 6–9.

A collection of thirteen Halloween poems that are funny and scary. The illustrations are as much fun as the verse. An easy-to-read book.

St. George, Judith. **The Halloween Pumpkin Smasher.** Illus. Margot Tomes. G. P. Putnam's Sons, 1978. 7–10.

Mary Grace has a make-believe best friend, Nelly. Nelly is brave, kind, and smart. Three days before Halloween Nelly and Mary Grace have to solve the mystery of the smashed pumpkins. Readers discover that Nelly isn't the only brave, kind, and smart person. The real pumpkin smasher is truly a surprise. (Picture book)

Schulman, Janet. **Jack the Bum and the Halloween Handout.** Illus. James Stevenson. Greenwillow Books, 1977. 6–9.

Jack the bum gets right into the act of begging on Halloween night. He discovers that UNICEF seems to be the magic word. How he learns the real meaning behind UNICEF is an engaging story for beginning readers. (Picture book)

Stevenson, James. **That Terrible Halloween Night.** Greenwillow Books, 1980. 5–8.

Mary Ann and Louie try to scare Grandpa on Halloween. He doesn't scare easily, not since that terrible Halloween night years ago when he went into the scary house with all the horrible creatures and came out an old man. Wonderful spurs for children's imaginations.

Vigna, Judith. **Everyone Goes as a Pumpkin.** Illus. by author. Albert Whitman, 1977. 6–9.

Emily has a gorgeous costume for the Halloween party. It is stolen from the bus seat as she rides the crowded bus to her grandmother's house. Happily, Emily discovers that going to the party as herself is the most fun of all. Softly colored illustrations. (Picture book)

Jewish Holidays

Aleichem, Sholem (translators and adapters Uri Shulevitz and Elizabeth Shub). **Hanukah Money.** Illus. Uri Shulevitz. Greenwillow Books, 1978. 6–9.

It is Hanukah. Father lights the candle and says the blessing. Motl and his older brother join the family activities, then enjoy themselves going to a relative's home to collect the expected gift of Hanukah money. Lively, detailed illustrations. (Picture book)

Cuyler, Margery. **Jewish Holidays.** Illus. Lisa C. Wesson. Holt, Rinehart and Winston, 1978. 8–12.

Pageantry, drama, and the recreative joy of present-day holidays that commemorate ancient acts of courage, love, and religious devotion are the stuff of this little volume. Simple, happy ink drawings illustrate the short readable chapters. Every major Jewish holiday is depicted, with a related and easy craft project for each.

Drucker, Malka. **Hanukkah: Eight Nights, Eight Lights.** Illus. Brom Hoban. Holiday House, 1980. 12–up.

The history, customs, and rituals of Hanukkah, the Festival of Lights, are treated in considerable depth. Related crafts, recipes, and puzzles are suggested. A valuable source book for middle graders with a glossary and index. Ink illustrations.

Greenfeld, Howard. **Passover.** Illus. Elaine Grove. Holt, Rinehart and Winston, 1978. 10–up.

The Passover holiday is described: how it is observed, what it means, its historical beginnings, its symbols. Simply-told stories are encased in an elegantly designed cover. Scratchboard illustrations capture a sense of timelessness, and top-of-page illustrations depict appropriate symbols. Very worthwhile.

Greenfeld, Howard. **Rosh Hashanah and Yom Kippur.** Illus. Elaine Grove. Holt, Rinehart and Winston, 1979. 8–12.

Rosh Hashanah and Yom Kippur, the most important of all Jewish holidays, are explained through text and black and white illustrations. All new terms are defined. An excellent book for acquainting children with Judaism.

Levitin, Sonia. **A Sound to Remember.** Illus. Gabriel Lisowski. Harcourt Brace Jovanovich, 1979. 6–9.

Jacov, a "not-too-bright" youngster, was chosen to blow the shofar or ram's horn for the Rosh Hashanah feast. Even though he practiced, not a sound would come; however, the kind Rabbi's plan works. Set at the end of the nineteenth century in an eastern Jewish settlement. (Picture book)

Suhl, Yuri. **The Purim Goat.** Illus. Kaethe Zemach. Four Winds Press, 1980. 7–10.

Braindel and her ten-year-old son live in poverty in a one-room cottage. Selling baked pumpkin seeds is their scant livelihood until they purchase a goat as another money-making venture. The goat disappoints them, but on the feast of Purim something wonderful takes place. Complementary illustrations.

Valentine's Day

Brown, Marc. **Arthur's Valentine.** Little, Brown, 1980. 6–9.

Arthur's secret admirer causes him embarrassment. Finally he figures out who it is and turns the tables on his Valentine. A funny animal story. (Picture book)

Nixon, Joan Lowery. **The Valentine Mystery.** Illus. Jim Cummins. Albert Whitman, 1979. 7–10.

Susan receives an unsigned valentine. Her only clue about the sender comes from two-year-old Barney who tells her the person wore watches on his tennis shoes. She must think about how a toddler talks in order to solve the mystery. (Picture book)

Quinn, Gardner. **Valentine Crafts and Cookbook.** Illus. Madeline Grossman. Harvey House, Publishers, 1977. 8–12.

A brief history of Valentine's Day and its interesting customs and easy-to-follow directions for creating cards, gifts, and special foods are included in this excellent resource book. Attractive illustrations.

Wahl, Jan. **Pleasant Fieldmouse's Valentine Trick.** Illus. Erik Blegvad. E. P. Dutton, 1977. 4–7.

The animals in the forest are not getting along, and Pleasant Fieldmouse decides to do something to bring them together again on friendly terms. He devises a plan which culminates on St. Valentine's Day. Black and white sketches. (Picture book)

Other Holidays

Barth, Edna. **Shamrocks, Harps, and Shillèlaghs: The Story of the St. Patrick's Day Symbols.** Illus. Ursula Arndt. Seabury Press, 1977. 10–up.

Another informative title added to Barth's holiday collection. Teachers and students alike will enjoy this well-written book that explains the origin and meaning of the symbols and legends associated with St. Patrick's Day. The index and annotated reading list will prove helpful to the young researcher.

Bunting, Eve. **St. Patrick's Day in the Morning.** Illus. Jan Brett. Clarion Books, 1980. 5–8.

Jamie Donovan proves to himself that he's not too young to march in the St. Patrick's Day parade. Illustrations authentically portray the Irish countryside and characters. Young readers easily relate to Jamie's aspirations and to the excitement of celebrating holidays. (Picture book)

Cheng, Hou-tien. **The Chinese New Year.** Illus. by author. Holt, Rinehart and Winston, 1976. 7–10.

Artful scissor cuts illustrate this informative account of the Chinese holiday that marks the beginning of spring. The festivities stretch over several days and include gift exchanges, special food, firecrackers, dances, and parades, culminating with the Lantern Festival.

Hathaway, Nancy. **Thanksgiving Crafts and Cookbook.** Illus. Hannah Berman. Harvey House, Publishers, 1979. 8–12.

Crafts, recipes, and a game centered around a Thanksgiving theme are collected in this volume. Simple instructions and black and white illustrations introduce projects such as dioramas, place cards, collages, puppets, and wall hangings. The author has also written *Halloween Crafts and Cookbook.*

Hopkins, Lee Bennett, compiler. **Beat the Drum: Independence Day Has Come.** Illus. Tomie de Paola. Harcourt Brace Jovanovich, 1977. 6–9.

The patriotic aspect of the Fourth of July and the fun of picnics, fireworks, and parades come to life in this collection of poems by poets ranging from Carl Sandburg to Shel Silverstein. Bright red and blue illustrations add to the enjoyment of the book.

Hopkins, Lee Bennett, compiler. **Merrily Comes Our Harvest In: Poems for Thanksgiving.** Illus. Ben Shecter. Harcourt Brace Jovanovich, 1978. 6–up.

The spirit and history of an American Thanksgiving are celebrated in twenty delightful poems. This anthology is fifth in a series of poems on specific holidays. A fine classroom tool. Brown ink illustrations.

Lobel, Arnold. **Frog and Toad All Year.** Harper & Row, Publishers, 1976. 6–8.

Five short stories relate the adventures of Frog and Toad during each season of the year and at Christmas. Humorous illustrations and an easy-to-read text make this third volume in a series about these two best friends another delightful book. (Picture book)

Madhubuti, Safisha L. **The Story of Kwanza.** Illus. Murry N. Depillars. Third World Press, 1977. 8–10.

Kwanza, a special holiday of thanksgiving for all that has been done and built during the year, was first celebrated in Egypt, known long ago as Chem, a great black nation. The holiday reaffirms the Africans' sense of self-determination.

Sharmat, Marjorie Weinman. **Griselda's New Year.** Illus. Normand Chartier. Macmillan Publishing, 1979. 4–7.

Griselda the goose wants to help her friends, but mostly she makes things a lot worse. When she tries to carry out her New Year's resolutions, her good deeds backfire. Big and bold drawings of some funny animals.

Williams, Barbara. **Chester Chipmunk's Thanksgiving.** Illus. Kay Chorao. E. P. Dutton, 1978. 4–7.

Chester Chipmunk is grateful for his many blessings at Thanksgiving time. Besides his large burrow and his new cloak, he has more than enough pecans for the winter. Inviting others to share his food is at first a disappointment and then a happy surprise. Delightful tan and brown illustrations in this good read-aloud book. (Picture book)

Collections

Alexander, Sue. **Small Plays for Special Days.** Illus. Tom Huffman. Seabury Press, 1977. 3–6.

Seven short and entertaining plays about popular holidays. Plays are written for two actors, but this number can easily be extended. Suggestions are given for easy-to-make costumes and props. An excellent resource book for the teacher of primary students.

Livingston, Myra Cohn, editor. **Callooh! Callay! Holiday Poems for Young Readers.** Illus. Janet Stevens. Atheneum, 1978. 8–12.

A collection of over eighty poems that celebrate holidays, including well-known and less famous poets and representing a time range from eleventh-century China to twentieth-century America. Contains something of the old and familiar, something of the new and fresh.

Quackenbush, Robert, compiler. **The Holiday Song Book.** Illus. by author. Lothrop, Lee & Shepard Books, 1977. 7–up.

One hundred familiar and lesser-known songs for holidays, including twenty-seven arrangements for easy piano and guitar. Martin Luther King's birthday is included, as is Passover, Pan American Day and Arbor Day. A useful reference for teachers, group leaders, and libraries.

Sarnoff, Jane. **Light the Candles! Beat the Drums! A Book of Holidays.** Illus. Reynold Ruffins. Charles Scribner's Sons, 1979. 8–12.

Teachers and children alike will enjoy this book of holidays and special events. Many famous characters are found in the text and material for a variety of ideas to be explored is found on every page. Colored and black and white illustrations.

Tudor, Tasha. **A Time to Keep: The Tasha Tudor Book of Holidays.** Illus. by author. Rand McNally, 1977. All ages.

With few words and beautifully bordered watercolor paintings, the author-illustrator describes traditional holiday celebrations in a New England household. A book for all ages to experience and enjoy.

Additional Holiday Books

Andersen, Hans Christian. *The Little Match Girl.* Illus. Blair Lent. Houghton Mifflin, 1968. 6–10.

Branley, Franklyn. *The Christmas Sky.* Illus. Blair Lent. Thomas Y. Crowell, 1966. 8–11.

Bright, Robert. *Georgie's Halloween.* Doubleday, 1958. 4–8.

Burch, Robert. *Renfroe's Christmas.* Illus. Rocco Negri. Viking Press, 1968. 7–10.

Carlson, Natalie Savage. *Befana's Gift.* Illus. Robert Quackenbush. Harper & Row, Publishers, 1969. 8–11.

Carlson, Natalie Savage. *The Family under the Bridge.* Illus. Garth Williams. Harper & Row, Publishers, 1958. 9–up.

Caudill, Rebecca. *A Certain Small Shepherd.* Illus. William Pène du Bois. Holt, Rinehart and Winston, 1965. 6–up.

Coombs, Patricia. *Dorrie and the Halloween Plot.* Lothrop, Lee & Shepard Books, 1976. 6–10.

Dalgliesh, Alice. *The Fourth of July Story.* Illus. Marie Nonnast. Charles Scribner's Sons, 1956. 8–12.

Davis, Katherine, Henry Onorati, and Harry Simeone. *The Little Drummer Boy.* Illus. Ezra Jack Keats. Macmillan, Publishing, 1968. 4–up.

Devlin, Wende, and Harry Devlin. *Cranberry Thanksgiving.* Parents Magazine Press, 1971. 5–8.

Domanska, Janina. *Din Dan Don: It's Christmas.* Greenwillow Books, 1975. 4–8.

Embry, Margaret. *The Blue-Nosed Witch.* Illus. Carl Rose. Holiday House, 1956. 6–9.

Ets, Marie Hall, and Aurora Labastida. *Nine Days to Christmas.* Illus. Marie Hall Ets. Viking Press, 1959. 4–8.

Gregorowski, Christopher. *Why a Donkey Was Chosen.* Illus. Caroline Browne. Doubleday, 1975. 5–8.

Heyward, Du Bose. *The Country Bunny and the Little Gold Shoes.* Illus. Marjorie Flack. Houghton Mifflin, 1939. 3–7.

Hoban, Lillian. *Arthur's Christmas Cookies.* Harper & Row, Publishers, 1972. 4–8.

Hopkins, Lee Bennett, comp. *Hey-How for Halloween.* Illus. Janet McCaffery. Harcourt Brace Jovanovich, 1974. 6–16.

Kahl, Virginia. *Plum Pudding for Christmas.* Charles Scribner's Sons, 1956. 4–9.

Lindgren, Astrid. *Christmas in the Stable.* Illus. Harald Wiberg. Coward, McCann & Geoghegan, 1962. 4–8.

Mariana. *Miss Flora McFlimsey's Valentine.* Lothrop, Lee & Shepard Books, 1962. 6–9.

Milhous, Katherine. *Appolonia's Valentine.* Charles Scribner's Sons, 1954. 5–9.

Milhous, Katherine. *The Egg Tree.* Charles Scribner's Sons, 1950. 6–8.

Moore, Clement C. *The Night Before Christmas.* Illus. Tasha Tudor. Rand McNally, 1976. 4–up.

Robbins, Ruth. *Baboushka and the Three Kings.* Illus. Nicolas Sidjakov. Parnassus Press, 1960. 5–9.

Robinson, Barbara. *The Best Christmas Pageant Ever.* Illus. Judith Gwyn Brown. Harper & Row, Publishers, 1972. 8–up.

Von Jüchen, Aurel. *The Holy Night.* Trans. by Cornelia Schaeffer. Illus. Celestino Piatti. Atheneum, 1968. 5–8.

Concepts

Alphabet

Asch, Frank. **Little Devil's ABC.** Charles Scribner's Sons, 1979. 6–9.

Little devils appear on each page in a humorous situation relating to a word associated with a given alphabet letter. Each page also shows the alphabet letter in uppercase and lowercase, decorated with tiny black and white drawings of objects. The sign language symbol for each letter is also included.

Chess, Victoria. **Alfred's Alphabet Walk.** Greenwillow Books, 1979. 4–7.

Alfred Animal puts off learning his ABC's; instead, he goes for a walk past assorted animals, the name of each beginning with a different letter. By the walk's end, he has mastered the alphabet. The use of several words per page, including adjectives, nouns, and verbs, makes this a challenging text. Outstanding illustrations.

Coletta, Irene. **From A to Z: The Collected Letters of Irene and Hallie Coletta.** Illus. Hallie Coletta. Prentice-Hall, 1979. 4–7.

Letters of the alphabet are introduced through a rhymed rebus on each page. A border of pictures around each rebus reinforces the sound of the letter. The two-color drawings are both entertaining and educational.

Crowther, Robert. **The Most Amazing Hide-and-Seek Alphabet Book.** Illus. by author. Viking Press, 1977. 5–8.

A manipulative book with flaps to pull or twist to illustrate each letter. The pages contain large bold block letters in black but colorful animals pop out from behind each one. To be used by an adult with the child, but a highly imaginative book worth that limitation.

Emberley, Ed. **Ed Emberley's A B C.** Little, Brown, 1978. 4–7.

Each alphabet letter is built in four stages by an animal, and each double-page spread shows objects the names of which use that letter but not always at the beginning of the word. Final pages note all the words, and arrows show the directions for making each letter. Vivid colors.

Fletcher, Helen Jill. **Picture Book A B C.** Illus. Jennie Williams. Platt & Munk, Publishers, 1978. 3–5.

This ABC book is just right for a child's first exposure to the alphabet. The large, colorful pictures are a joy to look at, and the rhymed text is fun to hear. The letters of the alphabet and all of the animals and objects introduced in the book are depicted on the end pages.

Hyman, Trina Schart. **A Little Alphabet.** Little, Brown, 1980. 4–7.

In this tiny alphabet book, each letter is delicately illuminated with objects and activities beginning with the letter. A checklist is provided on the endpapers.

Mack, Stan. **The King's Cat Is Coming!** Pantheon Books, 1976. 4–7.

A startling announcement that the King's cat is coming causes much concern and consternation among the villagers. They speculate as to the alphabetical characteristics it might possess. It might be an angry cat or a bashful cat, who knows? Cartoon-like illustrations add to the fun.

Merriam, Eve. **Good Night to Annie.** Illus. John Wallner. Four Winds Press, 1980. 3–5.

Flowers and animals from A to Z drift off to sleep in this attractive alphabet book. Little Annie with nightcap and candle is pictured throughout the book. Beautifully colored pages stimulate questions. Unusual end pages.

A Peaceable Kingdom: The Shaker Abecedarius. Illus. Alice Provensen and Martin Provensen. Viking Press, 1978. 3–up.

"Kingfisher, Peacock, Anteater, Bat, Lizard, Ichneumon, Honeybee, Rat" reads this rhymed menagerie in an alphabet book originally published in 1882. Through amusing and authentic pictures, the artists show the various animals taking part in the daily life of a Shaker community. A book to treasure.

Rockwell, Anne. **Albert B. Cub & Zebra: An Alphabet Storybook.** Thomas Y. Crowell, 1977. 4–7.

This alphabet book is presented as a wordless story about a bear cub searching the world for his abducted friend, Zebra. Full-color illustrations build visual literacy skills. An amusing vocabulary-building story completes the book.

Weil, Lisl. **Owl and Other Scrambles.** E. P. Dutton, 1980. 6–9.

In this unusual alphabet book, the letters of each word make a picture. Readers will enjoy figuring out the puzzles as they read from

A to Z. The scrambled illustrations may encourage young artists to try their own.

Wild, Robin, and Jocelyn Wild. **The Bears' ABC Book.** J. B. Lippincott, 1977. 4–7.

Fun-filled illustrations show three young bears rummaging and romping through a dump, discovering items A through Z. Readers can guess what the bears discover for each letter.

Yolen, Jane. **All in the Woodland Early: An ABC Book.** Illus. Jane Breskin Zalben. William Collins Publishers, 1979. 6–8.

An original song, complete with music, gives the first person account of a girl who goes into the woodland. She sees birds, animals, and insects from A to Z. Everyone tells her they are going a-hunting; in the end their hunt turns out to be a search for friends. Beautiful full-color drawings.

Color, Shape, Size

Anno, Mitsumasa. **The King's Flower.** William Collins Publishers, 1979. 4–10.

A single small red tulip shows the king, who always wants the biggest of everything, that biggest isn't necessarily best. Ink and watercolor illustrations highlight the book. (Picture book)

Asch, Frank. **Turtle Tale.** Dial Press, 1978. 4–7.

Turtle gets into trouble whether his head is in or out of his shell. Gradually he learns what a wise turtle must do. A brief story with simple illustrations that clearly outline the shapes familiar to the young child.

Brown, Marcia. **Listen to a Shape.** Illus. by author. Franklin Watts, 1979. All ages.

Outstanding color photographs of nature's handiwork depict the shapes that make up the world. The text is almost poetic in its descriptions. It invites children to observe the world more closely. One of several photographic concept books by this author-illustrator.

Crews, Donald. **Freight Train.** Greenwillow Books, 1978. 4–7.

Two concepts are introduced: colors and the various cars that make up a freight train. With only a few words, the ideas are presented using bold and handsome illustrations. The design of the book adds impact. 1979 Caldecott Honor Book. (Picture book)

Hoban, Tana. **Is It Red? Is It Yellow? Is It Blue?** Greenwillow Books, 1978. 4–7.

Bright colored photographs of ordinary objects in the city are matched in bold rounds of color at the bottom of each page. Children can look for six colors: red, yellow, blue, orange, green, and purple. Composition of the pictures is outstanding. (Picture book)

Kalan, Robert. **Blue Sea.** Illus. Donald Crews. Greenwillow Books, 1979. 3–5.

Little fish swims in the blue sea and is pursued by bigger and bigger fish. The progression of small to large fish shows the beginning reader the concept of relative size.

Lamperti, Noelle, et al. **Noelle's Brown Book.** New Victoria Publishers, 1979. 4–7.

A brown girl with friends of many races explores her world of brown things she loves. Photos are mixes with sketches in brown and black and white. Useful to teachers working with children in pride-building or in writing their own books.

Scarry, Richard. **Richard Scarry's Best First Book Ever!** Random House, 1979. 4–7.

As usual, Richard Scarry has hit the jackpot! Although not on a very sophisticated level, Huckle Cat and Lowly Worm's profusely illustrated adventures in learning about colors, counting, shapes, sizes, manners, etc., will appeal to children. (Picture book)

Wildsmith, Brian. **What the Moon Saw.** Oxford University Press, 1978. 4–7.

The Moon complains because she sees little of the world, so the Sun shows her many wonderful things. Large, colorful illustrations clarify the twelve pairs of opposites depicted. Familiar objects and animals are used as examples.

Counting

√Anno, Mitsumasa. **Anno's Counting Book.** Thomas Y. Crowell, 1977. 4–7.

In this wordless book many mathematical concepts are deceptively hidden in the natural everyday living situations. The child will discover one-to-one correspondences, groups and sets, and changes over time periods. Background information for the teacher is provided on the last page. The soft watercolor illustrations executed in naive style are appealing.

Bayley, Nicola. **One Old Oxford Ox.** Illus. by author. Atheneum, 1977. 7–10.

At first glance this is a counting book, but its uniqueness lies in the incongruous tongue-in-cheek illustrations of the tongue-twisting

rhyme; "five frippery Frenchmen foolishly fishing for frogs" are portrayed as alligators on the grounds of a French chateau. A handsomely designed, elegantly illustrated book.

Bridgman, Elizabeth. **All the Little Bunnies: A Counting Book.** Illus. by
author. Atheneum, 1977. 3-5.

A rabbit family performs daily tasks while counting to ten and back.
The simple rhyming pattern is pleasing to the reader. Pen drawings
are filled with gentle humor.

Farber, Norma. **Up the Down Elevator.** Illus. Annie Gusman. Addison-
Wesley Publishing, 1979. 4-9.

The fun begins in this counting book when a baker with a hot cross
bun gets on the elevator at one. At each stop more unusual characters
get on until they reach the tenth floor. Rhymed text and soft black
and white drawings add to this zany tale.

Ginsburg, Mirra. **Kitten from One to Ten.** Illus. Giulio Maestro. Crown
Publishers, 1980. 3-5.

The rhymed verse describes the adventures of a mischievous kitten.
Large, uncluttered illustrations provide the beginning reader satisfaction in counting bright objects. (Picture book)

Howard, Katherine. **I Can Count to 100, Can You?** Illus. Michael J.
Smollin. Random House, 1979. 4-7.

An unusual counting book that offers practice in counting several
ones, twos, or threes. Colorful and interestingly full pages work well
for interaction between child and adult or among several children.

Lasker, Joe. **Lentil Soup.** Illus. by author. Albert Whitman, 1977. 6-8.

Cardinal and ordinal numbers and the days of the week are concepts
used in this humorous story of a farmer whose wife could never
quite make the lentil soup as good as mother's, until she overcooked
it! Illustrations set the story in pioneer days.

Maestro, Betsy. **Harriet Goes to the Circus.** Illus. Giulio Maestro. Crown
Publishers, 1977. 5-7.

Colorful Harriet, the elephant, goes to the circus early to be first in
line. Mouse is second and Duck is third in a delightful development
of this number concept in words and pictures. Format and characters
are very appropriate for flannelboard storytelling.

Pavey, Peter. **One Dragon's Dream.** Bradbury Press, 1978. 5-8.

Ostensibly a counting book, this dragon's dream takes the reader to
a fantasy land where every animal and object is authentically detailed, sometimes in the expected habitat and sometimes surprisingly

out of place. The patterns, colors, and artistic composition of each double page are a source of visual delight and scientific information.

Space and Time Perspectives

Ferro, Beatriz. **Caught in the Rain.** Illus. Michele Sambin. Doubleday, 1980. 4–7.

Children delight in finding a variety of shelters when caught in the rain! The best is that little portable roof: an umbrella. The text addresses the children directly, while gentle, bright watercolor drawings induce a feeling of cheerful security. (Picture book)

Hoberman, Mary Ann. **A House Is a House for Me.** Illus. Betty Fraser. Viking Press, 1978. 4–7.

A kennel's a house for a dog, and a dog is a house for a flea, but "a house is a house for me." The rhymed text and detailed pictures will delight and stretch the imagination of young readers and listeners as they discover that "each creature that's known has a house of its own, and the earth is a house for us all." (Picture book)

Kessler, Ethel, and Leonard Kessler. **What's inside the Box?** Dodd, Mead, 1976. 5–7.

Something mysterious is inside the box. It has twenty toes and two ears. While the animals solve the mystery, the reader is introduced to such concepts as distance, near, far, time, yesterday, today, tomorrow. Easy to read and very funny.

Thurman, Judith. **I'd Like to Try a Monster's Eye.** Illus. Reina Rubel. Atheneum, 1977. 6–9.

A small girl tells about her view from three feet above sea level and wonders how things would look if she were an acrobat high above the crowds or a worm an inch underground. Drawings facilitate conceptualization of varying perspectives.

Trivett, Daphne, and John Trivett. **Time for Clocks.** Illus. Giulio Maestro. Thomas Y. Crowell, 1979. 6–9.

The author begins with simple concepts related to telling time and moves to complex notions. Lively cartoon penguins create clocks to illustrate the ideas. Experiments and activities are included.

Waber, Bernard. **The Snake: A Very Long Story.** Houghton Mifflin, 1978. 3–5.

The rippling green body of a snake, the main character, moves from page to page in this unique picture book. The simple text is illustrated with road signs, flowers, and telephone poles to reinforce the concepts of time and distance. A surprise ending awaits the reader.

Wakefield, Joyce. **From Where You Are.** Illus. Tom Dunnington. Childrens Press, 1978. 4–7.

Easy-to-read rhymed couplets and bold and colorful illustrations depict everyday things and events that are different when seen from various perspectives. Uses the word "unless" throughout.

Additional Concept Books

Anno, Mitsumasa. *Anno's Alphabet: An Adventure in Imagination.* Thomas Y. Crowell, 1974. 5–up.
Anno, Mitsumasa. *Topsy-Turvies: Pictures to Stretch the Imagination.* John Wetherhill, 1970. 5–10.
Burningham, John. *Seasons.* Bobbs, 1971. 4–8.
Carle, Eric. *1, 2, 3 to the Zoo.* World, 1968. 3–6.
Carle, Eric. *The Very Hungry Caterpillar.* Collins-World, 1972. 4–7.
Eichenberg, Fritz. *Ape in a Cape.* Harcourt Brace Jovanovich, 1952. 4–6.
Eichenberg, Fritz. *Dancing in the Moon.* Harcourt Brace Jovanovich, 1955. 4–8.
Falls, C. B. *ABC Book.* Doubleday, 1923. 2–6.
Feelings, Muriel. *Moja Means One: Swahili Counting Book.* Illus. Tom Feelings. Dial Press, 1971. 5–10.
Gág, Wanda. *The ABC Bunny.* Coward, McCann & Geoghegan, 1933. 3–6.
Hoban, Tana. *Circles, Triangles, and Squares.* Macmillan Publishing, 1974. 4–7.
Hoban, Tana. *Count and See.* Macmillan Publishing, 1972. 4–7.
Hoban, Tana. *Look Again.* Macmillan Publishing, 1971. 6–14.
Hoban, Tana. *Push-Pull, Empty-Full: A Book of Opposites.* Macmillan Publishing, 1972. 3–7.
Langstaff, John. *Over in the Meadow.* Illus. Feodor Rojankovsky. Harcourt Brace Jovanovich, 1957. 3–up.
Lewis, Stephen. *Zoo City.* Greenwillow Books, 1976. 6–9.
Mendoza, George. *The Marcel Marceau Alphabet Book.* Photos by Milton H. Greene. Doubleday, 1970. 6–10.
Oxenbury, Helen. *Helen Oxenbury's ABC of Things.* Franklin Watts, 1972. 4–7.
Reiss, John J. *Shapes.* Bradbury Press, 1974. 4–6.
Tudor, Tasha. *A Is for Annabelle.* Henry Z. Walck, 1954. 5–7.
Tudor, Tasha. *1 Is One.* Henry Z. Walck, 1956. 4–6.
Wildsmith, Brian. *Brian Wildsmith's ABC.* Franklin Watts, 1963. 3–5.

Social Studies

Careers

Anders, Rebecca. **Careers in a Library.** Photographs by Milton J. Blumenfeld. Lerner Publications, 1978. 6–8.

Full-page color photos accompany the opposite page summary of several different, but related, occupations in the field of library work. The job descriptions speak to requirements and training needed. New words are italicized. Another title in the Early Career Book series is *Careers in Photography.*

Demuth, Jack, and Patricia Demuth. **City Horse.** Photographs by Jack Demuth. Dodd, Mead, 1979. 7–10.

A spirited Tennessee Walker is brought to New York City to work for the police department. Black and white photographs combine with text to give an intimate look at Hannon's adjustment to city life, the places he patrols, and his friendship with rider Mike, a police officer. Good for class discussion.

English, Betty Lou. **Women at Their Work.** Dial Press, 1977. 9–12.

Twenty-one women of various backgrounds and ethnic groups tell why they chose and love their jobs, citing both the hardest parts and the best parts. Included are a jockey, an orchestra conductor, a chemist, a firefighter, a judge, and a carpenter. Black and white photos, large print, and large margins.

Fenten, D. X. **Ms.—Architect.** Westminster Press, 1977. 12–up.

While aimed toward females to encourage investigation in nontraditional careers, males would find this book useful also as it discusses architects' training and career blocks. Appendix lists colleges and universities offering programs. Part of a series.

Fowler, Bob. **Sports: Looking Forward to a Career.** Dillon Press, 1978. 10–12.

"What jobs does a general manager have?" "How many women work for pro football teams?" These are some of the questions asked and answered to inform the reader of the many positions available in sports. Excellent for those planning a career in this field. Black and white photographs; index included.

Goldreich, Gloria, and Esther Goldreich. **What Can She Be? A Computer Scientist.** Photographs by Robert Ipcar. Lothrop, Lee & Shepard Books, 1979. 8–12.

The authors describe the career possibilities in computer science by following a systems analyst, Linda Wong, through her day working with computers. A "What Can She Be?" career-lifestyle series book. Other titles include *A Legislator* and *A Film Producer.*

Harper, Anita. **How We Work.** Illus. Christine Roche. Harper & Row, Publishers, 1977. 5–8.

Vivid pictures and few words describe varieties of working conditions. Some people work alone, some work in a group; some work high, others low. A starter for thinking about variation in this important aspect of life.

Jaspersohn, William. **The Ballpark: One Day behind the Scenes at a Major League Game.** Little, Brown, 1980. 10–up.

A pictorial view of Fenway Park, home of the Boston Red Sox, is given through excellent black and white photographs. The reader discovers all the different people involved in preparing for a major league baseball game from grounds crew and food services to players and manager.

Lerner, Mark. **Careers at a Zoo.** Photographs by Milton J. Blumenfeld. Lerner Publications, 1980. 7–10.

Because zoos are special places, many people of different talents are required to operate them. With unnumbered pages and large print, fifteen occupational areas in zoos are described on one page while a color photo on the opposite page shows a worker doing that job. An Early Career book.

LeSieg, Theo. **Maybe You Should Fly a Jet! Maybe You Should Be a Vet!** Illus. Michael J. Smollin. Beginner Books, 1980. 4–7.

Different types of work are depicted in funny pictures and humorous rhymes. Jobs from flying a jet to being a vet are described. Colorful cartoon-like illustrations.

Matteson, George. **Draggermen.** Four Winds Press, 1979. 10–up.

Text and photographs follow the adventures of commercial fishermen aboard a modern trawler in search of cod, haddock, and yellowtail flounder off the New England coast. Includes information on different species, storms and wrecks, and the history of American commerical fishing.

Neal, Harry Edward. **The Secret Service in Action.** Elsevier/Nelson Books, 1980. 12–up.

Counterfeiters, hijackers, and assassins, both successful and unsuccessful, are among the many characters who people the pages of this fascinating story of the U.S. Secret Service. Included is a chapter on career opportunities within the organization. Illustrated with photographs.

O'Connor, Karen. **Working with Horses: A Roundup of Careers.** Photographs by Kelle Rankin. Dodd, Mead, 1980. 12–up.

Horses have been very helpful to humans for thousands of years. There are about ten million in the United States today, providing many interesting careers. The author interviews a blacksmith, a circus horse trainer, a jockey, a veterinarian, and others. Clear photographs.

Paige, David. **A Day in the Life of a Forest Ranger.** Photographs by Michael Mauney. Troll Associates, 1979. 8–12.

A real-life district ranger takes the reader through a typical day. Although containing only thirty-two pages, this treatment of a ranger's job is surprisingly thorough. Good introduction for career education. Part of the "A Day in the Life of . . ." series, other titles deal with an emergency room nurse, a TV news reporter, and a rock musician. Color photos; reinforced bindings.

Pelta, Kathy. **What Does a Paramedic Do?** Dodd, Mead, 1978. 10–12.

The history of emergency medical care is examined and the training and work of paramedics are explained. The precise, objective text is journalistic in style. One of a series by the same publisher.

Rennert, Amy. **Making It in Photography.** Photographs by Bruce Curtis. G. P. Putnam's Sons, 1980. 12–up.

The author presents several intriguing glimpses into different photographic occupations by describing the careers of actual people in the field. Included in appendices are lists of colleges that offer degrees in photography. Excellent book to stimulate interest in this career field.

Saul, Wendy. **Butcher, Baker, Cabinetmaker: Photographs of Women at Work.** Photographs by Abigail Heyman. Thomas Y. Crowell, 1978. 5–8.

Highlights of twenty-five different occupations, stressing women at work in traditionally male jobs. Easy text describes the job pictured and how people learn their work. Black and white photos depict old, young, black, white, homely, and attractive women: the real world. Contains good career awareness questions.

Seed, Suzanne. **Fine Trades.** Photographs by author. Follett Publishing, 1979. 12–up.

Descriptions and discussions of the specialized trades and the lifestyles of individuals who "add grace and beauty to all our lives." Included are a violin maker, an art conservator, an arborist, a chef, and others. The photographs express the technical as well as the aesthetic nature of the artisans' work.

Stilley, Frank. **Here Is Your Career: Airline Pilot.** G. P. Putnam's Sons, 1978. 10–up.

Airline pilots must undergo rigorous training and meet challenging tests of skill, courage, and quick thinking. Interviews with both men and women pilots attest to the demands and rewards of an exciting career. A very readable book.

Strong, Arline. **Veterinarian, Doctor for Your Pet.** Illus. by author. Atheneum, 1977. 7–10.

Simple text and clear black and white photographs follow the work of a veterinarian as she treats various domestic animals in her office. Important information for pet owners is included.

Williams, Barbara. **I Know a Salesperson.** Illus. Frank Aloise. G. P. Putnam's Sons, 1978. 9–12.

Written in conversational style, a young narrator tells of his twenty-one-year-old sister's career choice as a sporting goods salesperson in a department store. The book discusses filling out personnel applications, employee orientation training, and the secrets of selling success. Glossary; black and white line drawings.

Communication

Adkins, Jan. **Symbols: A Silent Language.** Illus. by author. Walker, 1978. 8–12.

The use of symbols from musical notations to weather maps, card games to international traffic directions is shown in intriguing illustrations and brief text. A discussion of trademarks is included with many commonly recognized symbols pictured.

Albert, Burton, Jr. **More Codes for Kids.** Illus. Jerry Warshaw. Albert Whitman, 1979. 8–12.

A sequel to *Codes for Kids,* there are twenty-five master code keys, over one hundred mystery messages, and over four hundred secret words. Codes involve numbers, spaced letters, and many other clues. Humorous drawings highlighted in orange add to the fun in this brain-teasing book.

Bielewicz, Julian A. **Secret Languages: Communicating in Codes and Ciphers.** Elsevier/Nelson Books, 1976. 8–12.

Fascinating lore about codes and ciphers, some secret, enable youngsters to learn about ways of communicating privately. Readers can test their growing cryptoanalytic skills with cryptograms scattered throughout the book as well as in the seven secret messages, with answers at the end. Black and white sketches; glossary.

Esterer, Arnulf K., and Louise A. Esterer. **Saying It without Words.** Julian Messner, 1980. 8–12.

Everyday signs and symbols are discussed as methods of communication. Chapters describe symbols concerning flags, trademarks, health, coats of arms, highway information, holidays, and international organizations. This interesting book piques children's curiosities for further study. Many drawings illustrate the symbols. Index.

Fisher, Leonard Everett. **Alphabet Art: Thirteen ABCs from around the World.** Illus. by author. Four Winds Press, 1978. 10–up.

Each of the thirteen alphabets is placed on a double-page spread with an English pronunciation indicated for each letter. Brief historical commentaries on the culture and the alphabet are given. Boldly executed in red with scratchboard drawings, this is a useful resource for art, social studies, and handwriting enrichment.

Fronval, George, and Daniel Dubois (translator E. W. Egan). **Indian Signs and Signals.** Illus. Jean Marcellin. Sterling Publishing, 1979. 8–12.

The nonverbal language used by Plains Indians is presented by concise text and hundreds of colorful illustrations. Other information includes trail markings, different types of signals, and body paint. Very useful for social studies units on Native Americans.

Myller, Rolf. **Symbols & Their Meaning.** Atheneum, 1978. 8–12.

Communication through the use of symbols is thoroughly discussed. The author explains and depicts symbols on subjects such as religion, traffic, music, flags, braille, morse code, and many others. Numerous illustrations add to the text.

Stewig, John Warren. **Sending Messages.** Photographs by Richard D. Bradley. Houghton Mifflin, 1978. 8-12.

People use many ways to communicate ideas. Written and spoken language are the most obvious, but body language (face change, stance, movement) also sends messages to others. Some people use special forms of nonverbal communication, such as dance and music. Illustrations and photographs add to the book.

Contemporary World Cultures

Allen, Thomas B. **Where Children Live.** Prentice-Hall, 1980. 6–9.

Colored pencil drawings present children in their home environments from different cultures throughout the world. Useful in primary social studies units.

Cole, Ann, et al. **Children Are Children Are Children: An Activity Approach to Exploring Brazil, France, Iran, Japan, Nigeria and the U.S.S.R.** Illus. Lois Axeman. Little, Brown, 1978. 8–12.

Excellent suggestions are given for activities related to the study of Brazil, France, Iran, Japan, Nigeria, and the Soviet Union. Written for children, the very readable instructions provide ways to explore the countries' geography, history, fine arts, customs, food, and language. Unique activities can be adapted to other studies. A superior resource.

Galbraith, Catherine Atwater, and Rama Mehta. **India: Now and through Time.** Houghton Mifflin, 1980. 12–up.

Views of India's past, its coping with recurring problems and its emergence as a nuclear power are skillfully blended together in a readable text with frequent complementary photographs. An informative, overall view makes this an excellent supplement. Map, bibliography, table of contents.

Hagbrink, Bodil (translator George Simpson). **Children of Lapland.** Illus. by author. Tundra Books, 1978. 7–10.

The lives of Norwegian Laplanders are followed from their wintertime tundra village through spring migration with their reindeer herd to summer life on the islands of the Arctic Ocean. The double page full-color pictures have abundant scenes, each described in a single column to the left of the picture. A beautiful, informative book.

Harper, Anita. **How We Live.** Illus. Christine Roche. Harper & Row, Publishers, 1977. 6–8.

An unusual, lively primer that entertains as it informs, as does its counterpart *How We Work* by the same author. Diverse life-styles and situations are presented as the reader begins to explore a complex world. Colorful cartoon drawings extend the brief, simple text.

Mangurian, David. **Children of the Incas.** Four Winds Press, 1979. 8–11.

Modesto Quispe Mamani, a thirteen-year-old Quechua Indian boy, lives in the highlands of Peru in South America. Life is hard in the small village but the family works together. Modesto hopes to become an engineer so he can help his people. Black and white photographs.

Musgrove, Margaret. **Ashanti to Zulu: African Traditions.** Illus. Leo Dillon and Diane Dillon. Dial Press, 1976. All ages.

Readers are given a mini-tour of the "Dark Continent" as they read and observe twenty-six African tribes from A to Z. The large, colorful pictures prepared in pastels, watercolors, and acrylics depict a family, their living quarters, artifacts, and a local animal. Carefully researched. 1977 Caldecott Award.

Rau, Margaret. **Our World: The People's Republic of China.** Julian Messner, 1978. 8–12.

One of a number of books about China for young readers by the author, this introduction emphasizes the way of life of the people. Part of the book is somewhat personalized by relating activities of a Tseng family of Peking. A picture map and black and white photographs augment the text.

Rau, Margaret. **The People of New China.** Photographs by author. Julian Messner, 1978. 9–12.

Each of the eight chapters of this readable, informative book centers on a particular village, town, or city in modern China. For a personal touch, each also focuses on the life and activities of a young person. Numerous black and white photographs.

Raynor, Dorka. **My Friends Live in Many Places.** Albert Whitman, 1980. 5–8.

Children from all over the world grace forty-five outstanding black and white photographs. Brief captions tell the location of the scenes. This is a beautiful collection that shows similar expressions in all manner of garb and locale. Good for social studies units as well as for browsing.

Singer, Julia. **Impressions: A Trip to the German Democratic Republic.** Illus. by author. Atheneum, 1979. 9–12.

Through text and photographs taken on trips in 1973 and 1977, the author presents personal experiences and observations of various aspects of life in the German Democratic Republic. The emphasis is on the people she met, something of their lives, thoughts, hopes. A personal approach and an easy style, including many conversational quotations.

Spier, Peter. **People.** Illus. by author. Doubleday, 1980. All ages.

While celebrating the uniqueness of individuals, the art and text explore various cultures' homes, foods, games, clothing, faces, and religions. Readers will appreciate the enormous diversity within the world's population.

Wiedel, Janine. **Looking at Iran.** Photographs by author. J. B. Lippincott, 1978. 8–12.

Although no book can hope to keep up with events in the Middle East, this brief overview of Iran's culture, history, geography, and economy will give young students some insight into the 1980–81 hostage crisis as well as a strong feeling of the sweep of history over an exciting and troubled land. Colorful photographs, straightforward writing.

Diverse American Cultures

Children's Writers and Artists Collaborative. **The New York Kid's Book.** Doubleday, 1979. 8–12.

Stories, history, games, puzzles, recipes, photographs, poems, addresses, pictures, illustrations, recommended places to go and how to get there are all part of this oversized, softbound celebration of New York City. Compiled by 167 children's writers and authors, this book is great fun and a valuable reference. Not just for New York kids!

Drescher, Joan. **Your Family, My Family.** Illus. by author. Walker, 1980. 3–5.

Families come in many styles and sizes. There are single-parent families, two-parent families, and other kinds. Sometimes grandparents take care of families, some foster parents care for children. What really makes a family is sharing and caring. An understandable book with humorous illustrations.

Frank, Phil, and Susan Frank. **Subee Lives on a Houseboat.** Photographs by Bruce Forrester. Julian Messner, 1980. 8–12.

For thirty years, the floating community of Sausalito has been growing into a little town of over 300 houseboats on San Francisco Bay. The book describes the life of Subee, one of the many children of Sausalito, who lives on Spicebox with her mother, stepfather, and family pets.

McCunn, Ruthanne Lum. **An Illustrated History of the Chinese in America.** Design Enterprises of San Francisco, 1979. 10–up.

This book traces the role of the Chinese in America from the 1800s to the present day. The language is clear and readable enough for a ten year old. The message of the shameful treatment of the Chinese is also clear and powerful. Many photographs lend credence to this history.

Meltzer, Milton. **The Chinese Americans.** Thomas Y. Crowell, 1980. 10–up.

This well-written account tells of the usually overlooked role played by the Chinese in the opening of the West, of the discrimination and violence that the Chinese have endured in this land of freedom, and of the fact that the Chinese were not permitted to become U.S. citizens until 1943. A powerful indictment of institutionalized racism, illustrated with black and white photographs.

Wolf, Bernard. **In This Proud Land: The Story of a Mexican American Family.** J.B. Lippincott, 1978. 10–up.

With black and white photographs and straightforward narration, the story of the Hernandez family is told. The parents, one son, and six daughters live in the Rio Grande Valley of Texas near the Mexican border. In summer they must travel to Minnesota to find work to supplement the family income. Life in migrant quarters and in the fields is pictured, as are the close, responsible relationships within the family.

Economics

Doty, Roy, and Leonard Maar. **How Much Does America Cost?** Doubleday, 1979. 10–up.

The federal budget is a road map of where we have been, where we are now, and where we should be going. Divided into sections, and explained in cents, not dollars, the budget is understandable and personalized. Readers can update and compare subsequent budgets with the one illustrated here.

Eldred, Patricia. **Easy Money Making Projects.** Illus. Kevin Pederson. Creative Education, 1979. 9–12.

There are plenty of things children can do to earn money by providing needed services or selling things. Finding a job one enjoys, doing it well, and being responsible are practical tips insuring customer satisfaction. A brief book, but filled with good advice; cartoon-style drawings.

Fodor, R. V. **Nickels, Dimes, and Dollars: How Currency Works.** William Morrow, 1980. 8–12.

Money, from barter to plastic, is discussed in an interesting and readable book. Many black and white photographs enlighten the concepts. Topics include the use of money by individuals and the Federal Government, international money systems, and investment concepts. Index.

Morgan, Tom. **Money, Money, Money: How to Get and Keep It.** Illus. Joe Ciardiello. G. P. Putnam's Sons, 1978. 10–up.

Explains how money can make or cost money, why interest rates vary, and how to organize corporations. A clear and humorously written book that provides information and examples. Utilizes knowledge of percentages.

Rockwell, Anne. **Gogo's Pay Day.** Doubleday, 1978. 7–10.

Gogo the clown discovers, after buying presents for his friends, that he doesn't have enough money left to pay his rent. Amusing, detailed illustrations emphasize Gogo's problems. This is a good resource book to introduce necessary facts about money management. (Picture book)

Sattler, Helen Roney. **Dollars from Dandelions: 101 Ways to Earn Money.** Illus. Rita Flodén Leydon. Lothrop, Lee & Shepard Books, 1979. 12–up.

This easy-to-read, practical guide suggests 101 ways to earn money. Indoor jobs, outdoor jobs, part-time jobs, and summer specials are described with directions for accomplishing them. Black pen drawings; index.

Schwartz, Alvin. **Stores.** Photographs by Samuel Nocella, Jr. Macmillan Publishing, 1977. 7–10.

Whether or not the reader is curious about stores, this book is fascinating with its black and white photos and diagrams, easy reading, and interesting bits of information. A day's work with thirty-seven businesses in a small town is described. Two unusual recipes and an index.

Seuling, Barbara. **You Can't Count a Billion Dollars & Other Little-Known Facts about Money.** Illus. by author. Doubleday, 1979. 8–12.

Marvel Comics No. 1 was sold in 1976 for $8,000, the all-time record for a single comic book. This and other unique, true facts about money and finances can be found in this amusing and informative book.

Weinstein, Grace W. **Money of Your Own.** E. P. Dutton, 1977. 10–up.

Some people seem to know instinctively how to manage money, but others must learn through experience and common sense. The book illustrates how to keep account of money spent, money earned, and money saved. Shopping and use of credit cards are discussed. Valuable supplementary book for home or school.

Food

Berger, Melvin, and Gilda Berger. **The New Food Book.** Illus. Byron Barton. Thomas Y. Crowell, 1978. 10–12.

Without food, there could be no life, but many people do not eat wisely or well. This comprehensive and readable book covers nutrition, diet, consumer tips, and foods of the future information. Each chapter could stand alone as the basis of a report. Easy experiments and recipes are included.

de Paola, Tomie. **The Popcorn Book.** Holiday House, 1978. 6–9.

The history of popcorn, how it's stored and cooked, plus other stories and legends about this foodstuff are delightfully told. Colorful, humorous illustrations.

Distad, Audree. **Come to the Fair.** Harper & Row, Publishers, 1977. 8–12.

An overall view of fairs is given in the accounts of several youngsters as they prepare and participate in the South Dakota State Fair, Huron, South Dakota. An interesting and detailed picture of the work and purpose of the 4H Clubs is revealed. Photographs.

Giblin, James, and Dale Ferguson. **The Scarecrow Book.** Crown Publishers, 1980. 7–10.

Scarecrows have always been necessary for farmers; they can be traced back 3000 years. The different types and materials used to construct scarecrows in different regions of the world are discussed. Directions are given for creating a scarecrow. Interesting photographs; bibliography and index.

Heilman, Grant. **Wheat Country.** Photographs by author. Stephen Greene Press, 1977. 10–up.

More than 100 beautiful photographs, supported by captions and informative text, tell the story of wheat from seed to silo. The quality of the pictures and text communicates the roles of land, machines, and people that combine to put bread on the table.

Jenness, Aylette. **The Bakery Factory: Who Puts the Bread on Your Table.** Photographs by author. Thomas Y. Crowell, 1978. 8–12.

This behind-the-scenes look at a large commercial bakery shows the processes involved in the production of bread and other pastries. Clear black and white photographs show the machinery and people at work as they mix vast quantities of dough into bread, rolls, and a huge wedding cake. A few simple recipes are included; index.

Mintz, Lorelie Miller. **How to Grow Fruits and Berries.** Illus. by author. Julian Messner, 1980. 8–12.

Interesting explanations are given for growing fruit trees and berry bushes in orchards and on porches. Information is included on purchasing, planting, pruning, and feeding. Pen and ink illustrations.

Penner, Lucille Recht. **The Honey Book.** Hastings House, Publishers, 1980. 8–12.

Beekeeping is discussed as an industry and the importance of honey is shown throughout history. Recipes for the use of honey in beauty care and cooking are provided.

Perl, Lila. **Hunter's Stew and Hangtown Fry: What Pioneer America Ate and Why.** Illus. Richard Cuffari. Seabury Press, 1977. 10–up.

This is an unusual approach to life in nineteenth-century America through description of the foods eaten by immigrant groups as they settled in various regions of the country. People, food, and environments are vividly described. Twenty recipes are included. A sequel to *Slumps, Grunts, and Snickerdoodles: What Colonial America Ate and Why.*

Perl, Lila. **Junk Food, Fast Food, Health Food: What America Eats and Why.** Clarion Books, 1980. 10–up.

This exploration of modern America's eating habits paints a grim picture of our overconsumption of sugar, fat, and red meat, and of the decline in quality and variety of food due to the large food corporations' preoccupation with the bottom line. However, the reader is offered some practical suggestions for beating the system, including twenty natural food recipes. A well-organized and highly readable book with a message of great import.

Rockwell, Anne, and Harlow Rockwell. **The Supermarket.** Macmillan Publishing, 1979. 3–5.

A young child takes a trip to the supermarket with his mother and helps to choose the groceries. Bright, colorful illustrations highlight the text.

Rockwell, Harlow. **My Kitchen.** Greenwillow Books, 1980. 3–5.

A child tells the story of how his lunch is made. Brightly colored objects found in the kitchen aid in preparing the food and eating it.

Selsam, Millicent E. **Popcorn.** Photographs by Jerome Wexler. William Morrow, 1976. 7–10.

The growth cycle of the ever-popular corn plant, which delights nibblers, is examined. For those who want to grow their own, the steps are clearly given. Close-up photographs in color and black and white provide detailed information and make this an effective informational book for home or school.

Shuttlesworth, Dorothy E., and Gregory J. Shuttlesworth. **Farms for Today and Tomorrow: The Wonders of Food Production.** Doubleday, 1979. 10–up.

The historical development of farming methods is given. Techniques that are used today are described and those that will become more important in the future are considered. An excellent addition for career information. Illustrated with photographs; index.

Watts, Franklin. **Peanuts.** Illus. Gene Sharp. Childrens Press, 1978. 7–10.

Do peanuts grow under the ground or above it? How are they used? This is one book of an informative series that gives the history and cultivation of selected foods. Fruits and vegetables that we take for granted are carefully explained and extended through photographs or sketches. Maps show locations of cultivation. Occasional recipes are offered. Index and glossary are appended. Other titles are *Corn, Oranges, Rice, Tomatoes, Wheat.*

Woodside, Dave. **What Makes Popcorn Pop?** Illus. Kay Woon. Atheneum, 1980. 8–12.

The history of popcorn and who uses it from Indians to present-day moviegoers is interestingly presented along with other little-known facts. The author offers several recipes, including a surefire no-fail way to pop corn. Black and white photographs and comical drawings.

Geography

Fradin, Dennis B. **Alaska in Words and Pictures.** Illus. Robert Ulm. Childrens Press, 1977. 8–12.

The story of Alaska is one in a complete series of books, one for each of the fifty states, which offers straightforward factual information useful for intermediate grade social studies reports. Geographic features and historic events are described and illustrated with many clear color photographs.

Lewin, Ted. **World within a World: Baja.** Illus. by author. Dodd, Mead, 1978. 10–up.

The great elephant seals, sea lions, elephant trees, pincushion cactus trumpet flowers, and more live in the private world of the Baja peninsula, part of Mexico on the Pacific. Text and black and white drawings are sensitive and create an aura of the place.

Radlauer, Ruth. **Mammoth Cave National Park.** Photographs by Ed Radlauer. Childrens Press, 1978. 8–12.

Mammoth Cave National Park, the world's longest cave, is described in an easy-to-read text with colored photographs of the rock formations, vegetation, and wildlife. Clear directions and map are included. The series is informative and a valuable extender for the social studies. Other titles include: *Acadia National Park, Bryce Canyon National Park, Glacier National Park, Haleakala National Park, Hawaii Volcanoes National Park, Mesa Verde National Park, Olympic National Park, Rocky Mountain National Park,* and *Zion National Park.*

Ronan, Margaret. **All about Our 50 States.** Illus. William Meyerriecks. Random House, 1978. 10–up.

A helpful reference tool that provides maps, pictures, and photographs. A summary is given for each state; various regions are shown with maps and photographs. Other information given includes state birds and flowers, state areas and populations, and time zones. For classroom use.

Schlein, Miriam. **Antarctica: The Great White Continent.** Hastings House, Publishers, 1980. 8–12.

What happens in far off Antarctica affects living things all over the world. Nutrients drift to northern oceans to feed the sea life. Its currents cool the world's oceans, and its ice sheet contains 90% of the world's water supply. A supplementary book for the classroom written in understandable language.

Handicaps

Kamien, Janet. **What If You Couldn't . . .? A Book about Special Needs.** Illus. Signe Hanson. Charles Scribner's Sons, 1979. 8–12.

Hearing and visual impairments, other physical handicaps, emotional disturbances, and learning disabilities are among the special problems discussed in this concise overview. The author introduces experiments that enable a child to imagine and understand how it feels to have a disability. Clear explanations aid children's understanding of people with special needs.

Larsen, Hanne. **Don't Forget Tom.** Thomas Y. Crowell, 1978. 6–9.

Beautiful color photographs sensitively portray the life of six-year-old Tom, who is mentally retarded. Tom's parents and siblings provide him with normal, affectionate family care. Compassionate and understanding.

Peterson, Jeanne Whitehouse. **I Have a Sister, My Sister Is Deaf.** Illus. Deborah Ray. Harper & Row, Publishers, 1977. 7–10.

A little girl tells about her younger sister who is deaf, and how everyday life is much the same to the sister as it is to others, with a few important exceptions. Everyday situations and feelings are described with affection and objectivity, revealing an understanding of the curiosity that hearing children have about those who live in a silent world. Sensitively illustrated with charcoal drawings.

Sobol, Harriet Langsam. **My Brother Steven Is Retarded.** Photographs by Patricia Agree. Macmillan Publishing, 1977. 7–10.

Beth is sometimes embarrassed because her brother doesn't look and act like everyone else, but she feels hurt when other children stare and laugh at him. Clear photographs add to a sensitive portrayal of a retarded child.

Sullivan, Mary Beth, Alan J. Brightman, and Joseph Blatt. **Feeling Free.** Illus. Marci Davis and Linda Bourke. Addison-Wesley Publishing, 1979. 10–up.

Based on the award-winning television series, the objective of the book is to provide opportunities for readers, both children and adult, to become more familiar and more comfortable with people different from themselves. Includes plays, problems, crossword puzzles, mysteries, and music; black and white photos and sketches.

White, Paul. **Janet at School.** Photographs by Jeremy Finlay. Thomas Y. Crowell, 1978. 4–7.

Color photographs and straightforward text give objective information about Janet, who uses a wheelchair or braces. Her condition, spina bifida, is explained with a diagram of the spine. Janet is shown as a wholesome individual, working and playing at home, in school, and camping.

Wolf, Bernard. **Anna's Silent World.** J.B. Lippincott, 1977. 6–9.

Six-year-old Anna is deaf, but seems to enjoy an active life. She cooperates wholeheartedly with her teachers in a regular private school and enjoys ballet lessons. The text and photographs combine for an empathetic story.

Religions

Asimov, Isaac. **Animals of the Bible.** Illus. Howard Berelson. Doubleday, 1978. 7–10.

Reminiscent of the beautiful illuminated religious manuscripts of the middle ages, each page tells of an animal mentioned in the Judeo-Christian Bible, with information about the animal and the reason for its inclusion. The sepia and gray paintings are accurately and artistically rendered. (Picture book)

Baylor, Byrd. **The Way to Start a Day.** Illus. Peter Parnall. Charles Scribner's Sons, 1978. 8–12.

Over the centuries people have celebrated the sunrise in various ways. Many are depicted here, with invitation to the reader to create a personal sunrise ritual. Text that is nearly poetic is set in handsome design and combines with the magnificent full-color illustrations to make this a superb book. 1979 Caldecott Honor Book.

de Paola, Tomie. **The Lady of ˙Guadalupe.** Illus. by author. Holiday House, 1980. 6–9.

This colorful picture book account of Our Lady of Guadalupe retells how Juan Diego, an Indian peasant, received the picture of Our Lady on his cloak, which can be seen today in Mexico City. Pictures are colorful and appropriate to the smooth-flowing text. Available in Spanish: *Nuestra Señora de Guadalupé.*

Greene, Laura. **I Am an Orthodox Jew.** Illus. Lisa C. Wesson. Holt, Rinehart and Winston, 1979. 6–9.

This explanation of customs of Orthodox Jews told by a young Jewish-American boy describes the rituals of Sabbath practices in the home, synagogue, and Hebrew Day School. Relationships with friends who are not Orthodox Jews are emphasized.

Shelter and Clothing

Gemming, Elizabeth. **Wool Gathering: Sheep Raising in Old New England.** Coward, McCann & Geoghegan, 1979. 7–10.

The history of wool gathering and sheep raising, as well as the development of New England's wool industry, are related in an interesting style. Excellent supplementary reading for the study of colonial New England.

Huntington, Lee Pennock. **Simple Shelters.** Illus. Stefen Bernath. Coward, McCann & Geoghegan, 1979. 8–12.

Eighteen kinds of shelters, from temporary to permanent, are shown in labeled black and white cutaway sketches. Text discusses questions concerning climate, materials, and living patterns of residents. Contains a glossary; may be useful in units on housing around the world.

Kenworthy, Leonard S. **Hats, Caps, and Crowns.** Julian Messner, 1977. 6–8.

Photographs illustrate this survey of headcoverings from around the world. The function of each hat or cap is stressed. Appropriate to the textbook format is the list of "things to do" at the end of the book.

Le Tord, Bijou. **Picking & Weaving.** Four Winds Press, 1980. 4–7.

In an interesting format and text, the raising and processing of cotton are explained, including harvesting, dyeing, weaving, and selling. A variety of finished products are shown. Illustrations are bright and informative. An excellent easy-to-read book for a unit on clothing.

Schaaf, Peter. **An Apartment House Close Up.** Four Winds Press, 1980. 5–8.

With a very brief, almost wordless text, black and white photographs contrast the inside and outside views of an apartment house. Hot water is depicted by the huge basement boilers and by the faucets of the bathtub. Similar pictures depict heat, windows, rooms, and elevators. An excellent book.

Siberell, Anne. **Houses: Shelters from Prehistoric Times to Today.** Illus. by author. Holt, Rinehart and Winston, 1979. 7–9.

The development of shelters from the caves to the unique solar-heated houses of today is simply traced in text and rust-colored drawings. The variety of dwellings of various cultural groups are presented in an appealing manner. An ideal supplementary book for primary social studies.

Watanabe, Shigeo. **How Do I Put It On?** Illus. Yasuo Ohtomo. Putnam Publishing Group, 1980. 3-5.

Bear demonstrates the wrong, then the right way of putting on shirt, pants, cap, and shoes. Simple and fun. Clear, humorous drawings.

Social Issues

Agostinelli, Maria. **On Wings of Love.** Illus. by author. William Collins Publishers, 1979. All ages.

The United Nations Declaration on Rights of the Child is beautifully illustrated with full-color interpretations of each premise. Includes the full text of the declaration. Useful for class discussion.

Berger, Terry. **How Does It Feel When Your Parents Get Divorced?** Photographs by Miriam Shapiro. Julian Messner, 1977. 8–12.

A variety of problems and emotions that young people experience when parents divorce and families separate are discussed. A preteen girl's questions and fears are described in the straightforward text. First person account with black and white photographs.

Berger, Terry. **Stepchild.** Photographs by David Hechtlinger. Julian Messner, 1980. 7–10.

The realistic concerns of a child whose divorced mother remarries. With black and white photos, brief sentences, and few words, the text adequately conveys David's worries. A timely topic.

Burns, Marilyn. **I Am Not a Short Adult! Getting Good at Being a Kid.** Illus. Martha Weston. Little, Brown, 1977. 10–up.

Information for children on what and who influence their lives is presented in readable fashion. Suggestions are given on how to make good decisions now. Excellent discussion material on life problems such as money, legal rights, TV and movies. A Brown Paper School book.

Curtis, Patricia. **Animal Rights: Stories of People Who Defend the Rights of Animals.** Four Winds Press, 1980. 12–up.

Seven animal defenders tell of their work to prevent the unconscionable cruelty to animals that occurs in this country and around the world: torture in lab experiments, neglect of pets, extinction of whales, painful trapping, torturous factory and farming practices, exploitation of animals for entertainment. Facts are documented. Informative and inspiring.

Hazen, Barbara Shook. **Two Homes to Live In: A Child's-Eye View of Divorce.** Illus. Peggy Luks. Human Sciences Press, 1978. 6–9.

Divorce is a difficult subject for anyone to understand, but to a child it is even more baffling and upsetting. This book explains the emotions of a little girl caught in the middle of a divorce. It is a sensitive and intelligent portrayal of a child's concern. The illustrattions are soft and subtle, lending a quiet feeling to the book.

Hyde, Margaret O. **Know about Alcohol.** Illus. Bill Morrison. McGraw-Hill, 1978. 8–12.

Alcohol consumption is presented as a fact of life, pleasant or grim, depending on circumstances. Readers are advised to learn about alcohol now, so they can make an intelligent decision on drinking later. Strategies are presented for responsible drinking, dealing with alcoholic friends and relatives, and coping with peer pressure. Sources for assistance and a bibliography are included.

Israel, Elaine. **The Hungry World.** Julian Messner, 1977. 7–10.

This excellent basic book with its haunting photos of hungry people explains in simple terms why hunger exists. New techniques of producing food like the "green revolution" and fish farms are discussed. Six suggestions, including writing legislators, are given. Possible topic for gifted program use.

Madison, Arnold. **Don't Be a Victim! Protect Yourself & Your Belongings.** Illus. Janet P. D'Amato. Julian Messner, 1978. 10–12.

Directed toward youngsters, this book gives practical suggestions for protecting their possessions, advice on baby-sitting, and hints for feeling and being safer. Operation Peace of Mind hotline number for runaways' use is given. Woodcut illustrations.

Seixas, Judith S. **Alcohol—What It Is, What It Does.** Illus. Tom Huffman. Greenwillow Books, 1977. 7–10.

This easy-to-read introduction gives the facts about alcohol: what it is, where it can be found, and its effects on the mind and body. Treats the use of alcohol as a matter of informed choice.

Seixas, Judith S. **Living with a Parent Who Drinks Too Much.** Greenwillow Books, 1979. 10–up.

Alcoholism, alcoholic behavior, and resulting family problems are described. The author advises children of alcoholic parents in dealing with these problems and offers hope for making their lives more productive and bearable. Hard questions are answered with great sensitivity and in careful detail.

Sobol, Harriet Langsam. **My Other-Mother, My Other-Father.** Photographs by Patricia Agre. Macmillan Publishing, 1979. 8–12.

Twelve-year-old Andrea, whose parents are divorced and remarried, tells how she feels about being a stepchild and of the advantages and disadvantages of having two sets of parents. Black and white photographs capture various key scenes from her life as part of a larger family.

Stevens, Leonard A. **Death Penalty: The Case of Life vs. Death in the United States.** Coward, McCann & Geoghegan, 1978. 12–up.

One of a series on Great Constitutional Issues, this book focuses on the Eighth Amendment that states that "unusual punishment" shall not be inflicted. The 1972 Supreme Court decision overturning the use of capital punishment highlights a discussion that includes a thoughtful, although biased, study of the issue.

Tobias, Ann. **Pot: What It Is, What It Does.** Illus. Tom Huffman. Greenwillow Books, 1979. 7–10.

An introduction to the basic facts about marijuana. The author notes that people who choose to use pot should know the effects and know about laws regarding its use. Illustrations and explanations are clear and easy to understand.

Transportation

Barton, Byron. **Wheels.** Thomas Y. Crowell, 1979. 4–7.

Very young readers are introduced to the development of the wheel from its first stages up to the present day. Because of the simplicity of the text and colorful illustrations, the nonreader will be able to follow the information presented. Excellent concept book for home or school.

Billout, Guy. **By Camel or by Car: A Look at Transportation.** Prentice-Hall, 1979. All ages.

Each double-page spread contains a brief text description and a handsome full-page stylized drawing of a mode of transportation. The narrative combines factual information with personal anecdotes from the author's childhood concerning camel, bicycle, motorcycle, car, truck, bus, subway, train, snowmobile, ship, balloon, aerial tram, plane, helicopter, and spaceship. Unique and useful.

Brown, Dee. **Lonesome Whistle: The Story of the First Transcontinental Railroad.** Holt, Rinehart and Winston, 1980. 12–up.

The story of the first transcontinental railroad is filled with the adventurous tales of the struggle to build the tracks from coast to coast. Mature readers.

Charlie Brown's Third Super Book of Questions and Answers: About All Kinds of Boats and Planes, Cars and Trains and Other Things That Move! Random House, 1978. 7–10.

Did Charlie Brown and Snoopy ever fly into outer space? Yes, they were nicknames for parts of the Apollo 10. What did the Mayflower carry prior to Pilgrims? Wine. It smelled quite sweet. Snippets of transportation information from prewheel days to the space age, plus excellent graphics, make this an appealing and worthwhile browser.

Dean, Anabel. **Up, Up, and Away! The Story of Ballooning.** Westminster Press, 1980. 12–up.

This interesting, comprehensive history of ballooning traces its development and includes well-known persons who experimented in this field. The use of balloons for weather instruments, space, and sports is discussed, including a look at their future potential. Glossary, bibliography, table of contents, and photographs and prints from the Smithsonian Institution are included.

Ditzel, Paul C. **Railroad Yard.** Julian Messner, 1977. 7–10.

A short book that explains how modern railroad yards operate. The clear photographs show the workers and equipment needed to keep the freight trains moving. A glossary of railroad terms is included.

Fisher, Leonard Everett. **The Railroads.** Illus. by author. Holiday House, 1980. 10–12.

This carefully researched book of the Nineteenth Century America series begins with the invention of the iron horse, which enabled the country to expand and to develop industrially. Names of several companies that are large corporations today are mentioned. Working conditions are described. Woodcut illustrations.

Hilton, Suzanne. **Getting There: Frontier Travel without Power.** Westminster Press, 1980. 10–up.

The many modes of traveling west in pioneer days are described in this book that traces the development of transportation. Houseboats, sailboats, canalboats, flatboats, and stagecoaches are included. Lists of supplies needed by the pioneers and even the slang of the period are recorded. A must for social studies. Photographs.

Italiano, Carlo. **Sleighs: The Gentle Transportation.** Tundra Books, 1978. 7–10.

As a child, the author-artist of this reminiscent picture book watched the sleighs moving through the Montreal streets. Twenty-three horse-drawn vehicles are pictured and described, along with personal notes and memories of these long-ago, graceful transports.

Lasky, Kathryn. **Tall Ships.** Photographs by Christopher G. Knight. Charles Scribner's Sons, 1978. 10–up.

A book inspired by the return of the tall ships to Boston Harbor for the Bicentennial, the text is enlivened with anecdotes and personal glimpses of the men who sailed the ships. Terminology is well defined. Striking black and white photographs.

Marston, Hope Irvin. **Big Rigs.** Dodd, Mead, 1979. 7-10.

If you already know what an eighteen wheeler is, you will find out more through the text and large photographs about the biggest kind of trucks on the highway, the tractor-trailers. What they haul, their emblems, and even the terms used by truckers on their CB radios are included.

Marston, Hope Irvin. **Trucks, Trucking and You.** Dodd, Mead, 1978. 10–up.

Beginning with the gripping true story of the daring rescue of one trucker by another, this book continues to claim the reader's interest throughout. Kinds of trucks, their uses, CB radio and truckers' jargon, various careers in trucking, and much more informs the reader and inspires liking and respect for truckers and trucking. Well illustrated with photographs.

Navarra, John Gabriel. **Superplanes.** Doubleday, 1979. 10–12.

For readers fascinated by air travel and planes, this book provides an introduction to commercial planes, airports, military aircraft, special aircraft, experimental aircraft. Well illustrated with many photos.

Pierce, Jack. **The Freight Train Book.** Carolrhoda Books, 1980. 4–7.

Black and white photographs and captions describe the various cars of freight trains, including locomotives, boxcars, tank cars, auto carriers, hoppers, flatcars, piggybacks, refrigerator cars, and cabooses.

Radlauer, Ed. **Some Basics about Vans.** Photographs by author. Childrens Press, 1978. 7–10.

Little homes on wheels with the motor and steering components built in are the topic of this book on vans. It gives the origin of the name, varieties of vans, and their uses for fun or work. Unusual interiors and exteriors are shown in full-color photos.

Reit, Seymour. **Sails, Rails and Wings.** Illus. Roberto Innocenti. Golden Press, 1978. 5–8.

Three sections of large full-color pictures move from early history to the future of ships, trains, and airplanes, aided by captions and a brief text. Although the busy pages could be termed cluttered from an artistic standpoint, this style intrigues children who enjoy poring over the detailed cross-section drawings.

Richards, Norman, and Pat Richards. **Trucks and Supertrucks.** Doubleday, 1980. 7–10.

There are about 29,000,000 trucks in the United States; practically any product can be carried by truck. Twenty-eight large illustrations appearing on left-hand pages are described in a clear, concise manner on right-hand pages. Five main types are emphasized. A Museum of Science and Industry/Chicago book.

Ross, Frank, Jr. **The Tin Lizzie: A Model-Making Book.** Lothrop, Lee & Shepard Books, 1980. 10–up.

For twenty-five years the Model T Ford, the Tin Lizzie, was the dream of most Americans. Four representative models can be made in miniature with cardboard and construction paper: the 1909 Touring Car, 1913 Pickup Truck, 1913 Runabout, and the 1914 Speedster. Clear, concise directions and illustrations. A transportation craft book.

Scarry, Huck. **Huck Scarry's Steam Train Journey.** William Collins Publishers, 1979. 7–10.

Soots and his dog Cinder take an imaginary journey and see famous old trains of Europe and America. The story is brief; more engrossing are the colorful, detail-filled illustrations of parts of trains, railroad yards, kinds of cars, and paraphernalia surrounding trains.

Snow, Richard. **The Iron Road: A Portrait of American Railroading.** Photographs by David Plowden. Four Winds Press, 1978. 10–up.

The story of American railroads is told through interesting anecdotes, including the familiar tale of Casey Jones. Highlighted by outstanding black and white photographs, this large, beautifully designed book focuses on the spirit of the American railroader. Its style makes it not merely a history, but a tribute to railroading.

Sullivan, George. **The Supercarriers.** Dodd, Mead, 1980. 12–up.

The development and use of carrier aviation are traced from its beginnings in the early twentieth century to the present. Technical treatment is balanced with accounts of life aboard the ships. Glossary.

United States History

Behrens, June, and Pauline Brower. **Algonquian Indians at Summer Camp.** Childrens Press, 1977. 6–9.

The Algonquian tribes had contact with the early Massachusetts settlers. This is an informative report resulting from a summer camp project that investigated life in the seventeenth century. It concerns the food, shelter, recreation, customs, and work activities of those who lived at that time. Excellent for study of early Massachusetts or Indian life. Colored photographs of live models.

Behrens, June, and Pauline Brower. **Pilgrims Plantation.** Childrens Press, 1977. 7–10.

Elizabeth and Daniel, Pilgrim children, are anxious to land and to get settled in America for the new year 1621. Their many experiences during the first seven years of the Plymouth Plantation settlement are concisely described in text and photographs. Gives an overall view of Pilgrim life.

Berg, Annmarie. **Great State Seals of the United States.** Dodd, Mead, 1979. 10–12.

The official seal of each state is shown in black and white, accompanied by a two- or three-page explanation of its symbolism, motto, and history. The text is enlivened by descriptions of occasional errors in design or controversies over possession. A valuable addition to the study of American history or of individual states.

Cheney, Cora. **Alaska: Indians, Eskimos, Russians, and the Rest.** Dodd, Mead, 1980. 10–12.

The fascinating history of Alaska includes its Indians, Eskimos, Russian adventurers, and even the latest newcomers, the pipeliners. The easily read text, which includes the true story of a ten-year-old boy who sailed with Vitus Bering, is complemented with attractive photographs. Excellent supplementary book for home or school.

D'Amato, Janet, and Alex D'Amato. **Algonquian and Iroquois Crafts for You to Make.** Julian Messner, 1979. 8–12.

Intertwined with facts on the life and customs of the Algonquian and Iroquois Indians are suggestions for craft projects. The clear instructions are accompanied by many orange, and black and white illustrations. Useful in social studies units.

Fisher, Leonard Everett. **The Factories.** Illus. by author. Holiday House, 1979. 10–up.

The Industrial Revolution is explained, focusing on the introduction of factories in the United States in the eighteenth century. By the end of the nineteenth century, factories had contributed to making the United States a major industrial power. Familiar names like Singer (sewing machines) and Kodak (cameras) are mentioned.

Fisher, Leonard Everett. **The Hospitals.** Illus. by author. Holiday House, 1980. 10–12.

The first part of the book describes health care institutions in the early 1800s. They are pictured as dark, dismal places where much suffering took place. The remainder of the book examines the improvements in medicine since 1850. One of the Nineteenth Century America series with handsome, intricate illustrations.

Fisher, Leonard Everett. **The Sports.** Illus. by author. Holiday House, 1980. 10–up.

The spirit and development of competitive sports in the nineteenth century are described. Physical strength and stamina were regarded as "musts." Baseball, tennis, golf, bare-fisted boxing, and others are included. Strong, detailed illustrations in black and white complement the vividly described, informative text. Index. One of the Nineteenth Century America series.

Freedman, Russell. **Immigrant Kids.** E. P. Dutton, 1980. 8–12.

Pictures and text combine to give the reader a clear and interesting view of the life-styles of the children who immigrated to America during the period of 1880-1920. An overview of home life, school, work, and play makes this a valuable book.

Hoyt, Edwin P. **War in the Deep: Pacific Submarine Action in World War II.** G. P. Putnam's Sons, 1978. 8–12.

A collection of Japanese and American submarine adventures in the Pacific during World War II. The tensions, successes, and failures of undersea warfare are explained in a straightforward style.

Loeper, John J. **Mr. Marley's Main Street Confectionery: A History of Sweets & Treats.** Atheneum, 1979. 10–up.

Nineteenth-century confectionery shops were wonderful places for all seasons and all ages and are part of America's history. Illustrated with old prints, the history of candy and other treats is traced. With the subject's built-in interest, this would be a useful resource for an enrichment project.

Lyons, Grant. **The Creek Indians.** Illus. David Kingham. Julian Messner, 1978. 10–up.

This well-written, informative history begins with the legendary birth of the Muskogee people, or Creeks, and ends with present government policy toward the Creek people who live as citizens of Oklahoma and the United States, no longer the unique, proud Creek confederacy. Effective black and white illustrations.

Madison, Arnold. **Lost Treasures of America: Searching Out Hidden Riches.** Illus. Dick Wahl. Rand McNally, 1977. 12–up.

Intriguing accounts of the history and legends of such lost treasures as Arizona's Lost Dutchman Mine, Jesse James' cache, and the burial chamber of Kamehameha. Not documented, the tales could motivate young readers to research further to separate fact from fiction. Index.

Mercer, Charles. **Statue of Liberty.** G. P. Putnam's Sons, 1979. 10–12.

The social, artistic, political, and economic forces of the times are skillfully interwoven in this lively tale of the adventures and mis-adventures of Miss Liberty, from her conception in the mind of the sculptor in 1865 to her installation in 1886. Illustrated with many stunning contemporary photographs and engravings.

Phelan, Mary Kay. **The Story of the Louisiana Purchase.** Illus. Frank Aloise. Thomas Y. Crowell, 1979. 10–up.

Historical figures including Thomas Jefferson, Robert R. Livingston, and Napoleon Bonaparte come to life in this interesting account of the purchase of Louisiana. Well documented and written in an interesting style, this book should prove an excellent supplementary account of this era in U.S. history. Black and white pen sketches.

Phelan, Mary Kay. **Waterway West: The Story of the Erie Canal.** Illus. David Frampton. Thomas Y. Crowell, 1977. 10–up.

An excellent account of the building of the Erie Canal, the book provides a vivid, readable picture of one segment of American history and engineering achievement. Black and white illustrations complement and enhance the text. Bibliography and index are included.

St. George, Judith. **The Amazing Voyage of the *New Orleans.*** Illus. Glen Rounds. G. P. Putnam's Sons, 1980. 8–12.

This lively retelling brings to life a true story from American riverboat history. Nicholas Roosevelt sets out down the Ohio and Mississippi Rivers to prove once and for all that steamboats can navigate the great rivers. Rapids, floods, an earthquake, fire, and Indian attacks hinder, but fail to stop, the 2000 mile voyage.

Schwartz, Alvin, editor. **When I Grew Up Long Ago.** Illus. Harold Berson. J. B. Lippincott, 1978. 8–up.

Recollections of 156 people who grew up between 1890 and 1914 paint a warm, human picture of life in America in the pre-World War I era. Comments are grouped into such categories as houses, clothing, and school. Humorous, touching, and instructive.

Simon, Hilda. **Bird and Flower Emblems of the United States.** Dodd, Mead, 1978. 8–12.

An excellent, quick reference source, this book provides information about each state's choice of symbolic bird and flower. Full-color illustrations by the author and an introductory essay concerning the use of symbols and emblems throughout history enhance the text.

Spier, Peter. **The Legend of New Amsterdam.** Illus. by author. Doubleday, 1979. 6–9.

The reader learns how the people of New Amsterdam lived, worked, studied, and played in the 1600s. The illustrations depict the vitality and humor found in this bustling town. The text ends with a detailed map and a surprise. Delightfully illustrated.

Steele, William O. **Talking Bones: Secrets of Indian Burial Mounds.** Illus. Carlos Llerena-Aguirre. Harper & Row, Publishers, 1978. 8–12.

Using objects found in mounds as clues, archaeologists can learn much about the daily life and burial customs of the people who built them so long ago. Exemplary black and white illustrations and a useful chronology are included. An excellent resource.

Strait, Treva Adams. **The Price of Free Land.** J. B. Lippincott, 1979. 10–14.

Reminiscent of the Little House books by Laura Ingalls Wilder, this book of true episodes involves another family's experiences as homesteaders in Nebraska in 1914. A strong sense of family unity continues throughout the story. Interesting photographs.

World History

Aliki. **Mummies Made in Egypt.** Illus. by author. Thomas Y. Crowell, 1979. 8–12.

Detailed descriptions include the process of embalming, the Egyptian beliefs about life after death, their funerary customs, and the structure of a pyramid. Aliki's colorful drawings, clear diagrams, and descriptive text add up to an extremely attractive presentation of a sometimes gruesome topic.

Gemming, Elizabeth. **Lost City in the Clouds: The Discovery of Machu Picchu.** Illus. Mike Eagle. Coward, McCann & Geoghegan, 1980. 9–12.

Hiram Bingham, a Yale history professor, discovered a lost city of the Inca Empire in 1911. The account of his expedition and the two preceding years is based on Bingham's personal descriptions. Conversations and fine writing bring the archaeological find to life. Glossary, timeline, list of museums, and bibliography appended.

Graff, Stewart. **The Story of World War II.** E. P. Dutton, 1978. 10–up.

The years from 1939 to 1945 were times of sacrifice, cruelty, and bravery. An overview of World War II from the beginning, the turning points, and the climax is clearly and concisely described for juvenile readers. Photographs and maps add to the interest of the account. Index included.

Halter, Jon C. **Top Secret Projects of World War II.** Julian Messner, 1978. 12–up.

An informative account of the secret projects and espionage missions that affected the outcome of World War II, this book is packed with factual data about such events as the Ultra secret, the strategy of lies surrounding D Day, and the development of the A-bomb. Maps and an annotated list of further readings included. Index.

Hoobler, Dorothy, and Thomas Hoobler. **The Trenches: Fighting on the Western Front in World War I.** G. P. Putnam's Sons, 1978. 12–up.

Photographs and first-hand reports lend credibility to this account of action on the European front during World War I. Those who survived the trench warfare and hand-to-hand combat lived amidst mud and filth for over three years while the German Army advanced through much of Western Europe. An index and list of further readings are appended.

Lasker, Joe. **Merry Ever After: The Story of Two Medieval Weddings.** Illus. by author. Viking Press, 1976. 8–12.

Although the text is geared to middle graders, the carefully researched illustrations can be enjoyed by all ages. Through the descriptions of two medieval weddings, one between a wealthy couple and the other between two peasants, the reader comes away with a clear idea about wedding rites, customs, and living conditions.

McMullen, David. **Mystery in Peru: The Lines of Nazca.** Raintree Publishers, 1977. 8–12.

Explorer Jim Woodman attempts to explain the mystery of the lines and pictures appearing in the desert plain of Nazca, Peru, by his theory of ancient hot air balloonists. Other theories are briefly mentioned. Photographs.

Meltzer, Milton. **All Times, All Peoples: A World History of Slavery.** Illus. Leonard Everett Fisher. Harper & Row, Publishers, 1980. 10–up.

Slavery through the ages and how it affected the various cultures is examined. Examples drawn from Rome, China, Egypt, and the United States demonstrate the life of the slaves and their continuing desire to be free. Black and white illustrations enhance the book with their intensity.

Meyer, Miriam Weiss. **The Blind Guards of Easter Island.** Raintree Publishers, 1977. 10–up.

The mystery of the giant statues on Easter Island is thoroughly explored. Legends and historical data are compared in a readable text illustrated with many fine color and black and white photographs. Maps are helpful. Quality of paper and print is unusually good.

Patterson, Geoffrey. **Chestnut Farm, 1860.** Andre Deutsch, 1980. All ages.

Large, expressive pictures of life on a typical nineteenth-century English farm are accompanied by a text that explains the various jobs done throughout the year by all members of the family, sometimes with the help of villagers. A small work of art in itself, this could be used in units on ecology.

Patterson, Geoffrey. **The Oak.** Andre Deutsch, 1979. 7–10.

Oak trees can live to be four hundred years old. Stretching from 1588 to 1978, this book describes an oak's life span in terms of the English history it mutely witnesses. Detailed double-page drawings, half in color, are an integral part of the presentation.

Perceval, Don. **From Ice Mountain: Indian Settlement of the Americas.** Northland Press, 1979. 8–12.

Using a point of view not usually given, the art and text tell of people who followed the reindeer across the tundra and began the settlement of the Western Hemisphere. It includes the history of the Europeans who came and conquered and the lives of the people today.

Roberson, John R. **China from Manchu to Mao (1699–1976).** Atheneum, 1980. 12–up.

The history of China is chronicled from the reign of Emperor Kang Xi. The author points out the influence of the Western culture on the Chinese as he describes the Opium Wars, Boxer Rebellion, and China's part in two world wars. Very readable source for social studies units.

Shapiro, Milton J. **Behind Enemy Lines: American Spies and Saboteurs in World War II.** Julian Messner, 1978. 10–up.

An honest portrayal of the adventures of spies and intelligence officers during World War II. The book explains the dangers that these brave men and women encountered in their daily lives behind enemy lines. The people are shown as human beings suffering both successes and failures in a quiet, courageous style.

Swinburne, Irene, and Laurence Swinburne. **Behind the Sealed Door: The Discovery of the Tomb and Treasures of Tutankhamun.** Sniffen Court Books, 1977. 10–up.

The finding of King Tut's tomb and its treasures are shown through outstanding black and white and color photographs. The very readable, large-print text and photograph captions will appeal to young readers.

Additional Social Studies Books

Baumann, Hans. *The Caves of the Great Hunters.* Rev. ed. Pantheon Books, 1962. 10–14.

Baylor, Byrd. *When Clay Sings.* Illus. Tom Bahti. Charles Scribner's Sons, 1972. 6–12.

Bealer, Alex W. *Only the Names Remain: The Cherokees and the Trail of Tears.* Illus. William S. Bock. Little, Brown, 1972. 10–up.

Denny, Norman, and Josephine Filmer-Sankey. *The Bayeux Tapestry: The Story of the Norman Conquest: 1066.* Atheneum, 1966. 10–14.

Epstein, Sam, and Beryl Epstein. *The First Book of Printing.* Illus. Laszlo Roth. Franklin Watts, 1955. 10–12.

Feelings, Tom. *Black Pilgrimage.* Lothrop, Lee & Shepard Books, 1972. 9–14.

Foster, Genevieve. *Abraham Lincoln's World.* Charles Scribner's Sons, 1944. 10–up.

Foster, Genevieve. *George Washington's World.* Charles Scribner's Sons, 1941. 10–up.

Foster, Genevieve. *The World of Captain John Smith, 1580–1631*. Charles Scribner's Sons, 1959. 12–up.

Jackson, Shirley. *The Witchcraft of Salem Village*. Illus. Lili Rothi. Random House, 1956. 9–12.

Johnson, Gerald W. *America Grows Up*. Illus. Leonard Everett Fisher. William Morrow, 1960. 10–14.

Lawson, Robert. *They Were Strong and Good*. Viking Press, 1940. 8–up.

Lester, Julius. *To Be a Slave*. Illus. Tom Feelings. Dial Press, 1968. 12–up.

Perl, Lila. *Slumps, Grunts, and Snickerdoodles: What Colonial America Ate and Why*. Illus. Richard Cuffari. Seabury Press, 1975. 8–12.

Phelan, Mary K. *Mr. Lincoln's Inaugural Journey*. Illus. Richard Cuffari. Thomas Y. Crowell, 1972. 10–up.

Roberts, Bruce, and Nancy Roberts. *Where Time Stood Still: A Portrait of Appalachia*. Illus. Bruce Roberts. Macmillan Publishing, 1970. 12–up.

Smith, E. Brooks, and Robert Meredith, eds. *The Coming of the Pilgrims*. Illus. Leonard Everett Fisher. Little, Brown, 1964. 10–up.

Spier, Peter. *The Erie Canal.*Doubleday, 1970. 8–12.

Biography

Barton, Peter. **Staying Power: Performing Artists Talk about Their Lives.**
Dial Press, 1980. 12–up.

Twelve performing artists, not yet famous but self-supporting and
devoted to excellence, tell about their lives and careers. The joy of
developing one's talents, the tough discipline, and the surmounting
of obstacles make inspiring and realistic reading for youth who are
interested in music, dance, and drama.

Blegvad, Erik. **Self-Portrait: Erik Blegvad.** Illus. by author. Addison-
Wesley Publishing, 1979. All ages.

Erik Blegvad's father, grandfather, and great-grandfather all possessed artistic talent, but it was Erik who really became an artist. He
tells the story from his boyhood in Denmark up to the present day
in text and exciting illustrations done in many styles. Good introduction to autobiography.

Brenner, Barbara. **On the Frontier with Mr. Audubon.** Coward, McCann
& Geoghegan, 1977. 8–12.

A partial biography of John James Audubon from the point of view
of his young assistant, Joseph Mason. In the format of a journal, the
narrator recounts the 1820 journey down the Ohio and Mississippi
Rivers to find new birds to paint. Illustrated with photographs and
reproductions of the artist's works.

Goodman, Saul. **Baryshnikov: A Most Spectacular Dancer.** Harvey
House, Publishers, 1979. 8–12.

Here's an exciting story about the twenty-six-year-old Russian ballet
dancer, Mikhail Baryshnikov, who defected to the United States. He
experiences incredible success from dancing on stage to making a
motion picture. Photographs dramatize his artistic vitality and blend
with insightful text about the world of ballet.

Lasker, David. **The Boy Who Loved Music.** Illus. by Joe Lasker. Viking
Press, 1979. 8–12.

Karl plays the horn in Prince Nicolaus's orchestra under the direction of Joseph Haydn. In order to persuade the Prince to let the court musicians return home at summer's end, Haydn composes a symphony with a surprise ending. Based on actual incidents, the tale is colorfully illustrated.

Scheader, Catherine. **They Found a Way: Mary Cassatt.** Childrens Press, 1977. 10–12.

This brief biography of Mary Cassatt (1844-1926) serves as an introduction to this American artist who achieved in spite of opposition. Being strong-willed, she was successful in having her own art shown among other Impressionists. Photographs of her numerous paintings of women and children are well chosen. Easy to read.

Sharon, Mary Bruce. **Scenes from Childhood.** E. P. Dutton, 1978. 7–10.

Colorful, primitive paintings portray the interesting childhood of Mary Bruce Sharon, an American artist. Brief descriptions written in the first person accompany the eye-catching illustrations that give the reader a glimpse of America in 1885. Toys, furniture, transportation, entertainment, art, and social customs are vividly portrayed. Some pictures require explanation and discussion.

Siegel, Beatrice. **An Eye on the World: Margaret Bourke-White, Photographer.** Frederick Warne, 1980. 12–up.

A selection of events in the life of Margaret Bourke-White from early childhood to her death from Parkinson's disease in 1971. A fine sampling of her photographs highlights the volume. Index and selected bibliography.

Zemach, Margot. **Self-Portrait: Margot Zemach.** Illus. by author. Addison-Wesley Publishing, 1978. All ages.

The autobiography relates funny anecdotes of Margot Zemach's youthful life with theater parents, her zeal to become an artist, and her marriage to another bright, struggling Fulbright student. The birth of each of their children is related to one of their children's books. Illustrated with the same delightful drawings that mark her award-winning books. One of a series of autobiographies of contemporary children's book illustrators.

Athletes

Aaseng, Nathan. **Eric Heiden: Winner in Gold.** Lerner Publications, 1980. 9–12.

This biography of Eric Heiden highlights his ice-skating career, but briefly tells his story from the time he received his first skates. Although Eric is featured, his sister's career is also described. Major coverage is given the 1980 Olympics at Lake Placid. Interesting book, well illustrated with photographs.

Aaseng, Nathan. **Winners Never Quit: Athletes Who Beat the Odds.** Lerner Publications, 1980. 10–12.

Short biographies of ten well-known athletes, including Bobby Clarke, Lee Trevino, Tom Dempsey, and Kitty O'Neil emphasize how each excelled in spite of handicaps and misfortunes. Numerous black and white photos help bring the sportspersons to life.

Allen, Maury. **Reggie Jackson: The Three Million Dollar Man.** Photographs by Louis Requena. Harvey House, Publishers, 1978. 8–12.

Reggie Jackson, who received a $3,000,000 contract from the New York Yankees, had a difficult childhood. This brief biography chronicles his life from his childhood in a broken home through his history-making three home runs in three swings in the 1977 World Series.

Allen, Maury. **Ron Guidry: Louisiana Lightning.** Photographs by Louis Requena. Harvey House, Publishers, 1979. 8–12.

This well-written sports biography traces the career of Ron Guidry, the New York Yankee pitcher who almost gave up before he finally was given the chance to prove his talents. Baseball fans will enjoy the easy text and many black and white photographs.

Belsky, Dick. **The Juice: Football's Superstar O. J. Simpson.** David McKay, 1977. 8–12.

An exciting biography of the boy from a San Francisco ghetto who once told Cleveland Browns' Jim Brown that he would break Brown's running record. In 1973, he did. O. J. Simpson eventually wins the coveted Heisman trophy, is unanimously voted All-American, and becomes professional football's highest paid player. Numerous photographs.

Burchard, Marshall. **Sports Hero, Jimmy Connors.** G. P. Putnam's Sons, 1976. 7–10.

Jimmy Connors learned to play tennis from his mother at a very early age. He was determined to succeed and dropped out of college to attain his goal. He became the world's number one tennis player in 1975. Large print, glossary, and photographs are included. Other Sports Hero biographies include Terry Bradshaw, Ron Le Flore, and Bill Walton.

Butler, Hal. **Baseball's Most Valuable Players.** Julian Messner, 1977. 9–12.

These five brief biographies of the players who won baseball's Most Valuable Player Award in 1974, 1975, and 1976 are written in a clear and interesting way. Included are Jeff Burroughs, Fred Lynn, Thurman Munson, Steve Garvey, and Joe Morgan. Provides a change of pace from longer, more detailed biographies.

Cohen, Joel H. **Joe Morgan: Great Little Big Man.** G. P. Putnam's Sons, 1978. 10–up.

A strong determination to become a real baseball player is evident in Joe Morgan's life. The title "little big man" is quite appropriate. His early life is briefly outlined while his career and participation in outstanding games are presented in detail. Photographs and index are included in this Sports Shelf Biography.

Devaney, John. **The Picture Story of Terry Bradshaw.** Julian Messner, 1977. 9–12.

Terry Bradshaw's persistence in his drive to quarterback the Pittsburgh Steelers to a win in the Super Bowl should inspire would-be football stars. Many black and white photographs.

Dolan, Edward F., Jr., and Richard B. Lyttle. **Dorothy Hamill: Olympic Skating Champion.** Doubleday, 1979. 9–12.

Eight-year-old Dorothy Hamill put on the $6.95 pair of Christmas ice skates, and the rest is history. The reader shares Dorothy's life from this point through the long practice hours, the nervousness, the compulsory figures, to her final triumph at the 1976 Winter Olympics. Black and white photos.

Dolan, Edward F., Jr., and Richard B. Lyttle. **Kyle Rote, Jr.: American-Born Soccer Star.** Doubleday, 1979. 8–12.

Although the major focus is on Rote's six seasons with the Dallas Tornado, much attention is given to Kyle Rote, the man, his personal goals and values.

Fogel, Julianna A., and Mary S. Watkins. **Andrea Jaeger, Tennis Champion.** J. B. Lippincott, 1980. 7–10.

In 1980 Andrea Jaeger became the youngest tennis pro ever. The first-person narrative, illustrated profusely with action photographs, gives an immediacy to the account of Miss Jaeger's tournament play.

Fogel, Julianna A. **Wesley Paul, Marathon Runner.** Photographs by Mary S. Watkins. J. B. Lippincott, 1979. 7–10.

Wesley Paul has been a runner for six of his nine years. The reader follows Chinese-American Wesley as he works to build up his speed and endurance for competing in the New York City Marathon, at which he hopes to set a new record. Black and white photos.

Gutman, Bill. **Great Baseball Stories.** Julian Messner, 1978. 10–up.

The glorious history of baseball with its remarkable catchers, home run hitters, and strikeout pitchers, and three outstanding teams of the past and present are brought together in this readable overview of the sport. Action photographs of the players enliven the stories.

Gutman, Bill. **The Harlem Globetrotters: Basketball's Funniest Team.** Garrard Publishing, 1977. 8–12.

The Harlem Globetrotters have been putting on funny shows for fans for more than forty years. The team won so many games at the beginning that something had to be done to encourage competition. This was why the comedy acts were introduced. Their history and activities are chronicled.

Gutman, Bill. **Modern Soccer Superstars.** Dodd, Mead, 1979. 10–12.

Profiles of famous soccer players including Pele, Kyle Rote, Jr., Jim McAlister, Shep Messing, Al Trost, and Werner Roth are written in an interesting and readable style for sports fans.

Gutman, Bill. **Superstars of the Sports World.** Julian Messner, 1978. 8–11.

Up-to-date brief biographies of Bobby Clarke, Julius Erving, Chris Evert, Franco Harris, and Pete Rose are written in a simple style for the young sports fan. Perseverance is an underlying theme in each account. Illustrated with photographs; index included.

Haskins, James. **Bob McAdoo, Superstar.** Lothrop, Lee & Shepard Books, 1978. 8–12.

Among the famous Americans born in Greensboro, North Carolina, the most recent is Bob McAdoo, superstar of the New York Knicks. At the age of four he started to shoot baskets. His supportive family encouraged his education and sports activities until he became a professional. Many photographs, glossary, and index included.

Higdon, Hal. **Johnny Rutherford: Indy Champ.** G. P. Putnam's Sons, 1980. 10–12.

Car enthusiasts will learn how one of the greatest drivers in auto racing has advanced in a most dangerous sport. Johnny Rutherford's life is traced from action in sprint and midget cars to his ultimate victory in the Indianapolis 500. Safety precautions and proper training are emphasized.

Jenner, Bruce, and R. Smith Kiliper. **The Olympics and Me.** Doubleday, 1980. 10–12.

Bruce Jenner, the 1976 Olympic decathlon champion, gives a brief history of the ancient games and describes several of the events. He then tells about his own training for and participation in the Munich Olympics, as well as his work with handicapped children who compete in the Special Olympics.

Laklan, Carli. **Golden Girls: True Stories of Olympic Women Stars.** McGraw-Hill, 1980. 9–12.

In 1904 when women were first allowed to compete in the Olympics, it was decried as "scandalous" and the "downfall of womanhood."

The dozen biographical sketches include information about the competitors' early lives and how they eventually became gold medal winners. Black and white photos show some then-and-now pictures.

Libby, Bill. **Superdrivers: Three Auto Racing Champions.** Garrard Publishing, 1977. 7–10.

An easy-to-read book about three men who made auto racing history. Roger Ward, Lee Petty, and Don Garlits are American racing car drivers.

Lipsyte, Robert. **Free to Be Muhammad Ali.** Harper & Row, Publishers, 1978. 8–12.

This is the story of a "champion." The book simply allows Ali to make statements about his own feelings toward life and the sport of boxing. It is direct and honest and well written. The last statement in the book may be the best summation: "Muhammad Ali once said, 'I don't believe all the stuff I say!'"

Mueser, Anne Marie. **The Picture Story of Jockey Steve Cauthen.** Julian Messner, 1979. 7–10.

The setting is Churchill Downs in Louisville, Kentucky when the reader first meets Steve Cauthen riding Affirmed in the Kentucky Derby. What follows is the story of his early years, captured in words and photographs. The many successes of this teenage hero are captivating. Easy to read. Glossary included.

Olney, Ross R. **A. J. Foyt: The Only Four Time Winner.** Harvey House, Publishers, 1978. 9–12.

This fast-moving story of the outstanding A.J. Foyt opens with the 1961 auto race at Indianapolis and concludes with the 1977 event. Why he has become so successful is apparent throughout the book. Illustrated with photos.

Olney, Ross R. **Janet Guthrie: First Woman at Indy.** Harvey House, Publishers, 1978. 8–12.

After brief highlights of Janet Guthrie's childhood, school years, and brief career as a physicist, the focus is on her struggle to be accepted in the world of auto racing and to become eventually the first woman to drive in the Indianapolis 500. Illustrated with photographs.

Phillips, Betty Lou. **Chris Evert: First Lady of Tennis.** Julian Messner, 1977. 10–12.

The story of Chris Evert from early childhood to her first victories at Wimbledon and Forest Hills. The emphases are on her relationships with her family, her schoolmates, and her tennis contemporaries. Indexed.

Robison, Nancy. **Kurt Thomas: International Winner.** Childrens Press, 1980. 7–10.

This short book tells of Kurt Thomas, the young gymnast who brought home the United States' first gold medal in forty-six years from the World Games in 1978. One of the Sports Stars books; other biographies in the series are about Nancy Lopez, Steve Garvey, Renaldo Nehemiah, Janet Guthrie, Walter Payton, Reggie Jackson, and Tracy Austin. Photographs.

Robison, Nancy. **Tracy Austin: Teenage Superstar.** Harvey House, Publishers, 1978. 9–12.

When Tracy Austin won the match at Wimbledon in June 1977, she encouraged aspiring youngsters and charmed the crowds attending the yearly event. This exciting biography will interest a wide range of readers. Many excellent photographs complete the text. Glossary of tennis terms included.

Rose, Pete. **Pete Rose: My Life in Baseball.** Doubleday, 1979. 9–12.

In this timely autobiography Pete Rose recounts events of his early life. The influence that his father exerted on his decision to become a hardworking ballplayer is evident throughout the story.

Schoor, Gene. **Babe Didrikson: The World's Greatest Woman Athlete.** Doubleday, 1978. 10–12.

Babe Didrikson Zaharias excelled in many sports including basketball, baseball, track, and golf. This remarkable woman won one silver and two gold medals in the 1932 Olympics and went on to win more golf titles than any other woman before being named the World's Greatest Woman Athlete of the Century in 1954. Her life, including her death due to cancer, is chronicled in this most interesting account.

Schoor, Gene. **Joe DiMaggio: A Biography.** Doubleday, 1980. 12–up.

"Once a Yankee, always a Yankee." That was the story of Joe DiMaggio's spectacular life as a baseball player. While still a teenager, he fell and injured his leg, which threatened to ruin his career before it had started. An interesting account of the "Yankee Clipper," illustrated with photographs.

Sullivan, George. **Modern Olympic Superstars.** Dodd, Mead, 1979. 8–12.

Biographies of 1976 Olympic Gold Medal winners Bruce Jenner, Sheila Young, Lasse Virem, Nelli Kim, Kornelia Ender and Alberto Juantorena. Brief stories provide background on the events leading up to the winning of the awards. Illustrated with black and white photographs; excellent portrayal of the qualities of a superstar.

Sullivan, George. **The Picture Story of Catfish Hunter.** Julian Messner, 1977. 8–12.

Catfish Hunter's career is followed from his childhood on a farm, where he used to practice pitching corncobs through a hole in the barn door, to his winning of the Cy Young Award. Anecdotes enliven this recounting of Hunter's life as a pitcher in the major leagues. Black and white photographs.

Sullivan, George. **The Picture Story of Nadia Comaneci.** Julian Messner, 1977. 7–10.

Winner of four gold medals at the 1976 Montreal Olympic Games, the first in Olympic history, Nadia Comaneci captivated her audiences and inspired young gymnasts throughout the world. Young readers will be impressed by her determination and dedication as she achieved success. Many photographs demonstrate her skill as a gymnast.

Tuttle, Anthony. **Steve Cauthen, Boy Jockey.** Photographs by Bruce Curtis. G. P. Putnam's Sons, 1978. 7–10.

A compact, easily read biography of Steve Cauthen, the young jockey who began his professional career at sixteen. This book also contains information about racing and about being a jockey. Well illustrated with many black and white photos.

Van Steenwyk, Elizabeth. **Stars on Ice.** Dodd, Mead, 1980. 10–up.

The biographies of outstanding figure skaters who represented the United States in the 1980 Olympics and other international competitions are told. Also included are biographies of former champions and possible future stars. The skaters comment on the regimen, sacrifices, triumphs, and heartbreaks. Several stories describe the overcoming of severe physical handicaps. Photographs.

Wayne, Bennett, editor. **Hockey Hotshots.** Garrard Publishing, 1977. 8–12.

This book tells about the men who have made the sport of hockey great. The short biographical sketches show the progress of modern hockey through some outstanding players' success in the sport. They include Howie Morenz, Maurice Richard, Bobby Hull, Bobby Orr, Terry Sawchuk, Glenn Hall, and Jacques Plante. Photographs.

Entertainers

Campbell, C. W. **Will Rogers.** Dillon Press, 1979. 9–12.

This account of Will Rogers relates that he was an Oklahoma cowboy of Indian descent who loved ranch life. He learned to combine his roping skill with entertainment to become a star of stage and screen and a noted humorist. He was world famous when he was killed in a plane crash in Alaska in 1935.

Cross, Helen Reeder. **The Real Tom Thumb.** Illus. Stephen Gammell. Four Winds Press, 1980. 8–12.

Tiny Charles Stratton attracted the attention of P. T. Barnum who renamed him Tom Thumb and made him famous. The book describes Tom's meetings with Abraham Lincoln and Queen Victoria, and tells the story of his marriage to Lavinia. The author conveys Tom's zest for life in spite of his frustration at having to live in a world of giants.

Edelson, Edward. **Great Kids of the Movies.** Doubleday, 1979. 10–12.

The names of famous child stars tumble from the pages of this book: Rooney, Garland, Temple, Taylor—all the great and near-great. Snippets of biographies are given, with the reminder that acting is not an easy life. Superficial, but fun for film buffs. Many photos.

Fortunato, Pat. **When We Were Young: An Album of Stars.** Prentice-Hall, 1979. 9–12.

When today's stars were young, they often had the same problems that face their young fans today: being shy, unathletic, too short, etc. Their dreams helped them overcome their problems. Young readers will enjoy learning more about The Fonz, Bruce Jenner, and Cheryl Ladd, among others, through quizzes, short biographies, and baby photos.

Hancock, Sibyl. **Bill Pickett: First Black Rodeo Star.** Illus. Lorinda Bryan Cauley. Harcourt Brace Jovanovich, 1977. 6–9.

Bill Pickett, a black cowboy born in Texas in 1860, became a legendary figure by introducing the art of bulldogging steers, performing with Will Rogers, and touring America and England in Colonel Zack's famous 101 Wild West Show before World War I. An easy-to-read book.

White, Florence Meiman. **Escape! The Life of Harry Houdini.** Julian Messner, 1979. 9–12.

Born in Hungary in 1874, Harry Houdini knew hard times in the U.S. as a child, leaving school in the fourth grade to work for a locksmith. Fascinated by magic and tricks, he became one of the world's greatest escape artists and magicians. Numerous black and white photographs augment the text.

Wilson, Beth P. **Stevie Wonder.** Illus. James Calvin. G. P. Putnam's Sons, 1979. 7–10.

Much of this fascinating biography of Stevie Wonder concerns his childhood. His first hit song, written at the age of twelve, called attention to his musical ability. This brief readable story gives insights into Stevie's motivation and creativity. Illustrated with black and white drawings. Large type letters.

Political Leaders

Davis, Burke. **Mr. Lincoln's Whiskers.** Illus. Douglas Gorsline. Coward, McCann & Geoghegan, 1978. 8–12.

When an eleven-year-old girl wrote to Abraham Lincoln suggesting that more people would vote for him if he grew whiskers, he took her advice. This appealing account of the incident brings into focus both the humor and sadness of Lincoln's character. Sepia and white illustrations.

Devaney, John. **Hitler: Mad Dictator of World War II.** G. P. Putnam's Sons, 1978. 12–up.

This well-written biography, authoritative and documented, covers Adolf Hitler's rise to power through brute force and his ability to influence people. His victories convinced his followers of his infallibility. The book takes the reader from Hitler's youth to his self-destruction in a bunker. Illustrated with photographs.

Faber, Doris. **Dwight Eisenhower.** Abelard-Schuman, 1977. 9–12.

Dwight Eisenhower's leadership qualities are emphasized, especially as they affected his military and political careers. An easy-to-read biography with suggestions for further reading and an index.

Fritz, Jean. **Can't You Make Them Behave, King George?** Illus. Tomie de Paola. Coward, McCann & Geoghegan, 1977. 8–12.

An entertaining biography of King George III, with funny and poignant everyday-life touches that enable the reader to see George as a person. We follow him from a bashful boy with turned-in toes to a senile old man with a wild white beard. Illustrations appropriately complement the text. Carefully researched.

Fritz, Jean. **Stonewall.** Illus. Stephen Gammell. G. P. Putnam's Sons, 1979. 10–up.

More mature readers will enjoy this well-written biography of the popular Stonewall Jackson. His complex personality is revealed in his early youth, his training at West Point, and his performance during the Civil War. Illustrated with a map and soft pencil drawings.

Fritz, Jean. **What's the Big Idea, Ben Franklin?** Illus. Margot Tomes. Coward, McCann & Geoghegan, 1976. 8–12.

This easy biography of the multi-talented Benjamin Franklin is done in the usual Fritz style: careful research revealing little-known but fascinating tidbits to give the subject flesh and blood. Notes at the end expand the text. Sketches in both black and white and color.

Morrison, Dorothy Nafus. **Ladies Were Not Expected: Abigail Scott Duniway and Women's Rights.** Atheneum, 1977. 8–12.

The efforts of the nineteenth-century feminist, Abigail Scott Duniway, who led the struggle for women's suffrage in Oregon, are recounted. As editor of *The New Northwest,* a women's rights newspaper, she wrote of injustice and hardship suffered by women. She traveled, wrote, lectured, and worked for forty-one years until, in 1912, the goal was achieved.

Schraff, Anne. **Tecumseh.** Dillon Press, 1979. 9–12.

Told in terms of United States history, not personal life, this biography recounts the life of Tecumseh, the Shawnee chief who was born in 1768 in the Ohio Valley. He united a confederacy of Indians and fought against the white man's encroachment on native land.

Van Steenwyk, Elizabeth. **Presidents at Home.** Julian Messner, 1980. 8–12.

Another volume for presidential buffs, this book shows the reader some familiar and not-so-familiar photographs of presidential residences. Accompanying the photos are brief biographies that include anecdotes associated with the houses themselves. A "How to Get There" section completes the book.

Religious Leaders

Douglas, Robert W. **John Paul II, The Pilgrim Pope.** Childrens Press, 1980. 6–9.

Pope John Paul II emerges as a very likeable youth, adult, and Pope in this brief, easy-to-read biography. His many talents find fulfillment in acting, intellectual pursuits, hiking, skiing, and canoeing. A map of the Vatican, a glossary, and a list of important events are included. Colored, glossy illustrations.

Edmonds, I. G. **The Girls Who Talked to Ghosts: The Story of Katie and Margaretta Fox.** Holt, Rinehart and Winston, 1979. 10–up.

Katie and Margaretta Fox, who lived during the last two-thirds of the nineteenth century, claimed that they were able to communicate with ghosts. Various investigators tested the Fox sisters, but none proved that they were frauds. The author concentrates on the early years of the women who started the Spiritualist movement in the United States.

Haskins, James. **The Life and Death of Martin Luther King, Jr.** Lothrop, Lee & Shepard Books, 1977. 12–up.

The first half of the biography of Martin Luther King, Jr., is devoted to his life from early childhood to maturity. The second half not only reports his death but also identifies various theories about the events leading up to the assassination, as well as questions yet unanswered. Bibliography and index.

Weil, Lisl. **Esther.** Illus. by author. Atheneum, 1980. 4–7.

The Bible Story of Esther is successfully retold for the young child in text and black and blue naive illustrations. Ahasuerus, the Persian king, was looking for a wife. Esther, a Jewish girl, was chosen. Through much strife she was able to save the Jews living in exile.

Scientists

Boesen, Victor. **Storm: Irving Krick vs. the U.S. Weather Bureaucracy.** G. P. Putnam's Sons, 1978. 8–12.

Irving Krick, who loves to forecast weather, has an eighty-five percent accurate prediction rate. The weather bureau does not exactly love him, but it is fun to find out how this meteorologist has achieved such phenomenal success. The biography describes how Krick has developed a method to produce accurate long-range weather forecasts.

Brown, Marion Marsh. **Homeward the Arrow's Flight.** Abingdon Press, 1980. 12–up.

The biography of Susan La Flesche, daughter of the last chief of the Omaha Indians, is the remarkable story of a spirited, quick-minded woman dedicated to serving her people. She overcomes sexual and cultural prejudices to become the first American Indian woman physician.

Cobb, Vicki. **Truth on Trial: The Story of Galileo Galilei.** Illus. George Ulrich. Coward, McCann & Geoghegan, 1979. 8–12.

The political aspect of science is as important today as it was in 1633 when Galileo Galilei was forced by the Inquisition to say that the earth does not move. The excitement of the explosion in scientific discoveries is conveyed well in this biography of the famous mathematician, physicist, and astronomer. Excellent, full-page black and white illustrations.

Epstein, Sam, and Beryl Epstein. **Dr. Beaumont and the Man with the Hole in His Stomach.** Illus. Joseph Scrofani. Coward, McCann & Geoghegan, 1978. 8–12.

This dramatic episode in medical history revolves around Alexis St. Martin who, when he was shot in the abdomen, had his stomach and lungs exposed in the wound. Even when the wound healed the stomach remained exposed. Dr. William Beaumont realized that he could perform scientific experiments on his patient. The result was fame for the doctor, a lifetime of employment for the patient, and new knowledge of the digestive system.

Epstein, Sam, and Beryl Epstein. **Secret in a Sealed Bottle.** Illus. Jane Sterrett. Coward, McCann & Geoghegan, 1979. 9–12.

Lazzaro Spallanzani, an eighteenth-century Italian biologist, is the focus of this biography. His discovery of the truth about microbe reproduction disproves the spontaneous generation theory and becomes a foundation for the work of future scientists.

Epstein, Sam, and Beryl Epstein. **She Never Looked Back: Margaret Mead in Samoa.** Illus. Victor Juhasz. Coward, McCann & Geoghegan, 1980. 8–12.

This brief, well-told biography of Margaret Mead covers the period of her life in Samoa preparatory to the writing of *Coming of Age in Samoa.* Children reading this book will gain not only an acquaintance with the lively and curious Margaret Mead, but also with the tasks facing an anthropologist exploring another culture.

Facklam, Margery. **Wild Animals, Gentle Women.** Illus. Paul Facklam. Harcourt Brace Jovanovich, 1978. 8–12.

The work of eleven women who study wild animals, both in zoos and in their natural habitats, is discussed. Short vignettes show the dedication, hardwork, and valuable research of these women in an important field of science. Black and white photographs, a bibliography, index, and list of organizations to contact are valuable supplements.

McGovern, Ann. **Shark Lady: True Adventures of Eugenie Clark.** Illus. Ruth Chew. Four Winds Press, 1978. 7–10.

This well-written biography provides girls with an unusual role model. As a child, Eugenie Clark spent Saturdays at the New York City Aquarium while her Japanese mother sold newspapers. She grew up to be a world-renowned ichthyologist, head of a marine laboratory, teacher, author, and fearless shark investigator.

Patterson, Lillie. **Benjamin Banneker: Genius of Early America.** Illus. David Scott Brown. Abingdon Press, 1978. 9–12.

A simple, highly readable biography of an intellectual leader of eighteenth-century America who looked on each day of life as an adventure in learning. Benjamin Banneker was a black man whose achievements were in the fields of astronomy, mathematics, and surveying. Well-chosen illustrations depict the highlights of his life.

Quackenbush, Robert. **Oh, What an Awful Mess! A Story of Charles Goodyear.** Prentice-Hall, 1980. 7–10.

The picture biography of Charles Goodyear describes the trials of the inventor from 1832–1841 when he was obsessed with finding a way to perfect rubber. Many apparent successes failed until a chance act brought a major breakthrough. Cartoon-like drawings add humor to the story.

Shapiro, Irwin. **Darwin and the Enchanted Isles.** Illus. Christopher Spollen. Coward, McCann & Geoghegan, 1977. 9–12.

Charles Darwin's exciting discoveries on his voyage around the coast of South America and to the Galapagos Islands are formulated into startling conclusions about how the earth and its creatures evolved into their present states. Darwin's character is clearly drawn; the context of family and national life and religious beliefs is interestingly presented.

Veglahn, Nancy. **Dance of the Planets: The Universe of Nicolaus Copernicus.** Illus. George Ulrich. Coward, McCann & Geoghegan, 1979. 10–12.

This well-written account describes the scientific study of the sixteenth-century astronomer Nicolaus Copernicus, who questioned the accepted theories of his day. Rebuffed by his peers, he continued his observations and writings about the motions of stars and planets. Only after his death was his work acknowledged.

Veglahn, Nancy. **The Mysterious Rays: Marie Curie's World.** Illus. Victor Juhasz. Coward, McCann & Geoghegan, 1977. 8–12.

This brief, carefully researched biography tells of Marie Curie's exhausting search for radium. The well-written text conveys the frustrations and joys that lay in this formidable task. The author develops both scientific knowledge and human understandings. The charcoal illustrations do much to illuminate this story of a brilliant and determined woman.

White, Florence Meiman. **Linus Pauling: Scientist and Crusader.** Walker, 1980. 10–up.

The only two-time American winner of a Nobel Prize, for chemistry in 1954 and for peace in 1963, has had a varied career. Recently a crusader for Vitamin C, Dr. Linus Pauling is a controversial figure in health and nutrition. The inspiring life story is illustrated with black and white family photographs.

Writers

Begley, Kathleen A. **Deadline.** G. P. Putnam's Sons, 1977. 12–up.

As a young girl, Kathleen Begley decided to become a newspaper reporter. At age eighteen she did. A ten-year period encompassing the late sixties through the mid-seventies is background for the young reporter who observed the nation's top news stories. An autobiography written in fast-paced, journalistic style.

Gleasner, Diana. **Breakthrough: Women in Writing.** Walker, 1980. 12–up.

Biographical sketches of Judy Blume, Erma Bombeck, Erica Jong, Jessamyn West, and Phyllis A. Whitney point up the personal feelings that consumed the writers as they struggled to succeed. The author's introduction sets the tone for this view of writer as woman. Illustrated with black and white photographs.

Johnston, Johanna. **Harriet and the Runaway Book: The Story of Harriet Beecher Stowe and** *Uncle Tom's Cabin.* Illus. Ronald Himler. Harper & Row, Publishers, 1977. 8–12.

From a very early age Harriet Beecher Stowe was intensely interested in the complex problem of slavery. The day-to-day experiences and impressions of her nineteenth-century life formed the basic structure of her book, *Uncle Tom's Cabin,* which brought the issue to the attention of many. Soft wash drawings enhance the text.

Morrison, Dorothy Nafus. **Chief Sarah: Sarah Winnemucca's Fight for Indian Rights.** Atheneum, 1980. 12–up.

The moving story of Sarah Winnemucca, the first Native American to publish a book in English, is based on her autobiography, newspaper accounts, reports to the Secretary of the Interior and the letters of Indian agents. This Paiute Indian woman, who lived in the 1800s, also started the first school taught and administered by Indians.

Naylor, Phyllis Reynolds. **How I Came to Be a Writer.** Atheneum, 1978. 10–up.

This autobiography recounts Phyllis Naylor's early experiences in grade-school writing through her successes of later years. Her problems and progress as a published author are detailed. Includes excerpts of books and photographs.

Roach, Marilynne K. **Down to Earth at Walden.** Illus. by author. Houghton Mifflin, 1980. 12–up.

Walden, Henry David Thoreau's setting for "an experiment in economy," comes to life as his day-to-day life is recounted. The building, food, clothing, and fuel are clearly described in text and pen and ink drawings. A fascinating and detailed account of this New England philosopher. Maps and bibliography appended.

Sanderlin, George. **Mark Twain: As Others Saw Him.** Coward, McCann & Geoghegan, 1978. 12–up.

This good introduction to Mark Twain contains a brief biography as well as chapters devoted to Twain's own opinions and the opinions of those who have written about him. Includes bibliographies and photographs.

Scheader, Catherine. **They Found a Way: Lorraine Hansberry.** Childrens Press, 1978. 10–12.

This carefully researched biography of Lorraine Hansberry relates her brief life, which is crowded with unusual achievements. She grows up in Chicago in a close-knit family. Her interest in writing leads to the writing of the popular play *A Raisin in the Sun.* Easy to read with attractive format.

Others

Ceserani, Gian Paolo, and Piero Ventura. **Christopher Columbus.** Random House, 1977. 7–9.

This brief biography is intriguing for the young reader because of the carefully drawn illustrations that supplement the text. Depicted are a scale drawing of the cross section of a ship, a map of the period, a chart of the crew, and plants of the New World.

Coerr, Eleanor. **Sadako and the Thousand Paper Cranes.** Illus. Ronald Himler. G. P. Putnam's Sons, 1977. 8–12.

This is a moving account of the final year of a real girl who developed leukemia ten years after exposure to radiation in the bombing of Hiroshima. Sadako Sasaki died before folding the thousand paper cranes that Japanese legend said would cure her. But school children place thousands of paper cranes under her statue every August 6, Peace Day.

Collins, David R. **Charles Lindbergh: Hero Pilot.** Illus. Victor Mays. Garrard Publishing, 1978. 7–10.

An interesting biographical sketch of Charles Lindbergh, the well-known aviator. His determination, skill, and courage are highlighted throughout the story and culminate in his successful solo flight from New York to Paris on May 21, 1927. Green and black illustrations complement the text.

Devaney, John. **Douglas MacArthur: Something of a Hero.** G. P. Putnam's Sons, 1979. 12–up.

A well-balanced portrayal of one of the United States' most controversial military leaders. Highlighted are MacArthur's roles in World War I, World War II, and the Korean conflict. Indexed.

Fritz, Jean. **Where Do You Think You're Going, Christopher Columbus?** Illus. Margot Tomes. G. P. Putnam's Sons, 1980. 7–10.

The story of Christopher Columbus is told in a chatty manner that suggests a personality filled with stubbornness and greed, seldom noted in other biographies. The facts are interesting; the asides are sometimes startling. Many colorful drawings add to the pleasurable reading experience. Notes and an index are appended.

Gauch, Patricia Lee. **The Impossible Major Rogers.** Illus. Robert Andrew
Parker. G. P. Putnam's Sons, 1977. 8–12.

Major Robert Rogers was a fighting hero of the French and Indian
War. The book deals with his life on and off the battlefield. The
theme of the book is that being any kind of hero is not easy.

Grant, Anne. **Danbury's Burning! The Story of Sybil Ludington's Ride.**
Illus. Pat Howell. David McKay, 1976. 8–12.

Sixteen-year-old Sybil became a heroine after riding alone to warn
her neighbors about the advancing British soldiers. The reader will
chuckle when the *real* reason emerges! The story is based on a
little-known episode during the American Revolution. Muted pastels
and greys add to the early American charm.

Greenfield, Eloise. **Mary McLeod Bethune.** Illus. Jerry Pinkney. Thomas Y.
Crowell, 1977. 8–10.

Mary McLeod Bethune's numerous contributions to education for
Afro-Americans are noted in this simply written biography. There
were no schools for black children near Mayesville, South Carolina,
where she was born. Laboring under many hardships, she obtained
an education and was determined to help others who were in unfortunate circumstances. Interesting pencil sketches.

Hoff, Syd. **Scarface Al and His Uncle Sam.** Coward, McCann &
Geoghegan, 1980. 8–12.

"Scarface Al" Capone bullies his way into the wealth made through
illicit liquor trade during Prohibition, confident that someday he will
run the country. But in Al's uneasy dreams, Uncle Sam tells him that
only the people can run the country. Humorously illustrated; good
for discussion of social responsibility.

Kherdian, David. **The Road from Home: The Story of an Armenian Girl.**
Greenwillow Books, 1979. 12–up.

This touching story of the author's mother tells the plight of the
Armenians in Turkey in the early 1900s. A young girl survives dreadful physical ordeals and terrible religious persecution. She is deported
and at the age of sixteen goes to America as a mail-order bride.
Poignant; for the advanced reader. 1980 Newbery Honor Book.

Koehn, Ilse. **Mischling, Second Degree: My Childhood in Nazi Germany.**
Greenwillow Books, 1977. 12–up.

This autobiography presents the atrocities of World War II from the
inside. Young Ilse did not know she had one Jewish grandparent
when she was forced to become a member of the Hitler Youth,
children who were treated harshly and unfairly as they underwent
vigorous, often cruel training. An important look at Nazism.

Paul, Frances Lackey. **Kahtahah.** Illus. Rie Muñoz. Alaska Northwest Publishing, 1976. 10–12.

The experiences are told of a real girl, Kahtahah, who lived and played in Juneau, Alaska, before the white people came. This collection of little stories tells of the families and lives of the people known as Tlingit Indians in the nineteenth century.

Sobol, Harriet Langsam. **Grandpa: A Young Man Grown Old.** Photographs by Patricia Agre. Coward, McCann & Geoghegan, 1980. All ages.

Karen, a seventeen-year-old girl, writes about her grandfather Morris Kaye as she sees him. He in turn writes about his life as he sees himself. Beautiful black and white photographs help tell this unusual story. Could provide introduction and discussion on the topic of aging.

Supree, Burton, and Ann Ross. **Bear's Heart.** J. B. Lippincott, 1977. 10–up.

The colored pencil drawings of a young Cheyenne warrior who was imprisoned in Florida in 1975 illustrate his tragic life story as he struggled to survive white domination, was chained in prison, and returned to the reservation, a brainwashed, educated Christian convert. The afterword by Jamake Highwater gives additional perspective to this account of indoctrination.

Collections

Ancona, George. **Growing Older.** E. P. Dutton, 1978. 10–up.

Interesting interviews highlighting the experiences of thirteen elderly citizens of the United States provide history in the making. Photographs of the subjects as young children are contrasted with current ones that depict them in their present situation. A definite motivator for getting children interested in their grandparents and family trees.

Bourne, Miriam Anne. **White House Children.** Illus. Gloria Kamen. Random House, 1979. 7–10.

The White House is the setting for excerpts from the lives of the children and grandchildren of Presidents Washington, Lincoln, Theodore Roosevelt, Kennedy, and Carter. Based on fact, these interesting anecdotes are presented in a simple flowing text. Line drawings complement the easy-to-read narrative.

Foote, Patricia. **Girls Can Be Anything They Want.** Julian Messner, 1980. 8–12.

While discrimination still exists, progress in women's rights is documented by fifteen women of varying ethnic backgrounds and occupations. Using large type and black and white photos, text tells of the women's early lives and struggles to reach their desired goals.

Harley, Ruth. **Captain James Cook.** Illus. Monroe Eisenberg. Troll Associates, 1979. 8–12.

Objective treatment is given to the life of Captain James Cook, a famous English seaman, surveyor, navigator, mapmaker, and discoverer of the Pacific Islands. Fictional tendencies are omitted and the reader is given a true picture of the times. Part of the Troll Adventurer's series, other titles include *Christopher Columbus, Eric the Red and Leif the Lucky, Ferdinand Magellan, Francis Drake, Henry Hudson, John Cabot and Son,* and *Vasco de Gama.*

Katz, William Loren. **Black People Who Made the Old West.** Thomas Y. Crowell, 1977. 10–up.

The spotlight is focused on the lives of thirty-five black men and women who were prominent in the growth of the middle and western United States, from Ohio to California, Wisconsin to Texas. Heretofore unpublished chronicles round out the reader's historical perspective. The short biographical sketches are interesting, entertaining, and at times inspiring.

Leone, Bruno. **Maria Montessori: Knight of the Child.** Greenhaven Press, 1978. 10–up.

Nineteenth-century Italy is the setting for this biographical sketch of a young girl who was determined to assist those in unfortunate circumstances. After becoming a doctor, Maria spent much time with children and perfected methods to teach them. This is one of the *Focus on Women Series* that highlights the determination, success, and failures of Indira Ghandi, Margaret Mead, Carol Burnett, Dorothy Day, Billie Jean King, and Rose Kennedy. Attractive format.

Schoder, Judith. **Brotherhood of Pirates.** Illus. Paul Frame. Julian Messner, 1979. 8–12.

In this realistic portrayal of life among the Caribbean buccaneers in the seventeenth and eighteenth centuries, the fine distinction is made between privateering and piracy. We also get a glimpse of political corruption. The "Brotherhood" included two women, as well as Captain Kidd, Jean Lafitte, Henry Morgan, and Edward Teach.

Additional Biography Books

Adoff, Arnold. *Malcolm X.* Illus. John Wilson. Thomas Y. Crowell, 1970. 6–10.
Aliki. *The Story of William Penn.* Prentice-Hall, 1964. 5–9.
Aliki. *A Weed Is a Flower: The Life of George Washington Carver.* Prentice-Hall, 1965. 5–9.
Braymer, Marjorie. *The Walls of Windy Troy: A Biography of Heinrich Schliemann.* Harcourt Brace Jovanovich, 1960. 11–up.

Bulla, Clyde Robert. *Pocahontas and the Stranger.* Thomas Y. Crowell, 1971. 8–12.
Chidsey, Donald Barr. *The World of Samuel Adams.* Elsevier/Nelson, 1974. 11–up.
Chukovsky, Kornei. *The Silver Crest: My Russian Boyhood.* Trans. by Beatrice Stillman. Holt, Rinehart and Winston, 1976. 11–16.
Commager, Henry Steele. *America's Robert E. Lee.* Illus. Lynd Ward. Houghton Mifflin, 1951. 10–14.
Cone, Molly. *The Ringling Brothers.* Illus. James and Ruth McCrea. Thomas Y. Crowell, 1971. 7–9.
Dalgliesh, Alice. *The Columbus Story.* Illus. Leo Politi. Charles Scribner's Sons, 1955. 6–9.
Daugherty, James H. *Daniel Boone.* Viking Press, 1939. 11–15.
D'Aulaire, Ingri, and Edgar P. D'Aulaire. *Abraham Lincoln.* Doubleday, 1939. 8–11.
Davis, Russell, and Brent Ashabranner. *Chief Joseph: War Chief of the Nez Perce.* McGraw-Hill, 1962. 11–14.
De Trevino, Elizabeth Borton. *I, Juan de Pareja.* Farrar, Straus & Giroux, 1965. 12–up.
Douglass, Frederick. *Life and Times of Frederick Douglass.* Edited by Barbara Ritchie. Thomas Y. Crowell, 1966. 12–16.
Fisher, Aileen, and Olive Rabe. *We Alcotts.* Atheneum, 1968. 11–15.
Forbes, Esther. *America's Paul Revere.* Illus. Lynd Ward. Houghton Mifflin, 1946. 10–14.
Franchere, Ruth. *Cesar Chavez.* Illus. Earl Thollander. Thomas Y. Crowell, 1970. 8–14.
Fritz, Jean. *What's the Big Idea, Ben Franklin?* Illus. Margot Tomes. Coward, McCann & Geoghegan, 1976. 6–10.
Galt, Tom. *Peter Zenger: Fighter for Freedom.* Illus. Ralph Ray. Thomas Y. Crowell, 1951. 10–14.
Greenfield, Eloise. *Rosa Parks.* Illus. Eric Marlow. Thomas Y. Crowell, 1973. 8–12.
Gurko, Miriam. *Clarence Darrow.* Thomas Y. Crowell, 1965. 11–14.
Haskins, James. *Fighting Shirley Chisholm.* Dial Press, 1975. 12–up.
Holbrook, Stewart. *America's Ethan Allen.* Illus. Lynd Ward. Houghton Mifflin, 1954. 10–up.
Judson, Clara Ingram. *Benjamin Franklin.* Illus. Robert Frankenberg. Follett Publishing, 1958. 12–up.
Latham, Jean Lee. *Carry On, Mr. Bowditch.* Houghton Mifflin, 1955. 12–up.
Lawrence, Jacob. *Harriet and the Promised Land.* Simon & Schuster, 1968. 6–10.
McNeer, May. *America's Abraham Lincoln.* Illus. Lynd Ward. Houghton Mifflin, 1957. 10–up.
McNeer, May, and Lynd Ward. *Armed with Courage.* Illus. Lynd Ward. Abingdon Press, 1957. 10–13.
Meigs, Cornelia. *Invincible Louisa.* Little, Brown, 1933, 1968. 10–14.
Meltzer, Milton. *Langston Hughes: A Biography.* Thomas Y. Crowell, 1968. 12–up.
Monjo, F. N. *Grand Papa and Ellen Aroon.* Illus. Richard Cuffari. Holt, Rinehart and Winston, 1974. 9–12.
Monjo, F. N. *The One Bad Thing about Father.* Illus. Rocco Negri. Harper & Row, Publishers, 1970. 6–9.
Moore, Carman. *Somebody's Angel Child: The Story of Bessie Smith.* Thomas Y. Crowell, 1970. 10–up.

North, Sterling. *Young Thomas Edison.* Illus. William Barss. Houghton Mifflin, 1958. 10–14.

Petry, Ann. *Harriet Tubman: Conductor on the Underground Railroad.* Thomas Y. Crowell, 1955. 12–15.

Rollins, Charlemae Hill. *They Showed the Way: Forty American Negro Leaders.* Thomas Y. Crowell, 1964. 9–12.

Sandburg, Carl. *Abe Lincoln Grows Up.* Illus. James Daugherty. Harcourt Brace Jovanovich, 1940. 11–15.

Sterling, Dorothy. *Captain of the Planter.* Doubleday, 1958. 8–12.

Syme, Ronald. *Geronimo: The Fighting Apache.* Illus. Ben F. Stahl. William Morrow, 1975. 8–12.

Syme, Ronald. *Nigerian Pioneer: The Story of Mary Slessor.* Illus. Jacqueline Tomes. William Morrow, 1964. 10–14.

Syme, Ronald. *Verrazano: Explorer of the Atlantic Coast.* Illus. William Stobbs. William Morrow, 1973. 8–12.

Terry, Walter. *Frontiers of Dance: The Life of Martha Graham.* Thomas Y. Crowell, 1970. 8–11.

Tobias, Tobi. *Maria Tallchief.* Illus. Michael Hampshire. Thomas Y. Crowell, 1970. 8–11.

Turk, Midge. *Gordon Parks.* Illus. Herbert Danska. Thomas Y. Crowell, 1971. 6–10.

Vipont, Elfrida. *Weaver of Dreams: The Girlhood of Charlotte Brontë.* Henry Z. Walck, 1966. 12–14.

Wibberly, Leonard. *Man of Liberty.* Farrar, Straus & Giroux, 1968. 12–16.

Wood, James Playsted. *The Life and Words of John F. Kennedy.* Doubleday, 1964. 9–12.

Yates, Elizabeth. *Amos Fortune: Free Man.* E. P. Dutton, 1950. 9–12.

Sciences

Aeronautics and Space

Berliner, Don. **Yesterday's Airplanes.** Lerner Publications, 1980. 7–10.

Outstanding color photographs and a minimum of explanatory text make this a good choice for space-minded readers. Three sections of information—classes of old airplanes, their restoration, and their enjoyment—provide a framework for viewing the topic of antique and classic airplanes.

Cipriano, Anthony J. **America's Journeys into Space: The Astronauts of the United States.** Illus. William Joffe Numeroff. Julian Messner, 1979. 10–up.

A chronicle of the events in the United States space program is highlighted by actual photography of the projects. Biographical sketches of the astronauts from Alan Shepherd to Vance Brand are included.

Coombs, Charles. **Passage to Space: The Shuttle Transportation System.** William Morrow, 1979. 7–10.

An examination of the "first reusable spacecraft" developed for travel in space, this book is well illustrated with numerous photos and drawings. Speculations for the future are given; a glossary and index are included.

Gemme, Leila Boyle. **The True Book of Spinoffs from Space.** Childrens Press, 1977. 8–12.

New products that were designed for the space program but that have been adapted for our more practical use are described with simple text and clear photographs.

Gemme, Leila Boyle. **The True Book of the Mars Landing.** Childrens Press, 1977. 4–7.

This is a first book of space exploration for beginning readers. Full-page illustrations and photographs of the planet Mars taken by the *Mariner* and *Viking* spacecrafts, many in color, are explained simply and clearly.

Mohn, Peter B. **The Golden Knights.** Childrens Press, 1977. 8–12.

The Golden Knights, a United States Army parachute team, open the air show and excitement builds as Leverett unfastens his seat belt to jump. What goes on in a jump school and how these performers are chosen are clearly explained. Glossy colored photographs add to the information. Other titles in the series include: *The Silver Eagles* (helicopters), *The Thunderbirds* (aerial demonstration team), and *The Blue Angels* (naval demonstration squadron).

Rosenblum, Richard. **Wings: The Early Years of Aviation.** Four Winds Press, 1980. 10–up.

A history of airplanes and their pilots is chronicled from the first attempts at flight to the World War II aces. Information on related topics such as blimps, air races, air circuses, and passenger service is included. The black and white drawings capture the excitement and thrill of flying.

Wheat, Janis Knudsen. **Let's Go to the Moon.** Illus. Bill Burrows. National Geographic Society, 1977. 7–10.

Spectacular photographs highlight this look at the Apollo 17's journey to the moon. Names and details of the flight are given only in the credits at the end of the book. The easy text is personalized so that young readers can gain a beginning understanding of space flight.

Wilson, Mike, and Robin Scagell. **Jet Journey.** Viking Press, 1978. 8–12.

From making the reservations to coming in for a landing, a jet journey is explained in detail. Photos, drawings, and diagrams explain how baggage is loaded, what keeps an airplane aloft, and what happens when the sound barrier is broken. Other books in this series include *Super Machines, Television Magic,* and *Space Frontier.*

Animal Kingdom

Animal Behaviors

Anderson, Mona. **Home Is the High Country.** Illus. David Cowe. Charles E. Tuttle, 1979. 12–up.

New Zealand's remote sheep raising country is the setting for six excellent true animal stories. The accounts, written in the first person, concern an outcast duckling nurtured back to health by a cat, a handsome kea bird who seems to enjoy being mischievous, puppies, possums, paradise ducks, and hedgehogs. Accompanied by six beautiful color plates.

Arnosky, Jim. **Crinkleroot's Book of Animal Tracks and Wildlife Signs.** G. P. Putnam's Sons, 1979. 7–10.

Excellent information presented in a lighthearted manner by Old Crinkleroot, who "can hear a fox turn in the forest and spot a mole hill on a mountain." Soft brown and black drawings are clear, attractive, and informative.

Arnosky, Jim. **A Kettle of Hawks and Other Wildlife Groups.** Illus. by author. Coward, McCann & Geoghegan, 1979. 4–7.

Simple, clear language describes the various societies such as a kettle of hawks, a swarm of bees, a school of fish, and others. Black and green illustrations. A worthwhile supplementary science book.

Berrill, Jacquelyn. **Wonders of How Animals Learn.** Illus. by author. Dodd, Mead, 1979. 10–12.

This exciting book describes how animals learn other than by instinct. Imitation, trial and error, and exploring are a few examples. Black and white illustrations.

Bethell, Jean. **Bathtime.** Holt, Rinehart and Winston, 1979. 4–up.

One rarely gets to see an okapi cleaning dust from one eye with its long tongue! Small children will delight in learning how birds and animals satisfy the basic need for cleanliness and comfort. Simple, clear text and unusual, fascinating photographs.

Blumberg, Rhoda. **Backyard Bestiary.** Illus. Murray Tinkelman. Coward, McCann & Geoghegan, 1979. 9–12.

Mythical animals contained in bestiaries of long ago are compared with today's real insects and animals. Habits of some creatures commonly found in backyards are so fascinating that they resemble the fabled rocs and phoenixes. A handsomely illustrated, intriguing book.

Craig, M. Jean. **Little Monsters.** Dial Press, 1977. 8–12.

Color and black and white close-up photographs of eighteen tiny "monsters" are fascinating. Beside each photo of bats, fish, spiders, and caterpillars, an easily read text tells actual size, food, habitat, and survival techniques of the creature pictured.

Friedman, Judi. **Noises in the Woods.** Illus. John Hamberger. E. P. Dutton, 1979. 6–9.

Suggestions on how to follow sounds in the forest by day and night are clearly explained. The more familiar sounds are identified in the text and in the soft, sensitive illustrations. Flying squirrels, raccoons, owls, and beavers are but a few of the animals described.

Hirschmann, Linda. **In a Lick of a Flick of a Tongue.** Illus. Jeni Bassett. Dodd, Mead, 1980. 7–10.

Tongues are handy devices for people, but even handier for animals who use their tongues to eat, groom, cool, and even heal their bodies. Humorous lines of poetry and three-color illustrations introduce many animals, along with some information on the wonders of their tongues.

Kessler, Ethel, and Leonard Kessler. **Two, Four, Six, Eight: A Book about Legs.** Dodd, Mead, 1980. 4–7.

This early concept book encourages the young to carefully observe, discover, and compare numbers of legs of people, animals, and insects that walk, hop, run, and jump. Especially appealing and informative are the illustrations, which match the brief text.

Kohl, Judith, and Herbert Kohl. **The View from the Oak: The Private Worlds of Other Creatures.** Illus. Roger Bayless. Sierra Club Books, 1977. 10–up.

This introduces the subject of ethology, the study of the way animals behave in their natural environments. Clear and simple phrases describe how animals see, touch, and smell differently from humans. References included are scientific, literary, and philosophical. The book makes readers realize what a small part of the universe they are.

Merrill, Margaret W. **Skeletons That Fit.** Illus. Pamela Carroll. Coward, McCann & Geoghegan, 1978. 8–12.

Beautiful illustrations and clear text blend together to make this a very special informational book about vertebrates. Explanation is given why the skeletal structure helps each animal to adapt to its environment. A vertebrate chronology, glossary, bibliography, and index are appended.

Rinard, Judith E. **Creatures of the Night.** National Geographic Society, 1977. 6–9.

Nocturnal animals and their after-dark activities are explained and shown in full-color photographs. Teacher's guide is available.

Schlein, Miriam. **Snake Fights, Rabbit Fights, & More: A Book about Animal Fighting.** Illus. Sue Thompson. Crown Publishers, 1979. 7–10.

Animals fight for territory, mates, and rank, but seldom injure each other seriously because they follow clear-cut rules of combat and surrender. The fast-paced text includes a lucid explanation of the survival-of-the-fittest theory. Beautifully illustrated with black and white drawings.

Van Woerkom, Dorothy. **Hidden Messages.** Illus. Lynne Cherry. Crown Publishers, 1979. 6–8.

When Ben Franklin found ants in the molasses pot, his lively mind devised an experiment to show that one of them could deliver a message to the rest. This and other experiments with the "hidden messages" of insects are described for very young scientists in this well-illustrated, easy-to-read book.

Animal Defenses

Brenner, Barbara. **Beware! These Animals Are Poison.** Illus. Jim Spanfeller. Coward, McCann & Geoghegan, 1979. 7–10.

The author stresses that some animals are poisonous and sometimes deadly, but emphasizes that they use their poison to defend themselves. The animals are classified by the means through which they dispense their poison, such as stingers, teeth, and fangs. Precise line drawings.

Freedman, Russell. **Tooth and Claw: A Look at Animal Weapons.** Holiday House, 1980. 6–9.

Staying alive is an animal's first concern. Weapons needed to do this include quills, sprays, teeth, claws, horns, poisons, and stingers. The electric eel shocks its enemies. Simple, straightforward writing and large print make this a valuable supplementary science book. Excellent photographs and index.

Ricciuti, Edward R. **Sounds of Animals at Night.** Harper & Row, Publishers, 1977. 8–12.

Selected animals are discussed and the special sounds they make at night are explained. This short book contains photographs of each animal in its natural setting.

Animal Habitats

Hess, Lilo. **Small Habitats.** Charles Scribner's Sons, 1976. 8–12.

Shiny little green lizards, intriguing horned toads, frogs, garden snakes, and turtles are a few of the pets for which a terrarium home can be made. Directions are given for plants, soils, rocks, and water to create the proper habitat for each animal. Many excellent photographs.

Hopf, Alice L. **Whose House Is It?** Illus. Leigh Grant. Dodd, Mead, 1980. 8–10.

One can never tell to whom a burrow belongs because after being abandoned by one occupant, another one comes along and a new cycle is begun. Vivid description of a burrow's design and building along with fine soft-pencil illustrations showing cut-away views add to the reader's interest.

Lauber, Patricia. **What's Hatching Out of That Egg?** Crown Publishers, 1979. 7–10.

The guessing game format of this informative picture book will appeal to the young reader. Text and striking photographs bring natural history clues close to the child for careful observation and include information on the ostrich, python, bullfrog, monarch butterfly, penguin, and turtle eggs. Index.

Lewin, Ted. **World within a World: Pribilofs.** Illus. by author. Dodd, Mead, 1980. 10–up.

The Pribilof Islands are in the middle of the Bering Sea off the coast of Alaska. Millions of fur seals and seabirds come in the spring to mate and rear their young. The lovely, sensitive black and white illustrations capture the island's world.

Nussbaum, Hedda. **Animals Build Amazing Homes.** Illus. Christopher Santoro. Random House, 1979. 6–9.

The construction and function of fifteen animal homes are described, including termites, spiders, frogs, crabs, ants, chimpanzees, and others. Each home is amazing and just right for the species. Two-color illustrations.

Pringle, Laurence. **Animals and Their Niches: How Species Share Resources.** Illus. Leslie Morrill. William Morrow, 1977. 7–10.

What happens when related animals in a wild community compete for food and space? A study of garter snakes, warblers, minnows, and rodents answers the question. This easy-to-read book offers a deeper understanding of the ecology of animals in various communities. Detailed wash drawings, glossary, suggested readings, and index.

Pringle, Laurence. **The Hidden World: Life under a Rock.** Macmillan Publishing, 1977. 8–12.

The unusual ecosystem of animals and plants that live under rocks is explored. The author describes where to look and what one will find in these hidden worlds. Excellent black and white photographs illustrate the text.

Birds

Amon, Aline. **Roadrunners and Other Cuckoos.** Illus. by author. Atheneum, 1978. 8–12.

The cuckoo is named for the sound it makes. Other members of this unusual species of birds are the South American hoatzin and the roadrunner. The different and sometimes odd characteristics of the cuckoo family are discussed in detail. Black and white drawings of each bird are included.

Arnold, Caroline. **Five Nests.** Illus. Ruth Sanderson. E. P. Dutton, 1980. 6–9.

Five different empty nests are pictured in the beginning: Who will care for the babies who are about to hatch? Brief chapters, written with easy-to-understand yet scientifically accurate text, describe contrasting species of birds' care of their young. Drawings are beautiful and meticulous. Indexed.

Brenner, Barbara. **Have You Ever Heard of a Kangaroo Bird? Fascinating Facts about Unusual Birds.** Illus. Irene Brady. Coward, McCann & Geoghegan, 1980. 10–12.

The author gives fascinating descriptions of several unusual and remarkable birds. The illustrations accurately depict these peculiar birds. Included are the puffin, the California condor, and the bowerbird.

Canfield, Jane White. **Swan Cove.** Illus. Jo Polseno. Harper & Row, Publishers, 1978. 6–8.

A summer in the life of a pair of swans is described for beginning readers. The illustrations reflect careful observation and make the text vivid.

Cole, Joanna. **A Chick Hatches.** Photographs by Jerome Wexler. William Morrow, 1976. 8–12.

The story of the growth of a chicken from fertilized embryo to hatching is told simply for young readers. The graphic black and white photographs are carefully integrated with the clear, concise text.

Freedman, Russell. **How Birds Fly.** Illus. Lorence F. Bjorklund. Holiday House, 1977. 10–up.

Comparing birds to airplanes and using what scientists have discovered through high-speed photography, the author presents fascinating facts on how birds fly. Elegant pencil drawings show the majesty of birds in flight.

Gans, Roma. **When Birds Change Their Feathers.** Illus. Felicia Bond. Thomas Y. Crowell, 1980. 6–9.

In simple text the author describes the different kinds of feathers that birds have, how they change them, and how feathers grow. Colorful detailed drawings illustrate the basic information.

Garelick, May. **It's about Birds.** Illus. Tony Chen. Holt, Rinehart and Winston, 1978. 8–10.

This book is packed with information that is easily comprehended and answers the questions many children have about birds: kind, size, eating habits, migration, and more. Numerous handsome duo-tone drawings.

Harris, Lorle. **Biography of a Whooping Crane.** Illus. Kazue Mizumura. G. P. Putnam's Sons, 1977. 9–up.

The life of a young whooping crane is interestingly portrayed from the time of the parent birds' care of the egg in Wood Buffalo Park, Canada, until maturity a year later, including the dangerous cross-continental seasonal migrations. Scientists' care protects this endangered species. Beautiful drawings in black and white.

Kaufmann, John. **Birds Are Flying.** Illus. by author. Thomas Y. Crowell, 1979. 4–7.

This attractive book on birds will be a welcome addition to the classroom because of its simple language and clear, accurately labeled diagrams. The functions of bones, muscles, and feathers and their part in the flight process are explained.

Morris, Dean. **Birds.** Raintree Publishers, 1977. 6–10.

The clearly written text presents interesting and precise information about birds. Many beautifully exact and well-labeled drawings convey information about how birds fly, build nests, and migrate. Difficult concepts are presented in a way that makes them accessible to young readers. A lengthy glossary and index are included.

Oxford Scientific Films. **The Chicken and the Egg.** Photographs by George Bernard and Peter Parks. G. P. Putnam's Sons, 1979. 8–12.

A life cycle description of the domestic fowl is supported by distinctive color photographs. Background narrative includes environmental and feeding information, mating, and egg-laying habits.

Schreiber, Elizabeth Anne. **Wonders of Terns.** Photographs by author and Ralph W. Schreiber. Dodd, Mead, 1978. 7–up.

A very complete explanation about the life and habits of a unique bird, the tern. The photographs give a graphic history of the tern from birth to maturity.

Scott, Jack Denton. **Canada Geese.** Photographs by Ozzie Sweet. G. P. Putnam's Sons, 1976. 8–12.

Illustrated with many excellent black and white photographs of Canada geese in flight or on the ground, this book provides much factual information about the life and habits of the geese. Migration, mating habits, rearing of goslings, and danger from hunters are discussed.

Scott, Jack Denton. **Discovering the Mysterious Egret.** Photographs by Ozzie Sweet. Harcourt Brace Jovanovich, 1978. 8–up.

Rich language and a profusion of exquisite photographs present the history and life of the egret, that lovely white bird that dwells with cattle and whose strange migratory habits have baffled ornithologists. A great amount of information is conveyed with artistry.

Scott, Jack Denton. **The Gulls of Smuttynose Island.** Photographs by Ozzie Sweet. G. P. Putnam's Sons, 1977. 8–up.

Smuttynose Island is a gull breeding ground off the New England coast. Through words and black and white photographs, the reader spends one breeding season with gulls, learning their survival threats and responses and other general information about gulls.

Scott, Jack Denton. **The Submarine Bird.** Photographs by Ozzie Sweet. G. P. Putnam's Sons, 1980. 10–up.

The cormorant, a fascinating bird, is presented through interesting bits of information including history, ecological niche, courtship and breeding rituals, diving ability, and use by fishermen. Clear, action-filled black and white photographs supplement the text.

Stemple, David. **High Ridge Gobbler: A Story of the American Wild Turkey.** Illus. Ted Lewin. William Collins Publishers, 1979. 10–up.

This story of a brood of Eastern wild turkeys through the first three years of their life is informational and readable. Illustrated with detailed black and white pencil drawings.

Zoll, Max Alfred (translator Catherine Edwards Sadler). **A Flamingo Is Born.** Photographs by Winifried Noack. G. P. Putnam's Sons, 1978. 6–9.

This small book uses black and white photographs of exceptional quality and composition to capture the life of a flamingo from the mating (pictured) to birth and several weeks after. The sparse text is packed with information.

Domesticated Animals

Clay, Patrice A. **Your Own Horse: A Beginner's Guide to Horse Care.** G. P. Putnam's Sons, 1977. 10–12.

Packed with information on buying, stabling, feeding, grooming, and caring for the horse, this book is a boon to prospective horse owners. Well illustrated with photographs. A glossary is included.

Davidson, Margaret. **Seven True Horse Stories.** Illus. Leo Summers and Sonia O. Lisker. Hastings House, Publishers, 1979. 7–10.

This collection of easy-to-read factual stories presents descriptions of the evolution of the modern horse. Ponies, mustangs, and donkeys are included. A fine introduction to other horse stories by Marguerite Henry. Includes index and bibliography.

Lavine, Sigmund A. **Wonders of Camels.** Dodd, Mead, 1979. 10–12.

In spite of their evil reputation, camels have long been useful to people, particularly in the Middle Eastern countries. This book, using black and white photographs and old prints, covers the facts and folklore of camels.

Lavine, Sigmund A., and Vincent Scuro. **Wonders of Donkeys.** Dodd, Mead, 1978. 8–up.

Delightful and informative, this volume tells how the donkey has been useful to humans, and discusses wild donkeys and donkeys as pets and show animals. Illustrated with photographs, old prints, and drawings.

Lavine, Sigmund A., and Vincent Scuro. **Wonders of Goats.** Dodd, Mead, 1980. 8–12.

The goat was one of the earliest animals to be domesticated. In addition to being a social animal, goats have been of great use to humans. They supply milk, cheese, fine wool, meat, skins, and in some countries have been trained to work. Excellent supplementary book with photographs.

Lavine, Sigmund A., and Brigid Casey. **Wonders of Ponies.** Dodd, Mead, 1980. 8–12.

Hippologists, students of the horse, tell us it is impossible to define a pony accurately. To be classified as a purebred, all of the pony's ancestors must be of the same breed and registered. Interesting facts illustrated with photographs.

MacClintock, Dorcas. **Horses As I See Them.** Illus. Ugo Mochi. Charles Scribner's Sons, 1980. 10–up.

Outstanding silhouettes of horses are so superb that they nearly overshadow the history and description of various breeds. The book gives information on uses of horses and literary allusions. A browsing book for some; an informative text for others. No index.

Scott, Jack Denton. **The Book of the Goat.** Photographs by Ozzie Sweet. G. P. Putnam's Sons, 1979. 11–up.

New opinions and images of the goat emerge with the reading of this book. The history, characteristics, habits, and usefulness of goats are discussed. Six popular breeds are explored and illustrated with black and white photographs.

Scuro, Vincent. **Wonders of Cattle.** Dodd, Mead, 1980. 12–up.

"How does a brown cow eat green grass and give white milk?" This question and many others are answered in this informative book. The many uses of cattle are explained and their value throughout many countries emphasized. Covers breeding, raising, dairying, and even discusses rodeos. Photographs, sketches, and index.

Steinberg, Phil. **You and Your Pet Horses.** Illus. Diana Magnuson. Lerner Publications, 1978. 7–10.

This brief informative guide answers the questions involved with having a horse for a pet. Different breeds are discussed along with the history, feeding, and care of horses. Also included are tips on how to ride. Black and white pictures, glossary, index.

Fish

Armour, Richard. **Strange Monsters of the Sea.** Illus. Paul Galdone. McGraw-Hill, 1979. 8–12.

The characteristics of many strange, frightening sea creatures, such as the Saber-Toothed Viperfish and the Deadly Stonefish, are described. Combined here is accurate information written in verse, blended with delightful action-filled drawings. Read aloud to find out about real, not mythical, monsters.

Brown, Anne Ensign. **Wonders of Sea Horses.** Dodd, Mead, 1979. 10–up.

The sea horse, like the catfish and dogfish, is really a fish. Yet it has a horse's head, chameleon's eyes, kangaroo's pouch, monkey's tail, and armadillo's armor! Here is fascinating information on varieties of sea horses, their history, behavior, and suitability as pets. The text is well illustrated with photographs and drawings.

Carrick, Carol. **Octopus.** Illus. Donald Carrick. Seabury Press, 1978. 6–up.

Superior text and paintings show the dramatic life of a female octopus as she obtains her food, escapes from the moray eel with one arm bitten off, accepts the exciting attentions of her mate, and cares for her multitude of eggs until, dying, she sees them hatch.

Carrick, Carol. **Sand Tiger Shark.** Illus. Donald Carrick. Seabury Press, 1977. 6–9.

A vivid picture of the life cycle of the sand shark is provided in picture book format. Biological information is reinforced by dramatic color illustrations. The fierce existence of the predator is emphasized.

Cole, Joanna. **A Fish Hatches.** William Morrow, 1978. 7–10.

Description and photographs, some close up and enlarged, provide life cycle information on a trout from egg to maturity. Excellent for science unit.

Fegely, Thomas D. **The World of Freshwater Fish.** Dodd, Mead, 1978. 10–12.

An overall view of the many varieties of freshwater fish—including characteristics, location and migration, feeding habits, coloration, and the effects of pollution—is provided by this informative book. Final chapters deal with creating a native aquarium and with the future. Profusely illustrated with black and white photos. Index.

Oxford Scientific Films. **The Stickleback Cycle.** Photographs by David Thompson. G. P. Putnam's Sons, 1979. 8–up.

A short introductory text describes the life cycle of this small freshwater fish. Enlarged color photographs portray each step in the cycle. They show the translucent egg, the embryo developing, the male caring for the nest, and the newly hatched young.

Shostak, Stanley. **The Hydra.** Illus. Jane A. Westfall. Coward, McCann & Geoghegan, 1977. 7–up.

The tiny hydra can replace its own worn-out cells or whole body parts. The photomicrograph illustrations in this book show hydras in almost every stage of development.

Frogs

Billings, Charlene W. **Spring Peepers Are Calling.** Illus. Susan Bonners. Dodd, Mead, 1978. 9–up.

The Hyla crucifer is a tiny frog that sings for its mate in early spring, jumps with incredible lightness, and titillates observers with amphibian antics. The life cycle of Hyla is described, and a how-to section on peepers as pets is included. Beautiful gray and white drawings.

Cole, Joanna. **A Frog's Body.** Photographs by Jerome Wexler. William Morrow, 1980. 7–10.

A frog spends part of its life in the water and part on the land. A bullfrog captures insects with its special flip-out tongue. These facts and more make this a good source for an animal study unit or science investigation. Diagrams and photographs.

Oxford Scientific Films. **Common Frog.** Photographs by George Bernard. G. P. Putnam's Sons, 1979. All ages.

Uncommon photographs tell the life story of the common frog. Full-page color photographs are accompanied by one sentence of text in attractively simple print. At the beginning is a brief information section. Beauty is combined with the scientific accuracy appropriate to nature study.

Insects

Conklin, Gladys. **Praying Mantis: The Garden Dinosaur.** Illus. Glen Rounds. Holiday House, 1978. 8–12.

By observing the praying mantis she keeps for a pet, the author is able to describe the interesting characteristics of this unusual insect. Information is also given on how to take care of a mantis. Black and white drawings.

Hoban, Brom. **Jason and the Bees.** Illus. by author. Harper & Row, Publishers, 1980. 6–9.

Jason encounters bees in his backyard tree and in the hives of Mr. Weiss, a neighbor and beekeeper. Sister Elsie nearly ruins Jason's new interest. Authentic information about bees is presented in story form. Well illustrated.

Hutchins, Ross E. **A Look at Ants.** Photographs by author. Dodd, Mead, 1978. 7–10.

Clear black and white photographs illustrate the physical characteristics, habits, and natural environments of various kinds of ants. The author, an entomologist, describes many fascinating features of these insects and discusses their place in the balance of nature.

McClung, Robert M. **Green Darner: The Story of a Dragonfly.** Illus. Carol Lerner. William Morrow, 1980. 7–10.

The master teller of life cycle stories makes the dragonfly's life a fascinating tale. McClung uses no anthropomorphism or cuteness; he tells a straightforward story that teems with the life and death escapades of a true nature story. Handsomely illustrated in black and white sketches.

Oxford Scientific Films. **Bees and Honey.** Photographs by David Thompson. G. P. Putnam's Sons, 1977. 8–up.

What goes on inside a hive of honeybees is clearly portrayed by exceptionally beautiful close-up photographs. The introductory text supplies background information on the habits of the honeybee. Young children who cannot read will be able to obtain meaning from the pictures.

Oxford Scientific Films. **The Butterfly Cycle.** Photographs by John Cooke. G. P. Putnam's Sons, 1977. 8–up.

Stages of the life cycle of a butterfly are clearly shown with color photographs. The introduction supplies background information for those who can read, while nonreaders can learn easily from the pictures.

Oxford Scientific Films. **Dragonflies.** Photographs by George Bernard. G. P. Putnam's Sons, 1980. 8–12.

Dragonflies are some of the oldest insects in the world. This unique book of photographs and brief text shows this species' physical characteristics and habitat.

Shebar, Sharon Sigmond. **The Mysterious World of Honeybees.** Photographs by Steve Orlando. Julian Messner, 1979. 7–10.

Susan and Tom visit their uncle and learn all about honeybees. The book, which includes a great deal of information about the life cycle of the bee, as well as the business of collecting honey, is profusely illustrated with black and white photos and drawings.

Lower Animals

Hess, Lilo. **The Amazing Earthworm.** Charles Scribner's Sons, 1979. 8–12.

A clear and simple book describing the characteristics and habits of the earthworm is filled with interesting facts. Large black and white photographs illustrate the text. Includes some experiments.

Jacobson, Morris K., and David R. Franz. **Wonders of Jellyfish.** Dodd, Mead, 1978. 8–12.

Black and white photographs highlight this concise discussion of these fascinating sea creatures. Both harmful and useful specimens are examined, as are the life stages and habits of jellyfish. Index, glossary, and annotated bibliography are appended.

Jacobson, Morris K., and David R. Franz. **Wonders of Snails & Slugs.** Dodd, Mead, 1980. 8–12.

Characteristics of a variety of snails and slugs, snails without shells, and their many uses are explained. Supplementary science book. Photographs, sketches.

Ryder, Joanne, and Harold S. Feinberg. **Snail in the Woods.** Illus. Jo Polseno. Harper & Row, Publishers, 1979. 6–8.

An easy-to-read book that gives a great deal of information about snails in a straightforward and interesting fashion. A life-cycle story.

Waters, John F. **A Jellyfish Is Not a Fish.** Illus. Kazue Mizumura. Thomas Y. Crowell, 1979. 6–9.

The reader will find enjoyment in this very informative book. The characteristics and functions of the jellyfish are described in text and in appealing black and colored washes. Emphasis is placed on the types to avoid.

Monkeys and Apes

Allen, Martha Dickson. **Meet the Monkeys.** Illus. by author. Prentice-Hall, 1979. 7–10.

This informational book describes the behavior, physical appearance, identifying characteristics, and natural habitat of thirty-two species of monkeys. The table of contents classifies them into four groups: Pre-Monkeys, New World Monkeys, Old World Monkeys, and Apes. Illustrations in color and black and white.

Amon, Aline. **Orangutan: Endangered Ape.** Illus. by author. Atheneum, 1977. 9–12.

A well-researched study of the great ape of the Far East. Chapters alternate between fiction and nonfiction. The fiction chapters recount the day-to-day activities of a mother orangutan and her offspring. The nonfiction chapters trace the orangutan from early history and myths to the present. Bibliography and index.

Kevles, Bettyann. **Watching the Wild Apes: The Primate Studies of Goodall, Fossey, and Galdikas.** E. P. Dutton, 1976. 12–up.

The stories of the research of three women primatologists working with chimpanzees, gorillas, and orangutans in their natural habitats: Jane Goodall in Tanzania, Dian Fossey in Rwanda, and Biruté Galdikas in Borneo. Some biographical material is included. Bibliography and index.

McDearmon, Kay. **Gorillas.** Dodd, Mead, 1979. 8–12.

This readable, well-organized, accurate look at the gorilla may change the reader's view of this animal. The physical characteristics and habits are described while photographs depict the gorilla in the wild and in captivity as a shy, gentle creature.

Meyers, Susan. **The Truth about Gorillas.** Illus. John Hamberger. E. P. Dutton, 1980. 6–9.

Here is an introduction to the life and characteristics of central African gorillas. Illustrations blend with text, informing the young reader about the importance of protecting this fierce-looking, yet gentle and rather shy primate. An easy-to-read index is included.

Michel, Anna. **Little Wild Chimpanzee.** Illus. Peter Parnall and Virginia Parnall. Pantheon Books, 1978. 8–12.

As Baby Chimp grows to be Big Chimp, he has basic life experiences that parallel those of human children. There is family care and affection as well as sibling jealousy. Authentic information on chimpanzees is given in text for beginning readers and in the many attractive drawings.

Michel, Anna. **The Story of Nim: The Chimp Who Learned Language.**
Photographs by Susan Kuklin and Herbert S. Terrace. Alfred A.
Knopf, 1980. 8–12.

Nim, the chimp, cooperates with an extensive research project and
proves his ability to communicate using a 125-word vocabulary.
Born in 1973, he is pictured in his infancy, first with his family and
then as a student. Easy text and photographs combine for a fascinating book for the young.

Rau, Margaret. **The Snow Monkey at Home.** Illus. Eva Hülsmann.
Alfred A. Knopf, 1979. 10–12.

This easy-to-read book describes the characteristics of the Japanese
macaque or snow monkey who lives farther north than other species
of monkeys. Information and research for this appealing informational book were obtained from the Jigokudani center in the
Japanese Alps. Bibliography and index included.

Teleki, Geza, Lori Baldwin, and Meredith Rucks. **Aerial Apes: Gibbons of
Asia.** Photographs by Geza Teleki and Lori Baldwin. Coward,
McCann & Geoghegan, 1979. 6–9.

This documentation of the Asian gibbon living in its natural treetop
environment is informative and interesting. The black and white
photographs that blend with brief text give the young reader a close-
up view of this wooly-haired aerialist.

Teleki, Geza, and Karen Steffy. **Goblin, A Wild Chimpanzee.** Photographs
by Geza Teleki and Lori Baldwin. E. P. Dutton, 1977. 6–9.

An average day in the life of Goblin, a young African chimpanzee,
is described. The primatologists, those who study the chimpanzee,
continue to be interested in Goblin since his birth in 1964. Feeding,
playing, wandering, and nesting are clearly described in words and
photographs. Picture map included. Excellent informational book.

Teleki, Geza, Karen Steffy, and Lori Baldwin. **Leakey the Elder: A Chimpanzee and His Community.** E. P. Dutton, 1980. 10–12.

A companion book to *Goblin, A Wild Chimpanzee,* this book is based
on observations made in Gombe National Park in Tanzania. The
aging Leakey is not the leader of the chimpanzee community, but
sets an example as community protector. The story covers the years
1968-70 when Leakey dies. Enlightening photographs.

Pets

Davidson, Margaret. **Seven True Dog Stories.** Illus. Susanne Suba.
Hastings House, Publishers, 1977. 7–10.

This easy-to-read book includes a brief history of remarkable feats
dogs have been trained to do. Outstanding is the story of Silver, a
collie who becomes blind, and Sascha, a dachshund who is trained

to be Silver's guide dog. Black and white illustrations. Index and bibliography included.

de Paola, Tomie. **The Kids' Cat Book.** Illus. by author. Holiday House, 1979. All ages.

Granny Twinkle has free kittens and lots of information about the history, lore, breeds, and proper care of cats. The soft color pencil illustrations of various historic periods add to the visual delight. Good with units on pets and their care.

Dunn, Judy. **The Little Rabbit.** Photographs by Phoebe Dunn. Random House, 1980. 5–8.

Sarah's Easter present is Buttercup, a white rabbit, who soon has seven bunnies of her own. Sarah's friends each get bunnies and the reader learns about the care and habits of pet rabbits. Large full-color photographs are fresh and appealing.

Ferguson, Giovonnia. **Handling Small Pets: Step by Step.** Illus. by author. Exposition Press, 1979. 9–up.

Instructions on handling six common pets. The text is well written with detailed drawings showing exact positions of the handler and the pet. A worthwhile book for pet owners.

Fox, Michael, and Wende Devlin Gates. **What Is Your Dog Saying?** Coward, McCann & Geoghegan, 1977. 8–12.

Fox, a noted authority on animal behavior, discusses the ways in which dogs use body language to communicate to humans. A clear question-and-answer format with many black and white photographs provides valuable information for young dog owners.

Fox, Michael. **Whitepaws: A Coyote-Dog.** Illus. Stephen Gammell. Coward, McCann & Geoghegan, 1979. 12–up.

Whitepaws is a coydog, the offspring of a dog and a coyote. Throughout his puppy months, his wild instincts often emerge. Finally, his child owners must decide what is best for their pet: domesticity or the freedom of a wild animal. Written by an authority on animal behavior.

Hess, Lilo. **A Dog by Your Side.** Charles Scribner's Sons, 1977. 8–up.

A thorough discussion of dogs including a brief history, explanation about purebreds and mongrels, information on well-known types representing the six official categories of dogs, and how to select, care for, and show a dog. Profusely illustrated with beautiful black and white photographs. Index.

Hess, Lilo. **Life Begins for Puppies.** Charles Scribner's Sons, 1978. 6–9.

The owner's Shetland sheepdog is pregnant when she is brought home from the animal shelter. Photographs are taken of the birth of the litter and the first eight weeks of puppyhood. The appealing pictures help tell the story of the dog's care and the training of her puppies.

Hess, Lilo. **Listen to Your Kitten Purr.** Charles Scribner's Sons, 1980. 6–9.

Kittens rescued from a sack in a stream introduce Mindy, a female cat. This book is an extremely well-illustrated plea on behalf of abandoned animals and the importance of spaying. Excellent introduction to the responsibility of caring for pets.

Huntington, Harriet E. **Let's Look at Dogs.** Doubleday, 1980. 8–12.

Hunting dogs, working dogs, dogs for the blind, and 101 breeds recognized by the American Kennel Club are discussed, with the special qualities of each mentioned. This informative, attractive book includes photographs.

Landshoff, Ursula. **Okay, Good Dog.** Harper & Row, Publishers, 1978. 6–9.

This easy-to-read book instructs the young dog owner on how to train a pet to sit, come, stay, and be housebroken. Humorous, instructive illustrations blend with text in emphasizing the use of gentleness, praise, and love in caring for a pet.

Leen, Nina. **Cats.** Holt, Rinehart and Winston, 1980. All ages.

In a black and white photo essay, brief captions relate the characteristics, folklore, and charm of cats. Exemplifying the outstanding photos and book design are two pictures placed side by side showing the remarkable changes in the pupils of cats' eyes, which account for their excellent vision. A browsing book that informs.

Pinkwater, Jill, and D. Manus Pinkwater. **Superpuppy: How to Choose, Raise, and Train the Best Possible Dog for You.** Illus. Jill Pinkwater. Seabury Press, 1977. 10–up.

The authors emphasize that making a dog what you want it to be is based on an understanding of the dog's personality, its feelings, and its reactions. Black and white illustrations. List of related free materials.

Sabin, Francene, and Louis Sabin. **Perfect Pets.** G. P. Putnam's Sons, 1978. 10–12.

This pet care book covers the more common pets with advice on selection, care, and housing. Information is included on insects (how to establish an ant colony and construct insect cages), birds, small mammals, water animals, amphibians, and reptiles. Photographs.

Schilling, Betty. **Two Kittens Are Born: From Birth to Two Months.** Holt, Rinehart and Winston, 1980. 4–7.

After the birth of Cassy's kittens, black and white photographs are taken daily for the first three weeks, and then frequently after that to show the kittens' growth and change. The animals are caught in delightful kittenish acts.

Silverstein, Alvin, and Virginia Silverstein. **Cats: All about Them.** Photographs by Frederick J. Breda. Lothrop, Lee & Shepard Books, 1978. 10–up.

Informative text and excellent black and white photographs present useful and interesting materials about cats. Not only is this a compendium on the care of cats, it is also a study of the cat in history, literature, psychology, and art. One of a series of the same authors' books about animals.

Silverstein, Alvin, and Virginia B. Silverstein. **Gerbils: All about Them.** Photographs by Frederick J. Breda. J. B. Lippincott, 1976. 9–12.

Gerbils, natives of Mongolia and imports to be used as research animals, make wonderful pets. Information is extensive and includes mating and care of these tiny animals. Black and white photographs. A fine guidance book for pet care.

Simon, Seymour. **Discovering What Puppies Do.** Illus. Susan Bonners. McGraw-Hill, 1977. 8–10.

The mother dog's behavior prior to the birth of her litter and the care required after their birth begin the book. Additional information tells the owner how to choose and care for a new puppy, its early training, required shots and other pet care tips. Soft charcoal illustrations.

Reptiles

Bare, Colleen Stanley. **The Durable Desert Tortoise.** Photographs by author. Dodd, Mead, 1979. 6–9.

At dawn the male tortoise leaves his shelter to seek food before the summer air becomes too warm. The physical characteristics and habits of tortoises are described in the text and complemented with clear photos. Possible extinction is discussed. A valuable addition for the science curriculum. Index.

Graham, Ada, and Frank Graham. **Alligators.** Illus. D. D. Tyler. Delacorte Press, 1979. 10–12.

Observations of early settlers are responsible for the many false notions concerning the habits and behavior of the alligator. Conservationists are determined to protect this useful but endangered species that has survived since the great age of reptiles.

Leen, Nina. **Snakes.** Holt, Rinehart and Winston, 1978. 9–12.

This introduction to the study of snakes includes thirty-nine species that are identified by habitat, habits, and the like. Of particular note are the outstanding photographs, many of which are unusual action shots. Bibliography and index are appended.

McClung, Robert M. **Snakes: Their Place in the Sun.** Garrard Publishing, 1979. 8–12.

A black racer snake suns itself after a chilly May night, then glides silently, hunting for food, to the meadow. Short chapters tell about the habitats and lives of common snakes. Profusely illustrated with photographs and drawings in both color and black and white. Excellent information resource. Indexed.

McGowen, Tom. **Album of Reptiles.** Illus. Rod Ruth. Rand McNally, 1978. 8–12.

Factual stories about crocodiles, cobras, sea turtles, lizards, and eight other common reptiles. Colorful full-page illustrations and small drawings, accurate in detail, extend the concepts. An introductory chapter, index, and pronunciation guide make this volume an excellent science resource. One of a series including *Album of Sharks* and *Album of Whales.*

Simon, Seymour. **Meet the Giant Snakes.** Illus. Harriett Springer. Walker, 1979. 8–12.

A Chinese legend tells the story of a giant Pa Snake that was large enough to eat an elephant. The anaconda can grow to be the length of a school bus, and that is not a legend. The anaconda, four types of pythons, and the boa constrictor are discussed. Excellent sketches.

Seals and Whales

Brown, Louise C. **Elephant Seals.** Illus. Nina Inez Brown. Photographs by Andrée Abecassis. Dodd, Mead, 1979. 8–12.

In simple language the life cycle, habits, and unique features of the elephant seal are interestingly presented. Nearly extinct by 1889 because they were discovered to be a source of oil, they have made a remarkable comeback. Photographs and sketches.

Grosvenor, Donna K. **The Blue Whale.** Illus. Larry Foster. National Geographic Society, 1977. 6–9.

The miracle of grace and intelligence evident in the gigantic seaborn mammals known as blue whales is depicted through life-like paintings and a well-written text. Other whales, penguins, and sea creatures integral to the lives of blue whales are included. End papers are vivid paintings of whales of the world.

Marko, Katherine D. **Whales, Giants of the Sea.** Illus. Bettye Rene Beach. Abingdon Press, 1980. 6–9.

Interesting facts about whales are written in an easy-to-read style. The muted blue illustrations add to the brief text. A good book for early science investigations.

Selsam, Millicent E., and Joyce Hunt. **A First Look at Whales.** Illus. Harriett Springer. Walker, 1980. 6–9.

This detailed information book describing the characteristics and habits of the whale has clearly labeled illustrations that assist and clarify the text. Need for the whale's survival is emphasized. Illustrations encourage the beginning reader to observe and classify these mammals.

Shaw, Evelyn. **Elephant Seal Island.** Illus. Cherryl Pape. Harper & Row, Publishers, 1978. 6–9.

The yearly visitation of elephant seals to Ano Nuevo Island in the Pacific Ocean is described in simple language for the young reader. The experiences of a male pup are described from birth until he is able to care for himself. An easy-to-read book.

Simon, Seymour. **Killer Whales.** J. B. Lippincott, 1978. 8–12.

This book helps to dispel myths about killer whales and describes their life in the open sea and in captivity. The clearly written text presents fascinating information about one of the largest and most intelligent animals in the world.

Strange, Florence. **Rock-A-Bye Whale: A Story of the Birth of a Humpback Whale.** Illus. by author. Manzanita Press, 1977. 8–12.

The birth of a humpback whale, one of nature's largest animals, is told simply. The brilliant monoprints help convey the motion and feeling of the sea environment.

Spiders

Lexau, Joan M. **The Spider Makes a Web.** Illus. Arabelle Wheatley. Hastings House, Publishers, 1979. 6–9.

This beginning reader's book describing the shamrock spider and how it spins a web almost every day of its life is very informative. Delicate line drawings enhance the text.

Oxford Scientific Films. **The Spider's Web.** Photographs by John Cooke. G. P. Putnam's Sons, 1978. 9–up.

Detailed photographs demonstrate how the garden spider and the net-throwing spider spin their webs and catch their prey. Background information is given at the beginning of the book. The beautiful step-by-step photographs are captioned.

Walther, Tom. **A Spider Might.** Illus. by author. Sierra Club Books, 1978. 6–up.

Fascinating and unusual facts about spiders encourage the reader to appreciate them more. Basic information is presented in simple, authentic text, illustrated with superbly detailed drawings of many kinds of spiders and their body parts. Index.

Wild Animals

Annixter, Jane, and Paul Annixter. **The Year of the She-Grizzly.** Illus. Gilbert Riswold. Coward, McCann & Geoghegan, 1978. 9–11.

An interesting and informational account of a she-grizzly and her cub in the Montana uplands is given. The ordinary search for food, the mating season, her new cub, and the constant encounters with her enemies make this an exciting and worthwhile book.

Bare, Colleen Stanley. **Ground Squirrels.** Photographs by author. Dodd, Mead, 1980. 8–12.

This book, done in narrative style and black and white photos, follows the complete life cycle of an engaging ground squirrel from the end of hibernation through mating and the new generation.

Barry, Scott. **The Kingdom of Wolves.** Photographs by author. G. P. Putnam's Sons, 1979. 10–up.

Wolves are described in a well-written, interesting text that bespeaks the author as a caring person. A strong argument is given against having wolves as pets or keeping them in captivity. Accompanied by outstanding black and white photographs, this is a book with sensitive impact.

Caputo, Robert, and Miriam Hsia. **Hyena Day.** Photographs by Robert Caputo. Coward, McCann & Geoghegan, 1978. 12–up.

Hyenas are shown to be well-organized animals whose daily routines and food-gathering techniques serve well their needs in the Serengeti Plains of east Africa. Large photographs show hyenas from nursing babyhood through predatory adult activities as the clan goes through the day from morning to preparation for evening rest.

Caras, Roger. **Coyote for a Day.** Illus. Diane Paterson. E. P. Dutton, 1977. 8–11.

A coyote finds a mate. Together they hunt, escape danger, and make preparations for the family they will raise together. The text and illustrations create a clear positive image of this beautiful, misunderstood creature.

Caras, Roger. **Skunk for a Day.** Illus. Diane Paterson. E. P. Dutton, 1976. 7–10.

Follow a skunk for twenty-four hours and have adventures and harrowing escapes that would leave a human exhausted, but are all in a day's work for the skunk. Large, realistic ink drawings in black and white vividly and accurately portray skunks and other woodland creatures.

Dinneen, Betty. **A Tale of Three Leopards.** Illus. Jennifer Emry-Perrott. Doubleday, 1980. 10–12.

Chui's two leopard cubs, Kali and Pesi, are born in the Nairobi Game Park in Kenya. Their playful day-to-day antics are described as they grow to maturity. One lesson they soon learn is the survival of the fittest in their predatory environment. Black pen sketches.

Ford, Barbara, and Ronald R. Keiper. **The Island Ponies: An Environmental Study of Their Life on Assateague.** Photographs by Ronald R. Keiper. William Morrow, 1979. 9–12.

' The ponies who live on Assateague and Chincoteague have been there for several hundred years. No one is certain of their origins. Their home is protected as public land and here scientists observe their living habits and their effect on the environment. A useful addition for an ecology unit.

Geringer, Laura. **Seven True Bear Stories.** Illus. Carol Maisto. Hastings House, Publishers, 1979. 7–10.

Young readers will meet many kinds of bears in this interesting, easy-to-read collection. Victor wrestled, Queenie danced, Teddy sang, and Grizzly Jack loved honey. Three other comic and entertaining stories are included. Informative introduction, index, and bibliography; black and white illustrations.

Griffiths, G. D. **Mattie: The Story of a Hedgehog.** Illus. Norman Adams. Delacorte Press, 1977. 10–12.

From birth in a hollow stump through her long life, Mattie is an adventurous hedgehog. Her relationship with humans is most interesting. Although hedgehogs are native to Europe, Asia, and Africa, but not the United States, this informative book will be enjoyed by all students.

Hamsa, Bobbie. **Your Pet Elephant.** Illus. Tom Dunnington. Childrens Press, 1980. 7–10.

Fascinating and scientific facts about the problems and pleasures of having an elephant as a pet include such items as the elephant's ability to bring in firewood. This Far-Fetched Pets series includes *Your Pet Beaver* and *Your Pet Bear.* The humor is delightful; the illustrations are loaded with fun. (Picture book)

Harris, Lorle. **Biography of a River Otter.** Illus. Ruth Kirschner. G. P. Putnam's Sons, 1978. 8–12.

An informational story of a mother otter's care and concern for her three cubs during their first year is complete with coverage of the otters' homes, food, protective measures, and pleasures. A valuable supplementary science book with meaningful brown and green illustrations.

Hopf, Alice L. **Biography of a Giraffe.** Illus. Patricia Collins. G. P. Putnam's Sons, 1978. 8–12.

Facts combine with setting to create an involving description of the life cycle of a giraffe. Black and white etchings contribute to the total work. A strong addition to the study of science or social studies in middle grades.

Hunt, Patricia. **Koalas.** Dodd, Mead, 1980. 7–10.

Teddy of Quantas Airlines is probably the best-known koala. The author describes the habits of these native Australian animals and the conservation efforts by that country to preserve this species of marsupials.

Lavine, Sigmund A. **Wonders of Marsupials.** Dodd, Mead, 1978. 8–12.

This informative book, which discusses some of the 248 species of marsupials, is divided into the various types: herbivorous, arboreal, phalangus, and carnivorous. Concern for the animals' survival in the future is expressed since they supply fur, leather, and pet food. Clearly presented with accompanying photographs. Index.

Lavine, Sigmund A. **Wonders of Mice.** Dodd, Mead, 1980. 10–up.

Zoologists have identified hundreds of species of mice. Rodents make up over half the living species of mammals. No matter which group they comprise—house, field, hunter, or climbing—they are fascinating creatures. The mouse lore section is especially interesting. Many photos and sketches.

McDearmon, Kay. **Rocky Mountain Bighorns.** Photographs by Valerius Geist. Dodd, Mead, 1980. 8–10.

Early Rocky Mountain explorers reported bighorns as plentiful as buffalo. Now fewer than 15,000 remain. Using both text and dozens of black and white photos, the reader learns about the bighorns' habits, enemies, and hazards to survival. Useful with ecology units.

Michel, Anna. **Little Wild Elephant.** Illus. Peter Parnall and Virginia Parnall. Pantheon Books, 1979. 5–8.

The habits of elephants are explored as the reader follows the life and training of a baby African elephant. Soft black and white sketches supplement the text. Good read-aloud book.

Michel, Anna. **Little Wild Lion Cub.** Illus. Tony Chen. Pantheon Books, 1980. 6–9.

The first two years in Little Lion's life are described in detail in the surroundings of his close-knit family. His mother's training, the search for food, his playtime, and encounters with other animals are depicted in gray-shaded drawings. An easy-to-read book.

Noguere, Suzanne, and Tony Chen. **Little Koala.** Illus. Tony Chen. Holt, Rinehart and Winston, 1979. 6–up.

Here is the amazing life of a koala bear in Australia, from birth, when, as a fly-sized pink speck, it smells its way to its mother's pouch, to the time of its independence more than a year later. Beautifully written and illustrated.

Oxford Scientific Films. **House Mouse.** Photographs by David Thompson. G. P. Putnam's Sons, 1977. 8–up.

Unusually detailed close-up photographs and objective information on the house mouse combine science and art. Included are photographs of newborn mice, mating mice, habitat, eating habits. Descriptive material develops the relationship with humans without overemphasizing destruction and human antagonism.

Oxford Scientific Films. **The Wild Rabbit.** Photographs by George Bernard. G. P. Putnam's Sons, 1980. 8–12.

This remarkable book depicts the wild rabbit with many outstanding colored photographs of the natural surroundings and the various developmental stages. Enjoyable at many levels of reading.

Rau, Margaret. **The Giant Panda at Home.** Illus. Eva Hülsmann. Alfred A. Knopf, 1977. 8–12.

Details of the panda's life cycle include facts of feeding, mating, and rearing of the young. Geographic and historic highlights are included.

Rau, Margaret. **The Gray Kangaroo at Home.** Illus. Eva Hülsmann. Alfred A. Knopf, 1978. 10–up.

A detailed report of a year in the life of a female kangaroo provides insight into special characteristics of the eastern gray kangaroo and of the other creatures and plants in its life community.

Rogers, Edmund. **Elephants.** Raintree Publishers, 1977. 8–12.

Outstanding color photographs highlight this look at the African elephant and follow one herd's daily trek through the tropical forest and grassland as the giant animals search for food and water. Glossary, further readings, and appendix are included.

Ryden, Hope. **The Little Deer of the Florida Keys.** Photographs by author. G. P. Putnam's Sons, 1978. 6–up.

A beautiful book that tells the story of the tiny key deer of Florida. The photographs are so clear, vivid, and lifelike that the reader almost feels a part of the deer's environment. Discusses the threatened survival of this species.

St. Tamara. **Chickaree: A Red Squirrel.** Illus. by author. Harcourt Brace Jovanovich, 1980. 8–12.

Here is a detailed chronicle of a year in the life of a red squirrel. Reaching maturity, this busy chickaree passes through winter days, mates when spring arrives, and brings up two sets of babies. Illustrations assist in describing the complex lives of these familiar animals.

Schaller, George, and Kay Schaller. **Wonders of Lions.** Illus. Richard Keane. Photographs by George Schaller. Dodd, Mead, 1977. 7–up.

Here is a well-written book about the proud lions of the Serengeti National Park in Africa. The authors give an accurate description of the lion's family life, hunting habits, and daily routine. Fine photographs show the lions at work and play.

Schlein, Miriam. **Lucky Porcupine!** Illus. Martha Weston. Four Winds Press, 1980. 6–up.

Porcupines are lucky to have protective quills, to be able to climb easily, run swiftly, float and swim, eat a variety of plants, and find cozy dwellings. Beautiful, accurate drawings.

Schlein, Miriam. **On the Track of the Mystery Animal: The Story of the Discovery of the Okapi.** Illus. Ruth Sanderson. Four Winds Press, 1978. 10–12.

Sir Harry Johnston, an Englishman of many talents, discovered the okapi about 75 years ago, probably the last-found mammal. The reader shares in investigative techniques natural scientists use for proper identification, making class, order, family, genera, and species more understandable. Black and white sketches.

Scott, Jack Denton. **Island of Wild Horses.** Photographs by Ozzie Sweet. G. P. Putnam's Sons, 1978. 8–12.

A beautifully written text combines with powerful black and white photographs to tell the story of the wild horses of Assateague Island. The book explores the history of this band and the life cycle of the horses, and introduces some of the problems involved in protecting the Chincoteague ponies today.

Scott, Jack Denton. **Little Dogs of the Prairie.** Photographs by Ozzie Sweet. G. P. Putnam's Sons, 1977. All ages.

Prairie dogs are accomplished diggers, engineers, and homemakers and are found only in North America. This content-rich book examines their society, enemies, characteristics, and history along with the ecosystem in which they precariously exist. Black and white photographs.

Silverstein, Alvin, and Virginia B. Silverstein. **Mice: All about Them.** Photographs by Robert A. Silverstein. J. B. Lippincott, 1980. 7–10.

Mice have a reputation for sneaking about, but most people have some sympathy for them. They appear in literature from Mother Goose to the Pied Piper of Hamelin. Should we get rid of them? Would this destroy the balance in nature? This book examines the habits, characteristics, and history of mice.

Van Wormer, Joe. **Squirrels.** E. P. Dutton, 1978. 8–12.

Various members of the squirrel family are briefly described and pictured in clear black and white photographs. Woodchucks, prairie dogs, marmots, and ground and tree squirrels are included. Traits of the species are given, such as color, size, range, and diet.

Williams, Barbara. **Seven True Elephant Stories.** Illus. Carol Maisto. Hastings House, Publishers, 1978. 7–10.

Jumbo, the name of an elephant in this book, is familiar to us because it means "big." Other stories include all kinds of elephants: circus elephants, work elephants, wild elephants, and royal elephants. The introduction provides background and recent research findings. This easy-to-read book includes index and bibliography.

The Young

Brady, Irene. **Wild Babies: A Canyon Sketchbook.** Illus. by author. Houghton Mifflin, 1979. 4–up.

Six species of wild animal babies are sketched from infancy to independence. The large, softly colored drawings are authentic in every detail, showing habitats and stages of growth, and are accompanied by stories about how the mothers care for their babies. Excellent for science lessons.

Davidson, Margaret. **Wild Animal Families.** Illus. Fran Stiles. Hastings House, Publishers, 1980. 8–12.

Unusual and interesting facts about different baby mammals are presented for the young science reader. Information is included on how they are born, fed, and protected, and how they play and learn. Simple text encourages further nature investigation of mammals.

Freedman, Russell. **Getting Born.** Illus. Corbett Jones. Holiday House, 1978. 7–10.

What newborns can do while less than one hour old is astounding! With fascinating text and black and white drawings and photographs, birth is documented from the time of egg fertilization in fish to hatching; live births of kittens, dolphins, and horses are also shown. Difficult words are written phonetically.

Freedman, Russell. **Hanging On: How Animals Carry Their Young.** Holiday House, 1977. 7–10.

Animals carry their young in many different ways. Some of the less common are included in this book. Black and white photos and the text explain how and for how long young animals are carried. Pictures invite lingering and looking.

Freschet, Berniece. **Moose Baby.** Illus. Jim Arnosky. G. P. Putnam's Sons, 1979. 4–7.

Five brief chapters describe the maturation process of a young moose. The reader learns what it eats, how it coexists with other animals, how it defends itself, and how it physically matures. One of the See and Read Nature Story series; the illustrations add much.

Freschet, Berniece. **Porcupine Baby.** Illus. Jim Arnosky. G. P. Putnam's Sons, 1978. 6–9.

This story observes the early experiences of a baby porcupine from birth to learning to protect himself from enemies. Pen and ink illustrations are amusing and informative. A nature story, simply and sympathetically told; a good read-aloud book.

McClung, Robert M. **The Amazing Egg.** E. P. Dutton, 1980. 8–12.

Detailed information about the eggs of mammals, reptiles, birds, amphibians, insects, and lower forms of animals is given, including their production, fertilization, and development. Black and white sketches and diagrams highlight the facts.

Miller, Jane. **Birth of a Foal.** J. B. Lippincott, 1977. 4–7.

The first three days of a newborn foal, a Welsh Mountain pony, are described in simple text and appealing black and white photographs. The foal lies in the soft grass and soon learns to stand on wobbly legs. Illustrations convey the wonder of birth and the mother's loving care for her young.

Rabinowitz, Sandy. **What's Happening to Daisy?** Harper & Row, Publishers, 1977. 4–10.

Gentle, full-page watercolor illustrations make the reader actually feel present as the mare Daisy gives birth to her foal. Joy and tenderness come into the pictures when Daisy licks her baby, nuzzles it to stand, and nurses it. Daisy is cared for by a young girl. A valuable life-concept book.

Shaw, Evelyn. **Sea Otters.** Illus. Cherryl Pape. Harper & Row, Publishers, 1980. 6–9.

A scientist studies two sea otters, Garbo and her pup Bo, living in the cold Pacific Ocean. Illustrations clarify the simple informative text. The reader can see how the mother sea otter cares for and teaches her baby to become independent. An easy-to-read book.

Weber, William J. **Wild Orphan Babies: Mammals and Birds.** Photographs by author. Holt, Rinehart and Winston, 1978. 9–up.

Factual information about the care of orphaned wild baby animals and birds is given by a veterinarian. He also includes how to tell if human care is needed and expläins government regulations and special precautions. Illustrated with many superb photographs.

Zoos

Grosvenor, Donna K. **Zoo Babies.** Photographs by author. National Geographic Society, 1978. 6–9.

A crocodile with a broken jaw and an appealingly ugly baby rhino are among the zoo babies presented in this volume of the very popular Books for Young Explorers series.

Hewett, Joan. **Watching Them Grow: Inside a Zoo Nursery.** Photographs by Richard Hewett. Little, Brown, 1979. 8–12.

From baby aardvarks through adult spider monkeys, Loretta feeds them, burps them, and changes their diapers in the zoo nursery. Told in diary form, with irresistible black and white photos, this is a hard book to put down.

Paige, David. **Behind the Scenes at the Zoo.** Photographs by Roger Ruhlin. Albert Whitman, 1978. 7–10.

Black and white and color photographs highlight this overview of zoo activity. Special emphasis is given to obtaining, housing, breeding, feeding, and caring for a wide variety of animals, including many who are endangered species. A glossary is included.

Shuttlesworth, Dorothy E. **Zoos in the Making.** E. P. Dutton, 1977. 10–up.

In addition to the residents of the zoo, the author looks at the operations and problems of zoos. Carefully researched information and exceptional photographs of outstanding zoos in the world complete this interesting book. Plans for the zoos of tomorrow are discussed.

Astronomy

Berger, Melvin. **Planets, Stars and Galaxies.** G. P. Putnam's Sons, 1978. 10–up.

This up-to-date overview of astronomy is written in a style suitable for the young scientist. What is known about the universe is clearly explained; recent discoveries, such as the rings of Uranus, are included. Black and white photographs and charts are helpful. Glossary and index.

Branley, Franklyn M. **Age of Aquarius: You and Astrology.** Illus. Leonard Kessler. Thomas Y. Crowell, 1979. 10–12.

The effects of objects in the sky upon Earth and its inhabitants are discussed from both the astrological and the astronomical points of view. Bibliography and index.

Branley, Franklyn M. **Sun Dogs and Shooting Stars: A Skywatcher's Calendar.** Illus. True Kelley. Houghton Mifflin, 1980. 12–up.

Americans see a man in the moon, Japanese see a rabbit, and Scandinavians see Jack and Jill. These and other fascinating facts, weather lore, and suggested experiments are given for the very scientifically gifted student. Black and white line drawings; divided by month and season.

Engdahl, Sylvia. **Our World Is Earth.** Illus. Don Sibley. Atheneum, 1979. 6–9.

An introduction to space for young children. Earth's place in the universe is expressed in poetic prose enhanced by effective double-page illustrations.

Jaber, William. **Exploring the Sun.** Illus. by author. Julian Messner, 1980. 10–12.

This articulate book on the sun is a valuable addition to the home or classroom. Beginning with sharp warnings on optical care in viewing the sun, the book continues with myths and historical opinions on the sun's makeup. Contemporary facts are also examined. Excellent photographs and drawings, glossary, and index.

Jobb, Jamie. **The Night Sky Book: An Everyday Guide to Every Night.** Illus. Linda Bennett. Little, Brown, 1977. 8–12.

Black and white drawings illustrate the many interesting facts about the stars, constellations, moon, and the zodiac. Instructions are given for projects about the night sky, such as how to find the constellations, how to make a simple astrolabe, and others. A Brown Paper School Book.

Kerrod, Robin. **The Mysterious Universe.** Lerner Publications, 1980. 7–10.

The question-and-answer format includes a great deal of information about space and our study of it. Planets, stars, and galaxies within the universe are explained and illustrated in full color. Appendices include a list of famous astronomers, names of the constellations, glossary, and index.

Knight, David C. **Galaxies: Islands in Space.** William Morrow, 1979. 10–12.

An introduction to our galaxy, the Milky Way, this book is well illustrated with photographs and diagrams. It also discusses other galaxies, their evolution and phenomena. Includes glossary and index.

Kuskin, Karla. **A Space Story.** Illus. Marc Simont. Harper & Row, Publishers, 1978. 4–7.

The planets are accurately described in a language the young child can understand. Curiosity is stimulated by the colorful illustrations and the double-page spread that presents the star patterns. An excellent informational book.

Simon, Seymour. **The Long View into Space.** Crown Publishers, 1979. 8–12.

An awesome look into space, starting with our nearest neighbor, the moon, progressing past the planets, through our galaxy, and ending up with galaxies so far away that they are barely visible through the most powerful telescopes. Interest is further stimulated by stunning black and white photographs, and a simple, straightforward text that at times achieves a poetic quality.

Simon, Seymour. **Look to the Night Sky: An Introduction to Star Watching.** Viking Press, 1977. 10–12.

Beginning observers are told how to look at the stars and how to understand what they see. The difference between astrology and astronomy is explained. A chapter is given to the explanation and use of the telescope. Information for further reading and research is included. Clear diagrams complement the text. Index.

Taylor, G. Jeffrey. **A Close Look at the Moon.** Dodd, Mead, 1980. 10–12.

What is on the moon? Are there any creatures living there? Is there any water? In the twentieth century there are answers to some of these questions. The easy-to-read text and easy-to-understand explanations will be enjoyed by many at home or at school. Clear photographs.

Zim, Herbert S. **The New Moon.** William Morrow, 1980. 6–9.

Specimens brought to earth from moon voyages, photographs, and powerful telescopes provide information about the earth's only natural satellite. Structural features of minerals found there are examined and explained; comparisons of earth and lunar features are made. Diagrams and photographs.

Conservation and Ecology

Brown, Joseph E. **Oil Spills: Danger in the Sea.** Dodd, Mead, 1978. 10–up.

Oil spills are shown to present a dangerous problem affecting life on our planet; the reader learns how oil is used, transported, and spilled, what oil spills do, how to stop them, and alternatives for future energy supplies. Illustrated wtih many photographs. Glossary and index.

Burt, Olive W. **Rescued! America's Endangered Wildlife on the Comeback Trail.** Julian Messner, 1980. 8–12.

A flock of whooping cranes was started when sandhill cranes adopted five whooping crane eggs. Four years later the flock has grown to seventy-four birds. Sea otters have been taken off the endangered species list. The people, strategies, and laws that made these and other ecological success stories possible are described in lively detail, accompanied by appealing black and white photographs and engravings.

Couffer, Jack, and Mike Couffer. **Salt Marsh Summer.** G. P. Putnam's Sons, 1978. 10–up.

Readers spend the summer of 1977 on the Back Bay of a southern California seaside marshland, with father and son Jack and Mike Couffer. Unparalleled photographs bring alive the narratives about birds, plants, and animals, as well as the efforts of naturalists and nature lovers to preserve the endangered wildlife environment.

Epstein, Sam, and Beryl Epstein. **Saving Electricity.** Illus. Jeanne Bendick. Garrard Publishing, 1977. 7–10.

This provocative, fact-filled book makes children aware and prepares them for the critical decisions they will face concerning conservation. A helpful index is supplied. Simple, clear illustrations show how electricity is generated. Basic information for a unit on electricity.

Fisher, Ronald M. **A Day in the Woods.** Photographs by Gordon W. Gahan. National Geographic Society, 1978. 7–10.

Harley and Joan learn that in the deceptive quiet of the forest lives a fascinating variety of animals, birds, reptiles, insects, and plants. Beautiful color photographs of sights rarely seen so closely expertly extend the teachings of the text.

Fodor, R. V. **Angry Waters: Floods and Their Control.** Dodd, Mead, 1980. 8–12.

The causes of floods are discussed: how they can be prevented and how they are forecast. The reader is given five basic rules to follow in case of a flash flood. Illustrated with photographs and diagrams.

Kavaler, Lucy. **The Dangers of Noise.** Illus. Richard Cuffari. Thomas Y. Crowell, 1978. 10–up.

A lively and lucid account of our machine age's noisy assault on our ears, our brains, and even our personalities. A concluding chapter provides young citizens with practical suggestions for saying *no* to noise.

List, Albert, Jr., and Ilka List. **A Walk in the Forest: The Woodlands of North America.** Illus. by authors. Thomas Y. Crowell, 1977. 12–up.

The forest environment, with all its elements, is discussed and analyzed in a question-and-answer format. Black and white photographs and drawings illustrate the diverse topics. The section devoted to projects to do in the forest is clear and sufficiently detailed. Students, teachers, and resource persons will find this a useful tool.

Millard, Reed. **Clean Air, Clean Water for Tomorrow's World.** Julian Messner, 1977. 10–up.

Causes of polluted air and water and possible solutions for pollution problems are examined. Appendixes include a glossary, lists of organizations and governmental agencies concerned with environmental problems and policies, a bibliography of suggested further readings, and an index.

National Geographic Society, editors. **Animals in Danger: Trying to Save Our Wildlife.** National Geographic Society, 1978. 6–9.

While the information presented about endangered species is brief, beautiful cheetahs, marmosets, sea otters, and other species are represented in very handsome photographs.

Newton, James R. **Forest Log.** Illus. Irene Brady. Thomas Y. Crowell, 1980. 6–9.

This basic science picture book introduces the natural world to the reader. A huge Douglas fir tree crashes to the ground and the process of decay is explained. Its value to the biological community is clearly depicted in text and excellent black and white drawings.

Pringle, Laurence. **Natural Fire: Its Ecology in Forests.** William Morrow, 1979. 9–12.

According to this book, forest fires aren't always bad. Some fires cause new seedlings to sprout, or clear the forest floor. Rangers and ecologists are learning more about this natural force and how it maintains the balance of forests. Excellent in an ecology unit.

Roth, Charles E. **Then There Were None.** Illus. by author. Addison-Wesley Publishing, 1977. 10–up.

A grim tale of the loss of species due to humans' assault on the environment. Included is the poignant story of Ishi, the last Yani Indian, illustrating the difference between a culture that lived in harmony with the earth and one that killed off bison, beavers, and passenger pigeons with little regard for the ultimate consequences.

Stuart, Gene S. **Wildlife Alert! The Struggle to Survive.** National Geographic Society, 1980. 10–up.

An overview of the main problems that wild animals face in our world today is discussed, including animal habitats, deadly substances in the environment, and the killing and sale of wildlife for commercial purposes. Excellent color photographs highlight the text. A classroom activities folder contains ditto masters, games, puzzles, and fact sheets.

Turner, Stephen C. **Our Noisy World.** Julian Messner, 1979. 9–12.

Loud, unwanted sound is noise. Nine activities/experiments help students learn more about noise, its effects, and what can be done about noise pollution. With well-captioned black and white photographs, a serious problem is dealt with in an understandable manner. Contains glossary and index.

Van Soelen, Philip. **Cricket in the Grass and Other Stories.** Sierra Club Books, 1979. All ages.

Five wordless stories are connected by simple objects. The plots deal with the exciting and violent life within the environment. The latter part of the book contains textual explanations of the stories. The format is unique and most interesting. Excellent for discussion; pen and ink drawings.

Wise, William. **Animal Rescue: Saving Our Endangered Wildlife.** Illus. Heidi Palmer. G. P. Putnam's Sons, 1978. 10–up.

Worldwide efforts to preserve endangered wildlife are discussed. The author describes species that have been rescued from extinction throughout the world and brings into sharp focus the interrelatedness of economics, food, changes in habitat, and breeding. For the good reader with special interests.

Earth Science

Bartenbach, Jean. **Rockhound Trails.** Illus. by author. Atheneum, 1977. 8–12.

Fourteen different types of rocks are described with anecdotes in this book that encourages young people to become rockhounds. Rules are included for safety and observing privacy, as well as practical suggestions for learning more about rocks. Packed with information and illustrated with pen and ink drawings.

Berger, Melvin. **Jigsaw Continents.** Illus. Bob Totten. Coward, McCann & Geoghegan, 1977. 9–12.

Plate tectonics, a new theory, explains the wonders of our changing world. Twelve giant plates comprise the entire surface of the earth. The moving of these plates is responsible for earthquakes and volcanoes. Clear drawings illustrate the text. Index included.

Burt, Olive W. **Black Sunshine: The Story of Coal.** Julian Messner, 1977. 8–12.

This introduction to coal begins with a simple explanation of the formation and evolution of America's most plentiful source of energy and continues with a close look at the mining industry. Safety and ecological concerns are discussed and the present and future uses of coal are explored. Index and glossary are appended.

Coburn, Doris. **A Spit Is a Piece of Land: Landforms in the U.S.A.** Illus. William Jaber. Julian Messner, 1978. 8–12.

Photographs and drawings highlight this introductory look at geology. Land features of each part of the country are explored; coastlines, lowlands, highlands, and valleys are discussed, followed by information on islands, caves and caverns, glaciers, and deserts. Index and maps aid the reader.

Cowing, Sheila. **Our Wild Wetlands.** Illus. Deborah Cowing. Julian Messner, 1980. 10–12.

Wetlands are formed when water is unable to drain off lowlands. The three forms—bogs, marshes, and swamps—differ greatly in appearance, plants, and animals. A map of the United States indicates these areas. Interesting, informative drawings complement the easy-to-read text. List of wetlands and index included.

de Paola, Tomie. **The Quicksand Book.** Holiday House, 1977. 7–10.

Jungle Girl sinks slowly as Jungle Boy carefully explains scientific facts about the quicksand into which she has fallen. He gives an illustrated lecture on ways to avoid quicksand and how to get out of it. Popular illusions are dispelled as Jungle Girl goes down, until the surprise ending. Colorfully illustrated.

Gans, Roma. **Caves.** Illus. Giulio Maestro. Thomas Y. Crowell, 1976. 6–9.

Like others in the Let's Read and Find Out series, this book presents a concept in picture book format. Simple text and clear illustrations provide a good introduction to the formation, past uses, and distinguishing characteristics of caves.

Goldin, Augusta. **The Shape of Water.** Illus. Demi. Doubleday, 1979. 8–12.

Water, the most common element on earth, regulates our lives and controls our environment. Simple explanations of the unique properties of water and experiments to study its molecular action enable readers to understand the basic scientific laws of our natural world.

Keen, Martin L. **Be a Rockhound.** Illus. by author. Julian Messner, 1979. 8–12.

Interesting, introductory information needed to begin a rock collection is written in a clear, concise manner. Facts about the identification of rocks, cleaning, and necessary equipment are given. A table of rocks and minerals is most helpful. Includes bibliography, index,

Code of Ethics of the American Federation of Mineralogical Societies. Black and white illustrations and photos.

Lye, Keith. **Our Planet the Earth.** Lerner Publications, 1980. 7–10.

A tightly packed, yet appealing format answers many questions about the earth, including theories on its origin, its physical features, and its resources. Full-color illustrations, a glossary, and index provide further information.

McFall, Christie. **Wonders of Dust.** Illus. by author. Dodd, Mead, 1980. 12–up.

Everywhere one goes there is dust. It comes from many sources; volcanoes, the soil, pollen, and even the sea send out dust particles. It presents a major concern in many areas of the country, especially for ecologists. Many meaningful photographs and sketches. Index.

McNulty, Faith. **How to Dig a Hole to the Other Side of the World.** Illus. Marc Simont. Harper & Row, Publishers, 1979. 6–9.

A youngster takes an imaginary trip through the center of the earth and learns about its internal structure. This informative and interesting text is matched with colorful illustrations. An excellent beginning science book for the young reader.

Mercer, Charles. **Monsters in the Earth: The Story of Earthquakes.** G. P. Putnam's Sons, 1978. 12–up.

The tragedy at Tangshan and the Great San Francisco Quake are recounted at the beginning of the book. The causes and effects of earthquakes are examined. Earthquake predicting is discussed, with the need for disaster planning stressed. Glossary appended.

Miklowitz, Gloria D. **Earthquake!** Illus. William Jaber. Julian Messner, 1977. 10–12.

This carefully researched informational book reviews some of the world's worst earthquakes and discusses their causes, ways to predict them, and what to do when one occurs. Black and white photographs, maps, charts, and drawings add graphic detail. A three-page glossary is appended.

Navarra, John Gabriel. **Earthquake.** Doubleday, 1980. 8–12.

Earthquakes' causes and effects make interesting reading for young science buffs. The author gives instructions on what to do if an earthquake occurs and many details of how scientists are measuring and tracking them.

Nixon, Hershell H., and Joan Lowery Nixon. **Glaciers: Nature's Frozen Rivers.** Dodd, Mead, 1980. 8–12.

Various kinds of glaciers are described and related to geographic areas. Included are valley, tidewater, retreating, piedmont, and outlet glaciers. The changes brought about by glaciers are described in text and with informative drawings and photographs. Background information on the ice ages is given and predictions for the future set forth.

Shedenhelm, W. R. C. **The Young Rockhound's Handbook.** G. P. Putnam's Sons, 1978. 8–12.

The novice rockhound will find helpful information in this book that explains the formation of rocks and minerals and describes their location, characteristics, and identification. Procedures for polishing and cutting minerals are also given.

Simon, Seymour. **Danger from Below.** Four Winds Press, 1979. 10–12.

This is an understandable and interesting discussion about earthquakes: how and why they occur, where they are most likely to happen, and how to stay safe when an earthquake hits. Informative photographs, graphs, and index are included. Text contributes to dispelling fears of quakes by sorting legends from scientific facts.

Thompson, Brenda, and Cynthia Overbeck. **Volcanoes.** Illus. David Hardy and L'Enc Matte. Lerner Publications, 1977. 6–9.

Many colored pictures help the young reader to interpret the simple text written in an easy-to-read style. Active and dormant volcanoes are described, listed, and the locations given. Maps are provided and new words are included. A First Fact Book.

Energy

Adams, Florence. **Catch a Sunbeam: A Book of Solar Study and Experiments.** Illus. Kiyo Komoda. Harcourt Brace Jovanovich, 1978. 12–up.

Sixteen projects dealing with the sun and its potential uses for energy await the young experimenter. Good information and diagrams.

Asimov, Isaac. **How Did We Find Out about Oil?** Illus. David Wool. Walker, 1980. 10–12.

Today's oil problem is focused upon in this book from the How Did We Find Out . . . ? series. The physical composition of oil, its development, and its importance throughout history are explained in an understandable style. Speculations are offered on oil's role in the future. Black and white drawings.

Bendick, Jeanne. **Putting the Sun to Work.** Garrard Publishing, 1979. 8–12.

Humans need to learn how to make better use of the vast amount of solar energy available. Five brief chapters of easily understood text tell what the sun can do, how to catch and use its energy, and some interesting classroom projects. Simple, attractive illustrations clarify the content. Indexed.

Branley, Franklyn M. **Feast or Famine? The Energy Future.** Illus. Henry Roth. Thomas Y. Crowell, 1980. 10–up.

This seventy-six-page book is filled with information on solar, hydrogen, and nuclear energy alternatives for transportation, houses, and electricity. It is useful for challenging academically gifted children. Black and white photographs and diagrams; list of further readings.

Brown, Joseph E., and Anne Ensign Brown. **Harness the Wind: The Story of Windmills.** Dodd, Mead, 1977. 10–12.

Windmills have been called symbols of sanity, and this book traces the windmill's role in history through photographs and anecdotes. (Did you know the Dutch gave them clothing and names?) Rising costs and finite quantities of fossil fuels now make this perfect ecological device worth a second look. Good for reports.

Dennis, Landt. **Catch the Wind: A Book of Windmills and Windpower.** Photographs by Lisl Dennis. Four Winds Press, 1976. 8–12.

Extensive photographs and drawings highlight this comprehensive coverage of the historic use of wind to pump water, generate electricity, sail ships, and grind grain. Free, nonpolluting, and available, windpower is regaining importance as a major source of energy after many years of disfavor. Bibliography, index, and sources of further information are appended.

Kettelkamp, Larry. **Lasers: The Miracle Light.** William Morrow, 1979. 12–up.

Uses and explanations concerning lasers make up this book. The ideas for laser, Light Amplification by Simulated Emission of Radiation, were developed during the 1950s, with the first operating model built in 1960. Highly technical information for interested and scientifically aware readers.

Lauber, Patricia. **Tapping Earth's Heat.** Illus. Edward Malsberg. Garrard Publishing, 1978. 7–10.

An extremely readable book about using the earth's heat energy to heat buildings and make electricity. A series of simple experiments clearly illustrates the scientific principles governing volcanoes, hot springs, fumeroles, and geysers.

Lewis, Bruce. **What Is a Laser?** Illus. Tom Huffman. Dodd, Mead, 1979. 10–up.

Explanations are given of laser beams, a special kind of light used in large and small tasks for common and uncommon purposes. Experiments are outlined, and descriptions and definitions are given for this newly discovered energy tool. Easy-to-understand examples.

Schneider, Herman. **Laser Light.** Illus. Radu Vero. McGraw-Hill, 1978. 12–up.

For the student interested in lasers, this book provides an extremely well-illustrated introduction and explanation. Some simple experiments are given. Index.

Engineering

Billout, Guy. **Stone & Steel: A Look at Engineering.** Prentice-Hall, 1980. 10–12.

Facts about historic bridges and landmarks from around the world are given. The unique illustrations, which are line drawings traced from photographs and then colored, add interest to the test.

Corbett, Scott. **Bridges.** Illus. Richard Rosenblum. Four Winds Press, 1978. 8–12.

This book makes the whole history of bridges and bridge construction exciting reading. Bridges from ancient times to the present are discussed. Pen and ink drawings of famous bridges of the world give the book an artistic feeling.

Englebardt, Stanley L. **Miracle Chip: The Microelectronic Revolution.** Lothrop, Lee & Shepard Books, 1979. 12–up.

The author traces developments in the electronics field that have led to production of the microelectronic chip. He describes how new technology has made possible minicomputers, digital wristwatches, calculators, and many other devices. For the mature science reader.

Kelly, James E., and William R. Park. **The Dam Builders.** Illus. Herbert E. Lake. Addison-Wesley Publishing, 1977. 6–9.

Many questions concerning the building of earthfill and masonry dams will be answered after reading this book. Types of dams and equipment are thoroughly explained. The design and construction of the dam are stressed rather than its function. Many illustrations clarify and extend the text.

Lewis, Bruce. **Meet the Computer.** Illus. Leonard Kessler. Dodd, Mead, 1977. 8–12.

In this introduction to computers, how they work, and their role in modern life, emphasis is given to the people who operate them. Easy-to-read style, clear explanation of terms, sufficient detail, and almost computer-like print combine to make this an enticing book.

Macaulay, David. **Underground.** Houghton Mifflin, 1976. 10–up.

Cutaway drawings and narration describe the immense complex of wire, pipes, and foundations under a large modern city. Construction methods and materials for subways, sewers, and telephone and power systems are described. Step-by-step procedure is shown. Excellent for social studies or art integration.

Malone, Robert. **The Robot Book.** Harcourt Brace Jovanovich, 1978. 12–up.

For anyone interested in robots, past, present, and future, this handsomely illustrated volume is a gold mine of information. The history and origins of robots are given; robots at work and robots in literature, art, and entertainment are explored; construction of robots and their future uses are considered. Excellent introduction to the subject.

Metos, Thomas H. **Robots A₂Z.** Julian Messner, 1980. 7–10.

This well-illustrated examination of the past, present, and future of robots is intended for younger readers. Famous mechanical creations of the past are introduced. Index.

Olney, Ross R. **They Said It Couldn't Be Done.** E. P. Dutton, 1979. 12–up.

Each of the ten chapters highlights a separate accomplishment of engineering believed to have been impossible. The lives and the works of those responsible for the Brooklyn Bridge, the Holland Tunnel, Mt. Rushmore and seven other feats are described. Photographs illustrate this book designed for mature readers.

Weiss, Harvey. **How to Be an Inventor.** Illus. by author. Thomas Y. Crowell, 1980. 10–up.

Practical advice is given on how to invent something from the first vague glimmer of an idea until a patent is sought and awarded. The author uses examples of his own cleverness to illustrate his points. Excellent black and white photographs, drawings, and humorous sketches.

Experiments

Cobb, Vicki. **More Science Experiments You Can Eat.** Illus. Giulio Maestro. J. B. Lippincott, 1979. 10–12.

The first book of experiments stresses using food to understand basic principles, while this one uses the principles to learn about food. Interesting experiments are written in an understandable style with listings of materials and equipment. Includes cottage cheese, cola, and pudding. Black and white illustrations.

Cobb, Vicki, and Kathy Darling. **Bet You Can't! Science Impossibilities to Fool You.** Illus. Martha Weston. Lothrop, Lee & Shepard Books, 1980. 8–12.

Science can be fun as shown by these sixty impossible tricks that are based on scientific principles. The reader who tries these tricks is bound to have a good time. Excellent book with carefully drawn illustrations to simplify some of the tricks.

Gardner, Robert. **Magic through Science.** Illus. Jeff Brown. Doubleday, 1978. 8–12.

The book explains how to do science experiments using materials found within the home. The photographs are clear and the step-by-step procedures are easy to follow. A young science buff would find it a helpful reference.

Simon, Seymour. **Exploring Fields and Lots.** Illus. Arabelle Wheatley. Garrard Publishing, 1978. 8–12.

This handbook provides an introduction to journals, observations, and record keeping. It includes simple projects to discover and record mini climates, effects of light on plants, and activities of animals in their habitat. Simple illustrations and texts.

General Nature Concepts

Anderson, Lucia. **The Smallest Life around Us.** Illus. Leigh Grant. Crown Publishers, 1978. 10–12.

The study of one-celled plants and animals, called microbes, is interestingly introduced in understandable terms. Excellent, detailed illustrations assist scientific explanation. Suggested experiments are clear and concise. A great resource for independent or small group study.

Berenstain, Stan, and Jan Berenstain. **The Berenstain Bears' Science Fair.** Random House, 1977. All ages.

Actual Factual Bear provides simply worded scientific generalizations as Papa Bear introduces his family to the concepts of machines, matter, and energy. Practical examples apply to basic things in the lives of modern children. Colorful cartoon-style drawings present a good-humored approach to knowledge. Fine motivation for a classroom science fair.

Borland, Hal. **The Golden Circle: A Book of Months.** Illus. Anne Ophelia Dowden. Thomas Y. Crowell, 1977. 10–up.

Evocative essays, invoking each month in turn, present the all-encompassing view of the golden circle of the year. Exquisite full-color paintings give the close-up view of the small unique plants associated with each calendar change.

Burns, Marilyn. **This Book Is about Time.** Illus. Martha Weston. Little, Brown, 1978. 10–up.

Fascinating bits of information about all aspects of time make this book interesting reading. Nearly every piece of information is reinforced by an intriguing activity that involves the child, either through imaginative thinking or acting. Topics range from railroad time to jet lag. A Brown Paper School Book with humorous drawings and diagrams.

Fisher, Aileen. **I Stood upon a Mountain.** Illus. Blair Lent. Thomas Y. Crowell, 1979. 6–9.

A young child speculates on how the world began after gazing at the beauties of nature. Many puzzling answers are offered by an old man, a woman, an Indian, and a young boy. An artistic arrangement of text and illustrations. A discussion starter for science and appreciation of nature.

Ford, Barbara. **Why Does a Turtle Live Longer Than a Dog?** William Morrow, 1980. 12–up.

Humans are included in this interesting discussion of the great variations in life spans of animals, birds, and insects. New research on cellular regeneration sheds light on aging factors and ways to extend life. There are many unusual photographs in this unique contribution to science studies.

Goffstein, M. B. **Natural History.** Farrar, Straus & Giroux, 1979. 3–5.

"Low trees hold fruit and vegetables lie warmly in the dirt or hide on vines." "Every living creature is our brother and our sister. . . ." The young reader or listener is gently reminded to celebrate and appreciate the joys of nature in simple text and clear, appealing watercolors.

Grillone, Lisa, and Joseph Gennaro. **Small Worlds Close Up.** Crown Publishers, 1978. All ages.

Using black and white micrographs, which are photographs taken through the scanning electron microscope, the authors show us familiar objects in new and unusual ways. Internal structures of the peppercorn, magnified sixty times, and chalk, magnified 16,000 times, are but two of thirty-one items revealing previously unknown beauty. Filled with fascinating facts and photographs.

Horsburgh, Peg. **Living Light: Exploring Bioluminescence.** Julian Messner, 1978. 8–12.

Children who marvel at the wonder of a firefly enjoy learning more about bioluminescence. In this readable book a variety of plants and animals that make their own light are described. Detailed information on collecting fireflies for scientific laboratories is included.

Hutchins, Ross E. **Nature Invented It First.** Photographs by author. Dodd, Mead, 1980. 10–up.

In each of the brief chapters a human invention is described, followed by an explanation of how plants and animals had the innovation first. The content is interesting and each example is clearly developed. Includes inventions such as electricity, flight, jet propulsion, chemical warfare, and crop cultivation.

Linsenmaier, Walter. **Wonders of Nature.** Random House, 1979. All ages.

Did you know that a newborn fawn has no scent at all? That the fierce crocodile lets a tiny bird pick its sharp teeth for food? That the black panther is really a black leopard and has yellow spotted babies? Here are many of nature's wonders, accurately portrayed in glowing colors and interesting text. Picture book format.

Pringle, Laurence. **Death Is Natural.** Four Winds Press, 1977. 7–10.

The relationship between life and death is highlighted; the dependence of one upon the other is clearly described. Questions are raised. How does the death of a plant or animal affect others of its kind? Striking photographs complement the text. Glossary, index, supplementary reading list included.

Rahn, Joan Elma. **Traps & Lures in the Living World.** Atheneum, 1980. 8–12.

The *femme fatale* firefly lures males of other species to their death by mimicking their special mating signals. The bolas spider captures her prey by tossing out an adhesive line. These luring and trapping creatures are described in clear and fascinating detail, along with the Venus's-flytrap, angler fish, and ant lion. Includes glossary, excellent diagrams and photographs.

Silverstein, Alvin, and Virginia Silverstein. **Nature's Champions: The Biggest, The Fastest, The Best.** Illus. Jean Zallinger. Random House, 1980. 7–10.

Maybe you think that you are the longest sleeper in the world, but it isn't so. One tiny dormouse observed in England slept for six months and twenty-three days. Twenty-five other plants and animals that have unusual characteristics are described. Large colored illustrations.

Simon, Seymour. **The Secret Clocks: Time Senses of Living Things.** Illus. Jan Brett. Viking Press, 1979. 8–12.

Some scientists do not not believe in biorhythms, but this attractive book offers the findings of research concerning "time sense." Clear examples observable in animals, plants, and humans are explained. Children will enjoy making their own biorhythm charts. Attractive illustrations, bibliography, and index are included.

Human Growth

Emotional

Albert, Burton, Jr. **Mine, Yours, Ours.** Illus. Lois Axeman. Albert Whitman, 1977. 3–5.

Children of different races and sexes engage in a limited exploration of themselves and things around them. They use words such as mine, yours, and ours to introduce the concepts of owning and sharing in a good-natured manner.

Ancona, George. **I Feel: A Picture Book of Emotions.** E. P. Dutton, 1977. 4–7.

A series of black and white photographs with one accompanying word to describe the emotion on the face. This is an introduction to the names of very familiar feelings and a good discussion-starter.

Berger, Terry. **I Have Feelings Too.** Photographs by Michael E. Ach. Human Sciences Press, 1979. 8–12.

Growing up is puzzling and children need help in sorting out their feelings about themselves and others. The everyday situations presented in this book offer ways to help children adjust in a complex world. Sensitive photographs extend the text. Discussion-starter.

Berkey, Barry, and Velma Berkey, compilers. **Robbers, Bones & Mean Dogs.** Illus. Marylin Hafner. Addison-Wesley Publishing, 1978. 8–12.

These are actual paragraphs written by children about their fears and frightening experiences, humorously and effectively illustrated with ink drawings. Readers will gain in self-acceptance and take comfort in knowing other people have fears. Excellent for discussion of feelings.

Bernstein, Joanne E. **Loss and How to Cope with It.** Seabury Press, 1977. 12–up.

Intended for the older youngster who is prematurely confronted with problems posed by death of a family member, the book is a helpful supplement for a child receiving personal counseling. Particularly valuable to the adult helping a child cope with loss are the bibliographies and lists of service organizations.

Bernstein, Joanne E., and Stephen V. Gullo. **When People Die.** Photographs by Rosmarie Hausherr. E. P. Dutton, 1977. 7–10.

Many questions frequently asked by children concerning death are answered in simple, honest, and understandable language. Why people die, afterlife, burial, and grief are all brought together as a part of the chain of life. Exceptional sensitive photographs.

Bradley, Buff. **Endings: A Book about Death.** Addison-Wesley Publishing, 1979. 12–up.

The physical and emotional aspects of death and dying are explored. The general American attitude toward death is compared with those of other cultures. Related controversial subjects of abortion, suicide, and euthanasia are considered forthrightly. References are made to how death is handled in great literature. Selected bibliography included.

Farber, Norma. **How Does It Feel to Be Old?** Illus. Trina Schart Hyman. E. P. Dutton, 1979. 6–up.

An old woman tells her granddaughter about the good and bad things of being old. The rhymed verse is realistic and tender and is eloquently complemented by the illustrations. A good read-aloud book.

Gallant, Roy A. **Memory: How It Works and How to Improve It.** Four Winds Press, 1980. 12–up.

A fascinating account of how the memory works is combined with information and exercises designed to improve the reader's memory. For mature readers.

Naylor, Phyllis Reynolds. **Getting Along with Your Friends.** Illus. Rick Cooley. Abingdon Press, 1980. 9–12.

Friendship is looked at from a variety of perspectives: how to make friends, how to be a friend, how to quarrel, and how to learn to look at yourself. A self-help book for children.

Schlein, Miriam. **I Hate It.** Illus. Judith Gwyn Brown. Albert Whitman, 1978. 4–7.

These humorous expressions of pet peeves and commonly encountered fears will help young children discover that negative feelings need not threaten their basic well-being, and that life isn't always so bad. Colorful illustrations.

Physical

Ancona, George. **It's a Baby!** E. P. Dutton, 1979. 5–8.

Photographs tell the story of Pablo from his birth until he walks. The spare narration works well describing the new life surrounded by his loving family. Excellent to use as follow-up to the how-babies-are-born books.

Berger, Melvin. **Disease Detectives.** Thomas Y. Crowell, 1978. 9–12.

As exciting as a mystery is this account of how scientists worked together to solve the riddle of the strange disease that struck the Legionnaires in Philadelphia in 1976. The work of bacteriologists, toxicologists and virologists is clearly presented, as is the complexity of the task that faced them.

Burstein, John. **Slim Goodbody: What Can Go Wrong and How to Be Strong.** Illus. Craigwood Phillips. McGraw-Hill, 1978. 10–up.

This uniquely illustrated book answers common questions about health and explains some of the many mysteries of the human body, including its ability to heal itself. It entertains as it educates children about their bodies.

Cosgrove, Margaret. **Your Muscles and Ways to Exercise Them.** Illus. by author. Dodd, Mead, 1980. 10–12.

Explicit and detailed drawings and text provide a knowledge of the body's muscle structure. The various kinds of important muscles and their relationships to bones are discussed. Emphasis of this science book is on how to use and exercise these body parts.

Doss, Helen. **Your Skin Holds You In.** Illus. Christine Bondante. Julian Messner, 1978. 8–12.

This introduction to skin, its properties and functions, provides interesting information about this vital part of the body. Hair, nails, warts, and moles are discussed, with suggestions for first aid and skin care. Photographs and drawings expand the coverage; glossary and index add to its usefulness.

Gross, Ruth Belov. **A Book about Your Skeleton.** Illus. Deborah Robison. Hastings House, Publishers, 1979. 4–7.

In an effective style and an attractive format this small book informs the young inquisitive child about bones and joints. "If you didn't have any bones, you would flop around like spaghetti." Attractive collage pictures.

Harris, Robie H., and Elizabeth Levy. **Before You Were Three: How You Began to Walk, Talk, Explore and Have Feelings.** Photographs by Henry E. F. Gordillo. Delacorte Press, 1977. All ages.

By following two children from birth until their third birthdays, the authors explain the steps all children go through as they explore their world, become mobile, and learn to communicate. Written with both children and adult readers in mind, the book succeeds in conveying much information without talking down.

Hazen, Barbara Shook. **The Me I See.** Illus. Ati Forberg. Abingdon Press, 1978. 4–7.

A fresh approach to the recognition of the parts of the body, the senses, and the functions of each. Rhymed text and pencil sketches enhance this book as it highlights the uniqueness of the individual. An excellent book for both parents and teachers.

Holzenthaler, Jean. **My Feet Do.** Photographs by George Ancona. E. P. Dutton, 1979. 4–7.

Full-page photographs of a small girl's feet, showing left and right, walking, running, jumping, and even tripping! The obvious joy of what feet can do is cleverly depicted. (Picture book)

Holzenthaler, Jean. **My Hands Can.** Illus. Nancy Tafuri. E. P. Dutton, 1978. 3–5.

The various skills that young children are capable of accomplishing with their hands are simply and attractively illustrated. Hands can button buttons and zip zippers. They can do good, they can hurt, and they can show others how we feel.

Marino, Barbara Pavis. **Eric Needs Stitches.** Photographs by Richard Rudinski. Addison-Wesley Publishing, 1979. 6–9.

This photodocumentary follows a young boy to the emergency room where he must get stitches in his cut knee. Medical terms and procedures are clearly explained as the nurse and doctor tell Eric exactly what they are doing. The book is a successful attempt to acquaint children with hospital procedures.

Shapiro, Irwin. **The Gift of Magic Sleep: Early Experiments in Anesthesia.** Illus. Pat Rotondo. Coward, McCann & Geoghegan, 1979. 10–12.

A graphic account of the search for a safe and effective anesthetic, and of the unseemly struggle among four men—two dentists, a doctor, and a scientist—to receive credit for the discovery of ether. The descriptions of pre-anesthetic operations will make readers thankful that they are living in the twentieth century.

Silverstein, Alvin, and Virginia Silverstein. **Cancer.** Illus. Andrew Antal. John Day, 1977. 10–up.

This overview discusses such topics as various types of cancer, possible causes and cures, advances in research, and cancer prevention.

Silverstein, Alvin, and Virginia Silverstein. **The Genetics Explosion.** Illus. Constance Ftera and Richard Erik Warren. Four Winds Press, 1980. 12–up.

An overview of genetics from Mendel to recombinant DNA and on into a future of both terrifying and fascinating possibilities is presented. Will genetic engineering unleash a deadly virus on the world? Or will it eliminate diseases like Tay-Sachs and hemophilia, or even make it possible for humans to grow replacement arms and legs? Clear presentation of an exciting subject.

Silverstein, Alvin, and Virginia B. Silverstein. **The Sugar Disease: Diabetes.** J. B. Lippincott, 1980. 8–12.

The symptoms of diabetes are discussed along with its history, diagnosis, and treatment. Implications for the future of current research are explained in an intelligent and sensible style.

Simon, Seymour. **About the Foods You Eat.** Illus. Dennis Kendrick. McGraw-Hill, 1979. 7–10.

What you eat turns into you. Tracing food from the time it enters the mouth, this sixty-one-page book is surprisingly thorough in discussions of digestion, food groups, nutrients, and calories. Black and white and pink line drawings illustrate well the simple, easy experiments. An excellent resource for nutrition education.

Skurzynski, Gloria. **Bionic Parts for People: The Real Story of Artificial Organs and Replacement Parts.** Illus. Frank Schwarz. Four Winds Press, 1978. 8–12.

The young scientist is introduced to new inventions in medicine to be used as replacement body parts. The working functions of the kidneys, eyes, ears, heart, arms, legs, and several other replacement machines are explained in detail. Some very unusual possibilities open to modern science today are explored.

Waxman, Stephanie. **Growing Up Feeling Good: A Child's Introduction to Sexuality.** Photographs by author. Panjandrum Press, 1979. 10–12.

A conversational text addressed to the child and numerous candid black and white photographs of children, teenagers, and adults discovering themselves and others in an atmosphere of love and responsibility set this book apart from the usual sex education texts that treat sexual development as a topic. The author frankly and sensitively discusses masturbation, puberty, making love, childbirth, families, and growing old. Certain content and illustrations may be considered too frank by some.

Machines

Adkins, Jan. **Heavy Equipment.** Illus. by author. Charles Scribner's Sons, 1980. 7–10.

Careful drawings with just enough detail to be understandable complement the brief informative text. This is a factual book that holds appeal for all children who are interested in the world of machines and construction. Large machines such as excavators, pipe layers, off-road trucks, and cranes are featured. Well designed.

Adkins, Jan. **Moving Heavy Things.** Illus. by author. Houghton Mifflin, 1980. 10–12.

"Never lift what you can drag, never drag what you can roll," advises the author. Clever people look for easier ways that are often simple and direct. Techniques from many workers and craftsmen offer suggestions and advice. Tools and procedures for lifting are presented in clear black and white illustrations.

Gardner, Robert. **This Is the Way It Works: A Collection of Machines.** Illus. Jeffrey Brown. Doubleday, 1980. 12–up.

Machines from zippers and coffeepots to nuclear reactors and solar heaters are described in detail with suitable diagrams, a note on the history of each one, an explanation of the scientific principle that makes it operate, and frequently a reference to its effect on the environment or its possible future development. Not an easy book, but one that provides much-needed information for various science and social studies units.

Gibbons, Gail. **Clocks and How They Go.** Thomas Y. Crowell, 1979. 6–9.

Everyone uses clocks. Curiosity about what makes them tick is pleasantly satisfied by the simple explanations and precise, brightly colored illustrations of this book. Basic types of clocks, ancient and modern, are discussed. Interesting to all ages; a good read-aloud book for younger children. Picture book format.

Gibbons, Gail. **Locks and Keys.** Thomas Y. Crowell, 1980. 6–9.

A picturesque accounting of lock and key devices is traced from the early ones used by the Egyptians to modern combination locks used on safes. Accurate drawings accompany the text.

Murphy, Jim. **Weird & Wacky Inventions.** Crown Publishers, 1978. 8–12.

A hat-tipping machine and a hair-cutting device are among the intriguing inventions from the files of the U.S. Patent Office. Illustrations are adaptations of the original drawings. A multiple-choice quiz format challenges the reader, who then turns the page for a detailed explanation of each invention.

Mathematics

Adler, David A. **Roman Numerals.** Illus. Byron Barton. Thomas Y. Crowell, 1977. 7–10.

This book simply and clearly explains the Roman numeral system. An amusing Roman stonecutter carefully clarifies this text. The young student is eased into learning the principles of Roman numerals by the use of coins, paper, cardboard, scissors, and a pencil. One of a series of Young Math Books.

Bitter, Gary G., and Thomas H. Metos. **Exploring with Pocket Calculators.** Photographs by Thomas H. Metos and Jeffrey T. Metos. Julian Messner, 1977. 10–up.

Clear, lucid descriptions are given of computing devices ranging from fingers and an abacus to modern calculators. Historical background and practical examples lend interest to this subject. For students who like to experiment with numbers, and for teachers and parents who want to expand modes of using numbers and mathematics.

Froman, Robert. **The Greatest Guessing Game: A Book about Dividing.** Illus. Gioia Fiammenghi. Thomas Y. Crowell, 1978. 8–10.

A light approach and lively illustrations in halftones and color add interest to this different math book. Dividing is certainly not formidable when choices are available on how to use remainders. Encourages estimating and common sense with examples from everyday life.

James, Elizabeth, and Carol Barkin. **What Do You Mean by 'Average'? Means, Medians, and Modes.** Illus. Joel Schick. Lothrop, Lee & Shepard Books, 1978. 8–12.

In Normal City, Jill is running a campaign for Student Council. To prove she is average, therefore representing everyone, she provides everyday examples of mean, median, and mode. Interesting illustrations and examples. Fun to read.

Mathews, Louise. **Bunches and Bunches of Bunnies.** Illus. Jeni Bassett. Dodd, Mead, 1978. 8–12.

Pictures of groups of rabbits and rhyming lines work together to reinforce the concept of addition in multiplication. The operations are given from one to twelve. Small figures, interesting activities; a worthy addition to a math collection.

O'Connor, Vincent F. **Mathematics on the Playground.** Illus. Eileen Strange and John Strange. Raintree Publishers, 1978. 7–10.

This easy-to-read book explores a range of mathematical concepts: counting, shapes, sizes. Children doing various activities are shown in colorful contemporary playground settings.

Peppé, Rodney. **Humphrey the Number Horse: Fun with Counting and Multiplication.** Viking Press, 1979. 6–9.

Clever thumbprint animals illustrate the multiplication tables up to 12 × 12. Once children have the directions in the book explained to them, they enjoy practicing on their own. Colorful, humorous illustrations invite creating new animals in the same style.

Riedel, Manfred G. **Odds and Chances for Kids: A Look at Probability.** Illus. Bill Kresse. Prentice-Hall, 1979. 8–12.

Taking chances is part of life. Learning to analyze chances helps individuals make intelligent decisions. In this introduction to probability, attention is given to problems of chance in science, politics, gambling, and everyday life. Diagrams, illustrations, and examples are provided for clarity and interest. Excellent for small group projects.

Riedel, Manfred G. **Winning with Numbers: A Kid's Guide to Statistics.** Illus. Paul Coker, Jr. Prentice-Hall, 1978. 8–12.

Short chapters deal with separate ideas and terms of statistics. Characters and problems pertinent to the age group contribute to high interest and readability. Cartoon-like graphs and illustrations illuminate the narrative. A useful classroom addition for math enrichment.

Segan, Ann. **One Meter Max.** Prentice-Hall, 1979. 4–7.

The Meter, Gram, and Liter families are members of the metric measuring system. Kid Kilogram measures things that are heavy.

Millie Millimeter measures things that are very small. Max Meter measures things that are long or tall. Meeting these families and their members helps clarify the metric system.

Sitomer, Mindel, and Harry Sitomer. **Zero Is Not Nothing.** Illus. Richard Cuffari. Thomas Y. Crowell, 1978. 8–12.

Introduces the concept of zero. Example after example is provided to illustrate the many functions of that special number. Lively black and white illustrations and ample margins contribute to an inviting format.

Srivastava, Jane Jonas. **Number Families.** Illus. Lois Ehlert. Thomas Y. Crowell, 1979. 8–12.

Members of a family always have at least one thing in common. For instance, John's family lives in apartment B. Basic number families are simply explained: odd and even, times, prime numbers, square and triangular numbers. Questions and answers are included. Animal families and ink blots, precise and whimsical, illustrate the concepts.

Srivastava, Jane Jonas. **Spaces, Shapes, and Sizes.** Illus. Loretta Lustig. Thomas Y. Crowell, 1980. 8–12.

Everything takes up space. Everything has volume. The concept of volume is explained with examples and illustrations. Easy-to-try experiments add interest and practical application.

Weiss, Malcolm E. **Solomon Grundy, Born on Oneday.** Illus. Tomie de Paola. Thomas Y. Crowell, 1977. 8–12.

Cartoonlike illustrations, varied printing style, question-and-answer format create an inviting well-paced discussion of an arithmetic puzzle. Everyday life examples of this puzzle, a finite arithmetic system, are given. Teachers can use these examples in learning stations and classroom activities. Youngsters can experiment independently with the ideas.

Zaslavsky, Claudia. **Count on Your Fingers African Style.** Illus. Jerry Pinkney. Thomas Y. Crowell, 1980. 8–12.

In an African marketplace people from various tribes indicate numbers with their fingers. The book is a fascinating melding of mathematics, culture, and language. Handsome pencil drawings give a strong sense of setting.

Meteorology

Beer, Kathleen Costello. **What Happens in the Spring.** National Geographic Society, 1977. 5–8.

Springtime becomes more meaningful than ever before as the reader peruses these expertly produced photographs of plants, animals, birds, and insects in their vernal phases. Colors and details, magnified at times, are bright and clear. The text gives interesting information in a way that is easy for young children to understand.

Davis, Hubert, compiler and editor. **A January Fog Will Freeze a Hog and Other Weather Folklore.** Illus. John Wallner. Crown Publishers, 1977. 8–12.

This collection of thirty rhymes about weather is delightful to read and chant. The black and white illustrations are handsome. An outstanding feature for children's further perusal is the set of notes that indicates the reliability and locale of the weather folklore. A fine blend of humor and weather science.

Hays, James D. **Our Changing Climate.** Atheneum, 1977. 10–12.

The author discusses the factors that govern climate and the effects of atmospheric changes on weather conditions. Among the fascinating topics are people's impact on climate and the impact of climatic change on people. Photographs, charts, and diagrams clarify concepts.

Oceanography

Cook, Jan Leslie. **The Mysterious Undersea World.** National Geographic Society, 1980. 8–12.

Outstanding color photographs of the undersea world are the chief feature of this handsome volume. The text deals with geographic features and ways of exploring the oceans. Attention is given to diving and snorkeling, sunken treasures, and aquariums. A teacher's guide with games and activity sheets is available.

Davies, Eryl. **Ocean Frontiers.** Viking Press, 1980. 7–10.

This colorful and informative book about the great ocean frontier discusses technical solutions to the problems of undersea exploration. The illustrations are clear; the book is filled with many exciting concepts. A most useful edition.

Jacobs, Francine. **The Red Sea.** Illus. Elsie Wrigley. William Morrow, 1978. 7–10.

The colorful history of this strategic waterway and its important role in the development of trade among Mediterranean civilizations is described in understandable language and pen sketches. The new scientific theory of plate tectonics is considered as a possible reason for the widening of the sea. Classroom use.

Jacobs, Francine. **Sounds in the Sea.** Illus. Jean Zallinger. William Morrow, 1977. 8–12.

In the underwater world sounds are made by rapidly moving currents, avalanches or mountain slides, and by the animals. The croaker and drumfish create unusual and distinctive noises. Marine catfish sound like stampeding cattle. Modern technology enables humans to listen to this world.

Physics and Chemistry

Arnov, Boris. **Water: Experiments to Understand It.** Illus. Giulio Maestro. Lothrop, Lee & Shepard Books, 1980. 10–12.

The author, a science teacher, presents simple experiments that demonstrate the properties of water. The directions are clear and the materials used are easily found in a classroom. A section on the relevance or application of each property is included following the experiment. Good step-by-step illustrations.

Branley, Franklyn M. **Color: From Rainbow to Lasers.** Illus. Henry Roth. Thomas Y. Crowell, 1978. 11–up.

A basic introduction to the world of color is presented very clearly. Included in the aspects of color are light waves and energy, the color spectrum, the physiology of the eye, current theories, and the psychology of color. Many drawings and colored illustrations simplify the text.

Fisher, David E. **The Ideas of Einstein.** Illus. Gwen Brodkin. Holt, Rinehart and Winston, 1980. 8–12.

Although this looks like an easy reader, its message is to older children, who may find the format too young. Nevertheless, it is a book well worth introducing, especially to precocious children who always want to know whether space is curved or straight, or whether they will be going backward or forward in time if they travel to the sun.

Gardner, Robert, and David Webster. **Moving Right Along: A Book of Science Experiments and Puzzles about Motion.** Illus. Tang Fung Cho. Doubleday, 1978. 10–12.

This comprehensive guide to the scientific study of motion contains clear explanations and many experiments that children can perform to study the phenomenon. Speed records are discussed, as are methods of motion in people, animals, and machinery.

Smith, Norman F. **If It Shines, Clangs & Bends, It's Metal.** Illus. Tom Huffman. Coward, McCann & Geoghegan, 1980. 7–10.

Many useful and decorative objects made of metal surround us daily. Silver, copper, aluminum, and iron are indispensable to us; without these metals we would live as cave dwellers. The origins and properties are described in clear text and illustrations. Simple experiments are included. Excellent for classroom use.

Plants

Adler, David A. **Redwoods Are the Tallest Trees in the World.** Illus. Kazue Mizumura. Thomas Y. Crowell, 1978. 7–10.

The giant redwood trees of California and Oregon are described in an easily-read text with excellent pictures and diagrams. Concepts are developed by using comparisons with objects familiar to children. Commercial use and conservation are discussed.

Busch, Phyllis S. **Cactus in the Desert.** Illus. Harriett Barton. Thomas Y. Crowell, 1979. 6–9.

Cactus plants usually live where little water is available. Long thin roots or short fat roots seek and hold water. Other adaptations of stems and leaves help retain life in harsh conditions. Drawings and diagrams in color and black and white.

Busch, Phyllis S. **Wildflowers and the Stories behind Their Names.** Illus. Anne Ophelia Dowden. Charles Scribner's Sons, 1977. 8–12.

A rare combination of historic, scientific, and visual information about sixty common U.S. wildflowers. The flowers and their parts are introduced. Scientific and common names are carefully traced with suggested methods for recalling common names. Illustrations are accurate, meticulously detailed, and in four/fifths actual size.

Dowden, Anne Ophelia. **State Flowers.** Illus. by author. Thomas Y. Crowell, 1978. 8–12.

A lovely book that describes the history and other background information of each state flower. The flower illustrations are precise and at the same time artistic. The book gives charm and excitement to a subject often neglected.

Dowden, Anne Ophelia. **This Noble Harvest: A Chronicle of Herbs.** Illus. by author. William Collins Publishers, 1979. 12–up.

Henbane, lovage, parsely, rue, thyme, betoney, monkshood, hyssop: the history and uses of these and dozens of other herbs are chronicled here. This is a book to be treasured for its fascinating information about medicine, magic, poison, dyestuffs, flavorings, and air fresheners of bygone ages, and also for its truly beautiful full-color illustrations.

Garelick, May, and Barbara Brenner. **The Tremendous Tree Book.** Illus. Fred Brenner. Four Winds Press, 1979. 6–9.

The tree, a most wonderful and useful plant, is presented in an exciting and dramatic way. Simple sentences make this a valuable tool for beginning readers. Colorful illustrations, bright and bold, encourage close observation of trees. A delight for all.

Lerner, Carol. **Flowers of a Woodland Spring.** William Morrow, 1979. 8–12.

For a few weeks in the early spring the forest floor is alive with the blossoms of wildflowers. The sun-loving plants bloom while the sun's light can still penetrate the canopy of leaves above. Detailed illustrations and life cycle descriptions.

Lerner, Carol. **On the Forest Edge.** William Morrow, 1978. 8–12.

Between the forest and the field there is a narrow strip that is the forest edge. In this strip live more plants and animals than can live in either full shade or full sun. Details, illustrations, and descriptions clarify this significant environmental concept. Excellent for an ecology unit.

Nussbaum, Hedda. **Plants Do Amazing Things.** Illus. Joe Mathieu. Random House, 1977. 7–10.

A resource book filled with funny and interesting facts about unusual plants, including those that give off light and those that walk. Illustrations are small but plentiful and assist text descriptions. Table of contents is an added bonus. A Step-Up-Book.

Selsam, Millicent E., and Jerome Wexler. **The Amazing Dandelion.** William Morrow, 1977. 8–12.

The dandelion is a most successful plant. From its strong tap root to its composite flower it has developed means to survive and spread. Handsomely illustrated with color and black and white detailed photographs, this well-written life cycle book is a worthwhile addition for plant study.

Welch, Martha McKeen. **Sunflower!** Dodd, Mead, 1980. 7–10.

The sunflower and its life cycle are described in easily-read text and bold black and white photographs. Good for classroom science work.

Williams, Barbara. **Hello, Dandelion!** Photographs by author. Holt, Rinehart and Winston, 1979. 6–9.

Here is affirmation of the charm and usefulness of the dandelion, one of nature's beauties that a child appreciates on sight. Interesting information, including some dandelion games. Delightful text and photographs.

Prehistoric Life

Aliki. **Wild and Woolly Mammoths.** Illus. by author. Thomas Y. Crowell, 1977. 6–9.

Mammoths, huge beasts like elephants, lived thousands of years ago. Their relics and pictures painted on cave walls show how they lived. Engaging illustrations depict these extinct animals as they were.

Carrick, Carol. **The Crocodiles Still Wait.** Illus. Donald Carrick. Clarion Books, 1980. 6–9.

This is a story of a fifty-foot-long prehistoric crocodile mother caring for and protecting her nest of eggs. When the young are newly hatched, she defends them from attacks by bird-eating dinosaurs and Tyrannosaurus Rex. Illustrations dramatize the interesting and imaginative account of this reptile's past.

Cohen, Daniel. **What Really Happened to the Dinosaurs?** Illus. Haru Wells. E. P. Dutton, 1977. 8–12.

Known facts about dinosaurs are presented and many conflicting theories related to their existence and disappearance are discussed. Black and white sketches aid description and explanation.

Eldridge, David. **The Giant Dinosaurs: Ancient Reptiles That Ruled the Land.** Illus. Norman Nodel. Troll Associates, 1979. 8–12.

One of four books in a series that studies prehistoric land, sea, and air reptiles and why they became extinct. Vivid physical descriptions, food gathering habits, and how scientists learn from fossilized remains are discussed. Colorful illustrations and pronunciation guides are included in each book. Other titles are *Flying Dragons, Sea Monsters,* and *Last of the Dinosaurs.*

Elting, Mary, and Ann Goodman. **Dinosaur Mysteries.** Illus. Susan Swan. Platt & Munk, Publishers, 1980. 8–12.

A series of questions about different dinosaurs and what happened to them are asked. The authors suggest answers to the mysteries and provide other interesting facts based on scientific research. A pronunciation guide for the dinosaur names is included.

Freedman, Russell. **They Lived with the Dinosaurs.** Holiday House, 1980. 7–10.

Starfish, horseshoe crabs, and cockroaches can be called living fossils because they are creatures who survived with little change from the time of dinosaurs. Time charts from 400 million years to 65 million years ago show when the creatures described lived. Characteristics that helped their survival are discussed. Black and white photographs.

Harvey, Anthony. **The World of the Dinosaurs.** Illus. Alan Male, et al. Lerner Publications, 1980. 7–10.

Although parts of the text may be difficult for some readers, the colorful illustrations and question-and-answer format of this volume will appeal to most children. A short dictionary of prehistoric terms, a glossary of dinosaurs, a gazeteer of dinosaur localities, and an index are most useful.

Knight, David C. **Dinosaur Days.** Illus. Joel Schick. McGraw-Hill, 1977. 6–9.

An easy-to-read general description of dinosaurs precedes the discussion of eighteen specific reptiles in the dinosaur family tree. Pronunciations, charts, and simplified drawings make this a very interesting book for young enthusiasts. Several theories concerning the disappearance of the giant animals are presented.

Porell, Bruce. **Digging the Past: Archaeology in Your Own Backyard.** Illus. Bruce Elliott. Addison-Wesley Publishing, 1979. 10–12.

This excellent informational book shows how archaeologists work and how readers can work in the same manner and evaluate their findings. Fascinating stories about the Dead Sea Scrolls and Black Death are included. Many appropriate pictures, maps, and diagrams in sepia tone illustrate the content. Addresses for materials and glossary appended.

Pringle, Laurence. **Dinosaurs and People: Fossils, Facts, and Fantasies.** Harcourt Brace Jovanovich, 1978. 8–12.

This book is not a typical treatment of dinosaurs. Instead, it investigates the problems people face in searching for dinosaur remains and then exhibiting them. It restates the theories of the Age of Dinosaurs and then permits readers to draw their own conclusions. Some very old myths are exploded.

Ricciuti, Edward R. **Older than the Dinosaurs: The Origin and Rise of the Mammals.** Illus. Edward Malsberg. Thomas Y. Crowell, 1980. 12–up.

The rise and development of mammals following the age of the giant reptiles is traced in an easy-to-read manner. The three eras, Paleozoic, Mesozoic, and Cenozoic, can readily be followed on the helpful chart at the beginning of the book. Black and white illustrations.

Rosenbloom, Joseph. **Dictionary of Dinosaurs.** Illus. Haris Petie. Julian Messner, 1980. 10–12.

A brief, informative introduction discusses the environment in which the dinosaurs lived. Each type of dinosaur is alphabetically arranged with a description and a black and white illustration. The meaning of its name, its type, and the period in which it thrived is given. Valuable for the classroom.

Selsam, Millicent E. **Sea Monsters of Long Ago.** Illus. John Hamberger. Four Winds Press, 1977. 6–9.

Information about prehistoric sea beasts is presented with clarity and style. Facts are meaningfully related to known things in youngsters' present-day life. Absorbing illustrations include full-color paintings, photographs of fossils, meticulous ink drawings, and a simple, attractive chart. Read aloud or use for research. Picture book format.

Selsam, Millicent. **Tyrannosaurus Rex.** Harper & Row, Publishers, 1978. 8–12.

The bones of the biggest meat-eating animal that ever lived on earth were excavated in Montana around 1900. This is a fascinating account of that project, and of the exciting, painstaking reassembling of the Tyrannosaurus Rex skeleton at the American Museum of Natural History in New York. Photographs, bibliography, and index are included.

Stuart, Gene S. **Secrets from the Past.** National Geographic Society, 1979. 10–up.

Beautiful colored illustrations highlight the text about mysteries of the earth's past. Information is included about pyramids, archaeological digs, Indians, lost cities, treasures from the sea, and other interesting puzzles. A classroom activity packet is attached, containing a poster, games, activities, and dittos for teacher use.

Unexplained Phenomena

Allen, Martha Dickson. **Real Life Monsters.** Prentice-Hall, 1978. All ages.

In 1917 a French naturalist announced that all the world's animals had been found. Since then the gorilla, Komodo dragon, and giant squid have been discovered. Accounts of these and the Loch Ness Monster, Big Foot, and the Abominable Snowman are written in a concise and easy reading style. Supplemented with pen sketches.

Caras, Roger. **Mysteries of Nature: Explained and Unexplained.** Harcourt Brace Jovanovich, 1979. 8–12.

Theories explaining eleven mysteries, and some puzzling natural phenomena, are presented. Included are the mystery of the stranded whales, the spitting cobra, the South African sea serpent, and other readable accounts. Illustrated with photographs.

Cohen, Daniel. **Missing! Stories of Strange Disappearances.** Dodd, Mead, 1979. 10–12.

This collection of six famous disappearances is surefire for young mystery fans. Included are the true stories of Dorothy Arnold; Judge Crater; Michael Rockefeller; the crew of the *Mary Celeste;* the bones of the Peking Man, and the Bermuda Triangle's Flight 19. Various theories and explanations are explored.

Cohen, Daniel. **Mysteries of the World.** Doubleday, 1979. 8–12.

This book should delight Forteans, those followers of Charles Fort (1874–1932), who love to collect odd bits of information. Ten unexplained happenings such as the Siberian explosion, cattle mutilations, human spontaneous combustion, and others are explained. Black and white photographs and sketches.

McHargue, Georgess. **Meet the Vampire.** Illus. Stephen Gammell. J. B. Lippincott, 1979. 10–12.

This book tells of vampires old and modern, east and west, horrible and more horrible, like Vlad the Impaler, the original Count Dracula. The last chapter provides possible explanations for vampires. Includes some gruesome black and white illustrations; not for the squeamish.

Mooser, Stephen. **Into the Unknown: Nine Astounding Stories.** J. B. Lippincott, 1980. 8–12.

A collection of nine mysterious cases that have been documented but not solved is presented. The author details the facts and offers several suggestions as to what might have occurred, but allows readers to draw their own conclusions.

Oleksy, Walter. **Visitors from Outer Space? Is There Life on Other Planets?** G. P. Putnam's Sons, 1979. 12–up.

Although unexplained phenomena have been reported since Old Testament times, only recently have people reported being abducted and questioned by humanoids. Many close encounters of all three kinds are described by responsible people. Ten pages of black and white photographs.

Roberts, Nancy. **Southern Ghosts.** Photographs by Bruce Roberts. Doubleday, 1979. 8–12.

Did you know Jimmy and Rosalynn Carter once lived in a haunted house in Plains, Georgia? This story, along with thirteen other short tales about haunted houses, phantom stallions, deadly bracelets, and other mysterious phenomena, is included. Large print and black and white photographs will invite lingering and imagining.

Snyder, Gerald S. **Is There a Loch Ness Monster? The Search for a Legend.** Julian Messner, 1977. 12–up.

In a detailed, balanced examination of the Loch Ness Monster legend, evidence both pro and con is given. Sightings are recounted; scientific expeditions and modern technological investigations are described. Many photographs add to the completeness of this well-done survey. Bibliography and index included.

Weiss, Malcolm E. **Gods, Stars, and Computers: Fact and Fancy in Myth and Science.** Doubleday, 1980. 12–up.

The author explores relationships between ancient myths and modern scientific explanations for such natural phenomena as volcanos, earthquakes, medicine, space, and human relationships to animals. A strong plea is made for ethics in scientific research. Human superiority over computer is firmly stated. Illustrated with photos and diagrams. Index.

Additional Science Books

Andrews, Roy Chapman. *All about Strange Beasts of the Past.* Illus. Matthew Kalmenoff. Random House, 1956. 10–14.

Asimov, Isaac. *Building Blocks of the Universe.* Abelard-Schuman, 1961. 12–up.

Baylor, Byrd. *The Desert Is Theirs.* Illus. Peter Parnall. Charles Scribner's Sons, 1975. 5–8.

Bendick, Jeanne. *The Shape of the Earth.* Rand McNally, 1965. 8–12.

Bendick, Jeanne, and Marcia O. Levin. *Take Shapes, Lines, and Letters.* McGraw-Hill, 1962. 9–12.

Bitter, Gary G., and Thomas H. Metos. *Exploring with Metrics.* Julian Messner, 1975. 8–up.

Branley, Franklyn M. *Air Is All Around You.* Illus. Robert Galster. Thomas Y. Crowell, 1962. 6–8.

Cole, Joanna. *A Calf Is Born.* Photos by Jerome Wexler. William Morrow, 1975. 5–8.

Eberle, Irmengarde. *Bears Live Here.* Photos. Doubleday, 1966. 8–11.

Elliott, Sarah M. *Our Dirty Air.* Julian Messner, 1973. 8–up.

Froman, Robert. *Rubber Bands, Baseballs, and Doughnuts.* Illus. Harvey Weiss. Thomas Y. Crowell, 1972. 9–12.

Gallant, Roy A. *Exploring the Weather.* Illus. Lowell Hess. Doubleday, 1957. 10–14.

George, Jean Craighead. *The Hole in the Tree.* E. P. Dutton, 1957. 6–8.

George, Jean Craighead. *"Thirteen Moons" Series.* Thomas Y. Crowell, 1967–1970. 8–up.

Gordon, Sol. *Facts about Sex for Today's Youth.* Illus. Vivien Cohen. John Day, 1973. 12–up.

Goudey, Alice E. *Here Come the Lions!* Illus. Garry MacKenzie. Charles Scribner's Sons, 1958. 8–12.

Henry, Marguerite. *All about Horses.* Illus. Walter D. Osborne. Random House, 1967. 8–12.

Holling, Holling C. *Minn of the Mississippi.* Houghton Mifflin, 1951. 10–14.

Hutchins, Ross E. *The Travels of Monarch X.* Illus. Jerome P. Connolly. Rand McNally, 1966. 8–11.

Knight, David C. *Harnessing the Sun.* William Morrow, 1976. 12–up.

LeShan, Eda. *Learning to Say Good-By: When a Parent Dies.* Illus. Paul Giovanopoulos. Macmillan Publishing, 1976. 8–up.

Milgrom, Harry. *Understanding Weather.* Illus. Lloyd Birmingham. Macmillan Publishing, 1970. 10–14.

Ravielli, Anthony. *Wonders of the Human Body.* Viking Press, 1954. 9–12.

Reed, W. Maxwell. *The Earth for Sam.* Rev. ed. Illus. Paul Brandwein. Harcourt Brace Jovanovich, 1960. 12–up.

Scott, Jack Denton. *Discovering the American Stork.* Photos by Ozzie Sweet. Harcourt Brace Jovanovich, 1976. 10–14.

Selsam, Millicent E. *Animals as Parents.* Illus. J. Kaupmann. William Morrow, 1965. 12–14.

Selsam, Millicent E. *How Puppies Grow.* Photos by Esther Bubley. Four Winds Press, 1971. 5–8.

Selsam, Millicent E. *Play with Seeds.* Illus. Helen Ludwig. William Morrow, 1957. 8–12.

Shuttlesworth, Dorothy. *Clean Air, Sparkling Water.* Photos. Doubleday, 1968. 8–10.

Weiss, Ann E. *Save the Mustangs!* Julian Messner, 1974. 8–up.

Zim, Herbert Spencer. *Dinosaurs.* Illus. James Gordon Irving. William Morrow, 1954. 8–12.

Sports and Games

Chess

Lombardy, William, and Bette Marshall. **Chess for Children, Step by Step: A New, Easy Way to Learn the Game.** Illus. John Schnell. Photographs by Bette Marshall. Little, Brown, 1977. 8–up.

Written by a chess Grandmaster, the book uses excellent diagrams, black and white photographs, and a pace suitable to making chess understandable. The authors explain how chess pieces are named, how they move, and many helpful hints. Includes both boys and girls in the photographs.

Pandolfini, Bruce. **Let's Play Chess!** Julian Messner, 1980. 10–12.

Unique in form, this book gives 616 numbered statements that explain the game of chess. The instructions begin at the most basic introductory level and move into an actual game with some thoughtful discussions about the play. The style is interesting with occasional analogies to literature or football.

Rosenberg, Arthur D. **Chess for Children and the Young at Heart.** Illus. Howard Berelson. Photographs by Marianne Groher. Atheneum, 1977. 8–up.

Eight- to ten-year-olds should have few difficulties with the chapters that identify the chess pieces and explain the basic moves in this step-by-step self-instruction manual. The elaboration on chess openings probably requires explanation by someone conversant with the game.

Cycling

Lindblom, Steven. **The Fantastic Bicycles Book.** Houghton Mifflin, 1979. 10–up.

This book is about bicycles: how to recycle them, fix them, and make things with bike parts. Lots of useful information for do-it-yourselfers or young inventors.

Monroe, Lynn Lee. **The Old-Time Bicycle Book.** Illus. George Overlie. Carolrhoda Books, 1979. 7–10.

It was a revolutionary idea: people could sit on two wheels, not touch the ground, and move! The evolution of bicycles, once called Boneshakers for good reason, is told briefly in large print and using colored sketches. Useful to show how inventions build on previous developments.

Murray, Jerry. **The Handbook of Motocross.** G. P. Putnam's Sons, 1978. 10–12.

Motocross is big business and a popular, fast-growing sport. This book teaches young readers how to ride and race motocross, as well as the importance of maintenance, safety, conditioning, and protective clothing. Black and white photos.

Pursell, Thomas F. **Bicycles on Parade: A Brief History.** Lerner Publications, 1980. 9–12.

Through the years bicycles have had an effect on road building and fashions. Bicycle shops were often inventors' training grounds. Bicycles old and new are discussed with black and white and color photos and sketches that add to the reader's interest.

Soucheray, Joe. **How to Repair Your 10-Speed Bike.** Illus. Kevin Pedersen. Creative Education, 1979. 9–12.

While not a complete technical manual, this book gives basic repair and maintenance tips on tires, wheels, pedals and chains, brakes, and derailleurs using a few select tools. Cartoon-style drawings; tongue-in-cheek style writing.

Yerkow, Charles. **Fun and Safety on Two Wheels: Bicycles, Mopeds, Scooters, Motorcycles.** G. P. Putnam's Sons, 1979. 12–up.

Much needed safety information is given to bicycle riders since statistics show that 30,000 riders are killed annually. Practical guidance includes proper dress, equipment and its functions, maintenance, traffic safety, and local ordinances. Written in an easy-to-read style. Index.

Flying

Berliner, Don. **Aerobatics.** Lerner Publications, 1980. 7–10.

The excitement of aerobatics, sometimes known as trick flying, is shown in excellent color photographs and a clear text that discusses the history of the sport. The specially designed airplanes are described as well as the men and women who fly them. Diagrams show some of the popular maneuvers.

Radlauer, Ed. **Some Basics about Hang Gliding.** Childrens Press, 1979. 8–12.

The hang glider is described in simple terms covering its construction and information on flying. Full-color photographs and authentic text make this a useful resource book.

Robison, Nancy L. **Hang Gliding.** Photographs by Bettina Gray. Harvey House, Publishers, 1978. 10–up.

The sport of hang gliding is thoroughly described, including the intricacies of the sport and the thorough, formal training required to participate. The importance of safety is stressed. Clear photographs contribute to the text.

Gymnastics

Dolan, Edward F., Jr. **The Complete Beginner's Guide to Gymnastics.** Photographs by James Stewart. Doubleday, 1980. 10–12.

Originally done by soldiers to develop combative skills, this ancient sport is enjoying new popularity. The book, filled with black and white photographs labeled to match printed instructions, discusses equipment, wearing apparel, and safety rules. Appealing to both sexes, it contains mostly beginner's stunts, with some intermediate ones. Short bibliography, good index.

Krementz, Jill. **A Very Young Gymnast.** Photographs by author. Alfred A. Knopf, 1978. 7–10.

An exciting story of ten-year-old Torrence York who is already the best gymnast in New York City. Through the text and excellent photographs, the reader is taken through her daily routine and becomes aware of her ambitions and struggles.

Murdock, Tony. **Gymnastics for Girls.** Plays, 1979. 12–up.

This informative book describes three forms of gymnastics in which girls can compete: Olympic artistic gymnastics, sports acrobatics, and modern rhythmic gymnastics. After a brief history of the sport, the apparatus, program, performance, judging, and scoring are clearly explained. Diagrams and photographs included.

Resnick, Michael. **Gymnastics and You: The Whole Story of the Sport.** Rand McNally, 1977. 10–up.

This clearly explains for the beginner the terminology used by the gymnast: balance beam, floor exercise, high bar, parallel bars, uneven parallel bars, rings, side horse, team gymnastics, trampoline, tumbling, and vaulting. Photographs clarify the text. Index included.

Sullivan, George. **Better Gymnastics for Girls.** Dodd, Mead, 1977. 10–12.

A photo-filled, technically accurate book on a popular subject that stresses grace, precision, and flexibility. The book is divided into sections on floor exercises, balance beam, vaulting, and uneven parallel bars. Contains glossary and sources of additional information. Olga Korbut and Nadia Comaneci are spotlighted.

Traetta, John, and Mary Jean Traetta. **Gymnastics Basics.** Illus. Bill Gow. Photographs by Don Carter. Prentice-Hall, 1979. 9–12.

This book stresses both the fun and safety aspects of gymnastics, as well as other benefits that include increased concentration, willpower, and physical stamina. Sketches of the movements are interspersed with black and white photos. One-page index included.

Hockey

Etter, Les. **The Game of Hockey.** Garrard Publishing, 1977. 8–12.

An easy-to-read discussion of the history, rules, and playing techniques of ice hockey includes play-by-play descriptions of important games. Information on famous players and the impact of the recent popularity of the game are highlighted by black and white photographs.

Gitler, Ira. **Ice Hockey A to Z.** Lothrop, Lee & Shepard Books, 1978. 6–up.

Important hockey information is packed into this book including anecdotes, rules and regulations, and advice to the hockey player. Photographs illustrate the text.

Olney, Ross R. **This Game Called Hockey: Great Moments in the World's Fastest Team Sport.** Dodd, Mead, 1978. 7–up.

Hockey is a fast, hard, exacting team sport. This book presents the players as competitive athletes who love the game, the challenge, and the danger of hockey. Each chapter introduces many complicated aspects of an exciting sport that is played throughout the world.

Williams, Lee Ann. **Basic Field Hockey Strategy: An Introduction for Young Players.** Illus. John Lane. Doubleday, 1978. 10–up.

Lucid explanations of both offensive and defensive strategy for girls' field hockey are clarified further by numerous drawings and full-page diagrams. Included also are pointers on equipment, conditioning exercises, drills, an appendix of rules, and a glossary. Particularly helpful are the several tips at the end of each chapter.

Horseback Riding

Krementz, Jill. **A Very Young Rider.** Photographs by author. Alfred A. Knopf, 1977. 8–10.

Photographs capture both the splendor of the horse show and the wearying routine for horse and rider that must precede a show. The rider is a dedicated young girl and the book expresses both her professional attitude and her youthful exuberance.

Pervier, Evelyn. **The Beginning Rider: A Common Sense Approach.** Illus. by author. Photographs by Melinda Hughes. Julian Messner, 1980. 10–12.

This book covers the basics of forward-seat riding and beginning jumping as well as care of the horse. The conversational style gives the reader the feeling of having a chat with an expert. Black and white photographs are well chosen and convey excellent detail; diagrams, index and glossary provide other important information.

Sholinsky, Jane. **In the Saddle: Horseback Riding for Girls and Boys.** Photographs by Dan S. Nelken. Julian Messner, 1977. 8–12.

In simple language and with informative illustrations, the author gives the basic information a beginning rider needs to know about the horse and tack, as well as how to approach, mount, dismount, sit, and ride the various gaits. Glossary is included.

Kite Making and Flying

Bahadur, Dinesh. **Come Fight a Kite.** Harvey House, Publishers, 1978. 10–up.

The excitement, fun, and techniques of kite flying are communicated by a master of kite making, flying, and the ancient sport of kite fighting. The text includes some descriptions of types of kites and their construction. Detailed guidance is given for launching and flying kites with or without wind.

Kaufmann, John. **Fly It!** Illus. by author. Doubleday, 1980. 8–up.

Instructions on how to make and fly kites, boomerangs, helicopters, hang gliders, and hand-launched gliders are simple. Each step is illustrated and detailed with excellent line drawings. The hints and suggestions provided to prevent problems with the different craft projects are invaluable.

Marks, Burton, and Rita Marks. **Kites for Kids.** Illus. Lisa Campbell Ernst. Lothrop, Lee & Shepard Books, 1980. 8–up.

Directions are given for making classic kites, space cruisers, and sky monsters. Construction tips, techniques, and a guide to flying are also included. Humorous detailed black and white illustrations enhance the text. Appendices include lists of supply sources and kite organizations.

Olney, Ross R., and Chan Bush. **Better Kite Flying for Boys and Girls.** Dodd, Mead, 1980. 9–up.

Good advice for flying kites, kite fighting, and making kites is combined with a short history of kites. Excellent photographs accompany the text.

Skating and Skateboarding

Bass, Howard. **Ice Skating.** Rand McNally, 1980. 8–12.

Many outstanding color photographs highlight this comprehensive volume that includes sections on speed and figure skating, ice dancing, ice hockey, and competitive skating. Recent champions are pictured and Olympic and other competition winners are listed. Techniques are shown, including a clear explanation of the International School Figures. Glossary and index are appended.

Bunting, Glenn, and Eve Bunting. **Skateboards: How to Make Them, How to Ride Them.** Harvey House, Publishers, 1977. 8–12.

Beginning with clear instructions for making your own skateboard, the book proceeds to a detailed explanation of various techniques of both simple and advanced riding skills. Safety is stressed throughout with special emphasis on equipment and approved riding locations.

Hess, Jeff. **Skateboarding Skills.** Illus. Kevin Pederson. Creative Education, 1979. 8–12.

Basic skateboarding positions and safety tips, along with consumer information about selection of skateboard blanks and wheels, are stressed in this short book. Magazines and books to help improve skateboarding techniques are listed. Cartoon-style drawings.

Krementz, Jill. **A Very Young Skater.** Photographs by author. Alfred A. Knopf, 1979. 7–10.

Katherine Healy is ten and has been skating since she was three. The camera follows her through her demanding, supremely disciplined schedule of skating and ballet classes, regular school, and special performances. A superbly photographed example of the personal determination and family support needed for a young skater to excel.

Olney, Ross R., and Chan Bush. **Roller Skating!!** Lothrop, Lee & Shepard Books, 1979. 8–12.

Enthusiasts caught up in the revitalized sport of roller skating will enjoy the many black and white photographs as well as the clear explanations of techniques, equipment, and trick maneuvers. A list of organizations, stores, and publications specializing in skating is appended.

Skiing

Church, Margaret. **Beginning Cross-Country Skiing.** Photographs by Laszlo Kondor. Childrens Press, 1979. 8–up.

A fine book to help the beginner learn how to ski cross-country.

Full-color photographs show equipment, dress, and proper skiing form. A valuable book for any novice skier.

Liss, Howard. **Skiing Talk for Beginners.** Illus. Frank Robbins. Julian Messner, 1977. 10–up.

A dictionary format is used to explain a variety of skiing terms and phrases. Although cross references are used throughout, some prior knowledge of skiing is necessary to understand most of the concepts. Difficult words are broken into syllables but accents are not given. Black and white line drawings.

Lyttle, Richard B. **The Complete Beginner's Guide to Skiing.** Doubleday, 1978. 10–up.

Specific instructions on moves and procedures for beginning skiers are given. The author also discusses equipment, safety, conditioning, and different kinds of skiing. A complete list of definitions and terms makes this a beneficial book to be used during the learning period.

Sullivan, George. **Cross-Country Skiing: A Complete Beginner's Book.** Julian Messner, 1980. 10–up.

The designation "A Complete Beginner's Book" fits this book precisely. There is enough, but not too much, information on history, ski design, wearing apparel, and technique. Appendices include ski areas, guide books, United States Park Services, and a glossary of ski terminology. Black and white photographs.

Soccer

Clements, David. **Soccer Tips.** Photographs by Gary Nichamin. Julian Messner, 1978. 8–12.

The simple and brief text sets forth the fundamentals of soccer for beginning players. Discussed are such topics as how to control the ball, techniques for passing, and goaltending. A glossary of terms and the rules of soccer are included. Photos or drawings illustrate each technique described.

Liss, Howard. **The Great Game of Soccer.** Illus. Bruce Curtis. G. P. Putnam's Sons, 1979. 8–12.

The growing popularity of soccer as an amateur and professional sport is traced, along with its history and famous players. Details of game skills, techniques, and rules are given and illustrated by many action black and white photographs. Glossary and index are provided.

Pollock, Robert. **Soccer for Juniors** Charles Scribner's Sons, 1980. 8–up.

Here is an excellent introduction to the game of soccer including basic skills, equipment, injuries, diet, and rules. Advanced skills and tactics are described in concise text and illustrated with good action photographs.

Scagnetti, Jack. **Soccer.** Harvey House, Publishers, 1978. 9–12.

Clear text and how-to photographs show player positions and demonstrate how the game of soccer is played. The history, equipment, and basic rules are included in this informational book.

Sullivan, George. **This Is Pro Soccer.** Dodd, Mead, 1979. 10–up.

Why soccer, one of the oldest sports in the world, has captured so many fans is explained along with background information on how it is played. A glossary, NASL records, and index are provided. Frequent photographs and diagrams help clarify the text.

Tennis

Huss, Sally Moore. **How to Play Power Tennis with Ease.** Harcourt Brace Jovanovich, 1979. 12–up.

Addressing persons who play tennis and wish to improve their game, the author, in a casual second-person style, promises immediate and dramatic results. Illustrated with humorous cartoonlike drawings. Glossary.

Lorimer, Larry. **The Tennis Book.** Illus. Elizabeth Roger. Random House, 1980. 9–12.

This very complete tennis book, including terms, people, rules, and playing tips, has been carefully arranged in an alphabetic format. A great help to young tennis enthusiasts.

Ravielli, Anthony. **What Is Tennis?** Illus. by author. Atheneum, 1977. 7–up.

Tennis is a sport of fast moves and graceful play. This book includes the history of tennis and how to play the game. The illustrations are artistic and helpful.

Volleyball

Lyttle, Richard B. **Basic Volleyball Strategy: An Introduction for Young Players.** Illus. John Lane. Doubleday, 1979. 12–up.

Precise instructions on playing techniques for volleyball are described in the text and black and white illustrations. A valuable book for the beginner and the more experienced player.

Sullivan, George. **Better Volleyball for Girls.** Dodd, Mead, 1979. 12–up.

Text and photographs clearly demonstrate the basic plan of the game and techniques for developing skill. A short history of volleyball and a glossary are included.

Thomas, Art. **Volleyball Is for Me.** Photographs by author. Lerner Publications, 1980. 7–10.

A young volleyball team learns the basics of the game. The text describes skills needed for serving, blocking, spiking, and passing. Readable text and good black and white photographs.

Water Sports

Bartram, Robert. **Fishing for Sunfish.** Illus. by author. J. B. Lippincott, 1978. 8–12.

This information-packed book explains basic facts about catching sunfish: equipment needed, best time of year, most likely spots, types of bait, and how to clean the sunfish. Nonsexist; a needed book on fishing.

Freeman, Tony. **Beginning Surfing.** Photographs by author. Childrens Press, 1980. 7–up.

A careful step-by-step introduction to surfing that shows equipment, training, and safety procedures. Clear, full-color photographs make this a most helpful book for any beginner.

Gleasner, Diana C. **Illustrated Swimming, Diving and Surfing Dictionary for Young People.** Illus. Stuart Goldenberg. Prentice-Hall, 1980. 8–up.

Facts about three popular water sports are given in dictionary format. Humorous illustrations add information and each definition is keyed with an easy-to-recognize symbol indicating the particular sport. Other topics in this illustrated dictionary series include gymnastics, ballet, auto racing, tennis, and skating.

Liss, Howard. **Fishing Talk for Beginners.** Illus. Leonard Cole. Julian Messner, 1978. 10–up.

Various fishing terms and phrases are discussed in dictionary format. Techniques of the sport as well as equipment and types of fish are discussed. Cross references and numerous illustrations further clarify the text.

Orr, C. Rob, and Jane B. Tyler. **Swimming Basics.** Illus. Bill Gow. Photographs by Emmett Wilson, Jr. Prentice-Hall, 1980. 8–12.

Fundamentals of swimming for beginners include instructions for the four basic strokes used in swimming competition and a guide for water safety. Excellent illustrations and photographs clarify and extend the text.

Various Sports and Games

Boccaccio, Tony. **Racquetball Basics.** Illus. Bill Gow. Photographs by Paul Jacobs. Prentice-Hall, 1979. 8–12.

Clear illustrations and detailed explanations are given on the sport of racquetball for beginning players.

Dexler, Paul R. **Vans: The Personality Vehicles.** Lerner Publications, 1977. 8–12.

The history of vanning as a sport and hobby is explained. Some vans contain genuine woodburning fireplaces; that and other facts are included in the discussion of the interior and exterior customizing. This is a book that is sure to be popular and lead to shared reading with other family members. One of a series on "Superwheels and Thrill Sports." Another book in the series is *Motocross Motorcycle Racing.*

Dickmeyer, Lowell A. **Baseball Is for Me.** Photographs by Camiel Kannard. Lerner Publications, 1978. 7–10.

The first-person narrator, a young enthusiastic sports buff, shares his experiences in learning fundamental rules and techniques. He is a Little League player and gets to meet a baseball hero. The realistic text is supported by exceptional photographs. Appealing for beginners. One of a series that includes books on basketball, fishing, ice skating, swimming, volleyball, soccer, and tennis.

Flanagan, Henry E., Jr., and Robert Gardner. **Basic Lacrosse Strategy: An Introduction for Young Players.** Illus. John Lane. Doubleday, 1979. 10–up.

The book outlines the fundamental skills needed to become a reasonably successful lacrosse player. The authors have drawn upon their personal experiences in coaching the game. Emphasis is on the thinking aspect. A solid basic resource.

Larson, Randy. **Backpacking for Fun and Glory.** Illus. John R. Henshaw. Harvey House, Publishers, 1979. 10–12.

This is a very thorough introduction to backpacking. It covers everything a beginner needs to know from how to cover blisters to which stove to buy. The photographs are clear and the explanations carefully worded to avoid misinterpretation.

Lorimer, Larry, and John Devaney. **The Football Book.** Illus. Charles McVicker. Random House, 1977. 9–up.

An appealing, informative A to Z encyclopedia about football. Outstanding players, coaches, and teams are included. Rules, equipment, and strategies are clearly described. Illustrated with diagrams, drawings, and photographs.

Olney, Ross R. **Modern Racing Cars.** E. P. Dutton, 1978. 12–up.

Racing cars such as Indy-types, formula one, sprint, stock, and midget are described, compared, and contrasted. Some historical information is included.

Poynter, Margaret. **The Racquetball Book.** Illus. Don Meyer and Terry Andrues. Julian Messner, 1980. 10–12.

A useful book for both beginning and experienced racquetball players. Included are such items as needed equipment, basic and advanced strokes, game strategies, and rules. Brief biographical sketches of some racquetball champions conclude the text.

Radlauer, Ed. **Some Basics about Running.** Childrens Press, 1979. 8–12.

Anyone can start running for fun and fitness by following these simple basic directions in text and pictures. Safety and equipment are emphasized. Photographs are in full color. One of the Gemini series that includes books about hang gliding, women's gymnastics, skateboards, motorcycles, bicycles, and water skiing.

Ribner, Susan, and Richard Chin. **Martial Arts.** Illus. Melanie Arwin. Harper & Row, Publishers, 1978. 8–up.

The authors give a history of the ancient Oriental martial arts from *Kung Fu* to *Ninjitsu,* explaining their development and techniques. The book traces the evolution of unarmed combat in terms of religion, national pride, and modern sport. Many unusual facts and stories are shared with the reader.

Robison, Nancy L. **Baton Twirling.** Harvey House, Publishers, 1980. 8–12.

History, types of batons, learning to twirl, and having fun with the baton are discussed in this book that has many black and white photos. Very few books are available on this subject.

Roddick, Dan. **Frisbee Disc Basics.** Illus. Bill Gow. Photographs by James Morse and Jack Roddick. Prentice-Hall, 1980. 9–12.

More frisbees are sold than baseballs, basketballs, and footballs combined. Fred Morrison is credited with the frisbee's invention. Spinning, curving, throwing, and catching the plastic disc are explained in this nicely illustrated book. It also has an index, lists record-holders, and gives the address of the International Frisbee Disc Association.

Rosenthal, Sylvia A. **Soap Box Derby Racing.** Lothrop, Lee & Shepard Books, 1980. 10–up.

One of the greatest amateur races, the All-American Soap Box Derby is an exciting event. The history of the derby, from its beginning in 1933 through the 1979 race, is well told with personalized anecdotes. Attention is given to girls who race in the derby.

Schumacher, Craig. **Frisbee Fun.** Illus. Kevin Pederson. Creative Education, 1979. 8–12.

Frisbee playing requires practice in order to acquire the proper techniques. The history and basics of throwing and catching are given. Readers are urged to invent games. The book is useful for science enrichment as gravitational, frictional, and lifting forces are what make the frisbee work. Cartoon-style drawings.

Siegel, Alice, and Margo McLoone. **It's a Girl's Game Too.** Illus. Lisa Campbell Ernst. Holt, Rinehart and Winston, 1980. 8–12.

Both team and individual sports are discussed in this compendium of sports talk. Beginning with a brief history of women's participation in athletics, the authors describe eighteen different sports giving complete scoring, rules, general and specific information about the players, fields, equipment, vocabulary, clothing, skills, and sources of further information.

Sullivan, George. **Better Basketball for Boys.** Dodd, Mead, 1980. 10–up.

The popular game of basketball is explained in depth, starting with the simpler aspects of ball handling, footwork, and passing. Photographs and diagrams illustrate the text. One of a series; related books are *Better Basketball for Girls, Better Football for Boys, Better Roller Skating for Boys and Girls.*

Sullivan, George. **Run, Run Fast!** Illus. by author and Don Madden. Thomas Y. Crowell, 1980. 8–11.

Regulated running can make us feel and look better. Sound advice on footwear, clothing, safety, and running form is given in brief sentences and paragraphs. Well illustrated with a mixture of black and white photographs and sketches.

Sullivan, George. **Sports Superstitions.** Coward, McCann & Geoghegan, 1978. 8–12.

After an excellent introduction, the author tells fascinating anecdotes of superstitious behavior by famous athletes in every major sport. Black and white photos.

Additional Sports and Games Books

Bunning, Jim, Whitey Ford, Mickey Mantle, and Willie Mays. *Grand Slam.* Viking Press, 1965. 12–16.

Coombs, Charles. *Drag Racing.* William Morrow, 1970. 10–14.

Epstein, Sam, and Beryl Epstein. *The Game of Baseball.* Illus. Hobe Hays. Garrard Publishing, 1965. 10–12.

Hano, Arnold. *Greatest Giants of Them All.* G. P. Putnam's Sons, 1967. 10–up.

Howard, Elston. *Catching.* Illus. Robert Osonitsch. Viking Press, 1966. 12–16.

Lindsay, Sally. *Figure Skating.* Rand McNally, 1963. 11–16.

Lipsyte, Robert. *Assignment: Sports.* Harper & Row, Publishers, 1970. 12–16.

Pickens, Richard. *How to Punt, Pass and Kick.* Illus. Fran Chauncey. Random House, 1965. 12–16.

Van Riper, Guernsey, Jr. *The Game of Basketball.* Garrard, Straus & Giroux, 1967. 8–11.

The Arts

Architecture

Haldane, Suzanne. **Faces on Places: About Gargoyles and Other Stone Creatures.** Viking Press, 1980. 9–12.

Vivid and dramatic photographs combine with an informative text to focus attention on gargoyles, those fascinating stone carvings that adorn buildings. The author skillfully uses myth and history to explain the significance and purpose of the carvings. Particularly fascinating is a detailed account of the construction of a gargoyle.

Macaulay, David. **Castle.** Houghton Mifflin, 1977. 12–up.

The fine pen drawings and knowledge about architecture make this a treasure of information on medieval life. The thirteenth-century castle rises from page to page along with a nearby town. The details of the castle's interior are fascinating. 1978 Caldecott Honor Book.

Macaulay, David. **Unbuilding.** Houghton Mifflin, 1980. 10–up.

The dismantling and moving of the Empire State Building is the focus of this fictional account. There is much humor in the story, but the sketches, diagrams, and textual explanations of the demolition of a skyscraper are accurate. Outstanding illustrations.

Circus

Walt Disney Productions. **Disney's World of Adventure Presents the Circus Book.** Random House, 1978. 8–16.

A Walt Disney version, illustrated in color, of *Toby Tyler* begins this volume that immerses the reader in the realities and delights of the circus environment. Included are interesting articles on P. T. Barnum, the Lipizzaner Stallions, how to be a clown, chimpanzees, and a Mickey Mouse circus adventure story. All drawings and photographs are in color.

Hintz, Martin. **Circus Workin's.** Photographs by author. Julian Messner, 1980. 10–12.

Most readers wonder how the big circus tent is set up and how it is dismantled. Circus life in general is explained and the expertise of certain personnel needed for a successful circus is described. Clear photographs and text.

Krementz, Jill. **A Very Young Circus Flyer.** Photographs by author. Alfred A. Knopf, 1979. 10–up.

This large appealing book in the A Very Young . . . series features Armando, a nine-year-old aerialist of the Farfan Family. The reader is taken through his daily schedule of work and recreation and is informed of the many skills necessary for his art. Outstanding photographs.

Dance

Berger, Melvin. **The World of Dance.** S. G. Phillips, 1978. 10–up.

The exciting relationship of dance to geography, climate, and historical events is clearly and interestingly shown from primitive dances to the hustle. Illustrated with photographs and pen and ink copies of ancient drawings. Excellent for studies of various cultures and history.

Davis, Jesse. **Classics of the Royal Ballet.** Coward, McCann & Geoghegan, 1980. 10–up.

Stories of six ballets, including *Swan Lake, The Nutcracker,* and *The Sleeping Beauty,* are told via brief text and many stunning black and white photographs of the Royal Ballet's interpretations. A book to be enjoyed by itself or as a splendid introduction to a live performance.

Dell, Catherine. **The Magic of Ballet.** Rand McNally, 1979. 10–up.

The fascinating beauty and challenge of classical ballet is presented through its history, technique, training, and the stories of great ballets and ballet companies. The expertise of the text, vividly enhanced by colorful photographs and drawings, make this a helpful book of authentic information for anyone interested in dance.

Diamond, Donna, adapter. **Swan Lake.** Illus. by adapter. Holiday House, 1980. 8–12.

Odette, the exquisite swan maiden, is betrayed by her princely lover when he is tricked into mistaking the wicked Odile for his beloved. A composite adaptation from several Russian texts, this book is beautifully illustrated with large double-page spreads in misty, shadowy tones of gray and white.

Elliott, Donald. **Frogs and the Ballet.** Illus. Clinton Arrowood. Gambit, 1979. 8–12.

Frogs doing pliés, entrechats, pas de deux, and pirouettes? Astonishingly, they are, in this improbable exposition of the five basic ballet positions, plus various steps and attitudes. The splendid illustrations and witty text will amuse and instruct balletomanes of all ages. A book to be shared.

Hansen, Rosanna. **The Fairy Tale Book of Ballet.** Photographs by Martha Swope. Grosset & Dunlap, 1980. 8–up.

Three best-loved classical fairy tale ballets are retold here and vividly illustrated with pictures by a famed photographer of famous dancers: American Ballet Theatre's productions of *Swan Lake* and *The Sleeping Beauty,* and the New York City Ballet's *The Nutcracker.* Good for class use with recordings of the ballet music.

Isadora, Rachel. **My Ballet Class.** Greenwillow Books, 1980. 6–9.

A beginning ballet student goes from the dressing room to class, through the technical routines and movements in the dance studio, and happily meets Father afterwards. She describes the happy feelings and the hard work. Full-page drawings are true to good ballet technique.

Jaffe, Evan. **Illustrated Ballet Dictionary.** Illus. Phyllis Lerner. Harvey House, Publishers, 1979. 8–12.

Famous dancers, ballet companies, and techniques fill this special subject dictionary. A short history of the ballet that precedes the alphabetical listings, coupled with the black and white illustrations, makes this a good reference source.

Krementz, Jill. **A Very Young Dancer.** Alfred A. Knopf, 1976. 7–10.

One of a series of books that focuses on a young person pursuing the arts, this gives a comprehensive look at the world of ballet. Written in the first person with minimal text, the photodocumentary stresses the pain and joy of a young girl chosen to dance with the New York City Ballet.

Merry, Suzanne. **Dancer.** Photographs by John Running. Charles Scribner's Sons, 1980. 12–up.

The true story of Celeste Jabczenski and her current life as a bright young trainee on scholarship with the junior performing ballet company Joffrey II is both informative and inspiring. Excellent photographs.

Thomas, William E. **So You Want to Be a Dancer.** Photographs by Ray Bengston and Machal Elam. Julian Messner, 1979. 6–up.

Nearly fifty brief topics directly related to the training and career of a show business dancer are interestingly discussed. Fascinating full-page photographs for the young reader. Helpful in career studies.

Walker, Katherine Sorley, and Joan Butler. **Ballet for Boys and Girls.** Prentice-Hall, 1979. 8–12.

This wide-ranging examination of ballet includes basic techniques, history, stories of individual ballets and performers, plus interesting details of backstage life. Good choice of black and white photographs.

Drama

Burr, Lonnie. **Two for the Show: Great Comedy Teams.** Julian Messner, 1979. 12–up.

Packed with information, this book describes the comedic elements that are unique to outstanding American comedy teams. Much history of American entertainment from vaudeville, radio, film, and television is contained in the engrossing chapters that move from Laurel and Hardy to Cheech and Chong. Numerous humor routines are excerpted. Includes glossary, chronology, bibliography.

Cahn, William, and Rhoda Cahn. **The Great American Comedy Scene.** Julian Messner, 1978. 12–up.

This survey of American comedy from the colonial theatre of 1700s to the present day introduces the highlights and headliners from minstrel shows, vaudeville, stage shows, radio, movies, and television. It also gives a brief introduction to and analysis of the changing concept of comedy. Lavishly illustrated with photographs.

Edelson, Edward. **Great Animals of the Movies.** Doubleday, 1980. 10–up.

A book for animal movie fans. Not only is there a behind-the-scenes peek at Lassie, Flipper, and Morris the Cat, but also a section on how they are selected, trained, and pampered. Numerous successes and fiascos are recounted in detail. Black and white photos.

Edelson, Edward. **Tough Guys and Gals of the Movies.** Doubleday, 1978. 12–up.

For young film buffs, this survey of movie actors from Bogart and Robinson to Hackman and Pacino provides a fast-paced overview of the "tough" hero tradition in films. One chapter is devoted to women. Numerous black and white movie stills.

Geis, Darlene, editor. **Walt Disney's Treasury of Children's Classics.** Harry N. Abrams, Publishers, 1978. 4–7.

Snow White, Pinnochio, Brer Rabbit, Bambi, The Lady and the Tramp, and twelve other classic and contemporary tales that were made into animated films by Walt Disney Studios are told. Each story is followed by an article telling how the movie was made. Beautifully illustrated with movie and studio scenes.

Quackenbush, Robert. **Movie Monsters and Their Masters: The Birth of the Horror Film.** Illus. by author. Albert Whitman, 1980. 8–12.

The text traces fifty years of horror films from Edison's *Frankenstein* to Hitchcock's *The Birds*. Eerie green, black, and white illustrations carry out the spirit of the text.

Simon, Seymour. **Creatures from Lost Worlds.** J. B. Lippincott, 1979. 10–12.

Imaginary worlds and creatures from Swift's Lilliput to Godzilla are discussed with deft humor. Authors mentioned include Edgar Rice Burroughs, H. G. Wells, Jules Verne, and Arthur Conan Doyle. Creatures from television and movies are depicted. Many black and white movie stills.

Fine Arts

Behrens, June. **Looking at Beasties.** Childrens Press, 1977. 7–10.

The fifteen glossy, colored reproductions of animals are simply explained. The time period for each picture and brief remarks about the artist are included. Animals portrayed are ibis, monster head on the prow of a Viking ship, serpent, lion, leopard, and others. Informational with a pleasing format.

Behrens, June. **Looking at Children.** Childrens Press, 1977. 7–10.

This fine collection introduces readers to famous paintings of children. The meaningful introductory statement tells how artists express their ideas and the media they use. Children of the past and present are brought to life in the glossy, colored reproductions. One of a series of art books.

Cober, Alan E. **Cober's Choice.** E. P. Dutton, 1979. 8–12.

An artist's sketchbook provides his personal and often humorous insight into the characteristics of such creatures as the bat, crow, falcon, skate, mandrill, skunk, rattlesnake, and others. Some of these are drawn from life, others are stuffed, and one is in a state of decay.

Fine, Joan. **I Carve Stone.** Photographs by David Anderson. Thomas Y. Crowell, 1979. 10–up.

Clear photographs and text supply a step-by-step account of changing a 300-pound marble block into an artistic sculpture. Sketches are made, clay forms are created, and finally the chisel is used. Available materials are listed for children who want to do their own carving.

Glubok, Shirley. **The Art of the Comic Strip.** Macmillan Publishing, 1979. 8–12.

The history of the modern comic strip makes interesting reading. The examples of early cartooning techniques give the reader an opportunity to see the progress in design, characters, and story lines. The book is an efficient reference and a fun experience.

Glubok, Shirley. **The Art of the Vikings.** Macmillan Publishing, 1978. 10–up.

History, folklore, and customs of the Norsemen are inextricably woven with explanations of their many treasures preserved today in metal and wood. Beautiful jewelry reflects the level of their cultural advancement. The information provided will complement the study of the Vikings. Photographs capture the strength of their art.

Goffstein, M. B. **An Artist.** Harper & Row, Publishers, 1980. 9–up.

Beautiful watercolor illustrations depict an artist trying to recreate God's world on canvas by using his talent with paints.

Henry, Marguerite. **The Illustrated Marguerite Henry.** Rand McNally, 1980. 8–12.

The horse stories of Marguerite Henry have always been a great favorite. This book pays tribute to the fine illustrations that helped her books come alive through the pictures. Wesley Dennis, Robert Lougheed, Rich Rudish, and Lynd Ward are the artists who are described. A very beautiful edition.

Holme, Bryan. **Creatures of Paradise: Pictures to Grow Up With.** Oxford University Press, 1980. 12–up.

A collection of color and black and white illustrations of animals as portrayed by famous painters throughout the ages. Artists included range from Chagall and Dürer to Kate Greenaway and Beatrix Potter. A companion volume is *Enchanted World.* Excellent introduction to art appreciation.

Price, Christine. **Arts of Clay.** Charles Scribner's Sons, 1977. 10–up.

The clay artwork of people throughout the world is traced from ancient times. Each pot is appealingly illustrated with pencil drawings. A helpful picture map locates the various types of pottery.

Proddow, Penelope. **Art Tells a Story: The Bible.** Doubleday, 1979. 10–12.

Biblical stories pave the way to appreciation of fine works of art representing a variety of art forms. Artists include Corot, William Blake, Ben Shahn, and Tintoretto. Legends of creation, Noah, Isaac, Jacob, Esther, and the Queen of Sheba are the inspiration for six of the stories. Photographs.

Proddow, Penelope. **Art Tells a Story: Greek and Roman Myths.** Doubleday, 1979. 10–12.

This is a new approach to mythology to help children appreciate literature and art. Twelve works of art by different artists that span the centuries depict the stories. The reader is introduced to different art forms including pottery, pen and ink, and oils. Illustrated with color and black and white photographs.

Music

Folksongs and Ballads

Bierhorst, John. **A Cry from the Earth: Music of the North American Indians.** Four Winds Press, 1979. 10–up.

A collection of Native American music that encompasses historical and regional differences. The book describes the creating of various types of songs and the differences between American Indian and European music. This is a fascinating and informative research guide that includes pronunciation aides, bibliography, source list, and an index to songs by area and tribe.

Gauch, Patricia Lee. **On to Widecombe Fair.** Illus. Trina Schart Hyman. G. P. Putnam's Sons, 1978. 10–up.

A glorious spirit of fun enticed people of eighteenth-century Devonshire to the annual Widecombe Fair. Seven old gentlemen *had* to get there, so they borrowed Tom Pearse's old grey mare, intending to return her. The tale is based on a folk song and on conversations with contemporary Widecombe dwellers.

Glazer, Tom. **Do Your Ears Hang Low? Fifty More Musical Fingerplays.** Illus. Mila Lazarevich. Doubleday, 1980. 3–5.

Fifty familiar and brand new fingerplays with piano arrangements and guitar chords are collected by a popular folksinger. The easy-to-read music and delightful illustrations provide hours of fun for young children.

John, Timothy, and Peter Hankey, editors. **The Great Song Book.** Illus. Tomi Ungerer. Doubleday, 1978. All ages.

Unknown and well-known traditional songs, with guitar chords, are divided into eight main sections ranging from songs of dance and play to nursery rhymes. The remarkable full-color illustrations make this a look-along as well as sing-along choice.

Langstaff, John, compiler. **Hot Cross Buns and Other Old Street Cries.** Illus. Nancy Winslow Parker. Atheneum, 1978. All ages.

This handsomely illustrated collection of old English street cries provides words and music with appeal for singers of all ages. A brief essay introduces the thirty street cries, some of which have been specified for singing at the same time: hot cross buns, strawberries, old rags for sale.

O'Hare, Colette, compiler. **What Do You Feed Your Donkey On? Rhymes from a Belfast Childhood.** Illus. Jenny Rodwell. William Collins Publishers, 1978. 7–10.

Skip-rope songs and street chants with a distinctly Irish vocabulary and flavor make up this handsome book. Notes at the end give some definitions. Both the full-color and black and white illustrations are haunting in their beauty and stylized suggestion of a child's eye view of Belfast life.

Raphael, Elaine, and Don Bolognese, adapters. **Turnabout.** Illus. by adapters. Viking Press, 1980. 7–10.

The old folksong about the husband and wife who decide to trade jobs for a day and end up being happy to return to their old jobs is delightfully adapted; in this case, the two are bears. Block print illustrations in orange, brown, and black are striking. Music is included.

Zemach, Margot, retold by. **Hush, Little Baby.** Illus. by reteller. E. P. Dutton, 1976. 3–5.

A distinguished illustrator gives an old lullaby a fresh interpretation after singing it to her own child for a year and a half. The familiar vignettes can be read aloud or sung; the music is included. Tempera illustrations depict the Victorian setting.

Instruments and Styles

Bailey, Bernadine. **Bells, Bells, Bells.** Dodd, Mead, 1978. 8–12.

"They have neither speech nor language, but their sound is gone out to all nations." From 4000 BC to our July 4, 1976 bell extravaganza, text and black and white photos cover bellringing, handbells, carillons, and famous bells like Liberty and Big Ben. Interesting, fact-filled book.

Busnar, Gene. **It's Rock'n'Roll.** Julian Messner, 1979. 6–12.

A fine and fairly complete chronological history of the music explosion of the fifties. The rock'n'roll artists are discussed and their contributions explained. The book has photographs of many groups along with lists of their songs. Index.

Prokofiev, Sergei. **Peter and the Wolf.** Illus. Erna Voigt. David R. Godine, Publisher, 1980. 8–12.

Outstanding illustrations grace this version of the classic musical story. The left page carries the story in large type with an instrument pictured next to a line of music. The right page is a large full-color scene of the adventure. A beautiful book.

Schaaf, Peter. **The Violin Close Up.** Photographs by author. Four Winds Press, 1980. All ages.

This stunning black and white photographic essay illustrating the parts of a violin and their relationship to each other will certainly enhance any child's appreciation of both the visual and tonal beauty of the stringed instruments.

Segovia, Andrés, and George Mendoza. **Segovia: My Book of the Guitar.** William Collins Publishers, 1979. 8–12.

Andrés Segovia shares his knowlege and techniques of playing the guitar for the beginner. Beautiful color photographs and excellent black and white photos and diagrams make this book a superior learning text. Also included are a dictionary of musical terms and thirteen pieces of music written by great guitar composers.

Plays for Children

Alexander, Sue. **Whatever Happened to Uncle Albert? And Other Puzzling Plays.** Illus. Tom Huffman. Clarion Books, 1980. 9–12.

These four original plays, each a mystery, are great fun. One play concerns a werewolf, one is a take-off on Sherlock Holmes, one a courtroom drama, and one a funny detective tale. Each requires few props. Simple enough to encourage children to act them out, funny enough to keep the interest of the audience.

Davis, Ossie. **Escape to Freedom.** Viking Press, 1978. 10–up.

This play about the young Frederick Douglass captures the drama, cruelty, and injustices of his early life. Eventually he escapes to freedom in the North and becomes an advisor to Abraham Lincoln. He was the first black to hold a diplomatic post, and one of the first to speak for women's rights.

Kraus, Joanna Halpert. **The Dragon Hammer and the Tale of Oniroku: Two Plays from the Far East.** Illus. Marisabina Russo. New Plays Books, 1977. 7–10.

These plays are designed as dramatic vehicles for children's groups and as an introduction to the art of reading plays. Simple production techniques suggested; charming illustrations can be helpful to young producers. Notes for parents and teachers included.

Mahlmann, Lewis, and David Cadwalader Jones. **Folk Tale Plays for Puppets.** Plays, 1980. 8–up.

Thirteen folktales from around the world have been adapted for use as puppet plays. The authors include production notes on what kinds of puppets to use, types of costuming, sets, props, lighting, and sound effects for each play. Includes The Gingerbread Boy, Baba Yaga, and others.

Young, Ed, and Hilary Beckett. **The Rooster's Horns: A Chinese Puppet Play to Make and Perform.** Illus. Ed Young. William Collins Publishers, 1978. 4–7.

The pourquoi tale tells why the rooster crows each morning and digs for worms. Directions are given for preparing and presenting a shadow puppet play. Published in cooperation with the U.S. Committee for UNICEF.

Additional Arts Books

Aliki. *Go Tell Aunt Rhody.* Macmillan Publishing, 1974. 4–7.
Audsley, James. *The Book of Ballet.* Rev. ed. Frederick Warne, 1968. 12–16.
Baylor, Byrd. *Sometimes I Dance Mountains.* Illus. Bill Sears and Ken Longtemps. Charles Scribner's Sons, 1973. 6–9.
Boni, Margaret Bradford. *Fireside Book of Folk Songs.* Arr. for piano by Norman Lloyd. Illus. Alice and Martin Provensen. Simon & Schuster, 1947. 10–16.
Borten, Helen. *Do You See What I See?* Abelard-Schuman, 1959. 5–8.
Carlson, Bernice Wells. *Act It Out.* Illus. Laszlo Matulay. Abingdon Press, 1956. 8–12.
Chappell, Warren, adapter. *The Nutcracker.* Alfred A. Knopf, 1958. 8–12.
Chute, Marchette. *Stories from Shakespeare.* World, 1956. 12–16.
Finch, Christopher. *The Art of Walt Disney: From Mickey Mouse to the Magic Kingdom.* Harry N. Abrams, Publishers, 1975. All ages.
Garson, Eugenia, and Herbert Haufrecht, eds.. *The Laura Ingalls Wilder Songbook.* Illus. Garth Williams. Harper & Row, Publishers, 1968. 9–up.
Glubok, Shirley. *The Art of the New American Nation.* Macmillan Publishing, 1972. 8–12.
Hawkinson, John. *Pastels Are Great!* Albert Whitman, 1968. 7–12.
Hofsinde, Robert. *Indian Music Makers.* William Morrow, 1967. 7–11.
Langstaff, John, adapter. *Frog Went A-Courtin'.* Illus. Feodor Rojankovsky. Harcourt Brace Jovanovich, 1955.
Langstaff, John. *The Swapping Boy.* Illus. Beth and Joe Krush. Harcourt Brace Jovanovich, 1960. 9–12.
Macaulay, David. *Cathedral: The Story of Its Construction.* Houghton Mifflin, 1973. 9–12.
Malcolmson, Anne. *The Song of Robin Hood.* Music arranged by Grace Castagnetta. Illus. Virginia Burton. Houghton Mifflin, 1947. 9–up.
Mills, Alan. *The Hungry Goat.* Illus. Abner Graboff. Rand McNally, 1964. All ages.
Price, Christine. *The Story of Moslem Art.* E. P. Dutton, 1964. 10–14.
Prokofieff, Sergei. *Peter and the Wolf.* Illus. Frans Haacken. Franklin Watts, 1962. 5–9.
Seeger, Ruth C. *American Folksongs for Children.* Illus. Barbara Cooney. Doubleday, 1948. All ages.
Sendak, Maurice. *Really Rosie: Starring the Nutshell Kids.* Music by Carole King. Harper & Row, Publishers, 1975. 8–up.
Spier, Peter. *The Fox Went Out on a Chilly Night.* Doubleday, 1961. 4–up.
Spilka, Arnold. *Paint All Kinds of Pictures.* Henry Z. Walck, 1963. 7–12.
Zemach, Harve. *Mommy, Buy Me a China Doll.* Illus. Margot Zemach. Farrar, Straus & Giroux, 1975. 5–8.

Language

History of Language

Arnold, Oren. **What's in a Name: Famous Brand Names.** Julian Messner, 1979. 8–12.

The first Frisbee was a pie plate from the Frisbee bakery. A man took a long lunch hour and overmixed some soap and the slogan, "It Floats!" was born. The author explains the naming and development of such products as the zipper, Levis, and Chiclets.

Glazer, Tom. **All about Your Name, Anne.** Illus. Demi. Doubleday, 1978. 8–12.

A delightful collection of information about such famous Annes as Raggedy Ann, Princess Anne, Annie Laurie, and Anne Morrow Lindbergh. The book includes a recipe for Potatoes Anna, a jump rope rhyme for Anne, and a "Song for Anne," written by the author. One of the All About Your Name series.

Greenfeld, Howard. **Summer Is Icumen In: Our Ever-Changing Language.** Crown Publishers, 1978. 10–up.

Using brief chapters this book gives an interesting introduction to the history of the English language. Topics such as early linguistic roots, the influence of the dictionary, altered word meanings, euphemisms, and slang are included.

Hazen, Barbara Shook. **Last, First, Middle and Nick: All about Names.** Illus. Sam Weissman. Prentice-Hall, 1979. 8–12.

Names have interesting stories and this book is packed full of short, fascinating bits of information about all kinds of names. Historical studies, coincidental quirks, and structural forms are discussed. Nearly every page has a humorous drawing or decoration. An excellent book for an interest center.

Schwartz, Alvin, compiler. **Chin Music: Tall Talk and Other Talk.** Illus. John O'Brien. J. B. Lippincott, 1979. 8–12.

From A to Y, examples of folk idioms active from 1815 to 1950 are given. Chin music is what people say when they sit around and talk. Many words are made up, such as "a snitch" for a small amount and "a do-little" for a lazy person. Glossary and source notes are useful.

Steckler, Arthur. **101 Words and How They Began.** Illus. James Flora. Doubleday, 1979. 7–10.

Common words from our everyday language and their derivatives are carefully explained and illustrated. An enticing book to enrich the vocabulary as the reader discovers that words like "hamburger" and "sandwich" were named after real persons. Ninety-nine other interesting facts.

Weiss, Ann E. **What's That You Said? How Words Change.** Illus. Jim Arnosky. Harcourt Brace Jovanovich, 1980. 7–10.

This introduction to the origin of common words is cleverly presented and written for the young reader. Used for enrichment or independent study, this book can help the student learn how the meanings of words have changed over the centuries.

Vocabulary

Banchek, Linda. **Snake In, Snake Out.** Illus. Elaine Arnold. Thomas Y. Crowell, 1978. 6–9.

Humorous and detailed drawings of an elderly lady, her snake, and her parrot illustrate the words "in, out, on, up, over, off, down, and under." The author presents a unique way to teach prepositions and provide fun in practicing reading.

Basil, Cynthia. **Breakfast in the Afternoon.** Illus. Janet McCaffery. William Morrow, 1979. 7–10.

Compound words are presented in guessing-game fashion; the answers are given when the page is flipped. More compound words are pictured than are mentioned in the text, adding to the challenge of the book. Bright pink, orange, and purple illustrations put this book in a superstar category.

Halsey, William D., and Christopher G. Morris, editors. **The Magic World of Words: A Very First Dictionary.** Macmillan Publishing, 1977. 6–9.

This first dictionary for early readers has nearly 1500 words and 500 brightly colored illustrations. A special alphabet page begins each letter section. Excellent format.

Hanson, Joan. **Plurals.** Lerner Publications, 1979. 7–10.

The rule for forming plurals is given in three sentences in the introduction. As the reader turns the pages, on the left page is an example of the singular form and on the right page is the same word in plural form. Humorous sketches add to the visual appeal. Also recommended is *Possessives: Words That Show Ownership.*

Krensky, Stephen. **My First Dictionary.** Illus. George Ulrich. Houghton Mifflin, 1980. 5–7.

This new addition to the American Heritage Dictionary line, includes over 1,600 main entry words, including the 500 most frequently used in children's reading materials. Every word used in the definitions is entered in the volume. Sample sentences illustrate words in contexts and further clarify their meanings. Full-color illustrations.

Kudrna, C. Imbior. **Two-Way Words.** Illus. by author. Abingdon Press, 1980. 6–9.

Common homophones and homographs are simply defined in this little picture book. The black and white drawings further aid comprehension.

Lippman, Peter. **Peter Lippman's One and Only Wacky Word Book.** Golden Press, 1979. 8–12.

These busy, labeled illustrations are designed to make middle graders giggle. An "Ugh Page" pictures a moldy cucumber, fish guts, and a dead mouse. Other pages detail the junk in a giant's pocket and CB radio talk.

Maestro, Betsy. **Busy Day: A Book of Action Words.** Illus. Giulio Maestro. Crown Publishers, 1978. 6–9.

Colorful pictures tell the story of an elephant and a clown who go through their busy day at the circus. Each page portrays the activity of the single word printed on it. The word is always a verb in gerund form: waking, marching, waving. Useful for models during language studies.

Miller, Carolyn Handler. **Illustrated T.V. Dictionary.** Illus. Michael Sporn. Harvey House, Publishers, 1980. 8–up.

Definitions of numerous TV terms from ABC to zoom are presented with clever black and white illustrations and easy-to-read text. A brief history of television and an explanation of the growth and popularity of this medium are also given.

Rosenbloom, Joseph. **Daffy Dictionary: Fun Abridged Definitions from Aardvark to Zuider Zee.** Illus. Joyce Behr. Sterling Publishing, 1977. 10–12.

This humorous, yet meaningful language skills book supplies numerous opportunities for development through word play. It provides the introduction to and practice for using more difficult dictionaries. Example: candidate (KAN-di-dayt), a fruit with a sugar coating (candied date). Black and white cartoon-like illustrations and index.

Writing

Barrol, Grady. **The Little Book of Anagrams.** Illus. Liz Vietor. Harvey House, Publishers, 1978. 8–12.

Children enjoy word anagrams where they rearrange letters in words to make new words. This book attempts something more complex, sentence anagrams. "A decimal point" can be reordered to read, "I'm a dot in place." "Hibernate" becomes "Bear's in." Useful for encouraging students to write their own word plays.

Bernstein, Joanne E. **Fiddle with a Riddle: Write Your Own Riddles.** Illus. Giulio Maestro. E. P. Dutton, 1979. 8–12.

This excellent writing enrichment book discusses eight basic ways of developing riddles. Teachers may despair about the finished products, but the writing process is what's important in this book. Very useful ideas; humorously illustrated.

Cassedy, Sylvia. **In Your Own Words: A Beginner's Guide to Writing.** Doubleday, 1979. 12–up.

A good source book for students who wish to express themselves through the medium of writing. The author addresses the areas of fiction, nonfiction, and poetry and suggests that skill in writing can be developed by attending to specific detail.

Greenfeld, Howard. **Books: From Writer to Reader.** Crown Publishers, 1976. 8–12.

Budding young authors, as well as those just curious about the techniques of bookmaking, are fascinated with the information found in this comprehensive volume. People and processes are emphasized, from the author's first idea through the writing, editing, printing, and binding of the finished book.

Morrison, Bill. **Squeeze a Sneeze.** Houghton Mifflin, 1977. 6–9.

The rhyme-maker man, sitting under a tree, suggests putting words together into new and funny rhymes, such as "Can you tickle a pickle for a nickle?" This clever book helps to develop a feel for words and encourages experimentation.

Tarbox, Todd. **Imagine and Make Up Your Own Book.** Todd Tarbox Books, 1977. All ages.

Children's writing is juxtaposed with dramatic black and white photographs to create a striking and imaginative book that may inspire children to make their own books.

Additional Language Books

Asimov, Isaac. *Words from History.* Illus. William Barss. Houghton Mifflin, 1968. 9–up.

Basil, Cynthia. *Nailheads and Potato Eyes.* Illus. Janet McCaffery. William Morrow, 1976. 5–8.

Kohn, Bernice. *What a Funny Thing to Say.* Illus. R. O. Blackman. Dial Press, 1974. 9–12.

Ogg, Oscar. *The 26 Letters.* 2d ed. Thomas Y. Crowell, 1961. 12–up.

Crafts

Costume Making

Gates, Frieda. **Easy to Make Monster Masks and Disguises.** Harvey House, Publishers, 1979. 8–up.

Directions for a collection of monster masks from materials such as paper, cloth, boxes, foil, foam rubber, and straw are given. Black and white illustrations.

Meyer, Carolyn. **Mask Magic.** Illus. Melanie Gaines Arwin. Harcourt Brace Jovanovich, 1978. 10–up.

Historical lore of masks as instruments of magic and celebration is interestingly told. Organized around seasons and holidays, the book can be used to bring memorable experiences into the lives of children. Directions for creating masks are explicit and clearly illustrated with ink drawings so that students can follow them independently.

Mooser, Stephen. **Monster Fun.** Illus. Dana Herkelrath. Julian Messner, 1979. 8–12.

Easy-to-follow directions using simple materials show the reader how to be transformed into a monster. Hints on how to throw a monster bash and transform a house into a chamber of horrors are given. Photographs and black and white illustrations.

Schnurnberger, Lynn Edelman. **Kings, Queens, Knights & Jesters: Making Medieval Costumes.** Illus. Alan Robert Showe. Photographs by Barbara Brooks and Pamela Hort. Harper & Row, Publishers, 1978. 10–up.

Published in association with the Metropolitan Museum of Art, this book provides clear, workable instructions for making medieval costumes. Handsomely illustrated with photographs of reproductions of museum treasures and children making and wearing costumes, it is a visual introduction to the world of the middle ages.

Sichel, Marion. **Costume Reference 7: The Edwardians.** Illus. by author. Plays, 1978. 12–up.

This volume is excellent resource material for students of costume design. Many details are included and the costume plates are excellent. Glossary, bibliography and index. A companion book is *Costume Reference 8: 1918-1939.*

Drawing, Painting, Printing

Ames, Lee J. **Draw 50 Buildings and Other Structures.** Doubleday, 1980. 10-12.

Step-by-step illustrations include the Empire State Building, the tower of Pisa, the Parthenon, an American Indian tepee, the Brooklyn Bridge, and a native house in Sumatra. The drawings are ambitious, but worth the effort. Based on the theory that "mimicry is prerequisite to creativity," this is one in a popular series of how-to-draw books. Also recommended are *Draw 50 Famous Cartoons, Draw 50 Famous Faces,* and *Draw 50 Dinosaurs.*

Emberley, Ed. **Ed Emberley's Big Orange Drawing Book.** Little, Brown, 1980. 8-up.

The author, in his unique style, has written another fun, easy drawing book with step-by-step instructions on how to draw people and animals using line and circle combinations. Illustrations in black and orange appropriately show off the numerous Halloween drawings.

Emberley, Ed. **Ed Emberley's Great Thumbprint Drawing Book.** Little, Brown, 1977. 7-10.

In a format made familiar by the artist's other drawing books, sketches show how simple thumbprints can be made into a variety of faces, animals, and other objects by adding lines, squiggles, and circles. Easy-to-follow directions and many examples encourage children to explore the technique.

Hawkinson, John. **Pat, Swish, Twist and the Story of Patty Swish.** Photographs by Sue Long. Albert Whitman, 1978. 6-up.

The first part of this book presents watercolor pictures of a small animal named Patty Swish. The reader may supply the words to the story. The second part gives information about materials for painting and demonstrates very clearly the technique of pat, swish, and twist with watercolors.

Pettit, Florence H. **The Stamp-Pad Printing Book.** Illus. by author. Photographs by Robert M. Pettit. Thomas Y. Crowell, 1979. 10-12.

Greeting cards, wrapping paper, stationery, and bookmarks are but a few items that can be created from inexpensive materials using a stamp pad and paper. The clear text along with photographs and diagrams combine to make this a handy, entertaining source for home or school. Index and sources of supplies included.

Rauch, Hans-Georg. **The Lines Are Coming.** Charles Scribner's Sons, 1978. 7–up.

Aspiring artists will enjoy the black and white drawings that demonstrate how simple lines, used in various combinations, make pictures. Perspective, shape, and shadow tell a story. Focus is on the power of the pen stroke.

Savage, Lee. **Aldo's Doghouse: Drawing in Perspective.** Coward, McCann & Geoghegan, 1978. 7–10.

The principles of drawing in perspective are illustrated in a step-by-step manner. Children will be interested in practicing the easy steps shown in this cartoon story. Home or school use.

Warshaw, Jerry. **The Funny Drawing Book.** Photographs by Dick Masek. Albert Whitman, 1978. 7–10.

Artistic shapes are given as a basis from which to draw. Attention is called to the fact that these basic shapes can be seen everywhere one looks. Step-by-step drawings are provided and many clear photos.

Paper Crafts

Borja, Robert, and Corinne Borja. **Making Chinese Papercuts.** Albert Whitman, 1980. 10–12.

The history of Chinese papercutting is told with beautiful illustrations of various intricate papercuts. Instructions are given for several beginning projects that the reader can try.

Comins, Jeremy. **Vans to Build from Cardboard.** Illus. by author. Lothrop, Lee & Shepard Books, 1978. 8–12.

Just the right book for the amateur builder; gives a brief history of van development and includes a metric conversion chart, suggested readings, and an index. Step-by-step directions for twelve types are given for building and modifying the basic cardboard van. Drawings and photographs clarify the text.

Hawkesworth, Eric. **Paper Cutting: Making All Kinds of Paper Shapes and Figures.** Illus. by author and Margaret Hawkesworth. S. G. Phillips, 1977. 10–up.

Through words and diagrams, directions are given for producing with simple materials two- and three-dimensional objects to use in storytelling. Included are the texts for nine traditional tales to tell.

Hou-tien, Cheng. **Scissor Cutting for Beginners.** Holt, Rinehart and Winston, 1978. 8–up.

Paper cutting, a simple and unique Chinese art form, is introduced in a very clear way with concise directions and illustrations. Each letter and number is shown in a series of easy-to-follow steps. A practical book for school or home.

Linsley, Leslie. **Decoupage for Young Crafters.** Photographs by Jon Aron. E. P. Dutton, 1977. 7–11.

Paint, paste, cutout paper designs, and varnish are the everyday materials needed to try one's hand at the craft of decoupage. Nine projects are shown in clear step-by-step photographs.

Norvell, Flo Ann Hedley. **The Great Big Box Book.** Photographs by Richard W. Mitchell. Thomas Y. Crowell, 1979. 10–up.

Sixteen suggestions for making playhouses, tepees, cannons, walkie-talkie helmets, and other play items are clearly described in this attractive craft book. Photographs and diagrams make the step-by-step directions clear to the builder. Children need assistance with the more difficult constructions.

Weiss, Harvey. **Working with Cardboard and Paper.** Illus. by author. Addison-Wesley Publishing, 1978. 10–12.

This useful book for older children introduces cardboard and its creative uses. How to cut, bend, and join cardboard is clearly shown in drawings and photographs. The last chapter explains how paper is made. A helpful tool for class projects.

Toy Making

Bourke, Linda. **Making Soft Dinos: A Dinosaur Craft Book.** Illus. Russell Burbank. Harvey House, Publishers, 1980. 10–12.

How to make dinosaurs from material or paper is presented with numerous illustrations. Clear and detailed text leads the skilled crafter through the somewhat intricate steps in making these delightful creatures.

Löfgren, Ulf. **Swedish Toys, Dolls and Gifts You Can Make Yourself.** William Collins, Publishers, 1978. 8–up.

Beautiful, quality handicrafts for which the Swedish people are noted are clearly illustrated in color. Background notes are supplied along with simple and clear directions for making the objects. Christmas, Easter, and other seasonal events are included. Many projects could be correlated with the study of Swedish folklore.

Wrigley, Elsie. **Soft Toys.** Illus. by author. Frederick Warne, 1977. 8–12.

Clear instructions are given for making simple soft toys from pieces of material or scraps of heavy plastic. The simple drawings picturing each step of the projects encourage readers to try this craft.

Woodcrafts

Herda, D. J., and Judy Bock Herda. **Carpentry for Kids.** Illus. William Jaber. Julian Messner, 1980. 10–up.

This concise guide containing eleven projects gives basic information about woodworking materials, hand and power tools, fasteners, and finishes. The book issues a safety warning and advises adult supervision. A good beginner's guide.

Torre, Frank D. **Woodworking for Kids.** Doubleday, 1978. 10–12.

This book discusses basic tools available in most homes and how to use them safely for woodworking and wood finishing. Step-by-step directions and plenty of photographs guide the beginner in simple projects. Included are ecology boxes, checkerboards, planters, and chopping blocks.

Weiss, Peter. **Scrap Wood Craft.** Illus. Sally Gralla. Lothrop, Lee & Shepard Books, 1977. 10–12.

The care and use of basic wood crafting tools is given and many interesting projects are suggested using scrap wood. Although the author emphasizes using wood scraps, the text serves as an excellent how-to-do-it book for beginning serious woodworkers.

Various Handicrafts

Arnold, Susan Riser. **Eggshells to Objects: A New Approach to Egg Craft.** Illus. by author. Holt, Rinehart and Winston, 1979. 10–12.

Craft artists who like to make decorations and homemade gifts can assemble the simple materials needed, follow the readable directions, and design their own eggshell art. Illustrations clarify the text. A variety of patterns is supplied. Index.

Berry, Roland. **Easy to Make Contraptions.** Harvey House, Publishers, 1978. 8–12.

After suggestions are given for finding needed materials, more than fifty interesting contraptions are described in clear, concise language. Helpful diagrams assist the project maker. Practice in metric system measurement is provided. Supervision not necessary.

Cramblit, Joella, and Jo Ann Loebel. **Flowers Are for Keeping: How to Dry Flowers and Make Gifts and Decorations.** Julian Messner, 1979. 10–12.

Flower lovers can enjoy the products of their gardens all year round with the many helpful suggestions offered in this book. How to dry and preserve flowers and other plants for bouquets and arrangements is discussed in text and illustrated with photographs and clear drawings. Practical homemade gift suggestions.

Crook, Beverly Courtney. **Invite a Bird to Dinner: Simple Feeders You Can Make.** Illus. Tom Huffman. Lothrop, Lee & Shepard Books, 1978. 8–12.

Instructions for constructing various types of bird feeders are given with sound suggestions for ease of building and for safety features. Some fine recipes are included and many terms and types of foods are defined. Clever informative drawings enhance this very practical and interesting book.

Feiden, Karen L. **Basket Weaving.** Illus. Sandra Little. Emerson Books, 1979. 10–up.

The traditional craft of basket weaving is explained and directions for some simple, practical, and decorative objects are given. Explanations of tools, supplies, and the unique properties of weaving materials are also included. Index, bibliography, and sources listed.

Fisher, Timothy. **Huts, Hovels & Houses.** Illus. Kathleen Kolb. Addison-Wesley Publishing, 1977. 10–12.

For budding builders and/or architects, this book gives directions on how to build houses made of cans, milk cartons, newspaper logs, snow, sod, and hay bales, among others. Windmills, greenhouses, and solar heating techniques are briefly discussed. Familiarity with some building terms would be helpful. Useful in gifted programs.

The Great Big Golden Make It & Do It Book. Golden Press, 1980. 7–up.

A craft book with something to do every day of the year includes magic tricks, games, puzzles, nature crafts, hobbies, art crafts, and science experiments. Each activity is ranked according to difficulty. Clear illustrations and concise directions.

Haas, Carolyn, Ann Cole, and Barbara Naftzger. **Backyard Vacation: Outdoor Fun in Your Own Neighborhood.** Illus. Roland Rodegast. Little, Brown, 1980. 10–up.

This unique craft book contains activity ideas planned for your own backyard. Games, nature projects, neighborhood gatherings such as ice cream socials, outdoor theatre, and county fairs are described. Numerous drawings add to the text.

Hodgson, Mary Anne, and Josephine Ruth Paine. **Fast and Easy Needle-point.** Photographs by Michael Pitts and Richard Fowlkes. Double-day, 1978. 8–12.

A helpful book for beginners with clear directions, diagrams, and photographs. Basic needlepoint stitches are given and twelve simple, attractive patterns are shown. The reader is guided into original designs for practical objects such as belts, pillows, and tennis racquet covers.

Miller, Lynne. **Make Your Own Thing: Games, Puzzles, Gimmicks & Gifts.** Illus. William Hogarth. Julian Messner, 1979. 10–up.

This book of instructions on how to make games, puzzles, and handicrafts presents many interesting and simple projects for young people. Numerous drawings highlight the text.

Roche, P. K. **Dollhouse Magic: How to Make and Find Simple Dollhouse Furniture.** Illus. Richard Cuffari. Photographs by John Knott. Dial Press, 1977. 10–up.

Detailed directions and clear sketches guide the hobbyist in creating dollhouse furnishings from scrap materials found at home. A useful book for teachers, parents, and children.

Ross, Laura. **Scrap Puppets: How to Make and Move Them.** Illus. Frank Ross, Jr. Photographs by George Dec. Holt, Rinehart and Winston, 1978. 9–up.

Four basic kinds of puppets are described: hand, rod, shadow, and marionettes. Materials used are mainly scraps or inexpensive items. The thirteen ideas presented are clearly explained and illustrated with diagrams and photographs. Ideal suggestions for folktale characters.

Simons, Robin. **Recyclopedia: Games, Science Equipment, and Crafts from Recycled Materials.** Illus. by author. Houghton Mifflin, 1976. 8–12.

A sampling of projects using materials that are usually discarded from homes or businesses is shown. Innovative and resourceful items to make include water clocks, pinhole cameras, prints, tops, flip books, and others. Developed by the Boston Children's Museum.

Thomson, Neil, and Ruth Thomson. **Fairground Games to Make and Play.** Illus. Chris McEwan. J. B. Lippincott, 1978. 7–10.

All the fun and excitement of a fair are brought to the reader in the brightly colored pictures of this attractive handicraft book. There are step-by-step illustrations showing how to construct toys, games, and other fun activities. A rainy day book for home or school.

Wiseman, Ann. **Making Musical Things: Improvised Instruments.** Charles Scribner's Sons, 1979. 8–12.

An extensive array of musical instruments made from easily obtainable materials is described in words and illustrations. Many different skill levels are represented but younger children may need assistance. Resource list.

Zubrowski, Bernie. **A Children's Museum Activity Book: Bubbles.** Illus. Joan Drescher. Little, Brown, 1979. 8–12.

This fun guide to the art of blowing bubbles includes how to make gigantic and unusual bubbles and bubble sculpture. Other books in this series include *Milk Carton Blocks* and *Ball-Point Pens.*

Additional Crafts Books

Bank-Jensen, Thea. *Play with Paper.* Translated by Virginia Allen Jensen. Macmillan Publishing, 1962. 6–12.

Cummings, Richard. *101 Masks.* David McKay, 1968. 8–14.

D'Amato, Alex, and Janet D'Amato. *Colonial Crafts for You to Make.* Julian Messner, 1975. 10–up.

Hirsch, S. Carl. *Printing from a Stone: The Story of Lithography.* Viking Press, 1967. 10–16.

Marks, Mickey. *Collage.* Photos by David Rosenfeld. Dial Press, 1968. 7–up.

Samson, Anne. *Lines, Spines and Porcupines.* Doubleday, 1969. 5–9.

Seidelman, J. E., and Grace Mintoyne. *Creating with Clay.* Crowell-Collier, 1967. 9–12.

Simon, Seymour. *The Paper Airplane Book.* Illus. Byron Barton. Viking Press, 1971. 8–12.

Weiss, Harvey. *Clay, Wood, and Wire.* Illus. with classic sculpture selected by the author. Scott, Foresman, 1956. 10–14.

Hobbies

Cooking

Blanchet, Francoise, and Rinke Doornekamp. **What to Do with . . . an Egg.** Barron's Educational Series, 1979. 8–10.

The author, an inexperienced cook, shares simple and nourishing recipes with her readers. Sequential pictures with clearly worded directives tempt the young cook. Table of contents and safety precautions are included. Other recommended titles in the series are *What to Do with . . . a Potato* and *What to Do with . . . Fruit.*

Cauley, Lorinda Bryan. **Pease-Porridge Hot: A Mother Goose Cookbook.** Illus. by author. G. P. Putnam's Sons, 1977. 4–7.

Stories and nursery rhymes inspired recipes for this cookbook. The up-to-date recipes are nutritious and delightfully matched with full-page pen and ink illustrations. A glossary of cooking terms encourages vocabulary development. Use to extend enjoyment and understanding of well-known fairy tales and rhymes.

Cooper, Jane. **Love at First Bite: Snacks and Mealtime Treats the Quick and Easy Way.** Illus. Sherry Streeter. Alfred A. Knopf, 1977. 9–11.

The recipes and format of this large cookbook are very attractive and appealing. Helpful information is given at the beginning of the book on how to get started and what to do while cooking. Recipes are indexed.

Gretz, Susanna, and Alison Sage. **Teddybears Cookbook.** Illus. Susanna Gretz. Doubleday, 1978. 8–12.

Recipes for Mooncake, Surprise Eggs, and Celery Trees are illustrated by brightly colored cartoons of bears at work preparing each dish. The twenty-three easy-to-follow recipes include snacks, salads, drinks, and desserts. Measurements are given in ounces and pints rather than tablespoons and cups. A table of equivalents is included.

Huang, Paul C. **The Illustrated Step-by-Step Beginner's Cookbook.** Illus. Joseph Daniel Fiedler and Michael McQuaide. Four Winds Press, 1980. 12–up.

Here is an excellent cookbook for the beginner. The author presents his cooking methods in detailed step-by-step drawings. Recipes are included for breakfasts, lunches, and dinners, along with a variety of different cuisines including Japanese, Chinese, French, Italian, and South American.

Katzman, Susan Manlin. **For Kids Who Cook: Recipes and Treats.** Illus. Edward J. Kohorst. Holt, Rinehart and Winston, 1977. 9–12.

Clearly written recipes, designed to follow the calendar year, are fun to make, good to eat, and ensure success. Both metric and standard measurements are used and cooking terms are defined. Most of the recipes have child appeal; kitchen safety is stressed. Contains puzzles, cartoons, jokes, and riddles.

Paul, Aileen. **The Kids' Diet Cookbook.** Illus. John DeLulio. Doubleday, 1980. 10–up.

Excellent nutritional advice is offered in this diet cookbook for young people. Suggestions for losing weight, counting calories, and keeping records are included, along with good low-calorie recipes. Easy-to-follow format.

Siegel, Alice, and Margo McLoone. **The Herb & Spice Book for Kids.** Illus. Gwen Brodkin. Holt, Rinehart and Winston, 1978. 7–10.

A recipe format, readable instructions, and interesting ideas combine to make this how-to herb book fun and informative. Four sections include gifts to make, crazy cure-alls (including one for removing freckles), food recipes, and instructions for growing herbs. Useful for home or classroom experimenting.

Steinkoler, Ronnie. **A Jewish Cookbook for Children.** Illus. Sonja Glassman. Julian Messner, 1980. 8–12.

Jewish cooking has a long heritage and each holiday has food associated with it. The celebrations are introduced and handed-down recipes appropriate to each are given, all in accordance with dietary laws. Cooking, safety tips, and measurements tables are provided. Thirty-six cooking terms are defined. Black and white sketches.

Walker, Barbara M. **The Little House Cookbook: Frontier Foods from Laura Ingalls Wilder's Classic Stories.** Illus. Garth Williams. Harper & Row, Publishers, 1979. 8–12.

Useful as a supplement to the *Little House* series, this cookbook also stands well alone as an interesting collection of information on pioneer cooking. Recipes are given for pioneer foods discussed in the Wilder books. Many quotations from those books are used relating to the recipes.

Watson, Pauline, and editors of *Cricket Magazine.* **Cricket's Cookery.** Illus. Marylin Hafner. Random House, 1977. 7–10.

An excellent cookbook for young cooks. Simplified recipes and directions (many set to a familiar melody for singing) are given for food that is both tasty and nourishing. Illustrations are delightful and helpful.

Zweifel, Frances. **Pickle in the Middle and Other Easy Snacks.** Harper & Row, Publishers, 1979. 6–8.

Recipes in this cookbook intended for the primary aged child do not require using a stove or knives. Simple, easy directions for preparing snacks kids will enjoy using such favorites as bananas, bologna, chocolate, and peanuts are provided. Colorful, easy to read.

Gardening

Herda, D. J. **Vegetables in a Pot.** Illus. Kathy Fritz McBride. Julian Messner, 1979. 9–12.

Using black and white photos and sketches, all phases of growing vegetables in a pot are shown. From selecting the container and preparing the soil to actual planting and care, each step is carefully demonstrated. Germination time and expected growth of twenty-eight vegetables and addresses of seed catalog companies are given.

Johnsen, Jan. **Gardening without Soil.** J. B. Lippincott, 1979. 10–12.

Hanging carrots, coleus cuttings, hydroponic tomatoes, summer vegetables grown in plastic "pillows": these are among the relatively simple and inexpensive projects described in this well-organized and clearly illustrated book. Most of the projects can do double duty in the classroom, adding both to the learning environment and the decor.

Kramer, Jack. **Plant Hobbies: A Beginner's Book of Gardening Projects, Principles, and Pleasures.** Illus. Berne Holman. William Collins, Publishers, 1978. 8–12.

While plants are essential to our survival, we can also enjoy their life-enriching qualities. Nineteen simple garden hobbies, plant experiments, and art projects, like weed weaving, are demonstrated in black and white sketches. Addresses of plant suppliers are given.

Kramer, Jack. **Queen's Tears and Elephant's Ears: A Guide to Growing Unusual Houseplants.** Illus. Michael Valdez and Robert Johnson. William Collins, Publishers, 1977. 9–12.

Sound advice for indoor gardening is given in a brief, readable text highlighting thirty-three unusual house plants. Each double-page spread gives a description with a black and white drawing of the plant and its namesake. Snake plants, Venus's flytraps, and kite orchids are some of the plants used. Index.

Lavine, Sigmund A. **Wonders of Terrariums.** Illus. Jane O'Regan. Dodd, Mead, 1977. 8–12.

All aspects of terrariums are discussed, from their origin to the unique creations that readers can make. Instructions for selecting containers and appropriate plants and for assembling the terrariums are given in clear terms with many diagrams and black and white photographs. A useful resource for indoor gardeners.

Paul, Aileen. **Kids Outdoor Gardening.** Illus. John DeLulio. Doubleday, 1978. 8–12.

An idea for growing initials in the garden and many other interesting garden projects are described. Materials, equipment, and directions are given for flower and vegetable gardens. Helpful diagrams complement the text. Planting chart and index are included.

Magic

Hess, Jeff. **Magic.** Illus. Kevin Pedersen. Creative Education, 1979. 7–10.

Magic depends on both the magician's skill and the audience's willingness to believe. The book gives a bit of magic's history and suggests ways to handle an audience, along with several easy tricks requiring some preparation and pratice. Cartoonlike drawings.

Kraske, Robert. **Magicians Do Amazing Things.** Illus. Richard Bennett. Random House, 1979. 7–10.

Six of the greatest tricks of magic are clearly explained in a format designed for easy reading. Among them are Houdini's walk through a brick wall, the Indian basket trick, and the floating princess. Appealing for young magicians, the book is well illustrated.

Kronzek, Allan Zola. **The Secrets of Alkazar: A Book of Magic.** Illus. Tom Huffman. Four Winds Press, 1980. 10–up.

A readable, well-written manual for aspiring magicians. Clear line drawings illustrate the tricks. Showmanship is the overall theme. The author presents general principles for doing tricks, points out the pitfalls, and shows how to do convincing illusions.

Reed, Graham. **Magical Miracles You Can Do.** Illus. Dennis Patten. Elsevier/Nelson Books, 1980. 8–12.

This book introduces the world of magic tricks, giving many hints on how to prepare the tricks and carry them out dramatically. The illustrations help the young magician see the steps to each illusion. A nice start for a future Blackstone.

Wyler, Rose, and Gerald Ames. **It's All Done with Numbers: Astounding and Confounding Feats of Mathematical Magic.** Illus. Carter Jones. Doubleday, 1979. 10–up.

Numbers and calculations play a significant role in magic, prediction,

and mindreading. Here are directions for magic tricks and explanations of why and how they work. Hints and ideas for practicing and
performing are also included. For beginning magicians and people
who like to read about numbers.

Models

Freeman, Tony. **An Introduction to Radio-Controlled Sailplanes.** Photographs by author. Childrens Press, 1979. 10–12.

Flying radio-controlled sailplanes is a growing hobby in the United
States. Here is an introduction to the sport written for the beginner
and describing the equipment and techniques necessary to operate
these models. Excellent color photographs encourage the reader to
try this sport.

Weiss, Harvey. **How to Run a Railroad: Everything You Need to Know
about Model Trains.** Thomas Y. Crowell, 1977. 8–up.

A model railroading guide to help the beginner construct an inexpensive train layout. The simple pictures and drawings are helpful in
planning and building train collections.

Weiss, Harvey. **Model Buildings and How to Make Them.** Illus. by author.
Thomas Y. Crowell, 1979. 10–up.

Careful directions and clear illustrations and photographs character-
ize this book on how to make model buildings. The two sections
deal with cardboard and wood. Tool requirements and procedures
are explained. Of interest to the future architect.

Photography

Laycock, George. **The Complete Beginner's Guide to Photography.** Doubleday, 1979. 10–up.

This helpful book from The Complete Beginner's Guide series clearly
describes how a camera works, how to select one, techniques for use,
and the developing of film. Many illustrative photographs show what
good pictures should look like.

Leen, Nina. **Taking Pictures.** Holt, Rinehart and Winston, 1977. 4–7.

An imaginative book for kindergarteners written by a famous
photographer who believes that photography teaches children to
observe and stretch their creativity. Basic photographic directions,
using items from the child's world, are shown in black and white
photographs. The author explains how to invent stories and make
backgrounds.

Levine, Michael L. **Moviemaking: A Guide for Beginners.** Charles Scribner's Sons, 1980. 8–12.

This simple guide to making movies is illustrated with excellent black and white photographs. Step-by-step directions from how to plan the story and rehearse it to techniques of filming make this a good aid for the young filmmaker.

Thurman, Judith, and Jonathan David. **The Magic Lantern: How Movies Got to Move.** Atheneum, 1978. 8–12.

The long and gradual development of the art of photography is traced in a simple manner through the text and many illustrations. When the book pages are flipped quickly, the silhouette of the acrobat in the upper right-hand corner demonstrates the principle of motion pictures. One picture flows into the next.

Various Hobbies

Ganz, David L. **The World of Coins and Coin Collecting.** Charles Scribner's Sons, 1980. 12–up.

This comprehensive volume on coins and coin collecting includes a general introduction to numismatics and information for the beginner on how to build a coin collection. For the serious collector it includes a chapter on investment. A complete list of sources, bibliography, and index are appended. Excellent illustrations and photographs.

Henriod, Lorraine. **Ancestor Hunting.** Illus. Janet Potter D'Amato. Julian Messner, 1979. 9–12.

Emphasizing each individual's uniqueness, this book is an excellent source for teaching or learning beginning genealogy. It has examples of pedigree, family group charts, and even how to rub a gravestone. Gives instructions on compiling information and makes suggestions for special projects. Black and white illustrations, glossary, and index.

Olney, Ross R. **The Amazing Yo-Yo.** Photographs by Chan Bush. Lothrop, Lee & Shepard Books, 1980. 8–up.

A fascinating history of the yo-yo from its beginnings in the primeval jungles to the modern yo-yo. Directions for basic manipulations plus numerous tricks are described and illustrated by black and white photos.

Sarnoff, Jane. **A Great Aquarium Book: The Putting-It-Together Guide for Beginners.** Illus. Reynold Ruffins. Charles Scribner's Sons, 1977. 10–up.

Thorough, detailed, and explicit information is given for starting an aquarium. Facts are interspersed with bits of advice and humor. The assortment of color and types, scientific drawings, and cartoons makes the subject appealing to youngsters.

Additional Hobby Books

Brown, Vinson. *How to Make a Home Nature Museum.* Illus. Don G. Kelly. Little, Brown, 1954. 10–12.

Cooper, Elizabeth K. *Science in Your Own Backyard.* Harcourt Brace Jovanovich, 1958. 9–12.

de Regniers, Beatrice Schenk and Isabel Gordon. *The Shadow Book.* Photos by Isabel Gordon. Harcourt Brace Jovanovich, 1960. 4–8.

Hobson, Burton. *Coin Collecting as a Hobby.* Sterling Publishing, 1967. 10–up.

Paul, Aileen. *Kids Gardening.* Illus. Arthur Hawkins. Doubleday, 1972. 9–12.

Powers, William K. *Here Is Your Hobby: Indian Dancing and Customs.* J. P. Putnam's Sons, 1966. 10–16.

Stein, Sara Bonnett. *How to Raise a Puppy.* Photos by Robert Weinreb. Random House, 1976. 6–10.

Wyler, Rose, and Gerald Ames. *Magic Secrets.* Illus. Talivaldis Stubis. Harper & Row, Publishers, 1967. 7–up.

Amusements

Curiosities and Wonders

Charlie Brown's Fourth Super Book of Questions and Answers about All Kinds of People and How They Live! Random House, 1979. 7–10.

Why do people celebrate Halloween? What games do Eskimos play? These and a variety of questions about people are answered in a readable style and in sufficient depth to satisfy the curious child. Peanuts gang cartoons and color photographs with index.

Ford, B. G. **Do You Know?** Illus. Harry McNaught. Random House, 1979. 6–9.

Do you know the largest land animal living today? Do you know how fast things go? Do you know that an acorn is a seed? Answers are supplied. Clearly labeled items and colorful illustrations combine to make this a valuable book.

Lopshire, Robert. **The Biggest, Smallest, Fastest, Tallest Things You've Ever Heard Of.** Illus. by author. Thomas Y. Crowell, 1980. 6–9.

When you talk, what word do you say the most? What mammal has the most children? (Answers: "I"; the pig, who can have thirty-four piglets at a time.) This easy-reading miniature Guinness Book of Records is bound to be fun for beginning readers.

McLoone-Basta, Margo, and Alice Siegel. **The Kids' Book of Lists.** Holt, Rinehart and Winston, 1980. 8–up.

This fun and zany list of kids' accomplishments includes unusual and outstanding feats, such as the first girl to pitch a no-hit game in Little League baseball and the boy who discovered the first doughnut with a hole. Black and white photographs.

National Geographic Society. **Far-Out Facts.** National Geographic Society, 1980. 8–12.

An array of unusual facts on plants, animals, manners, photography, history, and other topics is reported. For example, pigs can get sunburned like humans. Beautiful full-color photographs illustrate this zany collection of science miscellanea. A booklet of games and puzzles and a poster-size calendar are included.

Simon, Seymour. **Animal Fact/Animal Fable.** Illus. Diane de Groat. Crown Publishers, 1979. 7–10.

An archer fish aiming his bow-and-arrow, a wise owl holding a straight-A report card: which is fact, which is fable? Why? A flick of the page gives these and eighteen other answers in this witty and informative book for browsing. Outstanding full-color illustrations.

Sobol, Donald J. **Encyclopedia Brown's Record Book of Weird and Wonderful Facts.** Illus. Sal Murdocca. Delacorte Press, 1979. 8–12.

Did you know Santa Claus can spend only half of 1/10,000 seconds at each home? that 10 tons of space dust fall on earth daily? no one knows why dogs bury bones? An enjoyable collection of funny and fascinating trivia accompanied by humorous black and white drawings. Especially highlights children's feats.

Jokes, Puns, Riddles

Cole, William. **Knock Knocks: The Most Ever.** Illus. Mike Thaler. Franklin Watts, 1976. 9–12.

Puns, plays on names, and rib-tickling line-drawn cartoons that convey ideas are presented in this collection of familiar and fun knock knock jokes. The book stimulates imagination and listening acuity. Cultural and literary allusions extend interdisciplinary concepts.

Cunningham, Bronnie. **The Best Book of Riddles, Puns & Jokes.** Illus. Amy Aitken. Doubleday, 1979. 8–up.

"What did the irate circus owner say to the stubborn elephant? Pack your trunk and get out." Children enjoy repeating these jokes and riddles. An interesting foreword explains how riddles originated and that each country has its own tradition of riddles. Comic pen sketches.

Doty, Roy. **King Midas Has a Gilt Complex.** Doubleday, 1979. 8–12.

Puns fill this book. Each page contains several cartoons with gags in the word balloons. Some are riddles, some are jokes, and all are funny. Humorous black and white drawings are highlighted with orange and gold.

Doty, Roy. **Tinkerbell Is a Ding-a-ling.** Doubleday, 1980. 8–12.

This book of riddles, illustrated with action-filled, cartoonlike drawings, is funny in an extravagantly slapstick manner.

Henry, Sarah Ann. **The Little Book of Big Knock Knock Jokes.** Illus. David Ross. Harvey House, Publishers, 1977. 7–12.

Children will enjoy reading and sharing these knock knock jokes— some new, some old, and all silly. The pen and ink sketches add to the fun.

Keller, Charles, compiler. **Giggle Puss: Pet Jokes for Kids.** Illus. Paul Coker, Jr. Prentice-Hall, 1977. 7–10.

"If a dog loses his tail, where does he get another one?" Eighty pages are filled with jokes and riddles, old and new, about dogs, cats, and an occasional goldfish, flea, parrot, or turtle. A sure-fire hit, with appropriately cartoony illustrations. (Answer: "At the retail store, of course.")

Keller, Charles. **Still Going Bananas.** Illus. Hallie Coletta. Prentice-Hall, 1980. 8–12.

Accompanying this hilarious collection of riddles, wry wit, and puns are contemporary black and white line drawings that add to the fun. They depict people from a broad range of races, professions, and economic levels. For all lovers of laughter.

Keller, Charles, compiler. **The Wizard of Gauze and Other Gags for Kids.** Illus. Ken Mahood. Prentice-Hall, 1979. 8–12.

This collection of forty-five jokes is new to children, but quite recognizable to teachers. Joke books are always popular and this one is no exception. Several of the black and white drawings are quite clever.

Leonard, Marcia, and editors of *Cricket Magazine,* compilers. **Cricket's Jokes, Riddles and Other Stuff.** Random House, 1977. 8–12.

Well-organized into sixteen categories, *Cricket's* stuff is lots of fun for everyone, and useful for reinforcing reading skills. A surprise ending lets the reader view the antics of a performing cricket as the book pages are flipped backwards.

Lyfick, Warren. **The Little Book of Fowl Jokes.** Illus. Chris Cummings. Harvey House, Publishers, 1980. 6–9.

"What grows up while it grows down? A baby duckling." Crows, hens, ducks, eagles, pheasants, turkeys, and even jailbirds come to life in these humorous jokes for the young child. Each page has one or more pen drawings for more enjoyment.

McKie, Roy. **The Joke Book.** Random House, 1979. 7–10.

"How do you find a lost rabbit? Make a sound like a carrot." Knock knocks, elephant jokes, riddles, puns, and lots of old favorites are collected. Colorful illustrations add to the action and help the young jokester remember the punch lines.

Powers, Thetis, compiler. **The Little Book of Daffinitions.** Illus. Chris Cummings. Harvey House, Publishers, 1977. 7–10.

Children will enjoy such "daffinitions" as "Long distance: the best way to talk to a monster," and "Sassafras: what you shouldn't do to a 250-pound fras." This book could be a good springboard for writing.

Rosenbloom, Joseph. **The Gigantic Joke Book.** Illus. Joyce Behr. Sterling Publishing, 1978. 7–up.

According to the author, this collection of jokes places emphasis on wordplay. Included are over a thousand jokes from one-liners to elaborate story jokes, from classics every jokester knows to brand new ones. Simple black and white line drawings illustrate the humor. Readers will also enjoy *How Do You Make an Elephant Laugh?* by the same author.

Rothman, Joel, and Argentina Palacios. **This Can Lick a Lollipop: Body Riddles for Kids (Esto goza chupando un caramelo: Las partes del cuerpo en adivinanzas infantiles).** Photographs by Patricia Ruben. Doubleday, 1979. 4–7.

Young children interested in Spanish-English language will enjoy these body riddles. Parts of the body, black and white photographs, and a two-language text comprise this useful and fun book.

Seuss, Dr. **Oh Say Can You Say?** Beginner Books, 1979. 6–9.

A new addition to the author's other easy-to-read books, this collection of tongue twisters offers belly-laughs to all ages while firming up the skills of young readers. Electric colors and nonsensical creatures add to the hilarity.

Stine, Jovial Bob, and Jane Stine. **The Sick of Being Sick Book.** Illus. Carol Nicklaus. E. P. Dutton, 1980. 8–12.

It is never any fun being sick, but this book can help you laugh a little at the problem. Jokes, recipes, and a daytime TV Guide all help to bring out a good chuckle and a warm smile. When you're sick, that isn't always easy.

Thaler, Mike. **Never Tickle a Turtle: Cartoons, Riddles and Funny Stories.** Franklin Watts, 1977. 8–12.

This classroom-tested volume of cartoons, riddles, and wordplay about animals lends itself to a variety of language arts activities.

Thomas, Gary, compiler. **The Best of the Little Books.** Harvey House, Publishers, 1980. 6–9.

What is the best-educated insect? A Spelling Bee, of course! Limericks, tongue twisters, jokes, and anagrams fill this little book with many good laughs for children. Humorous pen sketches accompany most of the content.

Puzzles

Anno, Mitsumasa. **Anno's Animals.** William Collins, Publishers, 1979. 6–up.

Walk through the cool green woods with award-winning illustrator Anno and try to find the camouflaged animals. This wordless picture book is designed to sharpen one's perceptions and to develop visual skills.

Anno, Mitsumasa. **Anno's Italy.** William Collins, Publishers, 1980. 8–up.

The traveler goes on a delightful tour through Italy, past and present. The reader searches for the hundreds of images from myths, folklore, fine arts, architecture, and history in this country rich in culture. A unique imaginative experience in a wordless book.

Anno, Mitsumasa. **Anno's Journey.** William Collins, Publishers, 1978. All ages.

The reader journeys with the artist throughout northern Europe and views sights from fine paintings, folktales, Sesame Street, and religious legends. The artist continues to play with perspective and visual puzzles. Some stories unfold page after page. Drawn in the style of a Japanese scroll, this wordless book tells many stories.

Aruego, Jose, and Ariane Dewey. **We Hide, You Seek.** Greenwillow Books, 1979. 3–5.

The rhino and his animal friends are playing hide and seek. Prereaders can search the fanciful illustrations to find the camouflaged animals in their natural habitat.

Barry, Sheila Anne. **Super-Colossal Book of Puzzles, Tricks & Games.** Illus. Doug Anderson. Sterling Publishing, 1978. 6–9.

Super-colossal is the right term to describe this assortment of entertainment ideas for children or adults working with children. Lively puzzles, tricks, self-tests, pencil and paper games, quiet and party games are included. A must for home or school. Answers to puzzles and a guide to age suitability are appended.

Benjamin, Alan. **1000 Inventions.** Illus. Sal Murdocca. Four Winds Press, 1980. 8–up.

The unique quality of a flip book enables the reader to combine pages to make pictures of 1000 imaginative inventions. Good for stimulating creative ideas in language arts and art, or just for fun. Also recommended is *1000 Monsters* by the same author.

Bester, Roger. **Guess What?** Crown Publishers, 1980. 4–7.

Photographs depict three characteristics of each farm animal: horse, squirrel, duck, cow, chicken, and pig. These clues are followed by a complete picture with the answer below. Good for arousing the curiosity of the preschooler and encourages them to make associations.

Demi. **Where Is It?** Doubleday, 1979. 4–7.

This is an entertaining book of puzzles to captivate young and old. A box in the upper right-hand corner of the page contains an object; the observer must locate its duplicate among many colorful and similar objects. Some are easy, and some are difficult. Answers are included.

Emberley, Ed. **Ed Emberley's Amazing Look Through Book.** Little, Brown, 1979. 6–12.

Hot Lips Dragon and Curly Pig are among the creatures revealed when young readers follow the directions and hold each page up to the light. The unusual art technique is explained; it might present a challenge to older students interested in drawing.

Fixx, James F. **Solve It! A Perplexing Profusion of Puzzles.** Doubleday, 1978. 9–up.

An excellent section on the techniques of problem-solving introduces this stimulating collection of mathematical teasers, logical absurdities, word plays, and inventive games. While there is something for everyone, this is especially good for children who enjoy games of logic.

Most, Bernard. **Turn Over.** Prentice-Hall, 1980. 4–7.

A charming little book that invites one-to-one sharing. Each page has a question that can only be answered by turning over the page. Black and white ink sketches help teach such concepts as behind, turn over, and others.

Oakley, Graham. **Graham Oakley's Magical Changes.** Atheneum, 1980. All ages.

Thirty-two full-color, full-page scenes are cut in half horizontally, thus creating a flip book. Each half-scene lines up with the other to make unusual combinations. The flag pole bases once support flags, another time giant lamp shades, and still another time a huge wedding cake. A humorous, highly imaginative experience.

Peppé, Rodney. **Rodney Peppé's Puzzle Book.** Viking Press, 1977. 4–7.

The book consists of eleven puzzles, including jungle hunt, spot the mistakes, shapes and sizes, odd man out, help the farmer count, and others. The bold illustrations are brightly colored. Some are stylized, while others are personified.

729 Puzzle People. Illus. Helen Oxenbury. Harper & Row, Publishers, 1980. 8–12.

This heads-bodies-legs book has pictures of nine unique characters, each divided into three sturdy flip cards that can be alternated to make 729 different characters. A sentence part is on each card, making the same number of silly sentences possible. A fun-filled aid for sentence expansion lessons.

Vreuls, Diane. **Sums: A Looking Game.** Viking Press, 1977. 6–12.

A wordless book filled with pictured parts of whole objects. By putting the pieces together mentally and then turning the page, readers are able to see if their guesses are correct. This imaginative visual puzzle book is useful for developing perceptual and relational concepts.

Weissman, Sam Q. **An Apple to Eat or Cross the Street.** Prentice-Hall, 1980. 6–9.

The author describes fifteen common objects in uncommon ways: a banana as a boat, a hat as a monster, and a shoe as a house. Colorful drawings add to the humor. Useful in creative writing or drawing as imagination stretchers.

Additional Amusement Books

Bishop, Ann. *Noah Riddle?* Illus. Jerry Warshaw. Albert Whitman, 1970. All ages.
Gwynne, Fred. *The King Who Rained.* E. P. Dutton, 1970. 5–up.
Heaton, Alma. *Double Fun: 100 Outdoor and Indoor Games.* Brigham, 1975. 8–12.
Sarnoff, Jane, and Reynold Ruffins. *The Code Cipher Book.* Charles Scribner's Sons, 1975. 8–12.
Tashjian, Virginia A. *With a Deep Sea Smile.* Illus. Rosemary Wells. Little, Brown, 1974. 5–11.

Professional

Authors' Essays

Billington, Elizabeth T., editor and compiler. **The Randolph Caldecott Treasury.** Frederick Warne, 1978. Adult.

In this handsome collection of Randolph Caldecott's work, the author has carefully dealt with the growth of the artist's work rather than with the details of his personal life. Intriguing comparisons of certain landmarks are made: photographs of the buildings today placed beside Caldecott's sketches in the nineteenth century. An excellent book for studying the art of a master illustrator.

Commire, Anne. **Something about the Author: Facts and Pictures about Authors and Illustrators of Books for Young People.** Gale Research, 1980. 10–up.

This ongoing reference set now includes, with volume 18, biographical sketches of nearly 57,000 authors of children's books. Of these authors, contemporary and past, many are little known. The commentaries contain facts, sidelights, and book notes. Useful for the child who becomes intrigued with an author.

Hunter, Mollie. **Talent Is Not Enough.** Harper & Row, Publishers, 1976. Adult.

Compiled from a series of lectures, these essays on writing for children give insight into the craft of writing and into this particular author's philosophy and style. Hunter discusses technique, language, and genre as powerfully as she uses them in her books for children.

Rees, David. **The Marble in the Water: Essays on Contemporary Writers of Fiction for Children and Young Adults.** Horn Book, 1980. Adult.

A British author includes his first attempt at criticism in this collection of essays on ten American and eight English authors. The comments are sometimes scathing, sometimes praising, but decidedly non-American in viewpoint. Useful for contrasts.

Townsend, John Rowe. **A Sounding of Storytellers: New and Revised Essays on Contemporary Writers for Children.** J. B. Lippincott, 1979. Adult.

Essays on fourteen contemporary writers of children's books make up this extension and revision of *A Sense of Story*. Eight new writers are included: Nina Bawden, Vera and Bill Cleaver, Peter Dickinson, Virginia Hamilton, E. L. Konigsburg, Penelope Lively, and Jill Paton Walsh. Seven other essays are updated.

Bibliographies

Baskin, Barbara H., and Karen H. Harris. **Books for the Gifted Child.** R. R. Bowker, 1980. Adult.

The first third of this book reviews studies on giftedness, the education of gifted children, and reading experiences for the gifted. The remainder annotates approximately 150 books that are termed "intellectually demanding." Full-page discussions summarize and suggest why the books are particularly useful for high-ability children. Reading levels are placed in three groupings. A useful compilation. Indexes.

Baskin, Barbara H., and Karen H. Harris. **Notes from a Different Drummer: A Guide to Juvenile Fiction Portraying the Handicapped.** R. R. Bowker, 1977. Adult.

The bulk of this book is a well-annotated listing of selected children's books published from 1940–1975 that portray handicapped persons. Several chapters describe the state of literature on this topic. Subject and title indexes are included. Informative and usable.

Bennett, Jill. **Learning to Read with Picture Books.** Thimble Press, 1979. Adult.

This compilation of more than 100 picture books is annotated in a highly personalized style reflective of the author/teacher's use of the books with children from age four to seven. A choice listing.

Bernstein, Joanne E. **Books to Help Children Cope with Separation and Loss.** R. R. Bowker, 1977. Adult.

This is an excellent reference when selecting books for children about coping with separation and loss. Books chosen have contemporary, realistic themes, and are good literature. Selections are for children from age three through sixteen. Helpful indexes are included to facilitate use by teachers, counselors, librarians, and parents.

Bisshopp, Patricia, compiler. **Books about Handicaps for Children and Young Adults.** Meeting Street School/Rhode Island Easter Seal Society, 1978. Adult.

Annotations are especially informative in this compilation of books on handicaps. Certain books are unreservedly recommended, others are definitely not recommended, and many are characterized by both good and bad qualities. In all cases, explicit evaluative statements are given. Handicaps include auditory, visual, orthopedic, speech, mental, emotional, and learning disabilities.

Dreyer, Sharon Spredemann. **The Bookfinder: A Guide to Children's Literature about the Needs and Problems of Youth Aged 2–15.** American Guidance Service, 1977. Adult.

This work categorizes current children's books according to psychological, behavioral, and developmental topics of concern to children from two to fifteen. A unique split-page format permits the user to locate a subject and to find annotations for the books listed under that subject at the same time. All the forms in which the books are available are detailed; including Braille versions, Talking Books, audiovisual treatments, and paperback editions.

Fassler, Joan. **Helping Children Cope.** Illus. William B. Hogan. Free Press, 1978. Adult.

Stressful situations in children's lives, and books that might be useful in coping with these problems, are the focus of the book. Topics include death, separation, hospitalization, and life-style changes. The author is a child psychologist and a specialist in children's literature. The text is quite readable and gives many practical suggestions.

Gillis, Ruth J. **Children's Books for Times of Stress: An Annotated Bibliography.** Indiana University Press, 1978. Adult.

An efficient aid for teacher or parent in finding the right book at the right time to help a child through difficulty. Reviews are brief, but give information pertinent to selection. Books are located under subject headings; cross-referencing is complete. Valuable for helping children from preschool through sixth-grade levels.

Graves, Michael F., Judith A. Boettcher, and Randall J. Ryder. **Easy Reading: Book Series and Periodicals for Less Able Readers.** International Reading Association, 1979. Adult.

Here is an annotated bibliography of high interest, easy vocabulary books. Each review includes reading and interest levels, story synopsis, price, and an evaluative comment. Excellent tool to help choose the better quality book for the less able reader.

Greene, Ellin, and Madalynne Schoenfeld, compilers and editors. **A Multimedia Approach to Children's Literature, Second Edition.** American Library Association, 1977. Adult.

Approximately 1450 items, including books, films, filmstrips, and recordings, are annotated with full bibliographic information. The nonprint materials are based on children's books and are especially helpful for introducing books and for providing varied program formats related to literature. This edition contains materials received prior to 1976.

Harrah, Barbara K. **Sports Books for Children: An Annotated Bibliography.** Scarecrow Press, 1978. 10–up.

The purpose of this volume is to assist librarians and students in choosing sports books wisely, fitting both interest and reading ability. Eighty-nine sports, from the familiar to the more exotic, are listed. Fry reading levels, author and title indexes, and selected periodical guide are included.

Haviland, Virginia, editor. **Children's Books of International Interest, Second Edition.** American Library Association, 1978. Adult.

Outstanding American children's books that would be of particular interest to young people in other countries are listed here. There are approximately 350 books, culled from about 900 books suggested by earlier American Library Association committees as being worthy of translation and distribution abroad. A choice list.

Hinman, Dorothy, and Ruth Zimmerman. **Reading for Young People: The Midwest.** American Library Association, 1979. Adult.

Books of fiction, biography, and history dealing with Ohio, Indiana, Illinois, Iowa, and Missouri are annotated in this bibliography. Reading levels are grades four through ten. Other titles in the series include *The Great Plains, The Middle Atlantic, The Southeast,* and *The Rocky Mountains.* Extensive indexes of subjects and states.

Horner, Catherine Townsend. **The Single-Parent Family in Children's Books: An Analysis and Annotated Bibliography, with an Appendix on Audiovisual Material.** Scarecrow Press, 1978. Adult.

Following an analysis of single-parent family books for children is an annotated bibliography listing books written between 1966 and 1976. Indexing is separated into three categories: predominant parent, subject, and author. An appendix of audiovisual materials is included. An excellent resource for teachers and counselors, working with intermediate and junior high students.

Lass-Woodfin, Mary Jo, editor. **Books on American Indians and Eskimos: A Selection Guide for Children and Young Adults.** American Library Association, 1978. Adult.

More than 800 books for young people dealing with American Indians and Eskimos are listed. They are ranked good, adequate, or poor. Well-written summaries, age levels, and full bibliographic information are included. Each book was read by two reviewers. The introduction provides a fine statement on stereotyping. Index.

Lynn, Ruth Nadelman. **Fantasy for Children: An Annotated Checklist.** R. R. Bowker, 1979. Adult.

Approximately 1650 recommended fantasies are categorized under thirteen subject headings. Annotations are brief; quality ratings and bibliographic information are given for each book. Sources of reviews are listed. The ages range from preschool through secondary school. Out-of-print books are listed separately as are those available in the United Kingdom. Several indexes.

Maehr, Jane. **The Middle East: An Annotated Bibliography of Literature for Children.** ERIC Clearinghouse on Early Childhood Education, 1977. Adult.

Published prior to the hostage crisis in Iran, some of the listings in this bibliography are incomplete or contain errors, but the pertinence of the geographic area and the uniqueness of this compilation make textual inaccuracies less significant. The books are categorized by country as nonfiction, fiction, or folklore. Includes brief annotations and grade levels. Spiral bound.

Matthias, Margaret, and Diane Thiessen. **Children's Mathematics Books: A Critical Bibliography.** American Library Association, 1979. Adult.

Over 200 mathematics books for preschool through grade six are annotated with indications of content, activities, single or multiple concepts, accuracy, illustrations, writing style, and grade levels. Four quality designations are given. The book is divided into sections on counting, geometry, measurement, number concepts, time, and a general category.

McGovern, Edythe M. **They're Never Too Young for Books: Literature for Pre-Schoolers.** Mar Vista Publishing, 1980. Adult.

Extensive listings of books for preschoolers make up this bibliography. The fifty lists are divided into several age groups. Additional sections deal with the values and effects of using books with young children, general guidelines for selection, and suggestions for reading aloud. Complete bibliography.

Salway, Lance, compiler. **Humorous Books for Children.** Thimble Press, 1978. Adult.

This British compilation includes many books available in the United States and provides valuable discussions and comparisons within each annotation. A comprehensive index is appended.

Schmidt, Nancy J. **Supplement to Children's Books on Africa and Their Authors: An Annotated Bibliography.** Holmes & Meier Publishers, 1979. Adult.

This useful collection of children's books dealing with Africa has well-prepared annotations that give pro and con features of the books from an anthropological viewpoint. Biographical notes about the authors are included. The cutoff date for materials was summer of 1977. Many indexes are included.

Schon, Isabel. **A Bicultural Heritage: Themes for the Exploration of Mexican and Mexican-American Culture in Books for Children and Adolescents.** Scarecrow Press, 1978. Adult.

Written for teachers' use, the book discusses ways of teaching the culture of Mexicans and Mexican-Americans. The author recommends only a few of the books listed and gives specific reasons for not recommending the others. The reader's awareness is heightened by the author's guidance.

Schon, Isabel. **A Hispanic Heritage: A Guide to Juvenile Books about Hispanic People and Cultures.** Scarecrow Press, 1980. Adult.

Designed as an aid for librarians and teachers who are interested in exposing students to the cultures of Hispanic people. Annotations are provided and recommended books are indicated.

Stensland, Anna Lee. **Literature by and about the American Indian: An Annotated Bibliography, Second Edition.** National Council of Teachers of English, 1979. Adult.

Books for elementary-age children are singled out in this revised bibliography and are categorized for primary and intermediate grades. This very useful and comprehensive resource points out both good and bad features about the books. Introductory chapters are helpful in providing readers with an overview of Native American literature.

Tucker, Alan, compiler. **Poetry Books for Children.** Thimble Press, 1979. Adult.

Although many of the recommended books are available only in England, the evaluative annotations and comparative analyses are valuable resources for the American teacher. In addition to 109 separate entries, many other titles are discussed within the main entries.

White, Virginia L., and Emerita S. Schulte, compilers. **Books about Children's Books: An Annotated Bibliography.** International Reading Association, 1979. Adult.

Compiled to meet the professional needs of those interested in children and their books, this valuable tool has much to offer elementary teachers who wish to expand their use of books in the classroom. The careful selection of books falls into eight categories.

Wilkin, Binnie Tate. **Survival Themes in Fiction for Children and Young People.** Scarecrow Press, 1978. Adult.

Here is an excellent resource for selecting books that offer sensitivity to individual problems and to social issues of today. Picture books make up some of the selections. Busy librarians and teachers will find this valuable when suggesting individual student selections. Each book has a short annotation.

Yonkers Public Library Children's Services. **A Guide to Subjects & Concepts in Picture Book Format, Second Edition.** Oceana Publications, 1979. Adult.

Picture books are listed in fifty-five main subject categories. The groupings are especially helpful to primary teachers who want to find stories on specific topics. Cross-references are included. Covers books published prior to October 1978. Bibliography.

Criticism

The Arbuthnot Lectures: 1970–1979. American Library Association, 1980. Adult.

The first ten speeches presented in the Arbuthnot Lectures series are collected here. International in scope, the lectures deal with criticism and issues, bringing the new insights and new emphases to the field of children's literature that were originally envisioned when this series was created to honor May Hill Arbuthnot.

Davis, Enid. **The Liberty Cap: A Catalogue of Non-Sexist Materials for Children.** Academy Chicago Limited, 1977. Adult.

Essays and reviews of children's nonsexist materials are compiled from the two years of newsletters published in 1974–1976, offering thoughtful, perceptive commentaries that transcend the particular books and make statements about the topic.

Egoff, Sheila A., editor. **One Ocean Touching: Papers from the First Pacific Rim Conference on Children's Literature.** Scarecrow Press, 1979. Adult.

Speakers from ten countries who assembled at a Canadian conference shared their individual ideas on childhood and children's literature. Thirteen papers make up the international section while eight papers treat the specifics of children's literature in Canada. These thoughtful, in-depth essays are most insightful. Index.

Heins, Paul, compiler and editor. **Crosscurrents of Criticism: Horn Book's Essays 1968–1977.** Horn Book, 1977. Adult.

Articles expressing a wide variety of views concerning children's books make this an outstanding collection of literary criticism. This is similar to *A Horn Book Sampler* and *Horn Book Reflections,* compilations from earlier years. Thoughtful reading for teachers.

Lystad, Mary. **From Dr. Mather to Dr. Seuss: 200 Years of American Books for Children.** Schenkman Publishing, 1980. Adult.

A content analysis of 1000 American children's books published from 1776-1976 was conducted for information within the books concerning social characteristics that reflected the growth of the country. The chapters, arranged chronologically, relate the quantitative and qualitative findings of the analysis. A scholarly study presented in an interesting, readable style.

MacCann, Donnarae, and Gloria Woodard, editors. **Cultural Conformity in Books for Children: Further Readings in Racism.** Scarecrow Press, 1977. Adult.

Although many teachers and librarians may complain about the authors' "nit-picking" concerning adverse references to Native Americans, Asian Americans, Black Americans, and females, this analysis of approximately 150 children's books will do much to raise the consciousness of those readers who are able to take it in stride.

Meek, Margaret, Aidan Warlow, and Griselda Barton, editors. **The Cool Web: The Pattern of Children's Reading.** Atheneum, 1978. Adult.

Fifty essays by British and American specialists in children's literature deal with four themes: the relationship between the text and the reader's worlds, the role of authors, the literary criticism of children's books, and the ways teachers might move forward in the study of reading and literature.

Sale, Roger. **Fairy Tales and After: From Snow White to E. B. White.** Harvard University Press, 1978. Adult.

These first-person essays on selected old and modern classics of children's literature are written for adult perusal, not for teachers needing suggestions on using the books with children. The content is energizing; it theorizes that the books transcend childhood and offer inspired thoughts to be contemplated for a lifetime. Enjoyable reading.

Illustrations

Feaver, William. **When We Were Young: Two Centuries of Children's Book Illustration.** Holt, Rinehart and Winston, 1977. Adult.

This resource book for teachers of children's literature at the high school or college level traces the development of illustrations, with examples from early until modern times, from William Blake to Maurice Sendak. Art lovers, children's illustrations experts, and serious students will enjoy the magnificent colored plates.

Kingman, Lee, editor. **The Illustrator's Notebook.** Horn Book, 1978. Adult.

This compilation of information about the history and process of illustrating children's books is more than a collection of readings. The articles, all from *Horn Book,* have been edited and placed specifically, striving to show that the essence of the story must be entwined with the sensitivity of the artist. Illustrations from children's books extend the ideas.

Lanes, Selma G. **The Art of Maurice Sendak.** Harry N. Abrams, Publishers, 1980. Adult.

A singularly beautiful volume befitting the most distinguished contemporary illustrator of children's books, this is at once an intimate personal biography and a scholarly study of the sensitive development of an illustrator's style. Superb.

Larkin, David, editor. **The Art of Nancy Ekholm Burkert.** Harper & Row, Publishers, 1977. Adult.

Beautiful is the appropriate word for this collection of Nancy Ekholm Burkert's art. Many illustrations from her children's books are included. A brief biographical and critical commentary precedes the colored plates.

Puppetry

Currell, David. **Learning with Puppets.** Plays, 1980. Adult.

An excellent reference book on using puppetry as a teaching tool to develop language, reading, mathematics, and other skills. Step-by-step directions are also given for making hand, glove, shadow, and rod puppets, and simple puppet theaters and scenery.

Freericks, Mary, and Joyce Segal. **Creative Puppetry in the Classroom.** Illus. Katherine McCabe. New Plays Books, 1979. Adult.

Here is a good resource book on puppets for the teacher, librarian, nurse, camp leader, and parent. The authors discuss how to use puppets in numerous settings as well as how to make many different kinds of puppets.

Renfro, Nancy. **A Puppet Corner in Every Library.** Nancy Renfro Studios, 1978. Adult.

This text thoroughly describes how to organize and implement a library program, using puppets to effectively communicate with children. Puppets are used as library mascots, to teach library concepts and to tell stories. Informative photographs, diagrams, and directions are included for making puppets and stages. Many helpful resources are listed.

Renfro, Nancy. **Puppetry and the Art of Story Creation.** Nancy Renfro Studios, 1979. Adult.

Here are experience-tested and clever ways to create original stories, puppets, and dramatizations. Directions for making many kinds of puppets are given and illustrated with photographs and entertaining drawings. Tips are added for a successful puppet play production. Highly motivating; emphasis is on deaf children, but well applicable to all.

Storytelling and Booktalks

Baker, Augusta, and Ellin Greene. **Storytelling: Art and Technique.** R. R. Bowker, 1977. Adult.

This book covers story selection, preparation, presentation, and pro-

. gram planning in special settings, such as hospitals and outdoors, for children with special needs. The appendix outlines an inservice education workshop and sources for the storyteller.

Bauer, Caroline Feller. **Handbook for Storytellers.** American Library Association, 1977. Adult.

Here is the definitive handbook on storytelling. Suggestions abound for everything related to story programs including gathering an audience. Topics go beyond the classic forms to the use of magic, nonprint media, and music. Many sources of stories are given; sample programs for all ages are offered. Index.

Carlson, Bernice Wells. **Picture That!** Illus. Dolores Marie Rowland. Abingdon Press, 1977. Adult.

Twelve international folktales and stories are presented for reading or telling. Each is introduced by a game, verse, or audience-participation story. Following each tale are directions for craft activities that relate to the story. An excellent resource book for extending and appreciating folktales. Illustrations extend the understanding of the craft projects.

de Wit, Dorothy. **Children's Faces Looking Up: Program Building for the Storyteller.** American Library Association, 1979. Adult.

This book on various techniques of storytelling draws heavily from a rich background of folklore as a source for story material and programs. Suggestions on how to develop themes and extend them are given. Six sample programs are included. Excellent reference.

Gillespie, John T. **More Juniorplots: A Guide for Teachers and Librarians.** R. R. Bowker, 1977. Adult.

For each of seventy-two contemporary works of fiction there is a detailed plot summary, a brief discussion of theme, booktalk suggestions, sources of information about the author, and recommendations of other related books. Directed toward professionals dealing primarily with students in sixth through eighth grades.

Iarusso, Marilyn Berg, compiler. **Stories: A List of Stories to Tell and to Read Aloud, Seventh Edition.** New York Public Library, 1977. Adult.

Source materials and reference tools are brought together in this short softcover book that lists hundreds of stories and poems from many lands and on many subjects. Ideal for sharing with children during informal library programs. Useful for introducing children to the world's literature.

Leonard, Charlotte. **Tied Together: Topics and Thoughts for Introducing Children's Books.** Scarecrow Press, 1980. Adult.

Commentaries on books of related themes make a useful introduction to books for children. The sections are grouped into six topics: the outdoors, animals, holidays, family life, activities, and miscellany. A final grouping offers suggestions for parents, teachers, and librarians.

Pellowski, Anne. **The World of Storytelling.** R. R. Bowker, 1977. Adult.

This scholarly work is intended for adults interested in historical aspects of storytelling and the oral tradition out of which children's literature grew. The author encourages storytellers to share with the audience something of the culture and society within which the stories are told.

Peterson, Carolyn Sue, and Brenny Hall. **Story Programs: A Source Book of Materials.** Scarecrow Press, 1980. Adult.

This is a useful handbook of suggestions for using literature with toddlers (ages 2–3), preschoolers (ages 4–5), and primary grade children (ages 6–8). The sections deal with story programs, flannel boards, finger plays and action stories, creative dramatics, and puppetry. Patterns, music, and explicit directions are given. Index.

Schimmel, Nancy. **Just Enough to Make a Story: A Sourcebook for Storytelling.** Sisters' Choice Press, 1978. Adult.

The author shares practical tips on choosing, learning, and telling stories to audiences of varying ages. Citations for books and audiovisual media are given, as well as an excellent listing of seventy-one folktales with active heroine protagonists.

Spirt, Diana L. **Introducing More Books: A Guide for the Middle Grades.** R. R. Bowker, 1978. Adult.

This sequel to *Introducing Books* offers plot summaries, discussion suggestions, and related materials to be used with the books. Titles are grouped by nine themes that include making friends, developing values, identifying adult roles, and appreciating books. A valuable teaching aid for intermediate grades.

Teaching Methods

Applebee, Arthur N. **The Child's Concept of Story: Ages Two to Seventeen.** University of Chicago Press, 1978. Adult.

Reporting the results of his studies on the stories children tell and children's responses to stories they hear or read, the author offers a theory of the developmental stages of children's responses to literature. A scholarly text.

Butler, Dorothy. **Cushla and Her Books.** Horn Book, 1980. Adult.

This documentation of the importance of books in aiding the development of a severely handicapped New Zealand child is a testimony to the value of literature as a communication link. The story of the young parents and the extended family who worked diligently for the first four years of Cushla's life to bring her that link is heartwarming and courageous.

Butler, Francelia. **Sharing Literature with Children: A Thematic Anthology.** David McKay, 1977. Adult.

A textbook that uses a thematic approach and then subdivides into the more common genre divisions, this compendium includes a wide variety in the more than 160 selections that illustrate aspects of the themes. A section on explorations at the end of each chapter offers intriguing methods for using the literary selections.

Concannon, Tom. **Using Media for Creative Teaching.** Illus. Tegan Kenney. New Plays Books, 1979. Adult.

The creative uses of media are described in this slim paperback. The author suggests numerous innovative projects that he has used successfully with students; their appeal should encourage the most faint-hearted person's use.

Cullinan, Bernice E., and Carolyn W. Carmichael, editors. **Literature and Young Children.** National Council of Teachers of English, 1977. Adult.

Eleven essays concern the use of literature with preschool children. Topics deal with the kinds of growth that can be nurtured through literary experiences and the ways books and nonprint materials can be presented advantageously to children. In addition, a list of 100 best books and authors makes this a resource of continuing usefulness.

Favat, F. André. **Child and Tale: The Origins of Interest.** National Council of Teachers of English, 1977. Adult.

Results are described of a study that found relationships between Piaget's developmental stages and fairy tales by Andersen, Perrault, and the Grimms. Between ages six and eight, children's egocentrism and concepts of animism, causality, magic, and morality seem closely related to components and structures of age-old tales. A scholarly report.

Glazer, Joan I., and Gurney Williams III. **Introduction to Children's Literature.** McGraw-Hill, 1979. Adult.

This survey of children's literature offers practical suggestions for building literature units and a literature curriculum. A unique feature is the series of issues that juxtapose differing viewpoints on children's book topics. A readable introductory text.

Hopkins, Lee Bennett. **The Best of Book Bonanza.** Holt, Rinehart and Winston, 1980. Adult.

Creating exciting and lively environments for effective use of literature is what this bonanza is all about. Numerous tested activities are offered in a readable style. All types of classrooms can profit from this versatile treasury of the author's column in *Teacher* magazine.

Keysell, Pat. **Mime Themes and Motifs.** Plays, 1980. Adult.

An introduction to the art of mime and suggestions for its use with children, especially the deaf, is combined with numerous themes and suggestions on how to do the different motifs in mime. Excellent resource.

Lamme, Linda Leonard, et al. **Raising Readers: A Guide to Sharing Literature with Young Children.** Walker, 1980. Adult.

This stage-by-stage guide to using literature with young children, from newborn to beginning reader, is helpful for parents and teachers. The suggestions for sharing books are practical, intriguing, and worthwhile. An excellent addition to the books for parents concerning children's literature.

Monson, Dianne L., and DayAnn K. McClenathan, editors. **Developing Active Readers: Ideas for Parents, Teachers, and Librarians.** International Reading Association, 1979. Adult.

A collection of addresses, essays, and lectures by noted authorities in the field of reading makes up this monograph. Subjects include selection of books, library use, and involving children with literature.

Polette, Nancy, and Marjorie Hamlin. **Celebrating with Books.** Illus. Patricia Gilman. Scarecrow Press, 1977. Adult.

Holiday fun with books is the focus of this fine teacher's guide. For each of ten holidays summaries and activities for several books are listed. Directions are explicit; in some cases samples are given. A final chapter suggests how seasonal celebrations can be used to nurture independent study activities.

Reasoner, Charles F. **Bringing Children and Books Together: A Teacher's Guide to Early Childhood Literature.** Yearling Book, 1979. Adult.

This fourth in a series of teacher's guides offers suggestions for using twenty books with children from ages three to seven. Activities are geared to responding orally and answering by cutting and pasting, making X's, and drawing lines. Vocabulary development experiences are simple. Storytelling is emphasized; good practices in reading aloud are noted.

Shapiro, Jon E., editor. **Using Literature & Poetry Affectively.** International Reading Association, 1979. Adult.

Essays on using literature and poetry and examining children's attitudes toward reading have been written, selected, and published by reading authorities. Each article contains a bibliography of additional references.

Somers, Albert B., and Janet Evans Worthington. **Response Guides for Teaching Children's Books.** National Council of Teachers of English, 1979. Adult.

Suggestions for using twenty-seven books are given. The titles range from picture books to fully developed novels. Each guide is about three pages in length and offers discussion questions, various activities, and a list of related resources. The books are modern classics, all popular with children.

Sparkman, Brandon, and Jane Saul. **Preparing Your Preschooler for Reading: A Book of Games.** Schocken Books, 1977. Adult.

A helpful book for parents, teachers, and those involved in working with the very young child. Critical skills that lead to reading are stressed. Various types of games are described. Materials mentioned are readily available. Book and record list included.

Stewig, John Warren, and Sam L. Sebesta, editors. **Using Literature in the Elementary Classroom.** National Council of Teachers of English, 1978. Adult.

Six essays support the philosophy of using trade books to teach reading and language arts skills. Topics concern linguistics, vocabulary growth, literature study, visual and verbal literacy, composition, and reading comprehension. These articles are good examples of applying theory to practice.

Thomas, James L., and Ruth M. Loring, editors. **Motivating Children and Young Adults to Read.** Oryx Press, 1979. Adult.

Current articles on motivating children to read have been collected. Subjects include methodology, interests, selection, and nonprint media. The many practical ideas presented have been tested and are based on learning theory. Good resource.

Weisburg, Hilda K., and Ruth Toor. **Elementary School Librarian's Almanac: A Complete Media Program for Every Month of the School Year.** Center for Applied Research in Education, 1979. Adult.

Practical ideas to enliven the library program are suggested according to months in the school year. Bulletin board ideas, storytelling selections, art activities, authors' birthdates, and many facets of library operations are described in this readable text. Useful for teachers and public librarians, too.

Wilder, Rosilyn. **A Space Where Anything Can Happen: Creative Drama in a Middle School.** Photographs by Burt. New Plays Books, 1977. Adult.

This softbound volume contains an enthusiastic, detailed description of the values of creative drama. The author attempts to "re-create in print a living workshop experience." Packed with ideas and suggestions about "how-to-do-it."

Textbooks

Huck, Charlotte S. **Children's Literature in the Elementary School, Third Edition, Updated.** Holt, Rinehart and Winston, 1979. Adult.

This comprehensive textbook was updated to include books published from 1975–1978 and to revise briefly certain chapters and listings. The book gives an excellent survey of children's literature; the focus on teaching literature is an outstanding feature.

Sadker, Myra Pollack, and David Miller Sadker. **Now upon a Time: A Contemporary View of Children's Literature.** Harper & Row, Publishers, 1977. Adult.

Contemporary issues that are reflected in children's books are the focus of this textbook. Topics include altered family groupings, sex, aging, death, minority groups, ecology, war, and humor. A final section deals with controversy and creative ways of teaching literature. Extensive bibliographies; index.

Smith, James A., and Dorothy M. Park. **Word Music and Word Magic: Children's Literature Methods.** Allyn and Bacon, 1977. Adult.

There are four parts to this college textbook: one discusses the various genres and how literature relates to children's growth and creativity; another section focuses on authors; a third deals with many ways of using books with children; the final section lists resources for using books. Many suggestions for the college reader and extensive bibliographies.

Stewig, John Warren. **Children and Literature.** Rand McNally, 1980. Adult.

Several of the genre chapters in this comprehensive textbook have a section on sharing books with children that focuses on a particular mode of use: drama, storytelling, writing, art activities. The treatment is fresh and intriguing. Examples of good and bad literature are given; the content encourages discussion. A usable text.

Sutherland, Zena, and May Hill Arbuthnot. **Children and Books, Fifth Edition.** Scott, Foresman, 1977. Adult.

Many changes are included in this revision of the textbook, long a standard in the field. Chapters are reorganized to give a more specific genre approach. Focus is on major authors rather than a myriad of titles. New sections of books for early childhood and methodology are included.

Tiedt, Iris M. **Exploring Books with Children.** Houghton Mifflin, 1979. Adult.

Developed in part genre approach, part thematic unit, this textbook offers many interesting activities for the college student. Sections within each chapter suggest areas for further exploration, for research, and for additional reading. Written in lively style, the book is stimulating.

Directory of Publishers

Abelard-Schuman Ltd., c/o Harper & Row, Publishers, Inc., Keystone Industrial Park, Scranton, PA 18512

Abingdon Press, 201 Eighth Ave., S., Nashville, TN 37202

Harry N. Abrams, Publishers Inc., 110 E. 59th St., New York, NY 10022

Academy Chicago Limited, 360 N. Michigan Ave., Chicago, IL 60601

Addison-Wesley Publishing Co. Inc., Reading, MA 01867

Alaska Northwest Publishing Co., 130 Second Ave., S., Edmonds, WA 98020

Allyn and Bacon Inc., College Division, Rockleigh, NJ 07647

American Guidance Service Inc., Publishers' Building, Circle Pines, MN 55014

American Library Association, 50 E. Huron St., Chicago, IL 60611

Andre Deutsch, c/o Elsevier-Dutton, 2 Park Ave., New York, NY 10016

Atheneum Publishers. Dist. by Book Warehouse, Inc., Vreeland Ave., Boro of Totowa, Paterson, NJ 07512

Bahá'í Publishing Trust, 415 Linden Ave., Wilmette, IL 60091

Bala Books, 340 W. 55th St., New York, NY 10019

Barron's Educational Series, Inc., 113 Crossways Park Dr., Woodbury, NY 11797

Beaufort Books, Inc., 9 E. 40th St., New York, NY 10016

Beginner Books. Division of Random House, Inc., 400 Hahn Rd., Westminster, MD 21157

John F. Blair, Publisher, 1406 Plaza Dr., Winston-Salem, NC 27103

R. R. Bowker, Co., P.O. Box 1807, Ann Arbor, MI 48106

Bradbury Press. Dist. by E. P. Dutton & Co., Inc., 2 Park Ave., New York, NY 10016

Carolrhoda Books, Inc. Dist. by Control Data Arts, 474 Concordia Ave., St. Paul, MN 55103

Center for Applied Research in Education, Inc., c/o Prentice-Hall, Inc., P.O. Box 500, Englewood Cliffs, NJ 07632

Childrens Press, 1224 W. Van Buren St., Chicago, IL 60607

Clarion Books. Imprint of Houghton Mifflin Co., Wayside Road, Burlington, MA 01803

William Collins Publishers, Inc., 200 Madison Ave., Suite 1405, New York, NY 10016

Coward, McCann & Geoghegan, Inc., 1050 W. Wall St., Lyndhurst, NJ 07071

Creative Education, Inc., 123 S. Broad St., Mankato, MN 56001

Thomas Y. Crowell Co. Imprint of Harper & Row, Publishers, Keystone Industrial Park, Scranton, PA 18512

Crown Publishers, Inc., 1 Park Ave., New York, NY 10016

John Day Co., Inc. Dist. by Harper & Row, Publishers, Keystone Industrial Park, Scranton, PA 18512

Delacorte Press, c/o Dell Publishing Co., 1 Dag Hammarskjold Plaza, 245 E. 47th St., New York, NY 10017

Dell Publishing Co., Inc.,1 Dag Hammarskjold Plaza, 245 E. 47th St., New York, NY 10017

Design Enterprises of San Francisco, P.O. Box 14695, San Francisco, CA 94114

Dial Press, 1 Dag Hammarskjold Plaza, 245 E. 47th St., New York, NY 10017

Dillon Press, Inc., 500 Third St., Minneapolis, MN 55415

Dodd, Mead & Co., 79 Madison Ave., New York, NY 10016

Doubleday & Co., Inc., 501 Franklin Ave., Garden City, NY 11530

E. P. Dutton, 2 Park Ave., New York, NY 10016

William B. Eerdmans Publishing Co., 255 Jefferson Ave., S.E., Grand Rapids, MI 49503

Elsevier-Dutton Publishing Co., Inc., 2 Park Ave., New York, NY 10016

Elsevier/Nelson Books, 2 Park Ave., New York, NY 10016

Emerson Books, Inc., Reynolds Lane, Buchanan, NY 10511

ERIC Clearinghouse on Early Childhood Education, University of Illinois, 805 W. Pennsylvania Ave., Urbana, IL 61801

M Evans & Co., Inc. Dist. by E. P. Dutton, 2 Park Ave., New York, NY 10016

Exposition Press, Inc., 900 S. Oyster Bay Road, Hicksville, NY 11801

Farrar, Straus & Giroux, Inc., 19 Union Square, W., New York, NY 10003

Feminist Press, SUNY/College at Old Westbury, Box 334, Old Westbury, NY 11568

Follett Publishing Co. Div. of Follett Corp., 1010 W. Washington Blvd., Chicago, IL 60607

Four Winds Press. Div. of Scholastic Book Services, 50 W. 44th St., New York, NY 10036

Free Press. Div. of Macmillan Publishing Co., Inc., 866 Third Ave., New York, NY 10022

Gale Research Co., Book Tower, Detroit, MI 48226

Gambit, 27 North Main St., Meeting House Green, Ipswich, MA 01938

Garrard Publishing Co., 1607 N. Market St., Champaign, IL 61820

David R. Godine, Publisher, Inc., 306 Dartmouth St., Boston, MA 02116

Golden Press. Imprint of Western Publishing Co., Inc., Dept. M, 1220 Mound Ave., Racine, WI 53404

Stephen Greene Press, Fessenden Road, Indiana Flat, Brattleboro, VT 05301

Greenhaven Press, 577 Shoreview Park Road, St. Paul, MN 55112

Greenwillow Books. Div. of William Morrow & Co., Inc., Wilmor Warehouse, 6 Henderson Dr., West Caldwell, NJ 07006

Grosset & Dunlap, Inc., 51 Madison Ave., New York, NY 10010

Harcourt Brace Jovanovich, Inc., 757 Third Ave., New York, NY 10017

Harper & Row, Publishers, Inc., Keystone Industrial Park, Scranton, PA 18512

Harvard University Press, Customer Service, 79 Garden St., Cambridge, MA 02138

Harvey House, Publishers, 128 W. River St., Chippewa Falls, WI 54729

Hastings House, Publishers, Inc., 10 E. 40th St., New York, NY 10016

Herald Press, 616 Walnut Ave., Scottdale, PA 15683

Holiday House, Inc., 18 E. 53rd St., New York, NY 10022

Holmes & Meier Publishers, Inc., 30 Irving Place, New York, NY 10003

Holt, Rinehart and Winston, Inc., 383 Madison Ave., New York, NY 10017

Horn Book, Inc., Park Square Bldg., 31 St. James Ave., Boston, MA 02116

Houghton Mifflin Co., Wayside Road, Burlington, MA 01803

Human Sciences Press, Inc. Dist. by Independent Publishers Group, 14 Vanderventer Ave., Port Washington, NY 11050

Independence Press. Div. of Herald House, Drawer HH, Independence, MO 64055

Indiana University Press, Tenth & Morton Sts., Bloomington, IN 47405

International Reading Association, 800 Barksdale Rd., Box 8139, Newark, DE 19711

Jewish Publication Society of America, 117 S. 17th St., Philadelphia, PA 19103

Judson Press, Valley Forge, PA 19481

Alfred A. Knopf, Inc., 400 Hahn Rd., Westminster, MD 21157

Larousse & Co., Inc., 572 Fifth Ave., New York, NY 10036

Seymour Lawrence. Dist. by Delacorte Press, 1 Dag Hammarskjold Plaza, 245 E. 47th St., New York, NY 10017

Lerner Publications Co. Dist. by Control Data Arts, 474 Concordia Ave., St. Paul, MN 55103

J. B. Lippincott Co., c/o Harper & Row, Publishers, Inc., Keystone Industrial Park, Scranton, PA 18512

Little, Brown & Co., 200 West St., Waltham, MA 02154

Lollipop Power, Inc., P.O. Box 1171, Chapel Hill, NC 27514

Lothrop, Lee & Shepard Books. Div. of William Morrow & Co., Inc., Wilmor Warehouse, 6 Henderson Dr., West Caldwell, NJ 07006

Macmillan Publishing Co., Inc., Front & Brown Sts., Riverside, NJ 08370

Manzanita Press, P.O. Box 4027, San Rafael, CA 94903

Mar Vista Publishing Co., 11917 Westminster Place, Los Angeles, CA 90066

McClelland and Stewart, Ltd., 25 Hollinger Rd., Toronto, Ontario, M4B 3G2

McGraw-Hill Book Co., 1221 Avenue of the Americas, New York, NY 10020

David McKay Co., Inc., 2 Park Ave., New York, NY 10016

Julian Messner, The Simon & Schuster Bldg., 1230 Ave. of the Americas, New York, NY 10020

Meeting Street School, Rhode Island Easter Seal Society, 667 Waterman Ave., East Providence, RI 02914

William Morrow & Co., Inc., Wilmor Warehouse, 6 Henderson Dr., West Caldwell, NJ 07006

Mosaic Press/Valley Editions, Box 1032, Oakville, Ontario L6J 5E9

National Council of Teachers of English, 1111 Kenyon Road, Urbana, IL 61801

National Geographic Society, 17th & M Sts. N.W., Washington, DC 20036

New Plays Books, Trolley Place, Rowayton, CT 06853

New Seed Press, P.O. Box 3016, Stanford, CA 94305

New Victoria Publishers, 7 Bank St., Lebanon, NH 03766

New York Public Library, c/o Readex Books, 101 Fifth Ave., New York, NY 10003

Northland Press, P.O. Box N, Flagstaff, AZ 86002

Oceana Publications, 75 Main St., Dobbs Ferry, NY 10522

Oryx Press, 2214 N. Central Ave., Phoenix, AZ 85004

Oxford University Press, Inc., 16–00 Pollitt Dr., Fair Lawn, NJ 07410

Panjandrum Books. Dist. by Publisher's Group West, 5855 Beaudry, Emeryville, CA 94608

Pantheon Books. Div. of Random House, Inc., 400 Hahn Rd., Westminster, MD 21157

Parents Magazine Press. Dist. by Elsevier-Dutton Publishing Co., 2 Park Ave., Dept. JH, New York, NY 10016

Parnassus Press. Imprint of Houghton Mifflin Co., Wayside Rd., Burlington, MA 01803

S. G. Phillips, Inc., 305 W. 86th St., New York, NY 10024

Platt & Munk, Publishers. Imprint of Grosset & Dunlap, 51 Madison Ave., New York, NY 10010

Plays, Inc., 8 Arlington St., Boston, MA 02116

Clarkson N. Potter, Publishers Inc. Dist. by Crown Publishers, 1 Park Ave., New York, NY 10016

Prentice-Hall, Inc., Box 500, Englewood Cliffs, NJ 07632

Press Pacifica, P.O. Box 1227, Kailua, HI 96734

Putnam Publishing Group, 1050 Wall St., W., Lyndhurst, NJ 07071

G. P. Putnam's Sons, 1050 Wall St., W., Lyndhurst, NJ 07071

Raintree Publishers, Inc., 205 W. Highland Ave., Milwaukee, WI 53203

Rand McNally & Co., P.O. Box 7600, Chicago, IL 60680

Random House, Inc., 400 Hahn Rd., Westminster, MD 21157

Nancy Renfro Studios, 1117 W. 9th St., Austin, TX 78703

Rodale Press, Inc., 33 E. Minor St., Emmaus, PA 18049

Scarecrow Press, Inc. Div. of Grolier Educational Corp., 52 Liberty St., Metuchen, NJ 08840

Schenkman Publishing Co., Inc., 3 Mt. Auburn Place, Cambridge, MA 02138

Schocken Books, Inc., 200 Madison Ave., New York, NY 10016

Scholastic Magazines, 50 W. 44th St., New York, NY 10036

Scott, Foresman & Co., 1900 E. Lake Ave., Glenview, IL 60025

Charles Scribner's Sons, Vreeland Ave., Boro of Totowa, Paterson, NJ 07512

Seabury Press, Inc., Seabury Service Center, Somers, CT 06071

Sierra Club Books. Dist. by Charles Scribner's Sons, Vreeland Ave., Boro of Totowa, Paterson, NJ 07512

Simon & Schuster, Inc., 1230 Ave. of the Americas, New York, NY 10020

Sisters' Choice Press, 2027 Parker St., Berkeley, CA 94704

Sniffen Court Books, c/o Atheneum Pubs., 597 Fifth Ave., New York, NY 10017

Stemmer House Publishers, Inc., 2627 Caves Rd., Owings Mills, MD 21117

Sterling Publishing Co., Inc., 2 Park Ave., New York, NY 10016

Todd Tarbox Books, 2523 Ashton Rd., Jackson, MI 49203

Thimble Press, Lockwood, Station Road, South Woodchester, Stroud, Glos. GL5 5EQ

Third World Press, 7524 S. Cottage Grove, Chicago, IL 60019

Troll Associates, 320 Rte. 17, Mahwah, NJ 07430

Tundra Books of Northern New York, 51 Clinton St., Box 1030, Plattsburgh, NY 12901

Charles E. Tuttle Co., Inc., P.O. Drawer F, Rutland, VT 05701

University of Chicago Press, 11030 S. Langley Ave., Chicago, IL 60628

Vanguard Press, Inc., 424 Madison Ave., New York, NY 10017

Viking Press, c/o Vikeship Co., 299 Murray Hill Pkway., East Rutherford, NJ 07073

Walker & Co., 720 Fifth Ave., New York, NY 10019

Frederick Warne & Co., Inc., 2 Park Ave., New York, NY 10016

Franklin Watts, Inc., 730 Fifth Ave., New York, NY 10019

John Weatherhill, Inc. Dist. by Charles E. Tuttle, Co., Inc., 28 S. Main St., Rutland, VT 05701

Western Publishing Co., Inc., Dept. M, 1220 Mound Ave., Racine, WI 53404

Westminster Press, Order Dept., P.O. Box 718, Wm. Penn Annex, Philadelphia, PA 19105

Albert Whitman & Co., 560 W. Lake St., Chicago, IL 60606

Yearling Books. Imprint of Dell Publishing Co., Inc., 1 Dag Hammarskjold Plaza, 245 E. 47th St., New York, NY 10017

Author Index

Title Index

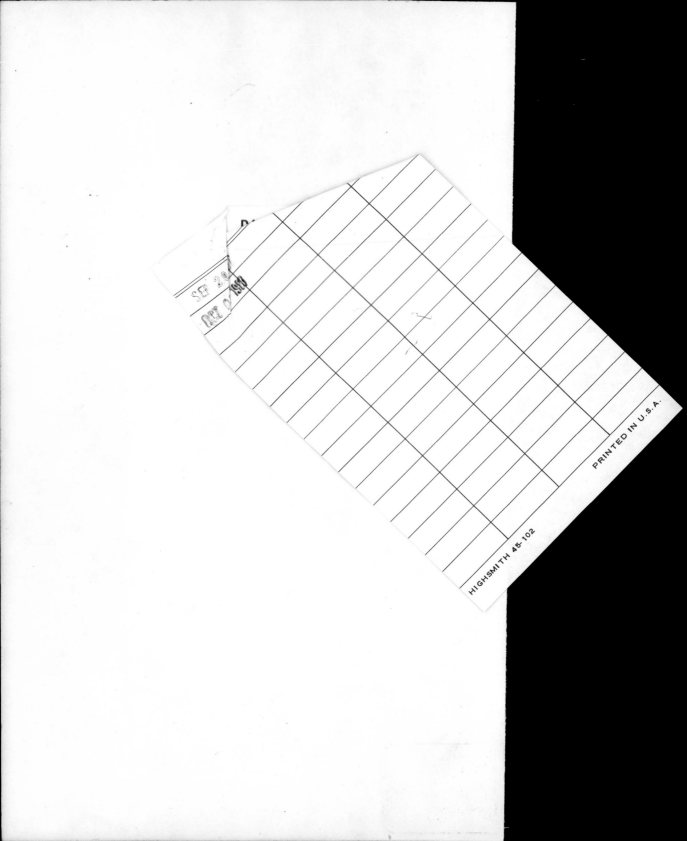

HIGHSMITH 45-102

PRINTED IN U.S.A.